Five Essential Steps
in Digital Video:
A DV Moviemaker's
Tricks of the Trade

FIVE ESSENTIAL STEPS IN DIGITAL VIDEO: A DV MOVIEMAKER'S TRICKS OF THE TRADE

International Standard Book Number: 0-7897-2615-7

Library of Congress Catalog Card Number: 2001093926

Printed in the United States of America

First Printing: December 2001

04   03   02   4   3   2   1

TRADEMARKS

All terms mentioned in this book that are known to be trademarks or service marks have been appropriately capitalized. Que cannot attest to the accuracy of this information. Use of a term in this book should not be regarded as affecting the validity of any trademark or service mark.

WARNING AND DISCLAIMER

Every effort has been made to make this book as complete and as accurate as possible, but no warranty or fitness is implied. The information provided is on an "as is" basis. The author and the publisher shall have neither liability nor responsibility to any person or entity with respect to any loss or damages arising from the information contained in this book or from the use of the DVD or programs accompanying it.

ASSOCIATE PUBLISHER
Dean Miller

ACQUISITIONS EDITOR
Angelina Ward

DEVELOPMENT EDITOR
Howard Jones

MANAGING EDITOR
Thomas F. Hayes

PRODUCTION EDITOR
Maribeth Echard

TECHNICAL EDITORS
Tony Marsh
Perry Mitchell
Jay Rose

TEAM COORDINATOR
Cindy Teeters

MEDIA DEVELOPER
Michael Hunt

INTERIOR DESIGNER
Anne Jones

COVER DESIGNER
Ann Jones

CONTENTS AT A GLANCE

CONTENTS

20 LIGHTING FOR DV   317

ABOUT THE AUTHOR

Denise Ohio is a writer, producer, director, DP, location audio technician, editor, and composer, and often does all of these jobs on her DV projects. In 1996, she made one of the first digital video features in the world. *Amazing World* has screened in film festivals in Montevideo, Montreal, Toronto, Paris, London, and Philadelphia. Ohio sold the home video rights to Northern Arts/Naiad in 1997 and pay-per-view rights in August 2000.

Between gigs as a marketing consultant, writer, DP, and camera operator, Ohio made *Family Business*, a documentary. Working as producer, director, DP, location audio mixer, grip, gaffer, editor, and soundtrack composer on the project, she shot DV and 16mm, and handled postproduction in her home video-editing suite.

In addition to making movies, she is a published novelist and has been compared to William Faulkner and Tennessee Williams. Currently, she is in preproduction on her next documentary/book project, *Verona*.

To find out more about her work, please visit `www.holytoledo.com`.

DEDICATION

To Catherine, always.

ACKNOWLEDGMENTS

My thanks to Sarah Johnson for being my pal and keeping me sane. Also thanks to Matt Lambert, John Bianchi, Peggy Gannon, Betty Marshall, Chris Beug, Shawn Telford, and Rich Phelps for all of your hard work on "Music Appreciation."

Also thanks to Neil Sussman for his bad jokes and sage advice, legal and otherwise. Thanks as well to Scot Charles and Peter B. Lewis for their insight into the dark arts of audio for motion pictures, Lanie McMullin for her expertise with movie permits, and Jeremy Brown for his knowledge of rental house procedures.

My gratitude to Perry Mitchell, Jay Rose, and Tony Marsh for their attempts to defeat my ignorance with their technical editing. And thanks to Angelina Ward, Howard Jones, and Sharry Lee Gregory at Que Publishing for their hard work.

Thanks to Bertel Schmidt, Eric Anderson, Bob Watson, Margot Roth, and Birgit Rathsmann for their patience and humor. Thanks also to Shooters Broadcast Services, Inc. (especially Dan Aschatz), Bexel Inc., Rick Belisle at Paragon Media, and Rich Fassio at Modern Digital.

My deepest thanks to my partner Catherine M. Minden, for her humor, intelligence, and patience. And for making me coffee in the morning.

TELL US WHAT YOU THINK!

As the reader of this book, *you* are our most important critic and commentator. We value your opinion and want to know what we're doing right, what we could do better, what areas you'd like to see us publish in, and any other words of wisdom you're willing to pass our way.

As an Associate Publisher for Que, I welcome your comments. You can fax, e-mail, or write me directly to let me know what you did or didn't like about this book—as well as what we can do to make our books stronger.

Please note that I cannot help you with technical problems related to the topic of this book, and that due to the high volume of mail I receive, I might not be able to reply to every message.

When you write, please be sure to include this book's title and author as well as your name and phone or fax number. I will carefully review your comments and share them with the author and editors who worked on the book.

Fax: 317-581-4666

E-mail: feedback@quepublishing.com

Mail: Dean Miller
              Que
              201 West 103rd Street
              Indianapolis, IN 46290 USA

INTRODUCTION

REMAKING MOVIES: THE DV PHILOSOPHY

So, you want to make a movie. Good for you.

The job of moviemaking can be broken down into sets of tasks. This book has done that in great detail. It's important to keep in mind, however, that although many of these tasks must be done simultaneously, many can be done serially.

The best examples of simultaneous tasks are during production. It's hard to light, shoot, run audio, and cover continuity by yourself. That doesn't mean it can't be done—it can, but usually it's easier to bring people in to handle these jobs so you can concentrate on managing their efforts.

Hollywood shows usually schedule all the jobs to be done simultaneously. There's a good reason for that—the cost of the money. A producer who borrows $40 million at a compounded interest rate of prime plus 5 percent is burning money just standing there. It's incumbent to get the product made and out the door as quickly as possible.

But you may not have those pressures. You can take more time making the movie you want to make, the way you want to make it. You can manage the entire process according to your strengths, taking time to write the script, develop the project, compose and record music, and so on. It's up to you.

Consider your strengths and your interests. What kind of movie do you want to make and what role will you take on? Consider your weaknesses. Ask yourself whom you can bring on to your show to handle the things you're not very good at.

Don't consider these roles strictly in terms of job description. For example, if you can't or don't want to run the camera yourself, you don't need a *camera operator* so much as *someone who has skill at running a camera*. It's a subtle but profound distinction. Don't rely on job titles to address the needs of your show: A person who calls himself or herself a camera operator may do that one job really well, but another person without the title may have the camera skills you need, as well as general lighting and continuity skills.

Also remember that anyone you choose to involve on your movie should be a team player and problem solver—the sort of person you can rely on. Making movies is difficult enough without throwing personality clashes and character flaws into the mix. Many moviemaking tasks don't require vast talent and skill. Although it's nice to have experience, most of the jobs are not so difficult you can't learn to do them as you go. Just remember to schedule for learning time.

One aspect you don't want to learn on the job is the business side of things— show business is 10 percent show and 90 percent business. Much of this book focuses on that side of moviemaking. I'm not suggesting we give up all artistic aspirations in favor of the profit motive. I am suggesting, however, that thinking about DV moviemaking as show business will help you protect yourself and allow you to retain control over your show.

Regardless of your budget or intent, the movie industry views all movies as product. Whether people will want your product determines its market value— how much they're willing to spend to get it. In these terms, a great short movie, truly brilliant and inspiring, is worth nothing if no one buys it.

But market value matters only if you're seeking financing or distribution. If you don't want to sell, don't. One of the great things about DV is that it's so inexpensive that many people can self-finance a DV movie without putting their financial health at risk. And whoever controls the money controls the show.

This is a very powerful idea: controlling the money by keeping the overall costs low. DV hasn't just lowered the overall cost of production, and the people who have picked up DV cameras haven't just challenged the bottom line. We've taken control of the process. We've challenged how and why movies get made.

DV isn't just a format—it's a new way of making movies.

Regardless of how you decide to make your movie, it still requires planning, planning, and more planning. And you plan based on these five steps.

HOW TO USE THIS BOOK AND DVD

I recommend you read *Five Essential Steps in Digital Video* from beginning to end.

Taking advantage of the experimentation and method that DV allows requires leadership and preparation. This book outlines some of the information you'll need to make interesting and intelligent choices across every aspect of your project. It also includes resources such as an annotated bibliography of books, articles, Web sites, and so on, so you can get more information and begin networking with other moviemakers.

I tend to think of moviemaking and computers as being inextricably linked. The computer is a crucial tool: You'll use it to budget, schedule, create contact lists, and write scripts, as well as edit the footage you capture with your DV camera. You can make movies without a computer, but having one can make it a whole lot easier. With this in mind, I included software tools and templates on the DVD that you may find useful.

The DVD also contains "Music Appreciation," a DV short produced by Holy Toledo Pictures, Inc., and a series of interviews with people in the business. They agreed to share their years of experience, suggestions, and tips to help your show succeed.

You have permission to use the documents in the Appendix and on the DVD, but not to redistribute them. Modify them as you need to and review them with an entertainment attorney to make sure you understand every part. This book is not a substitute for legal, financial, or business advice, but it will provide you with an understanding of the issues involved in making a DV movie. And visit www.holytoledo.com for updates and message boards about DV moviemaking.

STEP 1: DEVELOPMENT:
HUNTING AND GATHERING

OVERVIEW

Most people have heard about three aspects of making a movie—preproduction, production, and postproduction. So, why do I insist that there are five? Because there are:

- Development
- Preproduction
- Production
- Postproduction
- Selling

DEVELOPMENT

Also known as hunting and gathering, development is the time you need to determine what kind of movie you want to make and how you're going to make it, and finding the resources to get your movie made.

PREPRODUCTION

Preproduction done for DV movies is the same as it is for any other kind of movie. You must get specific tasks accomplished, such as script breakdown, scheduling, budgeting, hiring, firing, and the myriad of other tasks required prior to production.

PRODUCTION

This is what everyone thinks of when you say, "I'm making a movie." Production covers the execution of the planning done during development and preproduction. DV has some specific issues, especially regarding digital audio, that you need to know before shouting, "Action!"

POSTPRODUCTION

Postproduction (or *post*) for DV offers some exciting developments, but there are some basic things you need to do, such as organizing footage and gathering other material (such as music and sound effects), before beginning to cut the movie together. After you've locked the picture and handled your post-audio, there are some interesting choices you have before finishing that can help you set your movie apart from all the others.

SELLING

When it comes to selling, whom you know makes all the difference. You need to know whom to meet and how to meet them at festivals and markets, as well as how to promote a movie with an EPK (electronic press kit) and other tools. You also need to learn about motion picture distribution agreements and markets, Internet streaming, and self-distribution.

GETTING STARTED

Start with an honest assessment of why you want to make a movie. Ask yourself

- What is it about the project that gets me stirred up? Is it the story, an actor, or the idea of making a movie?

- What do I hope to achieve? If it's to get rich and famous, will DV moviemaking help me achieve that goal?

- What about a project will sustain me through the process of getting it made and sold? Where is my support system? Which people are always in my corner? Do I treat them with the kindness and respect they deserve? Will I continue treating them well through this project? How will I guarantee that?

- What makes me think I'm the one to do this project? Skills for moviemaking aren't limited to what happens on the set. I may be a great director but I've never managed anything, not even a hotdog stand. How do I know I can identify and solve problems and delegate responsibilities?

- What makes me think I can get it done? What evidence do I have? Am I flexible? Stubborn? Technically skilled? Have I got the stomach to fire people who may be my friends?

After you understand the entire process of moviemaking, your list will help you figure out where you'll need help. If you can't write, act, or run a camera, find someone who can. If you want to direct, maybe you should let someone else take on the responsibilities of running a set.

DEVELOPMENT

Development is your time to dream. It's the one phase in your project where you get to learn about, create, and commit to the Big Picture. One minute you're discussing cinematic motifs, the next tax advantages of a certain business structure.

During development, you attach key people to your project, analyze the market, create your production company, create a business plan, arrange your funding, get a script, promote your project, and a million other things.

Do this now, because if you don't have a plan, you will have a mess.

Most people believe that because DV equipment is relatively inexpensive, making a DV movie doesn't require planning. But every movie requires planning. The revolution of DV is putting high-quality equipment that can capture and manipulate high-quality images and sound into the hands of people like you and me, not skipping the best practices of moviemaking.

There are three questions you need to answer during development:

- Whom and what do you need to make your movie? How are you going to get all the stuff and all the people? How can DV work to your advantage?
- Who will produce the movie? What kind of business structure will you have in place?
- What kind of movie are you making and who will buy it? What's the market like?

This section covers the tasks required for development of a motion picture project. Chapter 1, "Who Does What: Job Descriptions," explains the most important project roles you may be taking on or hiring for. Chapter 2, "An

Getting Info

Every state has a film office or liaison, usually as part of the city or state office of economic development. These people are here to help—they want you to make movies and they want you to make them where you live. In addition to handling the permitting process, they have lists of motion picture professionals they're more than willing to share. You can also contact a local arts organization for further listings. Check the Resources section for more info.

Equipment Overview," is a quick introduction to some of the equipment you'll find on a DV set. This is an introduction. Later chapters will go into more detail. For now, get used to some of the jargon and start thinking about what you're going to need for your show.

Chapter 3, "I Mean Business," introduces you to motion picture business fundamentals, while Chapter 4, "Don't Tread on Me: Intellectual Property and Other Thorny Issues," discusses intellectual property as it pertains to motion pictures and producing. Chapter 5, "Who's Buying What: Surveying the Market," gives you an introduction to the markets and potential buyers for your show.

Chapter 6, "What Do You Got and What Can You Get?," helps you consider what you can buy, beg, and borrow for your project. Chapter 7, "Searching for a Script," gets into the nitty-gritty of locating a screenplay, while Chapter 8, "Writing a Script Yourself," walks you through the writing process.

The section ends with a set of checklists to help you plan and design your show.

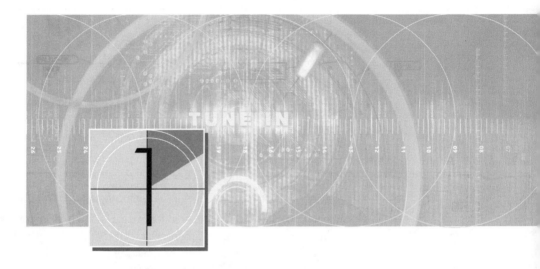

WHO DOES WHAT: JOB DESCRIPTIONS

People are everything. The right person with the right skills is more valuable than the most expensive equipment. Investors invest because of the people on a project, people work their magic on your project, and people buy your product.

There are more than 150 different departments on a major motion picture. That's a lot of people. Many have specialized skills necessary to any project. Others are managers, who watch to make sure their charges meet their schedules and budgets. Others are hangers-on, assistants, apprentices, and so on, trying to learn the business. If you need 150 different departments to make your movie, you're reading the wrong book.

But if you want to make your movie with DV and a small group of people, you're in the right place.

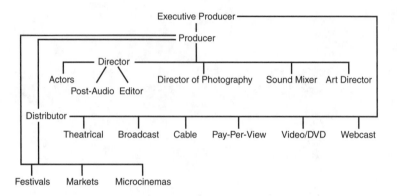

FIGURE 1.1

Movie project organization chart.

I'm a writer-producer-director-director of photography (DP)-editor. Most of the producers I know who are working with DV are hyphenates: writer-producer, producer-director, producer-actor, producer-director-DP, and so on. Some had little or no experience making movies until they started their own projects, and some have spent some time on Hollywood-style sets with specific and rigid roles, working as DPs, gaffers, 2nd assistant camera ops (2nd ACs), extras, production assistants (PAs), and other specialist titles.

But they all learned quickly that the key to being a producer is being a generalist. As a producer, you need to know all sorts of things, chief among them, what you can and can't do. And for everything you can't do, you'll have to find someone who can.

For example, I can't do straight makeup. I have no talent for it and I'm always afraid I'll poke someone in the eye. But someone has to handle an actor's makeup. My choices are to find a makeup artist or ask my actors to handle it themselves. I've found that the actors I work with prefer to take care of their hair, makeup, and wardrobe. As long as they know what they need for any given scene, they're happy to take responsibility for it.

Some jobs require individuals with specific skills and these are people you want to get onto your project as soon as possible. Some, such as your entertainment attorney, might never visit the set but will provide services every step of the way. Some, such as the DP, will work through prep and production, and be released after all the photography is completed. Others, such as the director, will be involved through postproduction.

You want to attach these people to your project as early as you can. *Attaching* someone to your project means he or she is more than happy to discuss signing a contract and working your show after you've obtained enough money to go forward.

Their résumés will go into your business plan, their expertise will help you estimate your budget and schedule, and their contacts may help you land a name actor or crucial investor.

Whether you hire someone with experience or not, be sure you listen to what these people have to say. Everyone brings something to the show. A lot of DV producers concentrate on the hardware and software of making movies, disregarding the people. But people are not trained monkeys. Those with experience can point out problems and opportunities that didn't even occur to you if you give them the chance.

I have a group of people I always call when I have a project. Some are in the movie business, some are legal and business advisors, and some are friends who are brutally honest. Although I don't always do what each recommends, I know I can rely on them to give me honest answers, new options, and candy. Candy is important. In addition to their expertise and ideas, I know I have an emotional support system—very important when undertaking any motion picture project.

You want people like this with you. Find them early, listen to them, and pay them as best as you can.

PRODUCER

The producer's job is to direct the project. The producer reports to the executive producer and when on the set, works for the director.

It's the producer's responsibility to make sure the show comes in on schedule and budget, and is a salable product at the end, and to squeeze every dime out of that product. That requires a lot of planning, clear communication, and the ability to say no and make it stick.

The producer also reaps a tremendous amount of credit. Although the public may applaud the actors and the critics may swoon over the director, without the producer, there is no show. This is your gig and you're in charge. Not only do you have the opportunity to do a good job, you give others the opportunity to do a good job.

The relationship between the director and producer is an interesting one. The director is hired, and fired, by the producer, but the director is the one in charge. The producer acts like the host of a party, making sure everyone is getting what they need in order to do what they need to do within the allotted time frame and budget.

If the shoot is dangerously close to going over budget or schedule, or the producer truly believes the show's salability is being affected, the producer has the responsibility to step in. Unfortunately, what constitutes a danger is open to the producer's interpretation, and sometimes what a producer interprets as a problem is really the producer's desire to direct.

Hire well and trust the people you hire. And remember that credits are the next best thing to money. You should be very reluctant to deal them out without getting something very valuable in return.

Producers come in all flavors. There's the producer who keeps the project moving. Then, there are executive producers, coproducers, line producers, associate producers—any kind of variation you can think of.

An *executive producer,* also known as The Money, is usually the person who has arranged financing. Sometimes a distributor, agent, or other entity will demand an executive producer credit.

You can usually spot an experienced exec on a set—they're dressed better than everyone else, keep out of the way, and keep their mouths shut. An exec's job is to hire well. If the exec has to come winging in to rescue the show, that exec did not fulfill this one responsibility. Inexperienced execs can wreak havoc. Because they're so used to having the producer's undivided attention, they'll demand it at the very moment the producer needs to be concentrating on something else. This is especially disastrous when the producer is also the director.

This happened on a project for which I was DP. Not only did the exec demand attention, he ruined takes because he wouldn't stay quiet. The tension was palpable. The producer-director was so busy paying attention to the exec, the rest of the ensemble would wait for an hour before he would direct a scene. He should've either told the exec to leave or handed over directing duties to someone else.

Coproducer can mean anything between the credit of line producer and producer. It may be shared producer responsibility or it may go to someone demanding it in exchange for the use of an important set or prop.

Line producers are involved in managing production. *Line producer* is a credit that actually goes to someone who used to be a unit production manager (UPM), only this UPM is so valuable the producer gives him or her the fancier title. Line producers tend to focus on the technical aspects of producing: who does what when. Often they're the bad cop to the director's good cop, taking the heat for decisions from the rest of the ensemble.

Associate producer credits can go to just about anyone who has made a major contribution to the production. Often a producer credit is given in exchange for money, service, or property. For instance, if someone has been given a screenwriting credit and won't share it, you can give the writer who polished your script an associate producer credit. It also may go to the person who is second in charge. I know some crew people who will take an associate producer credit when they're working several jobs on the set.

If you're the producer on your show and bring an associate producer on your project, be sure to make that person's responsibilities clear. I was on a shoot where the producer had an associate producer who wasn't sure what to do. When asked what her job was, the person responded differently every time, sometimes saying she was an associate, coproducer, and even once, an executive producer. This caused confusion, especially when she tried to give orders. It wasn't her fault. The producer had not made it clear what she was supposed to be doing. She became upset by how she perceived she was being treated (okay, we ignored her) and left the project soon after.

WRITER

The writer creates the script. The writer works for the producer.

It's a crucial job, so naturally writers are treated worse than dirt. There are very few jobs where someone without experience, skill, or talent can mess with the work created by someone who is experienced, skilled, and talented, without even the courtesy of asking.

One of the few places where working on a no- or low-budget DV movie can be attractive to a seasoned professional is in writing the screenplay. An experienced screenwriter may get the chance to be more involved with the development of a movie if she or he decides to work on a no- or low-budget DV show. This can be bad—the writer might meddle—or it can be very, very good. For instance, a writer who gets to know the on-camera talent may be able to shape or even create a character for an actor that really works to that actor's strengths.

When you're working with someone else's script, stick to the lines.

Changing another writer's work, unless you have permission, is not okay. Some writers would love a chance to become an integral part of the ensemble, using their talents to the greatest extent possible. Even for seasoned veterans, that's a new and valuable experience.

DIRECTOR

The director plans and executes the script. On the set, the director is the boss. The ensemble works according to the director's wishes and pace.

The director is responsible for the look and feel of the show, and is the creative leader and key decision-maker from prep to post. The director envisions, designs, and communicates the plan for the show: what it looks like, the emotional content of every moment, the performances—everything on the set and in postproduction.

There are a lot of decisions to be made and many directors delegate these tasks to others. But if there's plenty of time (or not enough money), he or she may prefer handling many of these responsibilities alone.

For instance, I handle my own casting. Nothing against casting directors, but sometimes I find an actor whose performance I really like but there's no place for her or him in my show. I can create a part, whereas a casting director can only do as ordered. Great examples are casting women in parts you'd normally think of as male, men in parts you'd normally think would go to women, and casting people of different ethnicities or different physical abilities in parts where those things are simply not an issue.

DIRECTOR OF PHOTOGRAPHY

The DP plans and executes the director's vision. The DP is hired by the producer, but works for the director.

Different DPs have different views on what their job entails. A DP should be able to translate the director's wishes visually and direct the eye in the frame. This includes knowing the emotional value of composition, camera angles, and camera moves. A DP should also be able to understand the script and director well enough to design the shoot for the most effective interpretation of the director's vision.

For a DV movie, a DP should be able to light, use the camera to capture an image, handle the lighting and grip equipment and crews, understand the resource requirements for the shoot, and know the limits of DV.

NAME TALENT

If you can get an A-list actor to star in your show, good for you. Get him or her attached to your project as soon as you can.

If you can't get an A-list, B-list, or even C-list actor, you may be able to get a name actor. There are lots of ways to define what a name actor is, but generally, a name actor is a person who people recognize either by name or face.

Actors are hired by the producer, but work almost exclusively with the director.

PUBLICITY AND BUSINESS

The publicity and support people work for the producer.

Your publicity effort will get and keep your name and project in the media. Your business efforts involve making sure your funds, contracts, and any other business and legal activities are covered.

On a no- or low-budget show, you may be handling your own publicity. Have copies of everyone's résumé, bio, and headshot filed and prepped, ready to be handed out at a moment's notice.

Your business office might be you, your company checkbook, and a box for receipts. With set payments, like paychecks, or location and permit fees, write the checks out ahead of time and keep them on you. I usually carry a folder or portable file box for extra contracts and releases, maps, schedules, contact lists, and so on, as well as several blank checks. Everyone on my set knows that if I okay a petty cash reimbursement, I need a receipt. No receipt, no reimbursement.

Get yourself an entertainment attorney immediately. Your lawyer is a key resource. She or he can explain the pros and cons of certain business structures, create contracts you'll need, make you aware of issues specific to your state, qualify investors, and so on.

If you're nervous about taxes, consider getting an accountant. In addition to making sure the government gets its share, your accountant may also be able to help you find investors.

DISTRIBUTOR

A *distributor* is a company that licenses a set of rights from you for your show to sell them to somebody else. A distributor becomes your partner in the effort to sell the show after a distribution deal is signed.

Distributors come in all shapes and sizes, but whether part of a massive multinational, or a single-operator shop, the distributor wants to buy from you at the lowest possible cost and sell for the highest possible profit.

The advantage of going with a distributor is market power. Distributors have relationships with theater chains, broadcasters, video/DVD rental shops, and retailers. They're not averse to throwing their weight around, especially when someone owes them money.

An independent distributor is one not regularly or substantially affiliated with a major studio. Most are members of the American Film Marketing Association (AFMA). Although some have production divisions, they don't have the financial resources of a major studio. When submitting a project, you must have some financing in place and be ready for principal photography.

Independent distributors usually distribute smaller movies, often to serve specific markets. Usually, they know their markets well and can tell you right off whether your show will sell to that audience. Unfortunately, independent distributors have limited financial resources to put into your show and a higher bankruptcy rate.

Now is the time to start contacting distributors about your project. A distribution deal prior to production gets you two things: money to make the movie and a little more persuasion with other investors. You can approach them with a deal in hand, making it easier for them to believe your show will get done and into the market to make some money. If you can get distribution for your project before shooting a single frame, you're doing well.

CONSIDER THIS

If you want to write, produce, direct, and run the camera, go ahead. If you want to produce and handle distribution, more power to you. There's no law that says you can't.

Approach moviemaking according to task rather than role. Many people believe they must hire one person for every possible task on a set, filling roles according to a list out of a book. They think they need a Best Boy because that's what's on the list. Especially on high-buck union shoots, the divisions between departments and jobs run deep. A grip will not hang a light, but will sit around cursing the darkness.

That said, assigning roles is handy for certain jobs, and I recommend that the preceding jobs have dedicated personnel assigned to them. Not only do the jobs require special skills, but also giving people responsibility usually gets you a better result.

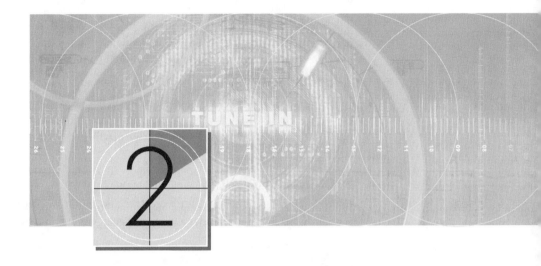

AN EQUIPMENT OVERVIEW

You need to know the basics about DV and motion picture equipment so you can make informed decisions in development and preproduction. The details regarding the DV technology, formats, and other tools are covered in later sections. For now, get comfortable with learning a new vocabulary and understanding the overall process of making movies.

YOU NEED IT WHEN?

Among the many decisions you need to make regarding your show is what you may want or need to buy versus what you can borrow or rent. Many DV moviemakers invest in equipment because they plan to make more than one show and the initial expense seems relatively small.

Decide soon whether you're going to be buying or renting the most important production gear, such as a camera, portable field mixer, and so on. Then consider when you'll be making your purchases. I have worked with producers who have purchased a DV camera the day before the shoot, giving the crew no time to get familiar with it before beginning work. This is not a wise strategy. Your crew needs a chance to learn the tools.

If you plan on producing and shooting your show yourself, it's even more important to get your hands on the equipment as soon as you can. You'll have plenty to do on the set without having to scramble for the user's manual.

The only time I suggest waiting to make a purchase is with your nonlinear editing system (NLE). Consider waiting until just before you need it to write that check. The market is still fairly volatile and prices are dropping all the time.

PRODUCTION GEAR

In production, you'll need tools for creating and capturing picture and sound on the set. This includes a camera, lights, rigging, and audio equipment.

DV Camera

The DV camera is what you use to capture sound and image.

A DV camera or camcorder (see Figure 2.1) is one that follows the digital video specs outlined in the DV standards document, the current version of which is IEC 61834, developed by the International Electrotechnical Commission (IEC). The IEC is a standards body related to the International Standards Organization (ISO) and the International Telecommunication Union (ITU).

FIGURE 2.1

Sony's DCR-VX2000, the heir to the venerable DCR-VX1000.

DV uses a 13.5MHz sampling rate and a Discrete Cosine Transform (DCT) compression scheme. A single image (spatial) or successive images (temporal) may have adjacent pixels that are the same value, so DCT compresses these pixels as one to save bit space. DV also gains some of its compression ratio by adding interfield (not interframe) compression of video images that don't have substantial motion.

DV audio accepts two channels at 16-bit 48kHz, or four channels at 12-bit 32kHz. DV information is carried in a nominal 25-megabit-per-second (Mbps) data stream. With audio, subcode (such as timecode), Insert and Track Information (ITI), and error correction, the total data stream comes to about 36Mbps recorded to tape.

Although digital video sample rates, color space, and tape width are standardized, camera and camcorder designs are not. This is one reason you see so many different models with varying features. For example, although DV can handle four channels of audio at 12-bit 32kHz, or two channels at 16-bit 48kHz, many of the DV camcorders and decks are limited to two 12-bit 32kHz channels or one 16-bit 48kHz channel.

Consumer, prosumer, and *professional* are categories of equipment developed by manufacturers based on the expectations of users. Consumer cameras tend to be small and lack manual control for certain features. Prosumer cameras are a step up in sophistication and have pro-level features, such as white balance and zebra stripes, but they're hidden within electronic menus. Pro equipment is fully functional, with all the bells and whistles easily accessible by exterior buttons and knobs. They also tend to have better lenses, more rugged housings, and bigger price tags.

Although many of the prosumer cameras lack certain desirable features, a variety of vendors offer add-ons to expand their functions. For instance, camera manufacturers use unbalanced stereo miniplugs for the audio in and out on many prosumer cameras. Several companies now offer audio boxes to make better use of DV's audio capabilities.

Armed with these add-ons, professional camera operators and broadcasters have purchased prosumer DV cameras. They not only get the quality they need, but also save themselves a bundle of money.

For more information on DV and other digital video formats, see Chapter 18, "Making Video Digital." For more information on common DV camera controls, see Chapter 19, "The DV Camera."

Lighting

Chief among the requirements for creating an image is carefully designing and executing your lighting. Lights come in various sizes and color temperatures, and lighting equipment includes reflectors and bounce cards. It also includes controls such as scrims, flags, dimmers, and so on.

The goal is to create an image that falls within the technical parameters of the equipment, while properly expressing the intent of the director.

For more information on lighting equipment and practices, see Chapter 20, "Lighting for DV" and Chapter 21, "Lighting Techniques."

Rigging

Rigging is anything you do to place equipment in a certain position. For the camera, you may use a shoulder mount, tripod, dolly, or jib arm. You may need a hostess tray or some other device to mount a camera on a car.

For lighting and lighting control, you may need a common piece of equipment called a *Century stand*, or more commonly, the c-stand. C-stands are remarkable tools with use limited only by your desperation. You may also use mafers, cardellinis, and other grip equipment.

Whatever you need to do, you can be assured there's a piece of rigging equipment to help you do it. There's even rigging equipment for shooting underwater, off heights, while parachuting—you name it, it's out there.

For more information on gaff and grip equipment and techniques, see Chapter 22, "Rigging."

Audio Gear

The goal of capturing sound on location is to get the clearest audio signal with the least amount of noise, recorded at the highest quality possible. Location audio gear comprises mixers, headphones, booms, microphones, and cables.

It's unlikely that a microphone mounted on your camcorder is going to capture your best audio in all situations. Prosumer DV cameras are often lacking in audio features, even though the format itself is loaded with them. The fullest-featured cameras have two modes of stereo sound: 16-bit for two channels or 12-bit for four channels. Most DV prosumer camcorders, however, give you one channel of 16-bit 48kHZ, or two channels of 12-bit 32kHz, and they use stereo miniplug connectors for audio in and headphones.

Fear not: If your camera has limited audio capabilities, there are plenty of vendors who offer inexpensive add-ons, so you'll be able to use pro audio equipment with your prosumer DV camera.

For more information on location audio, see Chapter 23, "Capturing the Sound."

POSTPRODUCTION GEAR

Postproduction means gathering all the materials for your movie and putting them together: footage and dialogue, animation, special effects, music, sound effects, titles, and anything else you may need. To do this, you need two kinds of tools: one set for assembling the video, and one for assembling the sound.

Cutting Picture: Hardware and Software

Your choices for editing software depend on your operating system. There are several demo versions of popular applications on the DVD for you to try.

DV uses a high-speed data transfer protocol officially named IEEE 1394. (Sony's version is called iLink, whereas Apple gave its version the catchier name of FireWire.) IEEE 1394 is the jack and the protocol that lets you transfer the DV data to your computer.

The DV specification includes frame-accurate device control and the ability to read and write digital video. An IEEE 1394 connection allows moviemakers using IEEE 1394-equipped DV camcorders and nonlinear editors (NLEs) to transfer the DV data stored on a tape into their computers with no generation loss.

Decide early on whether you're going to be working with an editor. If so, hire your editor early in the process and discuss exactly what kind of system the editor will be using. You don't want to walk in with a tidy box of materials only to find out your editor doesn't have compatible gear. Also, discuss rates now. It's easier to negotiate when you don't have deadlines looming.

If you're going to cut your show yourself, you need a fairly robust machine with as much RAM as you can afford, a card for transferring your DV footage to your hard drive, and plenty of storage space. One gigabyte of storage will hold about 4 minutes 45 seconds of DV video. Two gigs is about 9 minutes 30 seconds.

□ NOTE

NTSC and 29.97

NTSC is the broadcast standard in most of North America. Back when television used to be only black-and-white, TV displayed 30 frames per second, with each frame composed of two fields. The television cameras and sets first scanned the odd-number lines and then the even lines, and what you saw playing on your TV was an interlaced display. Video back then could be considered as 60 fields per second, coinciding with the alternating current from the power mains at 60Hz. For technical reasons regarding color and audio, NTSC was changed to 29.97 frames per second, or 59.94 interlaced fields per second. Different standards developed elsewhere in the world. One of the most common is Phase Alteration Line, or PAL, used in Europe. PAL has 25 frames or 50 fields

For more information on editing equipment, see Chapter 29, "Cutting Picture."

Post-Audio

After you have locked your picture, you'll go on to handle your post-audio work. Decide early whether you'll be handling this yourself or going to a post-audio house.

Usually, I organize material, place sound effects (called *spotting*), and create a scratch version for an audio engineer to follow. I take this material to a post-audio house in Seattle, not because they have fancy equipment, but because the engineer has better ears than I do. He knows what to listen for, how to add or subtract sound elements for a better effect, and often has good ideas.

If you decide to handle your post-audio yourself, you're going to need a way to deal with audio coming from a variety of formats.

If you want sound on a DAT or DA-88, you need an appropriate deck and a digital-audio workstation (DAW) or digital audio card in your system to handle the transfer of digital audio to your hard drive. If you want to use an analog format, you need some kind of analog-to-digital converter (ADC) hooked up to the outputs of the turntable, cassette deck, or reel-to-reel you need. Software is also required to handle the transfer or digitizing.

For more information on editing equipment, see Chapter 30, "Post-Audio."

FINISHING

After the picture and audio are locked, you may want to consider *video sweetening*, a combination of tape-to-tape color correction, clamping to legal colors, adding reference bars and tone, and adding titles.

Anyone who has worked with NTSC video knows that the initials stand for the National Television Standards Committee. It also stands for Never The Same Color. NTSC requires video color to fall within a certain standardized range. To make life more difficult, these NTSC standards are not the same as the standards for computer monitors or software. It's easy to cut a show that looks fine on your computer but horrendous on a TV.

Your show needs *legal colors*. Legal colors conform to the NTSC standards for TV broadcast. There are two ways to do this: Use a piece of software that will clamp your video or have it done while doing a tape-to-tape color correction.

In addition to making your video technically legal, tape-to-tape color correction sets the colors from shot to shot and scene to scene for a more consistent look, while cleaning up some video noise. You can have a postproduction house handle this, or use software. Color correction is processor-intensive and takes a long time.

You also need to add reference SMPTE bars and 1kHz tone to the head of your tape so the duplication house can set its equipment. Additionally, you need an 8-second countdown. Many NLE software applications have a utility that will create one for you.

SELLING

You need at least three masters of your show. A master is the completed motion picture, with bars and tone, legal colors, countdown, and audio split to two channels, the *dialogue track* and the *music and effects (M & E) track*.

The dialogue track contains all spoken words in the piece. The M & E track has all music, sound effects, sound beds, and any other audio. Splitting the audio in these two tracks allows broadcasters to dub the movie. *Dubbing* replaces dialogue in one language with dialogue in another.

One master will be vaulted. *Vaulted* means it's stored in a postproduction facility, duplication house, or film and video storage house. The vault is climate controlled and fireproof. You'll pay for the privilege of storing your show there.

One master is for festival screenings, and the third master will go to your duplication house, where you'll order 50–100 VHS copies for your marketing effort.

In addition to your masters and VHS dubs of your show, you're going to need support material, including a press kit. The kit contains the following:

- A one-page press release announcing the project with full contact information
- A 25-word pitch
- A two- to three-page treatment

per second, matching the 50Hz AC power coming from their power mains. You can't mix and match NTSC and PAL equipment and expect it to work together. Also, if you need a master for use in a country that doesn't use NTSC, you will have to get a standards conversion master made. Your duplication house will either be able to provide the service or recommend someone who can do it for you. For more information on finishing, see Chapter 31, "Finishing."

- Résumés of key personnel
- Two to three stills of the actors taken on the set
- Photocopies of any reviews or interviews

Some people also include an interview they've done with the director or lead actors that press people can crib from.

An electronic press kit (EPK) is a video about the project. It comes in a variety of forms, but the ones I've seen usually have a trailer, interviews with key personnel, and some behind-the-scenes footage.

For more information on selling your show, see Step V, "Selling: How to Keep Your Shirt."

BUYING EQUIPMENT

Most people who want to make DV movies want to buy a DV camera. Price versus power makes a lot of the prosumer cameras a very good value. But people rarely think about audio, lighting, and rigging equipment. Although you can always rent, you may want to purchase some key pieces so you'll always have them on hand.

Many DV moviemakers are also interested in purchasing a nonlinear editing (NLE) system with which to edit and otherwise manipulate image and sound. I understand the impulse. I own my editing suite. With the way I work, I couldn't afford to make DV movies any other way.

Following are some general guidelines about purchasing DV equipment you should consider while developing your project. Purchase and learn the equipment before principal photography and remember: If you purchase, you must maintain.

DV CAMERA PACKAGES: THINGS TO CONSIDER

You never just buy a camera. You buy a camera package. This includes the camera body, lenses, power supplies, batteries, cases, audio adapters, filters, monitors, tripods, and so on (see Figures 2.2, 2.3, 2.4, and 2.5).

DV camera. Consider what format of DV you want to work with: DV, DVCAM, or DVCPRO. That will often affect features and pricing. With consumer and prosumer cameras, *camera* means camera body and lens. For professional cameras, this means the camera body alone.

Lenses. If you want to use interchangeable lenses, you need a camera body that can handle that. Very few prosumer cameras have interchangeable lenses, so you may be looking at a pro-level camera. Fortunately for prosumer buyers, the lens that comes with the unit is versatile, so you may not

 NOTE

$$$

Figure out what you do and don't like by renting equipment at first; plus, you'll ease the strain on your wallet. There are other tools and lots of tricks that we'll go through in Step III, "Production: Action!"

need interchangeable lenses at all. Plus, third-party manufacturers make add-on wide-angle lenses for these cameras, although they're pricey.

FIGURE 2.2

Camera operator Matt Lambert with a JVC GY-DV500 on a Sachtler 18 fluid-head tripod with spreaders.

Number and size of CCDs. Get a 3-chip camera with the largest CCDs you can. A 3-CCD system uses a dichroic prism to split the light into red, green, and blue, expressed as *RGB*. Each color has a dedicated CCD chip for processing, so a 3-chip camera will give you better image quality. CCD size determines how many sensors are available for each RGB image. The more sensors, the more detail and the better the image.

1394 Input/Output (I/O). Don't get a camera without a 1394 input/output (I/O). The 1394 I/O allows you to transfer DV footage from your DV camera to your nonlinear editing system, and then back again. You can make digital clones of your master tapes from your camera to a separate deck if you need to.

FIGURE 2.3

Sound DSR PD-150 DVCAM prosumer camcorder.

Analog video I/O. Analog in and out is very handy if you need to transfer analog video to your DV system. Analog output is necessary if you want to use a field monitor, a highly recommended practice. (Monitors are discussed later in this section.)

FIGURE 2.4

Moviemaker Jeff Miner with his Canon XL-1.

Optical image stabilization (OIS). OIS uses mechanical elements in the lens to shape the image when the camera shakes. It's preferred over electronic image stabilization (EIS).

Viewfinder. Black-and-white viewfinders make focusing easier, which is why pro cameras have them. Most prosumer DV cameras have color viewfinders, and many now have LCD viewfinders. Although handy, LCD viewfinders are not reliable regarding color, focus, and other issues. If you want an LCD viewfinder, consider a camera that has a color LCD and a standard eyepiece viewfinder.

Zebra stripes. Professional and some prosumer cameras offer *zebra stripes*. Zebra stripes are electronic flags that show up in the viewfinder as horizontal lines across overexposed or saturated parts of an image. They look a lot like a zebra's coat. You adjust exposure until the stripes are minimized.

Manual control. You want to control as much of the image and sound as you can. Manual focus, exposure, and zoom are required. So is manual audio. Unfortunately, many consumer and prosumer cameras have an automatic gain control (AGC) that rides levels on your sound whether you want it to or not. Look for controls that you find easy to access and manipulate, and can do what you need to do.

FIGURE 2.5

JVC GY-DV500 DV camera. Courtesy Shooter's Broadcast Services, Inc., Seattle.

Power supplies. You'll want a rugged AC power supply. Some can power a camera and charge a small battery simultaneously. Batteries are the easiest way to power your camera, but you need at least enough for no more than two battery changes per shoot day and a charger. Consider battery belts for longer run times.

Cases. There are two kinds of cases you need: hard and soft. The hard case protects the camera and camera equipment within a hard-shelled box filled with foam. Soft cases are great for protecting the camera gear on the set. A good hard case protects your camera from just about anything, whereas a soft case protects it from dust, smoke, and some rain.

If you're going to be shooting in water, you need a specialty marine case to protect the camera. If you're expecting rain or snow, you may want to use a rain cape or rain jacket. If it's going to be cold, consider a heated soft case to keep the camera and camera operator's fingers warm.

Filters. Camera filters have two functions: to manipulate an image and to protect the lens. At minimum, you need a UV filter on every lens to protect the glass.

Monitor. Every time I shoot without a monitor, I end up dissatisfied with the image. Make your life easier by buying and using a good video field monitor—not an LCD screen, but a pro-level field monitor with a bluegun-only setting. You'll need batteries, charger, AC power supply, and a case for it. Make sure you have a cable and adapters to go from the camera's analog video out to the monitor's video in.

Tripod. Even a cheap one is better than none at all. Tripods consist of several parts: the head (that's what you put the camera on) and the sticks (that's the three legs). Spreaders keep the legs from folding up on themselves. Consider getting a fluid head if your budget allows for it. Fluid heads are easier to use, allow you to pan and tilt more smoothly, and are usually more rugged.

AUDIO GEAR: THINGS TO CONSIDER

Many people experience serious sticker shock when they see the prices for audio equipment. Sound is just as important as picture, so commit yourself to buying the best you can afford.

Like cameras, sound equipment should be considered as a package. The package includes a mixer, headphones, boom, microphones, and mic mount and cables. For some cameras, it may also include an audio adapter box.

Audio adapter boxes. Many prosumer cameras require a special adapter that allows you to plug in pro audio equipment. These adapter boxes fasten underneath most camcorders and provide two XLR mic/line inputs and one stereo output that goes to the miniplug of the camera. Some new prosumer DV cameras can handle pro-level audio feeds and do not require the adapter boxes. They need an adapter cable that converts from XLR female to stereo mini.

Mixer. Your location sound mixer on your sound crew will ride the level of the audio using a mixer (as shown in Figure 2.6), giving you greater control over the audio going to tape. The mixer should have enough inputs, generate phantom power and 1kHz tone for setting levels, and have stereo outputs. Be sure it's battery powered so you don't drag cable and to lower the chance of AC interference, resulting in buzzing on your audio track.

FIGURE 2.6

Shure FP33 field mixer.

Headphones. Not earbuds, but earphones. A good pair should be plugged into the DV camera and worn by the sound mixer on the set. You may want a second set for the boom operator.

Boom. A boom places a microphone in the best location to capture the best audio. They come in all sorts of sizes and prices. Many DV moviemakers use paint roller arms and other extending poles quite successfully.

Microphone. You need an external microphone with a fairly narrow pickup pattern. Shotgun and short shotgun (shown in Figure 2.7) mics are very useful. So are lavaliers. These microphones come in two types: dynamic and condenser. Dynamic microphones tend to be cheaper and not as sensitive. Condenser microphones are usually more expensive and very sensitive.

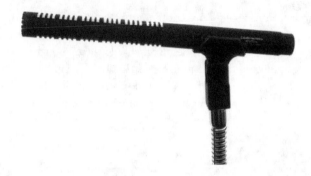

FIGURE 2.7

Audio-Technica 4073a short shotgun microphone.

Mic mount and cables. You need some kind of microphone mount so you can put the mic on the boom. The best kind is a shockmount, which floats the microphone to lessen handling noise. You also need lots of appropriate cable. (See Figure 2.8.)

FIGURE 2.8

Rycote modular suspension mount for shotgun microphones. This mount is set for mono use and has Rycote's Connbox to eradicate cable-borne noise.

LIGHTING AND RIGGING GEAR: THINGS TO CONSIDER

If you think there are a lot of options with cameras, wait until you see your choices with lighting and rigging equipment. I recommend you rent most of your lighting and rigging gear. It's expensive, heavy, and it has to be stored and maintained.

See Step III, "Production: Action!" for more details and techniques on lighting equipment.

Light kits. There are many types of lights. Start by considering a tungsten kit with three fixtures of various sizes and types.

Fresnel instruments have lenses allowing you to focus the light. They're very handy, but when you just need a lot of illumination, open-face instruments will do. Make sure it comes with stands, scrims, barn doors, and so on, all in one case. You also need extra lamps of two types: tungsten (3200 Kelvin) and daylight (5600 Kelvin). Make sure the kit is for motion pictures and has solid support equipment. Nothing can ruin your day like getting a hot light right on the noggin.

C-stands, grip heads, and grip arms. C-stands hold just about any piece of motion picture equipment, especially flags, scrims, and cucalorises. C-stands always come in handy, so you may want to get at least two with grip heads and grip arms.

Gels and diffusion. You need color correction gels and diffusion materials. Reflectors are always handy and you may want to consider getting a reflector holder to mount on a c-stand. You can also combine open-face lights with softboxes, egg crates, Chimeras, and other diffusion tools to make the light softer and more pleasing, especially on faces.

Flags, nets, and silks. Flags cut light completely, nets cut light partially, and silks diffuse light. Get a couple flags, one single and one double net, and a silk or two. As you work with the lights, place the flags, nets, and silks in and around the source to see what effect each has. Just be careful— although they're all treated, they will scorch and burn.

NLE: THINGS TO CONSIDER

You can buy or you can build. Either way, you need hardware and software to get DV footage in and out of the nonlinear editing system. See Step IV, "Postproduction: Directing the Movie," for more information on using this equipment.

Capture card. The capture card allows you to transfer to and from your DV source deck and your computer's hard drive. The capture card may be an interface, with the DV compression and decompression (codec) software based. It may be a hardware-based codec, with the same kind of processor and data handling as a DV camera. Hardware codecs are fast and expensive; software codecs are slower, but significantly cheaper.

Source deck. You can use your DV camera as a source deck, but that does place extra wear on the heads. Manufacturers offer various DV videotape decks you can keep with your editing system. They offer various functions at various price levels.

Capturing and editing software. Your choice depends on computer platform, available drivers for a specific application, and which one feels the most comfortable for you. Most editing applications allow you to control your DV deck, select what you want to transfer from a DV tape, and transfer it. Often a demo or light version of the application is bundled with the capture card or NLE system you buy. There are also several demos of editing software available on the enclosed DVD.

Hard-drive space. Two gigabytes of hard-drive space will hold about 9:30 of DV footage. If you have an hour to transfer, you'll need about 13 gigs. Having more than one hard drive is a good idea—you place the editing software and scratch disks (the place where the editing application will hold temporary files) on the main drive, and your audio and video files on another.

I MEAN BUSINESS

Show business is 10 percent show and 90 percent business.

There's plenty of room for creativity in business. Identifying opportunities requires some imagination, as does coming up with solutions for problems. And most of all, it takes a creative mind to put yourself in the other person's shoes.

Imagine you're an investor and a moviemaker approaches you for some cash. The moviemaker has no business card, no business plan, no script, and isn't even wearing a clean shirt. How can you take this person seriously?

As a producer, you're not just representing your project. You're representing yourself, your skills, your company, your future, and everyone working for you. You need to be professional. *Professional* doesn't just mean wearing a business suit and carrying a briefcase—although in some instances, that's exactly what you need to do. Professional is an attitude: You care about your potential partner's needs. You don't want to waste his or her time, so you've done your research, developed a business plan, consulted an attorney—in short, you've taken care of business.

Coming in prepared makes an excellent impression, one that says this investor, distributor, writer, or name actor can expect a fair, and potentially lucrative, business relationship with you.

There are a lot of business details that need to be taken care of in the development stage, such as forming a production company, drafting contracts, contacting possible buyers, and so on. It can be frustrating because you really just want to make a movie. But don't skip any of these details. You'll be happy you've taken care of them all in the midst of production.

YOU HAVE THE RIGHT TO AN ATTORNEY

I've worked with the same entertainment attorney, Neil Sussman, since 1996. In addition to knowing his business and the entertainment industry, Neil's smart, ethical, and has a cache of very bad lawyer jokes. Every time I hang up the phone after speaking with him, not only do I understand the issues and options of a specific contract or agreement, I'm reminded to think ahead and be clear about what I want. I also have another horrible joke to tell at cocktail parties.

You need an entertainment attorney. Do not ask your Uncle George the litigator or your neighbor Louise who works in tax law. Get somebody who knows his or her way around the entertainment minefield.

An entertainment lawyer can play a key role in helping you attach private investors to your project. They often have contacts with groups of investors who want to invest in motion pictures for tax-related purposes.

Entertainment lawyers are also crucial in equipping you with the contracts, agreements, and releases you're going to need for your project. Get them now while in development to give yourself time to read and understand every clause and provision. It's incumbent upon the producer to have and understand the correct contracts.

Your lawyer will also help you negotiate options on literary properties, as well as offers you get from distributors or other buyers.

To find a good attorney in your area, ask other moviemakers. You can't underestimate the power of a recommendation. Many bar associations have lawyer referral services to help you find an attorney and you can always ask lawyers you know. Check the listings from your local city or state film commission.

I also recommend Mark Litwak's *Dealmaking in the Film and Television Industry: From Negotiating to Final Contracts* as a guide to the various legal instruments you're sure to run across. Litwak also has an excellent Web site at www.marklitwak.com. For more listings, see Resources. When you meet with an attorney, ask

- How long have you been in practice?
- When did you begin focusing on entertainment law?
- Have you handled motion picture contracts before?
- What professional organizations do you belong to?
- What markets, festivals, and other industry events do you attend?

Check the local bar association and Better Business Bureau to see whether the attorney has had any complaints. To be doubly careful, check the county courthouse for any legal action taken against the lawyer or law firm. What you're looking for are the number of lawsuits and their outcomes, and what the attorney is alleged to have done.

The lawyer will undoubtedly ask you some questions about what your goals are and what your expectations are regarding hiring an attorney. Many have a one-page agreement explaining your obligations as a client that you may have to sign and another page describing what the attorney will try to do for you. You may have to give the attorney a retainer. Don't sign anything or hand over any money until you're sure this is the person you want to work with.

Personal chemistry and common ethical outlook play a part in this relationship. Pay attention to your gut—if you don't feel this is someone whose counsel you can trust, keep looking.

In the meantime, review the sample agreements in this book. Modify the forms as needed, and then take them to your lawyer to be vetted. Depending on your project and production company business structure, you may need other contracts, agreements, releases, and letters in addition to these:

DEVELOPMENT

- Partnership agreement—A written statement defining any partnership you form with anyone else for your project or company.
- Option and option execution agreements—Agreements to remove a literary property from the market while you develop your project. After development is complete, you execute an option to fully and legally license the audiovisual rights of the property.

- Shopping agreement—Similar to an option, but more informal, this agreement allows a producer to shop a literary property for a short period of time without defining compensation or any other terms.

- Screenplay submission agreement—An agreement signed by someone who sends you an unsolicited screenplay or treatment that he or she won't file a claim should you produce a similar movie without the writer's participation.

- Life story release—More extensive than the personal release, this release generally applies to people who are the subject of a nonfiction motion picture. Get this signed immediately.

- Product placement agreement—This agreement grants you permission, and sometimes money, to use a product in your show. If you want a product placement agreement, get your script in shape and reviewed. Approach the manufacturers early. They'll want to review your script before agreeing to anything.

- Trademark release—Go through your script one more time to see whether there are any props or items in set dressing for which you'll need a trademark release. Contact the trademark owner for a release. The owner may want to review the script ahead of time, so do this early.

- Screenwriting agreement—A contract to hire a writer to write a screenplay.

- Nondisclosure agreement—An agreement that goes to potential investors, subcontractors, and others, where they promise not to discuss the project with anyone except their advisers. Some writers will insist on a nondisclosure agreement before pitching to you. If so, walk the writer out to his or her car and wish him or her a pleasant drive home. Demanding this level of nondisclosure is a sign of the writer's inexperience and that may cause you problems later.

- Attachment letter or letter of intent—An informal one-page note that states an actor, director, executive producer, or anyone else will consider working on your project with you. It binds the person to nothing, but it's proof to potential investors that you've at least been talking with these people.

PREPRODUCTION

- Talent and crew contracts—After you've hired people, get their names on a contract defining compensation and other terms.

- Personal release—If someone walks into a shot and is identifiable, you'll have that person sign this release allowing you to use his or her image, voice, and so on.

- Location release—Permission to use private property or an exterior of a public building.

POSTPRODUCTION

- Master Recording License agreement—An agreement granting you access and permission to use a specific audio performance.

- Sync Rights agreement—An agreement granting you the right to synchronize music to picture.

- Soundtrack Licensing agreement—An agreement granting you the right to use a recording as part of a soundtrack album or collection.

FORMING A PRODUCTION COMPANY

Setting up a production company as a separate business entity is a good idea. Each business structure has advantages and disadvantages. Although federal rules apply across the board, states, counties, and cities may have additional regulations you have to follow. Talk with an attorney or accountant to make sure you understand the advantages and disadvantages, and what you'll need to set up your business.

Generally, these are the three most common business structures for production companies:

- Sole proprietorship

- Partnership

- Corporation

More general business information on business structures can be found on smallbiz.biz.findlaw.com/, www.nolo.com, and the IRS Web site at www.IRS.gov. See Resources for more listings.

SOLE PROPRIETORSHIP

A sole proprietorship is the simplest form and with it you and the business are the same. Business income and business losses are reported on your federal income tax return.

Establishing a sole proprietorship is inexpensive and relatively uncomplicated. In all likelihood, you'll have to get a business license, but be sure to check. If you're going to conduct business under a trade name, you may need to file an assumed name or fictitious name certificate. You can operate as a sole proprietor as long as you're the only owner.

The biggest disadvantage of a sole proprietorship is that you have unlimited personal liability. This means that someone can sue you and go after not only your business assets, but your personal property as well, such as your car, bank account, and house.

Advantages	Disadvantages
Easy and (c)(3) Corporation inexpensive to create.	Owner is liable for debts. Liability is not limited to the value of the business.
You have total ownership and control of the business.	More difficult to borrow money or obtain outside investment.
All the profits of the business belong to you, the owner.	All management responsibility is with the owner. You've got no one to share the burden.
No additional federal taxation on business profits.	
No periodic business reporting to the IRS or other government agency.	
Report business profits on your personal income tax form.	

PARTNERSHIP

If two or more people are going to own and operate the production company, you need to choose between establishing a *partnership* or *corporation*.

In a partnership, business ownership is divided between two (or more) partners. There are two types of partnerships.

The *general partnership* is the most common. In a general partnership two or more partners are fully involved in the operation of the business and all partners share both profits and liabilities.

A *limited partnership* provides for limited liability of the limited partners, meaning that their liability is no greater than the partner's investment in the partnership. Basically a limited partner provides all the capital and shares in any profits or losses, but is not actively involved in the management of the company. At least one general partner handles running the business and remains liable for all the debts of the partnership.

If you decide to form a partnership, write a partnership agreement. You can have a partnership without one, in which case you'd be governed entirely by either the Uniform Partnership Act or the Revised Uniform Partnership Act. But you want your partners to know exactly how they fit into the project and to stick to those roles.

Beyond the written agreement, the paperwork is minimal. You may have to file a partnership certificate to register your partnership name, and you may have to obtain a business license.

A partnership doesn't pay income taxes, but you must file an informational return that tells the government how much money the partnership made or lost during the tax year and how much belongs to each partner.

Limited partnerships have advantages. Limited partners can't interfere with the moviemaking process managed by the general partners. They also have disadvantages. SEC regulations are complicated, whether it's a public or private offering, and require research and expert advice from an attorney or accountant. In addition to federal filing, each state has its own regulations.

Advantages	Disadvantages
Easier and less expensive to create than other structures.	More expensive to create than a sole proprietorship or general partnership.
The partnership does not pay federal income tax. An informational tax return (IRS Form 1065) must be filed which shows income/loss to each partner.	Partners are personally liable for debts.
Liability may be spread among the partners.	Formation and subsequent changes in structure are complex.
Investment can come from the partners in the form of a loan. That creates interest income for the partners and a business deduction for the partnership.	Misunderstandings, different goals, and so on can weaken or destroy the partnership.
Partners report their share of profit or loss on their personal income tax returns.	If limited partners become actively involved in running the business, they lose liability protection.

Advantages	Disadvantages
Limited partners can't meddle.	Unless written into the partnership agreement, the partnership will dissolve on the death of a partner.
	General partners have unlimited liability. You may also be liable for the commitments of your partners.

LIMITED LIABILITY CORPORATION

The Limited Liability Corporation (LLC) blends the tax advantages of a partnership and the limited liability advantages of a corporation. State laws control how an LLC is created and the federal tax regulations control how an LLC is taxed. Owners of an LLC are referred to as *members*.

Members of an LLC have limited personal liability. The members risk only the individual member's share of capital paid into the business and any business debts that the individual personally guaranteed. That means any debts accumulated by the partnership are not the responsibility of a single member, unless that member guaranteed repayment of the debt himself or herself.

Nearly all states allow an LLC to be formed by just one person, although the LLC will not be taxed as a separate entity, like a regular corporation, unless you choose to have it taxed this way. Normally, you won't choose corporate-style taxation, but will have your single-member LLC report its profits (or losses) on your personal return.

If you have an LLC with two or more members, it will be treated as a partnership for tax purposes, with partners reporting and paying income tax on their shares of LLC profits. Unless you elect to have the LLC taxed as a corporation, the LLC reports its profit or loss on an informational return that notifies the IRS of how much each member earned or lost. Members will then report their individual shares of profits or losses on their personal income tax forms.

Advantages	Disadvantages
Owners have limited personal liability for debts even if they participate in management.	More expensive to create than a sole proprietorship or general partnership.

Profit and loss can be allocated differently than ownership shares.	Legal assistance is required to set up and the paperwork is complex.
	State laws may not match federal tax changes.
LLCs can choose to be taxed as a partnership or corporation.	The LLC dissolves if one of the owners dies or otherwise leaves.
No federal taxes, just like a partnership.	
No limit on the number of stockholders.	Some states require that an LLC have more than one member.
More than one class of stock is permitted.	
Business losses may be deducted on your personal tax return.	

C CORPORATION

If you're concerned about limiting your personal liability for business debts, you may want to set up your business as a corporation. Limited liability protects you from corporate debts that you haven't personally guaranteed, as well as from claims by people who are injured by business activities not covered by insurance.

A C Corporation requires that you file papers with the state and pay an incorporation fee. The corporation's assets and liabilities are separate from those of the owners. Because the assets are separate, some people retain copyrights to certain assets (screenplays, motion pictures, and so on) in their own names. If the corporation goes bust, the owner still owns the copyrighted material.

Federal taxation of corporations is complicated. Basically, a regular corporation is treated as a taxpayer separate from its investors and must pay corporate income tax. But a regular corporation may not have to pay any corporate income tax at all. In most incorporated small businesses, the owners are also employees. They receive salaries and bonuses that eat up all potential profits, so there's no taxable income left.

Structuring your business as a corporation is essential if you need to attract investors through a public offering. It's easier than it used to be. A small corporation can raise from $1 million to $10 million annually through a limited public offering.

Advantages	Disadvantages
Owners have limited personal liability for debts.	More expensive to create than partnership or sole proprietorship.
Shareholders (the owners) enjoy personal limited liability.	Tax returns require the help of an accountant.
Easier to obtain business capital than with other legal structures.	Double taxation on profits paid to owners.
Profits may be divided among owners and the corporation in order to reduce taxes by taking advantage of lower tax rates.	Recurring annual corporate fees.
The corporation does not dissolve upon the death of a stockholder or if ownership changes.	Business losses are not deductible by the corporation.
Owners can split potential profit among themselves, leaving none for the corporation to pay taxes on.	Paperwork can be a burden.

S CORPORATION

An S Corporation is owned by one person. It's easy to start, has little regulation, and the paperwork is fairly light. Electing to do business as an S Corporation gives you the limited liability of a corporate shareholder, but you pay income taxes on the same basis as a sole proprietor. As long as you actively participate in the S Corporation, business losses can be used as an offset against your other income.

Most states tax S Corporations the way the feds do: They don't impose a corporate tax, choosing instead to tax the shareholders for corporate profits. Some states do tax an S Corporation the same as a regular corporation.

Advantages	Disadvantages
Owners have limited personal liability for debts.	More expensive to create than a sole proprietorship or general partnership.

Advantages	Disadvantages
Owners report corporate profit or loss on their personal income tax returns. No federal income tax, and in most cases, no state income tax.	Legal assistance is required to set up.
Owners can use corporate loss to offset income from other sources.	Income must be distributed according to ownership share.
The S corporation does not dissolve if one of the owners dies or leaves.	More paperwork than an LLC having similar advantages.
Wholly owned subsidiaries are permitted.	Maximum of 75 shareholders.
Only one class of common stock is permitted (no preferred stock).	

501(C)(3) CORPORATION

Approaching some foundations, government institutions, and other grantors for funding requires nonprofit status, or at least a fiscal sponsor that has nonprofit status. Getting grants, however, is not the only reason to incorporate as a nonprofit. The organization is also tax-exempt and has personal liability protection.

The most common federal tax exemption for nonprofits comes from Section 501(c)(3) of the Internal Revenue Code, which is why nonprofits are called 501(c)(3). If your production company obtains tax-exempt status, not only is it free from paying taxes on all income from activities related to its nonprofit purpose, but people and organizations that donate to the nonprofit can write off their contributions.

Forming a nonprofit corporation usually protects the directors, officers, and members of the nonprofit from personal liability for the corporation's debts and other obligations. You can lose that protection if you or another corporate officer personally guarantees a bank loan or other debt the corporation defaults on, fails to deposit taxes or file returns, does something intentionally fraudulent, illegal, or stupid that causes harm, or mixes corporate and personal funds.

Unlike for-profit corporations, a nonprofit corporation cannot distribute any profits to its members, contribute money to political campaigns, or lobby. Many documentary moviemakers decide to form a nonprofit corporation to be eligible for certain types of grants.

Forming a nonprofit corporation is similar to forming a regular corporation. The difference is that you must also file federal and state applications for tax exemptions.

Advantages	Disadvantages
Corporation doesn't pay income taxes.	IRS can say no to tax-exempt status.
Contributions to charitable corporation are tax-deductible.	Full tax advantages available only to certain groups.

INSURANCE

Insurance is a fact of life. Depending on your project, budget, and business structure, you may want insurance to cover certain aspects of your show. The type of insurance and amount of coverage really depend on the kind of show you want to do, your sales goals, and your comfort with risk. Your attorney can help you assess what is right for you.

Equipment Rental. Rental houses require insurance on their equipment. For a set fee, the underwriter will cover loss, damage, and theft of rental equipment.

This is a good idea. I had a rented Sachtler tripod stolen off a beach. The thing was never more than six feet away from me and everyone was wearing bathing suits. I can only think of one place the thief could have hidden it and it makes me squirm. And not with delight.

The tripod's replacement cost was $2,500. My production insurance covered it, although it was like pulling teeth to get them to come across.

Your homeowner insurance policy may cover rental equipment, but check first. Rental houses will take just about anyone as your insurer, but your insurer may challenge a claim for a business loss if it's made on a homeowner policy. Talk with your agent and rental house before proceeding.

Comprehensive General Liability (CGL). CGL covers you if someone sues you, alleging injury or property damage caused by your negligence. If you want to shoot in public streets, parks, or other property, officials will require insurance to grant you a permit.

I know some producers who don't get CGL or permits, hoping their production company corporate status will shield them should something terrible happen. Whether you do this or not depends on your comfort with risk.

Completion Bond. This insurance guarantees that the movie will not have to cease production due to lack of funds. Banks and investors usually require completion bonds.

Errors and Omissions (E&O). E&O insurance protects distributors and broadcasters from claims based on any failure you made in clearing all of the elements in your show. They may require E&O before going forward with a deal. E&O insurance is expensive and you have to fill out an application to get it. Have your attorney review your script for anything that is defamatory or invades someone's privacy before you apply for E&O. You can solve these problems ahead of time, making the process easier.

When applying for E&O:

- Include a copyright report to show clear chain of title and do a title clearance.
- Have releases for everyone, as well as necessary music clearances.
- If you're using distinctive locations, get signed location releases.
- Secure agreements for everyone who provides material, goods, or onscreen services.
- Include your final shooting script.

The application is forwarded to underwriters who assess the risk, decide whether to issue a policy, and how much to charge you. If there's anything questionable on your application, the underwriters contact their lawyers, who in turn contact your lawyer. Your lawyer responds, and back and forth, until the underwriters offer you terms or reject your application.

Many producers don't bother with E&O until they have a deal that requires it.

There are other kinds of insurance and your insurance agent will know all about them. See the Resources section for listings of agents selling E&O and other insurance. You can also find agencies on the Internet or listed with your state's film commission.

SEE AND BE SEEN

Development is a good time to get involved in your local film and video scene. This includes attending festivals, attending meetings, readings, and screenings, and perhaps taking a few classes. You'll meet people of various levels of skill and experience, hear about all sorts of projects, and may even have the chance to work on a few no- or low-budget sets.

Television commercials (especially local nonunion shoots), corporate and industrial videos, and so on, are more good places to get experience on a set. You may even get paid for a couple days of work.

Don't limit yourself to this circuit, though. It's easy to get caught up in talking about movies and never making them. Reach out to people outside of the video and art communities, especially local media and small businesses. You'd be surprised at who wants to make a commercial or training video. Lots of people are interested in making shows for their community organizations—you can get some valuable experience and do a good deed. Moviemaking isn't for the shy, so get yourself out there.

You can also check some of the resources listed in Resources.

Create a contact list. Include all possible media outlets in your area, distributors you think would be interested in your show, the trade papers, and other print and online magazines about DV, independent movies, and so on. Make it a complete list with names, addresses, phone numbers, Web sites, and so on.

Watch the local shows broadcast from local stations for the names of producers. You can contact them directly. This is also true of local radio stations, especially public radio. A simple, sortable database will handle this material nicely. Code your list according to each category:

- Local press.
- Trade press. The trades and interested print and online magazines, user groups, e-mail lists, and so on. See the Resources section for listings.
- Distributors.
- Possible funders. Venture capital firms, investors, donors, rich relatives, and so on.
- Other. I usually include contact names of other producers, directors, and writers, as well as festivals and markets.

See the Resources section for listings that will help you develop each category of your contact list.

PR

Press releases can be handled in two ways: You can hire someone or you can write them yourself. If you decide to do them yourself, write each one ahead of time and have the envelopes stamped and addressed. Later, all you have to do is fill in the blanks, print the most recent, stuff the envelopes, and drop them in the mailbox. Plan a minimum of five mailings of press releases over the course of your show.

Your first press release should be an announcement about your company and your current project. Try to keep it to one page with a couple of quotes. Figure out the one thing that sets your project apart from all of the other DV movies you hear about. Geography? Location? Subject matter? There has to be something and that will be your hook.

The trick is to send out enough material to keep people interested without annoying them. Annoyance can be allayed by relevant, interesting, and entertaining information, so put some thought into your press releases. If a reporter thinks you might be an interesting interview, she or he might just give you a call.

WORK THE WEB

There are two kinds of contact you need to make: getting your message out to your potential audience and getting your message out to your potential partners. The Internet is instrumental to both of these endeavors.

- World Wide Web—If you don't have a Web site, get one. Register your domain name and use it on everything—your business stationery and swag. *Swag* refers to shirts, hats, and other stuff you give away. If you don't want to design your Web page, hire someone. A Web page is an inexpensive way to promote and keep promoting you, your company, and your project. Remember to put your press releases on your Web page. If you don't know how to create and maintain a Web site, consider trading video work in exchange for Web help.

- E-mail—Opportunity doesn't just knock. It e-mails. Opt-in e-mail is a great way to remind people of what you're doing and to build the kind of relationships that keep returning benefits to your show. Just don't spam.

- Online communities—Online communities are great places to find support and like-minded people. Lurk for a while to figure out whose opinion is actually relevant. A lot of information is useless and picking out the gems takes a bit of work. Consider building, supporting, or contributing to an online discussion group, newsgroup, forum, or chatroom for other DV moviemakers.

COLLATERAL

Imagine you need $35,000 from an investor. An investor is interested in your project and has asked to meet with you. You pitch with your whole heart a project that's ready and a company that's in place. It goes really well and the investor gives you a big smile when you shake hands before you leave.

Then she asks for your card.

A business card is often the first contact a potential partner has with you. It's your lead marketing piece and it makes an impression. If you're handing out cards obviously printed from your computer that are poorly designed and not even proofread, it says something about you. And it's not good.

If you don't think that investor isn't going to make a judgment based on that card, you're wrong. If she can't trust you to produce a decent business card, how can she trust you to make a motion picture? Your entire pitch is designed to remove any obstacle to a possible partner saying yes to you. Don't let a poorly crafted business card wreck it. The only thing worse is no card. It says you're not prepared.

Get your business stationery ready. Design it yourself if you're so inclined. You may be able to trade a screen credit for some design or print work. Make sure your contact information is correct and proofread everything before going to print.

You don't need four-color printing. Black ink on crisp stock with a bit of style says you mean business. And that's what people need to know.

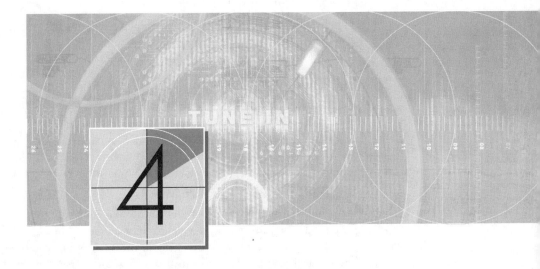

DON'T TREAD ON ME: INTELLECTUAL PROPERTY AND OTHER THORNY ISSUES

An attorney sells services; a camera manufacturer sells goods. Generally, when you sell a motion picture, you are actually selling licenses to certain rights protected by intellectual property law, granting access to the motion picture.

U.S. intellectual property law is guided in terms of the value or potential value of a work of intellectual property in the marketplace. That is what U.S. copyright law seeks to protect—not quality, reputation, or culture. If you think of intellectual property in these terms, a lot of the rules start to make sense: If what you do will harm the owner's pocketbook, you're probably infringing on someone's intellectual property.

Michael C. Donaldson has a terrific book, *Clearance and Copyright: Everything the Independent Filmmaker Needs to Know*, which covers these issues in depth and with style.

There are three types of intellectual property: patents, trademarks, and copyrights.

- A *patent* protects technical information and arises from a government grant.
- A *trademark* protects symbolic information, such as a brand or logo, and arises from use.
- A *copyright* protects expression and arises automatically upon creation.

PATENTS AND TRADEMARKS

It's unlikely you'll be filing patents during your show, but I know several DV producers who've built devices for motion picture use. After they finished making their movies, they refined the devices and sold them to other moviemakers. If you've done this, you may want to speak to a patent attorney (your entertainment attorney can recommend someone) about filing a patent and pursuing licensing or manufacturing.

A trademark or service mark is a brand name used by a business to distinguish its products or services from others. No one's required to register a trademark, although registration allows the trademark owner to receive triple damages and reimbursement of attorney's fees should the owner file a claim of infringement and win.

In *Clearance and Copyright*, Donaldson reasons, "You have every right to make a realistic film. Therefore, all the trademarks and product names that show up in a realistic scene are fair game. However, if the trademark or copyrighted work is a story point or if a lead character comments on the work, or if the camera lingers overly long on it, you should obtain permission."

So, if a product is onscreen for only a moment and not identified, and if no one mentions or uses it, you don't need a release. If you don't disparage the product in any way onscreen, you probably don't need a release. Remember to ask yourself whether your use could hurt the trademark's owner in the pocketbook. If it is, you might want to seek permission.

Please remember that I'm not a lawyer and you should speak with your attorney before proceeding. A release never hurts and your distributor or insurance company may require you get one for every identifiable product.

COPYRIGHTS

Copyright is the right to copy. The Constitution allows the creator of a certain work a monopoly on that work. The creator can exploit the work as she or he sees fit. Basically, you made it, you own it. Copyright protects original works of expression, such as plays, paintings, sheet music, recorded music performances, novels, software code, artwork, sculptures, photographs, choreography, and architectural designs.

The Copyright Act of 1976, the federal law providing for copyright protection, grants creators a bundle of intangible, exclusive rights to their work. These rights include the right to

- Make copies of a protected work
- Sell or otherwise distribute copies to the public
- Create adaptations and new works based on the original protected work
- Perform or display a protected work in public

To be eligible for copyright protection, a work must be

- Original
- An expression of the creator
- Of a nonutilitarian nature
- Fixed in a tangible medium of expression

If the work meets all four criteria, the creator automatically has copyright, whether it's registered or not. Since 1989, when the United States joined the Berne International Copyright Convention, a copyright notice is no longer required for a work to be protected.

Certain aspects of fictional works aren't subject to copyright protection. These aspects include

- Facts
- Writing style and individual words and phrases
- Literary devices
- Stock characters
- Events, scenes, situations, or details that follow from the theme or setting

The last comes from a legal principle called *scènes à faire*. This term means "obligatory scene," and copyright doesn't cover scenes that flow naturally from the general premise. *Scènes à faire* contain elements that necessarily result from the choice of setting or situation. For example, a sheriff confronts an outlaw.

NOTE

Product Placement

Trademark permission is closely related to product placement. *Product placement* means using a specific product in your movie in return for some consideration from the manufacturer. It's unlikely that an independent DV moviemaker would receive any money for product placement, especially from a large company. It's simply not worth the company's time to negotiate an agreement for a project that may never get wide distribution. Also, remember that theft is a real possibility. If you ask to use a product as part of a placement arrangement, you better make sure you can compensate the company if it's lost, stolen, or damaged. At minimum, though, you may be able to negotiate a trade-out, where you get permission to use the product onscreen in exchange for getting a supply of the product for the cast and crew.

The Resources section lists several product placement companies.

Scènes à faire, like material in the public domain, can be used by anyone, and can't be copyrighted. However, your expression of the scene in a fixed form is protected by copyright. If you write a script about a sheriff confronting an outlaw, that probably is protected.

Copyright registration is not mandatory, but it gives you the right to get attorney's fees and statutory damages up to $100,000 in an infringement suit. Regardless of registration status, if someone wrongfully uses your material covered by the copyright, you can sue, demanding compensation for economic loss and stopping further harm.

Generally, the people who create the works own the copyrights. There are three exceptions:

- An employer owns the copyright of a work created by an employee in the course of employment.
- A business or person other than the creator may own the copyright by purchasing it from the creator.
- A commissioning body owns the copyright in a creative work when the creator works as an independent contractor and signs a work-for-hire agreement.

The last point is important for producers. If you hire a writer to create a screenplay, you may want the contract to stipulate that this is a work-for-hire so you're sure that you own the copyright of the script.

PUBLIC DOMAIN

Most copyrights last for the life of the creator plus 50 years. If the work is a work-for-hire or is published anonymously or under a pseudonym, the copyright lasts between 75 and 100 years, depending on the date the work was published. When a work is not covered by copyright, it is said to be in the *public domain*.

Most works enter the public domain because their copyright has expired. When a work is in the public domain, it can be used by anyone without the creator's permission. Generally, the public domain includes

- Works no longer protected by copyright, including anything published more than 75 years ago
- Works in which no copyright ever existed, such as materials printed by the U.S. government
- Ideas, including procedures, processes, systems, concepts, principles, and discoveries

- Themes, titles, inventions, and typeface and industrial designs
- Facts or news of the day

To determine whether a work falls into the public domain, you may want to consider getting a detailed history of the work. Although you're free to search the records of the Copyright Office yourself, you may want to hire someone to create a copyright report for you. See Resources for listings of companies specializing in copyright reports.

FAIR USE

Because society benefits from the free exchange of ideas, unauthorized use of copyrighted materials is allowed when the use serves scholarship, education, or an informed public. This concept is called *fair use*.

Fair use is the exception, not the rule, to copyright law. There are very strict guidelines to determine whether your intended use falls under fair use, including

- Whether it's a competitive use
- The amount of the work you're using
- The nature of the material taken

Work used in the desire for commercial gain is unlikely to be considered fair use. Desire for commercial gain has a very wide definition, whereas fair use has a very narrow definition. Your status as a student or teacher has no bearing—if your use is for commercial purposes, it's not fair use. For example, a professor may be able to use a sound recording to illustrate principles of sound design in the classroom, but not in the trailer for her DV feature.

PEOPLE: PRIVATE AND PUBLIC

Have you ever wondered why characters in movies are rarely given last names? Or why they live in fictitious towns? Or why they work but you're never told where or what they do? It's to avoid a lawsuit by someone with the same name living in the same place and having the same job.

People clearing scripts get paid to do things such as look through phone books to see whether real people share the names and circumstances of fictitious characters. They do other things as well, but the idea is to make sure that there is no way any individual can file and win a claim based on invasion of privacy.

The *right to privacy* is the individual's right to control his or her person. The U.S. Constitution makes no mention of such a right, but the Supreme Court has said that such a right is implicit in both the Constitution and the Bill of Rights. You have the right to live without being subjected to unwarranted and undesired publicity—basically, the right to be left alone.

Go through your script and see whether a normal viewer could reasonably identify a real person based on what's in your movie. Pick up the phone book and see whether there are people or businesses with the same names as those in your show. Some people suggest using only a first name for your characters.

Other issues involve a reasonable expectation of privacy. A person at home taking a bath has a reasonable expectation of privacy. For you to shove a camera (preferably one in a watertight housing) into the bathtub is an invasion of that privacy. However, if that same person is taking a bath in a public street, that person can't expect the same level of privacy.

Producers of nonfiction movies, such as documentaries or historical shows, need to be very aware of the right to privacy. The best defense is a signed release for everyone on camera. Your attorney can discuss this and other issues with you at length.

LOOKALIKES, SOUNDALIKES, WALKALIKES

You may be tempted to hire someone who looks, sounds, or moves like a performer you couldn't get. Unless you're forthright about using a copycat lookalike, soundalike, or whateveralike, you could be in some serious trouble.

If you can't get the star you want, go in a different direction. Stars' faces, voices, styles, and so on have value in the marketplace and they have the right to protect their identities. Identity appropriation is a serious offense. When in doubt, don't do it. Even if you're not in doubt, check with your attorney before proceeding.

DEFAMATION AND SLANDER

Defamation is the dissemination of anything designed to injure someone else. *Libel* is defamation that is read; *slander* is defamation that is said.

While fiction moviemakers rarely deal with defamation, nonfiction producers need to be aware. If you're claiming that the movie you made is truthful, you'll want to have at least two sources of reference material for every assertion, especially for the really juicy stuff. Make sure the sources are independent of each other. Quoting a book that quotes a newspaper and quoting the newspaper isn't enough.

Defenses to a claim of defamation include

- Truth—Even if something isn't perfectly true, if you checked your facts and have a reasonable basis for believing they're true, you should be okay. Of course, people have different opinions on what is true, so do yourself a favor and recheck your material, especially anything inflammatory.

- Opinion—If what someone's saying is an opinion, make it clear that it's an opinion. Having someone start with, "Well, I think…" isn't enough. It has to be clear to a reasonable person that what's being said is opinion and not fact.

- Humor—If a reasonable person understands it's a joke, you haven't harmed someone's reputation. However, adding, "I'm just kidding," to the end of a flurry of insults is not a cover. Remember, reasonable people have different ideas about what is funny.

Being vindicated in court can hurt almost as much as being wrong. The point is to avoid going to court at all. Get releases for everyone and speak with an attorney about these issues so you understand what's involved.

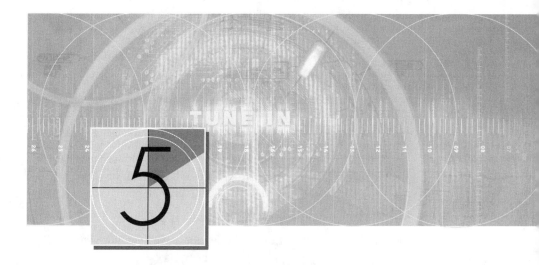

WHO'S BUYING WHAT: SURVEYING THE MARKET

Every movie has an audience, but not all of them have a market. The difference between the two is that an audience will watch, but a market will pay to watch.

The first question you need to ask yourself is whether there's a market for your show. If there is then there's bound to be a distribution channel. Whether you decide to do it yourself or go into business with a distributor, you'll be working those channels to generate revenue.

Hollywood Reporter, Daily Variety, Weekly Variety, Screen International, and the American Film Marketing Association (AFMA) have information about trends in the motion picture industry. The National Association of Broadcasters (NAB) sells directories and other research information about TV, radio, and other aspects of the broadcast industry. Cinemedia at www.cinemedia.com has an alphabetical list of Web sites with more information.

If you don't have distribution when your show is completed, announce that it is available in *Daily Variety, Weekly Variety,* and the *Hollywood Reporter.* Call them and they'll fax you a form. Fill it out and fax it back. They'll list your show alongside the big-budget flicks, along with your contact information and principal actors and crew.

See the Resources section for contact information and more listings.

After you know what kind of market your show may have, you can make some conservative estimates about potential revenue. Using this potential revenue as your guide, you can devise various production scenarios and budgets to see what makes sense financially for your show.

In addition to the directories, ads, and word of mouth about distributors, you may want to consider attending one of the film and video markets. These markets include

- American Film Market (AFM)
- International Film Financing Conference (IFFCON)
- Independent Feature Film Market (IFFM)
- Marché International des Films et Programmes pour la Télévision, la Video, le Cable et le Satellite (MIPCOM)
- Marché International des Programmes de Télévision (MIP-TV)
- Mercato Internazionale Filme e Documentario (MIFED)
- National Association of Programming Executives (NATPE)

Official reports from the markets are usually available and many independent film and video magazines run articles about the markets. If you decide to attend, read up on events from previous years and study the catalog. You probably won't be able to speak to every possible buyer, but you'll at least make contact with other people in the business. If you do pitch your project, follow the guidelines specified by the network or distributor. Don't hound anyone, and be sure to wear comfortable shoes, carry breath mints, and keep your expectations low. You probably won't sell anything—at least, not right away.

See the Resources section for contact information.

MARKET SEGMENTS

There are eight potential market segments for any show:

- Theatrical release, both general and art house
- Pay-per-view television
- Cable television

- Broadcast television, including public television
- Foreign markets
- Video, DVD, and other home-use formats
- Educational
- Internet

Each of the market segments has its own requirements and deliverables. You can find directories of distributors in the Resources section.

THEATRICAL RELEASE: GENERAL AND ART HOUSE

Wide-release theatrical means the multiplexes. Most of these screens are block-booked in advance by Hollywood studios. While not impossible, it is unlikely that an independent DV feature will get wide theatrical release. This may change—theater owners will run anything that will get paying customers in the seats.

Art house or specialty theatrical release may be possible, although you may have a problem if the theater has no video projection system.

If you want to work with a distributor seeking theatrical fiction features, find out whether it has videotape-to-film funds available or relationships with digital projection companies introducing new technology to movie theaters. Otherwise, you may have to bypass theatrical.

If you want to handle theatrical distribution yourself, be ready to devote at least a year of your life to delivering prints or projection dubs, posters, one-sheets, and ad slicks, all while constantly on the phone trying to convince reluctant theater owners to book your movie and reporters to write about it. It's a grueling job and you'll find out quickly why distributors demand so much of the money.

If your heart is set on showing your movie in a movie theater, you may want to consider four-walling. Four-walling is renting the theater yourself to project your show. You take all the risk, but you get to keep all the money from ticket sales. Concession stand money, however, goes to the theater.

Microcinemas offer another way to get your show to an audience. Microcinemas are usually set in the back room of a bar or coffeehouse. Customers may or may not pay an entrance fee to watch your movie. You get little or no money, but you may be able to sell VHS or DVD copies after the screening.

PAY-PER-VIEW TELEVISION

Pay-per-view may be interested in one-off independent features. There are two types of pay-per-view deals. The first is the better-known cable or satellite offering that's usually reserved for sporting events. The other is closed-circuit television (CCTV) often found in hotels around the world. I sold my feature, *Amazing World*, to a pay-per-view company during the summer of 2000. My deal was with a content provider for a hotel chain's CCTV system.

See the Resources section for listings and contact information.

CABLE TELEVISION

It's tough, but not impossible, for an independent show to air on cable channels. Your work will be edited for their time slots.

Cable channels such as the Independent Film Channel, Bravo, and so on claim to champion the work of independent moviemakers. Some cable channels, such as The Learning Channel and Discovery Channel, often work with independent producers whose shows fit their current lineups.

See Resources for contact information and more listings.

BROADCAST TELEVISION, INCLUDING PUBLIC TELEVISION

Commercial television has shown great reluctance to embrace quirky, independent shows of any kind. With so many channels available 24 hours a day, you'd think there'd be room. Unfortunately, broadcast stations would rather air reruns of *Gilligan's Island* than an independent offering. No disrespect to Gilligan, but honestly, how many hours a day do you need to watch him?

Public television may be available. Some public TV series or stations even offer coproduction or production financing. You'll find, however, that the competition is fierce, the money is small, and the tastes of programmers tend toward vanilla. Two public television shows that get national carriage and accept independent movies are *Through the Lens* and *P.O.V.*

Through the Lens will air your program and pay you nothing for the privilege. *P.O.V.* will pay you enough to cover the costs of your deliverables to them, such as E&O insurance, closed captioning, and so on. Independent producers are crawling all over one another to get a slot on these shows.

You can approach regional public television stations that carry independent work. WGBH in Boston, KQED in San Francisco, and WTTW in Chicago are known for their innovative programming.

Local PBS stations may also be approachable provided your movie has an identifiable regional interest. Call one of the station producers and ask.

ITVS, an independent entity outside of the Corporation for Public Broadcasting, offers funding programs to independent producers twice a year. These are not grants but distribution deals. They provide production funds in exchange for exclusive domestic television distribution rights and a piece of any other sale you may make.

See the Resources section for listings.

FOREIGN MARKETS

Foreign markets include theatrical, television, video and DVD, and so on, but are a separate category because of the unique challenges they present. Generally, unless you have existing contacts with buyers from foreign markets, you may want to consider leaving foreign markets in the hands of a distributor with experience.

Most independent moviemakers will approach an international sales agent with a script, director, budget, and cast in place. There are two types of sales agent. The first gives the producer a contract that guarantees the bankable portion of the budget. In return, the sales agent gets 20%–30% of foreign sales and equity on the back-end profits.

The other kind of sales agent can't guarantee the budget. But this person will take your package to film markets in the effort to raise production funds through foreign presales contracts.

VIDEO, DVD, AND OTHER HOME-USE FORMATS

There are many distributors who handle only video, DVD, and other home-use sales. Usually, they sell to a niche market, such as alternative lifestyles, health, hobbies, and so on. They're quite specific when it comes to what they're looking for and they know their market inside and out.

Amazing World was sold as a video deal to Northern Arts/Naiad. This deal gives me a piece of the cover price for every video sold and I received a small advance against sales. Many video and DVD deals take this same royalty shape, although usually there's no advance.

Other distributors handle video and DVD sales to large rental chains. These movies are intended for wider audiences, and often were originally slated for theatrical release.

See Resources for more information.

EDUCATIONAL

Unless you have experience distributing product to the educational market, I suggest you go to a distributor to handle these sales. Often, a distributor will put together a movie and educational guide for classroom use.

INTERNET

There are many Web sites that offer all kinds of movies, and with the exception of porn, very few have shown a profit. What does this say about the commercial value of Internet-based broadcast?

The outlook is grim.

But there are ways other than profit to measure value. Because the cost of DV compared to other formats is so low, and the quality and ease of use is so high, you can make movies you want to make without worrying about return on investment. Your movies can enter the free exchange of ideas without having to please a client or investor. You can make a movie for fun. You can experiment with the technology. You can take tremendous artistic risks and not have bill collectors coming after you. This is astounding.

Selling online is like any kind of selling: It's hard work. Online retailing deals with the same issues as any other kind of retailing, including packaging, pricing, payment, fulfillment, and customer service. Add to that the issues with e-commerce: payment acceptance, sales taxes, shipping and tracking, and security. If your core competency is making movies, do you really want to go into retail?

If you decide this is the way you want to go, you had better promote your movie and Web site. If you don't promote it, make sure you have another shirt because you're going to lose the one on your back.

Let's say you get the word out, and people actually start giving you money. What are you going to do when something goes wrong—say the dupe house makes a mistake and your customers get a porn show instead of your flick. You have to fix it. Not Chet in the warehouse. Not Janet from Customer Relations. You. And, at the moment, you're on location, trying desperately to get a crucial shot, while an irate customer screams at you through your cell phone.

Now that's a pretty picture.

But let's say you get that all solved and you even figure out an elegant way of handling shipping and returns. You could still lose.

You have competition.

Your competition isn't just the 15-year-old trying to sell her version of the ultimate light saber battle in claymation. (Actually, that sounds pretty cool. I'd buy that.) You're competing with Sony, Miramax, Universal—companies with dedicated staff to promote, market, and sell their products.

If you can identify a specific group of people with one shared interest, and this is what you made your movie about, you may have a niche product. For example, if you produce a show about making your own shoes from toner cartridges, there may be an online community actively seeking information about that subject. If you already have a presence on those e-mail lists, Web sites, or newsgroups, let them know you've made the flick and it's available. Gently.

Finally, selling online may be a last-ditch effort. You may have made a terrific show, but have no distributor interested. This happens a lot more often than people like to admit.

In this case, selling online really isn't a way to generate revenue. If you believe strongly in the work, or feel the message is worthy, you may want to take the financial hit just to get the movie out. Before launching an e-commerce site, however, examine the other online venues that handle retail. You'll get an idea of the scope of selling on the Internet by studying these models and an idea of just how much time and money you'll have to dedicate.

And remember that self-distribution is still distribution, which means a programmer may skip making you an offer. In addition to bypassing home video/DVD distribution, you may have lost a theatrical release, because theatrical distributors are hesitant to go from home-use to theater.

Be sure you include this distribution method in your business plan—it may entice that one dot-com millionaire investor.

ASPECT RATIOS, FILMLOOK, AND TAPE-TO-FILM: PLANNING AHEAD

You need to think about aspect ratios, filmlook, and tape-to-film transfers now because these issues affect your potential markets. For example, if you have every intention of going into theatrical release, you may want to shoot with a 16:9 aspect ratio. At the least you'll need a tape-to-film transfer, which means more money. Either you'll have to raise those funds yourself, or find a distributor willing to pony up the cash.

If you believe your show would do well on cable, pay-per-view, or video, DVD, and other home-use markets, you may want to run your video footage through a filmlook application. Perceived value of a show is definitely affected by format. You can fool some people into thinking you shot on film, not video, and that can affect their ideas about the kind of offer to make, but you need to consider this now.

ASPECT RATIOS

Aspect ratio refers to the width of the frame versus the height. Standard-definition television (SDTV) has an aspect ratio of 4:3 or 1.33:1. Currently, movies shot in a 16:9 aspect ratio, such as feature films, are broadcast or released to video or DVD in 4:3 or letterbox.

There is an international broadcast standard in place for high-definition television (HDTV). HDTV has an aspect ratio of 16:9, meaning it's 16 units wide by 9 units high. It's referred to as 16:9 because that's easier to remember than 1.78:1.

Eventually, everyone will watch movies originating on 16:9 formats on 16:9 televisions. Some producers are choosing to shoot in 16:9 now for future sales.

Other producers are shooting DV in 16:9 with the hopes of getting theatrical distribution. The DV material will either be transferred to film, which has an aspect ratio of 16:9, or projected at 16:9 in theaters with video projection systems.

Aspect ratio sample, starring my cat, Emily. The ratio is 16:9 on the left and 4:3 on the right.

If you're considering shooting your movie in 16:9 format now, be aware that there is a right way and a wrong way to do 16:9 DV.

16:9 THE RIGHT WAY

The right way is to use either a camera with 16:9 CCDs or an anamorphic lens or adapter.

Cameras with 16:9 CCDs can handle both aspect ratios. When in 4:3 mode, the camera reads a 4:3 image from the center portion of the 16:9 chips. When in 16:9 mode, the entire chip is used. In either case, the number of scanlines remains the same. Cameras with 16:9 chips tend to be more expensive.

An anamorphic lens has a cylindrical element that squeezes the image laterally, so that you get the tall, skinny pictures like images in a funhouse mirror. This squeezing allows the 16:9 image to fit in the 4:3 frame.

You then need to unsqueeze the image in postproduction with a digital video effects (DVE) processor or an NLE plug-in, or by embedding the appropriate codes into the data stream to tell the receiver that the image should be displayed in widescreen.

Shooting with an anamorphic lens allows you to generate video masters in whatever formats from your finished master with the least amount of image degradation. The downside is that you need to buy or rent an anamorphic adapter and field monitor. In post, you'll need a DVE, NLE plug-in, or flag in the data stream.

Also, if what you want is to just letterbox your movie, anamorphic isn't going to do it for you. You may want to shoot 4:3 and letterbox in post.

Optex (www.optexint.com) and Century Precision Optics (www.centuryoptics.com) have anamorphic adapters to fit several models of DV cameras.

16:9 THE WRONG WAY

The wrong way is to simply chop off the top and bottom scanlines of the image to get the widescreen picture. When you throw the switch, the horizontal angle of view doesn't change, but the image is cropped at the top and bottom compared to the 4:3 image. When displayed anamorphically on a monitor, the camera has digitally rescaled the lines to fit the entire raster, but 1/4 of the vertical resolution has been irretrievably lost.

The bad news is that most prosumer DV cameras do 16:9 the wrong way.

What's a poor DV producer to do, if he or she can't afford a true 16:9 or can't find an anamorphic lens?

Shoot and protect. *Shoot and protect* means using the entire, nonwidescreen 4:3 image, but protecting your distribution possibilities by keeping important visual information in the center or upper 3/4 of the screen. That way you have the full-resolution 4:3 image for use now and can upconvert and crop for HDTV later.

It's very difficult for me to judge whether shoot and protect has a profound effect on sales. I know many producers who are following shoot and protect, but there are vaults full of 4:3 material that is aired on network and cable television, and will undoubtedly continue to be broadcast when we all have HDTV. My feeling is that saying you were careful to shoot and protect to cover sales to a 16:9 format such as HDTV will give you credibility with distributors—as long as you truly shoot and protect.

FILMLOOK

Filmlook is a process of filtering video footage so it looks more like film transferred to videotape.

If you plan to use some kind of filmlook on your show, keep these ideas in mind:

- Light each shot with depth and modeling, using layers of light and shadow.
- Don't zoom.
- Lock down your tripod or, for a moving camera, use a dolly. No tilts or pans, especially artifact-riddled whip pans.
- Try out camera filters for a diffuse look. Some moviemakers prefer Tiffen Pro-Mist filters, such as the Black Pro-Mist #1 or Warm Pro-Mist 1/2. These knock off a bit of high-frequency detail and add a bit of halation around highlights, reducing hard-to-compress high-contrast edges.
- Reduce the image sharpness.
- Use only fades, cuts, and dissolves for transitions in postproduction.
- In post, adjust gamma and add fake 3-2 pulldown, gate weave, dust and scratches, film fogging, and so on. Be sure to budget your time and money.

TAPE-TO-FILM

Tape-to-film is a transfer process that takes your video footage and transfers it to film stock. The point of the process is to take footage either originating on video or created in a computer (such as special effects) and put it into a format most movie theaters can handle.

There are many different ways of doing this, ranging in price from expensive to very expensive.

The first step is to choose a standard. Although NTSC is the broadcast and production standard in most of North America, you may be able to use PAL equipment. PAL video has 25 frames per second (fps), closer to film's usual 24 fps. According to some transfer houses, better quality will result with PAL. PAL equipment can be expensive in the United States, so shop carefully.

You'll also have to hold off on creating titles until after the transfer is complete. Rolling titles, in particular, look terrible when transferred. Factor in time and money for creating titles either on film or as a separate step in the process.

Finally, you will need an image that is as close to 16:9 as possible. Either shoot and protect or, even better, get a pro-level camera with 16:9 chips.

You'll need more money to handle the format and extra equipment, postproduction, film internegative, printing, and shipping (film reels are heavy). Remember to budget in the extra steps and equipment, and arrange your postproduction schedule as well.

Begin contacting tape-to-film transfer houses now for information on exactly what you need to do. Every transfer house has its own recommendations. Check the Resources section for listings of firms that do tape-to-film transfers.

Keep in mind you'll only need a tape-to-film transfer if you have a theatrical distribution deal or are going to seek theatrical distribution. Few festivals require a tape-to-film transfer, so reconsider writing that big check if you're going the festival route.

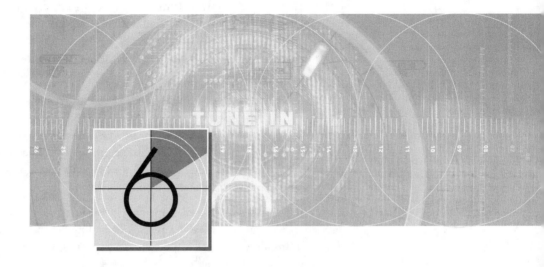

WHAT DO YOU GOT AND WHAT CAN YOU GET?

DV moviemakers are an ingenious bunch. We use props, tools, locations, and techniques Hollywood professionals wouldn't touch with a 20-foot carbon fiber boom pole. Some of the ingenuity comes from simply not having much money. A lot, though, comes from not knowing the accepted, and usually expensive, practices of the motion picture industry. Sometimes ignorance can be a blessing.

This doesn't mean there isn't planning involved. There is. At this stage of your project, you need to figure out precisely what you've got, what you're going to need to get, and where it's all going to come from.

Look out the window. What have you got right now that will help you define the setting, theme, motif, or characters in your story? What do you have that will make the entire process of making DV movies easier? What can you get that will give you a movie that looks different from others?

BORROWING COOL STUFF

I've known moviemakers who've spent inordinate sums on one item for one scene that ends up on the cutting room floor. If you want to make a movie that requires special sets, props, and so on, keep in mind that you're going to have to get all of this stuff somehow. If you already own it, great. If your friends have it, talk to them now about using their property.

You can go to clubs and organizations with special interests. For instance, Civil War reenactment organizations have many enthusiastic and knowledgeable amateur historians who may be interested in helping out as extras, consultants, or prop and wardrobe people. The Society for Creative Anachronism and renaissance festival participants may also have special knowledge and equipment, and be willing to work with you. The same holds true for local historians and museums.

Finally, you'd be surprised at how many people you know are actively interested in unusual hobbies and interests. One of my best friends collects and drives horse-drawn vehicles. She's an expert on these vehicles, as well as the horses and other animals.

Ask your friends and family. People's curiosity leads them to all sorts of places and most of them are more than happy to share their enthusiasms.

Start developing a relationship with these people now, not a week before you're about to shoot. Be clear about what you're asking. Don't assume because your friend will let you use her fancy sports car on one day, she'll let you use it again, or even that she'll let you mount equipment on it.

For example, for the DVD included with this book, I made a short DV movie called "Music Appreciation." In this story, one of the lead characters in "Music Appreciation" needed a nicer car than my truck. I asked a friend whether we could use her snazzy SUV. She was more than happy to let us, provided we didn't mount anything on it.

I had a coffeehouse lined up for "Music Appreciation," but I felt a theater would work even better. I'm working with a local historian on my current project, a documentary called *Verona: The Story of the Everett Massacre*, and I knew he has been involved in restoring an old local theater. I asked to use it. After chasing down the required people, we were given permission to use the theater for a nominal fee.

This brings me to the next point: Regardless of the size of your show, you're going to need a way to pay for it.

FINANCING

When it comes to movies, whoever controls the money controls the show. Your first option is to self-finance your project. Carefully assess your risk here. Only you know how deep you're willing to go into your own pocket. Make your budget and stick to it—it's easy to spend when you don't pay attention.

There is one big advantage to self-financing: You own the show. You can build a library without having to sign away your copyright. That's an important point.

You may need more money than you have immediately at hand. You have three choices: fundraise, borrow, or find investors.

FUNDRAISE

You have two choices when it comes to fundraising: Start holding bake sales (or the equivalent) or apply for grants. Essentially, both of these ways of raising money allow you to get funds without having to bring on partners or take on debt.

I know producers who have successfully raised funds for their projects by having parties and producing bands at local bars. It takes a while, but at the end, these producers have a small pot of cash for their projects.

The pool of available grant money shrinks a little more every day, whereas the number of people chasing it seems to get larger. It's not impossible for you to find grant money, but there are some tricks to make the next-to-impossible odds a little more in your favor.

Get a listing of all the appropriate grant organizations. See Resources for contact information and directories of grantmakers. Read through their brochures, Web sites, press clippings, and application packets thoroughly.

Find out whether the organization gives money to only nonprofit entities. If so, you have two options: form your production company as a nonprofit 501(c)(3) corporation or find fiscal sponsorship.

Fiscal sponsorship means an established nonprofit 501(c)(3) corporation is willing to sponsor you, your company, or project to make you eligible for certain kinds of funding. There are many organizations that offer fiscal sponsorship, such as the International Documentary Association (IDA) and the Association of Independent Video and Film (AIVF). There may be a local nonprofit media organization in your neighborhood that offers such sponsorship. Check your local film commission listings.

There usually is some kind of application and review process. If you're accepted for fiscal sponsorship, the sponsor will take a certain percentage of the funds you receive from grants, donations, and so on.

If the grant organization offers assistance with the application process, take it. The person taking your call knows what the organization is looking for better than you do and will guide you in that direction.

Follow every direction TO THE LETTER. Do not send more or less than requested and don't miss the deadline. You're being judged on how well you follow directions. Proofread every page and try to get someone to read your application materials before you send them.

LOANS

If people give you money for a project, it's either a loan or an investment. If it is a loan, it has an interest rate and you have to pay it back. If it is an investment, people expect to share in the profits. You can't get around an investment by calling it something else, such as *points*.

A point in this context is one hundredth of a percent. No matter how small that sounds, it's still a real thing. Unfortunately, many producers use the term "points" as a euphemism for "you'll never see a dime."

Credit Cards

Some moviemakers think that using credit cards to finance a show isn't borrowing. It is. I know two producers who have made their movies this way. One managed to make enough money from a distribution deal to pay off the debt; the other just keeps shifting it to low–introductory-rate credit cards.

Credit cards have three advantages. The application process is simple, you don't need to sign over collateral other than what you've purchased, and you can find credit cards with very low rates.

The disadvantage is that you'll be carrying debt. That debt is the amount you borrowed plus the cost of the money—the interest rate, fees, and so on that the credit card company charges you for borrowing in the first place. You want to factor in the cost of the money for any loan. The cost of the money can rapidly skyrocket due to the magic of compound interest. Get the amount high enough and you may not be able to borrow for life investments, such as a house or a college education. Miss payments and not only does your credit rating go down the drain, you may be forced into bankruptcy.

If you plan to purchase equipment, you can obtain financing from the dealer or manufacturer. For example, Sony offers consumer- and professional-level financing for its equipment, although I can't vouch for the interest rates.

Loans from Individuals

You can go to friends and family for personal loans. Just because you know them doesn't mean you shouldn't be professional. Sign papers specifying the terms of the loan and follow through. Do you really want your grandmother to think you're an irresponsible slob?

Banks

Banks loan money on assets. No assets, no loan. A script and finished movie are not assets. A distribution guarantee with guaranteed minimum payments is.

A producer licenses to a distributor specific rights to distribute a movie over a period of time. If the distributor guarantees a minimum payment, usually within two years of a typical seven-year distribution agreement, that's a distribution guarantee. You then borrow against those guaranteed funds for production money.

Distribution guarantees are difficult for independents to get. Basically, to get a loan you need to sell your show before you've made it. This will depend on your script, track record (if any), and star power. Star performers are almost required for any loan. That's why it's called a *bankable cast*.

Usually, the bank will require

- A synopsis
- A script
- Bios of everyone attached
- Chain of title documents
- A copy of the distribution guarantee
- A detailed budget
- A cash-flow chart
- Complete financial statements of all investors
- A security agreement putting the bank in first lien position
- An agreement between the distributor and the bank that the bank gets the producer's share of all money until the loan, interest, and costs are repaid
- A copy of the completion bond

You can't get a bank loan without a completion bond. A *completion bond* is an insurance policy that provides protection against over-budget expenses for the bank investing in the show. Rarely will no- and low-budget shows be able to get completion bonds because the bond companies figure it's simply not worth it. The overhead costs more than the typical 3%–4% fee based on the overall budget.

To get a completion bond, you need copies of

- The script
- The budget with minimum 10% contingency
- The production schedule
- The postproduction schedule
- A detailed special effects budget, if necessary
- All contracts with directors, actors, and producers
- All special contracts or agreements necessary for you to complete the picture

Talk with your attorney, accountant, and banker about loans and completion bonds before proceeding.

FIND INVESTORS

Money for independent motion pictures often comes from people outside of show business. You'll never really know why someone invests in your show. They may say it's a good investment or that they believe in the message, but it's just as often that they've always wanted to be in show business or they secretly want to be movie stars. Before approaching anybody, read Louise Levison's *Filmmakers and Financing: Business Plans for Independents*. It's a good guide for moviemakers considering finding investors.

When you're raising money from people, you're entering the field of securities. *Securities* can be membership units in a partnership, shares in a corporation, points, or anything else that expresses the person or business giving you money has a financial interest in your or your project's future.

Regulations regarding public offerings are relatively strict to protect less-sophisticated investors. Private offerings, however, are limited to investors considered sophisticated enough that they need less protection. Limit yourself to this group, along with some other requirements, and you may have a private offering.

Private offerings still require disclosure to investors, although you may be able to avoid the costly SEC provisions for public offerings. They're easier to set up, but you're limited to potential investors who are friends and business associates.

There are a few rules that should be followed when seeking out investors in any entertainment project:

- Make the investor realize that this is a very high-risk investment. Failure to make your investor aware of this could constitute fraud.

- The investor should realize that he or she might lose everything.

- Make sure it's a viable investment. If you don't get distribution before production, what's your plan?

You'll need certain things to appeal to investors, including

- An introduction
- A pitch
- A business plan

Introductions

You may be required to have someone qualified to approach potential investors, usually an attorney or accountant. You may also be limited to approaching only people you know. You'll probably start with them anyway. They may not know anything about moviemaking, but they may like you and sometimes that's all they need to write you a check. Ask your attorney or accountant for more information.

It's a good idea to have someone else introduce you regardless. If someone has turned down your project, always ask whether he or she knows someone who may be interested, and ask whether the person will make a call for you. Just remember that your conduct reflects on that person's recommendation. Be professional, polite, and persistent.

Pitches

Pitching is a time-honored tradition in show business. Basically, it means giving a quick summary of your movie in a way that's immediately appealing. A lot rides on the 25 or so words that make up your pitch. Develop one and try it out on people you know and trust. Hone it to a fine edge and rehearse it.

Try to stay enthusiastic about it—you'll be repeating these words over and over, so remember that your pitch is a reflection of you and your project.

BUSINESS PLANS

Whether you want to make one movie or ten, you'll need a business plan. If you're self-financing your project, a business plan is still a good idea. It helps you clarify exactly what it is you want to do and how you plan to do it. And should someone come along who wants to fund your project, you've got the important information at your fingertips.

Cicero said brevity is the soul of eloquence. Shakespeare said brevity is the soul of wit. Fran Lebowitz said brevity is the soul of lingerie.

You get the point: Your business plan needs to be concise. Imagine being handed a business plan that thuds when you set it on your desk. It's not likely you'll be perusing it any time soon. Any impression the hopeful moviemaker was going for will be lost because she or he didn't stop to think what it would be like to read anything that weighs more than a small dog.

Just because your business plan should be concise doesn't mean it should be content free. In 15–20 pages, your plan should be readable, substantive, truthful, and impressive to potential investors.

Your business plan may be the first impression an investor gets of you. You need to make it clear that you understand the business, you're a professional, and you're ready to go.

You don't need an advanced degree to write a business plan. But you need to do some researching and writing. Be sure to proofread carefully. One bad typo can ruin your whole plan. Organize it like this:

- Executive Summary
- The Company
- The Product(s)
- Business Environment
- Distribution
- Financing
- The Financial Plan
- Appendix

⌷ TIP

Include a cover letter on your business stationery with everything you send.

EXECUTIVE SUMMARY

The Executive Summary is an overview of the entire plan. Give a brief, honest description of your business and its distinguishing features.

Tell the reader what you're going to cover in greater detail in the later sections, including a brief description of your management team, DV projects, the motion picture industry and how DV movies are doing within it, the market for your show, distribution channels for DV movies, and how much money you have and how much you're asking for. Follow this with a summary of projected profit and loss over the next three to five years to give potential investors an idea of when they'll get their money back.

And remember to qualify any statements about future gain with words such as estimate and project.

THE COMPANY

Describe your company, including its history, location, and ownership structure. Describe the company's key players including their backgrounds and fields of expertise, as well as proposed additions to the team. Keep it short and put résumés in the appendix.

State what it is you want to do, such as the type of project you plan on making (short, feature, episodic on the Web, and so on), the budget, how long it will take, and what function the company will take, such as a production or distribution company.

Investors want to know where you're going to sell your product. Be as specific as possible and let them know that you expect to make money from distribution in theatrical or specialty film houses, foreign markets, cable cast, broadcast, wholesaling videotapes or DVDs, or selling directly to the consumer from a Web site.

THE PRODUCT(S)

Present a short, descriptive, specific overview of your show. If you have a script, use your one paragraph pitch for a plot synopsis and put a two- to three-page treatment in the appendix. If you don't have a script, say so and concentrate on what you do know, such as the genre and budget of the motion picture you want to make.

Disclose any assets that add value. If you have a name actor, director, or famous producer on board, mention that. If you've optioned an existing literary property, say so, and if it was a book, be sure to mention the book's sales history. Be sure to highlight your or your partners' experience in making DV movies.

If you have cash, partial funding, coproduction agreements, presales, soundtrack album deals, or any financial attachments, mention them now. You'll discuss them in greater detail in the financial section.

Finally, you'll need to give them your budget. A lot of producers just pick a number out of the air, or steal the information from someone else's project. Do a preliminary script breakdown and budget so you know what you're getting into. See Chapter 11, "Script Breakdown," and Chapter 13, "Locking the Budget," for information to help you create a preliminary budget.

BUSINESS ENVIRONMENT

The motion picture business is a crazy business. It's terminally hopeful and constantly transmogrifying. The influx of low-cost production tools such as DV cameras and editing equipment is merely another wrench among the works.

This part of your business plan discusses the state of the motion picture industry across distinct markets and how your show fits into them. These markets are

- Theatrical
- Pay-per-view
- Cable
- Television
- Foreign markets
- Video and DVD
- Educational
- Internet

Each market offers a potential revenue stream for every show, but be practical. If your project is destined for DVD, focus on that part of the industry. Include a brief explanation of how it works, reported financial data and projected sales, and how your project will get into the distribution channel. For example, will you approach existing distributors or will you market and sell the product yourself?

Each motion picture has specific production and distribution needs and has to be handled differently. Discuss only those markets relevant to your project. Identify the demographics of the market and include how you'll market to this audience. Your marketing plan includes how you'll promote your show and get it in front of your target market.

Although every producer I know thinks his or her show will appeal to every human being on the planet, the truth is that most movies have a limited audience. You must identify your movie's target audience, and explain to your investor who that audience is and how you'll make members of that target audience aware of your product.

Compare your project to the other motion pictures in the marketplace. Before you protest that your project is unique, all movies are unique. And before you say there's nothing out there like it, there is. It's better to know your competition, and how you'll differentiate your project, than blithely pretend otherwise.

By categorizing your project, you're explaining to the investor where your show falls in the distribution channel and general financing framework. If you're marketing a niche project with a small but enthusiastic audience, say so—production costs for DV are often so low that such niche projects can be nicely profitable. And if word-of-mouth gets around and others start buying, you may be able to do better than expected.

Because you've done your research and have identified your target market, you can suggest ways to promote your project to that audience. You don't waste time or money trying to get the attention of the people who aren't going to buy.

DISTRIBUTION

State exactly which distributor you're going into business with. Give a brief overview of that company, with additional information in the appendix.

If you haven't made a distribution deal, tell your potential investor exactly which distributors you've been speaking with and why you believe they are appropriate for your project. If you haven't been talking with any distributors, explain how you will find them—through film and video markets such as MIPCOM or MIP-TV, festivals, competitions, and so on.

If you're going to a producer's rep to place your project, say so. Explain who the rep is and how big a chunk of money he or she wants to do the job.

FINANCING

This section is where you offer your projected bottom line. Go through each market segment you feel applies to your project, compare sales numbers of recent DV movies with yours, and project your sales. Put supporting materials and the top sheet of your budget in the appendix.

Unfortunately, you're going to have a hard time finding hard numbers about DV movies. There just isn't much out there. Still, an honest comparison of what the industry is up to can point out opportunities. See Resources for listings of trade sources.

Be careful about what you promise. You may intend to presell territories, produce a soundtrack album, or publish books based on your project, but if you state them as facts, your investors will hold you to it. Unless you have commitments, contracts, and checks in hand, be careful about making such promises. But if you intend to pursue these sources of revenue, mention that.

THE FINANCIAL PLAN

This section offers a summary of projected profit and loss over the next three to five years, along with your reasoning for those projections. You have to forecast revenue and expenses, and the better your research, the better your guess. Remember to qualify everything by using words such as *estimate*, *may*, *projected*, and *intend*.

Explain every piece of money involved in your project. If you have in-kind contributions (gear, props, or labor), list them. If you have put in your own money, list that. If you have received grant money, list that.

Offer sales projections based on pertinent research from the *Hollywood Reporter*, *Daily Variety*, *Weekly Variety*, *Screen International*, and the American Film Marketing Association's listing of international sales. Limit the information to movies with similar budgets and subject matter. If you include the latest Hollywood $200-million extravaganza, you'll look foolish.

I don't know of anyone who's tracking data on DV movie sales on a regular basis. Luckily, independent moviemakers and distributors are generous when it comes to this kind of information. You can find out about the project, director, producer, and distributor by searching any of the print or online independent motion picture magazines.

Call up the producers and distributors and ask about sales. Not only will they tell you, this is also a good way to begin a relationship with a distributor and get familiar with that distributor's catalog.

Generally, you'll list the data you've gathered on sales of similar projects according to market segment. You will then offer your considered analysis of that data. Be honest—you're building a case for your project's success.

Even if you find movies that have only broken even or lost money, tell the truth and give your analysis of what happened.

Did they overproduce for the market? This means the producer spent too much money given the market for the motion picture. How will you remedy that? DV gives you a great advantage by lowering your production costs. Plus, if you buy your equipment, you can generate revenue by renting it out.

Did they underproduce for the market? That means they didn't spend enough money. For example, I know a producer who made a pilot TV series on VHS with very low production values. He had a great time, met some wonderful people, but never got the attention of a network. The people he was trying to sell to expected much higher production values than he delivered.

If your market segment is videotape and DVD sales, you'll need to project retail prices and generally, what your share will be if you make a deal with a distributor. Generally, you'll receive a royalty percentage that can range anywhere from 7%–13% of the cover price. Cover prices for videotapes range between $9.99 and $19.99, and DVDs retail for around $24.99, although it would be wise to research the most current pricing trends.

If your show costs more, explain why. In your marketing section, be sure to explain exactly how you're going to entice a customer to part with $79.95 for your show, even though similar products sell for less.

List your expenses based on your budget. Almost every producer I know just guesstimates what he or she needs. They need $150,000 because that's how much they need. Do it properly—make a preliminary budget. Don't be surprised if an investor asks to see the whole thing. You're going to look impressive if you have a copy immediately available.

Be clear about exactly how much you're looking for and what the investors get in return. Project potential sales and income across all market segments for 3–5 years out.

APPENDIX

The appendix should include contact information, letters of intent, copyright information, deal memos, option contracts, résumés of key management and cast, a two- to three-page treatment, and other pertinent documents that show how far along your project is. Don't include the script or the complete budget. If they want them, they'll ask.

PRELIMINARY BUDGETING: IF MONEY WERE NO OBJECT...

Someone who says money is no object is probably spending someone else's money.

Before you can make a budget, you need to have a script, script breakdown, and schedule. If you have no script, you need to get one. If you're seeking development funds, offer projected budgets for the movie you're going to make, but proceed with caution.

Many people pick a number out of the air when it comes to budgets. Don't do it. Although building a budget takes time, you really have to think about what it is you're trying to accomplish.

There are two ways to budget a show. The first is based on an assessment of how much you need: It requires you to fill out a budget thoroughly and to use that total when approaching investors. The other requires you to honestly assess how much money you think you can get, and then figure out how you should spend it.

I've done both.

Most no- and low-budget DV movies I know of use the how-much-can-you-get route. It's risky. Budgeting is based on your ability to schedule, not the other way around. I have been on shoots where producers decide that we'll do in four hours what really requires two days. Or the producer neglected to add in travel time, so the 10-hour day turns into a 16-hour day.

For your preliminary budget, first figure out how much you think you'll need. See Chapter 13 for more detail and line items. At this stage of a project, I budget as if I were paying full price for everything, the weather turns bad, and so on. Then, I multiply by two and have 20% contingency. I can trim, borrow, and beg later.

Budget items for a motion picture break down into categories: above-the-line costs and below-the-line costs. They're broken into these categories because that's where they fall on a budget sheet. Clever, eh?

Above-the-line is that part of the budget that covers the costs for the major creative participants: writer, director, lead or featured actors, and producers. These costs can be just about anything.

Below-the-line items refer to the technical expenses, location fees, extras, and labor costs. These are usually set costs. Tape stock is going to cost X. No agent is going to demand that tape stock get more money and its own trailer. Generally, the lower the budget, the higher the overall below-the-line percentage in the budget.

Many first-time producers make the mistake of thinking that because they have a sophisticated budgeting application, they can budget a movie. It's not the tool, but the person using the tool. If you're budgeting your show and you've never done it before, go through Chapter 13, "Locking the Budget." Think about all the factors that come into play.

Add up every item. Then, add in 10% to each line item for the stuff you forgot. Then, add 10% contingency to the overall budget. Then, keep your 10%–20% contingency line item as is. I suggest 20% contingency simply because if you spend everything, you've got nowhere to go. Studios build in overhead so they can rescue movies going over budget.

If you don't want to do a budget yourself, find an assistant director (AD) or unit production manager (UPM) to handle it for you. They should give you the most general schedule and terms, accounting for all contingencies. Remember, though, that a budget can't be final until your director has seen the schedule and the preliminary budget.

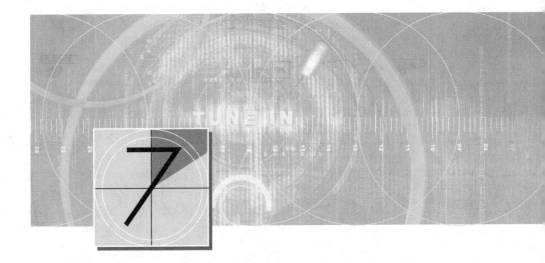

SEARCHING FOR A SCRIPT

If the movie you want to make is based on someone's life story, you need permission. If you want to make a movie based on an existing literary property, you need the audio-visual rights to the work. After you have control over the underlying material (book, article, life story, and so on) by optioning or outright purchase of the audiovisual rights, you can hire a writer to write a script.

You can also option an existing screenplay. More than 40,000 screenplays are registered with the Writer's Guild of America (WGA), while only about 400 features are produced in Hollywood every year. This is not a statement about quality, but I think the numbers suggest that there are people who want to get into writing for movies. You just have to find them.

You can hire someone to write a screenplay from an original idea or you can write the script yourself. I do, and know many other DV producers who do the same thing.

Often, it's the script that drives a person into producing. But be honest with yourself: If you have no talent for writing, find someone who does.

See Chapter 8, "Writing a Script Yourself" for information on writing screenplays.

LIFE STORY RELEASES

When you make a deal to portray someone in a motion picture, you must buy a bundle of rights, including protection from claims of defamation, invasion of privacy, and right to publicity. You may also be asking for cooperation from the subject and the subject's heirs, and access to letters, journals, diaries, and so on.

If the subject is deceased, many of the reasons for buying these rights disappear. Personal rights don't apply to the deceased. You can't defame or invade the privacy of the dead. Rights regarding publicity, however, may still apply depending on where you live. Your attorney will be able to help you with this.

Public figures have lives open to public scrutiny, so more of their lives can be portrayed without invading their privacy. Plus, public figures must meet a pretty high burden of proof to establish invasion or defamation—they have to show the moviemaker intentionally spread a lie or acted with a reckless disregard for the truth.

A life story release covers these issues. First, you and the subject must decide what rights will be granted. This may include remakes, sequels, and serializations, as well as the territory the grant covers, such as the world, North America, and so on. If you want access to other people in the subject's life, you'll have to get agreements from those people as well. Some financing and distribution agreements will require you to assign them these rights to get the deal, so be sure the release includes language to cover this.

Life story releases can be options or outright sale agreements. Usually, they include a reversion clause. Reversion clauses in any agreement provide that if the movie isn't made within a certain amount of time, all rights covered in the agreement revert to the person you're buying from.

You'll need language that discusses the consideration exchanged for the rights granted. A consideration is what distinguishes a contract from a gift. Although consideration is usually money, it can be just about anything. Usually for any release, I offer consideration of $1.00—and I pay it.

You can always fictionalize a true story by changing the names, locations, and other crucial identifiers so the public can't recognize the real people. You can then bypass the life story release.

There are other important issues regarding these agreements. Start with the life story release included in the Appendix and DVD of this book and modify it as needed. Just be sure to have an attorney scrutinize it and make relevant changes.

OPTIONING A BOOK, STORY, SCRIPT, OR OTHER PROPERTY

The most common way to get control of the audiovisual rights to an existing property is to option them. An option is the exclusive right to purchase something on fixed terms in the future. For motion pictures, an option means paying the person or entity controlling the audiovisual rights to take the property off the market for a length of time.

You can purchase outright the audiovisual or any other rights to an existing work, but an option is less expensive.

As a producer, you are trying to offer as little money as possible for the longest possible option term. I know several producers who regularly offer $1.00 for an option period of 18 months, renewable for another 12 to 18 months for another $1.00.

Why would a writer accept a buck? Because it's a buyer's market.

Before you write anyone a check, you need to make sure that you're dealing with the right person and that the property is free of encumbrances.

FINDING WHO CONTROLS THE WORK

To option an existing literary property, you must first determine who controls the work. It may be the writer, publisher, another producer, or someone else.

Some people suggest you try to contact the author, photographer, or other creator directly. Given the slight chance that person has ever dealt with a producer before, you'll probably be able to get a very good deal. At the very least, you may be able to get the creator on your side and that carries a lot of weight with agents and publishers.

Unfortunately, often the creators have no idea whether they control their works. This is especially true with music (which we'll deal with later in

NOTE

A Rose Is Not a Rose...

Film rights and *motion picture rights* are the same thing. I prefer *audiovisual rights* because it describes film, video, and any other motion picture technology that may come down the pike.

this book). You can spend a great deal of time in negotiation, only to find out you're talking with the wrong person.

I've had producers approach me wanting to option my novels. Each time, the producer contacted the publisher, who then passed the producer's name and number to me. Although I split ancillary rights with my publishers, the amount of money that could change hands was so small, the publishers didn't feel it was worth the effort. They asked only that I keep them apprised of any developments and let them know whether there was a contract offered.

This may be different for bestsellers, notorious topics, or famous authors. However, by the time regular people even hear about the latest hot properties, just about every right to that property has been sold off. Agencies and publishing houses feed material to big-buck Hollywood producers long before the work ever gets into print.

Still, you'd be surprised at what doesn't get optioned. If you love a book, article, short story, or other property and think it would make a great movie, go for it.

Start by contacting the publisher's Rights and Permissions department. They'll be able to tell you right away whether the property is available.

If the rights are available, you may be negotiating with the publisher, writer, or writer's agent. Whoever it may be, just be sure you're speaking with someone empowered to negotiate and make this kind of agreement with you.

FREE OF ENCUMBRANCES

Free of encumbrances means that the work hasn't been optioned or sold to anyone else.

An insurance underwriter may require a copyright report included with your application for Errors and Omissions (E&O) insurance. In that case, you need to do a copyright search. You, your attorney, or a company offering this service will research and create a copyright report showing whether the purported owner is not the copyright owner, whether the copyright has been sold or transferred, or whether any rights have been licensed.

Copyright reports apply only to material that has been registered with the U.S. Copyright Office. If you want to option a work published elsewhere or never published at all, you may have some difficulty finding a clear chain of ownership.

After you have determined that the work is available and that you are speaking with the right person, you can start negotiating an option/purchase or outright purchase agreement.

THE OPTION AGREEMENT

You've found the person empowered to negotiate. Be courteous and professional, tell him or her you're an independent producer, and ask what he or she wants in exchange for an option on the property.

If the seller wants more money than you have, don't give up. Usually the seller's position is negotiable—yours may be the only offer for the property, especially for obscure works. If the seller won't budge on the amount of money, walk away. If you just have to have the rights, get some serious concessions, such as a longer term, lower payoff, or other rights beyond the audiovisual rights.

Some of the most important provisions to an option agreement are

- **Definition of the work**—This specifies the work and includes any previous titles and copyright registration numbers.
- **Grant of rights**—This details exactly what the buyer is purchasing.
- **Grant of the option**—This includes the option price and first option period. As a rule of thumb, option prices are about 10% of the full purchase price, but it's negotiable. Sometimes a seller will give you an option for a nominal fee, such as $1.00. The option period can be an amount of time, but 12–18 months is common.
- **Rights of renewal**—This allows the buyer to extend the option for a specified period and an additional sum.
- **Terms for exercising the option**—This refers to the terms the buyer and seller have agreed on to purchase the rights optioned.
- **Purchase price**—This specifies the purchase price, either a flat fee or percentage of the motion picture's budget.
- **Additional compensation**—This covers any money, points, net profits, and so on the seller gets in addition to the purchase price.
- **Credits**—This spells out exactly what credit the seller will get.
- **Reserved rights**—If the seller wants to retain certain rights, they will be spelled out here.

The first option payment is usually *applicable*, meaning it counts as advance payment on the full purchase price. Payments made during the extension of an option, however, often are not applicable. Try to make all payments applicable toward the full price.

If the option expires, the seller retains the option money and the audio-visual rights as well. Some writers have repeatedly sold options on their works, making a tidy sum. I have a friend who bought a vacation house with the money from options of her mystery novels. If an option is exercised, however, the audiovisual rights belong to the buyer.

While negotiating the option agreement, you must also negotiate the purchase agreement. If you don't, you've just purchased a worthless option and no seller is obligated to sell on any terms.

There are other issues with option agreements. Your attorney can help you understand them to help you get the best deal possible.

THE LITERARY ACQUISITION AGREEMENT

A literary acquisition agreement is a contract to acquire the audiovisual rights to a literary property. Some of the most important provisions to a literary acquisition agreement are

- **Warranty of ownership**—The seller warranties that he or she is indeed the owner of the work, the audio-visual rights are available, and that the seller is empowered to negotiate this agreement.

- **Rights conveyed**—This specifies exactly what rights are being conveyed to the buyer.

- **Rights reserved**—This specifies exactly what rights the seller is reserving.

- **Right to make changes**—The buyer specifies that he or she may change the work according to the needs of the audiovisual work. This is standard. Sellers who can't stand seeing their work changed should either forgo selling audiovisual rights or become producers themselves.

- **Consideration**—This specifies exactly the terms of the purchase, including the purchase price and other money, profits, and so on.

- **Indemnification**—The seller promises that the work doesn't infringe on someone else's copyright or defame or otherwise injure anyone. This warranty means the seller promises to bear the burden of any litigation or damages incurred because of the seller's breach.

- **No obligation to produce**—This states that the buyer is under no obligation to produce the movie. This is an important clause, protecting you should you fail to pull together your project.

- **Reversion**—If the buyer fails to extend the option or make the movie, all rights revert to the seller after a period of time specified here.

- **Right to assign**—This allows the buyer to assign the rights to someone else.

Whatever you agree to, get it in writing. Make sure your entertainment attorney sees everything before you sign, and be clear about what you're asking for and your obligations.

THE INDEPENDENT MEMO

I've seen these only with independent projects. Basically, this memo deals with an informal agreement made between a writer and a producer. The writer agrees to take the property off the market for a very short period of time while the producer goes looking for financing.

All terms are to be negotiated later, dependent on the producer finding funds. Often, the property is a script that doesn't even exist yet. While the producer is pitching the idea to funders, the writer is feverishly writing.

These agreements are usually about a page long, often taking up three paper napkins from the local bar. I have no idea whether they have any legal standing. The people I know who have used them seemed pretty happy with the arrangement: formal enough, but not too formal, and very quick to execute.

Check with your attorney about this kind of arrangement before proceeding.

SPEC SCRIPTS

Spec scripts are screenplays written on the speculation that someone will buy them. They were not commissioned by anyone. Usually they are based on the writer's original idea, although sometimes a writer may have optioned or purchased the audiovisual rights to the work on which the script is based.

You can find spec scripts by letting people know you're looking for a script. You'd be amazed at what will come your way.

Try to give some kind of parameters of what you're looking for. If you want to make a romantic comedy, say so. Otherwise you'll be wading through stacks of the latest *Star Wars* rip-off. If the story needs to be set in a certain place (a town, in the woods, in a house), say that, too.

Use a submission agreement. It protects you from claims that you stole someone's idea. These are standard and there is no negotiation. Either the writer signs or you don't read the screenplay.

Your attorney can draw up an agreement or you can find a boilerplate version online. Just be sure the owner of that material gives you express permission to copy, modify, and use the document.

THE GREAT ORIGINAL IDEA

Some writers will come to you to pitch a script idea. The paranoia surrounding idea rip-off is palpable and some people will demand you sign a nondisclosure agreement before proceeding. This is a bit much for me, although I understand the impulse.

The writer may begin the pitch by saying something like, "Just to be clear, if you like the idea, we both understand that I get to write it." Give credit where credit's due. If you like the idea, negotiate with the person who pitched it. Although running around stealing people's ideas may not get you hauled into court, it brands you a creep.

If you have an idea for a movie but don't feel skilled enough to write a script, at least write a treatment. A treatment is a short version of your story. It may have some scenes written, or not. Just be sure to explain in detail who and what the story is about, plot twists, and other particular features. The more detail, the better.

Although ideas are not protected by copyright, copyright does protect the expression of those ideas in a fixed form, such as a treatment.

Protect the material by registering it with the Writer's Guild of America (WGA). You can register treatments or screenplays. Send them one 8.5"×11" unbound copy of the work with your full name and Social Security number along with the registration fee—$20.00 at this writing. The WGA will number and file the work for you. Registration is good for five years and you can extend it for another five if you pay another fee. Considering the protection and peace of mind, it's worth it. Plus, it's what the professionals do. See Resources for contact information.

You can also copyright the material. Contact information for the Copyright Office is also in Resources.

HIRING A WRITER: WHAT TO ASK FOR AND WHAT TO EXPECT

To hire a writer to write a script or treatment, you'll need a contract stating the services to be provided, when the material will be delivered, and for what compensation.

Hiring a writer is not like hiring anyone else on your project. Writers work alone, far away from the excitement of the set. Often, a writer is the first one to commit to a project and, especially if she or he isn't getting paid, is taking a huge risk that often goes unrewarded.

What do you do? Offer a working environment that a writer dreams about.

Treat the screenplay the way plays are treated in the theater—as sacrosanct. That doesn't mean the work goes unexamined, unrevised, or untested. Quite the opposite. You should fight about the script, but you need to fight fairly. Agree ahead of time who will be reviewing the script and whose feedback will be sought.

Bring the writer along for the entire process. The writer will be able to understand some of the difficulties inherent in making a motion picture and may understand some of your reasons for wanting changes. Some writers will enjoy the chance to work with directors and actors, developing characters, plot points, and themes—your actors may enjoy it, too. And having a writer on the set can be very helpful for continuity.

Sign a contract. This is a professional gig and you need to treat it professionally, regardless of compensation or lack thereof. Don't expect 47 revisions. First draft, one rewrite, and a polish are the standard. If the script needs more work, you need to address that in the contract. Either the writer will keep working for additional compensation, or you have the right to find another writer. Be clear about the terms. Set deadlines and pay schedules, whether deferred or not, and be up front about what you expect.

In return, the writer will expect you to respond promptly to any queries, give critiques quickly, offer fair compensation, and follow the schedule religiously. You are not to call every other day to find out how it's going, expect complete rewrites the next day, try slipping out of your financial responsibilities, or waste the writer's time with your nonsense.

Don't take credit for the script if you didn't write it. This happens so often, it's infuriating. If you came up with the story, take your Story By credit, but keep your mitts off the writer's credit. Look at the WGA's guidelines for determining credits prior to negotiating any agreement.

If it's just not working out, take action. Nobody likes getting the ax, but it's easier if it's done quickly.

If you hire a writer to write an original idea, you'll want a work-for-hire agreement that gives you the rights to the screenplay. If you hire a writer to revise an existing work, you will first have to option the material, and then hire the writer under a work-for-hire agreement.

WRITER AGREEMENT

A work-for-hire agreement for a writer is a contract that makes sure you're in compliance with U.S. copyright work-for-hire requirements. Some of the most important provisions of a literary acquisition agreement are

- **Terms of engagement**—This sets out the writing schedule in unambiguous terms. This section will also include options to hire the writer to handle a rewrite and polish. If you have this option, you can determine whether or not to continue working with the writer. This is good because some people are great at pitching, but lousy at writing. If you get a poor first draft, you can hire someone else to fix it.

- **Compensation**—The money, points, and other consideration the writer gets for doing the work. There are no typical fee schedules, though you can look at the WGA's guidelines for some ideas. Frankly, the writer will take what you offer or not work with you.

- **Credit**—There's always heartache when it comes to credits. Be careful about promising a certain credit unless you're funding your project. The WGA's guidelines for determining credits are a good way of handling this issue.

- **Ownership**—In a work-for-hire agreement, what the writer writes is yours. You bought it, you own it.

If you've hired a writer to write a script based on factual events, or if the writer has pitched a factual story, you may want to consider annotating the script. Annotating a script means citing source material for every relevant assertion in a screenplay. It's easier to do this as the writer is working, so decide whether you need this done right away. Coming back later requesting this information will get you one very unhappy writer.

Talk with your attorney before signing anything. Your attorney can draw up an agreement or you can find a boilerplate version online or in a book. Just be sure the owner of that material gives you express permission to copy, modify, and use the document.

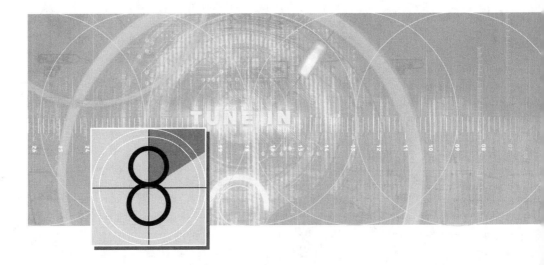

WRITING A SCRIPT YOURSELF

Syd Field and Linda Seger are justifiably famous for their books and articles on the craft of screenwriting. There are other books, as well as Web sites and articles, that discuss how to go about writing a screenplay. See the Resources section for listings.

Everything comes from your screenplay. It's your blueprint, the reference you use when making decisions about performance and technology. It's your touchstone. It's unlikely you'll have a level playing field with Hollywood in terms of money, special effects, or name talent. But you can compete when it comes to scripts.

Writing a screenplay requires talent, skill, and endurance. Why people think they can write scripts without ever writing anything more complicated than a grocery list is a bit mystifying. Still, there's nothing quite so humbling than to write and fail. You learn how hard it is to write anything, much less anything good, and develop a new respect for writers.

NOTE

Pay-or-Play

Pay-or-play refers to provisions in contracts that require producers to pay someone whether the movie gets made or not. Because there's no way to recoup the money if there's no product to take to market, and because the money is often substantial, many producers and studios will proceed regardless of what shape the script is in. They're betting that people will still pay for a ticket or video rental to see their favorite movie stars, or the merchandising will generate revenues even if the movie is terrible.

I am in favor of more respect for writers.

There's no reason to start production with an unfinished or incomplete screenplay. You probably won't have to deal with pay-or-play, so take your time to get your script the way you want it.

WHAT MAKES A GOOD SCRIPT?

I don't know. I do know that no one sets out to write or produce a bad script. Good screenplays (and good movies) seem to share certain characteristics.

- Verisimilitude
- Speed
- Structure
- Cohesion
- Intelligence
- Conflict
- Resolution
- Unexpectedness

VERISIMILITUDE

Verisimilitude is the making of a believable world. It does not mean realistic. Movies aren't realistic. Even nonfiction movies are manipulated to convey what the moviemaker deems relevant, important, or funny.

Verisimilitude functions as a way to make sure that people will continue to suspend their disbelief in favor of staying with the story. Every aspect of a movie is designed toward that end. For example, title sequences aren't in place just to fulfill contract obligations. They exist to ease a viewer from the struggles of the day into the world of the movie.

The made-up worlds of motion pictures require the careful management of appearances. This starts with the script that has believable characters. Not sympathetic characters. Not attractive characters. Believable characters.

SPEED

Screen life runs about four times faster than real life. Come in late and leave early. Give just what's needed and cut to the next scene. Hanging around watching irrelevant action is a waste of time.

Consider cutting any exterior shots of buildings, known as establishing shots. Why do we have them, especially on TV? People will say it's because the viewer will be confused as to where the next scene is taking place, but that's nonsense. Establishing shots exist to stretch out a show that has to fill a certain time period. Cut them.

STRUCTURE

Good movies, even experimental or conceptual, have structure, an underpinning that the moviemaker builds on from beginning to end.

I disagree that narrative movies are about characters changing. Characters can make life changes in an instant, but they mean nothing if not tested. The movie is about the test.

This is why I think movies are closer to fairy tales than novels. Fairy tales are about one moment: meeting the test.

Movies are about one moment. We throw in lots of decoration, such as subplots, comic relief, and special effects, but those are there mostly to fill time. It's hard to convince people to pay $10.00 for a three-minute movie. Everything in a movie is designed to get us to the test.

Getting the viewer to the test takes three acts for a narrative feature. The first act presents the rules: Here is the character (shown through action), here's the problem (often personified), and here's the solution to the problem (subtly conveyed in foreshadowing). Everything required later in the show is introduced in the first act. The more important the element, the closer it is to the beginning.

Action propels the character to the inciting incident. The inciting incident is what clues in the character that something is wrong. It's one thing that most people wouldn't even notice, except this character: the one thing for this specific individual, at this specific time of life, that can't be overlooked.

Yak will not deliver the goods here. Show it.

Problems are not easily solved in the movies. If they were, movies would be 15 seconds long. The second act is an adventure in complication. Complications arise through the character's effort, misperception, or misunderstanding.

These complications come about because the character reacts to the inciting incident in a profound way. Profundity in movies is purely subjective—water's only deep if it's over your head. Unfortunately, although the character knows something just isn't right, and may even know he or she has to change, the change has not been complete because the character hasn't been tested.

Toward the end of the second act, the character crosses a line. It may be physical, emotional, or spiritual, but once crossed, there's no going back. This is not limited self-awareness. The character finds a new resolve. The character makes a promise. The character is determined.

Then comes the third act. It runs 15–20 pages and begins with the climax. The climax is the test.

From the first frame of the motion picture, the story was heading for this moment. The lead character may win or lose, but the test is inevitable. What was foreshadowed is fulfilled.

Sacrifice is inevitable. Even if the character wins, he or she gives up something. It might be life or a way of living, a blissful state of unawareness, the girl, the boy, or the dog. That's up to the writer. How aware the audience is of the sacrifice depends on the kind of movie it is. Comedies may gloss over the sacrifice, whereas tragedies focus on it. It depends on your story.

Whatever you choose to do, the character must confront what is standing in the way—another character, a river, a spiritual lack, whatever. And through the character's own efforts, he or she must face the test.

The denouement is the landing. Depending on the kind of story you want to tell, it may wrap up loose ends or ease the audience out of the story.

COHESION

Every movie is one action. The main character wants one thing and either gets it or doesn't. That's it. Subplots expand or foil the main plot. They add dimension. If they don't, cut or revise them. Tell only what needs to be told—no more.

Usually, good movies don't cross genres. There may be elements of other genres present, but the movie picks its tone and stays with it. Transitions are tight—the story moves from scene to scene fluidly, without a jolt.

INTELLIGENCE

Leave out the stupid. I don't mean silliness or sophomoric humor. I mean the movies that assume we in the audience are too dumb to figure it out.

One of the reasons I dislike exterior establishing shots so much is that they seem to say that I don't have enough sense to know where I am. I feel the same way about shots that show signs, covers of books, or other writing. I don't need it, literally, spelled out for me, thanks.

As you revise your script, consider where you're being redundant, belaboring a point, or trying too hard to show how clever you are. We'll be much more impressed by a series of cuts that conveys a character's existential crisis than by listening to a character pontificate on Wittgenstein.

CONFLICT

This isn't the kind of conflict where someone is sitting there pondering. Conflict is given breath by the action of the lead or another character. Conflict puts the wind in the sail. Without the wind, the ship goes nowhere.

Tension comes from conflict, not the other way around. The needs of the characters—expressed by what they do, not what they say—propel the story forward. If you're adding scenes to make everything seem more dangerous and tenser to prop up the conflict, rethink.

The lead characters each want something. Sometimes the characters are barriers to each other; other times circumstances present hurdles. The characters must get through their respective conflicts through their own efforts. Not through divine intervention, luck, or because the script is 99 pages long and it has to end now.

RESOLUTION

Resolution does not automatically mean a happy ending. It's an easing of the tension created by conflict. The question *What will happen?* is answered.

UNEXPECTEDNESS

It's easy to go too far with the unexpected. You can go so far, you defeat your own efforts at verisimilitude.

The unexpected has boundaries set by the needs of the characters and expressed by foreshadowing. For example, if a character's primary motivation is ambition, show us (don't tell us) prior to the crucial moment when her ambition becomes a factor. We need that moment and we do pick up on the clues. We don't know we know, but when the ending comes, it feels right.

That's the trick. By the time the test comes, we know the character is going to do something, and usually we even know what form that action will take based on the genre and what's come before. But we don't know the concrete, specific, visual details.

SHOW, DON'T TELL

Your screenplay can be about anything you want as long as it's told through pictures. Your movie must show, not tell, through a combination of

NOTE

Lyrical and Experimental Movies

One of the nice things about DV is that you can produce screenplays that Hollywood would never touch. Short lyrical movies can be little gems. An experimental movie can be a discovery. They can be wonderful experiences, as well as wonderful movies. They can also be unintentionally pretentious, boring, and dumb as a box of hair.

If you want to make a movie of ideas then be sure you have one. And keep it short. Better to leave us wanting more than begging for less.

different images and sound cut together. A viewer responds to these combinations, adding to it the viewer's own imagination and experience.

By choosing and crafting combinations purposely, you manipulate the viewer into responding the way you want: with tears, anger, laughter, boredom, and so on.

A screenplay offers the director a map. The script is the path the director will take to achieve the desired effect.

As a screenwriter, you must craft a map that is clear, well-written, and can be made into a movie. You must show characters, themes, motifs, and plot for the director to interpret. Your script must be written so actors can become characters, DPs can design shots, post-audio people can design music and sound effects, UPMs can break down the script, and all the other people working on your movie can do their jobs.

Screenwriters labor so their work can be intentionally misunderstood.

YOUR WORKING METHOD

Regardless of your screenplay's subject matter, you need to figure out how you work. If you like to schedule your time then schedule it. If you like to work at night, work at night.

Just don't get caught judging the efficacy of a working method by how comfortable you are. Judge it by how much you get done and how good it is. You might hate getting up at 5 a.m., but if the work sings, you better set your alarm clock.

There are several other tricks you may want to consider using:

- Keep a pen and notebook by your bed. If you get an idea, write it down immediately. It'll be gone before morning.
- Read good books. Some of it may rub off.
- Talk with people you don't know. A lot of people who want to be writers hang out with other writers. Try hanging out with people in different lines of work and listen to them.

SCREENWRITING PHASES

There are several general phases a writer and script go through before getting into preproduction:

- Research
- A treatment or outline
- Characters

- First draft
- Rewrite
- Review
- Read-through
- Polish

RESEARCH

There are two levels of research. The first is researching the subject you want to write about and often uncovers a certain interesting fact that can bring authenticity and plot twist to the script. You can do research online, by reading books and articles, or spending time somewhere other than in your house or with your friends.

The other kind of research is to seek out information about screenplays. Study screenplays and the movies that came out of them and you'll find significant differences between the two. Even if you're directing and producing your show, your screenplay will change. People meddle. It's the nature of moviemaking.

Screenplays look different depending on the phase of the project. If you go to a bookstore that sells screenplays, you may find published scripts look a lot like published stageplays. Although these are helpful for reading, they're not helpful for formatting.

Screenplays have specific formats regarding margins, typestyle, and type size. Hollywood practice dictates you follow the accepted style. Interestingly, although people use different tools to write scripts, we're stuck following the same clumsy format. Supposedly, producers, studios, and others developed ways to estimate screen time based on this format.

This is nutty. I understand the need to estimate running time, but given the way movies are made in Hollywood, a feature's running time will be whatever the test audiences think it should be.

For example, you may have a page of dialogue that times out at exactly one minute. On the next page, however, is a single line: "The avalanche wipes out the town." How much screen time does the avalanche require? Two seconds? Fifteen seconds? Depends on the special effects budget and how much cheering or booing the test audience does.

A TREATMENT OR OUTLINE

Outlines and treatments are good places to start a script. Because action is character, focus on the plot: What happens? You may have some notes about the characters, but the point is to get the story down on paper.

I use a combination of an outline and index cards. The outline moves me quickly through plot points. If I'm struck with a certain piece of dialogue, a location, or prop, I put that in, too, but primarily, I concentrate on the order of events, asking over and over, "And then what?"

After I have completed the plot, I revise, adding subplots and ideas for minor characters. I also think about what kind of locations will add a bit of visual spice and clue me into the characters.

You can also use index cards. Every scene gets its own card. A scene is action that occurs in a specific place at a specific time. A scene may need different shots, but at this stage, concentrate on scenes. Order and reorder the index cards until you're happy with it. Place the sequences so plot twists fall at specific points in the story. Then place subplot scenes within those plot points, so they can have their own rise and fall within the main plot.

There are software applications that will allow you to do the same thing, but it's essentially the same: Order the scenes into sequences that fit into coherent plot points.

CHARACTERS

Pretend to be each character and ask yourself:

- Who am I?
- Where am I?
- What do I want?
- What's stopping me from getting it?
- How far will I go to get it?

Be specific. Concrete, original detail will help you create visuals and audio to express the action that will convey character.

Consider writing physical descriptions, short biographies, and backstories for the major characters. They can be as elaborate as you want, but this material is only for your use. It has no business in the script, so plan your time with care.

Action is character. A guy sitting in a room furrowing his brow over some great mystery is hard to make interesting. If a character wants love then what does love look like for that person? A hibiscus bush? A speedboat? What does the character do to get love? What does that action look like? How far will the character go? What's standing in the character's way?

When writing your dialogue, give your characters distinctive and consistent voices. A lot of screenwriters have characters that all sound the same. Even if they have the same backgrounds and ages, characters must sound different. Before you say that you know people who all sound the same, remember that movies are not real life. Characters who sound the same can be used for great effect, but make sure that decision is intentional.

Some people say you should only write about what you know. I say write where you find your interest. If you think steel-making is fascinating then immerse yourself in it. You'll have to be disciplined about cutting later, but for now, let your curiosity have its way with you.

Now start your first draft.

FIRST DRAFT

No doubt you've heard the saying, "Strike while the iron is hot." That applies to first drafts. Start writing while you're enthusiastic about the idea. Dig deeper, go further, toss in everything that pops into your head. Just keep going. The first flush of excitement is intoxicating and short-lived. I know many people who have stacks of scripts they started and never finished.

I'm a firm believer in striking *until* the iron gets hot. When it's no longer fun, but a grueling chore, keep hitting. The goal of a first draft isn't to dazzle people with your speed, cleverness, or talent.

The goal is to get it done.

For example, read the first draft of "Music Appreciation," located on the following pages.

REWRITE

After you have your first draft, start rewriting.

Show character, don't say it. Speeches are for dedicating birdbaths. Keep the plot moving forward and cut the yak. Your actors will convey their characters through action.

Don't try to write the way people talk. Nothing's quite so irritating as people trying to write dialect. If the character has an accent, make a note in the stage direction. Better yet, imply it in the character's name and brief description.

Keep stage direction short, using visually evocative words in the present tense. Nobody needs six paragraphs about how someone walks across the room. Brevity has power.

NOTE

What a Comedian

If you're writing comedy and there's a joke in the dialogue, place the punchline at the end of a character's line. That way, the audience won't laugh over the rest of the dialogue.

```
                      "MUSIC APPRECIATION"

FADE IN

INT. VET CLINIC — EXAM ROOM — DAY

Vet tech BONNIE, in surgical scrubs, pets a Great Dane
named WANDA. Bonnie's in her mid-thirties, and cute enough
to make even scrubs look good. MUSIC plays on a boombox.

Another tech, CARRIE, also in scrubs, walks into view,
reading a file. She pats Wanda on the head, then sets down
the file and begins the exam by looking at Wanda's eyes,
ears, and mouth. Wanda happily licks Carrie's face.

                        CARRIE
               First date with what's-his-name
               tonight, huh?

                        BONNIE
               I hate first dates.

                        CARRIE
               Everyone hates first dates.

Bonnie turns from the dog to arrange several instruments,
including a fecal loop, KY, swabs, and so on.

                        CARRIE
               Doesn't his job kind of give you
               the creeps?

                        BONNIE
               Why?

                        CARRIE
               It's creepy.

Bonnie hands Carrie the otoscope. Carrie looks in the dog's
ears.

                        BONNIE
               Somebody's got to do it.

                        CARRIE
               But you don't have to date him.
               Hope he doesn't order liver for
               dinner.



                              Music Appreciation - 1
```

FIGURE 8.1

Draft 1, page 1 of "Music Appreciation."

                         BONNIE
               We're not going to dinner. Just a
               concert. Folk music, I think.

     Carrie hand the otoscope back to Bonnie, who cleans it.
     Carrie continues the exam.

                         CARRIE
               With his job, you think he'd be a
               vegetarian. Is he?

     Carrie pats her front once, looking for her stethoscope.
     Bonnie hands her a pair from around her neck.

                         BONNIE
               I don't know. It's our first date.

     Bonnie turns off the MUSIC as Carrie puts on the
     stethoscope and listens to Wanda's heart.

     Bonnie uncaps a tube of KY and spreads it on the fecal
     loop. She caps the tube and puts it away.

     Carrie finishes checking Wanda's heart and scrawls
     something in the file. Bonnie turns the MUSIC back on, then
     snatches away the stethoscope and hangs it around her neck.

                         CARRIE
               You know, plain dead bodies I
               could handle—it's all the weird
               stuff you'd see…

     Carrie palpates Wanda's abdomen, then shivers.

                         CARRIE
               Yuck.

                         BONNIE
               You're being juvenile.

                         CARRIE
               It's gross.
                    (beat)
               Why is Wanda here?

                         BONNIE
               Owner's freaking out because she
               ate poop.

                         CARRIE
               Cat? Horse?

                                   Music Appreciation - 2

FIGURE 8.2

Draft 1, page 2 of "Music Appreciation."

```
                          BONNIE
                 Owner forgot to flush.

Carrie nods.

With the dexterity that comes from watching too many
medical dramas, Bonnie slaps the lubricated fecal loop into
Carrie's hand.

Carrie takes the loop, then steps behind Wanda and lifts
her tail.

EXT. COUNTY MORGUE — NIGHT

The sign glitters.

INT. COUNTY MORGUE — OFFICE — NIGHT

JOHN, the county Medical Examiner, glances at the mirror to
adjust a bright bowtie and smooth his hair. The same MUSIC
plays in the background.

He stares at himself.

                          JOHN
                 I hate first dates.

Turning from the mirror, John turns off the boombox,
extracts the CD, and slides it back into its case. He turns
out the light and closes the door.

EXT. QUIET CITY STREET — NIGHT

John's car goes by with John and Bonnie inside.

INT. JOHN'S CAR — DRIVING — NIGHT

John drives with his hands at ten and two. Bonnie sits in
the passenger seat, now wearing casual date clothes.

                          BONNIE
                 How was work?

                          JOHN
                 Mostly natural causes. One blunt
                 trauma, but that was an accident.
                 Routine.

                          BONNIE
                   (at a loss)
                 That's…good.


                                  Music Appreciation - 3
```

FIGURE 8.3

Draft 1, page 3 of "Music Appreciation."

A moment passes as they reach a stop sign. John fiddles
with his bowtie.

>   BONNIE
>   That's a nice tie.

>   JOHN
>   Thanks.

>   BONNIE
>   Don't see many men wearing bowties
>   anymore.

>   JOHN
>   I do a lot of leaning over.

He mimes leaning over. Bonnie, missing the joke, nods and
looks away.

>   JOHN
>   So, how about you? How was work?

>   BONNIE
>   The usual. Dogs and cats. Every
>   now and then someone brings in a
>   ferret, or a pet rat, maybe a
>   tarantula. We had a couple of
>   snakes in yesterday.

John shivers. He's creeped out.

>   JOHN
>   Ick. Snakes. The regular pets I
>   could handle, but the weird ones…

EXT. QUIET CITY STREET — NIGHT

John's car rolls through the intersection and out of view.

EXT. THE PLAYHOUSE — NIGHT

The lights from the marquee bounce off a deserted sidewalk.

INT. THE PLAYHOUSE — THEATRE — NIGHT

Ragged tables and chairs are crowded into the empty room.
On each table sits a basket of popcorn, untouched. On the
stage are a chair and a small table with a musical
instrument case resting on it. It looks like a very flat
coffin.

Music Appreciation - 4

FIGURE 8.4

Draft 1, page 4 of "Music Appreciation."

John and Bonnie sit uncomfortably at a table. John eats popcorn nervously. He offers her some. She takes a small handful. The SOUND of their chewing is huge. Both shift in their seats, pretending that the popcorn was not a mistake.

John turns to Bonnie and just as he's about to say, "Let's get out of here," the musician appears.

MAX VON HILDENFARBEN has a sense of importance to fit his name. His jeans are neatly ironed and his flannel shirt is buttoned all the way up. He opens the instrument case and extracts a very shiny saw and a little mallet.

John and Bonnie freeze.

Max settles into the chair and begins to play. The SOUND is excruciating, like bagpipes on Valium.

John and Bonnie are too horrified to move.

INT. CAR — PARKED — NIGHT

Still mortified, John and Bonnie sit in the front seat.

                    BONNIE
          I never knew people could do that
          with a saw.

                    JOHN
          Yeah. It was really…loud.

A moment passes.

                    BONNIE
          John?

                    JOHN
          Yeah?

                    BONNIE
          It was horrible.

Relief crosses John's face.

                    JOHN
          Oh, thank god. I thought, you
          know, we—

                                        Music Appreciation - 5

FIGURE 8.5

Draft 1, page 5 of "Music Appreciation."

```
                JOHN                              BONNIE
      —could go to this show and        He went on and on, it felt
      have something to talk            like he was playing for two
      about and there was that          weeks. I wanted to leave,
      popcorn and it was all            but nobody else was there
      crunchy—                          and—

                        BONNIE
              —I felt sorry for the guy.

                        JOHN
              I felt sorry for us.

      They both stop. Bonnie leans back in the seat.

                        BONNIE
              I hate first dates.

                        JOHN
              Me too.
               (beat)
              You said at the party you really
              liked music.

                        BONNIE
              I do. You said so, too.

                        JOHN
              I thought…

                        BONNIE
              I know. So did I. Something in
              common.

                        JOHN
              Yeah.

      They look at each other.

      Bonnie looks out the window as John starts the car. He
      slides in the CD with the same MUSIC Bonnie was listening
      to at work.

                        JOHN
              I'll take you home.

      She looks at him as he shifts into drive.

                        BONNIE
              Want to get some coffee instead?
```

Music Appreciation - 6

FIGURE 8.6

Draft 1, page 6 of "Music Appreciation."

```
John grins.

EXT. QUIET CITY STREET — NIGHT

John's car pulls away and out of view.

                    JOHN (OC)
              Can you believe he actually gets
              paid for doing that?

                    BONNIE (OC)
              What a terrible job.

They both laugh as the MUSIC goes up.

                                        FADE OUT
```

Music Appreciation - 7

FIGURE 8.7

Draft 1, page 7 of "Music Appreciation."

Don't include camera angles. That's not your job. Deciding what the camera sees is the director's job. If you need to emphasize a visual, maybe you ought to reconsider the scene. It should be apparent what should be given weight in the frame by the way the scene is written.

Consider your subplots. What is the subplot's relationship to the main action? Does it shed light on the main character's wants or needs? Does it add to the conflict?

Focus on key elements to get your first draft closer to a readable screenplay. As you rewrite, don't be afraid to use our friend the delete key.

You won't know how many rewrites you'll need until you do them. If someone has hired you to write a script, you're probably contractually obligated to deliver at least one rewrite. That doesn't stop you from doing more—just don't hand them over unless you're getting more money.

REVIEW

Find five people you trust. Not five people you like or five friends. Five people who will tell you the unvarnished truth. Ask these five people to read your script. If you feel uneasy, you can always ask them to sign a nondisclosure agreement, but remember that they're doing you a favor and not the other way around.

There are some online usegroups and messageboards that allow you to post your work for comments. See the Resources section for listings.

When you get the criticism, take notes and keep your mouth shut. It's not about you—it's about the work. You can whine about it later in the privacy of your own home. If you have specific questions about plot development or a character, wait until the person has finished before asking.

Some bars, coffeehouses, and film festivals offer staged readings of screenplays written by local writers. Check alternative papers and your local film commission. Staged readings can be helpful and harmful. Just because a screenplay reads well doesn't mean it will make a good movie. It's also very difficult for the audience to differentiate between the script and the performance. Some actors can interpret a character for good or bad, and some directors will emphasize the wrong things.

Sit still and listen to the performance. Take notes, and check to see how the audience is responding to the scenes. Listen particularly for dialogue

NOTE

Share the Pain

Some screenwriters have writing groups whose members read one another's work and critique it. If that works for you, do it. Just remember the quid pro quo—you have to read and comment on their work in exchange for them reading and commenting on yours.

that's too long or stilted. And no matter how much you want to jump to your feet to scream at someone, resist the temptation.

Give yourself some time before reviewing your notes, and then use what's helpful and ignore the rest. Revise as you see fit.

READ-THROUGH

After the movie has been cast, the director, producer, and actors will read through your entire script. They may recommend a bit of trimming or expanding, depending on who is in the room. You may or may not be invited to the read-through.

If not, the producer will contact you with notes. If you are, sit tight and listen. Often actors or a director will come up with a great bit or some improv that really works to the benefit of your script.

POLISH

After the read-through, you may be obligated to make changes for the director or producer. Sometimes the suggestions are good; usually they're just awful. Sometimes the changes qualify as another rewrite according to the WGA guidelines.

If you've fulfilled the terms of your contract and you're not required to do another rewrite, don't unless you're offered adequate compensation.

If you're the director and/or producer, polishing can continue right up until the moment you shoot a scene. Depending on the actors, I often work this way. It's fun, although learn how to say no, ask for the screen to be played as written if you're not sure about the changes, and keep good notes in your production script for continuity.

Personally, I consider all screenplays to be drafts until I've locked the fine cut. I'll continue to make changes as I work with the footage. That's just me.

The two leads I cast for "Music Appreciation" had worked together before and really enjoyed improvising. We discussed each beat and they worked from there. I also shaped the script more to match the actors' strengths.

Because I'd been searching locations ahead of time, I knew where we were going to be. I changed the script to match. You can see these changes in the second draft of "Music Appreciation," located on the following pages.

```
            "MUSIC APPRECIATION"

FADE IN

1.  INT. VET CLINIC - EXAM ROOM - DAY

Vet tech PEGGY, in surgical scrubs, pets a Great Dane named
WANDA. Peggy's in her thirties, and cute enough to make
even scrubs look good. MUSIC plays on a boombox.

BETTY, another vet tech also in scrubs, walks into view,
reading a file. She pats Wanda on the head, then sets down
the file and begins the exam. Wanda happily licks Betty's
face.

                    BETTY
          First date with what's-his-name
          tonight, huh?

                    PEGGY
          I hate first dates.

                    BETTY
          Everyone hates first dates.

Peggy turns from the dog to arrange several instruments and
slip on a latex glove.

                    BETTY
          Doesn't his job kind of give you
          the creeps?

                    PEGGY
          Why?

                    BETTY
          It's creepy.

                    PEGGY
          Somebody's got to do it.

                    BETTY
          But you don't have to date him.
          Hope he doesn't order liver for
          dinner.

                    PEGGY
          We're not going to dinner, just a
          show.

Peggy puts KY on a gloved finger.

                              Music Appreciation - 1
```

FIGURE 8.8

Draft 2, page 1 of "Music Appreciation."

> BETTY
> With his job, you think he'd be a
> vegetarian. Is he?

> PEGGY
> I don't know. It's our first date.

> BETTY
> You know, plain dead bodies I
> could handle—it's all the weird
> stuff you'd see…

Betty palpates Wanda's abdomen, then shivers.

> BETTY
> Yuck.

> PEGGY
> You're being juvenile.

> BETTY
> It's gross.
> (beat)
> Why is Wanda here?

> PEGGY
> Owner's freaking out because she
> ate poop.

> BETTY
> Cat? Horse?

> PEGGY
> Owner forgot to flush.

Peggy steps around Wanda and lifts her tail.

2. EXT. COUNTY MORGUE - NIGHT

The sign glitters.

3. INT. COUNTY MORGUE - OFFICE - NIGHT

JOHN, the county Medical Examiner, glances at the mirror to
adjust a bright bowtie and smooth his hair. The same MUSIC
plays in the background.

He stares at himself.

Music Appreciation - 2

FIGURE 8.9

Draft 2, page 2 of "Music Appreciation."

Turning from the mirror, John turns off the boombox, extracts the CD, and slides it into its case. He turns out the light and closes the door.

4. EXT. QUIET CITY STREET - NIGHT

John's car goes by with John and Peggy inside.

5. INT. JOHN'S CAR - DRIVING - NIGHT

Peggy stares out the windshield. She now wears date clothes.

John's hands are at ten and two, his bowtie peeking over the steering wheel. Suddenly, he points through the windshield.

> JOHN
> Have you ever eaten there? Great soy milkshakes.

> PEGGY
> You're a vegetarian?

> JOHN
> No, no, soy is so much better for you---

> PEGGY
> ---and it lasts forever.

The silence is thicker than a soy milkshake.

6. INT. EVERETT THEATRE - BALCONY - NIGHT

John and Peggy sit in a deserted balcony. The houselights are on, but it's dim. They shift in their seats, bump elbows on an armrest they both desert, as both hope their stomachs don't growl.

John drives with his hands at ten and two. Peggy sits in the passenger seat, now wearing casual date clothes.

> PEGGY
> How was work?

> JOHN
> Mostly natural causes. One blunt trauma, but that was an accident. Routine.

Music Appreciation - 3

FIGURE 8.10

Draft 2, page 3 of "Music Appreciation."

```
                    PEGGY
              That's…neat

Peggy looks out her window, then glances back. John, who
had been looking at her, misses her expression as he looks
out his own window.

He fiddles with his necktie.

                    PEGGY
              That's a nice tie.

                    JOHN
              Thanks.

                    PEGGY
              Don't see many men wearing bowties
              anymore.

                    JOHN
              I do a lot of leaning over.

He mimes leaning over.

Peggy laughs. Stops. Maybe that wasn't a joke.

                    JOHN
              So, how about you? How was work?

                    PEGGY
              The usual. Dogs and cats. We had a
              couple of snakes in yesterday. Did
              you know snakes can't unhinge
              their jaws? That's a total myth
              and boa constrictors have
              vestigial shoulders and hips,
              which means they once had legs, so
              maybe the serpent in the Bible
              really was punished by being
              banished to slithering on the
              ground, which isn't really so bad
              when you think about it and it
              brings up an interesting point
              about Biblical archaeology I saw
              this documentary on---

John shivers. He's dewy.

                    JOHN
              Have you ever been here before?
              They restored it all…


                                    Music Appreciation - 4
```

FIGURE 8.11

Draft 2, page 4 of "Music Appreciation."

> PEGGY
> Oh, no, yeah, it's…
>
> A moment passes.
>
> PEGGY
> I'm sorry.
>
> JOHN
> Oh---no---it's---what?
>
> The houselights drop.
>
> 7. INT. EVERETT THEATRE - STAGE - NIGHT
>
> The musician appears onstage.
>
> CLAUDE has a sense of importance to fit his name. He
> carries an instrument case and extracts a very shiny saw
> and a bow.
>
> Claude begins to play. The SOUND is excruciating, like
> bagpipes on Valium.
>
> John and Peggy are too horrified to move.
>
> 8. INT. JOHN'S CAR - PARKED - NIGHT
>
> John and Peggy sit in the front seat.
>
> PEGGY
> I never knew people could do that
> with a saw.
>
> JOHN
> Yeah. It was really…loud.
>
> A moment.
>
> PEGGY
> (delicate)
> What do I owe you for the ticket?
>
> JOHN
> Oh---a friend gave them to me.
> Don't worry about it.
> (pause)
> Did you like it?
>
> PEGGY
> Yeah, no, uh, yeah…
>
> *Music Appreciation - 5*

FIGURE 8.12

Draft 2, page 5 of "Music Appreciation."

```
A moment passes.

                        PEGGY
                  No. It was horrible.

Relief crosses John's face.

                        JOHN
                  He was awful. I thought, you know,
                  we—

        JOHN                              PEGGY
  —could go to this show and        He went on and on, it felt
  have something to talk            like he was playing for two
  about and it was all empty        weeks. I wanted to leave,
  and strange—                      but nobody else was there
                                    and—


                        PEGGY
                  —I felt sorry for the guy.

                        JOHN
                  I felt sorry for us.

They both stop. Peggy leans back in the seat.

                        PEGGY
                  I hate first dates.

                        JOHN
                  Me too.
                     (beat)
                  You said at the party you really
                  liked music.

                        PEGGY
                  I do. You said so, too.

                        JOHN
                  I thought…

                        PEGGY
                  I know.

They look at each other. It's hopeless, but now they can
make a graceful exit.



                                      Music Appreciation - 6
```

FIGURE 8.13

Draft 2, page 6 of "Music Appreciation."

Peggy looks out the window as John starts the car. He
slides in the CD with the same MUSIC Peggy was listening to
at work.

                JOHN
          I'll take you home.

She looks at him as he shifts into drive.

                PEGGY
          I have this CD.

                JOHN
          I listen to it all the time.

                PEGGY
          Me, too.
             (pause)
          Want to get some coffee?

John grins.

9. EXT. QUIET CITY STREET - NIGHT

John's car pulls away and out of view.

              JOHN (OC)
          I don't know what was worse---the
          beginning, the middle or the end--
          -

              PEGGY (OC)
          His poor neighbors. What a
          terrible job.

They both laugh as the MUSIC goes up.

                          FADE OUT

Music Appreciation - 7

FIGURE 8.14

Draft 2, page 7 of "Music Appreciation."

FORMAT

People think writing a screenplay requires a chair and some fancy software. They're half right. You will need a chair.

Often, people use specific screenplay applications because software is part of a suite of products that makes the preproduction process easier. For example, there may be a tool that allows online script breakdown, which another application uses as data for filling out breakdown sheets and budget items. That's handy, but you don't have to use it if you don't want to.

Sometimes the dedicated applications have tools that allow you to analyze the structure of your script more easily. There are low-tech ways to do the same thing that work just as well.

Regardless what tools you use, the script has to be formatted in a standard way. This format, although now past its practical use, is a secret handshake. It's one way people in the industry have to see how new you are. It's a way for script readers getting stuck reviewing unsolicited screenplays to skip over your work without so much as a glance.

Think it doesn't work that way? Guess again.

There are certain terms that come up frequently in a screenplay. These are not camera terms. It's not the writer's job to determine what the camera does. These terms are shorthand to better convey what you mean.

- ACTION means stage direction. What a character does or wears, or how someone or someplace is described.
- CHARACTER refers to any speaking part or character who performs a significant action.
- CONTINUOUS conveys simultaneous action. This includes phone conversations.
- CUT is a transition term. The director may choose to use a dissolve, wipe, or some other transition, but in a script, use CUT to signify a change in scene.
- DIALOGUE is what a character says.
- EXTRA is someone whose actions are not significant to the story. Usually, it refers to a warm body, atmosphere, a person in the background, and so on.
- FADE IN is the term signifying the beginning of a movie. Often a movie will start with a different kind of transition, but scripts always start with FADE IN.

- FADE OUT is the term signifying the end of a movie. Often a movie will finish with a different kind of transition, but scripts always end with FADE OUT.

- MONTAGE is a collection of images used to signify the passage of time. Usually there is very little or no dialogue within a montage. Montages are also used for dream sequences and to signify a change in a character's perceptions (for example, when a character has been drugged).

- SLUGLINE is the scene heading. One line that tells whether the scene is an INTERIOR or EXTERIOR, where the scene takes place, and what time it is. Here's an example:

```
INT.  -  EVERETT  THEATRE  -  STAGE  -  NIGHT
```

Standard screenplay format is described as follows:

Page margins

Top: 1 "

Bottom: 1 "

Left: 1.25 "

Right: 1.25 "

Sluglines

Left: 1.25 "

Right: 1.25 "

Flush left, 12-point leading on the top and bottom, single line spacing.

Action

Left: 1.25 "

Right: 1.5 "

Flush left, 12-point leading on the bottom, single line spacing.

Character

Left: 3.75 "

Right: 3.75 "

Character names are centered above dialogue. No leading, single line spacing.

Characters in your script must have their names all uppercase on first mention. After that, capitalize them as you would normally.

Dialogue is placed just below the speaking character's name.

Dialogue left margin: 2.75 "

Dialogue right margin: 2.5 "

Flush left, 12-point leading on the bottom, single line spacing.

Page numbers

Place the title and page number flush right in the footer. Some people place page numbers in the upper-right corner. It's up to you.

You can create a template in your existing word processor, use the template included on the DVD, or purchase a dedicated application.

Your screenplay should be photocopied single-sided, three-hole punch paper. The covers should be white cardstock front and back, with the title on the front in the center of the page about one-third of the way down from the top. Your contact information goes in the lower-right corner. Do not place a copyright symbol on the script, even if you have registered the work with the copyright office. An experienced member of your ensemble will know immediately just how inexperienced you are if you do this.

Put the entire script together using brass brads. Some people use two, others use three. It doesn't matter.

Different people format treatments differently. Generally, keep it as easy to read as possible. Keep the margins 1" to 1.5" wide, with the title and page number in the lower-right corner. You do not have to use three-hole punch paper, cardstock covers, and brads.

You can register your screenplay, treatment, or outline with the Copyright Office. I suggest, however, you do what the professionals do and instead register with the Writer's Guild of America. See Resources for contact information.

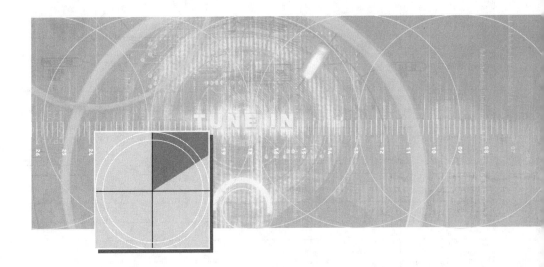

CHECKLISTS

Use the following four checklists to track all of your development activities for your project. Modify them according to your needs.

DEVELOPMENT PERSONNEL CHECKLIST

Position	Name	Date contract/letter signed
Producer		
Executive producer		
Coproducer		
Line producer		
Associate producer		
Unit production manager (UPM)		
Screenwriter		
Director		
Director of photography (DP)		
Name talent		
Entertainment attorney		
Publicist		
Distributor		

DV CAMERA KIT PURCHASE CHECKLIST

For each DV camera kit you're considering, fill out this checklist.

DV CAMERA MODEL _____

DV   DVCAM   DVCPRO

				Cost
Lenses	Inter-changeable	Noninter-changeable	Included?	
Additional lens	Type			
CCDs	Number	Size		
IEEE 1394 input/output				
Analog video input/output				
Optical image stabilization				
LCD viewfinder	Size			
Eyepiece viewfinder	Color	Black and white		
Zebra stripes				
Manual controls				
Switchable 4:3/16:9				
AC power supply				
Batteries	Number			
Additional batteries	Type	Number	Cable included?	
Hard case				
Soft case				
Filters	UV	Other		
Monitor Manufacturer	Size	Bluegun-only	Switchable 4:3/16:9	
Tripod head	Standard	Fluid		
Tripod sticks	Wood	Metal	Spreaders?	
			TOTAL	

CONTRACTS YOU MAY NEED

Contract/agreement	✓	Date signed
Development		
Partnership agreement		
Option and option execution agreements		
Shopping agreement		
Screenplay submission agreement		
Life story release		
Product placement agreement		
Trademark release		
Screenwriting agreement		
Nondisclosure agreement		
Attachment letter or letter of intent		
Preproduction		
Talent and crew contracts		
Personal release		
Location release		
Postproduction		
Master Recording Licensing agreement		
Sync Rights agreement		
Soundtrack Licensing agreement		

BANK CHECKLIST

For each bank you approach, fill out this checklist.

NAME OF BANK:_____**Date delivered:**_____

Item	✓
Synopsis	
Script	
Bios of everyone attached	
Chain of title documents	
Copy of title distribution guarantee	
Detailed budget	
Cash-flow chart	
Complete financial statements of all investors	
Security agreement putting the bank in first lien position	
An agreement between the distributor and the bank that the bank gets the producer's share of all money until the loan, interest, and costs are repaid	
Copy of the completion bond	
Other	

STEP II: PREPRODUCTION:
PEOPLE, PLACES, AND THINGS

OVERVIEW

Preproduction is the time to iron out all the issues prior to going into production.

You need to lock and analyze your script, break it down, lock your schedule, lock your budget, lock locations, hire and fire your ensemble, rehearse, and complete all the other tasks that can derail production before it begins.

This section focuses on tasks rather than roles. What's important is that everything get done, not who does it. Just be sure to give credit where credit is due. And have enough tricks in your pocket so if something does go wrong, you have options on how to fix it.

This section details the tasks and issues you need to cover for preproduction. Chapter 9, "Locking and Prepping Your Script," covers getting your screenplay ready to shoot. While dialogue may change, your script's basic sequence of scenes and locations does not. You want to get to this point as early as possible in the prep stage. Using this locked script, you break it down, identifying every element required for the shoot, and fill out breakdown sheets so you know whom and what you'll need and when.

Chapter 10, "Production Design," walks you through the process of planning and designing your project. This chapter helps you determine your color palettes, shot palettes, and other design decisions.

Chapter 11, "Script Breakdown," teaches you how to properly break down your production script and generate lists for your preproduction crew so you're prepared for your first shoot day.

Chapter 12, "Locking the Schedule," asks questions you need to answer to create a realistic shooting schedule. This is a very important job, but many producers hand it over to volunteers who don't understand the moviemaking process. Scheduling is not typing. Along with your director and DP, you should create a schedule that is practical, efficient, and realistic. Your show will live or die by this schedule, so be thorough.

Chapter 13, "Locking the Budget," teaches you how to create a realistic budget for your project. Every producer knows it's easy to bleed money making a movie. This chapter helps you get a clear idea of how much money you'll need, when you'll have it, and when you'll begin spending it.

Chapter 14, "Scouting and Locking Locations," helps you determine appropriate locations that will satisfy your director, DP, and sound mixer. Some producers wait until the last minute, but I think this is a bad idea. Often, people are letting you use their homes and businesses. Good manners and clear communication will help them say yes. Locking locations will also help make scheduling and creating callsheets easier.

Chapter 15, "Build the Ensemble," helps you figure out how to build your ensemble in front of and behind the camera. Hiring well is the key job for any producer, so you need to be clear about whom you need, when you need them, and what kind of contract they need to sign.

Chapter 16, "Storyboards, Shooting Scripts, Shot Lists, and Rehearsals," discusses ways to create a concrete representation of your, or your director's, vision of the final movie. The chapter also discusses how to get the most from your rehearsals, and ends with a discussion of the necessary preproduction contracts and releases you'll need for your show.

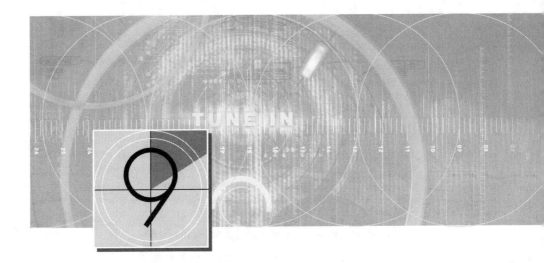

LOCKING AND PREPPING YOUR SCRIPT

As early as possible, lock your script. At this point, there should be only one version of the screenplay to ensure that everyone is literally on the same page.

You can always change lines or add or drop scenes, but make sure everyone knows what those changes are.

PREPARING YOUR SCRIPT

After your script is locked, you need to create a production script.

A production script is the script for the project. All changes and notes go in this script. I worked a set where everyone had a different version of the script. The schedule made no sense because the kids who did the schedule had yet another version. Suffice to say I did some yelling.

I usually have two versions of this script. One is a pristine master for photocopying. The other, however, goes into a three-ring binder, along with pens, pencils, a big eraser, and so on, that stays with me on the set. It gets mighty skanky. In addition to notes, shot lists, and hand-drawn storyboards, it gets studded with coffee rings.

To create a production script, first number every scene sequentially. This takes a bit of finesse. Many scripts have sequences that change locations or time of day, although the action is contained in one scene. You determine what is a scene by two factors:

- A change in location
- A change in time

For example, in "Music Appreciation," John and Peggy's reaction to Claude the saw player takes place in the balcony. That's a location change and needs to be noted in the production script. Mark the change in location, on any additional scenes, liked this::

7. INT. EVERETT THEATRE - STAGE - NIGHT

7A. INT. EVERETT THEATRE - BALCONY - NIGHT - CONTINUOUS

John and Peggy are too horrified to move.

8. INT. JOHN'S CAR - PARKED - NIGHT

If you later need to delete a scene, keep the scene number but note it as deleted to avoid renumbering scenes.

There may be changes and revisions to lines. Pages with changes are photocopied on color paper to distinguish them from original pages. The sequence is

- White
- Blue
- Pink
- Yellow
- Green
- Goldenrod

Mark dialogue changes with an (X) or (*) like this:

```
          BETTY
With his job, you think he'd be a
vegetarian.                           (X)


          PEGGY
I don't know if he's a vegetarian
or not. It's our first date.          (X)
```

Give your key people a copy of your production script. From now on, everyone uses it as the reference.

SCRIPT ANALYSIS

There are no accidents in scripts. Each screenplay is a closed system and everything about the movie comes from it. It's the director's job to know what's in the script to design and communicate his or her vision of the movie. Plus, the director and the producer need to create a coherent production plan based on the director's vision.

Everyone believes directors need only close their eyes and visualize the movies they want to make. But director preparation involves a great deal more. It starts with the discovery of the intrinsic order in every script, accomplished by a thorough analysis of the locked screenplay.

Without this analysis, you're going to have a hard time figuring out aesthetic, technical, and logistical issues.

There are two ways to begin your script analysis. You can approach it according to the smallest unit of each scene, called a *beat*, or the largest structural unit of the movie, the *story arc*.

Either way you start, the point is to understand how every part of the screenplay serves the conflict. I like to start with the beats: A good script contains only action and dialogue that reveal the conflict, and the pattern of smaller actions often presents excellent clues.

FIRST READ

The first read is to help you get a first impression. If you also wrote the script, try to set the screenplay aside for a while, and then go back for your first read.

Find yourself a comfortable chair and a clean copy of the screenplay. Read it all the way through. Don't worry about specifics. After you've finished, quickly write down the answers to these questions:

- How do you feel about the story?
- What about the story is important to you?
- What about it interests you?
- What is the script about?

Don't ponder the intentions of the writer, even if that's you. Concentrate on your immediate reactions.

SECOND READ

For the second read, find the givens. A *given* is specified in the screenplay and includes characters, objects, locations, time of day, and so on. This also includes what's inferred through dialogue and action.

For example, if the screenplay says a character is standing outside a house holding a coffee pot, the coffee pot is a given. If the character walks into the house in the next scene, you can infer the character is still holding the coffee pot.

Put a line through the stage directions, except those required to understand the plot. Circle any stage direction that refers to a character's personal objects or gives facts not in the dialogue. That will help you go a little deeper with the characters.

Look for evidence, follow the clues, and be strict in your interpretation of a fact. Just because a character says it doesn't mean it's so—you need circumstantial evidence. For example, a character who says, "It's a nice sunny day," could be telling the truth, trying to be sarcastic, delusional, or lying. It all depends on the context.

Draw a line through any notes about a character's emotional response. A character's state of mind is not a fact. Stick to what is in the script.

Finding what's given helps you in practical terms, because this is a good way to consider props, set dressing, wardrobe, and so on. Finding the givens also offers insight into characters and actions.

For every scene, write down the answers to these questions:

- What are the givens?
- What are characters' personal objects?

CHARACTERS

Each character is a bundle of wants expressed through action. Each has a motive. A motive remains the same throughout the movie and sets characters apart from one another.

Characters in the Story Arc

For every character, write down

- A description of the character based on the script
- A description of the character in your own words
- A backstory

A *backstory* is everything about the character that takes place prior to the beginning of the movie. It is a purely imaginative exercise, but it may help you dig into the script.

Don't get too involved in the backstory. Your actors will use their versions of backstory radically different from your own to frame their choices. The purpose of it is to help you understand the screenplay. If an actor has made choices you don't think fit the story arc, you can ask about those choices in an intelligent manner.

Characters Scene by Scene

Next, go back through the script. For every scene, write down the answers to these questions:

- What does each character say he or she wants?
- What does each character say he or she doesn't want?
- Is there a contradiction?
- What does each character do?
- How does this shed light on the characters' wants?
- How do personal objects shed light on the character?

There will be a lot of questions. You may or may not be able to answer all of them at this point, but your actors will.

You'll notice a pattern of action emerging for each character. If you don't, start thinking about how you can show through action what a character wants. You'll use this information when you begin designing your blocking.

BEATS

Scenes can be broken down into smaller units called *beats*. A beat signifies an emotional event. For example, a character walks into a room where another character is repairing a parachute. The first character asks,

"Where's the dog?" The beat is on the character who asks the question, but then changes to the parachute fixer, who replies, "I gave him to my sister."

The beat isn't that there's a question and then an answer, but in the emotional subtext beneath the dialogue. Depending on the context, exchanges such as the one above may be freighted with meaning. Beats are subtle when reading, but immediately recognizable when you see them. Your task is to find them in the script.

What happens between beats is like a game of emotional tag, where the beat signifies a character getting tagged when he or she undergoes an emotional change. Every scene has at least one beat. If a scene doesn't have one then what's it doing there?

One easy way to identify a beat is when a character changes the subject. For every scene, write down the answers to these questions:

- Where does the subject change?
- Who brings up the subject?
- What happens literally after the subject is brought up?
- What happens emotionally after the subject is brought up?
- How are the beats related?

Give each beat its own title so you can refer to them more easily.

You'll see patterns emerging quickly that will shed light on the characters, conflict, and resolution.

STORY ARC

In addition to the scene, character, and beat analysis you've done so far, you need to consider

- Conflict
- Inciting incident
- Complications
- Climax
- Outcome

Conflict

The conflict is what the movie is about. The center of any narrative movie is the struggle to resolve that conflict. The arc of the story exists as a way for the characters (and the viewers) to identify and resolve the conflict through action.

All action must be meaningful—meaningless action is motion. What separates action from motion is the relationship action has with the conflict. This is not plot. Plot is a series of events shaped by the action. Plot is a vehicle, nothing more. Action identifies conflict and resolution.

For example, many sex scenes in screenplays are meaningless. They're stuck into the show on the flimsiest pretext, and don't deepen the viewer's understanding of the characters or convey the conflict. This is a shame because sex scenes can be incredibly powerful—instead of using them as filler, consider exactly how a sex scene reveals the central conflict.

As the director, you must identify the conflict and relate all the action to it. Write down the answers to these questions:

- What conflict does this movie try to resolve?

- How is this conflict resolved?

- What does each character do in relation to this conflict?

You've just found your movie's action in terms of its conflict.

Inciting Incident

The inciting incident is the point where the character becomes aware of conflict. Often, the character lacks self-awareness about the kind of change, but action has propelled this character into conflict. The inciting incident must take place within the screenplay itself and can't come from outside the action. Write down the answer to this question:

- At what moment does the character commit, or become committed, to a course of action?

The inciting incident is usually at the end of the first act.

In "Music Appreciation," John and Peggy share an inciting incident, when each becomes committed to a course of action. That moment is when they sit down in their seats in the theater. Until then, either could have called the whole thing off. After they sit down, though, they're trapped: Not staying becomes more difficult than staying.

Complications

Complications usually fill the second act. They are meaningful only in how they further the conflict. Write down the answers to these questions:

- What are the complications?
- How do they relate to the conflict?
- What is the final complication?

The final complication is the crisis, the point when the movie's conflict must be resolved. Usually, the crisis is the last complication at the end of the second act.

Climax

The climax illuminates both the conflict and its resolution. It answers the dramatic question of what the movie is about. Write down the answers to these questions:

- What is the climax?
- How are the lead characters tested?

Very possibly, you will have to answer this question in several ways before you have answers that leave nothing of consequence out. What is of consequence is determined by the conflict inherent in the script.

The climax usually starts at the beginning of the third act.

Outcome

The outcome is the resolution of the conflict and a denouement. It allows the viewer to understand the resolution and move emotionally out of the show. Write down the answer to this question:

- What is the outcome?

The outcome happens at the end of the third act.

SEARCHING FOR PATTERNS

Go through your notes to seek out patterns. You can get more from every moment onscreen if you use these patterns effectively. Repetition has a lot of power, especially when used in a pattern of three. I call this *getting the triple,* and use it frequently. Basically, I set up a pattern, and then break it to signify a character's change.

Contrast gives the viewer a reference in which to compare characters, actions, motives, and so on. Thinking about contrast may help you make some decisions about how you want to present characters and scenes to the camera.

Take note of any elements that contribute as foreshadowing, especially in the first act of the script. You'll also notice *motifs,* recurring moments that underscore the meaning of a character, action, and conflict. For example, a character may always wear hats that shadow her eyes. A powerful visual cue, the hat may signal to the viewer that the character can't see clearly, until something knocks that hat off in the second act.

You may choose not to use the hat, but the idea may help you make other decisions.

By this point, you should have a stack of notes organized according to each beat in every scene. Your notes will help you understand and interpret every facet of the screenplay. This interpretation will inform every decision you make regarding your movie.

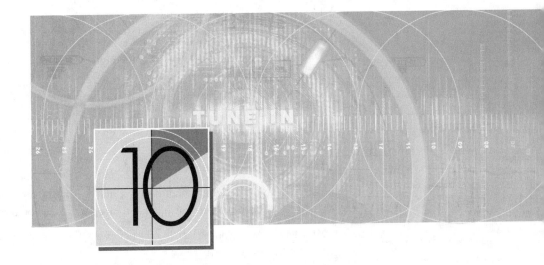

PRODUCTION DESIGN

Many DV moviemakers get caught up in the technical aspects of moviemaking to the exclusion of all else. It's an easy thing to do. But as the director, you must direct your ensemble so you can get what you need to put your movie together. Although it's nice to be able to speak the technical language of moviemaking down to the last detail, you can be more helpful to your crew by being prepared, knowing what you want, and communicating clearly.

The look of any motion picture is a combination of design and discovery. It is incumbent upon the director (with the help of the producer and DP) to have a design before getting on the set. Whether you use pencil and paper, a computer, or anything else, write and draw what you want. It will help you clarify for yourself and your ensemble what you're trying to achieve.

It's a fact: It's easier to change a plan than to start with nothing at all.

After the director has an analysis of the script, as discussed in Chapter 9, "Locking and Prepping Your Script," the director and producer can begin designing the production. Regardless of budget, they have to decide what will be presented to the camera and how.

Mise-en-scène is a French phrase that means "putting in the scene." It refers to all the visual elements presented for camera, including

- Blocking
- Framing
- Lighting
- Props, set, and set dressing
- Hair, makeup, and wardrobe

The mise-en-scène is designed according to the director's interpretation of the script. It is a combination that takes into account three concerns:

- Aesthetic—What does the director believe will best convey his or her reading of the script?
- Technical—What equipment is required, what locations are available, and what are the restrictions of using DV?
- Logistic—What issues regarding scheduling and budgeting come into play?

Many DV movies are developed for existing locations, wardrobe, and equipment. Designing for these requirements will save time, so keep these elements firmly in mind to help form a workable plan. Also, thinking about them ahead of time will help get the most out of each.

BLOCKING

Stephen D. Katz's books *Film Directing Shot by Shot: Visualizing From Concept to Screen* and *Film Directing—Cinematic Motion: A Workshop for Staging Scenes* are both good resources on blocking, staging, and camera placement.

Blocking is the relationship of actors to each other on the set. It can be a big move, such as the lead moving through a football stadium, or a small move, such as a character sitting in a chair. These moves help reveal the conflict of the story arc and the scene, as well as create transitions and interesting composition.

Blocking is different from *business*, which refers to individual moves an actor makes to convey character, such as fumbling with a toothpick.

Color Palettes

One of the least expensive and most effective techniques to raise production value is the use of color palettes. Wardrobe, sets, and lighting can have simple and effective color palettes used consistently across the show. For example, the lead may be limited to wearing shades of blue until a crucial moment, when she wears yellow.

Certain characters may only be seen in certain lighting designs. For example, a supporting character who offers crucial help may only be seen outside during magic hour or inside with shades of blue and orange.

Such designs help convey an emotional state and can help tie a show together.

Blocking is also different from *camera placement*. Camera placement refers to the relationship of the actors to the camera. Basically, if an actor moves, it's blocking. If the camera moves, it's placement.

As you read each scene, write down the answers to these questions:

- Who is moving?
- When are they moving?
- Why are they moving?

Some moves are strictly functional. It's a way of getting in and out of the scene. Functional blocking means using someone (often an extra or supporting player) to walk the camera into the scene or allow a real-time transition between beats.

Although functional blocking is handy, it usually isn't in the script and works more as an aesthetic choice for camera motion and placement.

Most blocking is written or implied in the script to visually express the conflict through the character's movement.

For example, a character becoming uncomfortable with a subject may cross the room to pick up a vase, saxophone, or hand grenade. The move makes the character's discomfort visual. Conversely, a character may feel great joy, but moves away from the person or thing he or she is reacting to because it's just too much to bear.

What's important to remember is that the moves are motivated by the beat and related to the conflict. Actors don't play plot points. Every action must reveal the conflict, and each bit of blocking must be motivated by the character's needs.

Blocking is about spatial relationships. Unfortunately, technical and logistical realities of the set may limit what kind of blocking can happen for any given scene. However, because you have a thorough script analysis, you can make blocking decisions that accommodate the limitations of the set, yet still convey what you need it to convey.

Sometimes as you visualize a scene, you'll see characters moving. Test this movement against your script analysis. Does it support your interpretation of the scene and the movie? If not, reconsider the blocking. Often the smallest tweaks will make it happen. Also, during rehearsal, your actors may be able to make it work through their knowledge of the characters.

You are not locked into reality when it comes to anything on camera. You have artistic license to make the moves work for the script. As director, your task is to reveal what the viewer sees when the viewer needs to see it.

NOTE

Body Wipes

A *body wipe* is when an actor crosses in front of the camera, offering the camera something to follow. The camera stops moving on the subject, while the actor continues out of frame. I also refer to it as a *walk-in* or *walk-out*.

Walk-ins and walk-outs are usually transitions between scenes. If you want to use a walk-in or walk-out, you may want to match the motion at the end of the scene prior, and the beginning of the scene following.

Another type of body wipe is used as a transition within the scene, often on a beat. You see them between a wide or medium shot to a closer shot. The shot tends to have the same angle of view, but different focal lengths. This body wipe allows you to edit during postproduction from the wider to the closer.

Common types of blocking include

- Entrance and exit
- Cross
- Lead-and-follow
- Circular

Entrance and exit means a character's entrance into or exit from the set. For example, three supporting characters may be sitting at a table when the lead walks in the door. Or two leads may be having an argument when one turns and stomps out of the room.

The team can also refer to a character's entrance or exit into the scene. For example, during a party, a character may leave one cluster of characters to join another.

A *cross* is when a character walks in front of or behind another character, or crosses the character's path. Crosses happen a lot in scenes, but it's easy to overlook their emotional power. Sometimes both characters are crossing simultaneously. A variation on a cross is a *lead-and-follow*. One character moves, and then another character moves. The characters may move in the same or opposite directions; they may even be on the same path.

Circular blocking means characters move in circular fashion. You see this most often with characters clustered at a table, often as a character goes from person to person.

FRAMING

Framing refers to how much the viewer sees of any given scene, as indicated in Figure 10.1. Each framing is called a *shot*.

Framing is determined by

- Camera angle
- Camera placement
- Lens focal length
- Depth of field
- Composition

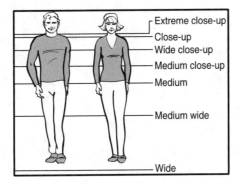

FIGURE 10.1

Basic framing heights.

For any given scene, any change of these factors constitutes a different shot. For example, if you take a two-shot, and then zoom in for a close-up, the close-up is a different shot.

Although framing helps you create good composition and the illusion of three dimensions, it's more important as a way to reveal action from different perspectives. In practical terms, multiple shots allow you to cover a blown line or missed actor or camera move. Multiple angles will also help you control pacing when you're editing your movie.

CAMERA ANGLE

Camera angles are determined by camera placement in relation to the action. Start by determining what you want to reveal.

Most camera angles fall into three categories: wide, medium, and close. Generally, wide shots give a sense of distance, sometimes grandeur. Often, wide shots are used to give the viewer a sense of geography.

Medium shots reveal some facial expression and body language, and can be useful when establishing the emotional relationships between characters. A *two-shot* is a common medium angle.

Close shots of a character's face are wonderful for subtle reactions. Close shots of action can be very dynamic.

Common camera angles are illustrated on the following two pages:

CLOSE-UP (CU): Tight on someone or something.

DUTCH: An angle that is intentionally crooked, sideways, or otherwise odd-looking.

FAVORING (FAV): Angling the camera to keep interest on a specific subject. Often a fairly close shot.

INSERT: A CU of something—a newspaper, set of keys, or another element of interest.

MASTER: A fairly wide angle that goes from the beginning to the end of the scene.

MEDIUM (MS): Usually refers to an angle from the waist up.

OVER-THE-SHOULDER (OTS):
The camera looks over the shoulder
of a character, usually FAVORING
someone else.

POINT-OF-VIEW (POV): The
camera sees according to someone's
point of view, although it can be the
POV of an object.

REVERSE (REV): The same angle
from the opposite direction.

SINGLE: Only one person, often
a CU.

TWO-SHOT: Two characters are
in the shot. You can also have a
THREE-SHOT.

WIDE (WS): A camera angle that goes
from head to foot or wider.

Generally, most movies use *line of action* or *axis of action* as a basis for establishing the visual geography of a scene. The line of action refers to an imaginary line running in front of the camera. The line of action allows you to retain continuity through a scene.

The line of action can be anywhere you choose, but often it's the eyeline between characters. The *180-degree rule* says that after the line is determined, the camera should be placed anywhere within a 180-degree semicircle based on that line. Any stationary shot that's on the correct side of the axis of action can be taken from three points within the 180-degree space (see Figure 10.2).

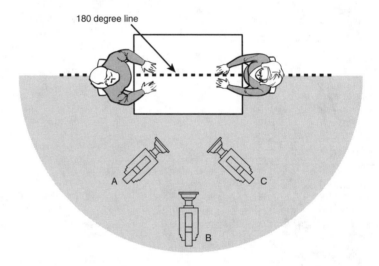

FIGURE 10.2

The 180-degree rule.

I call the 180-degree rule *working the triangle*. Working the triangle is a quick way of figuring camera angles for any scene on a line of action. Thinking in terms of the line of action can help you group your shots for efficiency and continuity.

One way to think about the line of action is to consider the viewer's geography of the scene. As with any geography, landmarks become very important. Give your viewers a reference and you can take them just about anywhere. After you've established who and what is where, you can shift as needed.

Line of action is helpful with stationary shots. The line of action can change. Just be sure to take the viewers with you. If a character moves, the line of action may shift. If a new character enters the scene, the line of action will shift. Consider cutting to an insert of an object. You can then work a different line of action. You can always dolly the camera to establish a new line of action. Just make sure your camera angles don't completely change direction without a landmark.

After geography is established, however, *line of motion* becomes the key principle to camera angles. Line of motion refers to the principal direction your characters are taking. Consider your camera placement in terms of the direction of motion, especially eyelines.

This thinking can help you avoid the worst continuity errors regarding screen direction. Viewers have become visually very sophisticated and many sequences, particularly action shots, can break the 180-degree rule and still "read." The crucial concept here is to set the scene's geography for the viewer.

CAMERA PLACEMENT

Camera placement means the camera in relation to the action. The camera placement can be stationary or in motion.

Stationary camera doesn't necessarily mean static. Camera operators will correct the framing as actors move through the scene. Static cameras are locked down, meaning that after you roll tape, the camera does not move.

Some camera motion happens for technical reasons. A handheld or Steadicam shot is often quicker to get because you don't need to lay down track or reset a tripod, dolly, or crane. But consider the reason for the motion in regard to the conflict: What are you trying to convey?

I use a camera in motion to convey a change in mood, introduction of a new element (such as a character), or as a transition. It's easy to get carried away with certain camera moves because, frankly, they're fun. There's something glorious about pulling off complex blocking combined with a complex move. But that's not a good enough reason. Every choice you make must be meaningful and motivated by the beat. Camera motion in particular can call attention to itself and push the viewer right out of the story.

Regardless of camera motion, camera placement is all in regard to the subject. As you visualize each scene, consider the apparent proximity of the camera to the action. What is the psychological distance between the character and the viewer? This will help you determine how far away the camera should be, as well as the focal length of the lens.

NOTE

Heights

Because actors come in all sizes, moviemakers have developed several tricks to make actors the right height. A common one is having a shorter actor stand on a box to make him or her taller. This is very common for love scenes. It also happens during dialogue sequences. There's actually a good reason for this: You may be limited in your framing and can't get a good composition or visual parity between characters because of height differences. For medium shots, such as two-shots, POV, and OTS, putting the shorter actor on a phone directory or box can help. Just be sure the actor is safe.

While taking your wide shot, try to block so the shorter actor is a little bit ahead and the camera is on that actor's side and a bit below eye level. Although the height difference is still there, it's not as distracting.

There are several common placements on the horizontal:

Horizontal placements

 Full front

 Three-quarter front

 Half front

 Three-quarter rear

 Full rear

There are three common vertical placements as well:

Vertical placements

 High    Eye    Low

There are several common terms for a camera in motion.

- CRANE—The camera is on a crane or jib arm and moving vertically. Cranes and jib arms are delightfully versatile tools and can be used for very short tracking shots. Generally, though, if you want to move the camera on the vertical axis—up, down, or diagonally—it's a crane shot.
- DOLLY—The camera is on a dolly and is tracking or moving horizontally.

- PAN—Moving the camera from side to side.
- RACK—Changing the focus of an image by moving the focus ring of the lens.
- STEADICAM—The camera follows the subject without using a dolly or other device.
- TILT—Moving the camera up and down.
- ZOOM—With the camera stationary, getting closer in or farther away from the subject by using a zoom lens.

As you analyze your script, you may visualize a distinct camera shot for a specific scene. Consider what makes it right. Often with DV shows, there just aren't the resources for grand camera moves, so while you may want to crane low to high, tilt down, dolly camera left, and rack focus on the lead character, chances are you won't have the time or the gear.

With a thorough script analysis, you can change up because of technical needs because you've figured out what's important in the scene.

LENS FOCAL LENGTH

Focal length refers to the angle of acceptance of a lens. The angle of acceptance is how much of an area a lens can see.

Wide-Angle Lenses

Wide-angle lenses deliver great depth of field so everything in the frame is acceptably in focus and camera bumpiness is minimized. Wide-angle lenses tend to have some distortion, especially of vertical lines, and exaggerate distances, so objects look farther away than they are.

These lenses also exaggerate perspective, making near objects seem larger and farther objects seem much smaller. This can be useful for a car chase sequence. Shooting with a short focal length or wide-angle lens will cause a vehicle coming toward the camera to appear as if it's going much faster.

Many DV prosumer cameras have wide-angle add-on lenses, as shown in Figure 10.3, to compensate for their standard zoom lenses.

Mid-Range Lenses

Mid-range lenses, or angle-of-sight lenses, have an angle of acceptance similar to that of the eye. Perspective, height, distance, speed, and changes in size are all similar to how you see. These lenses don't have extreme depth of field and tend to have backgrounds and foregrounds slightly soft, but this is not necessarily a negative.

They're useful for medium and close views.

FIGURE 10.3

Add-on wide-angle lens for Sony PD-150 and VX2000 prosumer DV cameras.

Telephoto Lenses

Telephoto lenses have a narrow angle of acceptance, with shallow depth of field. This shallowness isolates the image from the foreground and background, while visually flattening everything but what's sharply in focus. This compression of space can cause objects at varying distances to appear all crammed together.

Telephoto lenses are good for close shots and rack focusing.

Zoom Lenses

Zoom lenses change focal length without changing the subject-to-lens distance. Zoom lenses can change from fairly wide to telephoto focal lengths.

Many DV prosumer cameras are fitted with zoom lenses. Consider turning off the digital zoom because it often introduces electronic artifacts to the image. Many prosumer DV cameras can't focus through the zoom range, though, so if you need to zoom in, practice keeping the focus sharp and consider stopping down the exposure and adding more light for greater depth of field.

The zoom lenses on most prosumer DV cameras can only be controlled electronically using an electrical servo system. With some practice, you or your camera operator can become adept at varying the zooming speed. There are some add-on devices that can make this easier.

Using a zoom lens like a trombone is a sign of an amateur. Unless you have a reason for using them, try to keep zooms to a minimum. Combining a zoom with camera movement, such as a dolly or crane shot, or with an actor's motion, however, can give you a powerful image. Use the technique sparingly so as not to water down the impact.

F-STOPS AND DEPTH OF FIELD

Depth of field is the zone of acceptable focus in the field of view.

Depth of field is a function of the lens and the selected f-stop. The aperture of a lens is an opening through which light passes and is created by an iris inside the lens. Adjusting the aperture controls the amount of light that reaches the DV camera's CCDs.

The f number identifies aperture size, which is the ratio of the focal length of the lens to the diameter of the effective aperture. The *f* is an indicator of the amount of light passing through, so exposure settings are called f-stops.

Each incremental f-stop cuts the light reaching the CCDs by half. So, an f-stop of 4, expressed as f/4, lets in half as much light as f/2.8, and requires twice as much light to get the same exposure.

Depth of field is proportional to the f-stop. As the iris is set to lower f-stops, such as from f/5.6 to f/11, the depth of field increases. This is called *stopping down* the lens. Conversely, when you open up the aperture, such as going from f/11 to f/5.6, the depth of field decreases. Depth of field also decreases with an increase in focal length and with the distance of the subject to the lens.

You can think of it this way:

> The bigger the exposure number, the shallower the depth of field.

Also:

> The smaller the f-number, the greater the amount of light getting to the CCDs.

Controlling depth of field allows you to let foreground and background images fall out of focus. They become pleasantly soft, while the subject comes sharply into focus. Your viewers know exactly where to look.

If you design your project to have deep focus, with every detail sharp in foreground and background, your choices may not mesh with your technical and logistical requirements. Day exteriors may be fine, but night exteriors and most interiors may require a great deal of light to allow for greater depth of field.

Conversely, if you want shallow depth of field, your DP may need neutral density filters to cut down on the amount of light reaching the CCDs.

For example, outside on a sunny day, you or your DP may have to stop down to f/11 to get proper exposure. This f-stop will give you great depth of field, meaning that in addition to your actor or subject, the surroundings will be in focus. Your choices are to use neutral density filters (see Chapter 19, "The DV Camera," for a discussion of filters) or to use a longer focal length lens. See Figure 10.4 for an example of depth of field.

FIGURE 10.4

Example of depth of field.

If your camera has a zoom lens, you may be able to back the camera up, and then zoom in to get the same framing. Because of the change in focal length, you may be able to get enough of the surrounding area out of focus, while keeping your subject crisply in focus. These issues can be solved with discussion. Be clear about what you envision regarding depth of field and why. Sometimes a DP will offer a technical option that will enhance your artistic decision.

COMPOSITION

Usually, a director will not be concerned with issues about composition unless he or she is also the DP.

Composition for motion pictures involves the needs of the script, the limits of the set and gear, personal taste, and experience.

Generally, most human beings will search a landscape for a human shape, finding it more interesting than all the beauty of nature. A human face is of more interest than the back of someone's head, although people will look at the back of a head before a rock. It's how we are, and rules of composition come from human vision. The eye will be drawn to

- Higher before lower
- Larger before smaller
- Front before rear
- Brighter before darker
- Sharper before softer focus

The eye is drawn to elements moving

- Toward rather than away from
- Faster rather than slower
- Closer rather than farther

Generally, you compose each shot by giving weight to these areas of interest. Keep in mind the rule of threes, as shown in Figure 10.5. Imagine the frame divided into thirds horizontally and vertically. The points where the lines meet tend to be pleasing to the eye, so you may want to place the subject on the vertices.

FIGURE 10.5

Rule of threes.

Work the triangle to create dynamic composition. When framing your subjects, consider each as a point on a triangle as shown in Figure 10.6. Try to balance unequally sized objects, with the smaller objects combined against the larger. Shifting the camera a bit often helps to make the larger element smaller in the frame.

FIGURE 10.6

Working the triangle.

Also, especially in small rooms, placing the camera just a bit offside of the corner gives a greater sense of depth, as shown in Figure 10.7.

FIGURE 10.7

Working the corners.

LIGHTING

Harry C. Box's book *Set Lighting Technician's Handbook* is an excellent reference for many issues regarding lighting. In addition to in-depth discussions about electrical equipment, the book includes sensible discussions about lighting design.

We'll go into more detail about lighting tools and techniques you may be using in Step III, "Production: Action!" but for now, consider how light and shadow will support the story. Design according to those needs.

One hundred DPs will light the same scene one hundred different ways. Your job as director is to enable your DP to give you the lighting you need to support your story. Think about it now, away from the pressures of the set. For every scene, write down the answers to these questions:

- What's the time of day?
- What's the weather?
- Where does the scene take place?
- Where are we in the story arc?
- How should the viewer see each character?
- How does the character relate to light?
- What color and quality of light support the character's emotional states?
- Should the light include or exclude the character?

The lighting design may not be literal. It can be ironic, dark, buoyant, romantic, or any number of other moods. Light can be focused, bounced, gelled, shaded, diffused, broken up, and otherwise manipulated. Your DP will make choices about all of these based on the direction you give.

Generally, most lighting designs can be divided into *high-key* and *low-key*.

High-key designs have tones that tend to be brighter than medium gray. High-key lighting tends to have light falling off from foreground to background, and from the center to the top and bottom of the frame. Shading and shadows are very moderate. Color tends to play a significant role in conveying mood.

Low-key designs have lighting that is darker than a medium gray with large areas of shadow. Often, a character has only a slash of light across the face or body. Illumination is pooled and broken up with objects. Although color also plays a part in conveying mood, the emphasis is on contrast.

Many people use high-key for comedies, pastoral scenes, and a scene of warmth, and low-key for mystery, suspense, and danger. Depending on what you want, however, your emotionally charged scenes may have happy high-key lighting, whereas a scene with great gentleness may be lit with numerous shadows. It all depends on your interpretation of the script, your taste, your DP's taste, and your DP's skill.

If at all possible, consider the technical aspects regarding DV. Digital video has some limits regarding contrast that can drastically affect your lighting design.

Contrast ratio refers to the difference between the brightest and darkest point in the frame. The average exterior contrast ratio is about 150:1, but can go as high as 1000:1. Contrast ratios of interiors can range from 20:1 to 1000:1. But a DV camera can record a contrast ratio of only about 32:1. Peak white to black level is about five stops.

Recording a contrast range greater than a DV camera can handle causes highlights that will appear uniformly white or *blown out*. Darker tones will be uniformly black, or *crushed*.

This is not to say that blown-out or crushed video can't look interesting. It can. But as you make decisions about what you want your movie to look like, consider the lighting design of each scene in terms of DV's acceptable ratio.

Also, remember that every light requires a power source. This may seem obvious, but many DV productions are on locations with limited power. Night exteriors particularly require a lot of juice to power large lighting fixtures, so keep in mind these restrictions. You can resolve a lot of these technical and logistical issues with a thorough location scout, covered in Chapter 14, "Scouting and Locking Locations."

FLUORESCENT LIGHTING

Everyone I know has had to shoot under fluorescent lights. The high-key, flat light of fluorescent fixtures can be a blessing or a curse, depending on the types of fixtures and the requirements of the scene.

The first scene of "Music Appreciation" has Peggy being gently teased by her co-worker in the veterinary clinic. Peggy's trying to remain neutral about the guy she's going out with, so I chose to use the location's existing light. We changed all the fluorescent bulbs so they matched, I added three battery-powered fluorescents under the main shelves for a bit of blue and some additional contrast, and we gave Peggy a touch of key light on her face.

John's first scene shows him emotionally in the same situation as Peggy and also in a clinical setting, but a bit later in the day. We used existing fluorescents for him, but added some blue for when he turns out his office light and exits. We also lit a skeleton outside of his door with an existing halogen because I thought it was funny.

The theater interiors for "Music Appreciation" had different lighting. Initially, John and Peggy were going to have their conversation about their jobs in a moving car, but I changed that to the theater balcony. I wanted the focal point to be the missed connection between them, not John's driving skills.

I wanted this conversation to be both intimate and isolating. They're all alone, each with a stranger, in a great big place. I designed John and Peggy's conversation in the balcony to have a single, soft key light, a pair of rim lights to separate each from the background, the houselights up full, and a small light in a stairwell for additional depth.

PROPS, SETS, AND SET DRESSING

Generally, props are anything an actor moves. For example, a chair that a character kicks across the floor may be a prop, whereas a chair that a character sits in is part of the set.

Props listed in the script are meaningful to the action. Consider how you're going to show the significance of the object. You may want a close-up or an insert, so be sure to take note of that. That is a camera setup and needs to be factored into your scheduling.

Consider what kind of sets you want. Scenes are written explicitly for interiors and exteriors, but be sure the scenes fit the set. For example, a scene set in a suburban kitchen during the night may work better in the front yard during the day.

Set dressing refers to everything on the set that isn't moved by actors. Most no- and low-budget DV shows don't have the resources to build sets, but that doesn't mean the set can't be manipulated. Consider when the scene is taking place. You may be using a coffeehouse for the scene, and if it's after the morning rush, you can put cups and plates on tables.

You may not be able to bring in expensive furniture or knock out walls, but you can make decisions regarding what kind of place the character would live in and what condition it's in at any point in the story. For example, a character's living room may start out untidy, with all the furniture grouped around the television set. As the story progresses, the room gets cleaner, the room is lit more brightly, and the furniture is moved into a conversation area.

Keep your design simple and effective, with a consistent look that changes as required by the story.

Visual patterns, lines, and other shapes can convey certain moods. Jagged, broken lines can express tension, anxiety, chaos, or danger, whereas long, fluid curves can express sensuality or calm. A wall with stark geometric shadows feels very different from one with circles and curves.

Certain colors can convey certain responses in the viewer. A frame dominated by red can feel enclosed and suggest wealth, anger, eroticism, or simple warmth. Blues can connote cruelty, but they can also mean freedom, calm, and spirituality. The point is, whatever colors you use, design them to fit your vision of your movie.

Keep textures in mind. Surfaces bring detail to a scene. What do the characters have hanging on their walls? What kinds of floors are in their homes? What colors do you associate with each? What kind of roads do they drive down?

Try to visualize certain key colors, patterns, and surfaces for each scene. Something as simple as a bedspread, tablecloth, or curtain can make the whole thing work, but you need to plan.

See Chapter 25, "Props, Sets, and Set Dressing," for more information on these topics.

HAIR, MAKEUP, AND WARDROBE

Consider what the characters look like. What kind of clothes do they wear? How about hairstyles? Hair, makeup, and wardrobe, like props, are very important to actors, because they help actors develop their characters.

Your show may not have the resources to have intricate hair and makeup designs, or even people dedicated to these tasks. Your actors may feel comfortable handling all of this, but make sure they know what you're looking for.

The idea is to develop palettes for each character and scene that fit your interpretation of the script.

Try to group color choices to stay within DV's accepted contrast ratio of about five stops. That means pairing a character in all white with a character in all black can lead to some technical issues.

Also, keep in mind that there are some technical issues that may limit your designs. Specialty hairstyles, makeup, and wardrobe require time, so be sure to schedule accordingly. See Chapter 26, "Hair, Makeup, and Wardrobe," for more information.

And remember: Acting is not hair. Just because you dress someone up doesn't mean he or she can act the part.

STUNTS AND SPECIAL EFFECTS

Stunts and special effects don't fit into the no- or low-budget independent DV production style. They're dangerous, expensive, and time-consuming. You cannot rush a flying rig or mortar placement with any degree of safety. Even when done with the greatest care, explosions, hangings, knife fights, car chases, and other stunts and effects are still dangerous.

DV producers can't compete with the special effects teams of Hollywood. So, put your resources into what really matters: script, rehearsal, reasonable scheduling, editing, and music.

Still, many DV producers want to have stunts and special effects in their movies. Plan carefully. Most action and special effects sequences have many quick cuts, so plan on getting plenty of coverage. Consider using multiple cameras. It may save you time and wear and tear on your actors.

Keep in mind that the goal is to create an image that will be believable for the audience. If you stop being literal, you'd be surprised at how often you'll come up with clever ways to create a stunt or an effect that is safer, faster, cheaper, and looks better than the usual practice.

See Chapter 27, "Explosions, Gunplay, and Fistfights: When to Call In the Experts," for more information about this topic.

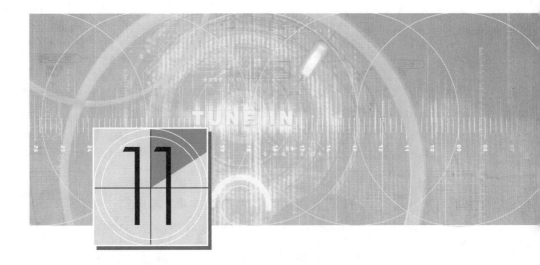

SCRIPT BREAKDOWN

A script breakdown means going through every single page of the production script and identifying what and whom you need. In addition to what's written, you have to imagine what else might be needed.

Because you brought your director and DP onto the project early, they should have an idea of what they want to do for every scene. Depending on your budget, what they want and what's actually going to happen are two different things. For now, as you do your script breakdown, use their notes to add information to your breakdown sheets.

Script breakdown is your chance to dissect your screenplay, understand how it works, and get a handle on everything that is going to have to happen to get the script produced.

You're deciding logistics: which scenes will be shot together, which scenes will require new camera setups, how much shooting will be done during the day and how much at night, and so on. As you gather this information, you will be better prepared to build a schedule that is efficient and cost-effective.

By grouping similar shots and scenes, you're going to save time and effort. Continuity in set dressing and lighting will be easier, equipment required for specific lighting setups or camera moves can be returned early, and locations you have for limited periods can be exploited to the fullest extent. Most importantly, though, you can release actors who have completed their scenes, rather than have them waiting around for two weeks to say three lines.

There are two steps in a script breakdown. First, every element of the script must be identified and color-coded. Then, this information must be entered into a breakdown sheet.

THE JOY OF COLORED PENCILS

Some people claim that using software is the best way to identify and catalogue script elements. I disagree. Although the old-fashioned way is time-consuming and painstaking, I've yet to find a piece of software that can imagine what's happening in the scene and what you're going to need.

Get a copy of the production script and write *breakdown script* on the top. Sharpen a pack of colored pencils. (Markers will bleed through.) Sit somewhere comfortable where you won't be disturbed.

Begin by determining script days. A *script day* is time according to the script. Script days are especially important for wardrobe changes.

For every category required for a breakdown, read the script through from beginning to end. Don't try to mark every element on each page in one pass or you'll miss something. People recommend marking all the elements at once, scene by scene, but I find reading through with one color pencil in hand at a time works better.

Note every question or concern in the breakdown script. You'll transfer this information to your breakdown sheets, but redundancy in this process is a good thing.

Page length is traditionally determined by eighths of an inch. An entire page is eight eighths (8/8). Take a ruler and measure the scene according to the lines, from the top to the bottom of the page, to determine scene length. It is possible to have a scene run nine eighths (9/8) or 14 eighths (14/8). I usually use the decimal value rather than the fraction—it just makes the math easier.

Color	Element
Red	Cast
	Speaking
	UNDERLINE the name of any character who utters a single word the first time they appear in a scene.
	Some scenes may not list everyone in them. You have to figure out if a character is there and if so, write his or her name on the script.
Yellow	Cast
	Silent Bits
	UNDERLINE characters who don't speak, but perform actions that forward the story.
Green	Cast
	Atmosphere
	UNDERLINE where actors are required to make a scene seem more real. You'll have to guess at how many you'll need and write that estimate in the breakdown sheet.
Orange	Stunts
	UNDERLINE any hazardous or potentially hazardous action.
Blue	Special Effects
	UNDERLINE all effects and practicals that must be created.
Brown	Sound Effects
	UNDERLINE all sound effects and note any prerecorded sound you may require.
Purple	Props
	UNDERLINE anything an actor has to pick up. Watch for implied props: A character holding a gun in scene 45 may still be holding the gun in scene 46, though it's not in the script. Note it on the page.
Black	**CIRCLE** all wardrobe information.
Black	**ASTERISK** all hair and makeup information.
Pink	Vehicles and animals
	UNDERLINE what are called picture cars. These are vehicles used by the principals. Atmosphere vehicles are all of the other vehicles in the scene. Count them up and write down the total of each on the breakdown sheet.
	Animals require a note in the Production Notes for a wrangler.
Black	Special Equipment
	BOX IN any instructions that fall outside the ordinary.
Black	**UNDERLINE** any production notes and write down your questions on the script.

FIGURE 11.1

Script breakdown guide.

Honestly, I don't know the reason for the use of eighths. I've seen these numbers referenced in production reports and scheduling, but I've never heard someone on a set say, "Hurry up! We have four and six-eighths pages to do today!" I've developed a system for estimating scene runtime for scheduling that I think is a bit more accurate and a lot less esoteric. See Chapter 12, "Locking the Schedule," for more information.

BREAKDOWN SHEETS

After you've completed the script breakdown, you fill out breakdown sheets, which isolate the elements in each scene. There are two ways to fill out breakdown sheets: by hand or with a computer.

BY HAND

Photocopy the breakdown sheet form onto white, yellow, blue, and green paper. You'll need at least 50 copies in each color. A sample form is included in the Appendix and on the DVD.

The colors signify different times and are an easy way to see when a scene is being shot.

- Yellow—Exterior Day
- White—Interior Day
- Green—Exterior Night
- Blue—Interior Night

Start with your first scene, picking the appropriate color sheet. Fill in the box with the marked elements in your script breakdown. Do this for every scene.

A *production board* is a tool for managing the information from the breakdown sheets to make scheduling easier. The production board holds strips of paper that contain relevant information taken from the breakdown sheets. The strips run vertically across the board.

Many people find production boards useful in scheduling. You can easily see what scenes can be grouped to make production more efficient. Many books explain in exhaustive detail how to best use a production board, and many stores sell production board supplies and software that mimics the production board method.

Day Ext.–Yellow
Night Ext.–Green
Day Int.–White
Night Int.–Blue

Scene number: _____
Date: _____

Script Breakdown Sheet

Page number: (Page number of the scene)

Title: _____   Int./Ext.: _____

Scene Number: _____ Scene name: _____   Day/Night: _____

Description: (One-line description of the scene)   Page count: (In 1/8ths of a page)

CAST— SPEAKING Everything underlined in RED.	CAST— SILENT BITS Everything underlined in YELLOW. STUNTS Everything underlined in ORANGE.	CAST— ATMOSPHERE Everything underlined in GREEN. Write in the number and circle it here.
SPECIAL EFFECTS Everything underlined in BLUE.	SOUND EFFECTS/MUSIC Everything underlined in BROWN	PROPS Everything underlined in PURPLE.
WARDROBE Everything circled in BLACK.	MAKE-UP/HAIR Everything asterisked in BLACK	VEHICLES/ANIMALS Everything underlined in PINK.
SPECIAL EQUIPMENT Everything boxed in BLACK.	PRODUCTION NOTES Everything underlined in BLACK.	

FIGURE 11.2

Sample breakdown sheet.

WITH A COMPUTER

I don't use a production board. Because the point is to manage information, I use a computer.

With the completed breakdown script in hand, I create a very simple table. I go through every scene, listing each element in the appropriate column.

Because I don't have extras, stunts, or other elements, I don't include them in my table. If I had one scene with one element in any of the missing categories, I would include it.

I then work and rework the table to generate a schedule before doing a mail merge from my breakdown table and into the breakdown sheets. I then photocopy the completed breakdown sheets onto the appropriate color paper.

For example, consider scene 1 of "Music Appreciation," shown in Figure 11.3.

This is a very simple database. I use the table as a basis for generating location lists, with complete addresses, location of parking, and even a snapshot of the exterior. You could also set up the table to generate callsheets for each person on the project with their contact information. *Callsheets* are forms that include who and what needs to be where when. For more information about callsheets, see Chapter 12, "Locking the Schedule."

On other projects, I've included my shot list and setups, as well as some storyboards, into each breakdown sheet. Because I produce, direct, and usually shoot my own projects, I'm the only one who needs to understand the information.

When you have other people involved, however, they can get derailed by too much information. There's no reason for your craft services person to know how many setups you're doing. All that person needs to know is what time, where, and how many forks to bring. Manage the information on a need-to-know basis.

If you decide to develop a relational database that's really slick, you can always share it with the rest of us. But remember: Development of anything for your show happens during development. You shouldn't beta test your application while in prep. Prep is about getting ready for the show, not tweaking software.

GENERATING LISTS

Use your breakdown table to generate an alphabetical list of every item regarding

- Props
- Set dressing
- Hair and makeup

- Wardrobe
- Stunts and special effects

An alphabetical list is easier to work with.

PROP LIST

Your prop list will give you everything you need to locate for your show. You can use your own stuff, borrow, rent, buy, or build. Often, you find what you need just by asking your friends. Depending on how complex your prop needs, you may have a prop shop where your prop crew can create whatever you need.

If you borrow props, you're probably going to have to let the owner on the set. If this person has some expertise in the prop's use or its historical period, this can be really helpful.

For simple props you feel confident won't be damaged or stolen, consider using the one-big-box technique. Gather the props early in preproduction and put them all in the same big box. Bring the box to the set, use what you need, and return the items to the box when you're finished. You return everything at the end of the shoot.

For special props and wardrobe, contact local chapters of the Society for Creative Anachronism, Civil War reenactment organizations, and so on. Horror props can often be found in the basements of Halloween fans, and many people are collectors of military memorabilia. Hobbyists are a great source of props and information.

If that doesn't work, garage sales and junk stores are good places to shop. Don't buy new if you don't have to.

For any expensive or dangerous props, be sure you have adequate insurance. Have someone on the set to handle and train actors on the use of dangerous props and animals. Specialty cars can be a problem. Many owners expect you to pay day rate for use of their vehicles, and won't let anyone else drive them.

You'll need someone with expertise to handle all dangerous props. Weapons, especially, can be lethal, even when dummied. Find a special effects coordinator with training and experience to handle these items and limit that person to that job when those props are being used.

See Chapter 25, "Props, Sets, and Set Dressing," for more information on these topics.

Location	#	Sc. Name	Desc.	P#	I/E	D/N	Count	Cast	Sound Fx/Music	Props	Wardrobe	Makeup/Hair	Veh./Animals	Spec. Equip.	Prod. Notes
Clinic	1	Vet Clinic	Wanda's exam	1	Int	Night	2.25	Peggy Betty	Pop song	Boombox CD case KY Swabs Latex glove	Peggy—scrubs Betty—scrubs	Light base	Wanda	Fluorescent sticks	Wanda Wrangler Existing location
Morgue	2	Morgue Insert	Establishing	2	Ext	Night	Insert								2nd Unit
Morgue	3	John's office	John hates first dates	2	Int	Night	.25	John	Pop song Door closing	Mirror Boombox CD CD case Concert tickets	John-suit and bowtie	Light base			
Street	4	Driveby	Driveby	3	Ext	Night	.125	Peggy John			John-suit and bowtie Peggy-casual date clothes		John's car		Road with a stop sign
Car interior - driving	5	Driving to the concert	In John's car on the way	3	Int	Night	1	Peggy John		CD CD case Concert tickets	John-suit and bowtie Peggy-casual date clothes	Light base Peggy-date make-up	John's car	Tow dolly 2nd vehicle Inverters Camera mount Light mount Fluorescent sticks	Road with a stop sign or light
Street	5 A	Theater Insert	Establishing	3	Ext	Night	Insert								2nd Unit

FIGURE 11.3
Sample production table for "Music Appreciation."

Location	Scene	Set	Title	No.	Int/Ext	Time	Length	Cast	Music	Props	Wardrobe	Make-up	Vehicle	Camera/FX	Action
Theater	6	Theater–Balcony	Snakes	3	Int	Night	.5	Peggy John Claude		Stage Chair Musical saw Bow Case Concert tickets	John-suit and bowtie Peggy-casual date clothes Claude-?	Light base Peggy-date makeup		Dolly	
Theater	7	Theater – Stage	The saw	5	Int	Night	.5	Peggy John Claude		Stage Chair Musical saw Bow Case Concert tickets	John-suit and bowtie Peggy-casual date clothes Claude-?	Light base Peggy-date make-up		Dolly	
Theater	7 A	Theater–Balcony	The reaction	5	Int	Night	.5	Peggy John Claude		Stage Chair Musical saw Bow Case Concert tickets	John-suit and bowtie Peggy-casual date clothes Claude-?	Light base Peggy-date make-up		Dolly	
Car interior–parked	8	Sitting in car	Oh the horror	5	Int	Night	2	Peggy John	Pop song	Concert tickets	John-suit and bowtie Peggy-casual date clothes John-suit and bowtie Peggy-casual date clothes	Light base Peggy-date make-up	John's car	Fluorescent sticks	Parked then pull out
Street	9	Happy ending	Outside the car	7	Ext	Night	.25	Peggy John	Pop song				John's car		Parked, then drive away

Day Ext.–Yellow
Night Ext.–Green
Day Int.–White
Night Int.–Blue

Scene number: **1**
Date: 3-17-01

Script Breakdown Sheet

Page number: **1**

Title: **"Music Appreciation"**

Int./Ext.: **Int**

Scene Number: **1**   Scene name: **Vet clinic**

Day/Night: **Day**

Description: **Wanda's Exam**

Page count: **2.25**

CAST– SPEAKING	CAST– SILENT BITS	CAST– ATMOSPHERE
Peggy Betty		
	STUNTS	
SPECIAL EFFECTS	SOUND EFFECTS/MUSIC Pop song	PROPS Boombox CD KY Swabs Latex gloves
WARDROBE Peggy-scrubs Betty-scrubs	MAKE-UP/HAIR Light base	VEHICLES/ANIMALS Wanda
SPECIAL EQUIPMENT Fluorescent stick	PRODUCTION NOTES Wanda wrangler Existing location	

FIGURE 11.4

Sample breakdown sheet for scene 1 of "Music Appreciation," generated from the production table.

SET DRESSING LIST

List set dressing requirements for each location. Add your production design and location scout notes from Chapter 10, "Production Design," and Chapter 14, "Scouting and Locking Locations," to this list. If you need to build any items, plan for time, space, and money to do a good job.

Somebody also needs to gather and track all the items required, and especially, make sure that everything gets back to where it belongs after every take. You can assign that task to someone, although often the producer or director will handle it. Discuss it ahead of time.

Always bring a collection of posters and other wall hangings to dress a bare wall. Make sure you have copyright clearance for any protected items. This collection can be used to dress up walls or unsightly areas.

See Chapter 25, "Props, Sets, and Set Dressing," for more information on these topics.

HAIR AND MAKEUP LIST

If you don't have any special requirements, you may not need to worry about hair and makeup lists. However, list them if you have any requirements that will affect continuity, budget, and schedule. You'll also need to consider what, how, and when you'll handle hair and makeup needs.

For example, if you require special effects makeup such as aging a character, you'll need to schedule enough time on the set. You may also want to schedule prep time and a technical rehearsal. Be sure to budget for the materials.

If your show requires unique hair techniques, such as authentic period styles, falls, sideburns, mustaches, and rental and styling of wigs, you may want to hire a professional hair and makeup person. He or she will handle these items, although you may have to negotiate budget.

Some actors have been trained to handle their own makeup for camera. Some, though, can only do makeup for stage and the result may be less than you hope for. Try to have a dress rehearsal so you can spot any problems ahead of time.

If you need a makeup artist, hire someone, or find a volunteer who is interested in the field. Do not assume you can just ask any woman on the set to take care of it. This has happened on numerous sets I've been on. An actor will need straight makeup done, the producer turns to a woman who is on as a PA and will tell her to do it. She may be really good at operating the boom, hanging lights, or driving a stunt car, but she'll get stuck combing people's hair and putting on mascara.

With special effects hair, makeup, and wardrobe, you may find people with a lot of skill to help you. Many people (including me) use Halloween as an excuse to make scary monsters out of friends and family. Many have a lot of skill and tools, and love doing this kind of work.

Find these people early and give them time to develop the special effects. Doing this well requires hours of effort and patience.

See Chapter 26, "Hair, Makeup, and Wardrobe," for more information on these topics.

WARDROBE LIST

Using your script analysis, make some decisions about wardrobe. You may not be able to specify every single item, but you'll have an idea of colors, textures, and condition of clothes you want your actors to wear. Start gathering specialty wardrobe such as uniforms or period costumes as soon as you can.

List wardrobe requirements on callsheets and have your actors write their wardrobe needs in their scripts. Some wardrobe decisions will be made on the set. Keep track of what the actors are wearing and consider taking pictures of every outfit.

Wardrobe can be a major source of continuity *blivets,* or mistakes. I was on a set where an actor forgot what he was wearing on a specific script day. He guessed at his outfit, didn't say a thing, and his scenes were shot with that wardrobe. He picked up his check and went home. No one noticed a problem with the dailies and it wasn't until two months later in postproduction that the continuity problem became apparent. The actor had left the country, so the only way to fix the problem was to recast the part and reshoot the scenes. The producer never finished that movie.

Some people will insist that having one person dedicated to wardrobe will lessen the chances of these kinds of mistakes. I'm sure that's true. Unfortunately, it still happens—big-budget motion pictures are plagued with the same sort of blivets.

Stop at the local library for some research. You need to be accurate regarding time, region, or job. Even for contemporary time, make sure you understand what's required. For example, military uniforms in movies often have ribbons, decorations, rank, and other insignia in the wrong places. With a bit of research, this is an easy fix. The same applies to police uniforms, vehicles, and tools.

For large projects, I've specified wardrobe according to script day on the breakdown sheet, and then cross-referenced that with a list for each actor. This is particularly helpful if someone's wardrobe changes—I need only be sure that everyone is wearing the right clothes for the correct script day, rather than revising each breakdown sheet. Do what works for you.

See Chapter 26, "Hair, Makeup, and Wardrobe," for more information on these topics.

STUNTS AND SPECIAL EFFECTS LISTS

If you have stunts or special effects, list what's going to happen and what equipment and personnel you'll need. Budget for materials and schedule build times. Consider scheduling technical rehearsals so you can see how things work. Also remember that you'll need sets of wardrobe. Stunts and special effects are often really messy and for continuity, your actors will need to change clothes.

See Chapter 27, "Explosions, Gunplay, and Fistfights: When to Call In the Experts," for more information.

LOCKING THE SCHEDULE

The best books on scheduling and budgeting for motion pictures are Ralph Singleton's *Film Scheduling* and *Film Budgeting*. He also has *The Film Scheduling/Budgeting Workbook*. Without question, these standout books will help you understand why things are done the way they are. You can also use the production scheduling estimating worksheet in the Appendix.

After you understand the purpose of breakdown sheets, strips, and production boards, feel free to use computer-based tools to make managing the data a little easier. But don't try it until you understand it.

I start on the schedule early because it gives me an idea of what kind of budget I need. Other people get a budget, and then schedule the other way. Whatever you decide to do, remember that schedule and budget go hand in hand. Changes in one will cause changes in the other.

A Good Guide to Scheduling People

You may want to check the employment requirements for unions and guilds in the motion picture industry. SAG, DGA, IATSE, IBEW, and others have specific rules about how many hours and days their members work, including turnaround time. You don't have to follow every rule, but it's a good place to start. See the Resources section for contact information.

Scheduling actually happens in two parts. The first is figuring out each task for every scene and how long it will take to accomplish. That's schedule as logic problem.

The second is figuring out in what order to shoot. This is where you can save time. That's realism in shooting schedules.

SCHEDULE AS LOGIC PROBLEM

For this part of scheduling, what you're trying to quantify is the amount of time it will take to shoot each scene.

This is where people talk about shoot ratios. A shoot ratio is the amount of footage you will get versus the amount of screentime the scene will actually take. For example, if the scene is one minute and you shoot eight setups (shots) with one take each, your shoot ratio is 8:1.

This is the way people figure out how much film stock they need. Videotape is cheap, so figuring out stock costs is relatively unimportant. What is relevant, however, is the amount of time you'll need to shoot those eight setups, including the number of takes each requires.

Each scene starts from the time you get to the set to the time you leave, making sure the location is exactly the way you found it.

Generally, for every scene you block, light, rehearse, and shoot, when you arrive on the set, the actors in a scene and key crew will first block the action. Blocking is figuring out where the actors will be going and what they'll be doing. These are very general moves—an actor may cross the room to pick up a bottle, but you're not locking the precise moment that happens.

The DP will then show the director the shot. If the director approves, the actors leave for wardrobe and makeup. Meanwhile, the DP will direct the crew to light the set. Some start lighting backgrounds while you're blocking, but the crew will put the key lights into place after blocking. That's how they know where to put them.

After the lights are in place, the actors return to rehearse the scene. This is where they adjust moves, business, and lines, making sure the right thing is said, and the right thing happens, at the right time. Camera and lights will be tweaked until the DP and director are satisfied.

If there's a complex camera move, you'll have a technical rehearsal so everyone knows what his or her marks are. Then you shoot.

Keep this in mind, and for every scene, ask yourself:

- How long is the scene?
- How many setups (different shots)?
- How long will each setup take?
- How many takes for each setup?
- How long will it take for the actors to be ready for the camera?
- How long will it take to dress the set?
- How long will the Foley, wild dialogue, and room tone take?

For every question, factor in the following:

HOW LONG IS THE SCENE?

- Time the scene during rehearsal so you know how long it runs.
- Blocking will take at least three times as long as the scene runtime.
- Rehearsal should be the same runtime, but factor in the number of on-set rehearsals.

HOW MANY SETUPS ARE THERE?

Usually shooting goes from the widest shot requiring the most coverage to the closest shots.

- In addition to a master shot, you will probably have at least one shot for every actor.
- Count two-shots, POV, and OTS shots.
- Every cutaway is another setup.

HOW LONG WILL EACH SETUP TAKE?

- Wider shots take longer to set up than close-ups.
- Complex blocking or camera moves will require more rehearsal time. There will be more blown takes and you'll need time to reset.
- Lights need to be set, focused, scrimmed, gelled, diffused, and otherwise manipulated.
- Butterflies, overheads, and reflectors may need to be placed.
- Moving shots, such as crane shots, take twice as much time as stationary shots.
- Driving shots take three times longer, whereas helicopter or other specialty rigging shots can take ten times longer than a tripod shot.
- Night scenes take at least twice as long as day scenes.

HOW LONG WILL IT TAKE FOR THE ACTORS TO BE READY FOR THE CAMERA?

- Simple makeup still takes time.
- Corrective makeup will take a bit longer.
- Special effects makeup can take hours.
- Simple wardrobe takes a bit of time.
- Specialty wardrobe (armor, spacesuits) can take ten times as long.

HOW LONG WILL IT TAKE TO DRESS THE SET?

- Reflective surfaces need to be moved or dulled.
- Furniture may need to be shifted.
- Windows need to be blocked or gelled.
- Personal photos may need to be removed.
- Props may need to be placed.
- White walls need to be covered or temporarily painted.

HOW LONG WILL THE FOLEY, WILD DIALOGUE, AND ROOM TONE TAKE?

- Foley may take an hour depending on the sound you're collecting.
- Room tone (an audio recording of the set with no one talking, shuffling, or coughing) takes a minimum of two minutes—one minute to tell everyone you're getting room tone and one minute to record the room tone.
- Wild dialogue (dialogue done without concern for picture) takes as long as the scene runtime.

OTHER CONSIDERATIONS

- Amateur actors, kids, and animals require more blocking time, more rehearsals, and more takes.
- Practical effects, such as lights being turned off, require more takes to get the actor and technical timing right.
- Especially in existing locations, circuits may be blown on a regular basis, even in the middle of a take.

For example, a scene taking one minute has two actors. You want a master shot and two close-ups, and there are no intricate blocking or camera moves. You estimate that each setup will have three takes. Getting the footage alone will require six minutes.

This doesn't include the time it takes for blocking, prepping the set, rehearsals, and glitches. Many of these things are done concurrently, but for your first schedule, assume it's all done sequentially.

It will take some time to answer all of these questions for every scene. Be sure your director and DP are involved here—DPs can often give you very exact answers.

Understanding how long each scene will take, from the moment you step on the set to the moment you leave, will help you figure out where you can save time and how you can order your scenes.

EIGHT DAYS A WEEK: REALISM IN SCHEDULING

At this point, you should be alarmed at how long it will take to shoot your movie. You may be able to cut back on the amount of time, but remember: Some things will take exactly as long as they take. If it takes an hour to get to the next location, it will take an hour. You can schedule 15 minutes' travel time, but that will make no difference.

After you know how long each scene will take, you can start ordering them in an efficient sequence. An efficient sequence means, specifically, an order that will allow you to get the most done in the shortest amount of time.

You'll have to balance what's efficient against aesthetic and logistical requirements. But now, focus on efficiency.

For example, usually the fewer locations you have and the closer they are to one another, the faster the shoot. You save time because you're not setting up and breaking down every scene, your power cables are in position, and there's no travel time.

To create a realistic shoot schedule, you need to keep in mind another set of factors. Start by grouping scenes according to these variables:

- Location
- Time of day (day or night shoot)
- Interior or exterior
- Scene number

Patterns will start to emerge immediately. Try to keep the scenes in order as much as you can—it's easier on everyone.

Location	#	Sc. Name	Desc.	P#	I/E	D/N	Count	Cast	Sound Fx/Music	Props	Wardrobe	Makeup/Hair	Veh./Animals	Spec. Equip.	Prod. Notes
Car interior—driving	5	Driving to the concert	In John's car on the way	3	Int	Night	1	Peggy John		CD CD case Concert tickets	John-suit and bowtie Peggy casual date clothes	Light base Peggy-date make-up	John's car	Tow doll 2nd vehicle Inverters Camera mount Light mount Fluorescent sticks	Road wit a stop sign or light
Car interior—parked	8	Sitting in car	Oh the horror	5	Int	Night	2	Peggy John	Pop song	Concert tickets	John-suit and bowtie Peggy-casual date clothes	Light base Peggy-date make-up	John's car	Fluorescent sticks	Parked, then pull out
Clinic	1	Vet Clinic	Wanda's exam	1	Int	Day	2.25	Peggy Betty	Pop song	Boombox CD case KY Swabs Latex glove	Peggy-scrubs Betty-scrubs	Light base	Wanda	Fluorescent sticks	Wanda Wrangler Existing location
Morgue	2	Morgue Insert	Establishing	2	Ext	Night	Insert								2nd Unit
Morgue	3	John's office	John hates first dates	2	Int	Night	.25	John	Pop song Door closing	Mirror Boombox CD CD case Concert tickets	John-suit and bowtie	Light base			
Street	4	Driveby	Driveby	3	Ext	Night	.125	Peggy John			John-suit and bowtie		John's car		Road with a stop sign

Location	Scene	Title	Description		Int/Ext	Day/Night	Pages	Cast	Sound	Props	Wardrobe	Make-up	Vehicles	Equipment	2nd Unit
Street	5 A	Theater Insert	Establishing	3	Ext	Night	Insert				Peggy-casual date clothes				
Street	9	Happy ending	Outside the car	7	Ext	Night	.25	Peggy John	Pop song		John-suit and bowtie Peggy-casual date clothes		John's car		Parked, then drive away
Theater	7 A	Theater-Balcony	The reaction	5	Int	Night	.5	Peggy John Claude		Stage Chair Musical saw Bow Case Concert tickets	John-suit and bowtie Peggy-casual date clothes Claude–?	Light base Peggy-date make-up		Dolly	
Theater	7 A	Theater-Stage	The saw	5	Int	Night	.5	Peggy John Claude		Stage Chair Musical saw Bow Case Concert tickets	John-suit and bowtie Peggy-casual date clothes Claude–?	Light base Peggy-date make-up		Dolly	
Theater	7 A	Theater-Balcony	The reaction	5	Int	Night	.5	Peggy John Claude		Stage Chair Musical saw Bow Case Concert tickets	John-suit and bowtie Peggy-casual date clothes Claude–?	Light base Peggy-date make-up		Dolly	

FIGURE 12.1

Sample production table for "Music Appreciation" according to location, day or night, interior/exterior, and scene number.

LOCATION

For every location, ask yourself the following questions:

- How long will it take for everyone to get to the set?
- How long will it take to get the gear staged?
- How long will it take to break down and tidy up?

How Long Will It Take for Everyone to Get to the Set?

- For every person you have in your ensemble—that's cast and crew—add five minutes to every location change.
- For every box of equipment, add five minutes.

How Long Will It Take to Get the Gear Staged?

- Stage your equipment in a place that is handy, secure, and out of camera view.
- Get camera mounts assembled and ready.
- Prep camera and audio equipment. Have all grip and gaffer equipment at the ready.
- Pull stingers (that's plugged-in extension cords) to the set for power, making sure to spread the electrical load.

How Long Will It Take to Break Down and Tidy Up?

- All gear must be properly broken down and stowed. Some lights must remain plugged in until they reach a certain temperature.
- Clean up, return items to their original position, and do an idiot check. An *idiot check* is sending a group of people through the location to collect forgotten items and make sure everything is tidy.

If you're using an existing location, keep in mind that you may be locked into certain dates and times. Start with those dates and schedule around them.

Remember, too, that you may need to go back for pick-ups. *Pick-ups* are reshoots of scenes or parts of scenes that have problems. Because you may need to do pick-ups, you need to be able to go back to the location. Keep it tidy and don't break anything.

TIME OF DAY

For every time of day, ask yourself the following questions:

- Does the scene or sequence require a certain time of day?

- Is there enough time between night and day shoots? This is called *turnaround* and can be a major problem if people don't get enough rest.

- How many meals do I have to supply? Remember that unions have specific requirements regarding breaks and meals—check their Web sites or ask local union reps for more information.

Does the Scene or Sequence Require a Certain Time of Day?

- If you require the scene or sequence be at dawn or dusk, you may have to spread production over several days to get all your coverage.

- Night shoots take one-and-a-half to two times as long as the same scene shot during the day.

Is There Enough Time Between Night and Day Shoots?

- Going from a night shoot that ends at 4 a.m. to a call at 9 a.m. the next day will result in an unhappy ensemble and diminishing returns. You need to schedule time off so people can recoup.

How Many Meals Do I Have to Supply?

- If call is at 6 a.m., you better supply breakfast. Assume each meal will last at least an hour.

OTHER VARIABLES

Now factor in variables such as

- Weather and seasonal changes
- Ensemble availability
- Equipment availability
- Location availability
- Special effects

Weather and Seasonal Changes

- Cold and wet slow everyone down. Plus, you may have equipment failures. Have protective and backup gear, and a contingency plan.

- Stay away from specific weather requirements for your exteriors. Move a rain scene indoors and show a window with water pouring on it and lightning flashes. Remember that this will take extra time to set up.

- If you must be outside, keep your shots close.

Schedule for "Music Appreciation"

The vet clinic was an existing location. The area where I wanted to shoot had no exterior windows, so we could be there at any time of day. I wanted to come in on a Sunday, when they were closed, but the owners preferred we come in on Saturday, when they worked a half-day. We got in at 2 p.m. Naturally, the vet had just had to put down a little girl's dog, and it was just horrible to come walking in on the middle of her grief. Poor kid. We used an office in the clinic for John's office. I had originally scheduled the theater for Sunday evening. The theater rep balked. Every other day was booked, so it was either the same Saturday or no go. The theater was 30 minutes from the clinic, so leaving and coming back wasn't an option because I wanted to shoot Peggy and John walking into the theater, which

Ensemble Availability

- If an actor is available for only a certain period, either shoot all those actor's scenes in one go regardless of location or recast.

- Some actors require several takes to get warmed up. Study your actors in rehearsal to find out.

- If a key crewmember is available for only a certain period, either lock in or rehire.

Equipment Availability

- It's faster and easier to shoot everything that requires a piece of specialty equipment, such as a dolly and dolly track, at one time, rather than breaking it down and setting it up for each scene.

- If a piece of equipment is available only on a certain date, or you can get it cheaper by using it then, lock it and schedule around it.

Location Availability

- If a location is available for only a certain period, either get it all in one go or find a different location.

- If a location has no secure area for equipment, factor in staging and breakdown for each day at that one spot, or find another location with a secure area.

- If a location lacks essential services, such as electricity, water, or bathrooms, factor in extra time to set up and break down those facilities.

Special Effects

- Even with rehearsals, the simplest fight sequences will take at least half an hour for every setup.

- Fake blood is messy. Factor in clean-up time.

Other Factors

- Certain props may be available for only a certain period. Lock in those dates and schedule around them.

- Setting up bullet ricochets and such takes longer than you think. You want to be careful—first, so they look good, and second, so no one gets hurt.

GETTING IT ALL TOGETHER

Now that you've figured out all the relevant information, start putting sequences together that factor in all the parameters. You know if people, places, and things are only available at certain times, so lock those into your schedule and arrange everything according to those limits.

Try to get all the simplest scenes at the same location grouped so they can be done right away. The fewer people in the scene, the faster it goes.

Group scenes that require extras on the same day or two so you don't have to worry about calling everyone to be sure they'll be there.

If you decide that you want to shoot a 120-page script in two weeks, keep in mind that you'll have to shoot at least nine pages a day to stay on schedule. It can be done, but you'll have to have a very experienced and well-paid crew and/or setups that are very, very simple.

DIRECTOR, DP, AND OTHER POINTS-OF-VIEW

Get your director and DP to review the schedule early in preproduction. They'll tell you whether it's going to work and even where you can save time. No schedule is set in stone and you can revise it if necessary.

SCHEDULING TIPS

Movies are shot out of sequence to save time. For continuity, try to schedule scenes in order. Sometimes, however, you end up shooting discontinuously as well. That means you get only one shot from a series of scenes. This often happens because you have an expensive piece of equipment that has to go back.

Keep your paperwork in order. When you've completed a shot and scene, mark it in your production script. All changes go in the production script.

You don't have to shoot out of sequence if you don't want to. If you believe your story would be better served by doing it in order, or if you have that kind of story, do it that way.

Some movies don't need to be shot in one go. If your story takes place over time, consider shooting it over time. There's no rule that says it all has to be done in 20 frenetic days.

Other tricks include

- Scheduling less-complicated scenes at the beginning. The ensemble will quickly figure out a working style and pace.
- Not scheduling 16-hour days.

(continued)
meant we had to get there in the evening. The shoot order for "Music Appreciation" hinged on the exterior car scenes. I knew they would take longer to rig. Plus, for safety's sake, I didn't want there to be excessive traffic. Those scenes went later.

The two inserts didn't require anyone but me.

Location	#	Sc. Name	Desc.	P#	I/E	D/N	Count	Cast	Sound Fx/Music	Props	Wardrobe	Makeup/ Hair	Veh./ Animals	Spec. Equip.	Prod. Notes
Clinic	1	Vet Clinic	Wanda's exam	1	Int	Night	2.25	Peggy Betty	Pop song	Boombox CD case KY Swabs Latex glove	Peggy–scrubs Betty–scrubs	Light base	Wanda	Fluorescent sticks	Wanda Wrangler Existing location
Morgue	3	John's office	John hates first dates	2	Int	Night	.25	John	Pop song Door closing	Mirror Boombox CD CD case Concert tickets	John–suit and bowtie	Light base			
Theater	7	Theater–Stage	The saw	5	Int	Night	.5	Peggy John Claude		Stage Chair Musical saw Bow Case Concert tickets	John–suit and bowtie Peggy–casual date clothes Claude–?	Light base Peggy-date make-up		Dolly	
Theater	6	Theater–Balcony	Snakes	3	Int	Night	.5	Peggy John Claude		Stage Chair Musical saw Bow Case Concert tickets	John–suit and bowtie Peggy–casual date clothes Claude–?	Light base Peggy-date makeup		Dolly	
Theater	7 A	Theater–Balcony	The reaction	5	Int	Night	.5	Peggy John Claude		Stage Chair Musical saw Bow	John–suit and bowtie Peggy–casual date	Light base Peggy-date make-up		Dolly	

Street	4	Driveby	Driveby	3	Ext	Night	.125	Peggy John		Case Concert tickets Claude—?	clothes Claude—?	John-suit and bowtie Peggy-casual date clothes		John's car		Road with a stop sign
Street	9	Happy ending	Outside the car	7	Ext	Night	.25	Peggy John	Pop song			John-suit and bowtie Peggy-casual date clothes		John's car		Parked, then drive away
Car interior - driving	5	Driving to the concert	In John's car on the way	3	Int	Night	1	Peggy John		CD CD case Concert tickets		John-suit and bowtie Peggy-casual date clothes	Light base Peggy-date make-up	John's car	Tow dolly 2nd vehicle Inverters Camera mount Light mount Fluorescent sticks	Road with a stop sign or light
Car interior - parked	8	Sitting in car	Oh the horror	5	Int	Night	2	Peggy John	Pop song	Concert tickets		John-suit and bowtie Peggy-casual date clothes	Light base Peggy-date make-up	John's car	Fluorescent sticks	Parked then pull out
Morgue	2	Morgue Insert	Establishing	2	Ext	Night	Insert									2nd Unit
Street	5 A	Theater Insert	Establishing	3	Ext	Night	Insert									2nd Unit

FIGURE 12.2

Sample production table for "Music Appreciation" in shoot order.

- Taking time off. Most independents schedule six days out of seven, giving everyone a day to do laundry and catch up on sleep.
- Not letting anyone leave. If someone wants coffee, send a PA. If someone wanders off to get fast food, you'll need an additional hour to get everything done.
- Not giving them a reason to wander off. Make sure the food is good.

TRICKS TO SAVE TIME

Most of the time movies run over schedule because they were never scheduled properly in the first place. You may be troubled by how much time it takes to make a movie, but you do have some choices.

- Cut shots needing greater set-up time, such as crane shots and those needing specialty mounts.
- Shoot fewer setups.
- Stay in one location for as much of the shoot as you can.
- Stay away from public areas that have lots of people around.
- If the script can stand the trimming, and the writer agrees, cut characters or sequences.
- Move everything indoors. Interiors with blocked windows are often easier to set up than night exteriors.
- Don't leave until you've gotten everything.
- Pre-rig as much as you can. While blocking and rehearsing, have the crew move gear to the next set at the same location, or start packing up to move. Just be sure they're quiet when shooting.
- Scout every location ahead of time with your key crew people.
- Rehearse ahead of time on the set.
- Have photocopies of floorplans so you can show people exactly where you want them.
- Keep equipment to a minimum. In addition to being secured, maintained, and rigged, all gear has to be managed.
- Limit special effects.
- Keep the hair and makeup people from fussing. Sometimes someone needs to be brushed up, but rarely between every shot.

INTERIORS, EXTERIORS, AND WHAT TO DO WHEN IT RAINS

The sets you use when the weather turns against you are called *cover sets*. Most DV moviemakers can't afford to have a location on-call in case of weather.

Try to schedule day exteriors with little or no dialogue first. You can always go inside if it rains, but if you've got one day left and it's still raining, you're in trouble.

Prepare for this eventuality by having a contingency schedule. Listen to the weather forecast and be ready to change if things aren't going your way. Schedule and locate the interiors either at or near where you'll be shooting exteriors. A few clouds usually won't cause too much trouble; neither will a few drops, as long as the lens stays clean and the actors are comfortable. But if it starts really raining, get the gear inside.

Go to your contingency schedule and start rigging for the interior scenes.

Sometimes you'll find a bit of inclement weather actually helps. As long as the equipment is adequately protected, you can get some scenes taken care of without too much trouble. Just be ready to hand your actors towels and hot coffee to keep them warm.

GENERATING CALLSHEETS

You'll need callsheets for every shoot day. You can use the blanks in the Appendix or the files on the DVD and modify them to fit your needs.

Callsheets contain only information for a day's work. They include the scenes, locations, cast and wardrobe, crew, special requirements or gear, any extra information regarding weather, parking, contact information, and call times.

The call time is when everyone is supposed to show up. Often the crew arrives earlier and stays later than the cast, but this isn't always true. Some people may need to be on set sooner or later, so include individual call times if necessary.

You can create callsheets for every shoot day during preproduction, but because there are always changes, it may be easier to do one every day during production. Do the first day's callsheet now and hand it out when people sign their contracts.

LOCKING THE BUDGET

While in development, you're chasing dollars. When nobody bites, you start whittling. A day here. A crewperson there. A piece of equipment. You're just trying to get a better-looking investment to funders. The money comes through, and you go into preproduction.

But you've got a problem: You don't have enough. There never is enough money—it doesn't matter what your budget is.

MONEY: HOW MUCH YOU NEED VERSUS HOW MUCH YOU GOT

It's an achievement to convince people to believe in you and commit to your project in the form of cash. In show business, people tell you they love you and your project, they promise to help, and they swear they'll come through, but that means nothing until they're committed—commitment takes the form of cash.

As mentioned in the development section, there are two ways to budget a show. The first is based on filling out a budget thoroughly and going after what you need. The second, more common with DV movies, is based on figuring out how much you can get, and then figuring out how you should spend it.

Either way, your budget sheets are the same. You have the dollar cost multiplied by number of units. It's basic math.

There are budget forms for your use in the Appendix.

Some budgeting software packages offer labor rate sheets based on current union scale. Plug in those numbers. You don't have to stick to them if you're not doing a union shoot, but you'll at least get an idea of what's typical.

Start calling rental houses for estimates on lighting and other equipment packages. Often, you can get package deals from rental houses, such as a 3-for-5 rate. A 3-for-5 is when you get the equipment for 5 days but are charged for only 3.

Having your director and DP onboard during development really helps because they can tell you what they want to do and what kind of equipment they'll need.

Tell the rental house people you're an independent. Call during early afternoon midweek, and try to go in ahead of time at least once. People in rental houses take a lot of abuse, so if you're polite, interested in their advice, and excited about your project, they'll treat you well.

BUDGET TIPS: SOMETIMES YOU HAVE TO BE TOUGH

Stick to your budget no matter what. If someone says, "Well, this is going to cost you more than we said it would," either make them stick to their word or leave. Here are a few budget hints:

- Make sure everyone knows what the budget limits are.
- No receipt, no reimbursement.
- Keep track of every dime.

Make all expenditures based on *production value*. If spending $5 gets you $20 of screen value, you might want to do it.

PLANNING THE MONEY FLOW

Cash flow sheets are reports you create to determine how much money you're going to need at any given time. I suggest you do two sets.

The first set covers each step of your project. Add up the lump sums for development, preproduction, production, postproduction, and selling. Dedicate these funds to each step and don't touch them. If you spend your postproduction budget, how are you going to finish your show?

The second set of cash flow reports is a week-by-week breakdown of funds. This is particularly helpful during production so you know exactly how much you have to spend. If you go over, it's better to know during a one-week period than at the end of a step. You may even be able to find the problem and fix it.

These reports can be in whatever form you want. Make them useful to you. If you have a UPM or production coordinator, be sure he or she creates, uses, and delivers these reports. If you have an executive producer or other partner, that person will probably want to see the reports as well.

SPEND, SPEND, SPEND

Most DV projects are self-financed. Often, people get into DV because they can afford to. They buy the camera and editing system and then pay as they go.

I think that's great.

Just because no one requires a budget, don't think you should proceed without one. It's easy to start throwing money at problems, especially during production. Don't. When people ask for cash, say no, unless there's an overwhelming reason otherwise.

Be honest with people about the finances. If this is a $10,000 shoot, tell them. If they want you to pay for things such as makeup, negotiate that ahead of time. My practice is to make sure no one is out of pocket because they're working for me, but I have specific guidelines about what I will and won't pay for.

Everyone on my shoot knows that if they carpool, I'll reimburse them for gas. If they have to buy wardrobe or makeup, I must approve the expenditure before the purchase and put a cap on what I'll pay—usually limited to a total of $10.

And unless you're seeking a distributor as an investor or a partner while in development, don't tell distributors what your budget is. It's none of their business.

TRICKS TO SAVE MONEY

- Don't pay more than the bid. If someone says it can be done for X, hold the person to it.

- Avoid kids and animals because they require special handling and are unpredictable.

- Arrange for actors to handle their own makeup and wardrobe.

- Avoid weather references in the script.

- Find locations you can use for free.

- Write the script around props and locations you have or know you can get.

- Consider deferrals as compensation, but don't offer if you have no intention of following through. That just makes you another jerk.

- Ignore permits, insurance, unions, guilds, and anyone else trying to stick their hands in your pocket. Do this with caution and recognize the risks you're running.

- Avoid complex camera setups.

- Avoid special effects.

- Avoid fancy camera moves or mounts.

- Avoid period pieces or scripts requiring elaborate wardrobe and makeup.

- Avoid actors insisting on trailers and special treatment. Egos cost money. Unless they're bringing you enormous value, it just isn't worth it.

- Don't skimp on food. People will judge the shoot on how well they eat. Happy people means better work. It'll save you money in the long run.

- Don't skimp on safety, especially regarding electricity. A properly trained electrician can patch into the grid so you're not blowing fuses every 15 seconds.

- Don't skimp on the script. It's the one place you can add enormous value for little cash.

- Don't skimp on rehearsal.

SCOUTING AND LOCKING LOCATIONS

You've got to go somewhere.

No location is perfect. A soundstage may be ideal, but you probably can't afford it. Your cousin's house may be great, but it's in the flight path. Your patio may be beautiful, but people walk by all the time and there's bound to be gaping.

The challenge is to balance aesthetic and technical considerations with logistics.

ASSESSING THE POSSIBILITIES

Take your script breakdown and generate a list of every location you need, interior and exterior. With your director and DP, talk about what the place should look like.

Now scout. You can always bring someone along who knows the area well, has a knack for charming people, and is enthusiastic about making a movie. Not only is the person pleasant company, he or she can hold the other end of the tape measure.

If you're going to be using public areas, an experienced location scout or location manager can help you with the permitting process. However, most people working on local film commissions are more than happy to walk through it with an inexperienced producer. For every location, you'll need to consider

- **Aesthetics**—Does the location look and feel right? Can you make it right with minimal effort?
- **Technical issues**—Does the location have the necessary infrastructure, such as power?
- **Logistics**—What type of resources are near to the location? How long will it take everyone to get there?

Regardless of where you go, you'll probably need a location release before you shoot a single frame. Start with the one included in the Appendix and modify it to your needs. You may want your attorney to take a look at it before proceeding.

AESTHETIC CONSIDERATIONS

All that's at stake here is that the place look right. Try to find more than one. And remember that often you can disguise the place with props and camera angles, making it look very different. Also, you can match different interiors and exteriors to get the best effect.

TECHNICAL CONSIDERATIONS

When you scout a location, take snapshots so you can remember the place. Also, bring along these tools to gather the necessary information:

- Still camera (digital or film)
- Compass
- Tape measure (electronic is helpful)
- Pad and pens
- Grid paper
- Circuit tester
- Flashlight

Consider using the location scouting worksheet in the Appendix.

Each location requires a thorough survey, taking into account technical and logistical considerations. Technical considerations include

- Access and parking
- Floorplan
- Available power
- Existing light
- Audio requirements

Access and Parking

Few producers take the time to see whether a location is easily accessible and has available parking. If you have to park an RV or grip truck, ask yourself where you'll put it and how you'll unload it.

Quickly sketch the area around the location. Use the compass to locate north and mark that on the sketch. Note entrances and parking spaces, as well as pick-up and drop-off points for carpools. Note any potential concerns regarding access. For example, if your lead actor uses a wheelchair, you may want to double-check that the elevator will be running on your shoot day.

Floorplan

Quickly sketch the location. Use the compass to locate north and mark every sketch.

- Sketch in roads, walls, doors, windows, power cables, and other features. If you're using an exterior, measure the distance from a public to the private area, such as the distance between a public sidewalk and a front door.
- Note how many people are around at this time of day. It's a good idea to return on different days and at different times to see whether anything changes.
- Note muddy ground and cracks in the pavement. This will help while loading and unloading, as well as designing shots in the area.
- Sketch the building and each room you want to use. Find the dimensions, being sure to note any features that may pose a problem for equipment, such as narrow hallways, low cabinets, and so on.
- Note surfaces. Bare walls may need to be covered. Dolly shots won't work well on thick carpet or cracked concrete. Concrete and linoleum reflect sound easily. Note any special treatment you'll need to protect floors, walls, and ceilings from special equipment.

- Note furniture and whether it may or may not be moved. Do the same thing with pictures, window treatments, and other items.

- Note appliances.

- Make sure which areas of the location you can use, inside and out. Don't forget parking lots or garages.

- Make sure you have room for craft services, makeup, wardrobe, waiting areas, and staging of equipment.

- Check whether the location allows you to shoot multiple angles.

Available Power

Ask whether there is enough power available at the location. For some reason, many novice producers overlook this.

I once had a producer who wanted us to shoot in a park. We had no permits, it was too late to drop a power line, and he had no budget for a generator. He thought we could just use the headlights from all the cars to light the scene. This kind of thing can work if there's no dialogue, the scene is short, and you can shoot at magic hour. But this was a pretty intricate sequence.

Suffice to say the sequence was shot in a parking lot.

You can bring a movie generator to power equipment, but they're expensive and often require a dedicated generator operator.

You can use a regular generator, but they're really noisy. Especially in the country, you can hear the distinctive putt-putt on your location audio tracks. Also, regardless of what kind of generator you want to use, you often have to have a generator permit for use in the city. See Chapter 22, "Rigging," for more information on generators.

Consider all available power sources.

- Note whether the voltage is 110 or 220.

- Sketch where the outlets are located and what kind each is. If you need 3-for-2 adapters (also known as *cheaters*), better to know now.

- Using the circuit tester, make sure the outlet is live and find out what circuit it's on. You'll probably have to spread the electrical load across several circuits.

- Get out your flashlight and find the circuit box. Engraved on each switch is a number, telling you how many total amps are available for that circuit. Because most existing locations will have things plugged in, this is not the number of amps you can use. You'll have to unplug everything or subtract 2–4 amps from the total available.

- Note any large appliances, cooling systems, or other electrical equipment in use.

Existing Light

Existing light means windows, fixtures, and any other source of illumination.

- For exteriors, consider streetlamps and any light coming from nearby windows.
- For interiors, sketch in all windows and doors and note dimensions. Be sure to have a compass point for every sketch.
- Sketch in all lighting fixtures, including type, and number and wattage of bulbs. Cheap fluorescent fixtures can wreak havoc, so be sure to note those.
- Note all floor and table lamps.

Audio Requirements

Jay Rose, DV audio guru and author of *Producing Great Sound for Digital Video*, writes, "As budgets go down, spend proportionally more for sound. If you plan audio properly, it's much more cost-effective than video."

Too often, locations are chosen based on what they look like without regard for what they sound like. Microphones can't be as selective as the camera. Although some audio problems can be solved on the set, many can't.

If your sound mixer is already attached to the project, include that person on the scout. Don't be surprised if he or she wanders around making funny noises and talking to walls.

If you don't have your audio tech on board, you can do some basic audio checks yourself. Don't be surprised to find yourself walking around making funny noises and talking to walls. You're listening for reflections coming from hard surfaces. As you walk around the room, you'll hear how sound changes according to how near or far a wall, bookcase, or other furniture is.

Although dialogue can often be repaired in postproduction by automatic dialogue replacement (ADR), or *looping*, in all likelihood, you won't be able to afford it. Get it right the first time.

If the scene depends on what people say as opposed to how they look, such as an interview, consider giving audio considerations priority.

- Close your eyes and listen.

- Note hard surfaces such as walls, floors, ceilings, and tabletops. They reflect sound.

- Pay special attention to central heating and air conditioning systems and vents. If you can't turn them off, you may have to remove the vent cover. If you can't remove the vent cover or otherwise minimize the noise, consider another location.

- Make sure appliances, especially refrigerators, freezers, and compressors, can be turned off.

- Listen for work noises coming from other areas. Typing and talking carry.

- Check drop ceilings. Many are open through the entire building and can carry more noise than you'd think possible.

- Listen for machine noise from nearby areas.

- Traffic noise can be particularly annoying during certain times of day.

- Airplane noise is also a problem, especially low-flying prop planes. Note whether you can hear them.

- Check for fire stations. If there's a chance an alarm will go off in the middle of a crucial scene, it will.

LOGISTICAL CONSIDERATIONS

Logistics play a critical role in location scouting. A place may be perfect technically and aesthetically, but if it takes three hours to get there, you may want to rethink using it.

I once had a producer who wanted to go up into the mountains for two weeks to shoot his feature-length motion picture. There was no water, toilets, electricity, or buildings. He thought we'd all just camp. That movie never got made.

In terms of logistics, note

- Location fees. Token money may be all right for a particular space, but don't go crazy.

- Overall cost for using the location. If you need to gel or black out windows, that will take time and money. If you need to rent a generator, that will cost time and money.

- Signs or other features that will have to be covered or removed.
- Where and how many bathrooms there are and whether drinking water is available at the site.
- The nearest grocery stores, hardware stores, and other establishments.
- Distance from home or hotel/motel and time how long it takes to get to the location.

EXISTING VERSUS CREATING SETS

Existing sets are cheap and usually authentic. Often, you just have to adjust a mirror and the set is ready. Unfortunately, they can also be a pain if there's not enough power or room, they're located in noisy areas, or people drop by to gape.

Soundstages can be wonderful. The ceilings are high, there's plenty of juice, they're quiet and private, plenty of parking, and usually have kitchens, bathrooms, and office space. There are makeup and dressing rooms. They usually have huge doors so you can move in construction materials, big props, and gear. Delightful.

Expensive.

Still, you can create a soundstage out of any large space. Warehouses are particular favorites and in some parts of the country you can rent them for very little money. Consider setting your story in a warehouse and you won't even necessarily have to build a set.

If you decide to create your own soundstage, be sure to budget for construction material. Even false walls cost time and money. Many warehouses are noisy and those made out of metal have enough condensation to make things a bit uncomfortable.

LEARNING TO HUNKER: MULTIPURPOSE LOCATIONS

You know you'll save money if you don't change locations. The trick is to get as many sets out of one place as you can. For example, one house can be one character's kitchen, another character's living room, the sacristy of a church, and so on.

Changes in lighting and camera angle are often enough to make the same room look dramatically different. Add a bit of set dressing and put the extras in certain clothes, and the whole place is elsewhere.

I've used the same house as business office, kitchen, living room, small sacristy, and fake TV studio. I've been on locations that have been used as a café, club, subdued bar, skanky backroom, and restaurant entrance.

You've seen many possible locations for your show. Now, consider where you can consolidate.

- Check basements and other rooms for possibilities.
- Driveways can function as parking spots.
- If a location has only one use, reconsider it. If you absolutely have to have it, consider using the rest of it for other scenes. Also consider using the exterior for scenes with no dialogue, but another interior for scenes with dialogue.
- Check local buildings for interesting architectural features. For example, a close shot of a minaret on top of a local restaurant may work as an establishing shot of a mosque.
- Any office can be made to look like another kind of office. Any home can be made to look like any other home. And sometimes offices can be made to look like homes and homes to look like offices. Changing sound effects in post really helps.
- Don't forget to look in back. Many buildings have interesting alleyways and yards.

PERMITS

Even if you hire a UPM, location manager, or location scout, it's the producer's job to make sure the permits are in place before shooting starts. In some places, the permit process will take 24 hours. In others, it can take weeks. Don't wait.

Permits are granted by the city through the film commission, county clerk, or city hall nearest to where you want to shoot. Contact them to get the details about the local permitting process.

Generally, if you are in a public area such as a street, park, or sidewalk, and if you need to put any piece of equipment on the ground, you need a permit. That's any piece of equipment—tripod, stinger, video monitor, dolly, anything. And don't think you'll be okay if you throw a power cord into a tree to get over a sidewalk.

Permit fees vary. In an effort to get more production companies to the area, many places waive the fees. Some film commissions will ask all kinds of questions, such as how many generators you'll be bringing in, what, if any, stunts you'll be doing, how many cars you'll be parking, and so on.

To get a permit, you may need

- A completed application, with application fee.
- Permit fee.
- Business license, requiring a fee.
- Proof of insurance.
- To flier everyone who will be affected by your shooting. This usually means homes and businesses on both sides of the block.
- A map of where you're shooting and a shoot plan listing scenes to be shot, exact locations, dates, and times, and remarks on equipment, personnel, and special considerations.

If a street has to be closed, you may have to apply for a closure permit. You may have to hire off-duty police officers as security guards. Street closure signs (see Figure 14.1) have to be in place 7–10 days ahead of time, and you must follow local traffic control regulations. If you need specific parking places, you may have to use parking meter covers to block them. Rental houses often have these items available.

FIGURE 14.1
Street closure sign.

National parks also require permits. See the Resources section for contact information.

If you shoot without a permit, be aware that you can be ticketed and fined. You'll have to file a permit application then and have to wait until it's approved before continuing.

BUILD THE ENSEMBLE

In addition to the people you attached to your project early, you'll need other people in front of and behind the camera. You'll be interviewing, auditioning, and hiring these people early in preproduction.

Be sure to make the chain of command clear. The chart in Figure 15.1 will help you explain to whom everyone reports and where the spheres of influence overlap. It will also help people understand their responsibilities to themselves, their crew, and the show.

Preproduction is the time you destroy the "Maginot Line" between cast and crew. By explaining basic principles—everyone must be motivated, good set behavior, and that everyone, in front of and behind the camera, is there to perform—you can build an ensemble that respects everyone's efforts.

Just remember that where you give responsibility you should give authority. Whether the person has experience or not, unless the situation goes horribly wrong, you need

NOTE

Run for Cover

Coverage is the term for all the footage you need to edit your movie together. Every scene has elements that need to be covered: wide, medium, and close shots. Make sure you cover every action, reaction, and piece of dialogue. Also, it helps if you allow actors and objects to complete an action. For example, keep rolling tape of an actor drinking from a cup until the actor completes the motion, or let a door swing completely shut before calling, "Cut!"

to back your people up. If you don't trust them, don't hire them. If you do trust them, don't ride them into the ground; protect them so they can give you their best efforts, and give them room to perform. Hire well and get out of the way.

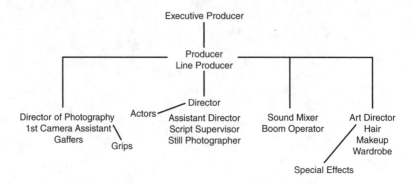

FIGURE 15.1

Motion picture production organization chart.

You're going to need people to handle tasks that can be grouped as follows:

- On-camera talent
- Camera crew
- Light and rigging crew
- Sound crew
- Art crew

You may also need a stunt coordinator and craft services provider, someone to take care of publicity or day-to-day business, as well as a script supervisor and other on-set personnel to help you get your show accomplished.

ON-CAMERA TALENT

The director, and only the director, directs the talent.

I admire actors. Everyone makes fun of them and for good reason—actors do a lot of strange things that we mere mortals find weird. But one of the reasons we make fun is, I think, because of envy. Actors can do things in front of other people that most of us can't. They can completely inhabit a pretend world and make it real. They act for us because we can't act for ourselves.

And as with writers, everyone relies on them to make the show come together. No one who watches your movie is going to comment on how great the audio is. If people are telling you how great the sets look, you have a big problem.

You can find actors everywhere. Some of them are members of the Screen Actors Guild (SAG) and make a living as actors. Some are semiprofessional, who work as actors but don't act for their primary means of support. Many of them are quite talented, but didn't pursue an acting career for personal reasons. Some are untrained or may be models who want to try acting.

The nice thing about working with trained actors is that they can often give the director what's required without a lot of handholding. They can handle their own makeup and wardrobe, and will even set up their props. Most of the trained actors I've worked with have offered to do these things—it really helps them develop their characters, get ready to work, and perform for the camera.

The nice thing about working with untrained actors, or people with little on-camera experience, is that they often bring a freshness to your show. They may require more takes, but sometimes after they've learned what they need to do, they deliver exactly what you need.

I like mixing trained and untrained actors. The untrained actors have an example of how to behave and the trained actors can challenge the untrained actors to dig deeper. Often untrained actors will give great responses for trained actors to work with and you get this combination of spontaneity and skill. Of course, it can also blow up in your face, or your choices in editing are limited because of blown takes and missed cues. It depends on how comfortable you are with the risk.

CAMERA CREW

The camera crew captures everything presented for the camera.

The camera crew is led by the DP. On larger film sets, the DP will have a camera crew made up of a 1st AC, a 2nd AC, focus puller, clapper-loader, and others. Often the DP won't touch the camera, but will instruct the camera crew to use certain lenses and filters on the camera, the gaffers about what kind of lighting is required for the scene, and grips to handle the cutters, flags, cranes, and dollies.

On smaller sets, often the DP will light and control illumination and handle the camera, with one assistant to help haul equipment and take care of the clapper and camera logs, and one grip/gaffer. The DP will then draft PAs or anyone else handy to help.

Some DPs will insist on bringing a grip or gaffer onto the shoot. If you can afford it, it's not a bad idea—an experienced grip or gaffer can help you keep things moving while the director and DP figure out the blocking.

LIGHT AND RIGGING CREW

The lighting and rigging crew works closely with the camera crew.

Gaffers arrange the lighting and electrical requirements according to the DP's direction. Gaffers handle and manage all the electrical equipment, from laying out feeder cable and electrical distribution to changing lamps. They are responsible for safely securing lights and stands during use, manipulating the light for direction, intensity, color, and quality, and wiring practical lamps, switches, and wall outlets on a constructed set, all while keeping an eye on light falling, blasting, leaking, and spilling on the set.

Gaffers usually have a good eye for lighting and knowledge of which lights to use for a given effect. Good gaffers can see balances of light and shade, correcting inadequate illumination, hot spots, over- or underexposures, odd shadows, and so on. Although gaffers are handy on a set, don't ask one to rewire your house. Few are licensed electricians.

Grips handle all nonelectrical lighting equipment. Whereas gaffers do the lighting, grips do the shading. Grips handle silks, flags, reflectors, jib arms, and other types of rigging. Grips rig camera mounts, move dollies, set cranes, lay tracks, and generally make it possible for the director to put the camera in more places than just on a tripod.

To maintain a chain of command, you can name someone as the head of the grips or gaffers as Key Grip or Key Gaffer. This person will act as a filter between the other grips or gaffers and report to the DP.

SOUND CREW

The sound crew captures the location audio.

There are usually two people in a sound crew: the sound mixer and the boom operator. Whereas the sound mixer makes sure the levels are correct during shooting, the boom operator gets the microphone on the boom in its correct place. Sometimes you may have a third person to pull cable, although you can always assign a PA to pitch in.

The sound mixer's sole purpose on your set is to make sure the proper levels are set for recording, the signal-to-noise ratio is acceptable, and the microphones get to their proper positions. Sound mixers should have familiarity with the entire editing and rerecording process. For instance, knowing that poor sound on a wide master shot can be replaced with the good, although perhaps not lip-synced, track borrowed from a crisp close-up.

Very few sound mixers possess more than the most rudimentary knowledge of audio circuitry. What they have mastered are the techniques of handling booms and fishpoles around lights, rigging, and cameras, all of which may be moving and shifting during the shot.

Although even location audio people will admit that theirs is the one job that can be redone in a studio, ADR (automatic dialogue replacement), or *looping,* is an expensive proposition for a no- or low-budget show.

Location audio people are hard to find. It's not a glamorous job, so few people go into it, and it's just hard enough that it takes a bit of time to understand what needs to be done. Someone who has never done any location audio can learn how to do it but it takes practice and some study.

I've learned that often the best way to solve this problem is to write a check. Especially with audio for digital video, the issues can be confusing—professional equipment mixed with prosumer and consumer gear can spell disaster when it comes to sound.

As you speak with postproduction people in your area, ask them to recommend someone. Often you can find a boom operator who wants to become a sound mixer and will work for little money for the experience. Sometimes you'll even find a location audio person who wants a chance to run a camera. In exchange for a bit of audio training, let her or him grab some inserts or second unit material. Just be sure everyone knows what the deal is—you don't want your DP getting into a snit—and do some camera and sound tests prior to your first day of production.

ART CREW

The art director plans and executes the look of the people, places, and things in the movie.

The art director is responsible for anything that has to do with dressing anything for presentation to the camera. This includes sets, props, wardrobe, hair, and makeup. Usually the art director works closely with the director and DP, and may have production designers, set dressers, prop masters, wardrobe people, and hair and makeup artists working for her or him.

On smaller sets, the art design may be done through a combination of what's on location, what props are necessary for the scene, and the director's intent. Everyone pitches in to dress the set and the actors handle their hair, makeup, and wardrobe.

If your show is a period piece requiring a massive amount of art design and management, you may want to bring in an art director. If you have valuable or dangerous props, you may want to bring in a prop master. If you have quite a bit of special effects makeup, you may want to bring in someone with the skills to handle the job. If you require food stylists, greensmen, or any other specialized art direction skill, an experienced art director will know whom to call. Otherwise, check your local film commission for listings.

The art director has an art crew to help dress whoever and whatever is going to be in the frame. This means the set, props, wardrobe, hair, and makeup. On smaller sets, anybody may be dragged in to help dress the set, especially if furniture has to be moved. Often actors prefer handling their own wardrobe, makeup, and hair, and will reset their own props for each take.

Makeup artists, especially those who handle hair as well, can be a great secret weapon on an independent set. They can help the actors develop their characters, use corrective makeup techniques to enhance the actors' looks, and keep all the makeup sanitary.

If you want to hire a makeup artist/hair stylist, ask around for recommendations and take a look at some portfolios. If at all possible, try to interview the artist/stylist on a set so you can see what kind of techniques and practices he or she uses. Good hygiene is crucial and one look at the makeup kit will give you a good idea of how this person feels about sanitary practices.

Be clear about what you want: If you need special effects makeup or someone skilled with wigs and hairpieces, tell the makeup artist. Some with experience in straight makeup may be looking for a chance to work with alien or gore makeup and may bring all that skill to you at an affordable day rate.

STUNT COORDINATOR

The stunt coordinator designs any stunts, sets stunt rigging, trains actors to do them if necessary, and will even take a fall for the show.

One of the reasons I like to work with trained actors is that they often know stage combat. They know how to handle fights and weaponry so it looks convincing and they understand that stunts are dangerous. Every time I see behind-the-scenes footage of motion pictures where people are playing with guns and knives, my stomach starts to churn. They might be props, but people can still get hurt or killed.

If you have stunts in your show, especially fistfights or gunplay, bring in a stunt coordinator to manage them. A disaster takes only one moment of carelessness.

CRAFT SERVICES

Craft services means the people who feed everybody on the set. This is an important job. Moviemakers, like armies, march on their stomachs. Make the effort to feed your ensemble with healthy food and have hot coffee and fruit juice always available. A can of pop and a tub of candy isn't going to cut it.

PUBLICITY AND BUSINESS

Be sure to have a still photographer on your set for at least one day. Photos are required for film festivals and distributors and it's better to get them now than to redo them later. I speak from experience.

SCRIPT SUPERVISOR

A script supervisor is responsible for script continuity. This entails noting screen and eyeline direction, actor business, and ad libs and flubs, making sure all the dialogue has been covered, and so on. The script supervisor needs to stay on book (keep the script in hand and read along with it), may run lines when an actor is doing a close-up, and, because he or she is standing on the set at all times, needs good shoes and an iron bladder.

OTHER TASKS

In addition to the preceding roles, you may want to consider bringing in others to handle what has to be done during every stage of your show.

Unit Production Manager

The unit production manager (UPM) prepares the script breakdown and schedule, establishes and controls the budget, supervises location selection, authorizes any changes in the shooting schedule because of inclement weather or illness, and manages logistics such as permits, insurance, security, and housing, meals, and transportation off the set. UPMs make sure everyone signs in and signs out, and delivers the paychecks.

Assistant Director

On large film sets, there's usually one person with a bullhorn. That's the AD. The AD keeps the set moving and needs knowledge of how much time a setup will take and a strong ego. ADs plan the day's schedule and are responsible for coordinating the action of every other department.

If you're bringing an AD onto your show, bring him or her on early. The AD is usually involved in preproduction with scheduling and budgeting, as well as other tasks, and can help you get everything ready to roll during production.

Production Coordinator

During preproduction, a production coordinator is working like mad to coordinate the show, and on some productions, a production coordinator may even hire the crew. During production, a production coordinator preps for the next day and disseminates important information. When the crew is at one location, the production coordinator makes sure the next is ready—sets, props, actors, extras, special equipment, and so on. He or she will also handle ordering supplies and expendables, book gear as requested, coordinate and distribute the shooting schedule, dispense petty cash, and keep the budget up to date.

Location Scout

A location scout finds and secures locations, getting written permission to use any number of places. It helps for a location scout to have a thorough knowledge of permit and insurance requirements, relationships with local authorities to keep the process going smoothly, and a mental file of interesting places a director may want to see.

Keep the chain of command clear and the lines of communication open. Remember that you must weigh the benefit of bringing people on against the costs. You must compensate them, feed them, transport them, and manage them. You also might have to fire them.

POSTPRODUCTION

Life sucks. And it's hard to edit.

That's why movies go into postproduction. Postproduction people organize, assemble, and manipulate the elements you've gathered. This includes logging footage, ordering transcripts (if necessary), cutting picture, creating titles, spotting sound effects, composing and recording (or locating existing music for) the soundtrack, recording voiceovers or narration, sweetening and mixing audio, finishing, mastering, and so on.

Many of these tasks are dependent on the kind of movie you want to make and the kind of repairs you may have to do. For example, not every show requires ADR, but you can be fairly certain that you'll want to edit picture. Listed here are the crucial postproduction personnel.

PICTURE

The editor takes all of your footage and cuts it into a movie, while working closely with the director. The producer steps in only if there's a risk of going overbudget or schedule, or the salability of the project is in danger.

AUDIO

The post-audio crew is made up of a sound designer, composer, musicians, studio engineer, and post-audio engineer. The sound designer will actually design what kind of sound should show up when. This may include existing or original songs, soundtrack beds, sound effects, and so on. The composer will compose the original music, including the soundtrack beds, which the musicians will perform and the engineer will record. If you have any ADR or a voiceover, the recording engineer will handle that, too.

The post-audio engineer will handle the audio sweetening and final audio mix. Audio sweetening is shaping the existing audio and adding new elements, whereas mixing is the final step of bringing the sound together.

MAKING CONTACT

One of the most daunting tasks for a first-time moviemaker is trying to find experienced people.

Start with your local film commission. Unfortunately, some film commission people are dismissive of DV moviemakers. This is unfortunate, but it's not an uncommon attitude. You'll find out that Hollywood producers will get access to places you can't.

Does it suck? Yes. Can you do something about it? Sure. Write to your local representatives and complain. Will you get what you want? Probably not this time, but maybe next.

Your local film board may have a cast and crew hotline where you can place a notice. They also usually have directory listings of local motion picture professionals. Start calling. Most will say no, but they may know someone who's looking for experience or wanting to try a new job. Often, an experienced grip wants to try being a DP, or a boom operator wants to be a sound mixer.

Send press releases, cast and crew calls, and announcements to local papers. Many will run them free. Ask other moviemakers and actors. You can even call local talent agents, managers, and casting directors. Often they have clients looking for more experience.

Go to local performances to see who's out there. Get involved with your local media arts organization, surf the Web, and poster local colleges or art schools. Regional and community theaters can bring you actors and stage technicians. Another really good trick is to get an article about you and your project into the local paper. Just make sure they print your contact information.

You can make a movie with an inexperienced ensemble. I recommend you have everyone buy and read this book and rehearse with the equipment a lot ahead of time. But consider making your life easier and bring on at least one experienced person in a management role. An experienced DP, gaffer, grip, or location audio person can make all the difference.

JUDGING RÉSUMÉS, HEADSHOTS, AND REELS

Sometimes you just know someone is going to do a great job. Other times, you're not sure. Go with your gut. Don't fill a job just because you need to fill it.

If you have camera or location audio skills, you can teach someone how to use the tools. Give yourself enough time in preproduction to go through the equipment with the person and make sure your schedule allows for extra preparation time. Be sure to run playback after the first take of every scene to make sure everything is technically okay.

RÉSUMÉS

Show business résumés are the stuff of fiction. Grand fiction. For acting résumés, usually

- *Starring* may be a starring role—check out the movie or show, although it can be *supporting* or *extra.*
- *Featured* means *extra.*
- *Principal* means a couple of lines—a *supporting* role.
- *Supporting* means *extra.*
- Listings without explanation mean *extra.*
- A character name and nothing else means an *extra.*

Theater roles are easy to check. Just look them up. Playing Hamlet in *Hamlet* is a lead role. A résumé loaded with network television and feature films credits probably belongs to a SAG actor. The actor may not want to work on a nonunion shoot. If the actor isn't SAG, then he or she is probably exaggerating.

Height and weight information means nothing. Ignore the age information and consider what age the actor could convincingly portray. Acting classes are often a good indicator that this is a person serious about the craft. Look for clues about geography. For example, an actor who has just recently left New York or Los Angeles may have a good reason for doing so—ask at the audition.

Depending on what job the person is looking for, crew résumés may or may not be a bit more truthful. Often, you'll find many crew people don't have résumés. The movie community is small enough that everyone knows everyone. Recommendations always carry weight. So do reels.

If someone recommends a crew person, ask

- How quickly does the person work?
- Is this person a leader or a follower?
- What other types of jobs can the person do besides the one you're asking about?

Just listen to how the person responds. Often, you'll get very important answers without having to ask a single question.

For people recommending DPs, ask

- Did you like the footage?
- How quickly does this person work?
- Does this person really want to direct?

Again, just listen. Hesitations are often very telling.

HEADSHOTS

Headshots are a standard tool for actors. Not having one is like a producer without a business card—it says this person is not professional.

Headshots are handy if you're looking for a specific type of look. You can quickly skim all the submissions. Keep in mind that they're supposed to be very flattering.

REELS

A reel, running about three to five minutes, is a collection of selected takes assembled on VHS tape. If the person doesn't have a reel, he or she may be new and simply hasn't shot enough material to create one. Ask for a sample copy of any completed work.

Some DPs don't have reels. I don't. When people ask for samples of my work, I hand over a copy of one of my movies, or direct them to my Web site to watch a short. Amateurish, I know, but I rarely work for anyone other than people who already know my work.

Don't accept this from a DP you don't know. If you like the person, ask for a work sample. If there is no work sample, ask for references. If there are no references, you may want to go another way.

The most common are reels from DPs. You don't have to be a DP to tell whether or not you like the work. Do you like the style? Are there any shots that match what you were thinking of for your story?

People will send you reels that don't belong to them. I had that happen once. I fired the DP after the second day of production. There's no way to guard against this kind of fraud except to call references. Asking for references is kind of unusual, but it's your show and you're the boss.

More actors are coming in with reels. Watching them will give you an idea of how the person comes across on camera, but remember that these are selected takes. And they won't tell you how many takes the actor needed to get a good one.

INTERVIEWS AND AUDITIONS

Interview potential crew people. Even if it's 15 minutes, this kind of contact is a good way to size a person up.

There are two kinds of auditions: scheduled and cattle call. Scheduled auditions are just that. The actor contacts whoever is doing the auditions and is assigned a time to show up. If you're handling the call, it gives you a good chance to preinterview the actor. You can find out a lot of things about people by the way they talk to someone who they think is just an assistant.

Cattle calls are just awful and they take forever. Basically, you put a call out for actors to audition. They sign a sign-up sheet and wait to come in.

Get some kind of audition space. Having people come to your house can be kind of creepy. Have two rooms: one where people wait and one where you actually do the interview or audition. Get someone in the room with the actors as they're waiting to direct traffic and make sure the casting sheets get filled out. There are sample casting and sign-up sheets in the Appendix.

Try to have a video camera for auditions. It will help remind you who is who.

RUNNING THE FIRST AUDITION

The point of an audition is to find out quickly whether you've found the right person.

You need actors who

- Are right for the part
- Take direction
- Are professional
- Are interesting to watch
- Can handle any material

Many actors have polished their audition pieces to a high gloss. Although they can be fun to watch, test the actors by directing them to change the tone, pace, or intent. See whether the actor changes up and stays with the change. You need actors who can vary their performances.

Keep auditions to 15–20 minutes. I always ask questions during scheduled auditions, but I don't cast in the typical way. I usually don't look for a specific physical type unless absolutely necessary. I look for chemistry, a willingness to try anything, a sense of humor, and knowledge of the world.

Because I usually work from my own script, I don't concern myself with sex or ethnicity unless necessary. Unless there's an overwhelming reason, I don't worry about age or able-bodiedness. I don't expect the part to be limited to those things.

A character is made in the collision of script and actor, guided by the director. Cast for collision, not by type.

CALLBACKS

After the first round of auditions, you must select actors who you think would fit certain parts and work well together. Do as many callbacks as you find necessary. There are two types of callbacks—separate and group.

At a callback, the actor will be working from *sides*. Sides are portions of the script. Make the sides available just before the actor is to audition. If auditioning separately, an actor will read the side with an assistant feeding lines.

I prefer group callbacks, combining certain actors with certain parts. Just be sure to tell them that this is what you're going to do and schedule at least an hour for chit-chat, study, and paperwork, as well as the audition.

Don't direct. Just let them go. It's amazing what happens. Some people fall apart. Other people you were considering for a small speaking role have excellent rapport with a lead. Some make demands on you, insisting on direction. That's a good clue about how needy they'll be on the set.

What you're looking for here is chemistry. Who works with whom, who is reacting and giving to other actors, and who is only tuning in to say a line. You can direct them to change roles and change pace, just to test the combination. But mostly watch, especially those not working the scene.

Actors are most truthful with other actors. Use that to your advantage.

HIRING AND FIRING: COMPENSATION AND CONTRACTS

No one works without a contract. No matter how tough the pressure gets, you can't let anyone hold your show hostage.

I worked a set where an actor held a movie hostage. The producer asked me what I thought he should do. I said, "Fire him. And let him walk back to L.A." That was obviously not the response he wanted. He asked another crewmember. The crewmember responded, "Fire him. And let him walk back to L.A."

Instead, the producer capitulated to the actor's demands. This was not a name actor bringing tremendous market value to the show. Even if he were, the time for negotiation was over. The contract should have been signed before the actor left home.

Generally, the contractor agreement should

- List compensation, including overtime.
- Give a job description.
- Give you ownership of the work performed.
- Give you the right to use likeness, image, voice, and so on.
- Explain legal remedies should the contractor fail to deliver.

Usually, the contractor will get a copy, credit, and meals regardless of the rest of the terms.

There are three general compensation contracts for everyone in your ensemble:

- Day rate
- Reduced rate plus deferral
- Deferral

Any of these agreements may include *points*, a fraction of a percentage of any profits.

DAY RATE

In the agreement, the contractor gets day rate compensation.

The term *day* must be defined. It may be 8, 10, or 12 hours. It may also be door-to-door, meaning the day starts when the contractor leaves home and ends when the contractor gets back. It may be set-time, meaning the day starts the minute the contractor steps on the set and ends when the contractor leaves. It may also include travel time. Discuss it ahead of time so there are no hard feelings.

The rate is negotiable. You will also have to discuss overtime, usually time-and-a-half based on an hourly rate, with a minimum. For example, if the contractor has 15 minutes of overtime, he or she receives an hour's pay at time-and-a-half. The contractor may want double time, being paid twice the day rate for working on weekends or more than five days per week, and also require mileage reimbursement, as well as other issues.

REDUCED RATE PLUS DEFERRAL

Like the day-rate contract, the reduced-rate agreement should define the term *day*.

The rate is negotiated for considerably less than the contractor's standard rate, with the rest deferred.

The deferral term must also be defined. In the sample agreements in the Appendix, all deferrals are to be paid when the motion picture has made back its cost, with a payment scheduled by the producer. In addition, all deferrals must be paid simultaneously. For example, the producer cannot decide to pay off one deferral contract without paying off the others.

Also, the percentage of payment must be the same for everyone. If the producer pays off 50% of one agreement, he or she must pay off 50% of all agreements. In exchange for the reduced rate and deferral, often the producer is giving the contractor points.

DEFERRAL

In a deferral contract, no money changes hands. The contractor is working for free, hoping to get paid when the show makes its money back.

If you have no intention of paying deferrals, don't offer them. Copy of the finished show, credit, and meals are often enough, especially for people new to moviemaking.

The sample contracts in the Appendix are for deferrals, but modify them to fit your needs and have your attorney review them.

UNIONS AND GUILDS

Depending on labor conditions in your state, you may be required to hire people who are union members. Check with your attorney.

If not, my assumption is that you're not a signatory to any union or guild agreement. If you are, you have very specific requirements you must follow on your set. The best source for information is to contact the union or guild. You can find contact information in the Resources section.

- For actors, contact the Screen Actors Guild (SAG).
- For extras, contact the Screen Extras Guild (SEG).
- For writers, contact the Writer's Guild of America (WGA).
- For directors, contact the Directors Guild of America (DGA).
- For gaffers and other lighting technicians, contact the International Alliance of Theatrical and Stage Employees (IATSE), International Brotherhood of Electrical Workers (IBEW), or National Association of Broadcast Employees and Technicians (NABET).

There are other unions who may also have requirements that you need to fulfill.

Keep in mind that if you're not a signatory, you're not responsible for meeting the requirements of the union or guild. Roughly, nonunion ensembles make half of the motion pictures made in the United States. If a union member decides to work on your show, that person is in violation of the union agreement, not you. The guild or union has no power in enjoining you from shooting, cutting, and selling your show.

If you decide to sign, these agreements cover in great detail almost every aspect of moviemaking, including

- Minimum wages
- Compensation for overtime, night, and weekend work
- Meal times and length of meal periods
- Job descriptions
- Travel obligations and distant location wage scale
- Hazardous work allowance
- Union dues and fringe benefits
- Insurance
- Arbitration procedures

You must be a signatory to work with name actors or directors who are guild members. Get a big enough name and a big enough budget, the costs of hiring union become less onerous.

Hiring union is no guarantee of quality. Even the unions will tell you so. If a union member screws up, shows up drunk, has a tantrum, or otherwise misbehaves, the union will take no action. Don't think it's never happened. It has and it will. And although most members are experienced professionals and worth every penny you pay them, some have been granted membership for volunteer work they did on behalf of the guild or the union. You think you're hiring experience and you find out you're not.

Union shoots are still expensive, regardless of the no- and low-budget agreements unions have created. In addition to fulfilling the employment requirements, including fringe benefits, pension payments, taxes, and others, it's incumbent upon you to make sure all the paperwork gets done. Often that means bringing in a payroll service or UPM you otherwise would not have hired to ensure you're in compliance.

Also, an agreement may hamstring a producer who gets a distribution offer. Some no- and low-budget guild agreements require that their members not agree to any set payment until a distribution deal is offered. After it is, the members can demand whatever compensation they want in order to sign off on the deal.

I understand that the point of a union is to protect its members from exploitation. I also understand that if a guild or union tries to create a less onerous set of agreements, some sleazoid producer will take advantage of it to screw someone out of fair compensation.

Unfortunately, although some unions and guilds have made efforts to work with no-budget and low-budget producers, their requirements are often still beyond the budget of many DV producers.

BUILDING THE ENSEMBLE

One thing to keep in mind while you're searching for people to work on your show: You can have people audition for a part or you can have them audition for the project. Regardless of whether they are in front of or behind the camera, in the office or editing suite, cast everyone according to how they fit into your vision of the project.

- Pay attention to your gut. If it feels right, it usually is. If it hangs over your belt, cut back on the mini donuts.
- Hire people you can yell at. They need to know that you're in charge.

- Where you give responsibility, give authority.

- Keep the psychodrama at home. If you are on the verge of an emotional meltdown, wait until you're away from the set. And don't indulge in gossip—while fun, it's a waste of time and energy.

- Follow the three-step rule. The first time someone messes up, take him or her aside for correction. The second time, politely correct him or her in front of others. The third time, though, yell. And consider firing.

- Creative differences are not always bad. Just make sure everyone fights fair by fighting fair yourself. As a producer, you'll be doing a lot of negotiating. Just remember to protect your director's vision.

- Don't lie.

- Don't steal.

- Don't letch.

For some reason, producers will hand out sides instead of complete screenplays to each member of the ensemble. This is a great way to make people feel less than appreciated. Give everyone a script. You want them to work with you—start by showing them your blueprint for the show so they can see where they fit in.

Schedule so your ensemble has room to discover and experiment, within reason. As producer, you must enforce the *within reason* part of this.

- Rehearse. Make sure your key personnel come to some of the rehearsals so they can meet the actors, get a sense of the director's interpretation of the script, and plan color palettes.

- Schedule an easy first day. Let people work at their best behavior and at the best level. There will be plenty of opportunities for panic, stress, and sleeplessness later.

Producers have a lot of jobs to do. While in preproduction, assess yourself once more. Are you detail-oriented? A risk-taker? Emotionally tough? If not, find a coproducer or line producer now to balance out your skills and personality.

On the set, people follow the pace and attitude of the director, but it's your personal authority that keeps the project moving. Let people do what they were hired for and don't meddle unless absolutely necessary. Stay out of the personality minutiae. Only step in when it's affecting the budget or schedule.

DESTROYING THE "MAGINOT LINE" BETWEEN CAST AND CREW

I'm sick of the line between cast and crew. It's so stupid. We're all there to perform. Nobody wants to be the one who screws up the take.

Everyone on a set has certain rituals and practices. We all make fun of actors who go through their exercises, but grips, DPs, and audio people have them, too. They just hide their preparations in a flurry of what appears to be technical activity.

On DV sets, there's a lot of mixing between cast and crew. I like that. I like when an actor offers to work production on the days he or she isn't performing. I like it when crew people offer to be extras in a scene. I love when someone from the crew improvs with a lead. Some of my favorite movie moments happen that way.

This doesn't mean an actor should start messing with the camera or a boom op should direct actors. I mean, however, that constant communication between both groups leads to a better result. And more fun.

Look after one another. Moviemaking is hard work and you're all in this together.

I have some advice for people in front of and behind the camera.

TO PEOPLE IN FRONT OF THE CAMERA

There's tremendous pressure when dealing with the technical aspects of motion picture production. Things happen that are outside the control of a producer, DP, or technician, yet the crew is supposed to soldier on.

Respect the work of the people behind the camera. They work just as hard, sometimes harder, than you. Often they don't get to sit down until the show's wrapped for the day. Don't be fooled by their grubby clothes: They're dedicated to doing a good job.

Please behave yourself.

- Getting drunk and passing out on the set isn't artistic; it's idiotic. If you're bored, offer to pull cable or run lines.
- Don't tell people how to do their jobs. Any actor who tells a DP where to put a camera deserves to get the camera in an unexpected, and uncomfortable, place.
- If you want to change your performance, please work it out in rehearsal. Unexpected yelling hurts the ears of anyone wearing headphones. Plus, it's no good in the recording.

- Before you ask for another take, remember that time is of the essence.
- Pick up after yourself. The crew isn't there to wait on you.
- Hit your marks. If it's not in the frame, it didn't happen.

Remember that the crew wants you to be great. They want you to be a star. You're representing them on camera and they need you to be prepared and give it your best. You don't have to be anybody's buddy—just be a pro.

TO PEOPLE BEHIND THE CAMERA

We all make fun of actors. Even actors make fun of actors. But enough's enough. Without them, we just have scenery.

- Protect your actors. They have to be rested and look right for the camera. They're representing you, so support them and be considerate.
- Protect your actors during nude scenes. Don't invite your friends to see the naked people. I fire crew who do this. If it's not necessary for you to be there, get out of the room.
- Keep your sarcastic remarks to yourself. Actors know when it's not going well and don't need your help to feel worse.
- Admit when you've made a mistake. If you need another take, say so. Better to be safe than have the producer crying. Usually.
- Alert the head of the department when you think something's wrong you can't fix yourself. This doesn't mean you whine about everything. It means you speak up when you can't solve the problem.
- Hit your marks.

If the actors want to help out, let them. Stage actors in particular often have lots of experience working in an ensemble. They often have technical skills and are willing to put them to work.

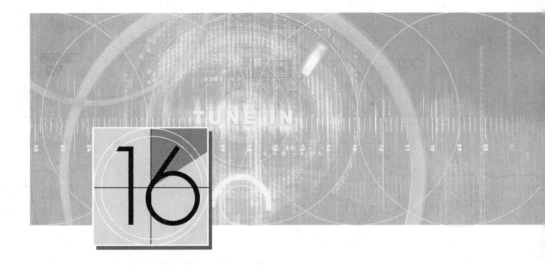

STORYBOARDS, SHOOTING SCRIPTS, SHOT LISTS, AND REHEARSALS

Storyboarding means producing sketches of the shots of your script. Shooting scripts are production scripts with camera shots, angles, and moves written in. There may or may not be storyboards. Shot lists are lists of each shot for every scene.

Usually, I use a shooting script that I've lined and a shot list. I write in the basic shots I want in the production script. I specify the camera mount and color palette I've chosen regarding lighting, and anything else I think is relevant. I then use a shot list to remind me of what I have planned.

I take these materials, as well as other notes and location reports, to rehearsal. When I use a storyboard in rehearsal, I get the chance to practice how to explain the shot to someone. It's a great test of my interpretation and design, and helps me think about how to guide the actors in developing their characters and beats.

See Chapter 10, "Production Design," if you need to review the terms for camera angles and camera in motion. These terms are the best way for you to explain what the shot should look like.

STORYBOARDS

I only sketch storyboards for specific angles or if there's a complicated sequence. Most of the time people see the sketch and laugh. I can't draw. I mean, I really can't draw.

FIGURE 16.1

Storyboard panels for scene 8, shots A, B, C, and D, "Music Appreciation."

Some people swear by storyboards. They can work out their ideas on paper and not on the set, saving time. They then use the storyboards as a quick way to communicate what they want. Some shoot only what they storyboard, covering only the material they need for editing.

Storyboards can help you visualize what your movie is going to look like. Professional storyboard artists draw beautiful renditions of each scene— truly beautiful illustrations. Unless you know how to wield pastels, or know someone who does, though, you may be drawing stick figures.

Start by going through your entire script, visualizing each shot and transition. Keep the drawing panels small and sketch in the first and last frame of each scene. Go back and fill in the intermediate frames. Write in a brief description under each storyboard of what's happening in the scene.

If you can't or don't want to draw, consider using possible wooden mannequins, Ken and Barbie dolls, or any other toy figurine as your characters, and take digital still photos of every shot. You can also use figures from clip-art collections.

Dump the shots into a storyboard template. You can draw in or use still photos of backgrounds if that helps you. Make sure you have scene number, shot, and brief description for each panel.

Make as many panels as you want. Detail depends on how much is required to get the point across. Storyboards are a tool, not an end to themselves, although given how much time is lavished on them, you have to wonder.

Storyboarding software makes the process easier by offering standardized terms and a library of figures for your use.

FIGURE 16.2

Screens of Storyboard Artist from Power Production Software.

Animatics is when you animate the storyboard. Depending on how complex you want to get, you can animate your storyboards using a GIF animator or Microsoft PowerPoint. Some software packages will animate your storyboards for you.

SHOOTING SCRIPTS

Shooting scripts have camera shots, angles, and moves written into the production script. There may or may not be storyboards.

I use a method known as *lining*.

LINING

With lining, you take a ruler and draw in the production script exactly what dialogue and business will be covered for each shot. For example:

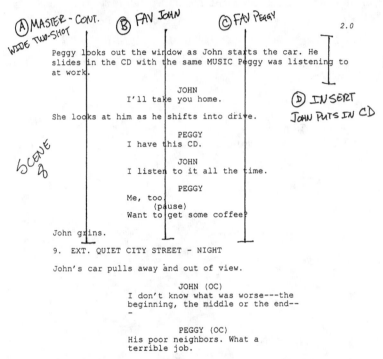

FIGURE 16.3

Lining a scene.

SHOT LIST

I create a shot list from my lined production script. Most people number the shots. For example, on the set the person slating says, "scene 8, shot 1, take 1." When slating added scenes, the person says, "scene 7A, shot 1, take 1."

On film shoots, the person slating each take is called a *clapper/loader*. There are no clapper/loaders on a video shoot, so the job goes to a second AC (if there is one) or a PA assigned to the camera crew.

I use letters instead of numbers for shots. I find it easier to distinguish takes this way. The slate goes, "scene 8, shot A, take 1." When slating added scenes, the person says, "scene 7A, shot A, take 1."

Lettered shots allow for a certain degree of consistency. For example, usually every "A" shot for me is a wide master shot. The ensemble learns this quickly and is able to think in terms of what the camera will see, helping everyone prep the set.

My shot list looks like this:

> 8-A. MASTER-TWO-SHOT
>
> 8-B. FAV JOHN
>
> 8-C. REVERSE FAV PEGGY
>
> 8-D. CU INSERT JOHN PUTTING IN CD

Using lining and shot lists is really quick and allows me to think in terms of coverage and shots.

REHEARSAL

The first rule of rehearsal is that you're allowed to say, "oops."

Rehearsal is the time to make mistakes, and through them, discover more about the characters, performances, and revelations about your screenplay's conflict. Give up any insecurity you have about how a director should behave or what a director should know. No one is infallible, especially directors. A little humility can help aid discovery and build trust.

No director can get a better performance out of an actor. Only the actor can do that. Your job is to help remove obstacles. This means removing the necessity for an actor to always be watching himself or herself—being audience as well as performer. The director is the audience. Give your actors your undivided attention. Be prepared, so they can trust you to know when they're on the right track. Listen to them and, when necessary, tell them to stop.

It's a balancing act.

The only downside to rehearsing is that there are too many choices. You can spend weeks going over the same fascinating aspect of one scene. As the director, it's your job to be disciplined.

First, set a schedule and stick to it. If you can rehearse on the set, excellent. If not, try to approximate the area, but don't lock any blocking. Often actors (and directors) can get hung up on the wrong details.

Plan how you want the rehearsals to develop. Actors don't play plot necessities. If they do, you've just wasted valuable screen time. Your actors don't imitate people. They create characters, based on the screenplay, through action. The essence of that action is conflict. Without it, there is no story.

Rehearsal is about finding the point of clash, testing it, and working it into concrete action. Actors, guided by the director, search out the moment in each scene when all the conflicting wants of the characters become meaningful in view of the central conflict.

Consider having a first reading with the entire ensemble. Make sure everyone knows this is not a performance. Introduce everyone, give a very brief overview of your plan of action for rehearsals, and then get it done. Stay on schedule. There's plenty of time for scene rehearsal later. This is the moment when you and the screenwriter give away the characters. Just hand them over to your actors. You hired them, so let them do their jobs.

All you need to do is be the perfect audience and guide when necessary.

For the rest of the rehearsal schedule, write a rehearsal plan, including

- What you want to accomplish in each rehearsal
- What each scene is about and where the conflict comes into focus
- The givens of each scene and your additions
- Backstories, or at least crucial backstory facts, for each character
- Each beat and what it means
- Props, hair, makeup, and wardrobe ideas and questions
- A blocking diagram

For your rehearsal plan, include scenes that follow the same line of thought, even though they may be set in different places. For example, conversations between characters may take place in a car, a store, and on a park bench. Rehearse these scenes together to uncover the cohesion of the scenes.

Prior to each rehearsal, review your script analysis notes for the scenes you're covering. Remind yourself of the possible meanings behind the lines and moves of each character. Most of directing is asking questions, so be ready to do so.

For your direction, keep it simple. And it's okay to give your actors permission. It's all right for them to try something new, slow down, speed up, get loud, get soft—whatever it is. Try to keep notes of what's working.

Improv is a great way to tease out the meaning of a scene or beat. That doesn't mean you can just float through. Improv works best when you can reflect any gains the actors make. Just stay disciplined. Actors are fun to watch and it's easy to get caught up in the performance.

If you have props available, use them. Sometimes actors will develop business with a prop that goes overboard. For example, a character picks up a feather duster and impulsively keeps dusting as he moves around the set. This can take the viewer's attention away from what's important, making the scene all about a feather duster. It's a fine balance between meaningful action and motion: Your actor will need your guidance here.

One of the best things about DV cameras is that you can set them up and roll tape without worrying about film processing and printing. Consider videotaping your rehearsals to get an idea of how things are working.

PREPRODUCTION CONTRACTS AND RELEASES

At this step in your project, you will now execute this series of contracts and releases:

- **Option execution agreement**—You must execute an option to fully and legally license the audiovisual rights of the property prior to principal photography.
- **Talent and crew contracts**—After you've hired people, get their names on a contract defining compensation and other terms.
- **Personal release**—If someone walks into a shot and is identifiable, you'll have him or her sign this release allowing you to use that person's image, voice, and so on.
- **Location release**—Permission to use private property or an exterior of a public building.

OPTION EXECUTION AGREEMENT

If you optioned an existing literary property, you will execute it on the first day of principal photography. Not only do you sign the contract and accept a short form to handle the copyright, you hand over a big check. No check, no deal.

Do not shoot a single frame until the agreement is signed.

TALENT AND CREW CONTRACTS

As soon as you know whom you want to hire, have him or her sign a contract. Some people will just make arrangements with the crew and bypass any written agreement, but I think that's a mistake. No one works without a contract.

PERSONAL RELEASES

Keep a stack nearby. Generally, if you can recognize the person onscreen, you need a release.

When you start shooting, you'd be amazed at who will come out to watch. Sometimes someone will do something great in the background of a shot. Get a PA to chase the person down to sign a personal release. Make sure the person gets a signed copy of the release and $1.00 consideration.

LOCATION RELEASES

As soon as you've found your locations, have the owners sign location releases.

STEP III: PRODUCTION:
ACTION!

OVERVIEW

Producing and directing are among the most terrifying and exhilarating experiences you can have. During production, you will have at least one moment when you'll want to quit and go home. Often, it's about a third of the way through, when there's still a lot to be done and you've run out of clean clothes. It's hard to keep your perspective, but you must.

The following chapters address how to stay focused on the work that needs to be done so you can make sure you get what you need.

Chapter 17, "Executing the Plan," covers the issues specific to making your vision come to life. Chapter 18, "Making Video Digital," is a detailed discussion of digital video, while Chapter 19, "The DV Camera," covers the most common camera controls, accessories, and techniques.

Chapter 20, "Lighting for DV," details common lighting equipment while focusing on the requirements for lighting an image for DV formats. Chapter 21, "Lighting Techniques," covers common problems and solutions, and offers helpful suggestions and tricks to get the most from even the smallest light kits.

Chapter 22, "Rigging," covers common grip and gaffer equipment to help you get the results you want safely, quickly, and inexpensively. Chapter 23, "Capturing the Sound," details the requirements for location audio for DV, including equipment, techniques, and tips. Chapter 24, "Renting Gear," explains some of the intricacies and common practices of working with a rental house.

Chapter 25, "Props, Sets, and Set Dressing," and Chapter 26, "Hair, Makeup, and Wardrobe," offer procedures for creating, using, and managing these elements of your show. Chapter 27, "Explosions, Gunplay, and Fistfights: When to Call In the Experts," details common stunts and special effects. Although a lot of them can be done by people with no experience, sometimes you need to hire help to get the best result safely.

The day before your first shoot day, make sure

- All equipment has been tested.
- All equipment is checked, packed, and pre-rigged on the set, at the location, or loaded into the production vehicle.
- All tape stock is purchased.
- Props, wardrobe, or other items have been rented or picked up.
- The first set is dressed.
- All members of the ensemble know their call times, which scenes will be shot, and precise directions to the set.
- Locations and craft services are locked.
- All contracts for production personnel have been executed.
- All paperwork, including production script, storyboards, phone lists, and so on, is packed and within reach.
- To get some sleep.

A lot of volunteers will show up on your first day of production. Excited about being in the glamorous world of show business, some of them will swarm around your set eating all the donuts. Usually, they hang out around the camera, trying very hard to look like camera operators, gaffers, and grips. Rarely do they help the location audio crew or offer to write a press release.

As the day goes on and the donuts disappear, these people start to evaporate.

Good.

Less is more.

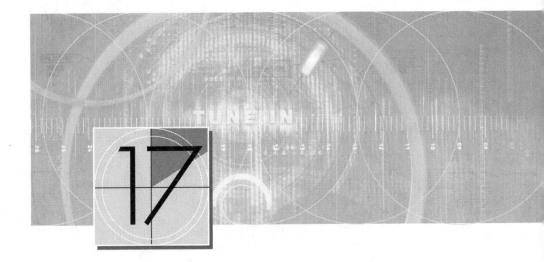

EXECUTING THE PLAN

In preproduction, you hammered out a plan for bringing
your movie to life. Production is all about executing that
plan so you have enough footage to make postproduction
go smoothly.

GETTING COVERAGE

The primary task of production is to capture footage that
can be edited with minimal continuity problems. For
every scene, you will need to cover various moves, objects,
or characters, so you can cut to them in editing to cover
errors and set the rhythm of the show. For example, let's
say you have a pie-throwing scene. You'll need a close-up
of an actor throwing a pie, and not just because pies are
funny. With enough coverage, you can cut back and forth
between close-up, medium, and wide shots to determine
pacing.

The second reason for coverage is to cover any mistakes in
a master shot, such as blown lines, missed business, or

TIP

Notetaking

A laptop computer always seems like a good idea on a set, but be absolutely sure you'll use it before hauling it along. Paper is cheaper, and you won't cry if someone loses your ballpoint.

discontinuity. You want to cover the errors in post by cutting away to a different angle—that's why these shots are called *cutaways*.

Communication is the first of three challenges to getting good coverage. The second is keeping track of changes. The third is protecting your ensemble to avoid burnout.

COMMUNICATION

A director doesn't just direct actors. He or she directs the entire ensemble. This means being very clear about what needs to be done and when it's been accomplished. Especially on the first day, it can be hard to gauge when a director is satisfied with a shot and ready to move on, so speak up.

No one can work until the director decides where the camera goes and what's going to be presented to it. The director must

- Be prepared
- Share the plan
- Let ensemble members do their jobs

Many directors underestimate the importance of clear communication when it comes to sound. Experienced sound mixers know that poor audio from a wide shot can often be replaced with sound from closer shots. Therefore, it's crucial that you tell the sound mixer ahead of time whether a wide shot is the only shot planned.

TRACKING CHANGES

The director and crew must keep track of screen distance, screen motion, and any changes to the plan. The best way to track changes to a scene is to note them in your production script. Record everything that deviates from the original: dialogue, blocking, camera motion, and so on.

This is particularly true for scene matching. If an actor must exit camera left instead of camera right as planned, your DP may want to match screen position and camera motion in the following scene.

You can assign someone the job of tracking changes and continuity. In addition to changes, this person will note specific business each actor does for the camera—for example, which hand an actor used to pick up a prop.

PROTECTING YOUR ENSEMBLE

No- and low-budget sets are under enormous pressure to get a lot done in a very short period of time. Take care of your people.

One of the best ways to save your actors' energy is to be clear about the shot's angle of view. You don't want them to burn themselves out when they're not even on camera. Help them save their energy for close-ups, when it's really going to count. Also, if you know you'll be interspersing other shots into a long master shot, there's no reason to spend hours trying to get that master shot perfect, which takes a long time to do and can wear down an ensemble.

Sometimes you may end up shooting submasters and close-ups. A *submaster* is a single shot of continuous action within a scene. Shooting this way is called *chasing a scene*. Chasing often happens with action scenes, complex moves, scenes with a lot of extras, or when the director just doesn't want to limit himself or herself to a certain kind of coverage. Be sure to keep track of every shot and be clear to your ensemble what you're doing. They need to save their energy.

SETIQUETTE

Many people who've never worked a set before are making movies. I think this is great. Unfortunately, some of the crucial practices that make working a set easier have been left behind.

First among them is chain of command. Just because no one is getting paid doesn't mean that no one is in charge. If you're a PA and you notice a problem, either solve it or tell one of the key personnel. For example, if you're assigned to the location audio crew and you notice a cable isn't in the right place, tell the sound mixer. He or she will then decide how to proceed.

Beyond that, good behavior on the set is a lot like good behavior in kindergarten:

- Saying "please" and "thank you" won't hurt anyone.
- Asking whether someone needs help is always good.
- If you messed up, admit it.
- Being quiet during a take does not mean whispering. It means not speaking or moving at all.
- Give credit where credit is due.

TO THE DIRECTOR

Being on a set is a test of character. You'll find out whether you can follow through. You'll find out whether you can handle adversity gracefully. You'll

TIP

Never let anyone start work without a signed agreement. Always carry extra copies of agreements and releases.

find out what's underneath your grand ideas about cinema, digital technologies, or desire for fame.

Your ensemble will take behavioral cues from you. If you waste time or are sloppy, your ensemble will waste time and be sloppy. If you're prepared, excited, and know what you want, they will respond in like manner.

Direct the Ensemble

Most crews on DV sets are a mixture of experience and inexperience. If you're working with an untried crew, you need to make sure people are taught how to best use the equipment. If that hasn't been taken care of during rehearsal, you need to take time to explain the gear before the actors arrive. Don't assume people know how to operate mixers, booms, and dollies.

However, if you're working with experienced people, tell them what they are supposed to do, but not how to do it. Unless you're a pro in the field, communicate what you want in terms of the result. If you want more shadows, ask for more shadows. Don't start moving lights or telling a grip where to set a cukie. Describe what you want and let your crew figure out the way to do it.

This applies to your actors as well. It's not the director's job to get a better performance from an actor; that's the actor's job. If you start performing the role, why did you bother to cast anyone but yourself? Don't act for them and don't line them. *Lining* is when you read the dialogue exactly the way you want the actor to perform it. Lining actors is like kicking them in the head. It hurts, it's foolish, and it leaves them too dazed to be of much use later.

Paid or not, if someone isn't working out, fire him or her. Do it quickly and as early in the schedule as you can.

Let Them Eat Cake

People judge how much their work is appreciated by their immediate needs. If your people are hungry, cold, and tired, it will be hard for them to work to the best of their abilities. Even if you're ahead of schedule and everything looks and sounds fantastic, they may not hear your praise for all the stomach-growling.

Mealtimes are the only time the crew gets to network, as well as clear their minds and put their feet up. No matter how far behind schedule you are, never cancel lunch. And never expect your ensemble to pay for it, either. It's professional etiquette for the production company to buy the food and drinks.

Make sure the food is good. Have caterers and craft services people give you samples before you hire them. Try to get one hot meal a day if your budget can handle it. For each location, keep a list of places that deliver. Sometimes you just need some kung pao chicken.

And make sure there's enough food. Movie crews, especially PAs, are like a swarm of locusts. Don't skimp on vegetables and bread. Keep a pot of coffee on and make sure to have all kinds of beverages in the cooler. Snacks are always good; just be sure people don't wander off to munch when they should be working.

Cross the Ts

Arrange transportation ahead of time. This doesn't mean you need to hire limos—just give some thought to how people are going to get to the set and where they'll park. Maps to each location are handy and take away any excuse for getting lost.

Put together a first-aid kit that includes sunscreen, aspirin, ibuprofen, antacid, bandages, disinfectant, tweezers, and anything else you may need. And borrow umbrellas from everyone you know and tuck them away in your car. Most people don't even think about umbrellas until after it starts raining.

Before you start production, it's helpful to give everyone a list of recommended items for personal use on the set. As long as people know they may want to bring water, a hat, a life preserver, and two bananas, they don't have a problem with it.

And finally, watch your scheduling to make sure people get enough rest. Productivity drops dramatically after 12 hours of work, and usually the worst accidents happen when people are sleep-deprived. It may make you sweat, but give people time off to recover.

WHAT TO EXPECT FROM YOUR CREW

If you've done your job, your crew should walk onto the set ready to go. They need to keep a few basic ideas in mind, though, to keep the interpersonal relationships productive.

To Inexperienced Crew: It's Not About You

Just because you are on a set to learn doesn't mean those with experience are there to teach you. Be quiet. Observe. Make yourself indispensable. The show isn't about you—it's about the director's vision. You're here to serve that vision. Anything beyond that is bonus.

Work the set. Network the breaks.

 TIP

Greening the Movies

Recycling is good for the environment. It's also good for the no- and low-budget producer. Reuse everything you can; recycle what's possible. For example, old clothes can become new wardrobe by dyeing or painting the fabric. Gift wrap often has an array of colors and textures that can be used in set dressing.

To Experienced Crew: It's Not About You

If you have an issue or concern, bring it up privately with the key, director, or producer. If an inexperienced PA is annoying you, deal with it. Too often, experienced crew people will say nothing, but just get progressively angrier until the yelling starts.

Follow the example of actors, who know that it always helps to make the other guy look good.

STARTING THE SHOOT DAY

Everyone should arrive at the time specified on the callsheet.

Begin the day by explaining briefly what scenes you'll be doing at that location. Show everyone exactly where copies of any storyboards, diagrams, and so on, are on the set, and ask everyone to all please check them before asking you questions. If possible, hand out callsheets for the next day when everyone is there. (You can also do this during lunch.)

Let your DP and sound mixer direct their people to begin unloading equipment and let them get to work. That work includes setting up and cleaning equipment. All batteries must be changed every new shoot day. Don't skimp on this. It's not worth trying to save a dime by not changing the 9-volt batteries in your field mixer, and then missing the perfect take because the mixer went dead. Make it the morning ritual (see Figure 17.1).

Prior to each scene, explain each shot to the DP and sound mixer. You need to tell them what the plan is: the scene, where you want the camera, a very brief description of the action, and the shots. Go over any changes to that scene.

Generally, you begin getting your footage by shooting the longest take. This is often the *master shot*, a wide shot that goes from the beginning of the scene to the end. Master shots serve a number of purposes. They allow you to lock lighting, blocking, and business and give you a single shot with the entire scene. They also establish continuity of dialogue.

For the master shot, instruct your actors to continue the scene even if they blow a line or move. Try not to repeat a master shot unless it's the only shot for the scene. They take a long time and can wear down your ensemble.

From here, move in for closer shots. Generally, you go from widest to closest on one side, and then get your reverse shots from widest to closest.

FIGURE 17.1

One of the first tasks of the shoot day is getting the battery chargers plugged in and charging all batteries.

Like many directors, I will depart radically from my shooting script if I find something more interesting. This does not excuse me from being prepared. Quite the contrary. I can only change up if I know what the scene is about, the screen placement of elements, and the screen motion of previous and following scenes.

It's your show, so follow your gut, but remember that it's easier to change a plan than to make it up on the spot.

BLOCK, LIGHT, REHEARSE, AND SHOOT

There's an accepted pattern to working the set. While the rest of the crew is unloading and staging equipment, setting up the craft services area, running to get coffee, and so on, the director, actors, and key crew people walk through the blocking.

BLOCK

Using blocking diagrams, walk through the actors' choreography with them. Often, a floorplan (as shown in Figure 17.2) will help make this process easier. Foreground and background action have to be blocked as well, so make sure either you, your AD, or DP handles that.

NOTE

Nothing to See Here

Everyone on your set should be working. This means no friends, groupies, or hangers-on. You don't have the time to manage them or the money to feed them.

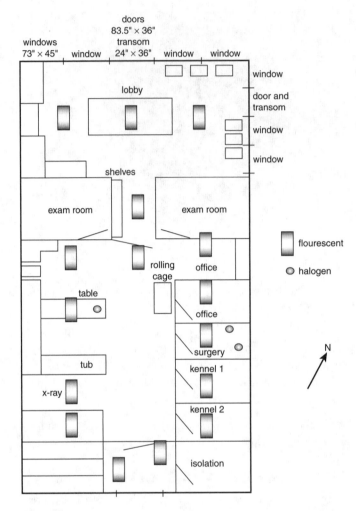

FIGURE 17.2

Clinic floorplan for "Music Appreciation."

After the actors and key crew understand the blocking, the actors will leave the set for hair, makeup, wardrobe, and other prep.

Make sure you designate an area for the actors' prep. Have at least one movie light there so they can apply makeup correctly. When they're finished, the director can discuss the scene, rehearse it, or have them run lines.

LIGHT

While the actors are prepping, the DP directs the crew in the placement of lights, flags, silks, nets, and other equipment. The DP will also see to it that the camera, mount, monitor, and other gear is in place. The sound mixer will prep equipment and may plant microphones. The camera will be cleaned and videotape loaded. Bars and tone will be recorded on the first minute of the tape, allowing the sound mixer and camera operator to set levels for their equipment.

After the lights are in place, the DP may ask for the actors to return to the set to double-check key lights and for the director's approval. On big-budget shows, stand-ins would take the place of the lead and supporting players. The DP may ask a crew member to stand in for the actors, but it's not absolutely necessary.

It's natural for directors and producers to get impatient with how long this takes, but try to stay calm. Good lighting takes time.

REHEARSE

After the set is lit and the camera is in place, the actors and director return to rehearse the scene. If you have complex camera moves or blocking, you may require several technical rehearsals so everyone gets the timing down.

Whenever the schedule is a bit behind, producers and directors have the impulse to skip rehearsals. Don't skip them, although you may want to consider rolling tape during them. I prefer to shoot rehearsals. Often, there's one great thing that happens.

Make sure everyone knows it's a rehearsal, though. The crew needs to see and hear what's going to happen so they can work out all the technical issues.

The slate should be readied. It should have the production and director's names, scene, shot, and take number. Use a dry erase marker and be sure to have a paper towel handy.

SHOOT

Some directors prefer to call their own shots. I do. Some prefer an AD or DP do it. Whatever you decide, just make sure that the person yells loudly and clearly so everyone knows exactly what's going on. A typical shot follows this call order:

1. When the director is ready, call, "Standby!"

   A PA or camera assistant will put the slate squarely in camera view.

2. When everyone has settled, call, "Quiet!"

FIGURE 17.3

Slate in the bag, ready for use. On the far right are several 400' cans of film. Bob Watson, the director-producer-camera operator was shooting video and film for this movie.

3. When the set is absolutely quiet, call, "Sound!" When ready, your sound mixer will respond with, "Speed!" "Check!" or "Ready!" Some location audio mixers won't require a cue. Their crew is always ready and will only call, "Standby!" if there's a problem.

4. Call, "Camera!"

   There's often a 10- to 15-second delay between the time the camera operator starts the camera and when tape actually rolls. When the camera is ready, the DP or camera operator will respond with, "Rolling!"

5. Call, "Slate!" or "Mark it!"

   The PA or camera assistant will call out the information on the slate. If you are using a backup audio recorder or shooting dual-system sound, that person will clap the slate sticks. Otherwise, it's not necessary.

6. Call, "Action!"

   The actors run through the scene.

7. When the shot is completed, call, "Cut!"

   Sometimes a director will interrupt a take in order to direct actors. Sometimes it's very quick and the director prefers that tape keep rolling. Sometimes, though, the pause turns into a meeting. The crew usually doesn't know what to do, but they will not stop the camera. Try to let everyone know what's up.

8. If the director wants another take, call, "Going again!"

9. If the scene is going to be shot again from the top, call, "Reset!" so all the props get back in position.

   Follow the call order until the director has what he or she wants.

10. After the director is satisfied, call, "Moving on!"

11. If you're staying on that set, call, "Hot set!" That means no one should touch anything presented to the camera unless told otherwise.

12. If it's a new scene, call, "New scene!" The actors will step off the set, and the crew will shift any equipment as necessary.

Sometimes the director will tell the crew to "roll at discretion." This means that the camera operator and sound crew will take footage as they see fit. I call this *poaching* and do it frequently. I'll ask for an *audio slate*, which means the sound mixer or boom operator will very quietly announce into the boom mic the scene number as tape is rolling. Often, you can get wonderful reactions and inserts, especially from inexperienced actors.

Poaching is also a good way to get *walla* and other audio. Walla is background sound—the murmurings of a café, office sounds, and so on. Walla is the basis for soundbeds in your show. You can also grab other, more specific audio. For example, if the director and leads have stepped away to discuss the scene, the extras may be chatting among themselves. You can pick up distinct voices that you can later use for post-audio.

NAKED PEOPLE

If it weren't fun to look at naked people, there wouldn't be any in the movies.

The only time I've heard lazy crew people argue about staying on the set to work is when the next scene has naked people in it. People who would leave in a New York minute to go nap will insist their presence is necessary and nobody should worry—they're professionals.

No one says it: Naked people can be a thrill. Many actors are very good-looking and in great shape—they're beautiful to look at. Face it, you and others in your ensemble may get a little excited in these circumstances. Don't fight it. Nothing wrong with a little thrill.

Now get over it.

You have two priorities for any love scene—getting the coverage and protecting your actors.

Make it clear from the beginning of the shoot that no one should invite friends to hang out on the set when you're shooting sex scenes. Doing so is grounds for dismissal. Be clear that you'll have a closed set on that day, so have a plan to pre-rig the next scene or location they can begin work on.

Block the scene with the actors in their clothes. Be very clear about what you need them to do, but like any directing, remove the emotional obstacles the actors may have regarding the scene. Take your time. I tend to speak quietly, but other people put on fun music and giggle a lot.

Get everything lit and close the set.

Closing the set means no one remains unless you say so. Have only key personnel there. The DP can run the camera. If not, the DP can set the shot, and then leave and let the camera operator take care of it. The sound mixer should be able to handle mixing and the boom. If you need a set dresser, have only one and ask that person to take care of any props. Same thing with makeup, hair, and wardrobe.

If you don't need them, send them away. No one stays unless you feel they are absolutely necessary to get the shot. If you're working with a producer, you may even need to send the producer away. If you're working with a director, you should very quietly ask if he or she wants you to remain; otherwise, lead the rest of the ensemble out.

One person should be in charge of the actors' robes. When "Cut!" is called, that person should be right there—the actors shouldn't have to scramble for something to cover themselves.

It's not a bad idea for the director to hand the robes to the actors. You can keep everyone at a proper distance, talk with the actors, and so on. It's very difficult to direct love scenes, especially love scenes that are explicit. You have to say things that can be difficult to say even in your own intimate circumstances. As the director, you need to retain the trust you've created throughout your shoot so your actors can concentrate on what needs to happen in the scene, not on avoiding someone being creepy.

When you're happy with the shot, let the actors get their robes on and call the crew back in to adjust the lighting for the next shot. When it's set, send them out again.

As the scene goes on, you and your actors may feel more comfortable having the entire ensemble stay. Whether or not you feel comfortable, let the actors suggest it. You can decide after that.

ENDING THE SHOOT DAY

At the end of the shoot day, call, "That's a wrap!"

Do not call wrap unless it really is the end of the day. Too often, DV moviemakers will call a wrap, and then decide they want another shot or scene.

Let your key crew people direct the breaking down of the set. If you're staying at a secure location, make sure all the gear is properly and safely stowed. If you're leaving, be sure the gear is safely and efficiently loaded into the production vehicle.

Finally, meet with your key crew people before you leave the set. Do not let anyone but the director, producer, DP, and sound mixer in on these meetings. If someone is hanging out, send him or her away. Iron out any personnel or technical problems, discuss the plan for the next day, determine any equipment requirements, and note any changes or discrepancies in the production script. This meeting should take no more than half an hour.

TIP

Do not leave the location until you have the footage and audio you need.

At least the producer and director should watch the dailies on the set or at home. If you want, include your key personnel. Get all the camera logs and videotape from that day and store them away from the set. Some producers think that continuing to shoot on the tape from the day before is cost effective, but it's not if you tape over the previous day's work.

If you plan to clone the original tapes, consider recording a VHS tape as well. It's an easy way to watch dailies without risking accidental damage to the production tape.

While you watch dailies, note in the production script any technical problems and script changes. Also, track what shots have been done.

If something doesn't work, you may have to schedule pick-ups. *Pick-ups* are reshoots of a scene or portion of a scene. Sometimes you have to shoot pick-ups because an actor was missing or the performance was off. It's easier in the long run if you take care of pick-ups as quickly as possible.

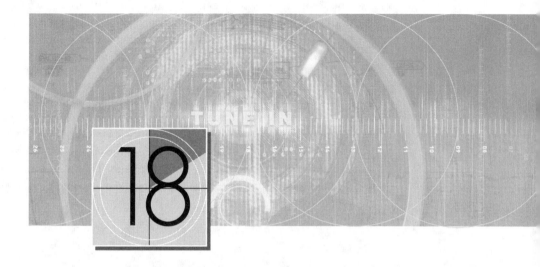

MAKING VIDEO DIGITAL

This is not an in-depth discussion of the engineering and quantum physics behind digital video, but an introduction to the fundamental aspects of DV technology. Knowing the rudiments of this technology may help you understand why DV cameras respond the way they do to certain situations. It will also help explain why DV camera models and decks have such a range of prices.

For a full discussion about DV and DV formats, see Adam Wilt's Web site at www.adamwilt.com. You can also find many useful articles at www.2-pop.com. For even more, see Arch Luther's and Andrew Inglis's *Video Engineering*.

Digital systems, including DV, convey information as a series of ones and zeros. A digital signal is resistant to noise, generational degradation, interference, and distortion.

There are two ways to digitize video images. The first is to handle it in a computer. A video card takes the analog signal from an analog format, such as Beta SP, turns it into ones and zeros, and writes it to the hard drive.

The second is doing it in camera. This is how DV works. The format itself has a standard for digitizing the analog video signal prior to recording to tape. Unlike an analog format, the material on the tape itself is already digital. When you take your DV footage and put it into your computer, you're not digitizing. You're transferring data.

No means of digital recording is perfect, but digital systems can recognize and correct bit errors. Error management attempts to hide a problem by making it not so noticeable. If the number of errors exceeds the limit, *error concealment* can reduce the visible effect of the errors. It may be concealed by using data from previous or following fields. The result is not guaranteed to be identical to the original, but the process is quick and relatively simple.

Before you can make video digital, the video signal must be created and conditioned.

"The natural world is an analog world," as my dad says. Life happens with depth, height, width, and time. To record images of this analog world requires a series of steps. And it starts when light and sound become electricity, as shown in Figure 18.1.

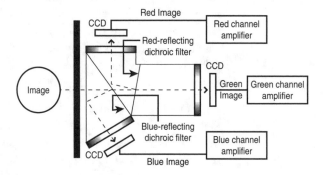

FIGURE 18.1

From light to electricity.

DV cameras create and condition analog video images in a series of defined steps. After the images are prepared, they're digitized and further compressed. These steps are

- Scanning
- Amplifying

- Sampling
- Digitizing
- Compressing

SCANNING

In a video camera, light from an image passes through the lens assembly. The lens assembly contains a lens and usually a low-pass filter.

The light from the image hits an optical beam splitter (shown in Figure 18.2), which separates the light from the image into red, green, and blue, or RGB. The beam splitter has two dichroic surfaces, each of which reflects light in one region of the spectrum while transmitting the rest. The image from each color is focused onto the sensitive surface of a charge-coupled device, or CCD, for that color.

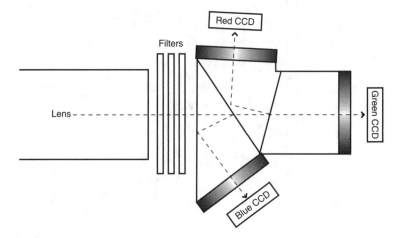

FIGURE 18.2

Beam splitter.

The CCD

A CCD is a collection of thousands of tiny semiconductors in an array of sensors. Each sensor, or charge-coupled array, is known as a picture element, or *pixel*. Each pixel converts incoming light into a charge directly proportional to the amount of light hitting it. In addition to creating a charge from light, each CCD can store it. Storage of a charge is fundamental to a charge-coupled device and is accomplished by using *potential wells*. These stored charges must then be transferred in an orderly fashion that matches the original image.

The three most common CCD architectures are frame transfer (FT), inter-line transfer (IT), and frame-interline transfer (FIT). All three use clock commands to execute their functions, as well as optical masks over the nonimage areas of the sensor arrays.

FT chips have a field storage area under the imaging area (see Figure 18.3). The picture shifts down directly through the active pixels into this storage area. Because active pixels are also shift registers, FT cameras use a rotating shutter to block light during the transfer. With these shutters, FT chips show no smear—but if the shutter fails in the open position, the image will smear.

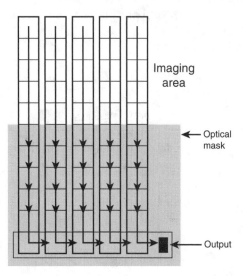

Imaging area

← Optical mask

← Output

FIGURE 18.3

The FT process.

To avoid using a mechanical shutter, the interline transfer (IT) architecture uses separate registers protected by an optically opaque mask. Charges accumulate in each element of the array. During the vertical interval, the charges are moved into the transport registers, and shifted out. The empty sensors capture the next set of charges while the information in the storage array is clocked out to create the video signal.

Because the sensing and shifting functions are separated, charge and storage structures can be optimized for their particular uses. The only significant limitation of IT imagers (see Figure 18.4) is *vertical smear*. Vertical smear occurs when extreme highlights in one storage register affect adjacent storage registers, creating a vertical line passing through the highlight.

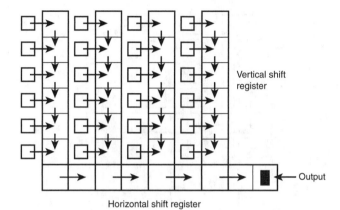

Vertical shift
register

Output

Horizontal shift register

FIGURE 18.4

The IT process.

FIT is the most sophisticated of the three. FIT moves the charge horizontally to an adjacent storage pixel, but then moves the charge vertically into a frame storage area. A row of selection gates between the image and storage areas are biased so charges in excess of a certain level are dropped before being transferred. FIT (shown in Figure 18.5) is still an expensive technology limited to high-end broadcast cameras.

Usually the image sampling in a CCD is at a higher rate than the subsequent sampling in the analog-to-digital converters (ADCs). If an analog signal is converted directly at the output of the CCD, it may need as many as 14 bits to allow accurate processing. 14 bits are not currently practical, so the gamma is compromised or some preprocessing must happen in the analog domain.

AMPLIFYING

The analog signals from the R, G, and B CCDs are expressed in voltages. These voltages can be affected by cabling, connectors, operating temperatures, interference, and so on, which need to be corrected. An 8-bit ADC has only 256 unique numbers, so each signal amplitude must be set so it doesn't exceed the ADC's acceptable range. So, from each CCD, each color channel is sent to an amplifier.

The ITU-R 601 standard specifies that black should correspond to level 16 and white to level 235, leaving headroom for errors, noise, and spikes. For color difference signals, 0 signal corresponds to 128 and full amplitude goes to 225 (see Figure 18.6).

NOTE

Aliasing

Aliasing occurs when sampling frequencies are too low to faithfully reproduce image detail— there just isn't enough information to complete the detail. There are different kinds of aliasing:

Temporal aliasing—A good example is when automobile wheels look like they're going backward. It also shows up in standards converters without enough temporal filtering.

Raster scan aliasing— You see twinkling on sharp boundaries such as horizontal lines. This is due to insufficient filtering prior to digitizing. You'll often see it when detailed images are compressed using cheap digital video effects (DVE) processors.

Moiré—This happens with high spatial frequencies. It can be minimized by a technique known as optical low-pass filtering. This filtering, in theory, should knock out all frequencies below a certain level, although in reality

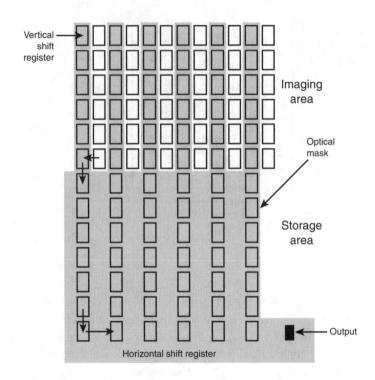

FIGURE 18.5

The FIT process.

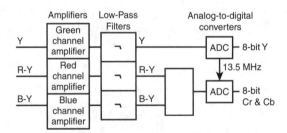

FIGURE 18.6

Amplifying the signal.

The signals then go through a low-pass filter to prevent the passage of information beyond the 5.75MHz luminance band limit and 2.75MHz chrominance, or color difference, band limit. If they do, aliasing could be visible in the picture. See the following for a more detailed discussion of aliasing.

RGB to Y, R–Y, B–Y

RGB is a component signal. Although video cameras produce RGB components and gamma-corrected values, it's not practical to digitize each signal individually. The RGB signals are converted into luminance Y and chrominance, or color difference, R–Y and B–Y, or U and V, signals at the input stage of the DV compression process, and are referred to as digital Y, R–Y, B–Y, or YUV systems. The conversion from RGB to Y, R–Y, B–Y allows a form of compression since the color channels are limited to one-half (for 4:2:2) or one-quarter (4:1:1) the bandwidth of the luminance.

In color difference component video, the first channel is luminance, Y. This is the intensity—the signal's brightness information with no color data. Y by itself gives a black-and-white picture. Because the human eye perceives brightness better than color, Y is sampled at full resolution. The other two channels are color difference signals, called R–Y and B–Y. These signify the difference between red and the luminance and the difference between blue and the luminance. The color difference channels can be mathematically recombined with luminance to give a full color picture.

Color subsampling is described by a trio of numbers. The first number tells you how many samples of luminance Y are taken per line. The second number tells you how many samples of each of the color difference signals R–Y and B–Y are taken on the first line. And the third figure tells you how many samples of each of these color difference signals are taken in the second line.

- In 4:1:1 sampling, the color difference signals, R–Y and B–Y, are sampled at one-quarter of the luminance sampling rate.
- In 4:2:0 sampling, the 0 means that R–Y and B–Y are sampled for every other luminance pixel on one line, and then for none of the luminance pixels on the next line, and so on.
- In 4:2:2 systems, color is sampled at half the rate of the luminance. Thus, you have one R–Y and B–Y for every two Y samples.

This subsampling is often done by first sampling everything with full resolution, and then averaging color values for adjacent pixels to produce the subsample. This approach has the advantage of reducing the sampling noise in the color channels.

Converting from RGB to Y, R–Y, B–Y saves an enormous amount of bandwidth. Digitizing a Y, R–Y, B–Y signal requires 16 bits (two bytes), as opposed to 24 bits (three bytes) for RGB, to represent true color. This color space conversion reduces the data to one-third of its volume without visible degradation.

the filtering isn't very efficient. Even with the filters, however, you may still see some moiré on complex patterns.

Some cameras are designed with spatial offset to compensate for aliasing. Usually, all three imagers (R, G, B) would be arranged so that equivalent pixels view the same area of the image. With spatial offset, columns of pixels of the green imager are shifted horizontally 50% of the width of a pixel.

The idea is to separate the R and B from the G sensors so their sideband phases are reversed. If the sideband amplitude of R and B equaled G, there would be complete cancellation and aliasing would disappear.

Spatial offset requires very tight tolerances, and even then it doesn't always work. An even better approach is to use more pixels, horizontally and vertically, than required for scanning.

Illuminating Luminance   Luminance, expressed as Y, is derived from the RGB signals and calculated as

$$Y = .299R + .587G + .114B$$

Digital systems such as computers use a luminance range of 0 for black and 255 for white. Some digital video streams define luminance by a 1–254 scale, with the values of 0 and 255 reserved for internal uses. Other systems use the ITU-R 601 digital coding standard, which specifies black to be set at level 16 and white at 235. These levels allow for some margin when converting to and from analog video.

Analog video, however, uses a different measurement: IRE (Institute of Radio Engineers) units. The electrical reference for white is generally defined as 100 IRE. Electrical reference for black, though, depends on what video format and standard you are using. For PAL, as well as the Japanese version of NTSC, black is 0 IRE. Unlike the rest of the world, black level in the United States is 7.5 IRE. This is referred to as *set-up* or *pedestal*.

Set-up is not recorded as part of the digital video signal and is only a function of the analog circuitry. Digital dubs between two pieces of DV equipment are not affected one way or the other—only when using analog equipment is set-up an issue. Check the manual of any DV equipment you want to use to see if it applies set-up to any analog out. If it doesn't, you will have to compensate by adjusting your field and waveform monitors and vectorscope to the appropriate IRE output. See Chapter 19, "The DV Camera," for information on using monitors.

Different IRE set-ups do not change the way the DV data stream defines black and white. DV and DV-based formats use the 16/235 luminance range. Black is just over 6% brightness, with an RGB color value of 16,16,16, and white is just over 92% brightness at 235,235,235. This is important to keep in mind when you know your show is going to display on an analog device, such as most television sets. If you create titles or have graphics outside these ranges, the images won't look how you want them to look and the video signal will not be considered "legal."

Chrominance   Black, gray, and white have no chrominance; color has both luminance and chrominance.

The R–Y and B–Y of Y, R–Y, B–Y express *chrominance*, or the color information relating to hue and saturation, but not the luminance of a color video signal. *Color hue* defines color on the basis of its position in the spectrum. *Color saturation* is the degree by which the eye perceives a color in relation to a gray or white scale of the same brightness.

Color video uses *additive color,* where red, green, and blue are added to form a range of colors. Equal voltage applied to all three phosphors will give you what looks like neutral grays or white. Black is the lack of color, so its voltage is at or near zero. (In NTSC, this is 7.5 IRE, but you get the idea.) The hue and saturation of most colors can be duplicated by combining these three additive primary colors of red, green, and blue.

For an indepth discussion of color theory and color systems, see Charles Poynton's Color FAQ at `www.inforamp.net/~poynton/notes/ colour_and_gamma/ColorFAQ.html#RTFToC1`.

SAMPLING

Sampling is the inherent process that allows digitization. An analog signal resembles a sine wave. Sampling reduces the infinite values of an analog image to a number that can be handled by the video system. Sample rates are not arbitrary. They're determined by physics and biology. According to the Nyquist theorem, a sample rate must be at least twice the highest analog frequency to enable accurate coding and decoding of the signal. Sampling at slightly more than twice the target frequency will make up for imprecision in components used for the conversion.

At this point in the DV process, the analog signals from the amplifiers are sent to a pair of analog-to-digital converters (ADCs). One ADC handles the luminance Y, and the other handles the color difference signals, R–Y and B–Y (see Figure 18.7).

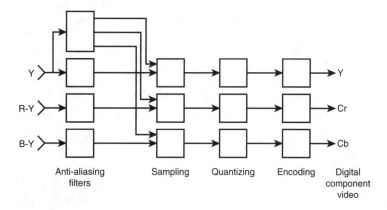

FIGURE 18.7

Converting from analog to digital.

In 4:1:1 video, the Y component is sampled 13.5 million times a second (13.5MHz), whereas the R–Y and B–Y signals are sampled 3.375 million times a second (3.375MHz). Human vision is more sensitive to brightness than to shifts in color so it makes sense to sample brightness (the Y component) more often than color difference (R–Y and B–Y) components.

Standard-definition TV (SDTV) is digitized to the ITU-R 601 standards of 13.5MHz sample frequency and 720 pixels per line. The sampling frequency of 13.5MHz was chosen as a common sampling standard for NTSC and PAL because it's an integral multiple of both. NTSC uses 525 lines with 59.94 fields per second and PAL has a 625/50 system. Both are a multiple of 2.25MHz, the lowest common frequency to provide a static sampling pattern for both.

Quantizing

Unlike an analog system, a digital system cannot always exactly represent the image intensity at any point. Instead, the value will be quantized. *Quantizing* is where the sampled amplitudes of the video waveform are converted into discrete values. When a value is quantized, it's fitted into the acceptable digital range between 0 and 255. Whereas some analog values will correspond exactly, others will be in between. These tiny errors are known as *quantization noise*.

Quantizing doesn't allow for ambiguity. Every pixel is assigned a value, and all the possible values in the series are determined by bit depth. Many current systems work with eight bits per image component per pixel. A *byte* consists of eight bits of data. An 8-bit byte can represent 256 different numbers in the range 0–255. So, with three bytes per pixel, an 8-bit digital video system can represent $256 \times 256 \times 256 = 16.7$ million different colors.

The eye can distinguish only about two million different colors, so an 8-bit system ought to work well enough. But some cameras and other systems use 10-bit or 12-bit per channel video for better contrast handling. The contrast is then corrected using gamma correction without increasing the quantization noise.

Encoding

Some compression may take place during quantizing. For example, a waveform divided into 256 values can be further divided and represented by 32 values. This is called *intraframe*, or *spatial*, compression because it reduces the data from within a single frame.

Interframe compression reduces the amount of redundant information from one frame to another. *Motion estimation*, one compression method, stores only the difference between one frame and the next. *Predictive interframe coding*, another method, compares the data of the current frame with past and future frames and records how long the data remains the same. Both further compress the images.

DIGITIZING: Y, R–Y, B–Y TO YCRCB

The ADCs precisely measure the amplitude of each sample. The numbers that have come out of the quantization process are decimal numbers that are converted to binary notation. The analog-to-digital conversion is complete. The digitized forms of R–Y and B–Y are referred as Cr and Cb.

Many computers use RGB processing, but DV and DV-based formats use YCrCb. This can be an issue when going from DV into a computer for image manipulation. For example, if you create a matte or title in an application such as Photoshop using full bandwidth RGB, be aware that you'll have problems getting it to look right. Some IEEE 1394 video capture cards have software that will perform the conversion as necessary. You can also buy plug-ins for certain nonlinear editors (NLEs) to handle the conversion. These transformations ought to be lossless theoretically, although in practice there may be small rounding errors.

See Chapter 31, "Finishing," for further discussion.

COMPRESSING

Video compression means the removal of data using mathematical formulas. Even with the filtering and sampling, the amount of data in the DV stream is still too large to be practical.

The DV compression process is complex and very difficult to simplify because it is adaptive. The process begins by removing unnecessary information. The video signal captured by the camera contains more data than is shown onscreen, called the *blanking area*. It is a spare area used for timing information based on the analog television standard. But DV does not digitize the horizontal and vertical blanking and sync intervals. It only digitizes the active picture area of 720×480 (NTSC) or 720×576 (PAL) pixels.

Next, DV uses *discrete cosine transform* (DCT), *adaptive quantization* (AQ), and *variable-length coding* (VLC) to further compress the video images.

Artifacting

Because of the amount and type of compression, DV exhibits certain kinds of artifacts. They come in three flavors: mosquito noise, quilting, and motion blocking. Other picture problems are dropouts and banding, which is a sign of tape damage or head clog.

Mosquito—Also known as *feathering* and *critters*, mosquitoes are compression-induced errors. Mosquito noise also shows up around fine detail on a diagonal and can usually be found around fine text superimposed on a nonblack background. White on blue seems to show it off best.

Quilting—Quilting shows up in long lines about 20° off horizontal and comes from minor discontinuities in the rendering of a diagonal. The only way to see quilting is to watch diagonals during slow pans.

Motion blocking—Motion blocking occurs when two fields are too different for

First comes *DCT blocking and shuffling*. DCT's blocking and shuffling doesn't compress the image, but transforms the data into a structure that makes it easier to tell what's significant from what isn't. The image is divided into 8×8 pixel blocks, each with four luminance and two color difference blocks. This divides the video frame into very small individual blocks or boxes (8,100 for NTSC, 9,720 for PAL), grouped in five columns called *macro blocks*. Five macro blocks are selected from five different areas of the image and assigned priority. This is the shuffling.

AQ and VLC do the actual data compression. The circuit first guesses at how much compression it needs to use for each DCT block: Information likely to need fewer bits is allocated less, and information that is near zero is discarded. If there's still too much data, the process goes through again, rounding off and discarding as much data as possible without damaging the image too much. This is essentially, in the simplest terms, how compression is enacted.

The information is then *deshuffled*, with the compressed data put back in the correct order and then recorded on the tape. The system will also do some error correction, where extra data is added to the data. This new information lets the system check that it has seen the data properly. If an error does occur, the system will correct it.

By the end of this compression process, only about 25 Mbits per second are going to be recorded on tape. What starts out as 384 bytes of data (8×8×6) is recorded into 77-byte receptacles with a 5:1 compression ratio.

During playback, the entire process is reversed. This includes adding a new blanking area.

NONSQUARE PIXELS

For NTSC, there are 486 active lines, each with 720 samples, of which 711 may be viewable due to blanking. So the pixel aspect ratio on a 4:3 screen is $486/711 \times 4/3 = 0.911$. The pixels are about 10% taller than they are wide. For PAL, there are 576 active lines, each with 720 samples, of which 702 are viewable so the pixel aspect ratio is $576/702 \times 4/3 = 1.094$. The pixels are 9% wider than they are tall.

It is important to know this when you're moving images between computer platforms and television systems, such as with a matte, title, or other graphic. If you're working with square pixels, such as in a graphics application such as Photoshop, you may want to set up your graphic to a 4:3 aspect ratio and then resize to the DV nonsquare pixel dimensions. That way, everything will have the correct dimensions.

DV AUDIO

Just as with picture, audio must be converted from analog to digital. This includes both sampling and quantization. With DV, audio data is not compressed, because there simply isn't as much of it compared to video. The audio is shuffled, error corrected, and then recorded to tape.

As with digital video, the Nyquist theorem applies. Digital sound must be sampled at twice the frequency of the highest pitch you want to capture. Human beings distinguish audio up to about 20kHz. The CDs you have are generally recorded at 44.1kHz, giving an accurate representation of almost all the frequency spectrum that we can hear. Most field recorders record at 44.1kHz or 48kHz.

DV supports two channels of AES/EBU digital audio at 16-bit 48kHz, two channels of 16-bit 44.1kHz, or four channels of 12-bit 32kHz. What's available to you depends on the camera and deck.

Bit rates apply to how much of a description you can give a sample. The mathematical relationship is always two to the power of n, with n referring to the number bits. This means 2 to the power of 12 (12-bit audio) would result in 4,096. This is pretty good. But 16-bit is better. Every sample in a 16-bit recording may be resolved, or rounded off, to one of 65,536 discrete amplitude steps. 16-bit recordings sound quite good to most of us.

The DV format standard allocates a fixed amount of space on the tape for the sound data, and 16-bit audio fills the entire space. The benefit of using 12-bit 32kHz audio is that it doesn't take up as much space on the tape. Because there is less data, you may be able to record more discrete audio channels than you would using 16-bit 48kHz, and some DV gear allows you to select up to four audio channels.

If you need to do multichannel recording like this, however, you may want to use dual-system sound for a better result. See Chapter 23, "Capturing the Sound," for information about audio for DV, dual-system sound, and other issues.

DV machines use unlocked audio that allows the sample number to vary according to the camera's or recorder's internal clock. This is a factor when you are insert editing (because unlocked audio isn't as precise, the insert may not work as well). It's also a factor when going back and forth from DV and other DV-based formats, such as DVCAM, that use locked audio. Locked audio specifies a precise number of audio samples for each frame. Some devices and nonlinear editing software may have a hard time handling both unlocked and locked audio at the same time.

the DV codec to compress together, so they must be compressed separately. Some fine detail is lost, showing up as a slight blockiness. You see it most often when the camera is locked down for a static shot and an object, especially a car, barrels by. Motion blur usually masks most of it, making it hard to see in most circumstances.

Dropout and banding— Dropout and banding, or *striping*, occurs when one of the two heads of the camera is clogged or otherwise unable to recover data. Just clean the heads using a standard manufacturer's head cleaning tape.

🔲 **N O T E**

IEEE 1394

IEEE 1394 is a standard communications protocol for high-speed, short-distance data transfer. Sony calls their implementation of IEEE 1394 i.Link, whereas Apple calls it the much-snappier FireWire.

Data stored on DV tape appears to reflect the packet structure sent across IEEE 1394, so you can make digital dubs between two cameras or videotape recorders (VTRs) and the copy will be identical to the original. You can also edit cuts-only over IEEE 1394 with no generation loss.

The real power of IEEE 1394 comes by combining it with a computer. With an IEEE 1394 board in your computer, you can transfer DV to and from a hard disk. This is a data transfer, with no digitizing. Usually, this transfer is done at full resolution, although there are some applications that allow low-resolution transfer. This is to save disk space,

WHAT'S ON THE TAPE?

DV tape moves past a rotating drum containing the record/playback heads. The drum is angled so that when the heads place the data, the rows of data (the collection of ones and zeros) are at an angle to the direction of the tape's travel. These rows are the *data tracks*, and this process is called *helical scanning*. Because so much data must be transferred to tape, the drum rotates at 9,000 revolutions per minute.

DV uses helical scanning to record the digital signal to tape. A single frame of DV has 10 tracks (one track for each 48 video scanlines) for one frame of NTSC video and 12 tracks for PAL. These tracks do not have successive sections of image. The 10 audio sectors can be divided into two, each of which can record two channels of 12-bit audio. Sixteen-bit audio uses all 10 tracks in NTSC and all 12 tracks for PAL for two channels of audio.

Four types of data are recorded onto tape: ITI data, audio data, video data, and subcode data. Separating each type of data is a gap that contains signals used for tracking.

- Insert and track information (ITI)—The ITI includes location information, track pitch, servo information, and the application ID of a track (APT). APT, repeated in all four signal areas, defines the internal structure of the track. ITI also includes whether the track mode is SP or LP.

- Audio—Audio includes the digital audio data and APT, as well as the recording time and recording mode.

- Video—Video includes compressed video data and APT, as well as the recording date and time, focus mode, AE mode, shutter speed, f-stop, and gain.

- Subcode—Subcode has the timecode, absolute track number, and APT. The absolute track number is a unique number for each track in the frame, expressed in a 23-bit code. This 23-bit code allows specifying unique addresses for 7 hours and 46 minutes of video, creating an index ID for quick searches.

DV FORMATS

The most expensive DV camera will *record* no better than the cheapest. This does not mean that the number and size of CCDs, quality of lenses, and other components are equal. They're not. They make a significant difference regarding quality of the image, and manufacturers offer a range of equipment at all sorts of price levels specifically for that reason. But the recorded video data is essentially the same, although there may be minor differences in the actual codecs.

All DV formats began and continue to evolve based on the DV standard.

DV

DV was created as a cooperative effort between Hitachi, JVC, Sony, Matsushita, Mitsubishi, Philips, Sanyo, Sharp, Thomson, and Toshiba. DV features 500 lines of resolution and component recording and supports timecode, separate video and audio insert editing, and direct digital in and output based on IEEE 1394.

The format uses 6.35mm (1/4") wide tape with two types of cassettes: a 4-hour-30-minute standard cassette (125 × 78 × 14.6mm) or smaller 1-hour or 1/2-hour mini cassette (66 × 48 × 12.2mm). The video recording rate is 25Mb/s.

Tape speed in SP mode is 18.81mm/sec (0.75"/sec.) onto a 4-hour-30-minute standard cassette (125 × 78 × 14.6mm) or smaller 1-hour mini cassette (66 × 48 × 12.2mm). DV in SP mode has 0.4 megabits per square millimeter. LP mode reduces the track width to 6.67 microns and extends recording time by 1.5.

DVCAM

DVCAM is Sony's proprietary DV variant that uses metal evaporated (ME) tape and differs from the DV format only in track pitch (15 microns) and tape speed (28.22mm/s). Sony claims the 15-micron track pitch is necessary for frame-accurate linear editing. In addition to using DVCAM cassettes, most DVCAM devices allow you to use DV cassettes. 4-hour-30-minute DV cassettes provide 3 hours of DVCAM recording. 1-hour DV mini cassettes provide about 40 minutes.

DVCAM gear will record two audio channels of 16-bit 48kHz or four channels at 12-bit 32kHz. DVCAM records audio in lock mode, which allows for precise insert editing.

DVCPRO

DVCPRO is a proprietary Panasonic Broadcast and Digital Systems Corporation format that uses metal-particle tape, an 18-micron track width, a tape speed of 33.813mm/sec, and native DV compression at 5:1 from a 4:1:1 8-bit sampled source. It uses 10 tracks per frame for NTSC and 12 tracks per frame for PAL, both using 4:1:1 sampling.

which is particularly handy when you're editing with a laptop or other computer without the storage for full-resolution DV. DVCPRO from Panasonic has a few differences, so a direct data interchange between DVCPRO gear and DV and DVCAM gear is not possible.

DVCPRO has two longitudinal tracks. One is for an additional analog audio cue track, and the other is a control track for near-instantaneous servo lockup and frame identification.

DVCPRO includes two locked 16-bit digital audio channels sampled at 48kHz. Both Linear Time Code (LTC) and Vertical Interval Time Code (VITC) are supported. The DVCPRO standard cassette holds 123 minutes of tape, but there is a newer, 184-minute tape now available using the same size cassette.

The DVCPRO datastream is different from DV. In DVCPRO, the compression process creates four adjacent luminance DCT blocks and two chrominance blocks in each macro block. The coefficient data is squeezed to fit the blocks with excess data slipped into any available space. Also, the header information is different.

It's impossible to have a direct data interchange between DVCPRO gear and DV/DVCAM, and some nonlinear editor systems are not capable of accepting or generating a compatible signal. The Society of Motion Picture and Television Engineers (SMPTE) has designated DVCPRO as the D-7 digital recording format. Philips-BTS also produces DVCPRO equipment under license from Matsushita.

DVCPRO-50

This variant from Panasonic uses a video data rate twice that of other DV systems at 50Mb/s. Sampling is 4:2:2 with compression of about 3.3:1. DVCPRO-50 also offers four 16-bit audio tracks. DVCPRO-50 uses the same DVCPRO tapes and transports as DVCPRO products, although a 93-minute DVCPRO-50 tape is available.

DVCPRO-50 uses two compression chip sets operating in parallel, each processing a 2:1:1 stream resulting in a 4:2:2 signal. The macro blocks of each of the 2:1:1 streams are structured like DVCPRO, but consist of two luminance blocks, two dummy blocks, and two chrominance blocks. Excess coefficient data has an entire block for overflow. The compression ratio is 3.3:1.

In addition to Panasonic, cameras and VTRs are available from Philips, Hitachi, and Ikegami.

DIGITAL-S

JVC's Digital-S also has a data rate of 50Mbps. Sampling is 4:2:2 with 8-bit component processing and compressed about 3.3:1.

Digital-S uses a more robust version of the 1/2 " SVHS cassette. Track width is 20 microns, and tape speed is 57.8mm/sec with a maximum recording time of 104 minutes, or 124 minutes if using thin tape. Audio is recorded in either two or four fully editable tracks at 16-bit 48kHz. Digital-S records to linear audio cue tracks, as well as a control track. There's also room for two lines of uncompressed video, useful for closed captioning.

The Society of Motion Picture and Television Engineers (SMPTE) has designated Digital-S as the D-9 digital recording format. Only JVC is supporting this format, although compressed data can be exchanged between DVCPRO50 and D-9 machines because they use an identical protocol.

PLAYING YOUR VIDEO

Until everyone has digital television, issues regarding analog video will remain a concern for DV moviemakers.

STANDARDS: NTSC, PAL, AND SECAM

Video in North America uses a standard called NTSC, named for National Television Standards Committee, and NTSC video operates at 29.97 frames/59.94 fields. Two other broadcasting standards are PAL (Phase Alternating Line) and SECAM (Sequential Couleur Avec Memoire). PAL and SECAM run at a sensible 50/25. PAL uses a subcarrier phase alternation technique that makes certain kinds of transmission errors less visible, whereas SECAM uses a luminance signal and two FM subcarriers to transmit color difference.

Although PAL and SECAM use a lot of common production equipment, including DV equipment, PAL and SECAM gear won't work with NTSC gear. So, if you sell your show to a country using a different standard, you will be obligated to deliver a master converted to the proper standard.

Each video frame of analog NTSC video in North America has an active picture area and a blanking area. The active picture area handles what you see, whereas the blanking area carries parts of the video signal that you don't. The *blanking level* is the beginning of the video signal information in the signal's waveform. It resides at a reference point of 0V, which is 300mV above the lowest part of the sync pulses. *Black level*, also called *set-up* or *pedestal*, is a reference black. Unlike the rest of the world, in North America black level is set at 7.5 IRE.

Set-up ensures a slight separation between the black that's displayed on the TV and the level of the blanked signal during horizontal and vertical retrace. Without this separation, early TV sets would show the retracing electron beam as a set of diagonal lines on the picture. With modern sets this is not a problem. We could drop set-up, and use 0 IRE, or 0mV as in the PAL world. But all the broadcast stations, production houses, post houses, and so on are set up for set-up. Plus, there are vaults full of programs with 7.5 IRE recorded in the signal.

In DV, as in all digital component systems, set-up is only a function of the analog circuitry and is not recorded as part of the digital signal. Digital dubs between two bits of DV equipment are not affected one way or the other.

Analog television has many types of sync signals, with different purposes. Coordination between cameras and display monitors is accomplished by vertical and horizontal sync. *Vertical sync* includes the *vertical blanking interval*, when the TV screen goes blank between the end of one field and the beginning of the second field. The vertical blanking interval may be used for a timecode, closed captioning, or other tools.

Horizontal sync (h sync) sets the electron beam to a locked position so that each line starts at the same place. The horizontal sync defines the time at which each line should start its scan and includes the *horizontal blanking interval*, the time between the end of one scan line and the beginning of the next. Vertical and horizontal sync are almost always combined into what is known as *composite sync*, often used in current video systems.

These sync pulses aren't necessary in digital applications. Instead, sync is indicated by the presence of two specific data words: SAV (Start of Active Video) and EAV (End of Active Video). SAV and EAV are reserved data markers and are used to start and end the sync blanking periods.

Only when the data must be displayed or recorded analog are sync signals required. They are re-created and reinserted to produce a signal that can be displayed on a standard video monitor or TV set.

INTERLACED AND PROGRESSIVE SCANNING

There are basically two ways to display video: *interlaced scan* or *progressive scan*.

Interlaced scan, shown in Figure 18.8 and used in standard television (SDTV) formats for NTSC, PAL, and SECAM, displays only half of the horizontal lines at a time. The first field containing the odd-numbered lines is displayed top to bottom. The electron beam is turned off and returns the beam to the top of the screen, where it's turned back on. This is followed by the second field containing the even-numbered lines drawn from top to bottom.

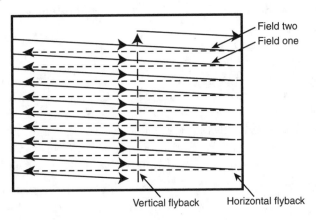

Field two
Field one
Vertical flyback
Horizontal flyback

FIGURE 18.8

Interlaced scanning.

This continues for every frame. Interlacing relies on phosphor persistence of the TV tube to blend the fields together into a seemingly single picture. While you're seeing 29.97 or 25 still images every second, they blur together to produce an illusion of motion, caused by a phenomenon known as *persistence of vision*.

The advantage of interlaced video is that a high refresh rate (50Hz or 60Hz) can be achieved with only half the bandwidth. The disadvantage is that interlacing reduces vertical definition to about 80% or 70%, known as the *Kell Factor,* of the noninterlaced image. The video is often filtered to avoid flicker and other artifacts.

Progressive scanning, used in computer monitors and digital television, displays all the horizontal lines of a picture at one time, as a single frame. The vertical definition equals the number of vertical lines for the active picture.

Nearly all current DV cameras use progressive scanning, but the fields are interleaved when the data is written to tape because most subsequent viewing devices, such as a television, require an interlaced scan. Some DV cameras do offer Frame Mode or Movie Mode options, but they don't really perform progressive readout on the chips. Instead, they appear to off-set the green CCD's timing by one scanline during readout. Basically, an even field from the R and B CCDs is blended with an odd field from the G CCD. This isn't true progressive scan, although the result can be kind of interesting to look at.

Timecode

Timecode is an electronic signal used to identify a precise location on media. With it you can identify individual video frames, as well as locate frames on digital audio tape (DAT) or any other recording system that uses it. Timecode is essentially a string of pulses or bits. On broadcast tape formats, timecode is recorded in SMPTE format with a 40-byte code containing two separate time frames in the form HH:MM:SS:FF, for hour, minute, second, and frame.

All of this sounds reasonable. So, naturally, it starts getting tricky with NTSC video. In *Producing Great Sound for Digital Video*, Jay Rose writes, "Prepare to be confused. Of all the techniques we use, SMPTE timecode is the most bewildering. What else can you expect of a system where 29 + 1 = 30 nine times out of ten, and 29 + 1 = 32 the tenth?"

NTSC video in North America runs at 29.97fps with 59.94 fields per second. SMPTE timecode format continuously counts 30 frames per second. *Nondropframe* timecode counts the exact number of frames in one hour, which is 108 fewer than would occur if the frame rate were exactly 30Hz. Nondropframe timecode isn't in sync with the wall clock. And that creates problems.

Dropframe timecode solves this by skipping or dropping two frame numbers per minute, except for minutes in multiples of ten. Dropframe doesn't drop anything. It's merely a way of counting.

Most DV cameras record dropframe timecode in a format similar to SMPTE, and it is simple to translate between them. Unfortunately, DV timecode won't show up as embedded into the video output. DV and DVCAM have their own timecode format recorded in the data.

DV data sent via IEEE 1394 has inherent timecode, and many decks also support timecode via LANC. *LANC* is a device control protocol found on consumer equipment. RS-232 is a computer port standard often found on consumer equipment for controlling equipment with a computer, whereas RS-422 is a serial device protocol that allows computers to control RS-422 equipment. That equipment usually uses SMPTE timecode and is frame accurate.

Some studio DVCAM decks also support the various forms of timecode for broadcast machines. One feature that distinguishes a professional deck from a consumer deck is the ability to lock the internal timecode generator to an external reference. If you need to set timecode at a specific time, you need a DV camera that will do that. If your equipment must accept external timecode in, you need equipment that has that option.

I use timecode strictly for media management. I don't offline/online footage and rarely need to recapture material from tape that has to be frame accurate. I use timecode, however, when organizing material by referencing the timecode for shot selection. I've also been on shows where shots are logged using database software that requires continuous timecode.

THE DV CAMERA

The camera is the primary tool of motion pictures. No camera, no show. Figure 19.1 shows a typical camera.

There are also many resources for information and comparisons of DV, DV cameras, and other DV equipment. First on my list is DV-L, an e-mail list run by Bertel Schmitt and Alexei Gerulaitis. You can subscribe at `www.dvcentral.org`. DV-L is busy, so if you can't handle umpteen e-mails on DV, you can check the archives.

DV.com has articles written by some of the most knowledgeable people on the topic. John Jackman has helpful information at his Web site at `www.greatdv.com`. In addition to DV, he has articles on lighting and the business of moviemaking. Hal Landen's Video University at `www.videouniversity.com` is also helpful.

The Golden List, put together by Ross Jones and posted online at the Desktop Video Guide at About.com at `http://desktopvideo.about.com/`, links to the major players on the Mac platform, and has reviews, FAQs, and other DV-related info. Richard Lawler's Silver List has information about DV on the PC platform at `http://www.well.com/user/richardl/SilverListFrameSet.html`. I also recommend a visit to `www.2-pop.com`. Terrific archives, nice people.

FIGURE 19.1

Sony DSR 300.

For information about any camera you may be using, start with the manual. That may seem obvious, but too often people skip reading the operating manual and then complain that the camera doesn't work.

You can get basic images by using the auto features of any camera. To really get the full use, though, I recommend working with the manual features. You can get great control over sound and picture with practice.

The extra mobility and small size of prosumer DV cameras lend themselves to all kinds of camera exploits. For example, the camera can sit on the ground for very low shots. I've driven a car over mine without having to worry about clearance. I checked obsessively with a tape measure before doing it, though.

Most DV cameras have tools for both recording and playing back footage. Camera manufacturers each have their own designs for the camera models they produce; some come with proprietary tools. All cameras, however, have certain shared features to handle capturing images and writing them to tape in digital format:

- Viewfinder
- Focus
- Exposure
- Contrast
- Color temperature
- Image stabilization
- Other image controls, including edge and skin detail controls
- Audio controls

Then there are extras for your camera you'll find very useful, including

- Monitors
- Power supplies
- Tape stock
- Add-on lenses
- Filters

VIEWFINDER

DV cameras come with all sorts of viewfinders. Prosumer cameras have color viewfinders and sometimes LCD screens. Pro cameras usually have separate black-and-white viewfinders. No doubt about it: Black-and-white viewfinders are better for critical focusing.

You can adjust your viewfinder to give you a better idea of exposure and color. See the section "Monitors" later in this chapter.

In addition to showing you the image, viewfinders should display basic information about the camera operation.

- A RECORD cue light or icon
- Battery indicator
- Tape remaining
- Shutter speed
- Gain level
- Contrast control
- White balance preset
- Filters

NOTE

Make It Automatic

Set up a pattern for cleaning and mounting your camera and recharging batteries. You should follow this ritual every time you use your gear. Make it automatic—it's the only use of automatic anything I recommend.

- Audio meter
- Fault indicators

On the set, the viewfinder belongs to the camera operator. Even the director should ask to look through it. Anyone who just walks over and looks through is not only guilty of bad manners, but may be jeopardizing your shoot. If that camera isn't locked down and falls, or the peeper accidentally readjusts a setting, the shot or the camera may be ruined.

If someone does it, a stern warning and temporary banishment to grunt work is called for.

FOCUS

Lenses accept and pass light through various elements and a controlled internal diaphragm called an *iris*. In addition to limiting the amount of light passing through to the imager, lenses are key to focusing that light correctly on the imager.

Keep your lenses clean. You can have a great camera, beautiful lighting, and a great performance ruined by a dirty lens. Use only photo-quality lens cleaner, tissues, and cloths. I recommend microfiber cleaning cloths that you can find at any photo shop. They're gentle and don't leave lint. Some people also recommend using canned air. That's fine, but don't spray the inner working of the tape transport. The pressurized air can knock the electronic components out of place.

Protect the front element of the lens with a skylight or UV filter. Use the sunshield to keep flare to a minimum, and cap the lens when the camera isn't ready to roll.

Focusing is usually done by looking through a viewfinder and turning a focus ring until you see the image is sharp. With consumer and prosumer cameras, the ring can be turned using autofocus or manual focus. As with most automatic features, autofocus is rather limited. It can be useful for grabbing shots, but in most instances manual focus is more useful.

In manual focus, you can select which part of the frame you want sharp. You can also manipulate the focus quite effectively.

Follow focus means changing focus according to the subject. For example, an actor walks into a room from the back, crosses, and sits down at a table. Depending on how tight the shot is and how shallow your depth of field, you may need to change focus to keep the image of the actor sharp.

Alternating focus means changing focus from one subject to another in the frame. *Transitional focus* means using focus as a transition, such as having the image go out of focus at the end of a scene, with the next scene beginning out of focus and gradually coming into focus. *Rack focus* is a type of alternating focus between subjects separated by depth. You focus on one subject, then the next, then either back to the original subject, or onto a third.

These focusing techniques can be difficult with some prosumer cameras. Cameras with autofocus lenses use more easily positioned internal focusing elements with lighter, faster, and cheaper focus servos. You'll know if your camera uses this kind of servo because the focusing rings have no marks on them.

In these cameras, the focus ring isn't connected to the focusing mechanism, but to a free-spinning ring attached to a sensor. Spin the ring and a series of pulses goes to the focus controller. Unfortunately, it's not linear. Turn the ring too slowly and nothing happens. Turn it quickly and you'll get a greater shift than if you turn it the same amount at a slower rate. That's why there is no way for the focus ring to have focus marks. You can't set marks or focus by scale with prosumer cameras, although you can use focusing techniques with practice and patience. Some prosumer cameras have a small button near the autofocus switch. When you press it, the autofocus snaps on momentarily. Keep your finger poised over it as you zoom, press it periodically, and you can get pretty good focus through the zoom range. Be aware, however, that some cameras have a button in the same position that forces the focus to the infinity position. Test it.

Alternating, rack, and follow focus are a lot easier on lenses with mechanical manual focus rings, such as those on pro cameras. These lenses use helical grooves in the barrels. Rotating the barrels creates friction as the barrels slide through the grooves. That friction plays havoc with autofocus. Moving the lens barrels requires good-size motors that need power to work and the lenses can't focus quickly enough to optimize autofocus algorithms.

If you have planned a lot of alternating, racking, or follow focus, consider using a camera that supports lenses with mechanical manual focus. Generally, you'll be looking at pro cameras and lenses. One common add-on for pro cameras is a *follow focus rig*. A follow focus rig allows the operator or a focus puller to control the focus manually more easily. The handwheel usually has a marker scale and is often taped to make sure the focus hits its marks.

Zoom controls have a similar problem. Many prosumer cameras have digital zoom features. Unless there's absolutely no other way for you to get close to an object, don't use them. The quality of the image is poor. For

NOTE

Cranking

There have been recent developments of video cameras that allow for changing frame rates. Several manufacturers now offer video cameras that run at 24fps to match the frame rate of film cameras. Many camera operators and DPs have said that you can definitely tell the difference between the frame rates, with the 24fps video having a more film-like motion.

If you want to shoot slow or fast-motion video, you may have trouble finding a camera that can be over- or undercranked. Both terms come from motion picture film cameras. *Undercranking* means lowering the frame rate. When the footage is played back, the result is fast motion. *Overcranking* uses a faster shutter speed and when the footage is played back, you get slow motion.

Usually, fast motion for video is created in post by removing selected frames in postproduction. Slow

manual zooming, you may get better results by using the rocker switch rather than the zoom ring.

If you're changing lenses, you may want to pay attention to back focus. *Back focus* is a mechanical adjustment in a camera that moves the imaging device relative to the lens to compensate for different focal lengths. Adjusting back focus means changing the physical position of the CCD or lens to achieve correct focus for all focal length settings. This is especially critical for a zoom lens.

When a lens does not hold focus at both ends of the zoom range, you may need to adjust the back focus. Unfortunately, not all lenses have a back focus adjustment. If you're having this problem, you may need to send your camera and lens for service.

Put the camera on a tripod and adjust your camera's viewfinder so it is in sharp focus. Set everything to manual and set a test pattern chart about 75 feet from the camera. If you don't have a test chart, use a page from a magazine. Otherwise, set the test pattern to the nominal subject distance for optimal focus tracking, which should be in the manual.

1. Open the iris to its widest aperture. If the illumination on the test chart is too bright for the open iris, reduce the light or move the chart to a darker area.
2. Set the zoom to extreme telephoto.
3. Focus on the chart.
4. Set the zoom to its widest focal length.
5. Loosen the back focus ring retaining knob and adjust the back focus ring until the chart is in the sharpest focus.
6. Repeat until the focus is consistently sharp at both ends. Tighten the back focus ring retaining knob.

Many prosumer cameras have built-in zoom lenses that work fine, although they usually don't hold focus throughout the zoom range, so the old standby technique of zooming in, locking focus, and zooming out and remaining in focus won't work. You'll be very glad you have a field monitor to double-check your focus, especially when you're tired.

EXPOSURE

Exposure is the way to relate log E (with *E* as the subject's luminance range) values to the acceptable range of the camera's CCDs. It's determined by the camera and requires referencing to a waveform monitor or zebra settings for best results.

What you're trying to do is properly expose the subject so the amount of light reaching the CCDs isn't so great that it clips or so low that the camera will try to compensate by adding gain to the signal.

Exposure can be defined as light intensity (I), determined by the f-stop, multiplied by the shutter speed (T).

$$E = I \times T$$

SHUTTER SPEEDS

In video, unlike motion pictures shot on film, changing shutter speeds does not affect the frame rate per second. For NTSC video, it's 29.97, while PAL runs at 25fps.

DV cameras have no physical shutter, but you can control the amount of time a CCD can be allowed to gather photons. With most cameras, a slower shutter speed results in either reduced vertical resolution or reduced effective frame rate, but a slower shutter allows for more light. You can get shots at 1/4 or 1/8 of a second that you wouldn't be able to get otherwise. These features are model dependent, however, so check the manual to find out what your camera can do.

I find the shutter speed of 1/30 pleasing in certain situations, despite the loss of resolution. Experiment with shutter speeds to find out what you like. Point your camera at some spinning object, like a fan, and start changing shutter speeds, and you can see what it does. Frame a fluorescent tube and see what happens when you use the highest shutter speed you can.

Just remember that changing the shutter speed in a video camera changes the amount of time light is allowed to get to the CCDs. It does not change the frame rate of the camera—29.97fps for NTSC and 25fps for PAL.

APERTURE AND F-STOP

An f-stop is the measurement of the aperture created when an iris inside a lens opens or closes. The smaller the number, the larger the opening. The larger the opening, the shallower the depth of field.

It is the reverse; the greater the number, the smaller the opening.

Technically, this is not correct. This are log values, meaning they're fractions: f/5.6>f/11, with f/5.6 being the larger number. But most people don't think of these as fractions…so fine. Change is made.

Many DV cameras have automatic light control, also called ALC, auto-iris, or auto-exposure. These servo control systems automatically open and

(continued)
motion is created by adding frames through interpolation in postproduction. Generally, the computer will create frames based on the material that was shot and put them in the appropriate place.

close the iris to ensure a constant output level to the camera. Some cameras have the auto-iris in the lens assembly, whereas others have the servo electronics contained in the camera with a four-wire connection made to the lens.

The auto-iris makes no judgment about what is important in the scene, but exposes for average levels weighted toward the center of the frame. You can often tell auto-iris is on because it hunts as you move the camera or subjects come in and out of view.

Learn to expose your images yourself. Auto-iris can help you figure out what your settings should be, but turn it off after you've made your decision. For example, if you're shooting in a kitchen with characters entering and exiting the shot, you can set your camera on auto-iris to see what its systems think the proper exposure would be. You can then lock in a setting using the HOLD button.

Most DV cameras seem to have an exposure sweet spot with an f-stop of 4 or 5.6 and shutter speed of 1/60. If the depth of field resulting from these settings fits your design and story, consider using them as the basis for your shots. Expose for the highlights, and then bring up shadow detail with additional lighting or reflectors.

Depth of Field

Depth of field is the range of acceptable sharpness before and behind the plane of focus in the final image.

Remember:

> The smaller the f-stop number, the shallower the depth of field.

Many prosumer cameras have 1/4" CCDs. These are small relative to film format sizes, and it can be difficult to get shallow depth of field. For better control

- Use neutral density filters to cut light so you can shoot at wider apertures.
- Use longer focal lengths. The longer the lens, the more shallow the depth of field. Longer lenses may also reduce contrast and color saturation due to atmospheric and other effects.
- Get some distance between subjects and background.

Gain

Video contrast is a range of light-to-dark values of the image proportional to the voltage difference between the black and white voltage levels of the video signal.

If there's not enough light, you, or your camera, can increase the gain of the video signal amplifiers to expose the image.

Automatic gain control, or AGC, usually increases the video signal in low light conditions. This control is applied to the gain of the video amplifier stage following the imaging device. It is usually related to ALC, auto-exposure, or auto-iris, so if the iris is open all the way and the video signal is low, the gain of the amplifier is increased.

Every +3db of gain gives you an additional 1/2 stop. Usually, adding gain will result in electronically noisy pictures. If there's no other way to get the image, however, then you should use it. If you like noisy video images (and sometimes they're absolutely right for what you're trying to convey) then use them.

Some cameras allow you to select negative gain settings. This reduces noise and is a way of controlling depth of field without using filters. If your camera allows it, set the gainshift to the negative gain for less electronic noise in the picture.

CONTRAST

The human eye can discern detail over a dynamic range, or contrast ratio, approaching 800:1. Even in high-contrast lighting, your eye can simultaneously extract detail from both bright and shadow areas very quickly. Unfortunately, an image that looks fine to your eye may record on your camera as overexposed or with too much contrast and lack detail in critical areas.

Film has a contrast ratio of about 8 f-stops, or about 256:1, while video can handle about 5 f-stops, or about 32:1. But exteriors can have a contrast ratio of 150:1, 1000:1, or even higher, while interiors can be from 20:1 to 1000:1.

If you go outside the bounds of DV's contrast ratio, your image may have highlights blown out and blacks that are crushed, leaving bright and dark areas with no detail in them. This is particularly true in digital formats, which allow you to only go 10% over the 100 IRE limit before the signal gets clipped.

Aesthetically, convention allows you some latitude regarding specular highlights. Most scenes will have some specular highlights, which represent the peaks of light that appear normally from reflections of shiny surfaces or points of light. If the specular highlights are very small, they can clip with little visual effect. They're an accepted part of the landscape, and most people don't worry too much about them unless they feel the highlight is infringing on the subject matter in the frame or causing smearing of the video image. While shooting "Music Appreciation," I drove my camera operator Matt Lambert a little crazy because I prefer to cut most specular highlights, while he prefers to let most of them go. I find them really distracting, and because I was the director, we followed my taste.

The best way to control contrast is by adding, removing, and modifying light. Using lighting and shading tools isn't only for dramatic effect, but to expose the image within the acceptable contrast range of the medium. See Chapter 20, "Lighting for DV," and Chapter 21, "Lighting Techniques," for information on tools and techniques.

Your decisions regarding contrast hinge not only on technical, but also aesthetic reasons. You may want blown out or crushed images. But make that decision intentionally, not out of poor practice. If you keep the images within DV's acceptable contrast ratio, you can always manipulate it in post. You can't usually fix it.

The best in-camera tool to use for checking proper exposure and contrast are zebra stripes. The best tools off the camera are field and waveform monitors.

ZEBRA STRIPES

Zebra stripes, or just zebra, are black-and-white striped patterns that appear in the viewfinder on overly bright areas of an image according to a preset reference. Other than a waveform monitor, zebra stripes are the only reliable way of telling whether or not your image is correctly exposed.

I've seen camera operators set f-stops based on how the picture looks in the viewfinder. Even if that viewfinder is properly adjusted, it's only a good approximation of exposure. The zebra stripes get you more precision. A waveform monitor will give you even more precision.

Many prosumer cameras have zebra stripes set to 100 IRE. Turn on the zebra stripes and look through the viewfinder. Open up the iris until you begin to see zebra on the brightest, hottest areas. Either stop down until the zebra pattern vanishes or knock down the hot spots by moving lights, or using flags, scrims, or other lighting controls. If the rest of the image is too dim, use fill lighting rather than opening the iris and overexposing the hot areas.

If you don't have the tools or time, consider shifting the camera and subject to get rid of the worst of the hot areas in the image. For example, if you have someone standing in the sun with a bright sky that the zebra indicates is too bright, consider moving the person under some shade, or place the subject in front of a background with other elements in it, such as trees or dark buildings.

Many pro cameras have dual zebra indicators, one at 100 IRE and another at 70 IRE–90 IRE. Because Caucasian skin highlights should expose around 80 IRE–85 IRE, and darker skin highlights should expose around 75 IRE–80 IRE, the 70 IRE–90 IRE zebra indicator gives a nice bracket for correctly exposing close-ups of people.

I know experienced television camera operators who only use the 70 IRE–90 IRE zebra. They figure that for their work, properly exposing faces is first priority, so they expose for people and let the highlights fend for themselves. If you can't control your lighting, such as in run-and-gun documentary shooting, you may want to follow this practice.

If you're on a set, however, you should take the time to expose the entire frame properly. At a minimum, use the zebra stripes and a good field monitor. For even better results, use a waveform monitor. See the following for more information.

COLOR TEMPERATURE

When a substance is heated, it gives off radiating energy, some of which falls in the visible spectrum (see Figure 19.2). That radiating energy is light.

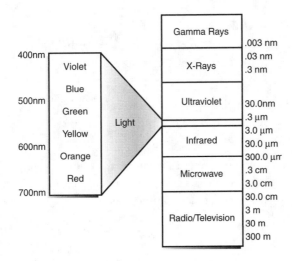

FIGURE 19.2

Only a small amount of radiation is visible to the human eye.

The spectral distribution of radiant energy from an incandescent body, known as a *black body* or *Planckian radiator*, is determined by its temperature expressed in Kelvins. This is color temperature. The higher the number, the bluer the color.

On the set, color temperatures are referred to as K. For example, tungsten has a color temperature of 3200K, whereas daylight is usually expressed as 5600K.

In the strictest terms, these Kelvin temperatures are not necessarily correct. The color temperature of tungsten lamps depends on the age of the lamp, the setting on a dimmer, how clean the lenses are, and so on. Daylight depends on time of day, atmospheric conditions, and other factors. However, these two color temperatures are the standards, and all motion picture lighting and color correction equipment are based on them.

Usually, people are not aware of differences in color temperature. Human perception automatically adjusts for sources of light. This phenomenon is called *approximate color consistency*. Approximate color consistency doesn't work for video. Mixed lighting will record and reproduce with distinct shades. Correcting, controlling, and manipulating color temperatures is a fundamental task of designing and lighting a scene and is discussed in Chapter 20, "Lighting for DV," and Chapter 21, "Lighting Techniques."

But you do have in-camera controls to correct color temperature. Two of the most important are *white balance* and *black balance*.

WHITE BALANCE

White balance is an electronic process for setting the relative gain of the color channels. The camera then uses the reference white to ensure color fidelity.

There are usually three ways to use white balance: using the camera's auto setting, selecting an in-camera color filter wheel, or setting white balance manually.

Many consumer and prosumer cameras use through-the-lens, or *TTL*, continuous white balance. Colors are sensed directly through the camera's lens with the camera's image sensor chips to make R–Y and B–Y signals. The camera sees the brightest object as the white and adjusts accordingly.

TTL color balancing is more accurate than external sensors. Cameras with TTL sensing have circuits that are a bit more sophisticated, and because the color sensing is done through the lens, the sensors only consider the image the camera sees, not ambient light around the camera.

Although auto white balance circuits are getting better and better, if you have mixed light, flesh tones may shift unexpectedly. Auto white balance, like most auto features, doesn't know your intent—when you pan from one subject to another, you may want the white balance to remain the same, but the camera may shift.

If your camera doesn't have a manual white balance, you can trick it into white balancing. You'll need something white—I've used paper, shirts, and white targets made from foamcore. See the following list for one method.

1. Set the white balance to AUTO.
2. Zoom into full-screen of a whitecard, or whatever you've got, under the illumination you will be using. For example, if you're in a room with incandescent lights, keep the card under the lamps.
3. Let the auto white balance adjust.
4. Set the camera to HOLD.

To set the color balance using a color filter wheel, select the camera's filter for INDOOR, usually a tungsten (3200K) filter, or OUTDOOR, usually a daylight (5600K) filter. Lock it in by selecting HOLD so it doesn't shift colors.

To white balance manually, put the white card in the scene under the light sources, and zoom in till it fills the frame. Some cameras require that you focus the white card as well. Press the white balance button. After it stops blinking, select HOLD to lock it in.

Different cameras white balance different ways. See your camera's manual for complete instructions.

BLACK BALANCE

Black balance adjusts the black levels of the RGB channels so that black has absolutely no color. Most modern cameras perform an automatic black balance when first switched on. Usually, you only need to do this if the camera hasn't been used in a while or if it has been through significantly different air temperature changes.

With black balance, the R, G, and B values of a black area are the same. Usually, you set black balance first so all the channels read the same when no signal is present, and then white balance. Cap the camera so no light enters. The image should be pure black. If it has a slight tint, either press the black balance button or change the gain to remove any color. This way when starting from the same equalized black level, a white input causes equal signal excursions in all three channels. Assuming channel gammas are equal, grays will stay gray regardless of their positions on the tonal scale.

After black balance is set, set the white balance.

IMAGE STABILIZATION

Many DV cameras have built-in image stabilization to smooth out shake and jitter.

Optical image stabilization uses a prism made by two glass plates separated by a high-refraction-index liquid mounted in the optical path. A sensor detects vibration and feeds data to servos that move the prism faces to compensate. When the prism changes, the light going through it is bent to keep the image stable as it reaches the CCDs.

Electronic image stabilization electronically transforms the image by repositioning the CCDs' active image areas so they can capture the image minus the shake.

Electronic image stabilization controllers look for motion in the image, and then decide how to reposition the image area. Either the image is then digitally zoomed to give the active picture room to move, or an oversized CCD allows a full-raster active area to be moved. Both methods have downsides: The images can suffer from motion blur and the controllers can be fooled.

If the area of the image being scanned doesn't have highlights or high contrast detail for the processor to lock onto, the stabilization can hunt in an annoying fashion. Slow camera pans may cause an electronic image stabilization system to see the move as a shake, and the stabilization system tries to compensate. You see an odd floating then almost a snap as the image centers itself.

You may or may not find your camera's image stabilization useful. For small jitters and shakes, both types can work well. For big moves, though, you may have to rethink what you want. There's no substitute for a good tripod. See the section on tripods later in this chapter. For more information on other types of camera support, see Chapter 22, "Rigging."

Adding a wide-angle or telephoto attachment can cause the servos of an image stabilization system to over- or undercompensate for vibrations, jitters, and jars because the shake seen by the prism is reduced by the wide angle and magnified by the telephoto. You may want to turn off the stabilization if you're using add-on lenses.

OTHER IMAGE CONTROLS

Resolution of a video image is determined by the CCD design and the video signal system. In addition to the controls already discussed, some cameras offer further image enhancement controls.

Sharpness control or *edge enhancement* takes the signal at the transition between different tones and pumps it up electronically to improve detail. You can also soften the edges, and some people find that look very pleasing. As you experiment with it, you'll see how sharp and more electronic you can make your images.

Contrast control allows you to set the contrast range of the image, while the *color control* lets you set the color saturation. Many people prefer a lower contrast, less saturated image. Work with these controls to get the look you want.

Some cameras offer a *skin tone detail* control that allows you to soften the appearance of faces. The effect is intended to reduce the appearance of facial lines. A circuit in the camera separates facial skin tone from all other colors and reduces detail in those tones. Skin color is usually selected by the camera operator, and the level of detail can also be manipulated.

One interesting effect with skin tone detail is the Amazing Melting Plastic Man, introduced courtesy of Adam J. Wilt and Bruce A. Johnson. Set Detail and Skin Tone Detail settings to maximum; then, flip the controls on and off. It's not at all useful, but you'll get a good idea of what these features are for. Start backing off the maximum detail settings and see if you like the result.

AUDIO

You can control audio by setting everything to automatic, but manual controls give you greater discretion, especially with external mixers and mics.

Your camera's audio inputs may be stereo miniplug or stereo XLR. Most pro cameras also supply phantom power through this connection, but check your manual. Also see Chapter 23, "Capturing the Sound," for information about location audio tools and techniques.

A competent location sound mixer will be able to help you decide how to configure these controls:

- Mic/line level
- Manual level
- Noise reduction
- Bass filter and limiting
- Routing to different tracks
- Headphone jack
- Audio return

If you're not using a mixer with a mono mic on prosumer cameras, you'll only get one channel of audio. Use a mono-to-stereo adapter to route audio to both channels. If you want to use more than one mono mic, you can use a dual-mono-to-single-stereo Y adapter. Both are available at Radio Shack. Either way, the audio will be at mic level.

If you're using a field mixer, use line level. Many mixers supply phantom power, which you should use to conserve camera batteries, and a test signal, which is used for setting a reference level for the mixer, camera, and headphones.

If you're using an adapter box, such as those from Beachtek or Studio One, the same rules apply. Attach the adapter and plug it into the camera. If you're using one mic without a mixer to one audio channel, turn down the volume of the other channel, or set the box to send the mono signal from the mic to both channels. If you're using a mixer, send a stereo pair into the adapter, with the adapter set to line level. Turn up the volume for both channels.

If you can use manual audio control in your camera, and you have a competent location audio mixer, use the manual control. Generally, you set your levels at –20 dB, giving yourself plenty of audio headroom to avoid peaking over 0 dB. 0 dB in digital audio is absolute zero—if your audio levels go over that amount, the result will be clipped and ugly. You won't be able to correct it in post. See Chapter 23 for a more detailed discussion.

Depending on your camera and audio equipment, you may not want to use the camera's bass filters and limiter. You can control these by using the microphones' bass roll-off and if necessary, the mixer's limiter. Your sound mixer would probably rather have this control, and it can be a lot more subtle if it's done off the camera.

While DV offers four tracks of digital audio, many cameras only allow you to use two 12-bit 32kHz or two 16-bit 48kHz. Set your camera to the highest sampling rate possible.

Your camera may allow you to assign audio routing to tracks one and two or tracks three and four. Depending on your post system, you may want to keep all of your audio on track one, or track one and two.

The headphone jack may require a stereo miniplug. I plug a small stereo minicable down the side of my camera and tape that cable down. This resists wear and tear on the itty-bitty jack. Your camera may have a separate control for headphone volume or an internal menu. Set the headphone levels to medium. Remember that raising and lowering the volume in the headphones has no effect on the incoming signal going to tape.

If you are using a mixer with test generator, set the level of the headphones while sending a test signal. The level should be about the same as a loud conversation—just verging on uncomfortable.

Some cameras have an audio return, which allows you to send audio from the camera back to the mixer. Audio return is especially handy if you're using an audio snake with two XLR cables from mixer to camera and one cable from camera audio return back to the mixer.

You can do something similar for cameras without an audio return using a miniplug in the camera and an XLR returning to the mixer. Plug the miniplug into the headphone jack and send it to the mixer's audio return in.

MULTICAMERA SHOOTING

Multicamera shooting means using more than one camera, and there are two ways to do it. The first has each camera recording to tape individually. You then select footage from all the material shot by each camera in post.

If you do this, use the same make and model of camera, if possible, and use the same settings for each camera. Keep good camera logs, label everything clearly, and be sure to slate each camera simultaneously. This will make organizing the material a lot easier in post. Consider using multiple cameras for action sequences and stunts—those things you just can't repeat for multiple angles.

The other type of multicamera shoot uses live switching. In addition to shooting with more than one camera, you'll be switching between them to determine which footage will be recorded to tape. Basically, you're shooting and editing simultaneously. Many events use live switching, such as sporting events, weddings, stage productions, and so on.

Most cameras used in live switching have only the camera and no video-cassette recorder, or VCR. I don't know of any DV cameras that don't have a VCR built in. Still, if you're on a budget, or can get the equipment inexpensively, prosumer DV cameras can work quite nicely.

Live switching requires

- Video mixer
- Two or more cameras
- At least one monitor, although one monitor per camera is better
- VCR
- Cables
- Sound mixer
- At least one microphone
- Tripods for each camera

Use the same make and model of camera, preferably three-chip with S-video out. Match all the settings and white balance each camera before shooting.

There are a number of low-cost video mixers on the market that take and send composite and S-video. Send the output from each camera via the out to the video mixer, and monitor the images using the monitors. Send the images from the mixer to the VCR.

Audio presents certain challenges. If you just need a performance, you can go directly from a local PA system, although it may be missing sound. Most PA systems are in place to reinforce the sound. For example, if you have a jazz band performing on stage, the vocalist may have a mic leading to a PA system, but the drums, sax, and bass probably won't because those instruments are loud enough. But check the PA—it may be what you need. If the house mixer is too far away, you can mic a speaker and get fairly good results, provided the house mixer tech knows how to run the board.

If the PA doesn't have a complete mix, you can plant mics in and around the area. Place them as close to the sources as you can, and lock them down to discourage thieves and as a defense against damage. Run cable from the mics to the audio mixer; then, send a stereo pair from the audio mixer to the VCR.

Cabling is the source of most problems. Heavier cables are usually better. A quality S-video cable may give you runs of 75 feet without requiring a distribution amp.

If you want to run multiple cameras yourself, you may need a remote controlled pan and tilt head on the tripods. Manufacturers offer inexpensive, yet powerful, heads for prosumer cameras. I've only used an expensive pan and tilt head once with a miniature video camera. I really enjoyed working with it, but pro pan and tilt heads are expensive. Unless you're going to be using them a lot, you may want to rent them.

For smaller prosumer DV cameras, you can use inexpensive auto pan and tilt heads. They are nowhere near as sophisticated, but they work surprisingly well with a bit of practice.

Two models are made by Bescor and Sunpak. Neither is quite at the level of professional remote pan and tilt heads, but they're cheap and with practice can give good results. I've used both on jibs and tripods in tight spaces.

VariZoom offers a considerably more expensive series of auto pan and tilt heads for cameras up to 15 pounds. The VZ-MC series pan and tilt heads have all the electronics necessary to drive the precision pan and tilt head into one small control housing.

Don't wait until the day of the event to figure it out. Practice with your switching rig to get best results.

MONITORS

A properly adjusted field monitor will help you make decisions regarding focus, framing, and exposure. A waveform monitor will help you achieve proper exposure, and a vectorscope will help you set proper color balance by giving you the exact levels of the analog video signal.

What you see on a field monitor, the levels measured by the waveform monitor and vectorscope, and the signals manipulated by a processing amplifier, or *proc amp*, are not the digital information recorded to tape. If you're sending video from the camera, such as with a field monitor, you're seeing images pulled prior to ADC and compression. If you're working in an editing suite and use these tools, you're dealing with a digital signal converted to analog by the VCR.

Still, these tools are very useful. Field monitors in particular are invaluable. You can see and correct errors prior to ADC such as poor focus, composition, and any problems associated with using auto settings.

Don't use a television set as your field monitor. TVs enhance the images they're given by contrast, color correction, and so on. Many sets are not set up properly and may be difficult to adjust for correct contrast and color. Also, TV sets have a raster that is smaller than the camera's. You're not seeing the entire image.

ADJUSTING YOUR FIELD MONITOR

Most pro field monitors have an *underscan control*. Most field monitors have a raster that extends slightly beyond the physical edges of the CRT screen, cutting off the outer edges of the picture. This is to ensure that images will always fill the display area of a typical television set. The underscan control will show you exactly how far off the visible area the image goes.

The *blue-gun-only switch* turns off the red and green guns of the monitor's cathode-ray tube (CRT), letting only blue show. Some manufacturers now offer a monochrome switch that turns on a monochrome tube when the blue-gun-only switch is depressed. Other manufacturers have monitors that route the blue signal to all three channels, giving a gray image with the solo blue channel source. Either way your monitor uses blue-gun-only, adjustments are made the same way to hue and chroma controls.

If your monitor does not have blue-gun-only, look through a Wratten 47a blue filter or a Kodak #47B gel from a local photo store. Imero Fiorentino Associates Inc., sells a Monitor Analyzer, a dark blue lens useful for making this adjustment. You can also use some blue gel, such as Rosco Deep Blue.

Attach your field monitor to your camera. Turn both on and let the monitor warm up. Block any reflections falling on the monitor screen. Set your camera to generate its color bars. There are two common types: SMPTE Color Bars and Full-Field Color Bars.

SMPTE Color Bars

SMPTE color bars for NTSC will be generated with black level at 7.5 IRE, and the white will be a gray bar at 80 IRE. For PAL equipment, the black level should be set at 0 IRE. (See Figure 19.3.)

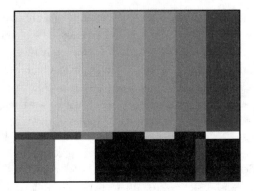

FIGURE 19.3

Black-and-white version of SMPTE color bars.

The SMPTE color bars are divided into three bands of signals as viewed on a color monitor. The top or first band contains the traditional seven—gray, yellow, cyan, green, magenta, red, and blue. The middle band contains the same colors in reverse order, with every other bar set to black. The third band contains the I, white, -Q, black, and PLUGE signals.

PLUGE, an acronym for Picture Line Up Generating Equipment, is used to adjust brightness. The PLUGE is the three black strips in the lower right. The left strip is superblack and set at about 3.5 IRE. The middle strip, black, is set to 7.5 IRE for NTSC. The third strip, dark gray, is above black at 11.5 IRE.

The white box in the lower left of the picture should be pure white on your monitor. The light bar at the upper left appears slightly less white. Adjust the contrast control until the white bar blooms. Turn down the contrast until the white bar just begins to respond. The darker of the two vertical stripes should merge into the background, and the lighter one should be barely visible. If it's not, turn the brightness up until it becomes just visible.

Turn on the blue-gun-only switch or hold up the blue gel to your eye to adjust the h; turn the Hue or Phase control. If the tint and color are adjusted correctly, you should see alternating bars of equal intensity. If not, turn the chroma or color knob until the gray bar at the far left and the blue bar at the far right are of equal brightness. Fine-tune the phase so the middle two bars match between upper and middle bands. Adjust until there is no visible difference between any of the blue bars in the first and second bands.

Turn the Hue knob until the cyan and magenta bars are of equal bright-ness. The gray, blue, cyan, and magenta bars should be of equal intensity. The yellow, green, and red bars should be completely black. Turn off the blue-gun-only and use the Chroma, Color, Chroma Gain, or Saturation knob to adjust the colors. Without a vectorscope, you can only approxi-mate the colors. I try to get a lemon yellow without anything looking overly saturated. Often, if everything else looks all right, the colors are fine.

Full-Field Color Bars

Full-field bars contain eight vertical bars from top to bottom. The bars are white, black, red, green, blue, yellow, cyan, and magenta (see Figure 19.4).

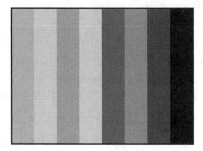

FIGURE 19.4

Black-and-white version of full-field color bars.

Turn on the monitor's blue-gun-only. All the dark columns should be equally dark, and all the bright columns should be equally bright. If the two outer bright columns don't match, turn the chroma on the monitor until they do. To adjust the inner bright columns, turn the hue until they match.

Adjusting the Viewfinder

You can adjust the image controls of your viewfinder to get a better idea of the image going to tape. Just remember that setting your viewfinder has nothing to do with the image going to camera. To adjust that image, you'll have to make changes to your camera's image controls.

1. Cap the lens.

2. Turn the contrast and brightness controls down until you have a very dark viewfinder.

3. Turn up brightness until you start to see the raster.

4. Turn on the camera's color bars.

5. Turn up the contrast until you see the bars properly. With SMPTE bars, you want to just barely begin to see the 7.5 IRE bar in the lower-right corner. If your camera doesn't generate SMPTE bars, try to get the best grayscale image you can.

This method is by no means perfect, but it may help you get a more accurate image in the viewfinder.

Attach your camera to a field monitor. Adjust the monitor properly; then, try to match the image in the viewfinder with the image on the field monitor. Save those settings in the camera.

If you always use a field monitor, consider turning down the viewfinder's color settings to make the viewfinder image as close to black-and-white as you can. It will help focusing.

WAVEFORM MONITORS

Even with a great field monitor, you may want to use a waveform monitor to get an objective, calibrated reading of the video levels.

The DV tape format doesn't record set-up (7.5 IRE) in NTSC. This should be added in the analog video output circuitry of the camera or deck, but set-up may be missing from a viewfinder or monitor out from a camera. Check your manual to see if your camera or deck adds set-up to its viewfinder and analog out signal. If it doesn't, adjust the monitors to 0 IRE instead of 7.5 IRE.

A *waveform monitor* is an oscilloscope that measures the voltage of an analog video signal and gives you a visual representation of the luminance of the picture. The video signal appears as a green trace waveform that superimposes the intensity graphs for every line of the video picture, one right on top of the other.

Traces at the top of the display correspond to brighter parts of the picture, and traces toward the bottom correspond to the darker. Objects to the left of the picture are represented by traces at the left of the waveform, whereas objects to the right are on the right.

In production, a waveform monitor monitors the signal levels of the picture. These levels must not exceed 100 IRE or drop below the black level of 7.5 IRE for NTSC or 0 IRE for PAL. Generally, every 20 IRE units is about 1 f-stop. If your image is clipping, try stopping down. If the blacks are crushed, try opening the f-stop, or add more light. You can also drop the shutter speed to let more light to the CCDs, if that won't adversely affect your image.

If you're getting images that are clipped and crushed, you have a problem with contrast. You'll have to bring in light and shading to correct your contrast and exposure.

Light faces usually fall between 60 and 80 IRE. Dark brown faces may be at 30 IRE–50 IRE. Faces in the +50–+80 range are generally considered to be properly exposed.

VECTORSCOPES

A *vectorscope* is a specialized oscilloscope used to check and align amplitude and phase of the three color video signals. The phase of the modulated chroma signal must be correct at all points in the signal chain, or else the signal will suffer hue and saturation problems.

With digital video, the vectorscope is less important than with analog video. For color balancing in postproduction, as well as broadcast and duplication, it can offer useful clues about the color content of an image.

The vectorscope displays and measures the chrominance of the video signal and is displayed in a way similar to a color wheel. The center of the wheel is neutral. The closer a color is to the wheel's center, the less saturated, or closer to white, it is. The farther out, the more saturated it is. A color can be dark and very saturated or light and unsaturated. Both white and black will make a dot right in the center.

Every point in a video image can be represented by Y, Cr, and Cb, with Y as luminance, and Cr and Cb as the color difference signals. The vertical axis of the vectorscope represents the Cr component, whereas the horizontal axis represents Cb. The vectorscope plots the two color components for every pixel in the image using these two axes.

The direction of a pixel's position on the scope represents the pixel's hue. The distance of the pixel from the center represents its saturation. Heavily saturated colors produce points on the vectorscope some distance away from the center, whereas all neutral colors, black, white, and all shades of gray produce a point exactly at the center.

If you pointed your camera at a white card, the vectorscope would display a dot in the center. If this dot is off center, the white card would not record as pure white, but with a tint.

To adjust the signal coming in from a camera or VCR, set burst to 0 using the Phase control. Turn the Phase or Hue control until the colors are lined up with their correct boxes.

If you're sending the image from a camera and the signal is still off, the camera may need adjustment. Adjust the camera's red and blue gain controls until the signals on the scope are dead center.

PROCESSING AMPLIFIERS

A proc amp can modify both the chroma and luminance values of the video signal. Usually, a proc amp is used with both a waveform monitor and vectorscope to ensure that the changes you are making are what you think you are making.

A proc amp lets you change the actual signal rather than just the display. Often, you'll find them between a source VCR and a record VCR in an editing suite. The proc amp allows you to adjust the luma and chroma of the video signal going from one deck to the other.

The proc amp can be an invaluable tool for correcting the color and luminance elements of an analog video signal. However, it must be used in conjunction with a waveform monitor and vectorscope for predictable results.

TIME-BASE CORRECTORS

A *time-base corrector*, or *TBC*, is used to synchronize a tape machine with other machines in a studio. This includes all the cameras, character generators, and special effects generators. Each device is genlocked to a master sync generator. If they aren't, the picture will break up and roll every time a cut is performed, and dissolves and fades would be impossible.

TBCs are also used to adjust color and video levels of the tape playback. The four controls used are basically the same as those found on a monitor. To set up a TBC:

1. Set up a waveform monitor with the black levels at either 0 IRE for PAL or 7.5 IRE for NTSC.

2. Turn on the TBC and use the control on the TBC marked Set Up, Pedestal, or Black Level to match the waveform monitor's black level.

3. Adjust the video level peak white to 100 IRE using the control marked Gain, Level, Video, or Luminance.

4. To adjust hue, turn the Phase or Hue control until the colors are lined up with their correct boxes.

5. Turn the Chroma, Color, Chroma Gain, or Saturation knob until the colors are in the boxes.

SIXTY SECONDS

After you've adjusted your monitor and audio levels, and your location audio crew have their equipment set to the correct levels, it's good practice to record 60 seconds of bars with reference audio tone at the head of every tape, provided the camera you're using can generate standard color bars.

An editor, an engineer, or a duplication house technician will check your tape for levels. They may use these references to set their equipment, or they may not. Some engineers set references to the standards reference and never look back.

Others will use your reference. The bars at the head of your tape are viewed first on the waveform monitor. The video level is adjusted so that the tallest bar just touches 100%. Black level is adjusted so that the black bars hit at the appropriate level, either 7.5% for NTSC, which is a dashed line just below the 10% line, or 0% for PAL. Chroma level is adjusted until it touches the 100% line.

On the vectorscope, six small boxes labeled R, G, B, Y, C, and M (red, green, blue, yellow, cyan, and magenta) will light up. When color bars from the head of your tape are displayed, instead of the ghostly waveform figure, you'll see six sharp dots. These dots are supposed to fall into the neatly labeled boxes. The phase on the TBC is rotated until the dots are in the boxes.

POWER SUPPLIES

The AC power supply that came with your camera should be treated with respect. Don't toss it around.

Some power supplies, especially for prosumer cameras, allow you to charge one battery on the power supply and one in the camera while powering the camera with AC. I prefer to use a separate charger, but that method will work in a pinch.

BATTERIES

Every piece of electrical equipment operates over a voltage range. When equipment is first powered up, the initial voltage may be as high as the upper-range limit. The voltage will begin to drop quickly during the first few minutes, and then continue to drop more slowly throughout the rest of the discharge cycle.

Establish the accurate voltage range of every piece of gear you want to power with batteries. You can look it up in the manual. If you don't have a manual, or the manual lists a single number, such as 12 volts DC, you'll have to figure out the voltage range. You can call the manufacturer and speak with an engineer and ask

- What is the lowest voltage I can use before quality or performance is adversely affected?
- What is the highest voltage I can use without causing damage?

There are many types of batteries you may run across. The most common are

- Nickel Cadmium (NiCad)
- Nickel-Metal Hydride (Ni-MH)
- Lithium Ion (Li-Ion)

Different battery types have different discharge curves. NiCads have a relatively flat curve and near constant voltage for most of the working range. Li-Ions have a more pronounced voltage drop.

Higher discharge currents will reduce the battery's life expectancy. Use batteries with capacities in watt hours at least twice the power rating in watts of the equipment. For example, a 25-watt camera will have very little impact on the life of a battery rated at 50 watt hours.

Nickel Cadmium (NiCad)   *Sintered/sintered* means both the positive and negative plates inside the battery have been impregnated with active material using a sintering process.

Pressed negative NiCads have a sintered positive plate and a negative plate with active material pressed onto it. While pressed negative NiCads may run up to 25% longer than sintered/sintered NiCads, the life cycles of pressed negatives are usually 30%–50% less. Pressed negatives tend to be more fragile and don't perform as well in higher-power applications.

High-porosity NiCads are based on a very high-porosity plate material called sponge metal. This great porosity exposes significantly more plate material to the electrolyte, and thus the battery appears to have the plate area of a larger battery with the associated greater capacity. These batteries behave like pressed negative batteries.

Nickel-Metal Hydride (Ni-MH)   Ni-MH batteries are popular because they have a higher capacity than NiCads and are virtually memory free, so these batteries do not need to be completely discharged before recharging. Manufacturers claim Ni-MH batteries have a long life, with 500–1,000 charge/discharge cycles, are lightweight, and are environmentally more friendly.

You can also remove the batteries from the charger and recharge them at any time. You won't get as much usage out of a battery that isn't fully charged, but you can do it with no adverse effects.

Ni-MH batteries can be damaged from heat by overcharging but this is easily avoided by using a high-quality, microprocessor-controlled battery charger, or a charger designed for Ni-MH batteries, and charging as directed.

Lithium Ion (Li-Ion)   NiCad cells have been the most advanced battery on the market for years, followed by Ni-MHs, which have a larger energy capacity than NiCads.

Rechargeable lithium ion batteries, though, have advantages over both. The Li-Ion battery is lighter in weight, 30%–50% smaller in volume, and has a longer lifespan. The self-discharge for idle batteries is also smaller compared to NiCad cells, which suffer a discharge rate of 20%–30% over a month.

The biggest disadvantage to lithium ion batteries is their cost. They are noticeably more expensive than either NiCad or Ni-MH batteries.

Using Batteries

Transport batteries in a fitted case or compartment and don't bang them around. The cell case can get dented, creating a permanent internal pressure point where the two plates are being squeezed together. Eventually, the separator breaks down, allowing a small leak of current, and the cell can totally discharge itself in a few days or even a few hours. The cell will give you a READY indication on a charger, although the battery remains in an imbalanced and unusable state.

Temperature changes affect battery life. Don't expose batteries to elevated temperatures, and keep them out of direct sunlight. In cold weather, keep batteries warm. If you're outside and have to carry them, put them inside your coat. Small slide-in batteries often used with prosumer cameras have more than twice the internal resistance and will be adversely affected to a far greater extent by cold temperatures.

Never put a cold battery on a charger. The battery may accept very little or none of the charge current, and it may even explode. Don't put a battery on a charger unless the label on the unit states compatibility by model number.

Keep adequate air circulation space between batteries when charging more than one battery at a time. Never group batteries so they're touching each other during charging.

Dispose of old cells properly. NiCads use mercury, lead, and cadmium, all classified as heavy metals. According to the Environmental Protection Agency, both mercury and lead can damage the central nervous system, especially in children. Return used cells to the manufacturers, or take them to a recycling center.

How Long and How Many?

When selecting a battery, use the *two-hour rule:* The battery must run the equipment for a full two hours. A battery is rated in ampere-hours (A-H) or milliampere-hours (mA-H). Typically, the stated rating is for a current of only 1/10 this value, so a 1A-H rating is actually measured at 0.1 amp. Because most camera batteries have about a one-hour duration, the A-H rating is usually pretty optimistic. *Capacity* refers to the total power a fully charged battery can deliver and is measured in watt hours. To determine the capacity of a two-hour battery for any application, take the power rating of the equipment you want to power and multiply by 2.

Factor in additional equipment, such as an on-camera light, battery age, and your recharging practice. Depending on the conditions, a battery may fail to provide even 1/3 of its rated power.

You can anticipate that you'll require one battery change for each piece of equipment over eight hours. The ultimate battery system is four batteries and one four-position charger.

Start the day with battery #1.

Mid-morning change to battery #2.

At lunch change to battery #3.

Mid-afternoon change to battery #4.

Many prosumer cameras have one-hour batteries. You'll need a lot of them, especially if you use your camera in full automatic mode. You can purchase battery belts from a variety of manufacturers for longer run times.

TAPE STOCK

It doesn't make sense to use cheap tape in an expensive camera. Tape is relatively inexpensive, and spending more for it is the one thing you can do to prevent dropout and other problems. Never reuse a tape. All it takes is for one dropout in a crucial shot to wreak havoc with your show. The

$10-per-hour cost for DV stock is far outweighed by the potential for disaster.

Buy more tape and use SP mode. LP mode is more sensitive to dropouts or alignment differences between decks than SP. DVCAM and DVCPRO were both developed using faster tape speeds to ensure better performance than DV for professional applications.

When the first DV cameras hit the market, there was an issue with using different brands of tape. That issue has been resolved, although it's still good practice to use the same brand of tape for each project.

Never leave tape stock in your car on a sunny day. Mark tapes immediately after you shoot, and use the SAVE slider so you don't record over anything valuable. Keep them in their cases and store in a cool, dry area. If you're keeping the tapes in very cold conditions, be careful to let them adjust to a warmer, more humid environment. I know a videographer who tapes dogsled races. He carries all his videotape in a bag right against his skin to avoid any problems with temperature changes.

STRIPING

It's standard practice to stripe all analog tape to lay down a control track. *Striping* means prerecording tape to get unbroken timecode. After a tape is striped, you then do all your recording and editing in INSERT mode.

DV has no separate control track, and new timecode is written each time you record because DV cameras and decks do not insert edit while recording. The timecode is written into a subcode area of the video track, unlike LTC, which runs along one edge. A DV camera does a full record and thus makes striping futile.

DV cameras pick up the timecode from the last frame that was played and carry on recording from that. If you fast forward or record to blank tape, the timecode starts again from zero.

You do want to avoid unbroken timecode, though, so you can batch capture in postproduction. Batch capture allows you to select portions of a tape by quickly scanning it, and then telling the computer to capture all the clips you've requested in one batch while you have some coffee.

Discontinuous timecode is caused by fast forwarding or playing beyond the end of previously recorded material. Ejecting and changing tapes is fine because the camera goes back and plays a couple of frames whenever you insert a tape to pick up the current timecode. Rewinding is fine. But if you need to watch something you just shot, use the End Search on your camera, or make it a practice to record some material after calling "Cut!" After you've watched the footage, you can then start recording without dropping timecode.

ADD-ON LENSES

Add-on lenses can work fine if they're of good quality. But you need to look out for vignetting at the widest angle. *Vignetting* is when the edge of an add-on lens or filter intrudes into the picture area, usually in the corners. Usually, you can only see the vignetting in the underscan mode of your field production monitor, and not in the action-safe area of the image. But if the lens is cheap or not set properly, the vignetting will cross into the action area and the viewer will see it.

Be sure to check the image in your monitor. You can always zoom through to a longer focal length to avoid the vignette.

Kenko offers two wide-angle adapter lenses. Century Precision Optics also offers wide-angle lenses for DV prosumer cameras. Sony also has an add-on wide-angle lens.

And remember, your boom operator needs room to place the mic. A camera with a wide-angle lens can always be tilted downward so that the frame is not filled with ceiling or sky at the cost of the audio.

FILTERS

The idea behind any on-camera filter is to manipulate an image prior to recording. The simplest filters change the spectral characteristics of light by absorbing certain wavelengths, allowing others to pass through. Others, such as neutral density filters, absorb all the light for an overall reduction in the amount getting into the lens. While filtering is used to correct exposure or contrast problems, it can also change the image in subtle, and not so subtle, ways.

The most common filters you'll find fall into five categories:

- Protective
- Neutral density
- Corrective
- Polarizers
- Creative

Filters can either be solid or graduated. A graduated filter has an area of optically clear glass and another area with the filtration. Some of the most common graduated filters are neutral density in various grades. They can be very handy for bright exterior shots.

Each filter has a filter factor starting with zero. The higher the number, the more light the filter absorbs. A filter with a factor of two requires opening the aperture by one stop, a factor of four means opening the aperture two stops, and so on.

Protective

Protective filters work specifically to protect the front element of the lens. I recommend you have a protective filter on every lens you use. You can get them in optically clear glass or use a sunlight or an ultraviolet, or UV, filter.

UV filters reduce the effects of excessive ultraviolet radiation. You can cut through some of the purplish haze in the sky created by ultraviolet radiation, which is especially useful for scenic exteriors. The weakest version of a UV filter is often called a skylight filter. Because the CCD sensors in DV cameras aren't very sensitive to UV radiation, this filter isn't good for much other than protecting the front of the lens.

Neutral Density

Neutral density filters, often referred to as *ND*, are used to control exposure by reducing the amount of light reaching the lens so you can shoot at a specific f-stop. Many DV cameras have built-in ND filters, and especially outdoors on sunny days, you may be using those filters often.

ND filters for use in front of the lens are referred to by their densities, which is the log of the opacity of the filter (the opacity is the filter factor). For example, a neutral density filter with a filter factor of two would be designated by its log, .3. A neutral density filter with an opacity of .3 has a filter factor of two, meaning you lose one stop.

Corrective

Corrective filters are used to color correct the image. I rarely see them on a video set, although they're often used to correct daylight film for tungsten and vice versa. Because video cameras allow white balancing, there's usually no reason for on-camera color correction. Most professional cameras still use minus-blue corrective filters with ND in the filter wheel to allow the electronic gain to work over a more restrictive range with better performance.

Polarizer

A *polarizer* transmits light in only one direction: perpendicular to the light path. This eliminates some unwanted bright areas or reflections, such as when looking through a glass window. Polarizers can also create dramatic skies, especially when the part of sky in question is about 90° away from the sun.

There are two types of polarizers: linear and circular. Linear polarizers can interact with beam splitters, semisilvered surfaces, and optical blocks in CCD cameras such as DV cameras. If a linear polarizer does not interact negatively with the image, it may interact with various subsystems on the camera, like exposure and autofocus.

Even if a linear polarizer works with one camera, it may not work well with another. You may want to buy a circular polarizer so you can use the filter with many different cameras. When you upgrade your camera, you won't have the added expense of buying a new set of filters.

A circular polarizer is a regular polarizer plus a 1/4-wave delay filter that rotates the polarization plane 90°. You can turn the plane until you get the effect you want. Polarizing filters can reduce glare, deepen a blue sky by cutting the glare of water vapor or dust in the atmosphere, and be used as a neutral density filter, losing two-and-a-half stops.

Polarizers are useful for a variety of things, but their effects change based on camera angle. If you pan, for example, you may see changes in the brightness of the sky depending on the angle of the sun. This applies to different angles of the same scene as well. Also, polarizers have the effect of increasing apparent color saturation—very effective with foliage, for example—because any reflective surface will be desaturated by reflected white light. A polarizer is very handy as long as you plan on how you're going to cut the scene together.

Creative

Creative filters can be broken into three groups. *Diffusion* includes contrast, frosts, nets, fog, and black-and-white dot filters. *Color* filters include solid and graduated tones beyond the corrective blue and orange. *Effects* filters include sunburst and star filters.

Diffusion filters are graded on a scale of one to five, with one as the lowest effect and five being the highest, although there are more subtle filters with grades of 1/8, 1/4, or 1/2. The grades pertain to how much the filter softens detail versus how much glow, or *halation*, it produces around highlights and how that affects contrast.

Contrast filters reduce contrast by spreading light from the highlights to darker areas. *Low contrast* filters usually effect images by keeping bright areas bright and the dark areas lightened somewhat. The more light there is, the greater the effect. There is no f-stop compensation, but you will see some halation around light sources or hotspots. This can be a problem for interiors.

Soft contrast filters reduce contrast by absorbing light, knocking down the bright area, but keeping the shadows dark. They will cause some halation. *Ultra contrast* filters lower the contrast uniformly through the image. Darker areas are lighter, but without halation.

Other filters that cause halation around highlights include frosts and mists. The higher grades tend to work best on strong specular light against dark backgrounds and also cause a haze over the entire image. The lower grades tend to leave blacks unaffected.

Mists tone down sharpness and reduce contrast by moderately lightening darker areas. They create halation close to the light source and often mute colors to a pastel. *Black mists* are more subtle than straight mists and definitely make colors more pastel.

Mists are really good for one thing: cutting down specular highlights. In shots where you don't have intense highlights on glass, chrome, and so on, all they will do is make the image slightly flatter.

White nets reduce blacks, while overexposed or white areas will bloom out. Fogs tend to reduce blacks, contrast, and saturation. Higher-grade fogs create halos around lights, but a double fog doesn't double the fog effect. It gives you a more noticeable glow around any lights in the image. If you can't afford to fog up a city street, a fog filter may be just the ticket.

Black, white, and color nets tend to desaturate the entire image, and some people find that look very pleasing. You can always give them a try.

Color filters tint the entire image. Common color filters are sepia, tobacco, straw, and coral. You may have better results shooting clean and changing colors in post. Sunburst and star filters are often used in still photography and produce flare lines from a highlight. Apparently, it's now standard practice for manufacturers to put a star filter in the clear position of filter wheels in pro cameras. Also, the optical antialias filter used on all CCD cameras will also produce a slight 6-pointed star effect. I don't think I've seen either color or sunburst filters on a video set, and I can't recommend them. Still, you can always experiment.

USING FILTERS

Choosing which filter and what grade depends on the shot, aperture, and any under- or overexposure. Generally, creative filters seem to work better on longer lenses and open apertures. You may have to use a variety of grades of a filter to match the effect for different focal lengths. Test first before committing. You'll also see that some filters mounted on the front of the lens are affected by spill and flares. Check all filter surfaces for any dirt or dust. Make sure they're placed properly. For graduated filters, such as neutral-density or color filters, make sure they're exactly where they need to be.

For circular polarizers, make sure the correct side is facing the lens. Unlike linear polarizers, circular polarizers must be mounted in correct orientation to the camera. There is a difference between the light entrance side of the filter and the light exit side. With screw-mount filters, this usually isn't a problem because the manufacturer correctly orients the filter in the filter ring.

If you want to use filters on the end of the lens, you'll need to know the size of the screw-on ring. Many prosumer DV cameras take a 52mm filter, but to be sure, take the camera to a local photo shop and try on different sizes of filter and step-up rings.

You may choose or have to use a matte box instead of screw-on filters. A *matte box* is an adjustable bellows attached to the front of the lens. A matte box protects the lens from flare and has several slots to hold square filters. Matte boxes are usually available for pro-level cameras.

To avoid vignetting with filters, you can use step-up rings. Step-up rings attach to a filter at a set diameter but have one end with a large diameter for larger filters. For example, you may have a 52mm UV filter on your lens. You could add a 52mm–72mm step-up ring and attach a 72mm neutral-density filter. If you need to, you could then attach a 72mm–77mm step-up with any additional filters.

In addition to on-camera filters, you may want to experiment with other tools. Shooting through a single net or white silk (see Chapters 20 and 21 for more information on these tools and how to use them) is a quick way to filter an image. You may want to experiment with putting panty hose on the lens, either on the front or on the back element for cameras with inter-changeable lenses. Panty hose and other similar items have mesh referred to as *denier*. Different denier and tints produce different results.

You can experiment shooting through optically clear glass smeared with petroleum jelly or other goop. Just keep the lens clean and don't ever use this stuff on the lens itself.

Not all DV cameras respond the same with every filter. Depending on the size of the chipset and its digital signal processor, what works well on one model may work poorly on another. Some prosumer cameras automatically crank up electronic detail to make up for less than ideal resolution for an image coming through a filter.

For example, a black mist filter that you put on to soften the image may cause the camera's digital signal processor to raise the detail more because the black mist is mistakenly identified as dirt. Cameras on autofocus may focus on the filter itself, especially if you're using mist and net filters.

Test first before committing.

CAMERA MOUNTS

It's tempting to do everything handheld, especially if your schedule is blown. Resist the temptation. Even a shoulder mount is usually better than straight handheld.

If you've planned your show for handheld shooting, use the widest angle lens. Narrow angles of view show more shake and jitter than wide angles. When you zoom in, the effect of any panning or tilting motion is magnified more than keeping the wide angle and moving closer.

Forget about holding a prosumer camera at eye level. Cradle it from the bottom, tuck your elbows into your sides, and crouch, resting the camera on your knee. If you need a higher angle, crouch on a higher surface, such as a table or counter. For moving shots, tilt the viewfinder up, hold the camera by the top handle, and cradle it underneath.

For low handheld angles, pull your knees up and rest the camera on them. Also, resting your camera on a sandbag will give you steadier shots than handheld. If you must be standing, you can also hook into the camera's tripod mount and attach a bungie cord from the hook to your foot so it's fairly tight. If it's too tight you'll be fighting with it; too loose and it won't work. This method can help you get smoother handheld pans.

Take a deep breath and relax your shoulders. Breathe into your belly, not your chest. Breathing into your chest causes your shoulders to rise and fall. You can see this gentle motion in many handheld shots. Breathing into your belly will minimize the motion, plus it's a more efficient way of breathing.

If you don't know how to breathe from your diaphragm, lie on the floor, put your legs up, and put one hand on your belly button. Now start singing. You'll soon realize you can control your voice better by breathing into your belly. That's what you want to do. If that doesn't work, take a singing lesson.

SHOULDER

Most of the television camera operators I know over the age of 40 have chronic neck, back, or shoulder problems from hauling, hoisting, and holding heavy cameras on one shoulder. The cameras are heavy. A friend of mine with a Sony DSR-300 says the camera weighs almost 25 pounds with all the options on it.

No matter how strong you are, standing eight hours with that much weight on one shoulder is exhausting. Shoulder mounts and padding will help keep the camera balanced and a bit more comfortable, but take care of yourself. If you need a rest, take a rest. People get hurt when they're working exhausted.

Even prosumer cameras get heavy. They can be especially difficult because there's no way to balance them. Shoulder mounts, such as the Mighty Wondercam, can help if you set them up properly, but they're not a complete solution.

A monopod is fairly easy to set up and can help stabilize your camera. But for best results, consider using a tripod.

TRIPODS

Tripods have three basic sections: the head, the sticks, and the spreaders.

Generally, cameras take 3/8" receivers that accept tripod heads and tripod plates. The tripod head mounts on the sticks with a receiver called a bowl that comes in different sizes depending on what kinds of head and sticks you're using. The most common is a 100mm bowl.

The spreaders attach to the feet of the sticks and will lock to keep the whole unit in place. When you're on a doorway dolly, load sandbags on the spreaders to help keep the tripod in place while moving. You can also wrap the strap of a field monitor case to the sticks to stabilize them.

You want a tripod that will adequately support the camera and all the add-ons and remain balanced. A good tripod costs money, but you can comfort the pain you're feeling by knowing that a good tripod will last for a very long time.

Fluid head tripods create friction that will help you pan and tilt more smoothly. You can also set the amount of drag for even more control over the moves. Almost all come with bubble levels. The best heads move on the horizontal for panning, move on the vertical for tilting, and have a way of leveling the head on the sticks. Some tripod heads allow you to roll the camera forward and back on a set of rods; others are specially designed for dutch angles.

Quick release plates attach to the camera. You then lock into the fluid head with the plate. Manufacturers have their own shapes of quick release plates. Always carry a spare in case you lose or break one.

The handiest tripod is a solid fluid-head tripod with spreaders and level bubbles that sets up quickly and is solid enough for your use. I have an inexpensive fluid-head tripod that can be very useful, but for critical work, I rent. Often, camera packages from rental houses include the tripod and head sized properly for the camera.

Some people prefer using a camera controller that is separate from the camera itself. You can mount this controller to the arm of a tripod or a shoulderbrace, or hold it in your hand. This makes shooting from a tripod a little more comfortable and is very useful when the camera is on a jib arm or a high tripod. VariZoom makes a variety of models. CoolZoom also offers smaller units. (See Figure 19.5.)

FIGURE 19.5

A CoolZoom unit. It's quite small and attaches to a tripod arm or shoulder brace quickly.

CAMERA STABILIZERS

I've used small Steadicams and Glidecams with prosumer mini-DV cameras. Using these mechanical stabilizers is often referred to as *flying the camera*. Although the results can be great, all three of the units I used were heavier than I expected. I found that a break between takes really helped.

Steadicams, Glidecams, and similar rigs have the camera mounted on a rigid sled supported at its center of mass on an arm or a pole (see Figure 19.6). The rig is counterbalanced with small weights and gimballed at or just above its center of gravity. The gimbal prevents the support from imparting twists, shakes, and bumps. They are either handheld or attached to an articulated arm and mounted on a body bracket or vest. There's a small monitor showing you what the camera sees, and you steer the camera by light touches near the gimbal. The trick is to balance the system so the camera will float in position as you move.

The SteadyTracker and similar systems use your hand as the mount and your wrist as the gimbal. I've never used one of these, although I have used a lightweight tripod to counterbalance a camera. When I have neither room nor time to lay dolly track, it can work for quick glides.

FIGURE 19.6
Bob Watson with a Steadicam rig.

There is another type of system that uses suspension to stabilize the camera. My friend Bob Watson has an Easy Rig he thinks quite highly of (see Figure 19.7). The Easy Rig suspends the camera within a harness, putting the weight on your hips, rather than on your shoulders. As Bob says, "If you can't hold the camera steady without it, this really won't help you, since you're still the support. But it really helps at the end of the day, when you've been carrying 20 pounds of camera. There's no hunchback fatigue because the weight is on your hips."

Another suspension system is the MarzPak. The MarzPak suspends the camera in a custom harness with a stretchy suspension cord attached to an adjustable mast that extends over your head. The creator of the MarzPak says it's great for event shooting, when you'd be handholding the camera for extended periods.

Take the time to properly balance the stabilizer and practice for better results. If you're sending your audio to camera and the camera is on the stabilizer, you'll have to consider the cabling while balancing. I usually gaff tape audio cables to my shoulder with just enough slack to minimize its effects, but I prefer to use dual-system sound. I send the audio from the mixer to a separate recorder and remove any audio adapter boxes, making the whole thing a bit lighter and easier to use.

For a discussion on using dual-system sound, see Chapter 23.

FIGURE 19.7

Bob Watson with an Easy Rig.

TECHNIQUES

The camera move needs to be motivated. If the viewer feels naturally motivated to shift gaze, the move will be almost invisible. One of the best ways to create this sensation is to design blocking and business in the frame that convey interest outside the frame. For example, an actor who looks across the room offscreen motivates a pan to whatever the actor is looking at.

When the subject doesn't motivate the move, the viewer assumes the director has done something necessary to show something specific and interesting. You can isolate certain objects or characters by dollying in or combining a tracking shot with a pan or tilt.

Even when the camera is in a static position, a camera operator will adjust framing to retain composition as actors and objects shift. Just like the actor, the camera operator has to commit to the moment because hesitation will call attention to itself. A confident move, even if it misses, can sometimes convey a sense of the scene that can be used as a transition.

Unless you have designed it otherwise, most moves seem to work best if started slowly, reaching a steady smooth speed, and then slowing to the end. This applies to pans, tilts, and zooms. Zooms need to be economical and rare. Panning or tilting with a zoom can often yield good results.

If an actor is shifting position through the scene and you're trying to keep that person in frame, zooming or backing away is enough to minimize the fishtailing camera. If it's not working, the director needs to ask the actor to stay on mark. The mark can be a bit of baby powder or chalk, a piece of tape, or a cardboard T.

Tracking shots meant to convey speed work well if there are elements in the foreground and background, such as trees, fences, shelves, and so on. Also, consider placing the camera fairly low with a longer focal length.

Communicate the move and rehearse before shooting. For more information on using other camera mounts, see Chapter 22.

SHOOTING COMPUTER SCREENS

The easiest way to shoot a computer screen is to use an LCD monitor. Turn off any image stabilization in the camera and use ClearScan if your camera has it. ClearScan is basically an infinitely adjustable shutter speed that allows you to match the scan rate of the computer monitor. If you don't have ClearScan, find out the refresh rate of the monitor, and set the shutter speed to an integral multiple of that rate. For example, if the refresh rate is 75Hz, set the shutter speed to 1/75 or 1/25.

If you can't set the shutter speed to a multiple, change the refresh rate of the monitor to match the shutter speed of the camera. On Windows computers, right-click anywhere on the desktop and select Properties. Click the Settings tab and select the Advanced Properties. Usually, there will be a drop-down list of Refresh Rate options.

Select a rate that matches your shutter speed, such as 60Hz for 1/60; then click OK. You may need to reboot for the new rate to take effect.

If this still doesn't work, you can use a converter box. They come in all prices, and there's bound to be one to suit your needs. Some have component, S-Video, and composite video ins. The converter box will allow you to zoom in on the computer image nicely.

PICK-UPS

Keep track of what you've done, review the footage, and schedule pick-ups as necessary. *Pick-ups* are reshoots of scenes you've done or shots you couldn't get because an actor or a piece of equipment wasn't available.

PAPERWORK

Camera operators must make sure the camera logs, with audio information, are filled in. Some DPs and producers will insist that camera settings be listed on the camera logs as well. If you need to do pick-ups, you can refer to the logs for the exact settings so you can match the footage. If this fits your needs, do it. Modify the sample camera log in the Appendix accordingly.

Some DPs and camera operators will mark camera positions on floor plans for every scene. I often do this to show everyone where the camera is going to be. If this sounds helpful, make sure you have a stack of photocopied floor plans so you can fill them out on the set.

CHECKLIST

CAMERA EXPENDABLES

Item	#
Lens cleaner	
Lens tissue	
Lint-free cloths for wiping off the camera body	
Canned air	
Videotape	
Extra internal batteries, if required	

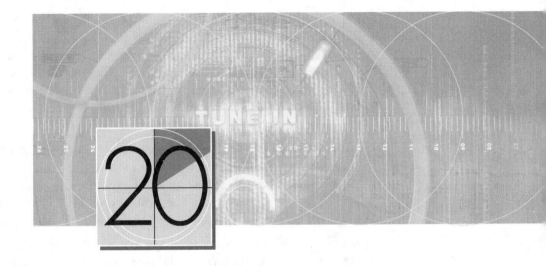

LIGHTING FOR DV

Lighting for any motion picture is a craft requiring ingenuity, taste, and knowledge of the medium. This chapter will briefly discuss motion picture lighting tools and techniques, but there are many books and Web sites that cover the subject in depth that you might want to read.

You'll also find the *American Cinematographers Manual* of great help in figuring color temperature, replacement bulbs, color correction, and other information on lights.

Film and video just aren't as flexible as the human eye, so DPs have developed a series of techniques to compensate. These techniques include the development of different lighting and shading instruments. To get the most use out of them, though, it helps to understand some basic things about light.

CHARACTERISTICS OF LIGHT

On the set, you'll be dealing with natural light, such as sun and fire, and artificial light, such as tungsten, HMI, fluorescent, arc, mercury, sodium vapor, and other sources.

Direct light is light coming from a source, such as the sun, a light unit, a desk lamp, and so on. On the set, it means specifically setting lights and reflectors to direct it where you want it.

Reflected light is light from a source that has bounced off a surface. The moon is a natural reflector. Whatever the reflector, the surface will absorb, spread, and diffuse the light depending on the reflecting surface's shape, texture, position, and color. Generally, the brighter the surface, the brighter the reflection. On the set, you'll consider reflected light coming from a subject, coming from the surrounding area, and as a tool to fill or illuminate dark areas.

Ambient light, also called *available* or *existing light,* illuminates an interior or exterior set before any other lighting is added. It may come from computer screens, neon signs, and so on, and be direct or reflected. Ambient light may need to be blocked, diffused, cut, or completely kicked out with additional lighting.

Light refers to both the fixture and the output, and the *lamp* is the bulb. Changing or replacing a lamp is called *relamping,* though some people refer to it as *reglobing.* PAR (parabolic aluminized reflector) lights have *globes,* but they're pretty much the same thing.

Every light source, whether direct or reflected, has these characteristics:

- *Intensity* of the source refers to the objective and measurable brightness in terms of luminance.

- *Quantity* of the source refers to the number, size, and type of instrument and its spread.

- *Quality* refers to beam cohesion. Spots tend to have a narrow, sharply defined beam; floods emit a wide light; and soft lights have diffused light. Reflectors, bounce cards, silks, and so on further diffuse the light.

- *Direction* of the source refers to the placement of the light beam.

- *Color* of the light according to its color temperature in Kelvins.

INTENSITY

The power rating of a light unit will help you determine just how bright that specific light is. You can use this information to help determine what result you'll get from a specific lighting unit. But on the set, you're mostly concerned with illumination—how much light is falling on the subject from a light source. And you'll also consider reflectance when correcting or minimizing specular highlights and using bounce cards and other reflectors.

Luminous objects, such as the sun or the burning filament of a lamp, emit light. *Luminous intensity* is the measure of a light source's capability to radiate light given in candelas. A *candela* is the luminous intensity of a black body heated up to the temperature at which platinum goes from a liquid to a solid state.

The eye has a varying sensitivity over the visual spectrum, being relatively insensitive to blue and to red light. Red and blue may make a deep impression on the viewer but, relative to yellow and green light, they need more watts of radiation to reach the brain. The candela is defined for only radiation at a single frequency of 540×1012, normally referred to as the corresponding wavelength of 555 nanometers.

The intensity of light of a luminous object stays the same no matter what. For example, the intensity of a star at the source is the same no matter how far away you are. This is also true of an HMI, a PAR, or a flashlight. What changes, however, is the level of illumination in relation to distance.

Illumination is luminous flux incident onto a surface—basically, the measure of brightness of a subject or set by an external light source. It is measured in footcandles or lux. One *footcandle (fc)* equals the total intensity of light falling on a surface with an area of one square foot placed one foot from a source point lit by one lumen.

One *lux* equals the total intensity of light falling on a surface with an area of one square meter placed one meter from a point source lit by one lumen.

You can convert between fc and lux by following these formulas:

> 1 fc = 9.29 lux
>
> 10.8 fc = 1 lux

Luminance is a measurement of reflected light, measured in lamberts. One *lambert* equals the brightness from a perfectly diffusing surface that radiates or reflects one lumen per square centimeter. A *lumen* is the unit of luminous flux equal to the luminous flux emitted per solid unit angle by a standard point source having a luminous intensity of one candela.

Most objects reflect only a percentage of the light falling on them. This property is called the *reflectance* or *reflection factor*. The reflectance is the ratio of reflected light to incident light in percentage. For example, a white object may have a reflection factor of about 92%, meaning it reflects 92% of the incident light. Shine 100 fc onto the white object and it will reflect back 92%, or 92 footlamberts.

A light meter measures the footcandle or lux scene by using a photosensitive cell that creates an electrical current when light falls on it. Increase the light and the current increases. The meter displays footcandles along an incremental scale.

QUANTITY

All light fixtures have an *illumination distribution curve*. It's measured by shining the light onto a flat wall to determine the beam coverage. Lighting equipment manufacturers offer these measurements to describe the characteristics of a lighting instrument.

Field coverage refers to the light's usable area, with the light no less than 10% of the peak value. *Beam coverage* is the area covered to within 50% of the light's maximum intensity.

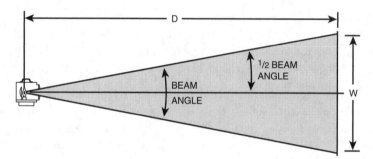

FIGURE 20.1

Beam coverage is the limit of the area covered to within 50% of the light's maximum intensity. Its area is at a level not lower than one stop from the light's center intensity.

Usually, a light with a narrow beam angle has throw. *Throw* refers to illumination in regard to distance from the lamp to the subject. Spotlights usually have greater throw than a floodlight of equal power.

Lighting equipment manufacturers include candela, beam angle, and so on with each product they sell. That may help you figure out how much light you can expect to get from a specific fixture, although you should automatically subtract 10%–15% of total light output because of aging and dirt. Most DPs, however, generally use a combination of familiarity with a certain light or type of light, lamp wattage, and knowledge of the light's quality, combined with the set, to determine lighting requirements.

Most lights are referred to in terms of lamp wattage. A 650w is a light with a 650-watt lamp, whereas a 1k has a one thousand–watt or one-kilowatt lamp. Keep in mind that the "k" in this instance refers to watts, and not color temperature.

Wattage is only an approximation of how much illumination you'll get. It can be misleading to talk about wattage if you don't keep in mind the type of light you're referring to. For example, HMI fixtures are relatively energy efficient and will give you about four times the light of a tungsten fixture of the same wattage.

QUALITY

Quality of light refers to beam cohesion. This means how diffuse the light is. For example, a spot has a hard, narrow beam, whereas fluorescents have a wide spread and diffuse light. Generally, the more diffuse, the less directional a light is. Also, the more diffuse, the less illumination.

Light quality is incredibly important and often makes the difference between a shot that works and one that doesn't. For example, if your show is a thriller, even, diffused lighting might not support the tenser beats of the story. If you use a harsher light with defined shadows, it might work aesthetically, but not technically. You'll need to add fill to light the darker areas. You don't have to illuminate them the same amount, but enough to get within DV's contrast ratio of 5:1.

Conversely, harsh light can ruin a scene. For instance, if you have two characters at the kitchen table eating dinner, you might want a softer, more even light to make the scene look realistic. You'll diffuse the light sources in a variety of ways so the light seems to wrap around people and objects in the shot.

This is a good exercise:

Get two friends, two white shirts you can get dirty, and a car. Go outside at night and turn on the car's headlights.

Sit one friend down fairly close to the headlight so the light strikes one side of his or her face. Make sure he or she is facing away from the opposite headlight. The light on your friend's face will look pretty harsh with hard shadows. Your friend will also probably complain about how bright it is.

Have your other friend hold one white shirt not quite directly opposite the headlight to reflect light to the darker side of your seated friend's face. The shadows will still be there, but the reflected light will fill the shadows somewhat so you can see some detail. This is called *bouncing light,* and the technique is often used to fill dark areas.

You also notice that the reflected light is much softer than and more diffused than the direct light.

Remove the shirt that is the reflector and lay it over the headlight so only one layer of fabric blocks it. The shadows will get softer because the light is more diffused, and it should be more even and pleasing. But the light is also less bright. To get the same illumination as from the direct light, your friend should move closer to the source.

Using diffusion material is also a standard technique in motion pictures. The materials tend to be flame retardant, but the technique is the same. To get a softer light, with less beam cohesion, you diffuse it. Anytime you diffuse a light, you cut its intensity and must adjust to get proper illumination, although usually you shift or add lights instead of the subject.

The other headlight, still unblocked, should be giving you a bit of back and background lighting, depending on how the headlights are angled. Have your second friend put the second white shirt over the second headlight. Try folding it so that different amounts of fabric fall across the light, and finally, have your friend stand in front and between the light so you can see what happens.

DIRECTION

The *inverse square law* states that the falloff of radiation from a point source is inversely proportional to the distance. As you move away from a light source, its output will fall off by half every time you double the distance. For example, when a light is 10 feet away from a subject with 4,000 lux, if you double the light-to-subject distance to 20 feet, you get only about 1/4 the original light, or 1,000 lux.

This isn't necessarily true with focusable lights, such as fresnels and spotlights. But keep this law in mind as you work with focusable lights.

Moving the light source is often the first option when solving exposure or contrast problems, yet many DPs overlook it. I've seen DPs dispatch PAs to the rental house for dimmers, when all they really needed was to back the light up a foot or two.

COLOR TEMPERATURE

Light is the part of the electromagnetic spectrum that the human eye can see, lying between about 400 and 700 nanometers. White light is a combination of all colors from the visible spectrum.

The intensity of a light source doesn't influence the Kelvin temperature. The Kelvin scale measures only color temperature, not the quantity of the light output.

The Kelvin scale applies only to light sources that are heated such as those listed in Table 20.1. Correlated Color Temperature (CCT) applies to arc-type sources or discharge lamps, such as fluorescent or industrial discharge lamps. For motion pictures, these light sources should have the CCT referenced when the accompanying Color Rendering Index (CRI) equals or exceeds 90.

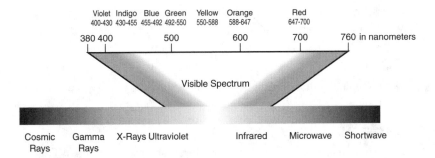

FIGURE 20.2

Visible light spectrum.

TABLE 20.1	APPROXIMATE COLOR TEMPERATURE OF COMMON LIGHT SOURCES
Source	**Color Temperature in Kelvins**
Candlelight	2000
Incandescents to 100w	2900
Quartz tungsten work lights	2800-3400
Tungsten	3200
Photoflood	3400
Daylight blue photoflood	4800
HMI	5600
Early morning sunlight	4300
Daylight	5500
Late afternoon sunlight	4300
Xenon arc	6000-6500
Overcast sky	6800

Mixed lighting refers to having light sources of different Kelvin temperatures. You'll know if you have mixed lighting by looking in your field monitor. The light from the window will look different from the light from a desk lamp, which will look different from the light from a fluorescent ceiling fixture.

Most people refer to color temperature in terms of daylight or tungsten, regardless of the light source. This shorthand, although not technically correct, is quite useful. What matters is being able to quickly correct any light to match the rest of the lights.

Color temperature is controlled inside the camera through proper filter wheel selection and white balance. Careful white balancing is essential to every scene, especially when other colors are introduced through creative use of gels and light sources. White balancing gives you correct rendition of colors, especially skin tones.

NOTE

Be Safe

Always wear gloves. They protect your fingers and the lamps. If you install a lamp with your bare hands, oils from your skin will deposit on the lamp's exterior. When the lamp is turned on and begins to heat up, those oils will burn hotter and can go through the lamp exterior to expose the filament. The lamp will fail suddenly and catastrophically, spewing molten quartz everywhere. Getting hit with molten quartz will seem fun compared to the lawsuit that inevitably follows.

Color temperature is also controlled outside the camera with color-correction gels on light sources.

TOOLS

There are many different kinds of lighting and shading instruments used in motion pictures. The following are just the ones I've used.

TUNGSTEN

Tungsten lights have a filament in the lamp that glows as it burns. They can be AC or DC and are usually 3200K.

Tungsten halogen bulbs for motion pictures use the halogen cycle. The halogen cycle carries evaporated tungsten back to the filament, increasing the life of the lamp and preventing any blackening. The halogen cycle requires temperatures of at least 250° C, which is why halogen lamps are made of quartz. Quartz can withstand such high temperatures.

Almost all incandescent lamps used in TV production are tungsten-halogen or quartz lamps.

Many small light kits for general use, such as the one illustrated in Figure 20.3, are made up of tungsten lights, stands, barn doors, scrims, spare lamps, and gels.

Fresnels are the mainstay of motion picture lighting and range in size from 100w to 10k.

NOTE

Too Hot

Make sure the power cord is not touching the light before you turn it on. If you smell something burning, chances are a light is responsible.

FIGURE 20.3

Arri kit. This kit has one 350w, two 650w, and one 1k fresnel lights. On the right and standing vertically is a roll of gels. In the back at the bottom of the open lid is a collapsed Chimera softbox.

Fresnels

Named for Augustin-Jean Fresnel, fresnel lights use fresnel lenses in the front of the lamp to bend diverging rays of light into a controlled beam. The lamp and reflector are mounted together inside the lamp housing and can be moved, giving you a tremendous amount of control over the output. Moving the lamp and reflector closer to the lens floods the light, whereas backing them away creates a spot, making it narrower and more intense. (See Figures 20.4 and 20.5.)

At full flood, a fresnel beam is relatively even, falling off quickly at the edges. To evenly light a room, you may flood each fresnel and overlap field areas about halfway, letting each light's edges feather into the next.

In many spotlights and fresnels set at spot, you'll notice in the middle a *hotspot* of 100% intensity. Hotspots present certain challenges you should correct with makeup, diffusion spray, or dots and fingers. Just be on the lookout for them.

Relamping fresnels isn't hard, but you need to pay attention, unplug the light from the power source, and always wear gloves. On smaller lights, the lamp plugs straight in. Be careful not to break the quartz from the porcelain base when removing it. Grab the base and wiggle it gently—that ought to do it.

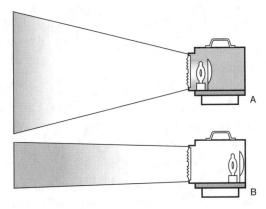

FIGURE 20.4

When the lamp and reflector are close to the fresnel lens, the rays are refracted into a wide beam. When the lamp and reflector are backed away from the lens, the rays are concentrated.

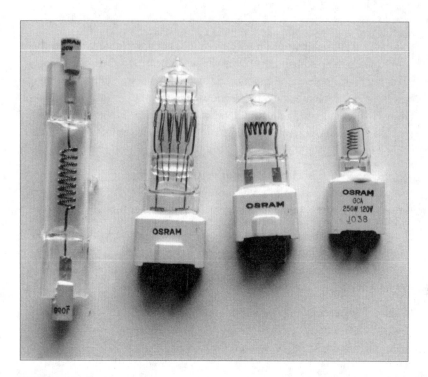

FIGURE 20.5

Quartz tungsten lamps from 1K, 650w, 600w, and 250w Arri fresnel fixtures.

Larger units have a screw in the lamp base. Loosen the screw, replace the lamp, and tighten it back up.

The fixture's performance will be affected dramatically if the lamp isn't seated correctly or the reflector is damaged or out of place. If there's a problem, replace the fixture. Try to mount larger fresnels with the base down and the lamp no more than 45° to vertical. Larger fresnels hung straight down will melt their reflectors.

Because fresnels are so common, often you'll hear people asking for a 650w or 1k, which assumes they want a fresnel at that wattage. They may also ask for a

- **Baby**—A 1k fresnel.
- **Baby-baby**—A 1k fresnel that is physically smaller than a regular Baby.
- **Betweenie**—A 300w fresnel.
- **Inkie**—A 250w fresnel.

- **Junior**—A 2k fresnel. *Junior* may also refer to a junior mount, such as 1 1/8–inch spud or pin, or any 1 1/8–inch female receiver.

- **Senior**—A 5k fresnel.

- **Tenner**—A 10k fresnel.

- **Tweenie**—A 650w fresnel.

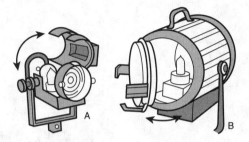

FIGURE 20.6

Relamping common fresnels. (A) The top of a pepper swings back on a hinge. (B) The lenses on larger units usually swing open like a door.

You may also come across *peppers*. Peppers are very small fresnel lights made by LTM Lighting, Inc. They range in power and you can place them easily in small spaces and are very handy for eye, back, and kicker lights. I love peppers.

Soft Lights

Soft lights produce diffused, shadowless light by aiming lamps at the inside of a white reflector set inside a box. The resulting light is even, diffused, and uncontrolled. Soft lights produce far less illumination than fresnels, so you end up using a lot of them. But it can be worth it.

Three factors affect the output of the light: the size of the source, the diffuseness of light, and the soft light's distance from the subject. Bring a soft light as close to the subject as you can for maximum illumination.

One common accessory to a soft light is an *egg crate*, as shown in Figure 20.7. Egg crates are like scrims for soft lights and it's best to keep them nearby. They get used a lot.

If you buy a set of used soft lights, you can repaint the interior. *Best boy paint* is white, heat-resistant paint that won't alter the color of the light. You can also use the paint for the inside of any homemade softboxes.

In addition to soft lights, you can use collapsible fabric softboxes from Chimera. Chimera softboxes are made of heat-resistant fabric in all shapes and sizes and will fit almost any fixture. You need speed rings to mount the softbox to the light, and always keep the ventilation flaps folded back so they don't get burned up.

FIGURE 20.7

Sliding an egg crate onto a Mole-Richardson Co. 750w Baby soft light, also known as a *zip light*.

Rifa lights from Lowel-Light Manufacturing, Inc., are a combination of softbox and lighting fixture in one. The light is mounted in a collapsible silver aluminized housing you can open to place gels.

You can always use the umbrellas included in some light kits. They're inexpensive but more difficult to set up and control because you're dealing with bounced light.

Other Softboxes

A Chinese lantern will give you wonderfully soft light. A Chinese lantern is a paper-covered-wire-frame globe into which a standard porcelain socket with a photoflood bulb is placed. Purchase photoflood bulbs from a photo shop. ECA photofloods are fairly common (3200K, 250w) and are available for about $4. Photofloods get hot, and they don't last very long, so you'll need a lot of them.

You can also use a string of white or clear Christmas lights. Leave them all bunched up as they're originally packed and slide them into the lantern. Either way, this kind of light is inexpensive, is easily rigged, and produces a soft light.

The downside to a Chinese lantern is that the light may spill, requiring you to set up flags for control. Also, the lantern itself is a fire hazard. Being made out of paper, Chinese lanterns are flimsy, easily torn, and not the most fireproof tool you could ever use.

Some manufacturers now offer Chinese lanterns made of fire-resistant material, although they're more expensive than the paper kind.

You can make softboxes using foam core, lumber, and diffusion materials. Be careful—the lights get hot and you can set stuff on fire. Be sure to mount a baby plate on the bottom so you can place your homemade box on a c-stand. You may also want to make it just a little bigger than 18"×24" or 24"×36". These are common sizes for flags, nets, and silks, and you can always slide the frame into your homemade box.

You can mount diffusion material on a frame and shine your light through it. I built a large frame out of lumber and hung an opaque shower curtain on it. I put four work lights behind it about four feet back and flagged them to control spill. The light had a really nice quality, although the shower curtain got really hot.

You may also be able to find quartz hobby lamps used by dressmakers and needleworkers. These lamps are treated with a coating to give them a color temperature of about 5000K.

Snoots are devices used to create a confined, narrow circular beam. You remove the barn doors from a fixture and replace them with these odd-looking things. Build a snoot using foam core with the black side in and diffusion about halfway between the bulb and the end of the snoot. Try different kinds of diffusion to get what you want.

You can make little snoot soft lights using an MR-16 bulb and a socket mounted on wood. MR-16 bulbs are pretty common: They're projector bulbs now found in track lighting and other household fixtures. You can find them in varying color temperatures and wattages. Be careful not to make something that will burn down the set. Black wrap will help control the spill. These fixtures are small enough that you can hang or clip them almost anywhere.

Open-Face

Open-face lights consist of a lamp and a reflector and use only on a reflector to focus the beam. Open-face lights are usually less expensive than lensed lights.

Prime fixtures have round faces and an adjustable reflector for greater control. They usually come with scrims and barn doors and have funny names. Some of the most common are

- **Blonde**—A 2k light also known as a *Mighty*
- **Redhead**—An 800w or 1k light also known as a *Mickey*
- **Teenie-Weenie**—A 650w light

Broads are very common in light kits and on sets. They consist of a double-ended lamp in a reflector. There is no lens, and the light is pretty harsh. They're good for bouncing against a ceiling, wall, reflector, or foam core, and in an umbrella or softbox.

The Tota-light from Lowel is one of the most common light units you'll see on an independent set. They are small, are inexpensive, and have a lot of power. You'll hear the call for a Tota almost anytime a set needs fill. Grab it, the stand, and a sandbag, and don't forget some black wrap to control spill.

Many people are using halogen worklights with 250w–1000w lamps as open-face light sources. You can change the clear lamp for frosted to make the light less harsh. Replace the switch with heavier duty switches and power cables. You can take off the safety cage, but whenever you use a quartz halogen light, never point it directly at a subject without some protective screen or glass in front of it.

The color temperature of the lamps is around 3000K–3200K, but it changes as they age. The stands are rugged enough; however, don't try to pole-vault with one.

You can bounce the light for fill. I've also used them to light deep background with a party gel. They don't have barn doors, although you could probably make portable barn doors with Duvetyn or black wrap and wire. Black wrap definitely helps control some spill and dissipate the heat.

Another homemade open-face light system is called a *bat strip*. A bat strip is a length of wood with porcelain sockets mounted on it. You use photoflood bulbs in the sockets. Be sure to mount baby pins to adequately support the strip and have your flags ready. Although bat strips produce a lot of light, you can't control it very well.

Bat strips are handy, but if you need a light source to fill large areas in a lot of scenes, it may be less expensive to rent or buy proper open-face lights.

HMI

HMI (hydrargyrum medium-arc iodine) lights are daylight-balanced to 5600K and give off beautiful white light. They come in a variety of sizes and wattages, ranging from the tiny Joker-Bug 150 from K5600, Inc., to monsters such as the LTM Super 12/18K HMI with its 24" fresnel lens.

HMIs are very efficient, making an HMI about four times brighter than a tungsten fixture of the same wattage. This is because incandescent bulbs such as tungstens dissipate 80% of their energy creating heat, whereas HMIs convert that same amount into illumination. (See Figure 20.8.)

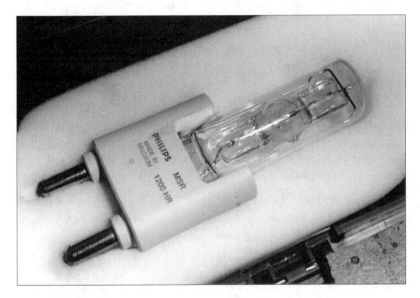

FIGURE 20.8

HMI lamp.

The main disadvantage of an HMI is the large, costly, high-voltage power supply you need to run it. Still, given its efficiency, color temperature, and high output, HMIs are very handy on location.

Smaller HMI fresnels such as a 200w, 575w, and 1200w are often used on interiors when daylight color balance is required. They can be plugged into a standard household outlet. HMI fresnels of 2500w, 4k, and 6k are often used in place of 5k and 10k tungsten to light interiors and for fill.

Large HMI fresnels have replaced carbon arc for large lighting applications. To cover wide areas, 12k and 18k HMI fresnels are mounted on booms and can light up an entire city block. They're also used with diffusion to create the effect of sunlit windows.

Portable HMI kits usually consist of a single instrument with a fitted case, a power supply, a stand, and accessories.

Attaching the head to the ballast isn't tricky as long as you're careful to have the ballast breakers off or the ballast unplugged before attaching any cable. Place the bulb in full spot position, away from the lens, to prevent thermal shock. Connect the cables, being sure the feeder cables are uncoiled and don't have anything crunching them. Before you turn on anything, you need to prepare everyone on the set. HMIs are very bright and you can startle or momentarily blind someone. Also, if the lamp explodes, you don't want anyone directly in front of the fixture.

Usually, whoever turns on the light calls, "Striking!" This warns people that the light is about to be ignited. What you want is to let people know that you're igniting the HMI, so get into the habit of calling out that lights are coming on.

Push the ON switch. The ballast will send a high-voltage charge to the head to create an arc between the electrodes in the lamp. After it's going, the ballast will bring the voltage level down to operating level. Give it two to three minutes to warm up.

HMIs have ultraviolet waves within their spectrums, so protection from these UV waves is necessary when using these sources. Sunblock for anyone handling these lights isn't a bad idea. (See Figure 20.9.)

PAR

PAR (parabolic aluminized reflector) lights are fairly simple HMI fixtures that use an assembly with globe, lens, and reflector all sealed together. An old-fashioned car headlamp is an example of a PAR bulb. The type of lens on the bulb determines the pattern and throw of the nonadjustable elliptical beam.

The globes come in various widths. If you need to adjust the beam, many PAR lights now have separate interchangeable lenses. Usually, PARs are mounted in groups and referred to by the number in a group. For example, a fixture with 3×3 PARs is called a nine-light.

The PAR is an efficient motion picture light. The raw beam pattern is not as smooth, but a PAR is great for diffusion and bouncing. They get very hot, so be careful when you rig them.

They're usually 650w. People often refer to any PAR 36 light as a FAY. A FAY light uses PAR 36 globes and a dichroic filter to correct for daylight. FAYs are handy for daylight fill.

FIGURE 20.9

HMI fixture. It has seen a lot of use, but it's still reliable.

You may also come across a Maxi-brute, which has nine 1k PAR 64 lights. A Maxi-brute lives up to its name—it has a lot of punch. Although they look awful when used directly on people, they work for window light and night fill.

FLUORESCENTS

Fluorescents belong to the group of lighting devices known collectively as *discharge lamps*. These are glass tubes filled with metal vapor, with electrodes at each end.

Fluorescents cast a soft light, use less power than incandescent lights, and run cool. They work well as long as they have flicker-free ballasts and color-correct tubes. Kino Flo was one of the first companies to make its own ballasts and tubes specifically for motion pictures. The phosphor blend of the color-correct tubes has a complete spectrum of light with a CRI of 95 with no green spike when used with Kino Flo ballasts.

Whatever size fluorescent light bank you need, Kino Flo probably makes it. Its color-balanced tubes enable you to mix the fluorescents with tungsten lights or HMIs without gel correction. It also offers tinted tubes for greenscreen work.

Fluorescents don't throw a narrow, hard beam, so they're often used in combination with other lights, such as fresnels or peppers. This combination is particularly useful for small areas with limited movement, such as interviews.

Flicker-free ballasts have become more common in commercial applications outside of motion pictures. If you're on a set with existing fluorescent lighting, open the fixture and see whether it has an electronic ballast built in. You can replace the commercial tubes with color-correct tubes from Duro-test. Get Optima 32 for 3200K and Vita-lite for 5600K. You can rent fluorescent tubes from the rental house if you don't want to buy them.

You can also use the better commercial-brand fluorescent tubes, such as Sylvania Cool White, to replace all the tubes in an existing location, and white balance to color correct with your DV camera. Table 20.2 lists the CRI temperature of common fluorescent lights.

TABLE 20.2 APPROXIMATE CORRELATED COLOR TEMPERATURE OF COMMON FLUORESCENT LIGHT SOURCES	
Source	Correlated Color Temperature in Kelvins
Daylight	6500
Design White	5200
Cool White	4300
Deluxe Cool White	4100
Natural White	3700
White	3500
Warm White	3050
Deluxe Warm White	2950

ON-CAMERA

In electronic newsgathering (ENG), for which quality is often secondary to getting a story, camera-mounted lights are sometimes used as a sole source of illumination. The result is often flat, direct light without a lot of depth.

On-camera lights are usually either tungsten or HMIs. The HMIs are most often called *sun-guns* and are very bright. They are typically powered by 12-volt batteries, often the same ones that power the camera.

Usually, you won't use a camera-mounted light on a set unless you want the look of TV news. An *obie* is an exception. An obie light is positioned directly above the lens, produces a minimal level of fill on the actors, and is used primarily as an eyelight.

You may find yourself using sun-guns on location. Although sun-guns are powerful, they don't last long on batteries, so be sure you have spare battery belts to power them. They're handy for lighting close shots where there is no other light source nearby.

PRACTICALS

A *practical* is any light that appears in a scene. This includes lamps, desklights, flashlights, candles, and so on. Using practicals in your show presents certain challenges. Almost always, if the practical is bright enough to illuminate an object, it will be blown out. If you dim the practical, the subject won't have enough illumination.

To get the exposure of practicals within the five-stop contrast ratio of DV, consider replacing all practical bulbs with 25w bulbs, putting all the fixtures on dimmers, and augmenting the overall illumination with more light.

You can treat each incandescent bulb. Spray black or brown streaks and tips heavily onto a cool bulb. You just wipe it off when you're done. If the bulb is bare, the streaks and tips will make the bulb look dirty and flyspecked.

Paint the side of the bulb facing the camera with barbecue paint from your local hardware store. Barbecue paint is used on barbecues and is more resistant to heat than regular paint. Screw in the bulb and mark which side faces the camera. Remove the bulb and take it to a well-ventilated place away from the set. Spray the camera-side of the bulb and let it dry. The painted side won't be so bright to the camera, but the unpainted side will still illuminate the set.

There's another, more destructive method, but it can give you nice results. Cut a hole in the back side of the shade. Line it with frost or opal diffusion and put it on the light. Swivel the hole in the shade toward the subject.

Finally, you can light the subject with another light, but make it look as if it's being lit by the practical. For example, if you have a lamp on in the scene, you could aim a diffused fresnel at it, being sure to control spill so you're not lighting the lamp itself.

Candles present their own problems. You can replace candlesticks with electric candles for backgrounds, but up close, there's no substitute for the real thing. You can use a contrast filter on the camera, but you may get unwanted halation. You can fill the rest of the room with very soft, diffused light color corrected as closely as you can to match the candle light.

For car headlights, put a dot of black tape on the face about the same size as the filament. It may still blow out, but you're getting within acceptable range.

Common Practicals

Household bulbs have a color temperature between 2600K and 2900K. That's pretty yellow, and you may want to gel to color-correct. Bulbs in wall sconces, chandeliers, candelabra, and so on have a smaller screw-in base, are usually fairly low wattage, and also have a warm color temperature. However, sometimes the color shift really works, and many DPs just leave it.

MR-16 bulbs are tungsten halogen, used in projectors, 3200K, and very bright. They're often used in track lighting fixtures and are pretty easy to find. There are screw-in type bulbs in 75w and 150w, whereas the track-lighting bulbs are 12-volt and need a transformer to work with AC. The VNSP MR-16 bulbs are bright, narrow, 3200K, and very useful for creating small pools of light.

Mushroom floodlights have a silver reflector inside for better throw. They come in 75w, 150w, 300w, and 500w, with a color temperature of about 2800K. You can also get these in 3200K. The R-40 size is the most common, and Lowel makes the K-5 kit with sockets, mounts, and barn doors for R-40 bulbs.

CONTROLLING COLOR TEMPERATURE

To correct the other lights, you'll need color-correction gels. Rosco International (www.rosco.com) and Lee (www.leefilters.com) have extensive Web sites that list all their color-correction gel products. Knowing what gels to use in different situations will help you solve many tricky lighting problems.

There are two types of color filters. *Absorption* filters, such as gels, absorb unwanted portions of the spectrum, including the infrared heat from a tungsten lamp. Gels that block a large portion of the infrared will deteriorate more quickly than a filter that allows it to pass. For example, a deepblue gel will fade and age more quickly than a light-yellow filter when used with a tungsten light source.

Interference types, such as dichroic filters or dichroic mirrors, reflect the unwanted portions of the spectrum instead of absorbing them. Dichroic filters last longer because they do not absorb the infrared and do use glass as their base. Because they use glass, though, they'll break if you drop them. They also tend to be expensive.

Gels come in rolls of 4'×25 'and sheets of 20"×24 " and 10 "×12 ". You can buy a packet of various color-correction and party gels, as well as diffusion. Fluorescent color-correction gels also come in sleeves you slide over the tube. Common color-correction gels include

- CTO (Color Temperature Orange) in full, half, quarter, and eighth grades corrects daylight to tungsten.
- CTB (Color Temperature Blue) in full, half, quarter, and eighth grades corrects tungsten to daylight.
- Plus Green in full, half, quarter, and eighth grades corrects tungsten or daylight to fluorescent.
- Minus Green in full, half, quarter, and eighth grades corrects fluorescent to tungsten or daylight.

Put pieces of tape in the corners of gel sheets and mark the gel type in the upper-left corner. When hanging gel using pushpins or tacks, push through the tape to save the gel.

A common use of gels is in interiors to match tungsten sources with an exterior source. For example, if a large window provides the most illumination, you can white balance the camera to 5600K and put blue CTB on your lights.

But you could do it the other way. You can get CTO combined with neutral density in a single gel, known as an 85, that converts 5600K to 3200K, while reducing the total illumination. Rosco also makes large, rigid acrylic panels, known as Roscolex, that are durable and easily reused. They're good for permanent or long-term window correction, but they're a bit hard to transport and store.

Party Gels

Gels not used for color correction are referred to as *party gels*. The most common are saturated reds, blues, and yellows. Using these gels is a way to introduce color into the scene or simulate realistic sources, such as firelight, moonlight, and so on.

CONTROLLING LIGHT AND SHADOW

Placing a light is only half the battle. Now you have to control it. Unwanted light is called *spill*. The light can be *taken down* by using diffusion, nets, flags, scrims, or dimmers, or by using black wrap or barn doors to cut the light. The light may also be *wasted* by changing the angle of the fixture.

Generally, anytime someone on a set talks about something being too *hot*, that person is not talking about coffee. He or she is referring to too much light in a single area.

Tools for controlling light fall into two categories, on the light and off the light.

ON THE LIGHT

On the light tools include the following:

- Barn doors
- Scrims
- Diffusion
- Gels
- Filters
- Black wrap
- Dimmers

Barn Doors

Barn doors are adjustable black metal flaps that slide onto the face of a light fixture (see Figure 20.10). When the fixture is put away in a kit or set up in the staging area, the barn doors close to protect the lens. When the fixture is in place and on, they mask off unwanted light to prevent spill.

Barn doors typically have two rectangular and two wedge-shaped leaves. The smaller leaves fold in first. You can close barn doors to create lines and patterns as eyelights or as texture on a wall. Barn doors are also handy as a place to clip gels and diffusion.

Barn doors provide a soft edge to the perimeters of the light. For a more defined edge, use a flag.

Scrims

Another way to control the intensity of light is with scrims. A *scrim* is a frame of stainless steel wire. By using single- or double-thickness scrim over a light, its intensity can be cut by 30%–60%.

Scrims with a green ring have a loose weave and are called *singles*. A scrim with a red rim and tighter weave is called a *double*. Half scrims cover half the rim and affect only half the beam. They can be either single or double, as shown in Figures 20.11 and 20.12.

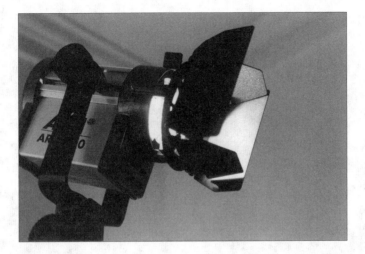

FIGURE 20.10

Arri fresnel with barn doors.

A set of scrims usually has a single, two doubles, a half single, a half double, and a gel frame. There are quarter and graduated scrims, but they're usually not part of the standard set.

Diffusion

Diffusion on the light comes in rolls of 4'×25' and sheets of 20"×24" and 10"×12". There are many kinds of diffusion, and every DP will prefer one over another for different situations.

- *Light Grid*, in full, light, and quarter grades, is reinforced diffusion material that is similar to the silk used in butterflies and overheads. It can be sewn and grommetted, and is ideal for tenting and large-area diffusion.

- *Tough Spun*, in full, light, and quarter grades, comes in various densities. Spun softens edges but keeps the beam shape. It's an excellent general-
purpose diffuser with a tough, heat-resistant base.

- *Frost* is relatively dense and creates an even soft, shadowless light. If you need to use multiple lights, you can use them with a Frost or Soft Frost to create a large-area soft light. Half Soft Frost is similar but less dense.

- *Tough Silk* spreads the light beam in one direction to create a slash of light.

FIGURE 20.11

Single and double scrims are made for the individual light. For example, a scrim from a pepper won't fit the scrim for a 1k.

FIGURE 20.12

Single and double scrims.

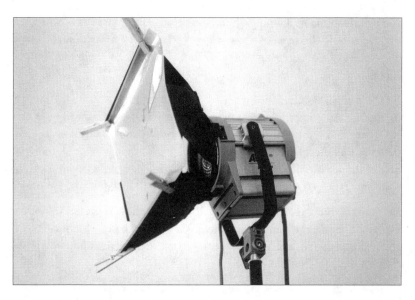

FIGURE 20.13

Arri fresnel with diffusion and gel pinned to the barn doors.

To set the diffusion, use C-47s to clip the flame-retardant diffusion to lights and crank the light to full flood. (See Figure 20.14.)

FIGURE 20.14

Clipping diffusion to barn doors.

Rolls of diffusion are often used in frames, butterflies, and overheads. See the following for more discussion.

Dimmers

Brightness can be reduced in incandescent lights by decreasing the voltage to the lamps with dimmers.

Household dimmers are plugged in between the light and the power supply. Household dimmers of 650w–1k are often used. Socket dimmers, handling bulbs of no more than 150w, screw in between the bulb and the socket.

As the electrical current is increased, more resistance is created within the filament, increasing the heat. Decreasing the electrical current lowers the resistance and reduces the heat. Unfortunately, this also affects color temperature. When the heat is low, the filament gets more amber. A rough rule of thumb is that for every one-volt drop in the voltage to an incandescent light, the color temperature is reduced by 10K.

Because the human eye can detect a 200K color shift in the 2000K–4000K range, a light can be dimmed by only 20% without having a noticeable effect on color balance. You'll have to color correct if you dim more than that.

A household dimmer (see Figure 20.15) works by interposing resistance on the wire in series with the light. A *variac* dimmer is an autotransformer. A variac doesn't use resistance but uses coils to induce a current, controlling the voltage. You can dim HMIs and fluorescents if you use high-frequency dimmable ballasts operating above 40kHz. These are readily available at a rental house.

FIGURE 20.15

A household dimmer used in-line with a light.

OFF THE LIGHT

The most common lighting control instruments are

- Flags
- Single nets
- Double nets
- Silks

Flags have black handles, single nets have green handles, double nets have red handles, and silks have gold handles.

Pieces of flame-retardant material are stretched onto frames that are usually 18"×24" and 24"×36". Smaller versions of these instruments are referred to as *dots* and *fingers*.

A couple of empty frames can be handy, although you can always make frames with lumber and baby plates. See Chapter 22, "Rigging," for more information about grip equipment. You can hang just about anything on these frames, but remember that most material is NOT flame retardant. Use caution when placing your homemade flags.

Other common lighting control tools specifically for motion pictures include

- Butterflies and overheads
- Dots and fingers
- Cukies
- Reflectors

You'll also see moviemakers using

- Visqueen
- Car window tint
- Fog machines

Flags

Flags, also called *cutters* and *gobos*, consist of any type of opaque material that can block and sharply define the edges of the light source mounted on a frame. One common material is Duvetyne, a heavy black cloth treated with fireproofing material, which is used for blacking out windows, making teasers, hiding cables, and hundreds of other uses.

Flags are generally either clipped to stands or attached to the outer edges of barn doors. The farther away they are from the light source, the more sharply defined the light cutoff will be. Moving a flag closer to or farther away from a light source will feather, or soften or harden, the shadow on the surface.

A *topper* is a flag set up above a light to control spill on the top part of the scene. A *bottom* or *bottom chop* is a flag used to keep light off the floor or the lower part of a scene.

Flags are also made out of black wrap, created and shaped, as needed, from double or triple layers. Black wrap is aluminum foil with a heat-resistant matte black finish. It's used as a heat shield on lights to prevent spill and between a flag and a light to prevent the flag from getting scorched. It comes in sheets and rolls. I recommend you buy a roll. Always leave it wrinkled for heat dissipation.

Controlling a soft light can be difficult. The effectiveness of flags, as wells as nets, silks, dots, fingers, and cukies, varies according to the quality of the light and how close it is. The closer the flag is to the light, the softer the shadow. The closer to the subject, the harder the shadow.

Whereas you might use a net on a fresnel, you'd probably use a flag on a soft light. And to be effective, the flag must block the direction in which the light is traveling and not just a portion of the light. You may be using large flags to achieve this or even building a *teaser*, which is a length of Duvetyne attached to 1"×2" on 1"×3" lumber (see Figure 20.16).

Nets

Nets are a type of scrim used to cut light. Nets are wired frames with black mesh cloth called Bobbinet. Bobbinet also is available in rolls for darkening windows.

A *single* has one layer of material and will reduce the light about 30%. A *double* has two layers of material and will reduce the light about 50%. See Figure 20.17.

Nets are great for shading light, especially when the set has dark and light colors. You'll use nets especially as you place more lights and need to control brightness.

You can also use scrim material to knock down light from larger sources. RoscoScrim is black on one side and silver on the other. It's really handy for cutting light from a practical light that's in the scene.

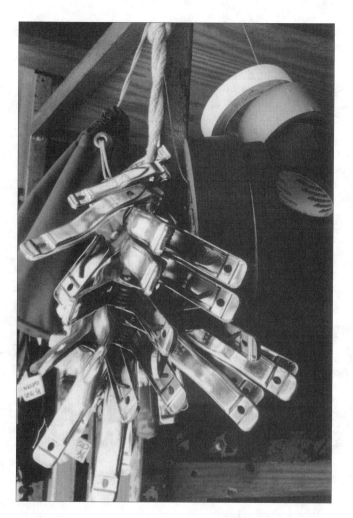

FIGURE 20.16

The ubiquitous grip clip has a lot of uses on the set. One of the most common is clipping flags together to create shapes of shadow.

Go to your nearby fabric store and get some organza and netting material in white, black, and any other shades that suit your fancy. Organza is used for veils, and netting has all sorts of uses. These materials are not flame retardant, so keep them away from hot lights. They work wonders everywhere else, and the material is cheap. You can also pick up black felt for blocking windows, muslin for overheads, and green fabric for greenscreen.

Another handy diffusion material available anywhere is a white, plastic garbage bag. Just keep it far enough from the lamp to avoid melting. I also like to use shower curtains and curtain sheers. Keep this stuff off the light.

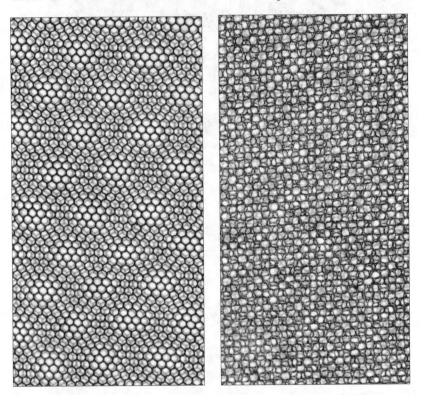

FIGURE 20.17
A single net (left) has one layer of material while a double net (right) has two layers of material.

Silks

Silks are also a type of scrim. A silk is a frame of diffusion or reflective material, formerly real silk, now artificial material. Silks reduce and diffuse light. The most common color is white, but you may see lavender. I have a black silk I've used when lighting night scenes to raise overall illumination without making it obvious that a light source is present.

Butterflies and Overheads

A *butterfly* has assorted flags, nets, silks, and diffusion, used for light control. They come in various sizes, the most common being 4'×4', 5'×5', or

6'×6', with clamps so they can be mounted in a grip head, as shown in Figure 20.18. The frame is made of tubes that you assemble and then stretch the material over. A 12'×12', or 20'×20' may be called a butterfly kit, but it's really an *overhead*.

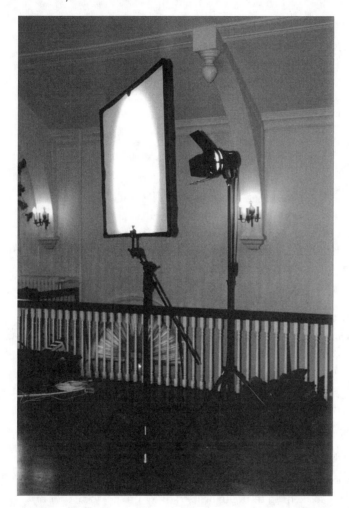

FIGURE 20.18

Butterfly with silk and light.

In addition to flags, nets, and silks, you can use diffusion for butterflies and overheads. Grid, spun, frost, and white diffusion are just like the diffusion you clip to a light, only larger. *Silent diffusion* is a special diffusion material that doesn't rattle when caught by a breeze. It's not as heat resistant and should never be used directly on the light.

You can also use fabric other than silk for great effect. Muslin, both natural and bleached, is inexpensive and durable and can be used as a reflector or diffuser.

A butterfly or an overhead kit may or may not include a griff. A griff, short for *grifflon*, is made of three-ply, high-density rubber. The material is attached to a frame and used as either a soft reflector or to cut or soften direct sun. It generally comes in three sizes: 6'×6', 12'×12', and 20'×20'. You can always use griff for rain protection.

When using a butterfly or an overhead, be sure it's secured with sandbags or guy lines tied to stakes in the ground. A slight knock or soft breeze can send it flying, so make sure it's secured safely.

You can build butterflies and overheads with lumber. Be sure to mount baby pins on the sides so you can lock into a pair of c-stands and attach gussets in each corner. Reinforce any Duvetyne, muslin, silk, or net material by hemming the edges and consider putting rivets along the sides. Make it a couple inches smaller than the dimensions of your overhead so when you tie it onto the frame, you can pull it tight.

Dots and Fingers

Dots and fingers are miniature flags, nets, and silks. Dots are circular, and fingers are rectangular. Although flags, nets, and silks usually affect the entire beam, dots and fingers change only a certain part of it. For example, if there's a reflection on someone's bald head, you could use a dot to cut the reflection.

Dots come in 3", 6", and 10" sizes, whereas fingers come in 2"×12" and 2"×14". They have long handles and are easily fitted into grip heads.

Cukies

Cukies can be fixed to the light itself, most often a focal spot or Leko. (A Leko is an ellipsoidal reflector spotlight, usually used in theaters. You may or may not find them on a movie set.) They also can be large sheets of wood or foam core set in place using clamps and c-stands.

The idea behind using a cukie is to break up large patterns of light into more interesting shapes.

You don't necessarily have to buy cukies. You can make them or use what's on hand. I've thrown light through Venetian blinds, doorways, windows, and pallets—as long as it doesn't burn, you can use just about anything. One of the most common cukies is called a *branchaloris*. A branchaloris is a limb found on the ground or cut from a tree or shrub and held in front of a light by a grip. If necessary, the grip will make the branchaloris subtly wave as if being blown by the wind.

If you have a patch of sunlight you want to break up, consider using camouflage netting. You can get it at army surplus stores very cheap and hang it wherever you need it.

Reflectors

Reflectors reflect light. The light tends to be uncontrolled and diffused. The closer the light source is to the reflector, the brighter the reflection.

Reflectors usually have two sides. The sides may be diffused, silver, gold, black, white, or just about anything else. They can come as one piece or modular sets, with varying frames and materials. You can purchase or rent reflectors, or make them.

- *Showcard* is a white artists' cardboard that's easily cut and formed. You can find it at artist supply shops and department stores in 2'×4' sheets.

- *Bead board* is a styrofoam reflector in 3/8", 1/2", or 1" widths. It comes in 4'×8' and 4'×4' sheets.

- *Foam core* is one of the handiest materials you'll use on a set. It has polystyrene sandwiched between paper. You can find it in 4'×8' sheets, or even smaller, at craft stores. It comes white on white, meaning both sides are white, and white on black, with one side white and one black. You can use the black side for negative fill.

Negative fill is a way of removing reflected light. For example, an actor is sitting at a table with a white tablecloth. When you go in for a close-up, you see the white tablecloth is reflecting light under the actor's chin. You can put a piece of black foam core down to get rid of that reflection.

I have a foldable reflector with a special arm attachment so I can mount it easily to a c-stand. It works great, looks good, and folds into a small package for easy transportation. Modular reflector kits are not terribly expensive, and you can often rent a modular kit from a rental house.

Making reflectors is pretty simple. You can use just about anything—just watch it so it doesn't start burning. A look around your local warehouse hardware store will yield all kinds of things you can turn into reflectors, cutters, and cukies.

Reflecting sunshades for cars are also handy for reflecting and bouncing light. Consider getting a couple of sheets of 4'×8'×3/4" foam like they use for insulation on the sides of new houses. Cut the sheet down the middle vertically and horizontally so you have four sheets 2'×4'. You can tape these together so they fold up and use them for bouncing work lights.

If you use two 4'×4' sheets, you can bend them into a V shape to make them stand up. This shape is more efficient than just a flat white surface. You can also use it to flag unwanted light on location.

Regardless of what kind of reflector you're using, cover the reflecting surface with light to get the maximum bounce onto your subject.

Visqueen

Visqueen is a plastic that comes in a variety of thicknesses. You can get the .006mm in 20'×100' rolls. Visqueen is good for blocking windows, creating light tents, and fitting under things if the scene requires making a big mess.

Good substitutes are plastic garbage bags. You can just tape them up. Felt from a fabric store is also useful for blocking windows.

Car Window Tint

Car window tint is cheaper than neutral density gel and a lot easier to find. Auto parts stores carry different types. Stay away from the ultra-dark kind, and experiment with the orange and gray tints. I have six rolls of various kinds I always take with me.

Do not put it on lights and don't use the kind with adhesive. Use the kind that goes on with water. Fill a spray bottle with water from the location. Some people use a drop of soap as well. Spray the window and apply the tint, smoothing it with a squeegee. Trim carefully with a razor knife.

Don't forget to wash the windows after removing the tint.

Fog Machines

Fogging or smoking the room allows you to add diffusion in the air for added texture. In this case, you don't want to see the fog. If you need fog effects, please see the section on fog special effects in Chapter 27, "Explosions, Gunplay, and Fistfights: When to Call In the Experts."

Use light-catching fog to reduce color saturation and bring up black tones that you have underexposed. Fogging works best indoors with no wind, but it can work outdoors. Blow in more fog than it appears you will need and let it waft and settle before rolling camera.

According to the National Institute for Occupational Safety and Health (HETA 90-355-2449), glycol and water fogs are among the safest theatrical effects you can use. The amounts of chemicals used in the fog are low, and the chemicals are benign.

That being said, some people may be sensitive to the mix, and some may have a slight drying of the mouth and eyes. Glycols are hygroscopic and bind with water, making the air drier, though the drying effect is limited and doesn't last long.

Fog can also be created by forcing water at a very high pressure (usually over 1000psi) through a tiny nozzle with a sharp rod in it that breaks the droplets of water into tiny sizes. The water then hangs in the air, just as natural fog does. There is nothing unnatural or hazardous about this system, although things will get a bit damp.

Cracked-oil foggers crack mineral oil into tiny droplets 10–20 microns in diameter, which is sprayed through a high-pressure nozzle into the air. The health hazards of a cracked-oil system depend greatly on the grade of the mineral oil.

You can also use cryogenic fogs, made from dry ice and liquid nitrogen. Make sure you're in a well-ventilated area so you don't deplete the oxygen. Condensation from the carbon dioxide or nitrogen will cover surfaces, so be careful with electrical equipment and walking around—you can slip. Plus, you can freeze an essential body part if you're not careful.

Finally, this smoke doesn't last very long (it will hang around for a bit and looks pretty good) and it stinks, but if the area is small, you can always burn some toast in the toaster. For very small areas, you can use a humidifier or burn incense.

EXPENDABLES CHECKLIST

Local grocery and hardware stores	Number and type	Cost
Spare or replacement incandescents and fluorescents		
Artist board		
Bead board or Styrofoam sheet		
Black and white garbage bags		
Spray bottle		
Squeegee		
Streaks and tips (you can always go to a beauty supply shop)		
Tacks and pushpins		
Visqueen		
Hobby shop or fabric store		
Camouflage netting		
Felt		
Muslin (bleached)		
Muslin (unbleached)		
Netting (black, white, other colors)		
Organza (black, white, other colors)		
Silk (white)		
Automotive supply store		
Car window tint		
DC tungsten hand spot		
Motion picture supply shop		
Spare lamps for light units—if not supplied by rental house		
Black wrap		
Bobbinet		
Diffusion in a can		
Duvatyne		
Foam core		
Photo supply shop		
18% gray card		
Photoflood bulbs		

GELS AND DIFFUSION CHECKLIST

	Full	1/2	1/4	1/8
Correction Gels				
CTO				
CTB				
Minus Green				
Plus Green				
Straw				
Party Gels				
Mixed sheets				
ND, 85, and Scrim				
ND .3				
ND .6				
ND. 9				
ND 1.2				
85 ND .3 (ND with CTO)				
85 ND .6				
85 ND .9				
Roscolex panels				
Roscoscrim				

	Full	Light	Quarter
Diffusion			
Light Grid			
Tough Spun			
Frost			
Soft Frost			
Half Soft Frost			
Tough Silk			

ELECTRICAL LIGHTING EQUIPMENT CHECKLIST

	Number	Pick-up from	Pick-up date	Return date
Tungsten fresnels with barn doors, 5-piece scrim set, gel frame, scrim bag or box, power cables				
10k Studio				
10k Big Eye				
10k Baby Tenner				
5k Studio				
5k Baby Senior				
2k 8" Junior				
2k Baby Junior				
2k Studio Junior				
650w				
lk Baby Baby				
420w Pepper				
300w Pepper				
200w Pepper				
200w Midget/Tiny/Mini				
100w Pepper				
Tungsten soft lights with egg crate and power cable				
8k soft light				
4k soft light				
4k zip				
2k super soft				
2k zip				
1k zip				
750w zip				
400w soft				
Chimera with speed rings				
Rifa kits				
Chinese lanterns				
Photoflood bulbs with ceramic sockets				
Christmas lights				

Tungsten open face with barn doors, 5-piece scrim set, gel frame, scrim bag

2k Mighty Mole				
2k Blonde				
1k Mickey Mole				
1k Red Head				
650 open face				
1k Molette				
2k Molette				

Tungsten Area Lights

10k Sky Pan				
5k Sky Pan				
2k Sky Pan				
6k Chicken Coop				
2k scoop				
1k scoop				

Tungsten PARS

1k Mole with barn doors and scrim set				
1k PAR cans with gel frame and bail block				
6-lite				
MaxiBrute (9 PAR 64s)				
Dino (24 PAR 64s)				
9-light FAY				
6-light FAY				
4-light FAY				
2-light FAY				
1-light FAY				

HMI fresnels with barn doors, 5-piece scrim set, gel frame, scrim box, magnetic ballast, 2 50' head cables, ballast feeder cable

18k				
12k				
6k				
4k				
2500w				
1200w				
575w				

200w				
Electronic ballasts				
12k Clear glass lens				
HMI soft lights with egg crate, magnetic ballast, 2 50' head cables, ballast feeder				
6000w soft				
2500w soft				
1200w soft				
575w soft				
Electronic ballasts				
HMI PARs with barn doors, 5-piece scrim set, gel frame, scrim box, magnetic ballast, 2 50-foot head cables, ballast feeder cable				
6k PAR				
4k				
2500w				
1200				
575w				
400w				
200w				
Sun Guns				
Sun Gun				
30v NiCad battery belt				
AC power supply				
Dedos and Spots				
Leko				
250w Dedo Cool kit				
100w Dedo kit				
150w Dedo kit				
Fluorescents				
Wall-O-Light (10 bank)				
4' four bank				
4' double bank				
4' single bank				
2' four bank				
2' double bank				
2' single bank				
12v single 15" kit				
12v Mini Flo kit				

12v Micro Flo kit				
DC Fluorescent sticks				
Dimmers				
Variac				
Plate				
Hand dimmer				
Kits				
R-40				
Arri kit				
Lowel kit				
Other				
Fog machine				
Fog juice				
Dry ice machine				
Cyclorama strip				
Flicker box				

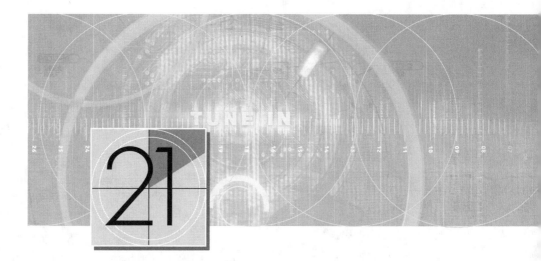

LIGHTING TECHNIQUES

Lighting causes more heart palpitations than any other technical practice of moviemaking. It always takes longer than anticipated; the tools are heavy, hot, and often expensive; and there always seems to be some sort of hocus-pocus going on with proper placement.

The technical purpose of lighting is to get proper exposure within the contrast range of the medium—in this case, DV.

The aesthetic purpose of lighting is to set the subject apart from the background to direct the viewer's eye in the frame. By directing the eye, you're showing the viewer what's important.

Technically, how you use lighting instruments and shadowing tools depends on

- Quantity of light required for proper exposure and contrast
- Quantity of light required for depth of field

- Creating a comfortable environment for the actors to perform
- Your budget
- Your schedule
- The amount of power available

The technical side of lighting is bound by the laws of physics; you can't break them even if you want to. But physics doesn't apply to aesthetics. Insisting there are aesthetic laws is like insisting twelve-tone music is the *only* music. It's just not so.

That said, there are rules. These are conventions that have developed through years of practice and are not in place to make your life more difficult or to keep moviemaking a mysterious, highly ritualized activity (or are they?). They're a way for moviemakers to communicate without having to reinvent lighting or calling attention to the techniques. It is a failure of the moviemaker to make the technical aspects of moviemaking an issue for the viewer.

In Chapter 10, "Production Design," you figured out what it was you wanted the viewer to see for each beat of your show. You answered these questions:

- What's the time of day?
- What's the weather?
- Where does the scene take place?
- Where are we in the story arc?
- How should the viewer see each character?
- How does the character relate to light?
- What color and quality of light support the character's emotional states?
- Should the light include or exclude the character?

Conventional practices will help you combine these aesthetic needs with the technical requirements.

For example, if the scene is a night interior, you usually don't just turn off all the lights and shoot in the dark. The camera won't see anything, and you'll end up with radio. Conversely, you'll have a hard time convincing people it's night if everything is lit up as bright as daytime.

The convention is to light using blue-gelled sources—the viewer will accept the blue as moonlight. You have other choices to make, but you get the idea: The conventions give you an excellent place to start lighting.

SEPARATING THE SUBJECT

Separating the subject from the background allows you to further control what you want the viewer to look at. It also allows you to add some depth to the overall image. Generally, you can separate the subject from the background by

- Using color to separate the subject
- Using contrast to separate the subject

USING COLOR TO SEPARATE THE SUBJECT

You can use an in-camera filter to change the look of the image. For example, a 3200K filter used outdoors will make everything very blue, with skintones that look very pink. You can manipulate the color by adjusting the color balance and contrast controls. You can also white balance to a card that isn't white.

You can use party gels to paint color in an area or form little pools of color in the background, or a hard light to really hit wardrobe that may be very vivid or very bland. You can also use overall color to convey mood. For example, you choose to use color correction that's a little warm or cooler in tone.

Of course, wardrobe and set design play a large role in separating elements within the frame. See Chapter 25, "Props, Sets, and Set Dressing," for more information.

Reaction to color is subjective and often influenced by culture. When using color, keep in mind:

- Many colors have a certain feel to them. Reds and oranges are considered hot, whereas blues feel cold.
- The eye sees objects that are red as closer than objects that are blue. You can design to use this to great effect.
- Color effects are relative. Surround a warm tone with cooler tones and vice versa for greater emphasis.
- Balance colors according to their complementaries. The complementary of red is green, the complementary of blue is orange, and so on. Hotter colors usually require less physical space than cooler colors.
- Prolonged exposure to one color seems to decrease sensitivity, although the complementary color will evoke an increased response.
- A small area of saturated color can throw off your composition by continually attracting the eye. Balance these colors within the frame by working the triangle, and keep the strong color with the subject.

USING CONTRAST TO SEPARATE THE SUBJECT

Lighting ratio and contrast ratio are inextricably linked. Whereas *contrast ratio* is the difference in brightness between the lightest and darkest areas of the image, *lighting ratio* refers specifically to the amount of light on the subject and the light of the surrounding area. Here are some ratios:

- 1:1—flat lighting
- 2:1—one f-stop
- 3:1—one and two-thirds f-stops
- 4:1—two f-stops
- 8:1—three f-stops

A contrast ratio of 2:1 may be barely noticeable to the eye, but is very noticeable on tape. You'll see the difference between subject and background lighting with a ratio of 4:1, but it will be very noticeable when recorded.

Three-point lighting uses three light sources of different intensities to model the subject. These three lights are the key, the fill, and the backlight:

- **Key**—The main light source. Usually a lensed light.
- **Fill**—Often a soft light positioned in front of the subject to fill in shadows, cutting contrast and illuminating detail on the subject.
- **Back**—Also called a rim light, usually a lensed instrument of less wattage than the key and placed behind the subject to add the illusion of depth and separate the subject from the background.

Generally, each light is above the subject at about 45 degrees, with the key and fill in front of the subject and the rim behind. The key is about 45 degrees off the subject on one side and the fill light 45 degrees on the other side. The back light is placed behind the subject, with a tight beam aimed right at the back of the head. This creates a rim of light. If it's placed too low, the back light will be picked up by the camera. If it's too high, it will spill over the top of the subject's head, lighting the tip of the nose.

(These angles are approximations—if you start here, you can adjust to fit your story and the subject.)

I think three-point lighting is a place to start lighting your set. You usually end up placing other lights to add dimension and enhance the style of the image. These lights include background lights, spot highlights, kickers, and eyelights:

- **Background lights**—Illuminate the set or background to create the illusion of depth. Any type of light can be used as a background light as long as it is fairly even. If the background has detail or texture, put it on the same side as the key. Hitting drapery with a narrow slash of light is common background lighting, as is my favorite, shining the light through Venetian blinds.

- **Spot highlights**—These accent a portion of the set with a pool of light or color. Usually, a spot highlight is created with a tight beam. It may be in place to replicate a reflection, to create the illusion of spill from an offstage area, or as a pool along a wall or floor. Practicals with MR-16 lamps in them can be used as spots. Aim them toward wall art or bookcases, and make sure they're not so hot that they distract from the subject.

- **Kickers**—Kickers are usually spots used for modeling the subject. They're placed on the fill side of the subject to accent the shoulder and side of the subject's face. Kickers are also used to get rid of distracting shadows. If your set has been lit with fairly even fill, you may not need to worry about kickers until you go in for medium and close shots.

- **Eyelights**—Eyelights are wonderfully effective, painterly touches to an image. Often the key works as an eyelight, adding a twinkle to the eye, but you can set up your lights to place your eyelight separately. It won't take much—eyes are quite reflective. You can use a small bounce card or tiny, color-correct light just above and to the left or right of the camera. Unless you can see the subject's eyes clearly, don't worry about placing an eyelight until you go in for close-ups.

Consider using different shapes for different effects, and try to stay away from having more than one. Unless you have a practical to explain it, such as candles on a birthday cake, more than one eyelight gets really distracting.

If you have practicals, you'll need to take those into account as well.

LIGHTING FOR MOVEMENT

Lighting for motion pictures often involves lighting for movement. You can pool lighting according to important beats reflected in the blocking (for example, a specific moment when an actor stops to react to something).

Generally, there are two types of lighting practices:

- Lighting the subject first, then the set
- Lighting the set first, then the subject

Whatever you do for one will affect the other. For example, if you set your lights for your subject, the fill may take care of the set without any additional lights. If you light the set, the subject may not need anything additional.

Generally, for shots where either the subject or camera is moving, I tend to light the set first. When the subject and camera are stationary, I light the subject first.

I also light the subject first for interviews or when I have limited equipment. I'll light the set first when I know the entire area is going to be presented to the camera, there's going to be a lot of camera motion, or there's a window on the set. I like shining light through windows and will even change a camera setup so the light from the window can be fill or a background pattern.

For some reason, some moviemakers are hesitant to cheat the lights for close-ups. Cheating for lighting, or anything else, is when you adjust for a better image. A close-up may have a slightly different array of light for better exposure when you cheat, but the viewer usually won't even notice. Another common cheat is with blocking—an actor standing at a counter may shift a little bit so the shot has better composition.

When you go in for a close-up, take the time to adjust the key, back, and eyelight on your subject. That extra 15 minutes can really make a difference.

COMMON PROBLEMS AND SOLUTIONS

Mixed lighting means having multiple sources of light with different color temperatures. A common scenario is a room with incandescent lamps and exterior windows. The lamps are around 3200K, and the light through the windows is 5600K.

To correct mixed lighting, balance the camera to the dominant light source and color-correct the other lights to the dominant source.

Pick a reference—the predominant light source. Determine the Kelvin temperature or CIR of the reference. You can use a color temperature meter or a vectorscope, although it's more common to use a field monitor. You'll be able to see right away the color temperature of various sources.

Determine the color temperature of all other light sources. Gel the lights to match the reference.

This sounds pretty straightforward until you factor in time and money. Gelling all your tungsten fixtures will cut total illumination and take time, and may require a lot of gel you don't have. It may be easier, faster, and cheaper to gel the window to match tungsten. You can use neutral density gels; ND gels with color correction, such as CTO; fabric; or car window tint.

White balance the camera and make sure you have it the way you want it. There may be more adjustments, or the DP may want to gel something differently to separate the image for greater effect.

After you've been working with lighting for a while, you soon learn certain light sources have certain color temperatures. You'll also find that although the Kelvin scale has a precise meaning in science, it's used more often as shorthand when lighting for motion pictures. Rarely will you hear people refer to CIR or MIRED values.

This applies to gels as well. You'll learn that you'll usually be calling for the same color-correction gels over and over, usually CTO or CTB for balancing to tungsten or daylight in all their fractions, or Plus and Minus Green when working with fluorescents.

To eliminate unwanted reflections, you can mask them with cellophane tape, dulling spray, or a little Arrid XX spray-on deodorant. You may want to remove the shiny object entirely.

For glass in picture frames or mirrors, you can stick something behind it to change the angle. A wad of tape or a paper cup will often do the trick. It might look funny to you, but look in the field monitor and you'll see it's just fine. Just be sure someone is holding the picture or mirror as you're doing this.

PROBLEM: TOO MUCH LIGHT

Specular light is highly directional, focused light, whereas a *kick* is a shine or reflection on it from another object. You can control specular highlights and kicks by taking away the offending object, diffusing light sources with diffusion on the light, softboxes, silks, and so on.

You can also use diffusion spray. It looks like morning dew on a surface. Spray it on where you need it, and then when you're done, clean it off with a warm, moist towel. You can also use hair spray or Arrid EXXtra Dry.

Specular highlights are common and you have to make some decisions about what you will and won't make efforts to get rid of.

Interiors

Exterior windows are often the source of too much light for interiors. If you never show the window, close the curtains or cover the window with Visqueen or garbage bags.

If you need that illumination, you'll have to control the light and color-correct any mixed lighting.

If the light faces north or south and no sunlight comes directly into the room, and it's the only light in the scene, just make sure you're within the five-stop contrast range. If there's too much illumination, curtain sheers cut and diffuse light beautifully.

If there's still too much light, use a piece from a roll of neutral-density gel by applying it to the inside of the window. Mist the glass with a spray bottle filled with water and a dash of soap, apply the gel starting in an upper corner, and smooth it with a squeegee. You can also tack or tape it. If the windowsill is a light color, you may have to age it using streaks and tips to make it less bright.

Streaks and tips is temporary hair coloring. In addition to changing the look of an actor, you can use it on cool lamps and bulbs to cut down the amount of light they emit. You can also use streaks and tips on surfaces to age them. See Chapter 25 for more information about using streaks and tips with set dressing.

If you don't have any rolls of neutral density gel, you can also use car window tint. Apply it the same way. You can keep adding layers of ND gel or tint, but be sure it's securely fastened—it may peel itself off the window at a crucial moment of the scene.

If the window isn't in the scene, you can tack or tape white organza or netting from the fabric store on the window. If the window has curtain sheers, close them. You can double up on the organza and netting until you've cut the light down quite a bit, but only if you don't see the window. Doubling up the organza will cause a noticeable moiré pattern. The netting isn't as bad, but it can cause moiré as well.

If the window isn't in the scene, but you're getting a lot of direct sunlight, you can use translucent vellum tracing paper. It comes in rolls.

If you have other light sources in addition to the window, decide which to color-correct. If you have a roll of CTO, it may be easier to gel the window. If you have sheets of CTB, you'll color-correct the lights. Clip the sheets to the light so the color temperature matches that of the window. If you have practical lights in the shot, you'll have to color-correct them, too.

Incandescent practicals will probably be blown out. Color-correct if necessary, and replace the bulbs with those of a lower wattage, such as 25 watts. Clip ND gels to the inside of a lampshade or globe, and use dimmers. Dimming incandescents works well until you start getting really low. The light starts to get quite red, so be ready to gel to correct. You can also turn off the practical and hide a small light inside it. I've used tungsten movie lights, as well as off-the-shelf battery-powered fluorescents and even flashlight lamps taped to common 9-volt batteries, although I had to wrap them in blue gel. Some people will use streaks and tips if they have to.

If you have existing fluorescents in the shot, you'll need to replace existing tubes with daylight-correct tubes. If you don't have color-correct tubes, replace them with high-quality consumer fluorescents so the illumination is consistent. Gel them with the appropriate blue and Minus Green gels to match daylight. You may need further correction, but check the *American Cinematographers Manual* for a table of common fluorescents and correction gels.

You may decide to gel the window with Plus Green to match the fluorescents. Apply it the same way you do ND or car tint.

If the room gets direct sunlight, you'll have a hard time controlling the amount and placement of sun pools and beams. If the scene is short, make sure your exposure is correct and the image is within the five-stop contrast ratio, and then get it.

If you have to show the window at some point but it gets direct sunlight, you can fake it. Shoot the camera angles that include the window at the time of day you want. After you have that footage, block the window, and then put a lighting unit and cukie in the shape of the window in the same area, with the illumination falling onto the set.

This sounds easy, but it isn't. It will work for close-ups, though.

You can also place a light in a light tent on the outside of the window. Enclose the exterior of the window in Duvetyne, Visqueen, or any other opaque material hung on c-stands, PVC pipe, or anything else you can find. The tent must be large enough to accommodate the light, stand, any flags, and the person setting it up. Make sure there's enough circulation and clearance between the fixture, structure, and tent, or you may have material, or someone's house, getting scorched, melted, or burned.

You can also wait until night, when you have the problem of not enough light.

Exteriors

Exteriors often have too much light. Neutral-density filters on the camera will limit the amount of light getting to the CCDs, and that may solve the problem.

If you have the budget or access to the equipment, you can block out the sunlight using an overhead, faking the sun with a battery of HMIs. It's expensive and time-consuming, but if you want to do it, do it.

Early morning and late evening are the best times to shoot most exteriors. The light hasn't reached full illumination, so you can get some fairly wide shots that will expose properly. Often, mist in the air diffuses and softens the light, also cutting illumination. You still may get hotspots from specular light reflecting off glass or structures with white walls, but that may be acceptable.

Magic hour is a gift from the sky. There are two: The first is from dawn until full light, and the second is the time just after sunset until the sky loses its luminosity. (Consider just after sunset to mean the time when people start turning on their car headlights.)

Both last about 20–30 minutes. It's not easy to shoot a sequence over several days during magic hour. Clouds, smog, and other factors change the light from day to day. But shooting during magic hour really is magical. Colors seem iridescent, and everyone and everything seems beautiful.

Another problem is contrast. Your choices are to cut the bright areas or lighten the dark areas. Either way, you're dealing with large areas you need to control. You can use different kinds of contrast filters on your camera. If you don't have filters, or don't like the way they look, you can use a filter, or an overhead or a butterfly, with a flag, silk, or net.

Unless there's absolutely no way to avoid it, stay away from direct sunlight from 11 a.m. to 3 p.m. The light is so direct, your actors will have unsightly shadows on their faces.

If you can't avoid it, get out the overheads and reflectors. Use nets on the overhead to reduce light, silk to diffuse and reduce it, and reflectors to bounce the sunlight to the opposite side of the face as fill. Tie down each corner with 1/4" hemp secured to a sandbag or a stake pounded into the ground. The slightest breeze will start it wobbling.

Consider using the sunlight as side or backlighting, and filling with reflected light or HMIs. If the actors are close enough to the HMI, it can work, although it will get uncomfortable.

You'll need to cheat your close-ups if you do this. It would seem logical to get the first actor with the sun as a rim or backlight, and then on the reverse, get the next actor with the sun as a key light, but that looks strange. Shoot both with the sun as a backlight.

Consider shooting in the shade. You might get some hotspots from dappled sunlight, but they might be acceptable. Just watch the backgrounds to make sure you're within the five-stop contrast ratio. A good trick is to put a net between the actors and a sunny background, far enough back so the camera won't pick up the net's pattern, but not so far you see the framing. Place one edge on the ground and hide it, and then tilt the top toward the actors like a lean-to.

You might be able to combine time of day and shade. For example, having your characters walk down the street after 3 p.m. under full-leafed trees might work, although test first before committing.

If an overhead is too bulky in a wooded area, you can stretch netting between trees. Window screen netting will work, too. If you have a lot of footage to shoot in a single forested area, consider building chicken-wire and lumber frames to support sheets of muslin or artificial silk. These contraptions should be placed in a small clearing between shaded areas and secured thoroughly. Use a fog machine to smoke up the dark parts of the image. The light will fall on the smoke, raise the illumination level, and lower the contrast.

Many people will just expose for the shaded areas and let the bright areas fend for themselves.

It's unlikely you'll be able to start turning on light fixtures to compete with the sun, but you can bounce sunlight. You can use shiny boards, griff, reflectors, foam core—just about anything. You can park a white grip truck in a good spot and bounce sunlight into entryways. That may raise the illumination just enough.

Remember, though, that standing in the sun and getting hit with reflected sunlight can get very uncomfortable for your actors.

CLEVER TRICKS

Magic Gadgets, Inc., builds special boxes you can plug lights into to get special lighting effects. If renting a Magic Gadgets box is outside your budget, consider using some of these tricks.

To mimic firelight, aim a redhead with an orange gel away from the actors toward a massive reflector. Shake the reflector, aiming the light onto the actors. Add burning sound effects and you have fire.

To mimic television or computer screen light, use a light with a blue gel and wave a piece of paper in front of it to create a flickering effect. You can also put the light on a dimmer and dial the dimmer back and forth.

Tape a mirror with clear tape. Smash the mirror. Bounce a light off it onto the subject and wobble it. It looks like the reflections on water.

On gray days, you can use HMIs to mimic sunlight. The light from the cloudy skies will act as a diffused fill. Concentrate on lighting faces, and shoot in the early morning or late afternoon. The result can be quite beautiful.

Backlight rain for best effect.

LIGHTING GUIDELINES

These are my guidelines to lighting:

- Light must be motivated.
- Where you don't put a light is just as important as where you do.
- Every light you add brings new problems.
- Use entrances and exits.
- Dark scenes need light.
- Bright scenes need shade.
- Light only what the viewer needs to see.
- If you're going to break the rules, really break them.

LIGHT MUST BE MOTIVATED

Motivated lighting means developing a logic for all the light in a frame. The sources can be real or imagined: the light from a window, candles on a cake, ambulance flashers—identify it and use it consistently.

For example, you can send light through a cukie in the shape of Venetian blinds to hit a back wall of a scene. You are implying that the room has an exterior window through which light is falling through the blinds.

Another example is having light coming from upstairs, with the rungs of a staircase shadowing the back wall. You can then fill these shadows with light from a softbox that has been heavily gelled with blue or purple.

Sometimes the viewer will accept a frame that's evenly lit but apparently unmotivated. For example, filling a dark room with diffused, blue light conveys the idea that it's nighttime. We all know it doesn't really look like that, but this is an accepted convention.

WHERE YOU DON'T PUT A LIGHT IS JUST AS IMPORTANT AS WHERE YOU DO

Have you ever watched a scene in a show with areas of the set brightly lit for no apparent reason? It looks like someone is going to walk over there, but no one ever does. It's just a bright, distracting spot pulling the viewer's attention away, similar to many community theater lighting designs for productions of *Our Town*.

Avoid the *Our Town* syndrome. Pools of light and color are great, but keep the intensity below that of the key. The key is where you want the viewer to look.

EVERY LIGHT YOU ADD BRINGS NEW PROBLEMS

Less can be more. There's a tendency to keep adding lights to correct problems that occur when you keep adding lights.

When you call for a light, train your crew to bring the light, stand, sandbag, and scrims. They should also bring a c-stand with a grip arm and sandbag for setting shading tools. Consider having a dimmer on every light, and keep the black wrap handy.

USE ENTRANCES AND EXITS

Windows in particular are great places to shine lights. You automatically have motivated lighting with a bright window. Watch the contrast, and consider how you can manipulate the angle of the light for best effect.

Consider lighting partially opened doors and the end of hallways. You have to pay attention to the level of illumination so it doesn't intrude on the lighting on the subject, but these are great ways to add depth and paint with color.

DARK SCENES NEED LIGHT

Darkness in movies doesn't mean there's no light. It usually means that the brightest light doesn't fall off gradually, but abruptly. The surrounding areas are still lit, but at greater than a 2:1 ratio. Just keep it within DV's five-stop contrast ratio.

For night exteriors, consider shooting during magic hour. Turn on interior lights and car lights to enhance the feeling that it's night. Consider gelling lights with blue. For interior lights, use a straw gel. If you don't want backgrounds falling to black, use a cukie for patterns of light and dark.

Keep your shots pretty close. Wide shots require a lot of light. You're heading into 10k and larger lights for background lighting, which means you'll need a generator. You'll also need a 2k or 5k for key, with some reflectors for bouncing. The big light works as a backlight to give the subject a strong rim and separate the subject from the background.

Spray the area with water, especially roads and exterior walls, creating bright reflections. These will give texture and raise the overall light level.

Consider using a 12v spotlight that you can buy at an auto parts store. They're narrow and pretty harsh, but they pack a lot of punch. Gel and diffuse or bounce them.

If you really need fill light, there are many battery-powered HMIs available. Sun guns work great, although you'll have to diffuse them heavily and bring a lot of battery packs.

BRIGHT SCENES NEED SHADE

Lights are cut, diffused, and shaded to add depth to the image. If you can adjust your blocking so your actors move into shade, you may have better results. Get out the overhead with some diffusion, and get ready to bounce.

LIGHT ONLY WHAT THE VIEWER NEEDS TO SEE

When you watch a scene, you can often tell what's going to happen because certain parts of the frame are lit. For example, a doorway has a pool of light hitting it at about face height. You can almost bet that someone will be standing there before the scene is over.

When it's done well and the lighting is subtle, you don't realize it's lit until someone steps into it. (Also, you'll ignore it in favor of a strong performance. Viewers will ignore a lot of things to watch an interesting, powerful performance.)

If your set and lighting design allows it, don't hide the key lights. For example, if someone is walking under pools of light down a hallway, that person can stop right on the edge of the light for the beat. It won't be perfect, but when you go in for a close-up, you can bounce the overhead light to the actor's face for fill.

If you key light for motion, your subject will be properly exposed and the entire frame composed and within the contrast range of DV.

IF YOU'RE GOING TO BREAK THE RULES, REALLY BREAK THEM

All technical and design decisions for your show are at the mercy of your story. If blown-out windows and crushed blacks convey what you are trying to convey then use them. If flare and whip pans support the story you're trying to tell then do that.

However, make sure your choice to use mixed lighting, dutch angles, or other "incorrect" techniques is a choice, not done out of ignorance or sloppiness. Then go forth.

Have the courage of your convictions.

RIGGING

Rigging is everything you do to put equipment where it needs to be. This includes placing lights, flags, nets, silks, overheads, cameras, and just about anything else you can think of (see Figure 22.1).

There are many types of grip equipment. Whatever you may need, someone has probably created it. A good resource or explanation of grip equipment and techniques is *The Grip Book* by Michael G. Uva and Sabrina Uva. The best way to learn it, though, is to use it.

On big-budget sets, different departments take responsibility for staging, maintaining, setting, and breaking down specific equipment. On most no- and low-budget sets, though, often grips are gaffers, assistant directors, gophers, and therapists. The primary task is to get the gear where it needs to be, and then stage, set up, adjust, repair, and break it down.

Start with load-in. Load-in and load-out are a combination of brute force and planning. If you have a doorway dolly, use it for loading equipment in and out. Use the wheels on the cases, and ask for help with the heavy stuff.

FIGURE 22.1

Grip truck with flags, silks, and nets in front. Courtesy Shooters Broadcast Services, Inc., in Seattle.

Assign a staging area for all the equipment. You'll need areas for

- Lighting equipment
- Camera and camera support
- Location audio equipment
- General tools, such as stingers, tape, ladders, and so on
- Props and set dressing storage and creation
- Wardrobe, hair, and makeup
- Production office
- Craft services

Power cables have to be placed, batteries need to go on chargers, and worklights must be set up where needed. Be sure to have at least one stinger in the wardrobe, hair, and makeup area.

After watching the blocking and reviewing the shot list and lighting design, the DP will confer with the light and grip crew about what's going to happen. Some DPs just point and say, "Light this. I want it kind of yellow." Others give very specific instructions about exactly what they want in terms of tools.

When someone calls for a certain light, that means bring the light with barn doors, stand, scrim bag, appropriate gels and diffusion, and a stinger. You'll probably also need a c-stand with grip head for flags, nets, and silks, as well as sandbags.

Camera support starts with the tripod. The camera operator may set it up alone, but an extra pair of hands can be welcome. Be ready to bring in the monitor with fully charged batteries or a stinger. If a dolly is needed, bring the dolly and track. For a jib arm, bring the arm and counterweights.

When you're done with something, it goes back to the staging area. Lights especially should be *head wrapped*: the stand fully lowered, the cord coiled, barn doors closed, and scrims removed and back in the scrim bag. Always keep scrims with the light.

Generally, the location sound crew will look after the audio gear. Still, it doesn't hurt to offer assistance, especially if they don't have much experience.

STANDS, MAFERS, AND OTHER GRIP EQUIPMENT

Take some time to learn how to handle the most common grip equipment. Different types of stands, clamps, and other tools are easy to use after you get the hang of them, and they are very rugged. You may even want to invest in some pieces of grip equipment because they don't depreciate in value the way cameras and other electronic equipment does. Don't go overboard, though. Your local grip house will be happy to rent you everything you need.

STANDS

Light stands and other rigging generally have two kinds of mounts: baby and junior. *Baby* refers to 5/8" studs and their receivers. (A *baby* can also be a 1k light or a light that's smaller than the standard size.) Baby stands have two or three steel risers with baby studs on the top riser for mounting equipment with baby receivers, such as smaller lights (less than 2k) and grip heads.

Junior refers to 1 1/8" pins and receivers found on larger lights and equipment. Junior stands are beefier than babies, with two or three risers and a junior receiver on the top riser (see Figure 22.2). You can use an adapter pin, called a *spud*, to adapt a junior stand to a baby stand.

A *rocky mountain* stand has one leg that can be adjusted in length separately from the others. They're very useful for steep or uneven surfaces, stairs, and so on.

FIGURE 22.2

Junior receiver with a baby pin that can be swung up and locked into place.

Rolling stands have wheels and snap brakes that can be handy on a flat surface.

Blade stands are light and fold flat. They're often included in light kits and are best with smaller lights because they're rather flimsy. Figure 22.3 shows some racked blade stands.

Some stands have removable legs, making them easier to pack and store. I have several I carry in a hard-shelled golf club case. The case has wheels and is large enough for the collapsed stands, but not so big I can't handle it alone.

FIGURE 22.3

A rack of bladed light stands. These are a bit beefier than the stands included in kits, so they can hold heavier lights and grip equipment.

To protect floors from scratches and gouges from stands, put crutch tips on the feet. Small stands use 3/4" and large stands use 1 1/4" tips. You can also use cup blocks, which are wooden blocks with an indentation in the center in which to place the feet of stands. Cup blocks will also stop the stands with wheels from moving. You can find crutch tops and cup blocks at the local hardware store.

Using Light Stands

Extend the legs and lock them into place. Set the light on the stand and tighten the knuckle (see Figure 22.4). Carefully loop the power cable on the knuckles down the length of the stands to take some strain off the cable. Always have at least one leg pointing in the same direction as the light for extra stability.

A sandbag is then hung, not shoved or leaned, on the rung of the stand leg (see Figure 22.5). Depending on the physical size of light unit and how much traffic there is, you'll use one to three sandbags per stand. A good rule of thumb is one sandbag per extended riser. You can get sandbags from your rental house—often they'll include sandbags in your kit whether you ask for them or not.

You may also hang lights using a variety of grip equipment on a light grid or truss. A *light grid* is often found on a soundstage or studio. Basically, it's a permanent ceiling support for lighting and power cords that connect each light to a dimmer. A *truss* is a movable light grid made up of lengths of triangular metal structures that hook together. You often find them at concerts. Trusses are handy for spanning a large area.

FIGURE 22.4

Mounting an HMI with baby receiver on a baby stand.

FIGURE 22.5

The correct way to hang a sandbag on a stand.

C-STANDS

Like a lot of people who make movies, I have become very fond of the c-stand. C-stands, or *century stands*, are devices designed to make your life on the set easier. They consist of a stand with various types of legs and bases and a grip head, or *gobo*, that grips equipment of various sizes. One important piece of equipment used with a c-stand is a grip arm. A *grip arm* is a length of tubing with another grip head attached to one end. It enables you to extend lights, flags, nets, silks, and cukies wherever you need to. Figures 22.6, 22.7, and 22.8 show some of the parts of a c-stand.

FIGURE 22.6

The grip head attaches to the c-stand. Equipment is then clamped in.

Always place the longest leg of the stand under the extended arm to help stabilize it. Sandbag the legs using the one-sandbag-per-riser rule.

The knuckle of a c-stand should always be on the right, so when a weight, such as a flag or cukie, is set, the head will tighten and not slip. Avoid setting the stand with a long length of arm going backward into traffic. Someone is bound to run into it. If it's unavoidable, use a Styrofoam cup or tennis ball on the end.

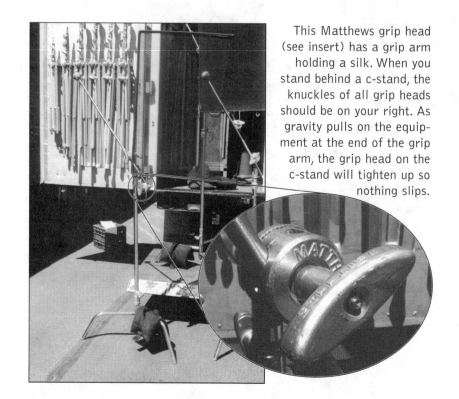

This Matthews grip head (see insert) has a grip arm holding a silk. When you stand behind a c-stand, the knuckles of all grip heads should be on your right. As gravity pulls on the equipment at the end of the grip arm, the grip head on the c-stand will tighten up so nothing slips.

FIGURE 22.7

This c-stand holds a single net. A Styrofoam ball is on the end of the grip arm to warn people that it's sticking out, and a sandbag is in place.

PARALLELS

Parallels are a portable scaffolding used as a lighting or camera platform. They're made of lightweight steel tubing and fold for easy storage and transportation. They assemble quickly and can be safe if set up with caution. I recommend you have an experienced grip with you if you need to use parallels.

Parallels must be set up and used on level ground. It can be hard to tell what's level, so use a plumb line or bubble level. You can stack them one on top of another, but don't stack more than three. Tie off all four corners to spikes pounded into the ground, and be careful. Distribute the weight evenly on the platform, especially when people start hauling up equipment. Secure all light and c-stands with ratchet straps, and tie the power cables to a vertical post.

Make sure you have safe ladders and use the buddy system: Someone holds whenever someone else goes up or down. Use a tag line, too. A *tag line* is a rope attached to the top of the parallel you use to hoist light equipment. Rope off the area beneath the parallel to stop people from walking too closely underneath it, and don't drop or toss anything off the platform.

MAFERS AND OTHER GRIP GEAR

A *mafer* is a small adjustable clamp with a baby stud, which can be interchanged with a variety of accessories (see Figure 22.8). They're great for setting a light where you otherwise couldn't. I've used them on deck trim, edging, rails, and so on. If the mafer doesn't fit what I want to clamp onto, I use a cardellini, shown in Figure 22.9.

FIGURE 22.8

Mafer clamp. I have a set of 5/8" pins of various lengths I had a friend make to use with my mafer clamp. I clamp the mafer to something solid, then select a pin of appropriate length, and lock that into place.

A *cardellini* has a baby pin on one side and wide grip for clamping almost anywhere. Spin the handle to tighten it.

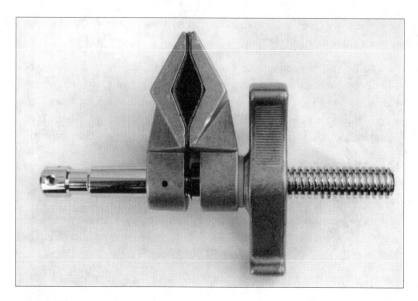

FIGURE 22.9

A cardellini clamp.

A *gaffer grip* is a big clamp with rubber teeth. You can quickly snap it onto something such as a railing and then attach small lights to the baby pins on it. I've used them to hold foam core (although the gaffer grip leaves marks in the surface) and clamped that into a c-stand.

A better tool for reflector sheets is a *platypus* or *duckbill*. This is a holder that clamps onto foam core or bead board so you can mount it on a c-stand. The clamp is a pair of wide, smooth grip surfaces.

A *baby plate* is a steel plate with a baby pin welded onto it and four holes for mounting. They're used for mounting lights or grip heads on a wall, box, or other surface. They're usually either a 3" or a 6" plate. A *baby plate female* is the baby receiver on a welded plate.

Other common grip tools include *apple boxes,* which are reinforced plywood boxes of various heights used anywhere something needs to be higher (see Figure 22.10). You can also attach a baby plate or receiver to an apple box quickly using drywall screws if you need to mount a light really low. The smallest is known as a *pancake* because it is nearly flat.

FIGURE 22.10

Apple box waiting for use.

DOLLIES AND JIBS

Camera motion is a very powerful way to direct the viewer's eye. As mentioned in Chapter 10, "Production Design," the eye is drawn to elements moving

- Toward rather than away from
- Faster rather than slower
- Closer rather than farther

By moving the camera, you can better direct the viewer's eye. Dollies and jibs are the most common platforms for moving the camera.

DOLLIES

Tracking shots can introduce a subject or location by revealing details or portions to the viewer. They can also reveal relationships between characters or a character's response to a piece of information or situation.

You can track slower, faster, or at the same speed as the subject; run parallel; track in or track out; move in front or behind the subject—pretty much anywhere you want to go. There are different kinds of mobile camera platforms. The dolly might have angled or grooved wheels to run on track or might have pneumatic tires that run directly on the ground or floor. The dolly may be a simple platform on which you set a tripod, or it may have a camera mount and seats. The dolly may have a motor for lifting camera, camera support, and operator. Common models are made by Fisher and Chapman, though there are certainly others. There are many different makes and models, but the most common dollies you'll see on a no- or low-budget set are

- Camera dolly
- Doorway dolly
- Western dolly
- Crab dolly

Camera Dolly

A *camera dolly* has a set of wheels that attaches to a tripod. The wheels may be separate or connected to a spreader. Most have some kind of braking system (see Figure 22.11).

Doorway Dolly

A *doorway dolly* is rectangular with four pneumatic tires, one in each corner. One pair of wheels can be steered while the dolly is pushed or pulled. It can be fitted with track wheels for use on a straight track. A doorway dolly (shown in Figure 22.12) is narrow enough to fit through a standard doorway. You can add sideboards for a larger platform. Doorway dollies are usually covered with nonslip carpet and have at least one recessed tie-down loop. If your tripod doesn't have a spreader on which to put a sandbag, you can tie down the tripod for extra stability.

In addition to being a camera platform, doorway dollies are often used to haul equipment.

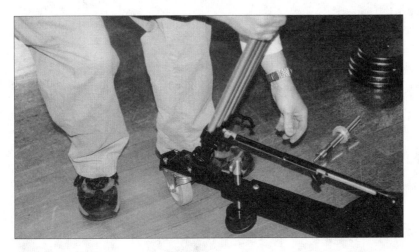

FIGURE 22.11

Locking the tripod onto a camera dolly.

FIGURE 22.12

A doorway dolly with sideboards and pneumatic tires.

Western Dolly

Western dollies are a lot like doorway dollies, but are wider, longer, and have larger wheels, so the ride is a bit smoother (see Figure 22.13). A Western dolly can be fitted with track wheels to run on curved track. The push bar can be mounted on any side and this can be quite convenient. In addition, you can flip the platform of a Western dolly over. This allows the platform to ride higher off the ground for greater clearance. This is great for bumpy ground.

FIGURE 22.13

Western dolly with pneumatic tires. The push bar tilts to make it easier to handle.

Crab Dolly

Crab dollies are common on larger sets. They're compact, sturdy, reliable, and have three-way steering: rear, crab, and circular. Crab dollies are designed so the front and back wheels have independent steering. This allows you to make much tighter turns, as well as "crab" the dolly diagonally or horizontally. They do require a smooth surface or track for best results.

You'll often find a Fisher 10, Fisher 11, or Chapman Pee Wee dolly on the set. They're handy, inexpensive to rent, and come with a variety of useful accessories. The best way to figure out if you need one is to go to your local grip and lighting rental house and ask a tech to show you the dolly kit. The first thing you'll notice is how the tech will crab the dolly out of its storage area over to you. He or she is just showing off. These dollies are fun to operate, although you'll need some practice to make your moves look smooth.

Using a Dolly

Track needs to be placed and leveled. Check it with a carpenter's level and use wedges if necessary. Generally, PVC pipe is fine for straight runs for dollies with angled skateboard wheels, such as the homemade platforms (see Figure 22.14). Just be sure to bring along some Lemon Pledge as lubricant for the track.

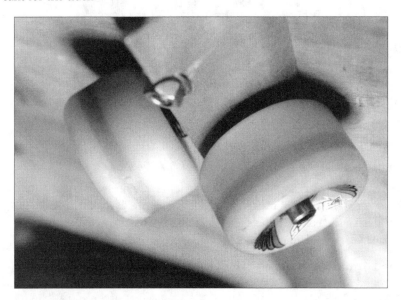

FIGURE 22.14

Dolly wheels angled to run on track.

Metal tubing works works better than PVC and is best with straight runs and curves. If you want a tight curve or a circle, your best bet is square metal track. Make sure the dolly can handle both the track and the radius of the curve.

You can make your own dolly and track using common materials from a hardware store, but there are advantages to using professional equipment. It's more versatile, tends to work better—and if you rent rather than buy—quite affordable.

After the track is in place, get the camera operator on the platform, and with eye to eyepiece, run the length. The camera operator will quickly see whether the track is level enough for the move. If not, level, wedge, and adjust. Put the dolly in the start position, and rehearse the move for speed and marks. Use tape on the floor so the dolly grip can see each position.

Use baby powder to stop wheels from squeaking down the track. Some people use Lemon Pledge to stop the squeaks on PVC track, although you need to spray oil or silicone on metal track. Dirt won't stick if you use silicone spray.

Figure 22.15 shows a doorway dolly in action.

FIGURE 22.15

Running a doorway dolly on the set of "Music Appreciation."

Place the monitor on the dolly where the camera operator and dolly grip can see it. If you require AC power for the monitor or camera, make sure you have someone pulling cable so you don't run or trip over it. You'll want your sound crew to handle their cable as well.

If the surface isn't smooth, has really thick carpet, or when you have a ground slope and you want the camera to remain level, you'll need a dance floor. A *dance floor* is built with 3/4" A/C plywood that is smooth and level. The A side is free of flaws and goes face up. Some grips insist on using only birch 3/4" plywood, although it's more expensive. What you want is plywood that is strong, smooth, and rigid enough for your use.

Use the plywood, wedges, and cinderblocks, and be sure to bring a carpenter's level for best results. You can then lay the track over it, or freewheel if you have the room.

You can buy, rent, or build a dolly and track. You can also use existing tools, such as a wheelchair, for a tracking camera. I've clamped small cameras to hand trucks, handheld a camera on a moving platform normally used to move diesel engines, and hung on for dear life while two friends ran the length of a warehouse pulling a dolly used to haul pallets. I've also dolly gripped for other people using camera, doorway, and crab dollies; office chairs; and a wheelchair.

It's easier to do tracking shots using the right tool, but if you can't afford one, look around. You'd be surprised at what will work. Just be careful and rehearse.

JIBS

Jibs and jib arms are mechanical devices on a dolly, tripod, or other supporting gear, counterweighted to hold a camera for an increased range of motion. Basically, you use a jib arm for crane shots.

Most of the inexpensive jibs use weightlifting weights as the counterbalance. The jib arm is locked to length, mounted on the tripod or riser, and then balanced for the camera.

Some jibs allow you to use the head over- or underslung. *Overslung* means the camera is on top of the head. *Underslung* means the head is locked beneath the end of the jib arm and the camera placed in it, allowing the camera to go lower. I've recently seen jib arms for prosumer cameras that clamp onto the handle running along the top of the camera.

Make sure any jib arm you want to use will accept the weight of your camera fully loaded. If you're using your own tripod, make sure it can handle the weight of the jib arm, counterweights, and camera, plus a little extra. And make sure the jib arm fits the tripod bowl size. Otherwise, rent a different set of sticks or a complete jib rig.

Have a camera assistant, grip, or PA on the weighted side of the jib when you're attaching or removing the camera. When balanced, the camera and jib arm should stay exactly where you put them. Place the monitor nearby—looping the case handle around the base of the tripod will both stabilize it and let you tilt the monitor up so you easily can see it.

Figure 22.16 shows a Porta Jib waiting for use.

You can rent big cranes with hydraulic lifts, seats for director and camera operator, and other fancy accessories. If you need one, and can afford it, by all means use one. Cranes take time to set up properly, and if you're going to go to that expense, it makes sense to have an experienced operator handle the rig for you. It will be safer and a better use of time.

SASH CORD, SANDBAGS, AND C-47S

Sash cord is white cotton rope. Common weights are #6, #8, and #10. You can also get #4 weight *Mason line*, which is white, or *trick line*, which is black, to tie up stingers. Bring along a collection of bungee cords and S-hooks.

FIGURE 22.16

A Sony DSR-300 on Porta Jib, set up on a camera dolly, waiting for the monitor. This rig was ideal for the set—the wooden floor was very smooth and the camera operator was able to track in almost any direction to follow a dance performance.

All the cord, bungees, and S-hooks allow you to quickly secure anything you need to tie down on the set. Learn how to tie a bowline and a square knot. Never walk away from a knot if you're not sure about it. See Figures 22.17 and 22.18, and practice.

When hanging lights from a light grid, from a truss, or on a pipe or an existing structure, use safety or grip chain. *Safety chain* loops around the light grid and light bracket to keep the light from falling if the clamp should fail. Safety chains save lives. You can use sash cord if you have to, or even lengths of dog leash with a ring and a snap on each end. Just use them.

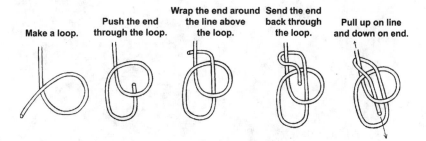

FIGURE 22.17

The bowline is used for anything that's a dead hang.

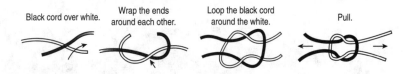

FIGURE 22.18

Square knots are most often used for bundling cables and the pieces from disassembled overheads and butterflies.

You'll also find a use for bungee cords and ratchet safety straps. Keep a collection in your production vehicle or tucked away in the staging area.

Sandbags (see Figure 22.19) are required to steady light stands, c-stands, and just about any other kind of small stand you'd need to secure. They're also handy for adding extra weight to camera dollies so the dollies will move more smoothly across the floor or down the track.

Clothespins, nicknamed C-47s or *bullets*, are used to attach gels and diffusion to lights (see Figure 22.20). Get the wooden clothespins with the metal springs. The springless ones are useless and the plastic ones will melt.

FIGURE 22.19
Big pile of sandbags.

FIGURE 22.20
A C-47 holding diffusion on a barn door.

CAR MOUNTS

Figure out whether the car must be moving for the shot. You can get away with marking the car's position and then lighting and framing for that place. Shut off the engine and put the car in neutral. You'll need a couple of people to push the car and the actor will then brake to bring the car to a smooth stop on the mark. It's easier said than done—rehearse first.

Have the driver pull into the shot with the window rolled down. For the passenger, just move to the other side. Put your boom operator in the back seat and out of sight, and watch out for shadows.

This is a very common technique. Why do so many Hollywood movies show scenes with actors in cars who have the side windows rolled down? Because framing through an open window is the easiest way to handle the shot.

Try to do these shots at magic hour or close to magic hour for nice, even lighting. Use an HMI for fill, and put some reflective mylar on the dashboard to kick light on the actors' faces. You can get a space blanket or even some of that shiny silver and gold wrapping paper.

You can also cover a piece of foam core with the same material and slip it into the back seat as a backlight. Just keep it out of view. If there isn't enough room for the foam and the boom operator, you can either plant mics on the actors or have a PA step to the back of the car holding a big reflector.

Watching someone handle a piece of 4'×8' foam core or a butterfly on a windy day can be a source of amusement. It can be very frustrating to get the reflector into a solid position, but at least you're laughing.

I like to use small household fluorescent sticks for backlight. You can tape them right onto the back of the seat and turn them on. You may have to cut them with netting and gaffer's tape, but it works.

For front shots, you can shoot right through the windshield. Overcast days are the best in terms of light, but even with a polarizer, you may simply have too much reflection to get a usable image. Consider pulling the car under an overhead, or even better, a leafy tree.

SHOOTING INTO THE CAR

Every city, county, and state has its own rules regarding picture cameras. In some areas, the authorities just don't care what you mount on a vehicle as long as you're within the legal height and width restrictions. Others, however, will cite you for negligence if you're cruising in a vehicle rigged for picture. Check before you start strapping things to the hood of a car.

No movie is worth someone getting hurt or killed. Practice safety, and spend extra time making sure everything and everyone is protected and being careful.

I recommend you consider hiring an experienced grip to get camera mounts properly and safely rigged. You can get great results, and it can be worth the extra expense to get it done right. Also, consider renting a tow vehicle to pull the picture car and hiring an experienced driver.

If you don't want to do that, consider hiring a rental house to rig the mounts on the picture vehicle. If you want to handle this yourself, be safe. In addition to the usual tension from being on camera, you're blocking the driver's view. Use a tow bar, tow dolly, or trailer with an experienced driver. Stay on quiet streets. And there's no need for speed because moving shots that are angled almost perpendicular to the road give the illusion that a vehicle is going faster than it really is. Making your depth-of-field using ND filters as shallow as practicable will further enhance the illusion.

Test before committing to any of this. Hook up your mount, strap it down, and drive down a deserted road to see whether it's safe and it works.

When you're shooting for real, keep in mind that onlookers will make fools out of themselves. I've been waved, shouted, and hooted at, and flashed once. In addition to being annoying, you don't know what the other drivers are going to do. Be careful.

Take time to rig the picture car. Everything must be in place and secured with two points of contact: the mount and a safety strap or chain attached to the vehicle itself.

There are a variety of ways to rig the shot. Each one involves placing the camera, placing lighting equipment, and placing audio gear.

Consider using a vehicle with tinted windows or put some temporary window tint into place. You can always use neutral-density gel on the glass, but be sure it's secured completely, or the gel may ripple when the vehicle moves.

The most common shot is done handheld from the back seat for a two shot. You can use a reflector for backlighting, and fluorescent sticks can be useful. Just watch out for flare and unevenness. A variation is to put a 2'×4' through the window for extra stability, and either lean or mount the camera on it. Pad the ends of the board so you don't scratch anything.

I recently used two nylon straps on the end of a piece of slotted electrical channel I bought at a local hardware store. I trimmed the channel to four feet and then beveled and padded every edge to protect the vehicle from scratching and gouges. I hooked the adjustable straps to each end and closed them in the rear side doors of the vehicle. My VX-1000 was mounted to the channel through one of the slots with a wingnut. It worked all right, but next time I'll use a bungee cord from the channel to my foot or somewhere low in the vehicle for extra stability. And I don't think I would try this with anything much heavier than the VX-1000.

Many DV cameras are so small, you can mount them on the dashboard. You'll need a wide-angle lens and probably have to tuck the camera in the corner, but for pick-ups and other large vehicles, that may work.

If you need a shot of just the driver, you can handhold the camera in the front passenger seat. The monitor goes on the floor and the boom op and sound mixer in the back. Some camera operators jam themselves between the seat and the dashboard. I like to sit sideways with my knees up or a sandbag on my lap as camera support, and keep my upper body relaxed so I'm not fighting the motion of the car.

If the car is really small, you may not have enough distance between the subject and the front of the camera. You can try resting the camera on your shoulder against the window, but that still may not be far enough. You can unroll the window and shoot through it from a second car, or mount the camera to the side of the vehicle and unroll a window to get the shot.

If the vehicle, such as a pickup, has large sideview mirrors on adjustable frames, you can mount a small camera on them. This will get you a single from either side, but you may not have any vertical space for correct framing. You can try putting a small tripod head on and mounting the camera to that. Just be sure to strap down the camera and mount to make sure it's secure. You'll have trouble lighting the interior—fluorescent sticks hidden on the dash may help.

If you have a very small prosumer camera, you can use a window mount. These are small tripod heads on a padded clamp that attach to a window. You then bungee cord the camera to the car body. You'll still have a problem with getting enough light on the subject.

Also, newer cars have curved windows, and you still may not have enough distance between the lens and the subject, so this just may not work. I used one for *Amazing World*, but we were in a 1968 Mercury Marquis convertible. The car was huge, the windows were almost completely flat, and the top was down.

The windshield was raked and curved, so we tucked the shotgun into it and aimed at the actors. There was the cushion of silence—even with the engine running, you could hear them perfectly. When coasting, it was as if we were in a moving isolation booth.

You can use a *hostess tray*. A hostess tray attaches to the side of the vehicle and offers a platform for mounting the camera. It has padded surfaces for resting on the vehicle and straps for attaching it. If you've never used one, hire someone to mount it for you. You can damage the vehicle if it's not done correctly.

You can affix a tripod to the front bumper of the car and latch the camera onto the tripod. Add a second point of contact by strapping down the tripod and the camera separately.

Visual Departures, Ltd., makes a series of suction-cup mounts that are really handy. One is shown in Figure 22.21. I have two small ones that I use all the time. Get an appropriate size. Mount the camera to the suction cup, and then mount the suction cup to the front of the vehicle, using bungee cords as safety straps. This is a down-and-dirty way of handling the problem—you're really limited on where you can put the camera because of the odd angles, but it will work in a pinch.

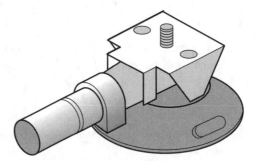

FIGURE 22.21

An SM-3 from Visual Departures, Ltd.

There is the old standby of getting in the back of a truck and driving in front of the picture car with the actors, and then shooting through the front windshield. You'll have to run dual-system sound or dub in the dialogue, but it works. Just keep your hands off the zoom.

I built a small support structure for this technique with a 2'×4' and two pairs of foundation lifters. The lifters are used to lift the foundations of houses or level a deck and are made of steel. I drilled three holes into the 2'×4' for a knob with the proper screw for a tripod head and then attached a lifter on each end and between the knob holes. All the ends were padded to prevent scratching.

I locked in the board by turning the lifters until they fit snugly to the inside of the bed of a pickup truck, right over the rear axle, and then dropped the second pair of lifters for extra support. I used a three-axis fluid head so I could level the camera at the head, instead of trying to level the board.

Some people place a sandbag or big pillow on the hood of the picture car and then secure the camera with cord, ratchet straps, and lots of tape. That can work, although you may want to pad the rope and straps, as well as the bottom of the sandbag, with foam.

You're going to have to light these setups. Lighting in a car is similar to lighting any interior with an exterior light source. You have to deal with contrast ratio, proper exposure of the subjects, and color temperature, only now in a tiny interior area that's moving.

Consider choosing a road with plenty of background backlit by the sun. You can also try positioning the vehicle so sunlight falls into the subject's lap. Put reflectors on the dash and one on the subject's lap to act as a kicker to the subject's face. When the car moves under shadows, the bounce will as well, and this gives a realistic look. This technique might also save you from having to rig lights.

You can roll up a DC-powered fluorescent in a bunch of diffusion, muslin, or silk and mount it on the inside. You can even ask the actors to hold it on their laps. Just keep it out of the shot. Kino-Flo also has some mini-flo fixtures that can be handy because they're pretty small. You can also hide some household DC fluorescent sticks.

You can safely attach lighting equipment to the hood mount, as well as a camera for any front shooting. Hood mounts come in a variety of configurations, but generally, they need to be strong enough to hold the gear under stress, be padded anywhere they contact the vehicle, and may have suction cups and ratchet straps to secure them.

Have the rental house mount it on your picture car or, at least, pay them to show you how to do it.

I've made hood mounts for small cameras using electrical channel and suction cups. All my ratchet straps are padded with pipe foam, as is the edge of the electrical channel. I place the channel and suction it on the hood or even the roof of the vehicle. With the ratchet hooks attached to the frame, I ratchet it down, mount a three-axis fluid head to the bar, and mount the camera to the head. Everything is then strapped down.

Whatever mount you use, ratchet it to the fender and frame of the car for safety. Pad the ratchets and use a furniture blanket so you don't scratch the paint.

You'll need power for the lights. HMI ballasts can be finicky with inverters, so check it out at the rental shop to make sure it will work. Don't forget the spare fuses.

You can also lock down a putt-putt to the back of the vehicle and power lights that way. If you're using a tow vehicle, put the putt-putt on it. It'll be loud, so side shots may be difficult with the windows rolled down.

If you're using an HMI, the ballast can be strapped to the fender, placed in the trunk, or placed on the floor of the back seat. Safety-chain the light to the hood mount.

You can also cantilever a light, especially if the car already has a roof rack. Mount pipe, Speed-Rail, or a 2'×4' securely to the roof rack and use mafers or cardellinis to mount lights. Just make sure you have two points of contact on everything and nothing is sliding around. Run the light cables to the back of the vehicle to power them. Audio is an issue. You've got the engine running, air whooshing from vents, and with a window rolled down, you're going to get noise that may just be unacceptable. Plan to do ADR in post. This can be a real problem with long-dialogue scenes.

If you have a lot of dialogue in a moving vehicle, consider getting a tow bar, tow dolly, or trailer.

A *tow bar* attaches to the front of the car. Some people always use them because the pulling vehicle controls the picture car. The actors can concentrate on acting and not on driving. Just tell the driver not to steer the vehicle. You can damage the car and the tow by forcing it this way. You still need the hostess tray and hood mount.

You drive the front tire of the vehicle onto a *tow dolly*. The tires are locked on, and the picture car is towed. A tow dolly will raise the front end about

12–14 inches, so if you're thinking about shooting out the back of the tow vehicle, make sure you've got the height.

You can drive the picture vehicle onto a *trailer* as well, but all four tires are locked on. You can place the camera pretty much wherever you want as long as it is secured to the trailer and vehicle. You can mount the lighting equipment on the hood mount or the tow vehicle. The director sits in the tow vehicle with headphones and a monitor. The sound crew may be in the vehicle, although your sound mixer can plant mics easily. Because the engine isn't running, you can get great audio this way.

If you're on the back of a truck towing a vehicle, make sure there are sturdy sideboards or Speed Rail to protect people from falling out. And remember: In some states this is illegal. Check with your local film commission.

A *low-boy* is a special dolly that rides on the street (if you're towing the picture vehicle) or trailer (if the picture vehicle is on a camera trailer), allowing you to place a camera that's aimed into the vehicle on a platform alongside. You can move from the front to the back of the passenger compartment and back again. If you're considering using a low-boy, hire an experienced grip and driver, make sure your permits are in order, and be careful. The low-boy is moving at the same speed as the picture and tow vehicles, but without the protection of safety cages or seat belts.

Vehicles with four-wheel or rear-wheel drive may be damaged by towing. Even in neutral, the transmission is still winding up, and pressure builds that can damage the transmission. Be careful not to go too fast or too far. It may be best to unhook the transmission cable before towing. Just be sure you hook it back up before trying to start the car.

GAFFER'S TAPE AND SNOT TAPE: OTHER HANDY TOOLS

Gaffer's tape is a heavy fabric tape that tears neatly in the direction of the weave. It's used just about everywhere, and although it's expensive, it's worth it. White *camera tape* is handy for labels. *Paper tape* has less adhesion than gaffer's tape, but it's cheaper. The most common colors are black and gray, although you can get others. Tie the tape to a loop of sash cord and hang it nearby, as shown in Figure 22.22. The handle of a dolly and the knuckle of a c-stand are good spots.

J-Lar is a transparent tape used to splice gels together. One roll will usually last for a while. *Snot tape*, or 3M transfer tape, is a sticky film used for mounting gels in frames. It's also great for taping small props into place.

Blu-tack is a claylike substance that can be bought in drugstores and stationery shops. It is normally used to stick things like posters on walls. It's not terribly sticky, so it's easy to clean up, handy, and cheap.

Butyl is window weld ribbon sealer you can get at an auto parts store. It comes in various widths, and you use it for putting gels on car windows. The butyl will make sure the gel doesn't rattle, but be careful with it—this stuff really sticks, especially if you also use the Butyl Primer from 3M. I don't like it, but some grips I know use it all the time.

FIGURE 22.22

Rolls of tape on sash cord. You can hang them on a dolly c-stand or light stand for easy access.

Also bring along cellophane tape, which is good for covering shiny edges. Duct tape is handy, too, although you shouldn't leave it on because it turns into a gooey mess. Electrical tape is good for insulating wire splices, comes in a variety of colors, and is great for color-coding cables.

MAKING THE MOVE

Executing moves requires rehearsal and communication. Make sure everyone understands what's going to happen, as well as what the camera will be seeing. Your audio crew, in particular, will appreciate knowing this information.

Mark your positions so the dolly grip can see exactly where the nearest tire should end up. I don't recommend using sandbags at the end of the move.

You can run right into them, ruining the shot and giving the camera operator and dolly grip a bit of a jolt.

Be careful with jib arms. Make sure someone is on the counterweighted end to control any movement. Make sure it's balanced and marked with something bright so everyone can see it, and don't forget to rehearse.

A moving camera needs composition. Consider where your marks are for the dolly or crane, and be sure to compose well and have some action within the frame. Nothing too big, but enough so if you have to cut away for pacing, you can.

Make the moves smooth. Especially with a dolly, you can creep along the line of motion before ramping up to full speed. If your dolly grip can see the monitor, he or she can make slight adjustments for better composition, but make sure you discuss this before getting the shot. I was on a dolly with a grip who decided the camera should be elsewhere than where I had told him I wanted it. He ignored both my instructions and my signals, so I grabbed a doorway to stop him from moving anymore.

That kind of behavior does not engender trust or a good working environment.

WATTS, VOLTS, AND AMPS: HOW MUCH POWER?

Set Lighting Technician's Handbook: Film Lighting Equipment, Practice, and Electrical Distribution from Harry C. Box is an excellent resource for understanding electrical systems on the set. Although most of the information applies to sound stages and larger sets, a lot of what he conveys applies to shows using existing power on location.

What will be helpful is a fundamental understanding of electrical power, including

- AC and DC
- Power units and how they relate to one another
- Meters and what they measure
- Using existing power
- Tie-ins, line drops, and generators

AC AND DC

There are two types of power sources: alternating current, or AC, and direct current, or DC.

Alternating current or AC—Supplied by the power company, an AC generator, or with a transformer on a DC power supply, AC has a hot lead and

NOTE

Average Effective Volts

While the voltage may be 120 or 240, you should find out the average effective voltage of service in your community. It may be 110 or 115, or 210, 220, or 230 volts. Check with the power utility.

Generally, a typical room in a house will be using 5-7 amps in general circuits, excluding electrical devices such as stereos, television sets, computers, and so on. You'll need to factor in these appliances to find out the total amperage of the circuit available for your use.

a grounded lead. Although the grounded lead is also called the *neutral wire* and the *common*, it is not the same as a grounding wire. The direction of the flow, or *polarity*, of the circuit alternates from positive to negative and back again. In the United States, AC operates at 60Hz 120V, whereas elsewhere it operates at 50Hz 240V.

During each cycle, the voltage of a 60Hz 120V goes from 0 to +170V, then goes back to 0, reverses polarity, goes down to –170V, and back to 0. This happens 60 times a second, fast enough that the filament in a lamp has no time to dim, resulting in a constant glow. To get an effective voltage of 120V requires 170V.

Direct current or DC—A DC power source from a battery or a generator has a positive terminal and a negative terminal. Electrons flow from the negative to the positive. The polarity never changes, and the current maintains a constant voltage.

To convert from AC to DC, you need a rectifier. To convert from DC to AC, you need an inverter.

MEASURING ELECTRICITY

There are three basic units DC of measure for electricity:

- **Wattage**—The total amount of power being delivered is measured in watts. Watts are the product of amperage and voltage, and measures the amount of work being done.

- **Voltage**—The force is measured in volts, usually expressed as V. For example, 12V, 120V, and so on.

- **Amperes**—Current, the rate of flow of electrons, is measured in amps. In practical terms, amps represent the amount of power being drawn from a circuit.

To determine available power, apply the *West Virginia rule*:

$W = V \times A$

W = watts

V = volts

A = amps

In the United States, voltage is 240V or 120V. In most homes, the volts are 120. During your location scout, you should have located the circuits and circuit box for your location. You should know what kind of voltage is available per circuit as well as how many amps.

You can figure out how many amps a light needs by calculating

Watts/volts = amps

Generally, electrical outlets for homes in the United States are equipped for 15–20 amps per circuit, although that circuit may include outlets with other devices on it. Industrial electrical circuits may go up to 30 amps, but a single outlet may still be capable of only 20 amps.

Add up all the lights you are using, and see whether you are exceeding the capacity of the circuit.

If you switch all the lights on at the same time, the power surge will probably blow a fuse or circuit breaker. Turn on the lights one at a time. Don't try to operate cameras, computers, or VCRs from that same circuit. The lighting equipment may depress the voltage and cause the other gear to act unreliably.

If you're using equipment that has capacitive properties, such as electronic ballasts and electronic dimmers, or inductive properties, such as magnetic ballasts, you'll have to figure the power factor to calculate the load correctly.

Tungsten lights have neither inductive nor capacitive properties, but just create resistance in a circuit. A purely resistive circuit has a power factor of 1.0, or 100%. This is known as *unity power factor*, and watts/volts = amps will give you the correct load.

When a load involves coils, such as in a transformer or magnetic ballast, inductive reactance lowers the power factor to less than 100%. Inductance opposes the flow of current, causing it to lag behind voltage. With voltage and current out of phase, more current is required for the same amount of work.

If a circuit has a piece of equipment on it with capacitive properties, such as some electronic ballasts and electronic dimmers, capacitive reactance produces a power factor of less than 100%. Capacitive reactance causes current to leak voltage, which once again produces reduced efficiency.

To calculate power factor

$$pf = \frac{\text{rated wattage}}{\text{volt–amperes}}$$

pf = power factor

For single-phase circuits

Volt–amperes = volt×amps

For three-phase circuits

$$\text{Volt–amperes} = 1.732 \times \text{volts} \times \text{amps}$$

The power factor is usually written on the equipment. If it is, you can figure actual amps by

$$\text{rated wattage}/120 \times \text{pf} = \text{required amps}$$

METERS

Meters and testers come in all shapes and sizes. You can get them from a local hardware store, an electrical supply company, or an online motion picture equipment shop.

A voltmeter measures voltage. Touch the two probes to the terminals of a circuit, being sure not to touch the poles with your fingers. The voltmeter will indicate the voltage, which is very handy for figuring out how much power the circuit is running.

To test Edison outlets, use a circuit tester. You can quickly find out whether the outlet is hot, the polarity is correct, and the ground is present. Just plug it in.

A line frequency tester measures the frequency of an AC circuit in an Edison outlet. Plug it in to find out the frequency in Hz. Remember that frequency of power mains in the United States is supposed to be 60Hz, whereas elsewhere it's 50Hz. Make sure you have the correct frequency for your equipment.

To find out the amperage of a circuit, you can check the number on the circuit breaker located in the circuit box. You can also use an amp probe. The amp probe has two curved fingers that close around a single, insulated conductor cable. It measures the strength of the magnetic field created by the current running through it, which is proportional to the amperage running through the wire. The reading is in amps.

A continuity tester works only when the cable or component is disconnected from the power. Use one to find a break in the line. If the line is continuous, the tester will beep, light up, or otherwise indicate it.

You can get a single digital multimeter to measure AC and DC voltage, detect continuity, and measure resistance.

USING EXISTING POWER

Give some thought to where you need power and how you'll get it there. If you're plugging into existing wall outlets, track down what else is already plugged in. You may think you've got 15 amps available on a circuit, but you don't know the homeowner's stereo system is using it.

Most homes and commercial buildings use single-phase, three-wire AC to provide 120V or 240V power from three wires. Most tungsten and smaller HMIs use 120V, although large HMI ballasts and PARs may require 208V, 230V, or 240V. Some lighting arrays require 277V. There are many different ways to wire circuits for motion picture equipment. If you need big lights or many lights requiring lots of power, hire an experienced gaffer who can do it safely. The skill is worth the money.

If you need 240V, you can get it from single-phase three-wire AC. If you need 240V and there are no correct outlets available, bring in a gaffer or an electrician to wire an outlet. Make sure it's correctly marked.

With AC, you can complete a circuit by touching a hot wire while standing on the ground. With DC, you must complete the circuit by touching the positive and the negative wires at the same time. This is why DC-powered lighting equipment is used around water.

If you have AC-powered lights in a bathroom, near a swimming pool, and so on, make sure you plug into a circuit with a ground fault interrupter, or GFI. Also called ground fault circuit interrupters, residual current devices, and earth leakage detectors, a *ground fault interrupter* is a protective device either in a specially designed circuit or in a 120V outlet that detects current fault much smaller than would trip a normal circuit breaker. It's designed to protect people against shock current in the event of a fault.

If you're in an area with running water that has GFI outlets, use them or replace the existing one. You can even build a GFI outlet box with parts from the local hardware store.

MORE POWER: TIE-INS, LINE DROPS, AND GENERATORS

If your location doesn't have enough power for all your equipment, you do have options. You can tie in, order a line drop, or use a generator.

A *tie-in* taps into the power mains by temporarily tapping into the main service of a location. It's illegal in many areas and dangerous in all. Check with your local authorities, and if it's allowed, you'll probably need a permit. You can get killed tying in, so hire a pro to handle it. A *line drop* is an extra power line from the power mains brought to the site. Your local utility company will do it for you, but it will cost, and you'll want an experienced electrician to set up a panel box with main breakers from the meter so you can draw power. A line drop is a designated circuit with sufficient amps, doesn't burn fuel, and is silent.

You can use a generator, known on the set as a *jenny*. You can use one that's not designed for motion picture use, but keep in mind that generators are noisy. Even ones specific for motion pictures can still cause problems. Often, generators for home use don't have regulators to keep the power consistent. You may end up with flickering, dimming, or discoloration from changing wattage. Motion picture generators are electronically governed to be very reliable for use with HMIs and maintain voltage with great precision.

Although you might think you're saving money using your uncle Jerry's generator, it might not be worth the headache. It will probably be loud, so you'll spend more time placing and silencing it, and it might not provide consistent power to keep your lights running properly.

I made a documentary called *Family Business* about a 74-year-old diesel machinist. I spent a week in his shop, shooting film of him machining engine blocks and replacing rods, cylinders, and other parts. I've seen what happens to the insides when you use poor fuel or don't bother to keep the engine properly maintained. Who knows what condition your Uncle Jerry's generator is in? If it falls apart on your shoot, Jerry's going to expect you to repair or replace it.

I've used a putt-putt, a small generator adapted for motion picture use, for background lighting at night. It was a lot easier to do that than run hundreds of feet of cable through the woods. I was on my own property and didn't require a permit, but I told my neighbors ahead of time what I was doing. I can't stress enough the importance of letting people know what you're planning—most will leave you alone to work as long as they know what's going on. Some will even come over to see whether you need help or offer use of their bathrooms, barns, and electrical outlets. My neighbor, Bob, even helped pull cable just for the fun of it.

At the very least, good manners never hurt anybody.

Remember that you may not be able to run a generator in certain areas or at certain times of the day. Find out the regulations, and get your permits taken care of.

If you use a putt-putt, be sure to shut off the fuel valve when you move it so you don't flood the carburetor. Be sure it's on level ground, or you'll have fuel intake problems. Tuck it behind anything you can find to help block the noise.

Decide whether you want a gas- or diesel-fueled generator. Gas generators are quieter and lighter but can generate no more than 60kW or 500A and use more fuel. Gas is also flammable, and you may not be allowed to use it in certain areas.

Diesel generators are heavier, reliable, low maintenance, and efficient. They can turn larger alternators, generating more power, and the fuel is combustible rather than flammable, meaning it's safer. Unfortunately, diesel generators are sensitive to poor-quality fuel, which can block the diesel fuel injectors, and hard to start when cold. They also tend to be louder.

In addition to putt-putts, you can get tow plants that mount on trailers and range from 200A to 2400A. The smaller ones use gasoline engines, and the larger use diesel. You can also rent tractor-mounted plants with greater fuel capacity, or generator cars and trucks.

You'll need a distribution system from the generator to the set. The system comprises feeder cable, distribution boxes, disconnects, and other components for reliable and safe use. See Box's book for an in-depth discussion of cabling a generator properly, as well as other issues about electrical systems on the set.

Keep in mind, too, that while generators solve one big problem of not having enough power, you need to budget for renting the equipment, as well as hire someone experienced to run it. You also need to schedule accordingly. Locating the generator and laying cable takes time. You can pre-rig, as long as you have a plan drawn up for your electrician and crew.

Make sure you have enough fuel. There's nothing quite like the sputtering and darkness of running out of gas. And don't think it never happens.

And remember: This equipment should be fenced off to prevent people from accidentally making contact with conductive material.

STINGERS, CHEATERS, AND OTHER ELECTRICAL DOODADS

A *stinger* is a single extension cord that's plugged in and ready for use. You can buy industrial extension cords or rent them. If you rent a grip tuck, chances are the cabinets along the outside of the truck bed will be crammed with them.

Wire size is numbered according to the American Wire Gauge sizes. For wire numbered from 18 AWG to 1 AWG, the smaller the number, the bigger the wire.

Cable larger than 1 AWG are numbered 0, 00, 000—written 1/0, 2/0, 3/0—and spoken of as "aughts" or "otts," as in "one aught, two aught, three aught." Multiconductor cable is labeled by the gauge and then number of conductors. For example, 12/3 means 12 is the gauge and 3 is the number of conductors.

If you are connecting or disconnecting the power cord to a light, please, please make sure the power is off. Arcs and sparks can make your hair stand on end and ruin your whole day.

A cable that's taut is an accident waiting to happen. Use the appropriate-length cables. Cable from a light should coil in a figure eight on the floor near the stand, so when the stand is moved, the cable plays out from the top. If you've got lights rigged to pipes or other structures on the set, leave a couple loops hanging on the structure.

When connecting cables, you can use a stress knot to prevent kick-out. *Kick-out* is when cables accidentally get unplugged. You can either loosely knot the two cables or use a strip of Velcro or sash cord. I've also used ponytailers (see Figure 22.23). Also called *hairballs*, these are ponytail holders with two plastic balls on them you can buy just about anywhere. I use them primarily with audio equipment, but they're handy all over the place (see Figure 22.24).

FIGURE 22.23
A ponytailer.

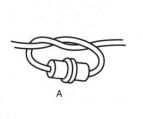
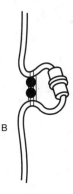

FIGURE 22.24

(A) shows simple strain relief for a stinger that will prevent kick-outs. (B) uses a ponytailer for the result. The ponytailer is quicker to put on and take off.

All cables should be coiled clockwise. Stranded copper wire has a natural twist and coiling counterclockwise works against the twist.

After the lights are on, it's good practice to touch the cables to see whether anything is overheating. They should be warm, but if they're hot, something's wrong. Replace the light and mark it to have the cables replaced.

Don't use a damaged extension or power cord. Male and female Hubble Edison plugs are great for replacing the damaged plugs. If you're running multiple cables through holes or over walls, or otherwise snaking them across the room, label the stingers at each end to make your life easier.

If you're blowing fuses, there's something wrong. Either there's a short in a socket, plug, or fixture, or a problem with the way the load is distributed. Recheck what you have plugged into the circuit and redistribute as necessary. Do not replace the fuse with an oversize fuse or a penny. You can start a fire.

A *cheater*, shown in Figure 22.25, or ground plug adapter is used to adapt grounded plugs to ungrounded plugs. They're also called *ground lifters* and *two-for-threes*. You can find them at any hardware store.

Power strips are handy as well, but make sure you're not loading up too much equipment, and don't gang sensitive electrical equipment on the same strip as lights.

Cube taps are used for plugging several low-amp lights into one outlet, with 15 amps maximum.

GETTING WIRED

If you want to make small lights or rewire practicals, you're going to need some bits and pieces. If you rent prop practicals, they'll arrive with bare wires, so you'll have to put plugs on them. If the lamp, fixture, or sconce is UL listed, you can wire them up easily.

Zip cord is #18 household lamp cord used for rigging small lamps and practicals. It's 18 American Wire Gauge and may NOT be used with anything electrical having a ground. It's rated for 10 amps maximum, so don't over-amp. Keep the runs no more than six feet—resistance in zip cord is so high that the cord will burn up before the breaker is tripped.

Get a spool of it, as well as a wire cutter and wire stripper.

FIGURE 22.25

Cheaters. Cheap and handy.

Quick-on plugs are made to be used with zip cord only and you can find them at any hardware store. Quick-ons stab the zip cord with copper spikes, so you don't have to use screw terminals. An *Edison plug* is an ordinary household plug with two flat blades and a ground pin. An *in-line tap* is a female Edison socket that can be spliced onto #18 zip cord without tools. *In-line switches* are plug-in 15-amp switches on the power line. They can be handy for lights mounted in such a way that it's difficult to get to the switches and for practicals (see Figure 22.26).

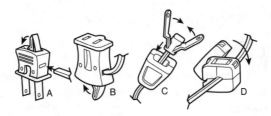

FIGURE 22.26

(A) Male quick-on, (B) female quick-on, (C) another male quick-on, and (D) an in-line tap. You can usually find these at any hardware store.

INVERTERS

If you have to use power from a vehicle, you'll need an inverter. You can buy an inverter from an auto supply shop or rent one from the rental house. Some inverters have fans in them, so you can't put them inside the vehicle because you'll hear it on your audio track. They can go in the trunk or be strapped to the fender.

Try to get an inverter that makes a "squine wave." This is what Tripp-Lite calls the waveform on some of its inverters. Instead of a square wave made from switching DC back and forth, it's an approximation of a sine wave. Magnetic HMI ballasts are fine with it.

Because the inverter is adding an additional load to the vehicle's electrical system, it's not unusual for the battery to slowly drain to the point where the inverter shuts down. Use a vehicle that runs well and has a strong alternator and battery. Don't forget to have the car running when you're tweaking lights. And get spare fuses for the inverter and the car.

Inverters can be dangerous to an electrical system. The amperage required for 12v is very high, whereas an average car alternator/battery combination can't handle anything more than 800 watts for an extended time. A 1k inverter at full load is far more than the cables can handle, and you can set your car on fire.

If you're not comfortable rigging electrical equipment inside a vehicle, find someone who is. This is not the kind of thing you want to guess at. Often car enthusiasts can help you rig just about anything safely for a number of vehicles. They can be very helpful in figuring out how to get the amount of power you need safely from a DC system.

OTHER RIGGING EQUIPMENT

You need good leather gloves. Everyone on the set who handles lights and grip equipment should have at least one pair, along with a retractable utility knife or Leatherman.

Furniture pads or furniture blankets are quilts used to protect furniture when you're moving it. In addition to protecting furniture and equipment on the set, you can use furniture pads to deaden sound. If your sound mixer is getting a lot of reflected audio, he or she can hang up the furniture pads and anything else soft and squishy.

Rubber matting is used as heavy and durable floor mats that cover power cables when they cross heavy traffic areas. You can also use commercial carpet runners in the same way. Legal milk crates are the ones that haven't been stolen. You can store rolled-up sheets of gel and diffusion in them, as well as other bits and pieces.

You're going to need a tool belt and toolbox. Keep the tool belt with you. Tuck the toolbox in a handy place on or near the set. The tool belt should have

- Grip clips
- C-47s
- Flashlight
- Gloves
- Pen
- Permanent marker

The toolbox should have

- Amp probe
- Battery-driven drill and drywall screws
- Circuit tester
- Continuity tester
- Crescent wrench
- Digital multimeter
- Levels and plumb line
- Line frequency tester
- Machine oil
- Needle-nose pliers
- Pushpins or tacks for putting up gel, scrim material, and light-blocking material on doors and windows
- Scissors
- Screwdrivers
- Soldering iron and flux
- Spackle knives
- Tape measure
- Voltmeter
- Wire cutters
- Wire stripper

Lexan is plastic sheeting that comes in different weights and sizes used to protect the camera and camera operator from explosions or messes. You can get large sheets of 4'×8', but especially for protection from explosions, make it at least 1/2" thick. If you need to cut it, use a carbide-tipped blade on a circular saw and be careful.

EXPANDABLES CHECKLIST

3/4" A/C Plywood (if necessary)		
Arrid XX spray-on deodorant		
Baby powder		
Blu-tack		
Bucket		
Bungee cords		
Caulk and caulking gun		
Cellophane tape		
Chalk (kids' sidewalk chalk works fine}		
Cheaters		
Clothespins (wood)		
Cotton towels		
Crutch tips		
Cube taps		
Duct tape		
Grip clips (Pony clips or equivalent)		
In-line switches		
In-line taps		
Lemon Pledge (if necessary)		
Machine oil		
Mason line		
Mylar or shiny wrapping paper (gold and silver)		
Paper towels		
Ponytailers		
Power strips		
Quick-on female plugs		
Quick-on male plugs		
Ratchet straps		
Safety chain (short dog leashes will work)		
Sash cord		
Spackle		
Spool of 18# zip cord		
Sponge		

Spray silicone (if necessary)		
Tacks or pushpins		
Trick line		
Wedges for dolly track		
Window cleaner		
Wooden cup blocks		
Wood filler		
Zip cord		
Automotive supply store		
Butyl		
Inverter		
Motion picture supply shop		
Camera tape		
Canned air		
Gaffer's tape		
J-Lar tape		
Paper tape		

RIGGING EQUIPMENT CHECKLIST

	Number	Pick-up from	Pick-up date	Return date
C-stands				
C-stands with rocky mountain leg				
Rolling stands				
Light stands				
Junior steel three-riser				
Junior steel two-riser				
Junior Low Boy				
Junior aluminum three-riser				
Junior aluminum two-riser				
Baby Low Boy				
Baby aluminum three-riser				
Baby aluminum two-riser				
Mombo-Combo four-riser				
Cinevator				
Super Crank				
Crank-O-Vator				
Wheel sets				
Mafers				
Cardellinis				
Baby plates—male				
Baby plates—female				
Gaffer grips				
Duck bills				
C-clamps				
Furniture clamps				
Spuds				
Apple boxes				
Sandbags				
Dollies				
Camera dolly				
Doorway dolly with sideboards and pneumatic tires				
Skateboard wheels for doorway dolly				

Western dolly with sideboards and pneumatic tires				
Skateboard wheels for Western dolly				
Crab dolly				
Track: PVC				
Track: metal tube				
Track: metal square				
Jibs				
Jib arm with counterweights and head				
Jib mount				
Car mounts				
Hostess tray				
Hood mount				

CAPTURING THE SOUND

One of the best resources on audio for DV is Jay Rose's book *Producing Great Sound for Digital Video*. You can also check Jay's Web site at www.dplay.com and his columns on audio for video at www.dv.com for more information.

Also, check Fred Ginsburg's articles at www. equipmentemporium.com and www.camerasound.com. The articles are detailed and helpful, covering just about every issue regarding location audio. Both he and Tom Hamilton are great resources.

Cinema Audio Society at www.ideabuzz.com/ cas/ also has a journal and online discussion that's a treasure trove of techniques, ongoing issues, and audio trivia. The archives are online as well.

Most motion pictures in the United States are made using location audio, with sound recorded simultaneously with the picture. Not every moviemaker uses synchronous sound. Some European moviemakers continue to shoot all their footage without sound or MOS and then add their dialogue in a recording studio using a technique called *looping,* or *automatic dialogue replacement* (ADR). Although ADR can often save a line, don't count on it to rescue an entire scene. ADR is time-consuming, expensive, and difficult.

See Chapter 30, "Post-Audio," for more information on ADR.

Most DV shows, however, use sync sound. One big reason is that audio is recorded onto the videotape along with picture. This form of moviemaking is called *single-system sound. Dual-system sound* is when you record audio to a separate device, such as a Nagra, DAT, or MiniDisk (MD), and sync it up in post.

You may use dual-system sound when the camera is too far away or otherwise unavailable to record audio. For example, I've used dual-system sound to record scenes taking place in moving cars and when there's a lot of dialogue in a large room. Just be sure to use clapper sticks. If they're unavailable, have someone clap his or her hands on camera. It makes syncing the audio easier.

DV's excellent audio capabilities make single-system sound a viable option. Unfortunately, too many DV producers think of location audio as an afterthought—if they think of it at all. For no- and low-budget motion pictures, however, location audio can make or break the show.

Consider hiring an experienced location sound mixer. He or she will often have gear and the knowledge to use it. An experienced sound mixer understands the entire moviemaking process and knows when audio from one take can be substituted or repaired in post.

If you don't want to hire, take the time to train someone in the basics of location audio.

CREW

If you've hired a sound mixer, he or she will show up with a sound cart full of fascinating gizmos. If not, let that person figure out ahead of time your show's necessary equipment. He or she will give you a list to take to the rental house. If there's a problem, let the sound mixer know in advance.

Your sound mixer may handle mixing and operating the boom both. He or she may also grab someone from the crew and teach that person how to be a boom operator. Don't interfere unless there's a problem.

If you're going to assign the jobs of sound mixer and boom operator to your crew, don't delegate them to someone just standing there. It seems like the people who are energetic, smart, and competent get grabbed to work camera crew or hang lights. Don't have a dud doing your sound. Don't have a dud on your crew in the first place, but especially, don't assign the laziest, least capable person to handle your audio. It's too important.

Take two of your crew over to the sound cart, teach them the equipment and techniques, and let them take it on. Get playback often until you're satisfied they're handling the job. Do not assign them to anything else but audio. They can help on load in and load out, but don't expect the person running the boom to dress the set. They need to concentrate on blocking and rehearsals.

The sound mixer will watch all audio levels, keep an eye on boom placement and shadows, and judge the quality of the sound. Quality is determined by levels and amount of noise. It's also judged by consistency. There are three aspects that the sound mixer must be attentive to:

- Consistency within the shot
- Consistency between shots within the scene
- Consistency between scenes

Most of these decisions will come from the sound mixer regarding equipment, mixer settings, and mic placement. In addition, the sound mixer needs to understand the postproduction process, so he or she can make informed decisions about when to speak up about a take's audio.

The boom operator must be attentive to mic placement and boom shadows. Make sure the boom op has headphones—there's no way he or she can know whether the take is good, or adjust for errors, without hearing the sound.

The boom op takes direction from the sound mixer; the sound mixer takes direction from the director. That's how it's supposed to go.

If there's a problem with the take, encourage the audio crew to speak up. Sound mixers in particular must fight to get good mic placement, as well as other improvements for the good of the sound, and you want them to. Sound mixers don't ask unless they truly believe there's a problem, so believe them. And make sure your DP knows that "Loop it!" is rarely a good response to an audio problem.

MAKING WAVES

Sound is a pressure wave. Waves have four major properties that distinguish one from another:

- *Amplitude* is the amount of pressure change. Sounds with high intensity (louder) have high amplitude.

- *Frequency*, given in Hertz (Hz), is a measure of the number of waves from crest to crest that pass a point in a given amount of time. One hertz, or 1Hz, means one wave passes every second. A 1kHz tone has 1,000 crests passing a given point in one second.

- *Wavelength* is the length of a wave, measured in units of distance, such as nanometers, feet, or meters. It's easiest to remember the *lower longer* rule: Lower frequencies have longer wavelengths.

- *Speed* means how fast the wave is traveling, determined by multiplying the frequency times the wavelength. Often the speed of a type of wave through a specific medium is constant, such as the speed of sound through air at a given temperature.

A decibel (dB) is a logarithmic ratio of two signals or values related to human hearing or vision. The use of logarithms makes the math easier, but don't forget that big changes are reflected by small numbers. For example, a voltage boost of 6 dB may not seem like much, but it makes the signal twice as strong.

Keep in mind the there is no absolute level in dB—you have to know the reference. Zero on a mixer may not match the zero of your recorder, so be sure to check that each is set to a single reference tone.

Decibels may refer to power, voltage, current, sound intensities, and so on.

LOCATION AUDIO PRIORITIES

The first priority of location audio is to get usable dialogue, with correct levels and a very high signal-to-noise ratio (S/N). *Signal-to-noise ratio* refers to the amount of desired audio versus the amount of undesired audio. For example, if there is unavoidable background noise on the set, the audio crew wants to get the mic in the best possible location to get the cleanest audio, such as dialogue, mitigating somewhat the unwanted environmental noise. Noise also includes interference and other noises on the line, all of which the sound crew has to consider. If getting a high signal-to-noise ratio is impossible, the sound mixer and boom operator will at least record a guide track for looping, or ADR.

The second priority is to match the perspective of the camera angle. Matching picture requires a trained ear to get a realistic audio perspective. For example, wide shots tend to have sound that includes reverberations and other sound characteristics of the room. Close-ups tend to have the microphone very close. A close-up with a wide sound may strike the viewer as odd. A trained sound mixer will notice and be able to compensate for differences with proper microphone placement.

The third priority is to collect room tone from every single location. Room tone, or *presence*, is 60 seconds of air recorded onto tape with everyone and everything in place and silent. Room tone is used in postproduction as a way to smooth over cuts in dialogue.

Finally, the sound mixer is concerned with recording any sound effects for the scene. Decide in advance what kind of post-audio requirements you have. If you're going to a post-audio facility, you can save money by bringing in your own sound effects. Discuss the post needs with the sound mixer before you get to the set.

AUDIO ISSUES FOR DV

Audio for DV is a combination of the usual location audio tools, such as microphones, mixers, boom poles, and so on, and the cameras themselves.

Most pro-level and some prosumer DV cameras offer two channels at 16-bit 48kHz or four channels at 12-bit 32kHz audio. Other prosumer DV cameras have one 16-bit 48kHz channel for mono sound or two 12-bit 32kHz channels for stereo, and some allow four channels of 12-bit 32kHz audio. If your camera allows you to switch, go with the 16-bit 48kHz in mono or stereo.

Most audio signals handled by pro equipment (such as mixers) are amplified at a high enough level to avoid circuit or cable noise. Professional sound equipment is often rated at +4 dBu line level and operates at a nominal signal level of about 1.25 volts. This is called *line level*.

Consumer equipment is often rated –10 dBV with a nominal signal level of about .3 volt. The only time you should have to worry about –10 and +4 voltages is when you have to interconnect consumer and professional equipment, such as hooking up a field mixer to a prosumer DV camera.

Most prosumer DV cameras have mic-level ins. To feed line-level audio from a mixer into a camera, reduce the signal by 30 dB–50 dB. Some

NOTE

Clear Dialogue Is the Goal

You can easily add background sound and reverb in postproduction. It's often difficult to remove it. Get the cleanest sound you can.

mixers have a switch to reduce their outputs from line to mic level. Some add-on boxes, such as the Beachtek DXA-4, also have switches.

Otherwise, insert an attenuator, also called a *pad,* between the output of the mixer and the input of the camera. Don't use a cheap one. If you're not using an adapter box with a built-in pad, manufacturers such as Shure and Audio-Technica make line-to-mic pads that will work.

Many prosumer cameras lack audio meters or have meters that are hidden from the sound mixer's view. Manufacturers have created add-on meters, and they may help. Key to this issue is to make sure you talk with the camera operator about your sound levels.

STEREO MINIPLUGS

Many DV cameras have an external mic input through a 1/8" stereo miniplug. The stereo miniplug is just awful. It's fragile, rarely fits snugly into the camera, is susceptible to hum and drop-out, and offers no strain relief for the cable.

The signal flowing through is also unbalanced. A balanced audio signal is one that is independent of ground, can travel long distances with no quality loss, and is relatively impervious to hum. A balanced audio line runs within a three-wire cable with two leads and a grounded shield. The two identical conductors carrying a signal of opposite polarity let the input circuit resist hum. Usually, balanced audio cables have XLR (think of the mnemonic: eXternal, Live, and Return) connectors.

Most, if not all, pro audio gear uses balanced outputs. Most prosumer DV cameras have unbalanced, miniplug inputs. To feed professional balanced microphones with XLR connectors into a camera with a stereo miniplug requires some kind of adapter.

The adapter should pad down the output of the mixer from line to mic level and take care of any bias voltage on some prosumer cameras.

If you are using only one mic, you may be able to use an adapter cable that will put the mono mic signal onto both camera tracks. Some of the new digital cameras just need an adapter cable that converts from XLR female to stereo mini. However, some off-the-shelf adapter cables are wired incorrectly. Research thoroughly what kind of cable you'll need.

XLR adapter boxes operate as transformers to drop input impedance, have two volume controls to manipulate the left and right channels, and have a way to ground the connection between audio gear and the camera. These boxes attach to the bottom of the camera and provide for one or two XLR inputs, switchable for mic or line level, and mono or stereo.

If you need an adapter box, attach it to your camera, plug it in, and leave it connected. This will lessen the wear and tear on the stereo miniplug.

Consider putting a rubber band around the miniplug cable going into the miniplug. This will help ensure a snug connection and provide some relief from cable strain. Use right-angle connectors with in and out for more strain relief and to reduce the chance of the cable getting broken on the set. Never allow long cables to tug directly on the miniplug of the camera.

MICROPHONES

Microphones come in all kinds of shapes and sizes. Generally, though, they can be categorized according to their directional patterns:

- **Omnidirectional**—Omnidirectional mics are more or less equally sensitive to sounds coming from all directions.
- **Bidirectional**—Bidrectional mics have a bipolar pattern with the mic responsive to sounds from two directions. These are rarely useful on a DV set.
- **Unidirectional**—Unidirectional mics are sensitive to sounds coming primarily from one direction. These are most common on a motion picture set. There are three types of unidirectional mics:
  - Cardioid
  - Supercardioid
  - Hypercardioid

The cardioid pattern vaguely resembles a heart shape. Mics using a cardioid pattern are sensitive to sounds over a wide range in front of the mic, but relatively insensitive to sounds coming from behind. The cardioid pattern is too wide for most production situations.

Supercardioid mics have a narrower sensitivity pattern than cardioid mics. When a supercardioid is pointed toward a sound source, off-axis sounds are rejected. Shotgun mics are a type of supercardioid mic. They're the handiest mic on most sets because they're directional and provide good pick-up.

Off-axis means that sound is outside the mic's primary pick-up area. This doesn't mean it won't be recorded—it may be. But unidirectional microphones are accurate only for sound directly in front. Sounds striking the mic from the rear or sides will be affected.

Hypercardioid mics have a very narrow angle of acceptance. Off-axis sounds will be rejected, which is good. Unfortunately, this also means that the boom operator has to constantly readjust the microphone placement.

DYNAMIC AND CONDENSER

In a dynamic microphone, sound waves hit a diaphragm attached to a coil of fine wire suspended in a magnet's magnetic field. Sound waves hit the diaphragm and move the coil, causing a small electrical current that corresponds to the original sound waves. These waves are amplified and recorded.

Dynamic microphones are very rugged and less expensive, but they're just not as sensitive as condenser microphones. If you have to blow something up, use a dynamic mic to capture the sound.

Electret condenser microphones have a permanent electric field created by the material of the mic capsule. Sound waves cause a light diaphragm to move in the electric field, causing shifts in the electrical charge. Electrets require some kind of power supply, often a battery, and are used in lavalier microphones.

Many common shotgun mics, such as the Sennheiser ME-66 and Audio-Technica 815/835, used on a DV set are electret. They're inexpensive and work well for many applications.

In a condenser mic, an ultrathin metal diaphragm is stretched tightly above a piece of metal or ceramic. A power source maintains an electrical charge between these elements. Sound waves hitting the diaphragm cause fluctuations in the electrical charge.

The audio signals created by these fluctuations, and those in electret mics, are quite low, so they're amplified by a mic preamp contained in the mic housing or in an outboard electronic pack. This amplification brings the signal up to traditional mic levels to survive the cable run. These preamps require power that can be supplied from batteries or an AC power supply.

Phantom power is the power supplied by a mixer for condenser mics. Phantom power tends to be more consistent than that of batteries, so often the quality of the audio is better. Use phantom power when you can.

Phantom power almost always uses XLR connectors and fully balanced wiring between power source and mic. NEVER plug an unbalanced mic, cable, or adapter into a phantom-powered input or you'll damage the equipment.

On any set, you'll see a variety of microphones. The two most commonly used are shotguns and lavaliers.

Shotguns

Condenser shotgun microphones can come in a variety of sizes, pick-patterns, and prices. Generally, they have great reach and a narrow pattern, allowing you to boom a shotgun as close as possible to the sound while remaining out of frame. Shotgun microphones have tight unidirectional pick-up patterns for better off-axis rejection.

The downside is that the narrower the pick-up, the more critical the placement of the microphone becomes. Also, an inexperienced boom op or sound mixer can be fooled into thinking a narrower pick-up will completely reject unwanted sounds at the side of or behind the mic. This isn't necessarily so. Depending on the volume and distance, these sounds can be louder than the audio you want, plus they have a funny coloration that can be distracting and hard to repair. Scenes involving tricky blocking, multiple actors, or an inexperienced sound crew might be better served by a mic that does not require as critical a targeting, even though you won't have as much reach.

Lavaliers

Lavaliers, or more commonly, lavs, are either planted or worn on the body. I love lavs. They're just so darn cute. Unfortunately, they can be a bit fragile. Someone dropped my Sanken COS-11 and crushed the mic element. $300 later, it's working fine again, but now no one touches my lavs unless I tell them to.

Rigging lavs on people requires time and tact. You may have to ask actors to loosen their clothes, so take them aside, away from potential gapers.

The microphone capsule itself can be secured either outside of or hidden under wardrobe. Connector and cable always go under wardrobe.

Lavs outside of clothing can be mounted using clips that look like tie clasps. Loop the mic cable in a "J" through the hinge of the clip. Make a little circle with the cable behind the clothing and catch the jaws of the clasp for strain relief.

See Figure 23.1 for examples of lavalier microphones.

NOTE

Monitor

Always monitor the audio at the recording device. It may sound good from the mixer and no peak lights are flashing, but you may still be driving your recording device too hard. Plug into the recorder—camera, DAT, or computer—for the best result.

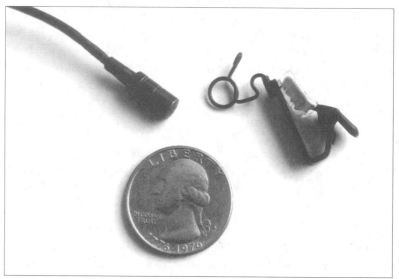

FIGURE 23.1

Sanken COS-11 and Sony ECM-77 lavalier microphones.

The rest of the cable is hidden under the clothes. Put the XLR connector in a convenient place, such as a pocket or taped to the lower leg, so you can disconnect quickly for the actor's convenience. Run mic cable as usual.

External lavs can be made less conspicuous by matching them to wardrobe. Color small strips of tape or foam windscreens with markers to subdue the appearance of the mic head and clasp. Alternatively, small patches of felt or cloth can be used to cover the mic.

However, don't cover the little holes. Those are critical to the design of any mic. If you block them, you'll hurt the sound.

Hiding a lavalier completely under clothing requires more care and attention. You can place them under the collar or high on someone's chest.

Take two strips of tape and fold them into triangles with the sticky side out. Sandwich the mic in between two sticky triangles of tape and mount it. Tie the cable with some thread for a bit of strain relief and tape it down. Press the clothing to the top triangle to stop it from rubbing against the mic.

If the actor is wearing a bra, mount the lav on the front inside, right over the chest. The bra acts like a shockmount.

Use the triangle method to rig a lav on skin as well. Clean the area with alcohol pads or Sea Breeze and cotton pads. The person may want to shave, but it's not necessary unless we're talking about a lot of body hair. Use surgical tape for the triangles.

You can mount a lav in a shirt pocket, but you'll have to make a little hole in the back for the cable. Another trick is to tuck a lav inside a glasses case in the pocket. You can also snip the end off of a pen and mount the lav inside.

Don't mount a lav near jewelry, especially beads. You'll end up with clicking sounds that will drive you crazy. Tape down all clothing that may rub against the mic capsule. Form a loop in the cable near the mic for strain relief, and then apply a few lengths of tape along the cable. Use double-faced tape or sticky triangles to immobilize clothing as necessary, to keep it from rubbing.

MIC MOUNTS

Microphone mounts offer a way to rig a mic onto a boom. There are several different kinds. Microphone clamps are usually made of plastic and metal and don't isolate the mic from vibration. Because they're cheap to make, you may get one with any mic you buy. It's better than nothing, but there are other, and better, options.

A good shockmount will isolate your mic and eliminate a lot of handling noise. One of my favorites is the Audio-Technica 8415. It's reliable, is easy to use, handles all sizes of shotgun mics (except the really long ones), and isn't outrageously expensive.

NOTE

Mounts and Thread Sizes

There are three different mic mount thread sizes: 3/8", 5/16", and 5/8". The 5/16" thread used to be the standard for motion picture location audio but has been replaced with 3/8". If you have a boom or mount with a 5/16" thread, use an adapter to make it 3/8".

The 5/8" thread is for mic stands and goosenecks. Most mic clamps are threaded for 5/8", although they may come with a 3/8" insert adapter.

Moving up the scale in terms of quality and price are pistol-grip shock-mounts.

Pistol-grip shockmounts are usually designed for specific microphones. Some of the shockmount manufacturers also offer short mounting yokes instead of pistol grip. These shockmounts are more fragile than the cheaper ones, but are quieter and more efficient, especially with longer shotguns.

Pistol-grip shockmounts are designed to take blimp windscreens. You can use a foam windscreen on most interiors, but for exteriors, you'll want a blimp (see Figure 23.2).

FIGURE 23.2

Rycote Windshield blimp on a pistol-grip mount. This is a nice zeppelin and pistol grip combination often available from rental houses.

There are two types of wind noise that will affect your location audio. The first is *acoustic*, wind noise that's part of the environment, such as wind in trees. There isn't much you can do about this. You can *roll off*, or filter, low frequencies and that will help a bit. Just get the mic as close to the actors as possible so dialogue dominates all the audio.

Contact wind noise is wind that strikes the diaphragm of the mic. It causes distortion and audio breakup and can't be fixed in post. Fortunately, wind-screens were designed to handle this kind of noise.

The simplest windscreens are *pop filters*. Pop filters are either thin foam or metal mesh. Their purpose is to block exhalation from a performer, known as *pops*. Pops also occur when people make certain sounds, such as the letter P. If the lav comes with a foam or mesh windscreen, use it to protect against pops.

Thicker foam windscreens will protect shotguns against light breezes. Slide the foam windscreen down the length of the mic, and then slip it out so there's about an inch or two of empty foam on the end. You can also check to make sure the windscreen isn't covering the mic's roll-off switch.

Your shotgun mic should always have a foam windscreen on at all times, even indoors, to protect from noise created from air coming from central air, open passages, and boom handling. A foam windscreen also protects the mic from dust and impacts.

The basic blimp windscreen has an outer mesh shell that slows down approaching air, while trapped air within the blimp itself continues to slow the moving air. For locations with a lot of wind, you can protect the mic from wind noise even more by using the foam windscreen on the mic, inside the blimp. Just make sure there's plenty of airspace between the foam and the inside of the blimp. Don't let the foam touch the blimp.

You can also use a synthetic fur *windsock* or *furry* over the blimp, as shown in Figure 23.3. The fur will disperse the oncoming wind, cutting down on wind noise.

FIGURE 23.3

Not a shih-tzu, a furry.

MIXERS

A mixer isn't just for a large number of inputs, but for controlling one or two. Unless your sound mixer has experience and matched microphones, stay away from multiple microphones on the set. They can often lead to phase problems.

A good mixer should have

- Two to four inputs
- Some equalization (EQ)
- Lots of input gain
- Slate mic
- Talk-back for communication with the boom operator during a take
- Audio returns for the boom op
- A 1kHz tone oscillator for setting reference levels

Battery operation is imperative. Clean AC is often hard to come by on a set, and electrical connections may cause ground loops and other noise.

Generally, there are two types of mixers you'll find on a DV set: field mixers and mixing boards. Regardless of the type of mixer you want to use, if you've never used one, spend time with the unit, practicing with and learning about all its features before the first day of shooting.

FIELD MIXERS

Field mixers, as shown in Figure 23.4, are designed to be portable, offer the maximum number of features in the smallest possible package, and use DC power. They often take 9-volt batteries you can buy anywhere, and manufacturers offer cases and carabineer clips to make carrying and using them easier. They're rugged and, especially the high-priced units, add very little noise to the signal.

MIXING BOARDS

I'm seeing more mixing panels on sets these days. One simple reason is that both Mackie and Behringer (see Figure 23.5) make excellent pro-level boards at a third of the cost of a field mixer. Mixing panels can also be used in other mixing situations, when a field mixer wouldn't be appropriate.

Mixing boards are not as portable as field mixers, although many are very lightweight, and you need to bring an inverter and a battery belt for DC power. They usually don't have a tone generator, although they usually offer more inputs with phantom power and more channels.

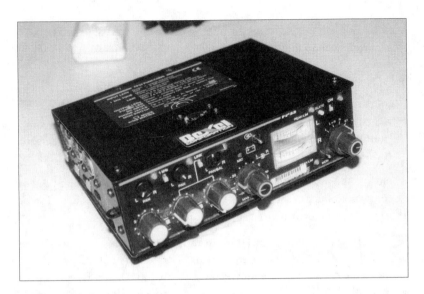

FIGURE 23.4

Shure FP-33 field mixer, courtesy of Bexel, Inc.

FIGURE 23.5

Chris Beug on the set of "Music Appreciation," cabling up a Behringer 1604A mixing board.

Both field mixers and mixing board use potentiometers, or *pots*. The mixing board has sliders that some people find easier to use than the rotary controls on field mixers. I use my mixing panel for interviews and rent field mixers when I'm on long shoots.

BOOMS

Camera-mounted mics are noisy, rarely have a narrow enough pick-up pattern, and lack reach. They usually wind up picking up sound of someone in front of the camera along with background directly behind the person.

You need to isolate the sound you want from the background and ambient as much as possible. The best way to do this is to boom a supercardioid or hypercardioid microphone as close to the sound source as possible. You do this by attaching the mic to a shockmount on a boom pole.

The closer the boom mic is to the actor, the more of the actor's voice you will capture. Although the mic will also pick up prop noises, footsteps, traffic, reflections off nearby surfaces, crew coughing, and other noises, sounds fall off rapidly with distance, so by getting closer to the actor, you'll hear proportionately more of the voice.

Boom poles are usually aluminum or carbon fiber and come in many lengths. An 8-foot boom may be long enough for nonfiction interviews, whereas a 15-footer is best for fiction moviemaking when you need to reach across the set.

Good booms are inexpensive to rent and should be seriously considered for many shows. A pole should be lightweight, but not to the point of bowing under the weight of a mic, shockmount, and windscreen at full extension. Struggling all day with a bending fishpole will wreak havoc on your boom operator's back and make him or her cranky to boot. I speak from experience.

Some booms have internal cables, which can be very handy. Just be sure the boom op keeps the cable taut within the pole while booming and the cable is of excellent quality.

Many people will make a boom pole from paint roll extension rods and other objects from a local hardware store. Experiment if you want, but make sure there's no handling noise from the boom itself.

The idea of booming is simple. Hold the mic over and slightly in front of the actor and pointed toward his or her mouth. Get as close as physically possible without being in the frame. Sounds easy until you actually do it.

Your front arm should be the strongest. It acts as the fulcrum to support the pole above your body. Use your rear arm to steer and rotate the boom to cue the microphone properly. Extend the pole further than what you need for the shot and hold it closer to its center of gravity for counterbalance.

Grip the pole firmly but not tightly with your fingertips. Some boom operators wear gloves to reduce handling noise.

Avoid the Y position, with your arms extended up and to the sides. This puts a lot of the load on your upper arm muscles. Stand like an H, with your arms straight up. Protect your lower back and keep your knees slightly bent. The H position allows you to reach in or out with the boom to follow the action quickly and smoothly.

You can hold the boom at chest level, provided you have the height. Keep your inside arm rigid to carry most of the weight straight down. The outside arm does the steering. I know a boom operator who's pretty short. She seeks out anything she can stand on so she can hold the boom at chest level. I've seen her on counters, apple boxes, truck beds, and stacks of telephone directories. She even brings her own little stepladder. Not a bad idea.

Tape the junction where the microphone connects to the boom cable, and check all of your connections along the path to make sure everything is snugly connected. Have a bit of slack in the cable between boom and microphone.

The cable can also bang against the pole. If it's an internal cable, loop it around your finger or thumb and keep the line snug. You can also tape the cable where it exits the pole.

For an external cable, wrap the cable around the boom several times and attach it to the length of the boom using ponytailers. The balls should all be on the same side. They can either be facing the same direction as the front of the mic or all facing the back. Just make sure they're going the same way so it's easy to see which way the mic is pointing when it's in the zeppelin. Keep the cable tight on the pole with your steering hand.

Whatever type of boom or method you use, just make sure the cable isn't swinging around. Always keep a couple of loops on a carabineer, Velcro loop, or ponytailer on your belt. This will prevent cable from dropping or rubbing against the floor.

Place the mic by dropping it into the frame and then slowly pulling up until it's just out of view. Your sound mixer or camera op will tell you when you're out. Find some reference points on the set so you know exactly where your line is.

Most supercardioid mics don't sound very good when they're not aimed directly at the actor, so watch the rehearsals and blocking carefully. If you have no experience, or the blocking is complex, you may want to use a short shotgun with a more forgiving pick-up pattern.

When there is more than one actor in a scene, you move the boom mic during pauses between lines. The goal is to be about the same distance from every actor for every move. Occasionally, actors will step on one another's lines and overlap their dialogue. If you can't swing the boom in time, consider staying with one actor for one setup, and then concentrate on another actor during subsequent setups.

For some scenes, you may have to boom from a direction other than above. If there's a lot of headroom in the shot, the lights are illuminating the ceiling, or the ceiling is really low, you can point the mic from underneath or from the side. The sound will have a different quality, however, so try to boom in the same manner for every scene. This will help make postproduction easier.

Booming from below can often give a voice more bottom end and energy, especially if the actors are whispering.

HEADPHONES

Without a reliable way of monitoring audio, you will never know what you are getting. Many headphones, particularly cheap ones, are poorly engineered or designed for listening to music. Get sets that are designed for location audio.

Headphone ear cups come in three styles: supra-aural, circumaural, and inside the ear. Supra-aural are an open design, circumaural are closed, and in-the-ear are earbuds or Walkman-style headphones. You can use earbuds and cheap headphones, but it's better to use a proper set of circumaural headphones to completely shut out all sound and stop audio bleed. *Audio bleed* occurs when the sound from headphones or speakers is picked up by the mic.

Enclosed headphones will stop the sound from escaping onto the set, plus they're more comfortable. Eight hours of wearing earbuds hurts.

Always monitor the record deck rather than the mixer. It's the only way to know whether there's interference, ground loops, and other problems. Also, that's one way to ensure all the audio cables are plugged into the camera.

CABLES

Most professional location audio equipment uses XLR connectors with three pins. There are other types of audio connectors, however, such as RCA and 1/4" stereo and mono plugs. RCA jacks are often found on equipment that doesn't require tremendously long runs, such as most consumer equipment.

Quarter-inch stereo and mono plugs, as shown in Figure 23.6, are common as cables for electric guitar, basses, and keyboards. But you will find 1/4" connectors on a set: Headphones often have 1/4" connectors. There are two types. A stereo connector has a ring, tip, and sleeve, whereas a mono has only a tip and a sleeve.

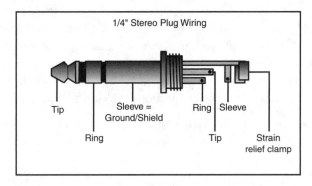

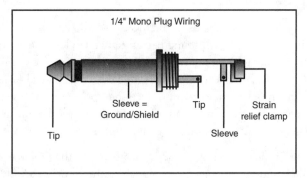

FIGURE 23.6

Quarter-inch mono and stereo plugs.

□ NOTE

Gunshots

Don't expect to use dialogue recorded along with on-set gunfire. Even if you do a great job avoiding distortion from the gun blast and are able to hear the dialogue, the sound of the gunshot won't sound right. Blanks don't sound like real bullets.

Your choices are to lose the dialogue, make sure the dialogue doesn't run over the gunshots, shoot takes with the actors not firing the weapons, or record the dialogue wild after each setup and hope you can slip it in during post.

The gunshots will in all likelihood be replaced in postproduction.

If you want to record gunshots, turn that mic down and consider using a limiter to protect your ears, gear, and track. Also consider using a dynamic mic rather than a condenser. A dynamic mic is more rugged. Get at least one rehearsal before going to camera and be careful.

(Stereo TRS 1/4" jacks are also sometimes used as balanced mono ins and outs on some mixing boards, especially those from Mackie and Behringer. Plugging a stereo Y-cable into a stereo TRS output like this will give you two mono signals that are out of phase. Because you want to avoid audio that's out of phase, don't use splitters. If you need more inputs, get another mixer.)

You can get adapters, but adding them is a last resort. Every adapter offers one more place for noise to get into the signal.

Many audio cables are color-coded for stereo. Follow the *red is right* rule: A red audio connector goes into the right channel. Consider tagging the connectors with color tape so everything gets plugged into the correct place.

You'll need XLR cables of varying lengths. *Audio snakes* are combined cables, such as a left and right XLR and miniplug for headphones, in one package. They often come in lengths of 75'–100' and can really keep the audio cabling tidy.

Keep cables clean, dry, and well aligned, without bent pins or loose pin connectors. Wipe them down with Armor All or a similar product to keep them pliable. Mic cables can sit in wet grass or water, but the connectors must be kept dry. If you're in rain or snow, or getting repeatedly hit by water from a hose, wrap the connections in electrical tape to protect them.

You may also want to consider getting a lightweight, mobile, location sound cart. Park the cart on the edge of the set in full view and earshot of all the action.

WIRELESS

Wireless systems have a place in the location audio bag of tricks. Generally, a wired mic will sound better than a wireless one. Wireless rigs have a dynamic range more limited than wired systems and use sophisticated electronics, such as companders, to get acceptable audio. These additions, as ingenious as they are, introduce their own problems, such as noise and RF signal cancellation. In addition, interference will continue to be a challenge as the radio spectrum continues filling up.

Sometimes, though, a wireless mic is the answer to the problem. For example, if the boom op can't get close enough to the actors in a wide or medium wide shot, you may just want to get out the wireless. Other times, the director wants a shot in a public place with improvised dialogue or a really important interview. The people on-camera keep moving closer and there are no cutaways planned. ADR will be difficult, or even impossible, so get out the radio mics.

In a wireless system, a mic's audio signal is converted into an RF signal and transmitted to a receiver somewhere on the location. The audio from the receiver goes to the mixer, and then to the camera or other recorder. Wireless or radio microphone systems are made up of the following:

- Microphone
- Small transmitter the microphone is plugged into
- Short antenna attached to the transmitter
- Receiver set at the same frequency as the transmitter
- Antennas attached to the receiver
- Cable from the receiver to the mixer, and then camera or other recorder

There are two types of wireless mics: self-contained and two-piece. Self-contained units tend to be handheld mics with transmitter, power supply, and antenna. A two-piece wireless unit has a mic connected to a separate transmitter that can be hidden under clothes, clipped to a belt, strapped to a leg, or dropped in a pocket.

You can plug almost any mic into a transmitter. A wireless boom mic gives you the sound quality of a large condenser mic with the flexibility of radio.

Unfortunately, good wireless systems cost dough. Great ones cost serious dough. If you need a wireless system, consider renting. It won't be cheap, so make sure you need it. Budget for batteries. Wireless mics go through 9-volt batteries fast. Most receivers use one to three batteries, whereas transmitters use one battery every few hours. A fresh 9-volt battery puts out around 9.30 volts, and you'll replace them when they drop to about 8.5 volts. Consider an additional $10–$12 per unit per day for your batteries.

Look for these features in any wireless setup:

- **UHF**—Wireless mics originally ran in the upper part of the *Very High Frequency* (VHF) TV band, using broadcast channels 7–13 but now interference is often a problem. Modern circuits can handle the *Ultra-High Frequency* (UHF) range above TV channel 14, although it costs more to build equipment for that part of the spectrum. The higher frequency allows broader audio channels for better fidelity. Plus, UHF uses a smaller antenna, so it's easier to wire the actors, mount a receiver, or use special directional antennas.

NOTE

Companding Troubles

Although companders are
great, they can also cause
problems. In a quiet
room, shake a bunch of
keys, moving them gradu-
ally closer to the mic. If
the keys don't sound like
keys, but crunchy like
crushed potato chips, the
compander may be mis-
tracking high frequency
transients.

Tape a lav to the center
of a wooden table with
nothing else on it. Gently
thump the table with your
fist. Do you hear a satis-
fying *thump* or a *thump-
zzz*? If it's not a clean
thump, the compander
may be mistracking low
frequencies.

If it's your wireless system, get it fixed before
using it. If it's a rental,
return it immediately.

- **Diversity reception**—Diversity receivers use multiple antennas. Any time one antenna is not picking up a clear signal, the other will. Circuitry within the receiver will instantly select the stronger and clearer of the two signals. *True diversity* uses two radio frequency circuits. This system monitors the radio signal level from each circuit and uses the stronger signal.

- **Frequency agility**—Transmitters and receivers used to be controlled by crystal oscillators. Now, instead of crystals, frequency-agile wireless rigs have precisely controlled oscillators that can be set to several different operating frequencies. This is great because even UHF is getting crowded.

- **Companding**—Wireless systems with a compander have a compressor on the transmitter and precisely matched expander on the receiver. The result is greater dynamic range with less noise.

There are several manufacturers who make excellent, low-cost wireless rigs. See Audio-Technica www.audiotechnica.com, Lectrosonics, www.lectrosonics.com, and Sennheiser, www.sennheiser.com, for information about their products.

USING WIRELESS

G. John Garrett and Jay Rose have an excellent article on using wireless rigs that I highly recommend. See "Dialog Unplugged: The Art of Wireless Mics" at www.dv.com/magazine/2000/1000/garret_rose1000.html.

It has been my experience that weak batteries account for most of the problems with wireless systems. Using fresh batteries will eliminate some of the more common problems, such as weak transmission.

Wireless transmitters can be hidden just about anywhere. Common places include the waistband, the inside pocket of a jacket or coat, the small of the back, inside a pant leg, around the ankle, under an armpit, or the inside of a wig or hat. A cloth pouch with a Velcro tab can be very convenient, especially if the pouch has an elastic strap. Be sure it's necessary to mount the transmitter on someone. You can always tuck a transmitter out of view on the set if the actor or subject isn't moving around too much.

If you have to mount the transmitter directly on skin, don't just tape it down. Clean the skin with Sea Breeze or an alcohol pad and use surgical tape. Use a barrier, such as an unlubricated condom or sandwich bag, to prevent moisture from getting into the transmitter.

Check your level out of the transmitter; then tape down the controls before mounting. Stuff the top of the condom or bag with absorbent material and tape the whole thing shut, letting only the antenna and mic cable stick out.

Your audio can't be better than it is at the transmitter. If the transmitter input is noisy, there is nothing you can do later to fix it. It really helps to work with the wireless rigs before you get on the set so you know what kind of range and idiosyncrasies the transmitter has.

Set the transmitter gain during an early technical rehearsal and ask the actors to give you delivery similar to what they're going to do in the scene. Turn the screw until the limiter just starts to turn on at the loudest point of the dialogue and then back off a bit. If the level from the transmitter is too low, add gain at the mixer. If you set the transmitter gain too high, it triggers the limiter, resulting in ugly sound.

Never allow the mic line and the antenna to cross. It's okay if the mic line loops on itself, but don't let that happen to the antenna. Keep it rigid— you can put a rubber band on the antenna's tip and safety pin the rubber band to clothing. Tape tends to loosen as actors move, so check the rigging as often as you can. Also, moisture absorbs radio frequencies, so if necessary, you may want to slide a piece of surgical or other rubber tubing over the antenna to protect it.

An antenna is a transducer that converts radio-frequency (RF) fields into alternating current (AC) or vice versa. There are two types: the transmitting antenna, which is fed AC and generates RF, and the receiving antenna, which receives RF and delivers AC.

Although the antenna on the transmitter is short, hiding it can be a challenge. Don't let it curl or bend—it has to stay straight for the best performance—and try not to run antennas directly against the skin. Sweat can absorb the radio signal, reducing the transmission range.

Good antenna placement is crucial to eliminating drop-outs and reducing the chances of interference. Antenna alignment usually involves some sort of compromise, especially when you're trying to hide transmitters, but try to keep the antennas in matching positions with line of sight.

Keep the antenna path short and transmit through as few obstacles as possible. If someone is standing between transmitter and receiver, ask that person politely to move. You may end up asking more than once.

Antenna polarization is another factor affecting range. Basically, *antenna polarization* refers to the radiated energy from an antenna that varies with the direction from the center. Keep the transmitter and the receiver antennas going in the same direction horizontally and vertically. If the receiver

NOTE

Double Your Power, Double Your Fun

Double the power level and the signal increases 3 dB. Halve the power level and the signal decreases 3 dB.

Double the distance from transmitter to receiver and the signal level decreases 6 dB. Halve the distance from transmitter to receiver and the signal increases 6 dB.

has two antennas, angle them into a V. Keep line of sight between the transmitter and receiver antennas, and if you have to, go higher. You can mount the receiver on a ladder or c-stand out of view.

Keep the transmitter on the receiver side. If the transmitter has to pass through the actor's or subject's body, the signal will be absorbed, cutting the range. Don't forget to check behind the set—sometimes the best spot for a receiver is behind the actors, not in front. If an actor or a subject is moving around a lot, you can have a PA carry the receiver.

Remote Antenna

Most wireless rigs come with *quarter-wave whips* mounted to the front or rear of the receiver. The quarter-wave whip is called that because its overall length is 1/4 that of the RF signal wavelength. Most of them will work just fine. If you need more range, you may have to use a remote antenna.

If you need to go remote, replace the quarter-wave whip. Quarter-wave whips are low impedance and don't have a proper ground plane other than the chassis of the receiver. Because a ground plane is the other half of the antenna, using a quarter-wave whip is actually worse than using no antenna because the antenna feed will pick up extraneous RF.

Replacement antennas can be divided into omnidirectional and directional antennas. Usually, an omnidirectional antenna will do the job.

Directional antennas have a pattern that provides high gain in the front and rejection at the back of the antenna. One common type is the yagi. *Yagis* have one active element, have narrow frequency coverage, are forward directional to about 60° and provide up to 5 dB of gain. They look like a miniature version of a rooftop TV antenna. If you use a directional antenna, be sure it's matched for the frequency range and input impedance of the receiver, and be sure to aim it at the transmitter for best results.

Pay attention to your cabling. A *transmission line* is any cabling used to transfer an electrical signal between equipment. This includes antennas. Coaxial cable gives the best results for antennas. For maximum transfer of energy, the impedance of the coax must match the antenna and the receiver. Almost all communications equipment is designed to be 50W with the exception of television, which is either 300W or 75W. Use the 50W. The recommended coaxial cable for this application is RG-58A/U.

Multiple Wireless

Often you're faced with having to use multiple wireless mics. You can use multiple wireless rigs, but every transmitter must have a receiver on the same frequency, and each receiver/transmitter must be on a different frequency. Cable from the receivers into a mixer to be controlled, just like the signals from standard mics.

Generally, every diversity receiver on your set should have its own set of antennas. However, you can use several receivers on one set within the same frequency range using an RF distribution amp, or *splitter*. To make this system work, every receiver on the antenna requires a split, and every time a split is made, some signal is lost. An *active splitter* is a powered device that splits and amplifies, whereas a *passive splitter* just handles the splitting. Selective filters are also used to further protect from interference.

A *quad box* consists of four individual receivers in a compact case that includes a splitter, one or two antennas, and a power supply. Quad boxes are convenient, but sometimes you'll get better performance by separating the receivers and placing them closer to the action.

Multiple wireless mics may present problems. Actors close to each other may generate a buzz in the wireless system, so set the frequencies as far apart as possible. Another problem is spurious emissions, occurring when transmitters radiate unwanted frequencies. They can be reduced through filtering and using well-constructed transmitter housings. A good housing is one molded piece of metal, and while small round holes are okay, there shouldn't be any slits for radio frequencies to escape through. A tight transmitter is also less susceptible to outside interference and just more durable.

If you rent a wireless rig or quad box, rent a good one. The cheap ones just aren't worth the trouble.

AUDIO ON THE DV SET

First, put fresh batteries in everything.

Watch the blocking. If the director or DP hasn't already done this, one of them will explain how the scene is going to be shot. The boom op can rehearse mic placement as the sound mixer will determine whether the audio crew needs to make any changes to the audio gear for the scene.

MOUNTING THE GEAR

Mount all the equipment. Sometimes, the director will request that the actors be rigged with lavs. You may not use the hidden mics, but it's easier to just do it and not argue.

If you're using an Audio-Technica 8415 or similar mount, use the *over-under technique*. Spread the rubber bands on one end wide so they cross one another, and slide the mic in. Do the same thing on the other end. It will keep that mic in place.

You must use some kind of windshield, even indoors. Shotgun mics are so sensitive that the air rushing by the mic as you move it can cause noise. If you have a zeppelin, mount the pistol grip on the boom, slide the mic carefully into place, and seal it up. If you don't have a zeppelin, use the foam windscreen. Slide it all the way onto the mic, and then pull it back, leaving about one inch of air between the end of the mic and the windscreen.

You'll know the windscreen is out far enough when it clears the roll-off switch on the microphone. I usually pinch the tip with my thumb and forefinger to make sure there's enough room.

If you have no windscreen, use some cheesecloth that you can get at any grocery store. Just keep winding it around the mic until it's covered. Be careful to tape the side of the mic away from the actors, and don't cover the holes. That can destroy its directionality.

PLUGGING IN

Talk with the camera operator about your method for plugging and unplugging your cables. Don't just walk over and do it. Some camera operators are very protective of their gear and for good reason. If that camera takes a tumble, that might be the end of the show.

Plug in your mic and headphone cables. The sound mixer and boom op usually end up handling the audio cables, so keep everything tidy. If you need help, get a PA to be your cable puller.

SETTING LEVELS

In analog recorders, if you go over zero, the distortion will be gradual and may not even be noticeable. In digital audio, zero is absolute zero. There's no forgiveness. The maximum record level on a digital audio recorder is expressed as 0 dBfs, or *0 decibels at full scale*. 0 dBfs is the loudest you can go with digital audio. If the signal goes over zero, it *clips*, or distorts. The distortion is immediate and ugly. You need *headroom*, a little bit of margin, so if someone gets loud, your signal doesn't go past zero. With digital audio levels, it's much safer for levels to be on the low side.

One of the best ways to figure out at what level your DV camera will perform best is to test it. Set up your audio rig and record normal dialogue, whispers, and shouts. Try them at different settings. You may even be able to do this during rehearsal in preproduction.

Play the audio back on the editing system and see which works best without distorting.

If this is the first time you've been confronted with a DV camera or the audio equipment, and there isn't time for testing, drop the audio into auto and see where the levels fluctuate. The automatic gain control, or AGC, will kick in, so try to do this without long pauses.

Switch back into manual audio and set levels based on that test. This technique isn't as good as a full test, but it's better than running at AGC.

You may also need to set up your audio equipment so everything is within acceptable levels. The meter on your mixer and the meter on your camera measure different things. The 0 dB on your mixer's meter is often expressed as 0 VU, with VU standing for *volume units*. Even if your audio hits 0 VU, you still have some room on an analog mixer for peaking. Not so with digital.

You want to match up your mixer's meters with the camera so you don't have peaking anywhere along the signal path and so you can keep an eye on your levels from the mixer. That way you don't have to constantly hover over the camera, dodging the camera operator, to make sure nothing is clipping.

Because loudness is subjective, you need a standardized reference. The reference tone that plays with the color bars for digital equipment is a 1kHz sinewave. That's your reference tone.

Turn on both the camera's AGC and the mixer's tone generator. Set the mixer controls so its meter reads 0 VU, making sure that no single rotary control or slider is cranked to maximum.

Pay attention to how the camera meter responds while on auto. It's the best indication you have of what the manufacturer thinks is the best level for that device. Set the camera back on manual and adjust the camera's volume control for the level the AGC indicated. It should be around –20 dBfs. If your camera isn't calibrated to decibels, set it to the nominal 0 VU. This is not 0 dB, which should be the top of a digital meter, but should be well below the top of the meter.

If you're using a mixing board, you'll also have to set the preamp for each mic. Set the slider or rotary and trim control for each mic to zero. As the actor or subject speaks, bring up the slider or rotary control. Fine-tune by adjusting the rotary trim pot for that mic until you're getting peaks just over 0 VU on the mixer's meter. It usually doesn't take much. Now back off a bit with the slider or rotary control.

You'll continue to adjust levels as the actors rehearse. Be sure to play back the first few takes to make sure everything is set correctly. Listen for crackles, pops, and squeaks—these are signs that the level is clipping somewhere along the audio chain.

Setting the recorder for –20 dBfs should give you 20 decibels of headroom. Unfortunately, some camera manufacturers use cheap analog circuits, so you can't be absolutely sure until you've tried the equipment and settings. Pay attention and ask for playback until you're satisfied or the director orders you to move on.

Defeating AGC

Many DV cameras have AGC. These devices will automatically set the gain to record audio, and if there's a pause in the dialogue or an interview, the AGC will pump up, looking for something to record. As soon as someone starts talking again, the AGC will drop. You can hear the AGC pump and wheeze throughout the audio. It's really annoying and hard to cut when you're editing.

AGC is the equivalent of an auto-iris. Shut it off. Manual control is preferred. You'll be able to keep your audio within the dynamic range of the recording system, adjust the levels to suit the subject, and maintain consistent sound over a number of shots or takes.

If you can't turn off the AGC, one trick is to set your manual volume control low through a Beachtek or other attenuator and send in the signal from the mixer. This forces the AGC to maximum, eliminating the wheezing and pumping. Make sure you route to both channels or the AGC will kick in.

Forcing AGC can result in more noise from the camera's preamp. It's really up to you whether the pumping from the AGC is more annoying than the noisy preamp.

You do have another option: dual-system sound.

DUAL-SYSTEM SOUND

Many DV moviemakers use dual-system sound as a solution for noisy camera sound or nondefeatable AGC.

In addition to cleaner audio, another big benefit of dual-system sound is how much more freedom the audio crew has. Because the sound mixer may not have to keep a cable between the mixer and the camera, he or she can move anywhere to get the best audio. This is especially true for wild dialogue and sound effects. The sound mixer can poach during a rehearsal or off the set without having to bother the camera operator.

Because the audio recording is separate from the camera, the sound mixer isn't limited to the audio specs of DV. He or she doesn't have to worry about defeating AGC, camera and handling noise, or noisy preamps. Also, the audio can be recorded at higher bit and sampling rates.

Still, there's some extra work involved. You will need a bit more time for each take, the sound mixer MUST keep accurate sound logs, and you'll spend more time in post syncing audio with picture. Budget your time and money accordingly.

First figure out how you are going to handle post so that you know for certain that the systems you use work with your system. You may have excellent location audio recorded with a Nagra, an analog system, but have no way to digitize it other than the standard sound card that came with your computer. If you want to transfer digital audio into your computer and remain in the digital domain, you'll need a card in your computer that will allow you to accept the recording format.

Remember, too, that DV accepts 16-bit 48kHz stereo audio. If you want to master your audio to higher bit and sampling rates, you'll need to master to a different format.

Going Wild

You can use any audio recorder—it doesn't have to be digital, have timecode, or have any other bells and whistles. As long as it runs at a constant rate, it will work. You'll want to pay attention to the quality of the audio —why run dual-system if you don't gain anything by it?

Use clapper sticks at the head of every shot as a sync point. You may also want to mark the end of every shot, especially for a documentary. Hold the slate upside down, call the shot and take number, and clap. This is called a *tail slate*.

In post, you line up the picture and the claps. People who work with film have been doing this for years, and it works nicely, even though it takes time.

Two of the most common recorders on the DV set are MiniDisks (MD) and DATs. None of the consumer or prosumer DV cameras offer timecode, video sync, or genlock inputs or outputs. Neither do MD or consumer DAT recorders. However, all of them have fairly precise internal digital master clocks.

Unfortunately, at some point the master clocks in the camera and recorder will lose sync with each other without a shared time reference. There's no way to predict when—it varies depending on your equipment. Still, MD and consumer DAT can work fine with short shots or shots that are really wide. Also, if you have complex camera moves, especially with a Steadicam or similar stabilizer, a couple of these little recorders rigged directly to your actors can work in lieu of a wireless system.

MD and DAT   MD uses a data reduction scheme called Adaptive Transform Acoustic Coding, or ATRAC. This is a data-reduction algorithm that now seems to work quite well, especially for typically limited dynamic range audio such as dialogue and ambient. While MD may not sound as good as DAT, it is much better than analog cassette.

Unfortunately, most of these recorders have either no recording level adjustments or recording levels that can only be adjusted while in pause. Also, MD does not have nor does it support any kind of timecode. There's no simple way to plug in pro mics and mixers. MD uses stereo miniplug ins and outs, poor metering, and a rather delicate construction.

Still, MD recorders can be handy, since they're relatively inexpensive and small. You can slide one into someone's pocket and clip a lav to a collar with minimal fuss. You may also want to look at the HHB MDP-500 professional MD recorder at `www.hhbusa.com` and read Dan Brockett's review of this recorder at the LAFCPUG Web site at `www.lafcpug.org/review_mini_disc_rec.html`.

A digital audio tape, or DAT, recorder works in similar fashion as helical scan video systems. The tape is drawn from the cassette by the tape transport and wrapped around a record and playback head rotating at a high rate of speed. This drum lays the digital audio data in a series of diagonal lines for high information density on tape. A servo system keeps the spinning head and linear tape transport locked together using an internal crystal oscillator.

Most consumer DAT recorders don't accept external timecode, so you must rely on the recorder's ability to play back correctly using an internal clock.

Many consumer MDs and DATs have AGC and noisy preamps as well. While your sound crew may have more mobility, you're not really gaining much in audio quality.

If you want to use an MD or a consumer DAT recorder, you may want to look at the MDReport and MDReport Junior at the PMI Audio Web site, `www.pmiaudio.com/mdreport.html`. These boxes give you additional professional features.

Using Timecode

Timecode marks every single recorded frame and allows you to sync between recorders. If you decide to use dual-system sound on your set, decide whether you want to use timecode. First, make sure your recorder and DV camera take a sync reference. No use getting timecode audio equipment if you can't match up audio to picture using timecode.

Timecode, while very useful, is not a requirement for dual-system sound. The mobility you gain running dual-system is lost when cabling audio recorders and cameras to a single clock source. However, if you need higher bit and sampling rates, or multitrack recording with a DA-88 or other multitracker, you may as well save yourself some effort and use timecode.

Basically, timecode is fed from one device, the master, to a second device, the slave. The slave device follows the timecode transmitted by the master. There are several different ways to generate timecode, but the one you'll probably run into on a DV set is jam sync.

Jam sync allows the slave to compare incoming timecode with code written to the slave's track that was generated by a built-in or outboard synchronizer. The slave device will search for the correct spot on the track and then adjust speed until its code equals the master code. When it's in the right place, usually you'll get some sort of indicator, such as an LED coming on, indicating that sync is locked.

Jam sync refers specifically to a synchronizer's ability to generate code if something happens to the timecode from the source. This keeps the devices running and in sync. Timecode accuracy can be affected, but if the drop-out is for a short period, jam sync works fine.

To use jam sync (or any timecode mode), first make sure the timecode format is exactly the same across all the devices. Use the camera as the master and jam sync all other devices to it, although you can also use an independent master clock to camera, recorder, or smart slate. This can be very handy for multicamera shoots. Rejam code every three to four hours to maintain the lock, and if possible, feed the camera the same audio to your audio recorder as a backup.

You'll get better quality audio by using a good field mixer with your recorder. Although some DAT field recorders have stereo inputs and phantom power, their preamps can be noisy, and they just don't give you the same amount of control. Also, make sure you have enough stock and batteries.

EQ AND OTHER TRICKS

Equalization, or EQ, was created to remove unwanted frequencies or correct other problems in an audio signal. But like everything cool, people began experimenting with it and discovered new ways of manipulating sound for certain effects.

On a set, EQ is handy for plant mics and lavaliers. You can equalize their sound to match the main boom mic, but it's easier to do this in post. If you're getting some rumble, use the bass roll-off switch on the mic because it's more subtle.

Do not try to use EQ to match audio from set to set or shot to shot. I've seen it done, usually by people who claim expertise in location sound mixing because they've run the mixer for their friends' bands. It's not the same thing.

Other than using the bass roll-off on the microphone, or a bit of tweaking for a really windy day, your goal is to get the cleanest sound you possibly can. You can always EQ the audio in post.

MULTIPLE MICS

Phase cancellation, which results in low-level and hollow-sounding audio, occurs when two or more mics pick up sound from the same audio source. Because the sounds arrive at the mic at slightly different times, they end up being out of phase and, to various degrees, cancel each other out. When multiple mics are used on a set, there are four things you can do to reduce or eliminate the resulting phase cancellation:

- Turn down mics any time they are not needed.
- Place mics as close as possible to sound sources.
- Use directional mics.
- Use an automated mixer.

If you're running only two mics, send each to its own channel. For example, during interviews for nonfiction projects, I have my Audio-Technica 4073 short shotgun on an Audio-Technica 8415 shockmount mounted on a carbon fiber boom clamped onto a c-stand. The mic is placed just out of camera view above and in front of the subject, with the mic point right at his or her mouth.

I then rig a lavalier, either my Sanken COS-11 or Sony ECM 77, on the person. Both mics are sent to my Behringer 1604 mixing board, where I pan the boom mic hard right and the lav hard left, separating them on two different stereo channels. If one of the mics fails or the signal peaks on one channel, I have the other as a backup. I don't bother EQ'ing the lav—if I need to match, I do that in post.

The boom operator should wear headphones to monitor the entire mix, not just the boom mic. If there are problems, especially with phase cancellation, the boom operator and sound mixer must both respond immediately.

GETTING THE TAKE

While the set is being lit, the sound mixer will send reference tone from the mixer as the DP sends color bars from the camera to set up the monitor. The DP will set camera audio levels. When everyone is happy with the levels, record 60 seconds of bars and tone.

The sound mixer should adjust headphone levels so that the reference tone sounds as loud as a loud telephone conversation. Dialogue is not the same as tone, so normal dialogue at correct levels will sound comfortably distinct.

During rehearsal, the sound mixer should direct the boom operator in mic placement, as well as let the DP, gaffer, or grip know whether there's an avoidable problem with lighting.

The sound mixer should get room tone from every single location before the first take. Although you can grab pieces of room tone in post, it's good practice to get it separately. I prefer getting tone before the first take because it helps calm people down. I also prefer that my sound mixer be a bit assertive regarding audio requirements, but I'm unusual in this. Most directors would rather the sound mixer ask permission first, and the sound mixer should be prepared to be rejected. It doesn't make sense, but it happens. When everyone is in place and permission given, the sound mixer will scream, "QUIET, PLEASE! ROOM TONE! DO NOT MOVE! DO NOT TALK! BREATHE OUT OF YOUR MOUTH! ROOM TONE STARTING NOW!"

The camera operator will get the recorder going, slate with the scene number, and record for 60 seconds. The sound mixer will then call, "CUT! THANK YOU!"

Many sound mixers will get room tone after the scene, but many people leave the set or are concentrating on moving equipment for the next setup and shift around too much. Doing it first also helps you teach the entire ensemble that when someone calls for quiet, that means QUIET.

If there's a problem with a take, the sound mixer should speak to the director or AD immediately. This should be done quietly, not shouted across the set. For some takes, especially wide master shots, the sound mixer may know the director is going in for close-ups and other cutaways. It may not be necessary to redo the master shot just for audio.

When the scene is completed, the sound mixer may request a *wild take*. This means the audio is recorded without regard to picture. The boom operator will move in very close to the actors to record optimal levels. The idea is that if the director has the dialogue, he or she may be able to replace the poor recording with the optimal one.

Make sure the actors re-create their blocking, business, and delivery. You won't get lip sync, but you may get some good material that can save you a reshoot later. If the problem is prop noise, request that the actors not use the props. And remember: "Loop it!" is rarely an acceptable solution to audio problems.

The sound mixer and boom operator may also request sound effects recording. Many sound effects can be added later, but a set may have a certain sound to it, and sound effects recorded there will match the feel and tone. Slate them with the scene number. The sound mixer can elect to record all of the sound effects for that location in one shot. It all depends on the sound mixer's practice and what the producer and director want to do.

LOCATION AUDIO TRICKS

Prosumer cameras can be very sensitive to the presence of any AC grounding problems, especially when there's a video monitor nearby. This is less of a problem when the video monitor is powered from batteries, but not in all cases. If you hear a buzz and have already checked all your connections, try switching your monitor to DC.

Power cords can create hum and interference. Fluorescent lights can also cause an annoying buzz. Listen carefully to find any problems, and correct them before the first take. Sometimes all you have to do is move the mic cable away from power cords.

Shut off refrigerators, freezers, air compressors, and other equipment. Just remember to turn them back on. You can do this by leaving the crew car keys in or on the equipment. Shut off the central air. If you can't do that, you may be getting noise from air turbulence around the vents, so remove the vent covers to minimize the noise. That should do it, but if it's still too loud, you may even have to block the vents.

Whenever a room has smooth, unbroken walls or uncarpeted floors, reverberation can be a problem. Cut sound reflections by sticking couch cushions, blankets, and other cushy material around the room. Throw a sound blanket on the floor if the actor has to walk around. Put a piece of foam core on the desk if the actor is going to put something down.

If the actors are walking on an uncarpeted floor, consider putting foot foam on their shoes. Foot foam is adhesive backed, thin neoprene rubber that can be cut and stuck on shoes, glasses, or anything else. Dr. Scholl's footpads are also a good substitute.

To protect the furry, empty a full can of ScotchGuard onto it for rain protection. In heavy rain or when using fire hoses, put a condom over the microphone.

Be aggressive with mic placement. Get in there. Sometimes you have to be a bit demanding to get the best placement. If the producer gets annoyed, well, you did your best.

Don't use booms telescoped to full length. Extend each section as far as it'll go, and then slide each section back a few inches before locking it. The joints will have greater strength and won't creak (see Figure 23.7).

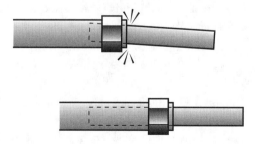

FIGURE 23.7

Boom joints should always overlap.

Also, the clutch that locks the sections can wear out. Put a layer of plumber's Teflon tape around the threads.

To hide or plant a mic, tape one to the back of a prop or set dressing, such as a vase or napkin dispenser. Listen to the mic before the take to make sure the levels are good and everything is on axis.

OTHER AUDIO GEAR

If the director wants to monitor audio, you can rig another set of headphones. Just be careful when the director yells cut and barrels toward the actors to discuss what just went wrong. The headphones or cable can get yanked hard enough to break.

- **Walkie-talkies**—I use consumer walkie-talkies that work fine. They're very small, come with headsets for hands-free communication, and work well. Be sure they're locked to the same channel and have their ringers turned off. You can always rent pro walkie-talkies.

- **Furniture blankets**—Furniture blankets are padded pieces of fabric used to wrap furniture when moving. They're great for cutting sound reflections, and because they have grommets, you can easily hang them. You can rent them from a rental house or buy them at a local hardware store. If that fails, use some quilting material from your local fabric store.

- **Audio adapters**—Get an array of RCA to 1/4", 1/4" to miniplug, and other adapters, and keep them in a small plastic box.

- **Cotton gardening gloves**—Cotton gloves are cheap and can cut down on handling noise. The cotton palms will pad your hands so you can slide the boom without making noise.

- **Ponytailers**—Ponytailers from Goody can be opened or closed with one hand and are ideal for holding cable or keeping mic wires from rattling. Get at least two dozen and keep some on hand at all times.

- **Carabineers or Velcro hook-and-loop straps**—These will handle extra loops of cable. Get one for the sound mixer and one for the boom op.

- **Small flashlights**—Flashlights are handy no matter your job or where you are. In addition to lighting dark basements, you can use a small one to light the side of a camera or other recorder to make sure the connectors are getting into the right places. You can also use the flashlight for practice sessions with untrained audio crew. Have them extend the boom and try to keep the light on the actor's mouth. This is a great way to audition boom op candidates.

EXPENDABLES

Just about everything for audio operates from batteries. Even if you have enough AC and proper adapters, try to run equipment off of batteries in order to avoid the risk of AC-induced noise. Noise travels along electrical wiring, even when the outlets are on different circuits. Also, you can move a little faster if you don't have to worry about pulling cable.

Many field mixers use 9-volt batteries. Separate power supplies for mics also use 9-volt, as do Comteks and popular wireless mics. Walkie-talkies may take 9-volt, AA, or AAA batteries. Other equipment will have other particular battery requirements. Always have a spare dozen of every battery standing by.

Discarded batteries from the sound cart are fine for most consumer devices, so you can use them in walkie-talkies or flashlights. Just don't use them in your audio gear.

Purchase all of your batteries from a reputable supplier. Check some with a battery tester you can get from Radio Shack to ensure that they are fresh and putting out full capacity.

Other items that you will need include

- Cloth camera tape (all colors)
- Gaffer's tape
- Surgical tape for rigging lavs and cables to skin
- Alcohol prep pads or cotton pads and Sea Breeze for cleaning skin prior to rigging lavs and taping cable to skin
- Rubber bands
- Safety pins
- Markers
- Flashlight
- Pocketknife
- Mini-tool kit
- Static Guard for clothing when planting lavs on people
- Ace bandages for rigging transmitters under pants
- Canned air
- Condoms for waterproofing mics and wireless

PAPERWORK

On most DV sets, the sound mixer rarely fills out an audio log or a sound report. He or she may call notes to whoever is handling the camera log, but don't expect the information to get recorded unless the director insists on the practice. The sound crew can always record important information into the slate mic at the head or tail of the take.

For sets where the sound mixer knows there's going to be a problem editing the dialogue, insist that the information get into the camera log. Consider noting takes, or portions of takes, with good sound. This will help the editor find usable audio.

Have all wild takes, walla, room tone, and sound effects noted in the camera log. It will be easier to track.

RENTING GEAR

You don't have to buy every last piece of gear manufactured to make movies. That's a waste of resources. Keep your purchases to a minimum. For the rest, you can go to your local rental house. You can find them in the phone book under Video Equipment Rentals, through your local film commission listings, or on the Web.

Rental houses fall into three categories:

- Film equipment
- Video equipment
- Grip and gaffer equipment

Film equipment houses generally specialize in film cameras, lenses, and other gear. They may have some video equipment and a small selection of lighting, audio, gaff, and grip gear. Although you may not be renting from them, it's good to know what they have in case you have to.

Video rental houses specialize in video equipment. They usually have a selection of lighting, audio, grip, and gaffer equipment. Many houses focus on high-end professional analog equipment. They have Beta SP cameras and decks and work most often with local television stations and production companies doing commercials, corporate, and similar types of shows.

They're bringing in more DV equipment, although it's taking a while. It's hard for the owners of these shops to know where to invest. Some of the video houses are focusing more on the DV format. They have a selection of DV cameras and decks for you to choose from.

Grip houses rent grip, lighting, and gaff equipment that will rent you a single light or enough equipment to fill a soundstage. They also offer grip trucks—panel vehicles with gear packed on specially designed shelving for easy access. Sometimes they sell gear and expendables, such as gels and gaffer tape, as well.

MAKING CONTACT

After you have an idea of the equipment you're going to need, call the rental houses in your area and schedule appointments. Call midweek in the afternoon, when things are usually pretty slow. If at all possible, tour the facility to see what they have and what kind of services they offer.

I always go to the rental house a few weeks before renting anything. Bring your equipment wish list and tentative shooting schedule. Discuss with the sales rep and technicians what you need and why you need it. Often they'll suggest other equipment in place of or in addition to what you have listed. Pay attention. Sometimes they want you to rent higher-priced gear. Sometimes, though, what they suggest will be easier and cheaper for you in the long run.

If they're not busy, many rental house people will show you how to put together the gear and how to operate it. Many people who work in rental houses like independents and think what we do is interesting. Others may throw some attitude—they probably *will* throw attitude—but who cares? The quality of your show is not dependent on the rental house workers' collective opinion of you.

I try to maintain a professional attitude and don't pretend I know what every little clip and doodad is for. Often rental technicians are fairly knowledgeable, and there's usually at least one person who knows what's what.

TIP

Mohammed Goes to the Mountain

If you don't live near a rental house, or want a piece of equipment you can't get locally, many rental companies will ship equipment, at extra cost, anywhere you need it. Shipping charges are paid by the renter. Ship everything one-day air. You'll pay more for shipping but save on the rental.

PRICING AND DEALS

Don't expect the rental house to let you walk out with anything if payment hasn't been arranged.

Every producer pleads poverty, even the ones with big budgets. Be honest about what you can afford. Rates are based on daily rental.

Rental houses often have 3-for-7 deals: You pay for three days, but you get the equipment for a week. You can often get a discount at certain times of the year. A lot of shows go into production in spring and summer. If you can handle the weather changes, consider shooting in fall or winter.

Some rental companies offer discounts for long-term rentals. Ask about them. If there's no discount, or it's not sweet enough, consider quick turn-around: Pick up and drop off everything as soon as you're done with it. You save money and you don't have to haul around dolly track or a jib arm that you don't need.

Ask about travel day discounts. Travel days are days when you have the equipment, but it's being transported to the location and you can't use it.

Finally, keep in mind that it's easy to overlook the value of convenience. Although grip trucks may seem expensive, they make production more efficient by keeping everything organized and safely stowed. They have hydraulic lifts to make loading and unloading easier, saving wear and tear on your crew. The little grip trucks aren't hard to drive, but be sure you budget gas money.

Most rental houses will require that you show proof of insurance. If you request it in advance, your insurance company will fax a certificate of insurance to them. If you don't have an insurance provider, the rental company should be able to provide the name of one.

Some rental houses also offer house insurance billed as a percentage of the daily rental fee, multiplied by each calendar day that the equipment is in your possession. Others require a steep damage deposit for uninsured productions. Finally, some rental houses will waive insurance costs if one of their employees is on your crew.

WHAT TO GET, HOW TO GET IT, AND WHEN

Rental equipment comes in packages or as separate pieces. Generally, you get enough gear to make the thing work.

For example, camera packages usually come with the camera, lens, power supply, battery charger, tripod, and plate. They may or may not include a field monitor with power supply, batteries, and charger. Be sure to ask.

Light packages usually include the fixtures, stands, scrims, barn doors, cables, and some gels. They should have spare lamps, but ask to make sure they're included. Some kits may include a couple of dimmers, but ask what's in the package. If the kit doesn't have complete gel or diffusion sets, you'll need to get some. You may find some black wrap, but you'll probably need more.

Tripods almost always come with heads, although you have to ask for spreaders. Dollies may or may not come with track. Jib arms may or may not come with tripod legs. If you're renting a car mount, the day rate usually doesn't include mounting it. Unless you know what you're doing, have the rental house technician mount it on your picture car or you may end up with big scratches on your Aunt Edna's new Chevy. This applies to other specialty mounts as well.

You'll have to request grip equipment as separate pieces. C-stands usually come with grip heads and arms. At least one should have a rocky mountain leg. Consider getting some mafer clamps with spuds, cardellini clamps, and anything else you need. You have to ask for individual reflectors, butterflies, and overheads, specifying the size and material, although more rental houses are offering modular kits.

Flags, nets, and silks, as well as dots and fingers, may or may not come in a variety of sizes and loaded in a large box on wheels (see Figures 24.1 and 24.2).

Smoke and fog machines usually come with fluid. Dry ice machines don't include dry ice. You may be able to get some from your local grocery store, although you should check ahead of time.

Audio equipment usually doesn't come in a kit, although the rental house usually includes audio cables for free. You may have to ask for specific adapters, but don't expect the rental house to have adapter boxes for prosumer DV cameras. Wireless systems usually include one microphone, transmitter, and receiver, although you need to request better antennas. Field mixers often require 9-volt batteries you'll need to supply.

You can never have too many stingers. And try to get at least one sandbag for every light and c-stand.

FIGURE 24.1

Flag boxes are great, though heavy, and carry an array of flags, nets, and silks of various sizes. Courtesy of Bexel, Inc.

FIGURE 24.2

Flag box and rack of c-stands in a grip truck. Courtesy of Bexel, Inc.

Special equipment, such as cranes, Fisher microphone booms, portable scaffolding, and so on, should come complete. Don't consider using this equipment without an experienced crew.

PICK-UP

You don't pay for the equipment until you actually use it. However, if the gear is in high demand, you may need to give the house a deposit to lock in a reservation. If you lock in, you pay whether you use the gear or not. If your plans change, let the rental house know as soon as you can.

Usually, you can pick up the equipment in the afternoon of the day before and return it on the morning after the shoot. If the rental house is closed due to holiday or weekend, you don't pay. A Saturday rental is usually a one-day rental but covers Friday afternoon to Monday morning.

Before you leave the rental house, check the rental package to make sure you have everything. Even the best houses will forget a crucial cable or adapter. It's a pain, but unpack each piece and make sure everything's there and operating. Better to find out a battery charger is missing now, than when you really need it.

Test the gear, especially cameras and audio equipment. The rental house will not be liable if the equipment didn't work properly.

Make sure all the stands have the correct pins for the equipment. If you have junior stands and lights with baby receivers, make sure they give you adapter pins.

All the batteries should be charged. Usually, there's a piece of camera tape over the elements with the recharge date on them. This is a good practice. Try to follow it as you recharge batteries in the field.

Be sure to get a signed agreement regarding the rental terms, cost, check-out and return times, and terms of liability. It should list every single item you're renting. Keep this piece of paper with you and use it when you double-check for return at the end of your shoot.

Finally, get an emergency contact number.

MANAGING THE GEAR

Whether you bought or rented, someone is going to have to manage the gear. For lighting and electrical, this job is handled by the *best boy (electric)*. For grip equipment, it's done by the *best boy (grip)*. For the camera, it's the camera crew or DP.

You may or may not need two people handling the gear—it depends on how much you have. Usually, the person with the most experience, often a DP or grip, will take charge and get everything packed and into the production vehicle just fine.

Just be sure each piece gets returned to its proper case with all the correct accessories. It needs to be stowed safely, yet easily accessible to the crew. Lamp replacements and repairs have to get done quickly.

Many independent producers use their cars as production vehicles. Often, the car is too small and the producer has to come up with a complicated arrangement to get everything in. Everybody waits until the producer is available to load up. This is not a good use of the producer's time.

Vans, RVs, and pickup trucks are very handy. Two-door sports cars are not. It may seem like a minor matter, but just think about packing all this stuff up at the end of a very long day.

Consider how you're going to get the gear where you need it. Most gear, rental or not, comes in large, and heavy, shipping cases. Make sure they're all on wheels and have a hand truck available.

I know producers who bring unpaid volunteers onto their shoots just to help with load-in and load-out. The volunteers stand around for 12 hours doing nothing until it's time to go. They usually don't come back the next day.

Keep track of your rental contracts. Some producers create equipment sheets and have the best boys list any repairs or replacements separately.

If a piece of equipment should stop working, inform the rental house immediately. Arrange replacement or return the item, making sure you're credited with the early return.

DROP OFF

When you're finished with the equipment, load it up, using your rental contract as the checklist. The rental technicians will unpack and check their list to make sure everything's where it should be and that nothing is broken.

If something's missing, notify your insurer immediately. If it was stolen, your insurer will require you to file a police report. If you haven't done that already, do it now. Contact your insurance representative for further instruction.

The rental house may require you to reimburse it while you wait for your insurer to reimburse you. This is a drag—your post-production funds are tied up because your insurer can't handle its responsibilities. To avoid this situation, stay on top of your insurance agent. You may find yourself calling every week for two months before you receive a check.

PROPS, SETS, AND SET DRESSING

In Step II, you generated lists of props you will need and ideas for set dressings. In production, these seemingly small details can lend authenticity and character to your movie's aesthetics—or become a logistic and artistic nightmare. When it comes to props, sets, and set dressing, once again simplicity and organization are key to your show's success.

PROPS

Obviously, you'll want to borrow as many props as you can, and out of necessity there are some you will have to buy. But other props can be easily and inexpensively made as long as you give yourself enough time to get them done. Often, you can make a prop by modifying an existing item. You can always sculpt objects from urethane or Styrofoam. Papier-mâché is inexpensive, safe, and relatively quick. Determine how durable the item has to be before choosing a material.

There are many books and Web sites devoted to the subject. See Resources for listings.

CASTING PROPS

You can create molds and cast replicas of an object. Thurston James's *The Prop Builder's Molding & Casting Handbook* is a good resource on casting objects, although there are many other books and Web sites on the topic.

Props can be molded and cast using a variety of materials. There are three basic steps:

- Finding and preparing a model
- Creating a mold
- Making and finishing a cast

You can use an existing model or create your own using modeling clay or other materials. Spend time creating the mold. A good mold is often the difference between a realistic prop and an unrealistic one.

Soft casting materials, those that remain soft even after curing, include latex, neoprene, silicone, and some urethanes. Plaster, polyester resins, and fiberglass are considered hard casting materials.

If you need any fake body part, DO NOT, UNDER ANY CIRCUM-STANCES, use plaster to create molds of living tissue. There is a proper way to create molds based on living tissue using alginate and other safe materials. Alginate is manufactured from seaweed and is safe, very fast setting, and won't adhere to anything.

See Chapter 27, "Explosions, Gunplay, and Fistfights: When to Call In the Experts," for tips on special effects makeup, including appliances.

Mold making and casting are really fun. Give yourself plenty of time to practice and be mindful of safety. Some of the materials require or generate heat, so wear protective clothing, and because some materials give off fumes, work in a well-ventilated area.

BREAKAWAY FURNITURE

Chairs and tables can have their legs removed and reattached with a touch of glue, toothpicks, tiny wood wedges, and so on. The lightest blow will dislodge them. Styrofoam and balsa wood are often used to create breakaway props as well. You will probably need more than one of any prop that will be broken. For example, if an actor breaks a prop chair during the master shot, you will need a matching chair for the next shot.

Remember that even with breakaway props, actors are still hitting each other. Choreograph and rehearse before proceeding.

BREAKAWAY GLASS

Some stunt performers, wearing protective gear and with years of experience, will jump through real glass. The glass is prepped with a tool called a glass breaker, which is a small spring-loaded arm with a sharp metal tip. Glass breakers are rigged to the bottom of the glass and triggered a fraction of a second before the stunt performer goes flying through it.

There are safer, and cheaper, alternatives. Any trained special effects coordinator or stunt technician will be able to help you decide on the best course of action.

You can purchase breakaway glass sheets and props from a theatrical or special effects supply store. Check your local film commission directory or see Resources for listings.

You can also make breakaway glass props. Sugar glass has been used to make many different types of objects. The idea is based on rock candy recipes and you can search cookbooks for ideas. Most sugar glass props have flaws in them, such as air bubbles and flow lines. If the prop will be substituted at the last moment, it may not matter.

If you decide to make your own breakaway glass props, wear protective clothing, including leather gloves and apron, and a face shield. The sugar mixture must get to 300° Fahrenheit, whereas resin gets to 400° Fahrenheit.

The materials get quite messy, so try to keep everything as tidy as possible.

Sugar glass is not your only option for breakable props. For example, picco resin and other materials may serve your needs better. And props that are supposed to look like china can be cast using paraffin wax and painted on the surface. Keep the paraffin object in the refrigerator or freezer until the very moment of use to keep them brittle. They shatter nicely.

GUNS

If you are using guns in your show, you have a number of options, some of which are quite safe and relatively inexpensive. This is one area in which you can use Hollywood's established practices to your advantage.

There are three types of prop guns used in a movie:

- Practical
- Nonpractical
- Replicas, dummies, and rubber

Sugar Glass

1/2 cup water

1/2 cup light corn syrup

1 3/4 cup granulated sugar

Food coloring to tint the glass (you may want a hint of blue to fake clear glass)

Cream of tartar

Crisco, Pam, or other releasing agent

You may want to use a candy thermometer for best results.

Cover the inside of the mold with a releasing agent.

Bring the water to a boil, add the food coloring and corn syrup. Stir in the sugar until dissolved. Sprinkle in some cream of tartar and bring it to a gentle boil at 220° Fahrenheit. Let boil until the sugar is at the hard crack stage, about 300° Fahrenheit. Watch it so it doesn't burn.

Pour into the mold. For panes of glass, you can use a greased, flat metal cookie sheet or a large pan lined with baker's parchment. Let cool.

There are many armorers and suppliers of these and other prop weapons. See the Resources for listings. See Chapter 27 for information on special effects that mimic gunfire.

Practical

Practical guns are real guns that fire blank ammunition. If you intend to use practical guns—and there's no reason on God's green earth why you would—hire a special effects coordinator who is a firearms expert as your gun wrangler.

Blanks are dangerous. Although no bullet comes out on firing, superheated gases come out of the barrel that can set fire to sets, props, or wardrobe. Grains of gunpowder can embed themselves in skin, and brass from the shell and cardboard wadding can travel at incredible speeds. Blank guns should never be fired at anyone. If you want the effect of someone being targeted, have the actor aim offside and set the camera angle to create the illusion.

If a weapon will be discharged, make sure everyone on the set has earplugs.

Even if you won't be firing blanks, have your special effects coordinator teach your actors how to handle the weapon safely. Walk through rehearsals with the actors pointing their fingers and saying, "Bang!"

After the rehearsal is completed, the gun wrangler will load the weapons and hand them to the actors for the take. When the director calls, "Cut!" everyone freezes until the gun wrangler has gathered all the weapons back. Between takes, each weapon must be checked to make sure there are no jams.

Don't let anyone play with these weapons. A casual attitude toward safety will lead to injury.

Nonpractical

Nonpractical guns are real guns that have been deactivated so they can't fire anything. Many suppliers make nonpractical weapons with tungsten pins pressed into the barrels that can't be drilled out. These guns look good, work very nicely, and are so safe you can fire them directly with no safety hazard. Absolutely nothing exits the barrel. These guns are called "suicide guns" because you can use them for suicide scenes.

Many modern weapons have special designs to eliminate any flashing when a bullet is fired. This is often the opposite of what a moviemaker wants. If you need flashes, consider using a strobe light, especially for machine guns.

Replicas, Dummies, and Rubber

Replica guns are highly detailed in plastic or metal. Often, they function mechanically, but they don't fire. They're good for action sequences where there is no firing. Dummy guns are just the shell. They're often referred to as *holster fillers*. Rubber guns are good replicas and are used for stunts or when the actors need to run.

You can make some realistic-looking weapons by painting plastic cap guns. You can find detailed plastic cap guns with removable clips, working triggers, and so on in places like Wal-Mart, K-Mart, Target, and so on. You'll have to paint over the bright "toy" colors, but that's not too hard if all you need are black weapons. Your first step is to wash the plastic weapon with warm water and dish soap. You may want to use an old toothbrush to scrub the detailed areas. Use #600 grit wet sandpaper to score the plastic a little, helping the paint adhere to the prop.

Primer is an initial coat of paint specially formulated to provide a strong bond between paint and plastic. Common acrylic lacquer primers include Dupont 30-S or 131-S. Use the primer right out of the bottle and on the thick side, working it in the cracks. Let it dry completely.

Paint or spray a solid base coat of black over the entire weapon and let it dry. Buff with a soft cloth. Cover with a flat clear acrylic lacquer. Alternate layers of black paint and clear lacquer until it looks right. After the lacquer is thoroughly dry, it can be gently sanded with #2000 grit 3–M sandpaper.

Combining pieces of different models is one way armorers create unusual weapons for Hollywood movies. If you require such a weapon, you may be able to do this yourself. Just be sure to give yourself plenty of time to create the prop and don't expect it to fire anything.

SETS

Most DV producers use existing sets, usually because it's cheaper. But just because you're in a real place doesn't mean you have to settle for what's already there. Sometimes all it takes is to shift a chair or coffee table, and the room looks exactly right for the character.

It may be cheaper for you to build a set because you only create the side that will be seen by the camera. Every piece will be *wild*, meaning it can be moved in and out of position. Moving set pieces is called *flying in* or *flying out*, because the set flats are often on cables and rigged to a pulley system, much like a stage production.

You'll need a larger area if you plan to create and use a built set, as well as the time to do the work and money for materials. If you're on a soundstage or in a warehouse, this may work just fine. The best places for creating sets are high-ceilinged lofts, office spaces, and warehouses. If the place is already decorated, you can use it as one set, and then add and subtract elements to create other sets. You have room for lighting equipment, small cranes, and rigging set pieces.

You can always build false walls in existing rooms. Any basic carpentry or remodeling book can get you started, and you may want to check out some books on set building. Many cities, counties, and states require that false walls be built to code, so check with your film commission for information.

Be sure the false walls are secured tightly. Budget for materials as well as time. Using screws, rather than nails, makes building and breaking down go a lot faster. You also can salvage any plywood, drywall, and 2'×4's for the next set.

Surfaces and finishes on false walls can be an issue. You can use cheap paint, but it may not reproduce correctly on videotape. Theatrical supply shops sell paints and other finishes that are color correct, resist heat, and go on quickly. You can often dilute the paint or finish with water and still get a good result. Wallpaper goes on quickly and is a good option for making a new set out of an old one. You can create floors with cheap floor tiles and double-stick tape, while you can find window treatments and other materials at secondhand stores and junkyards.

Building a set requires good building techniques. Make sure there's adequate ventilation, safety guards on power equipment, and room to get the job done. Keep in mind that you'll need at least one vehicle to haul all of these materials, as well as large doorways and elevators in and out of the location.

In addition to making everything safe, spend carefully. Try not to buy new if you can help it. You can often find materials free if you look. For example, a producer I know used wooden pallets as a sidewalk outside a saloon for a Western he was making. Not only did the pallets look right, they sounded right.

If you build a false wall, be sure you keep enough room on the set for lighting equipment and camera gear. Even small DV cameras take up space when on a tripod. Start adding members of your ensemble, and a large basement can get very crowded.

Exteriors can be difficult to create. If you have an interior set with exterior windows, consider using a backdrop to make it more interesting. You can use front or rear projection systems, or a single still backdrop.

Some backdrops are like giant transparencies that you backlight. Some manufacturers offer sampler packs with cityscape backdrops in day and night for most major American cities. Expect to pay a lot for them. See the Resources section for listings.

You may be able to hire a local artist or art student to paint scenery for you. These pieces can work quite nicely, especially if you're seeing the piece through a half-curtained window. Be sure to budget for fees and materials, and keep in mind that this will take some time to execute and set up. You can paint the background yourself or use a greenscreen and chromakey in the image you want. See Chapter 27 for more information on this technique.

SET DRESSING

Set dressing means manipulating the surroundings and objects of every set. Set dressers, known as the *swing gang*, are responsible for the picking up of these items and dressing sets, everything from selecting and placing ketchup bottles to planting shrubs.

One common problem with using existing sets is created by white walls. When illuminated, a white wall can be so bright that it will affect the limited contrast ratio of 5:1 of DV. Also, bare walls can be dull to look at.

Consider bare walls as an opportunity. Numerous times, people will automatically cover a white wall, whether the wall is illuminated or not. A wall that has a shadow on it isn't white anymore—it's a shade of gray or yellow. That shade can add depth. Textured walls in particular can be great if lit well. You can paint a bare wall with light, conveying mood through a cukie of blinds, bushes, or the light through a window during the rain. Use fill light with blue or maroon to color the shadows.

If you need to change a white wall but have no wall hangings, or the scene requires a blank wall, you can use temporary hair tint in a technique called *aging*. Carefully spray on streaks and tips, being careful not to spray any on nearby fabric. Be sure to test an area of the surface before aging it. It can be cleaned off with soap and water.

Don't be afraid to use common materials to create uncommon set dressing. You can fake marble, granite, and other surfaces using kits from local hardware stores, and many tricks have now become popular DIY home-improvement techniques, such as rag rolling, sponging, and applying shelf paper. Just don't put the lights too close since the heat can ruin your home improvement efforts.

You can create stained glass window effects by gluing gels on clear Plexiglass. You can also paint a stained glass window on sized seamless muslin. (*Sizing* means to prepare fabric or another surface for painting by filling its pores with starch or animal glue.) Apply the colors in layers till it looks right, using black paint for the "leading" of the window. The trick to making such effects look real is to backlight them and try not to get too close.

EXPENDABLES AND TRICKS

Carry small jars of spackle and wood filler in case you need to make a repair. Bring tape of various kinds and a staple gun. White caulk is useful, too.

Have diffusion spray or Arrid XX spray-on deodorant on hand. They can be sprayed on reflective surfaces to dull them. Flashlights and strings of Christmas lights can be handy for set dressing, as can be shapes made out of Scotchlite, a highly reflective material.

For exteriors, don't be afraid to use the side of a grip truck as a reflector or flag. You can control large amounts of spill with some judicious parking.

HAIR, MAKEUP, AND WARDROBE

Hair, makeup, and wardrobe are crucial for actors. Wardrobe helps them clue into the characters, whereas hair and makeup get them in the right frame of mind. You don't have to have lavish prep facilities but at least have a comfortable location with plenty of color-correct lighting and mirrors. Try to have running water and allow time for actors to prepare themselves. The more relaxed they feel, the better the performance.

EVERY DAY IS A GOOD HAIR DAY

Most actors will know exactly what they need to do to have great hair. Just give them time and a location to do it, along with mirrors and good light.

If your actor needs his or her hair tinted, temporary hair color is best done using streaks and tips. Streaks and tips can be found in any drugstore, as well as theatrical supply shops. The tint comes in a variety of colors. Test to make sure you have the shade you need. Apply hair tint before applying makeup. You can touch it up after the makeup is on.

Other times, you may need special effects hair styling. To make hair lie flat against the scalp so you can put on a bald cap or wig, soap the actor's hair. To do this, soak a bar of soap in some water overnight. Add the soapy water to the hair in sections, drying it with a hair dryer as you go. You can get the same effect with a hair resin, such as Gafquat. Because Gafquat washes out in the shower, there's no problem with residual glue on the hair.

You can find Gafquat online and at beauty supply stores.

If you have special hairstyling requirements, such as complex braids, wigs, falls, toupées, false facial hair, and so on, consider hiring a pro. Wigs, in particular, need to be styled and set properly to look good. Makeup and hair artists really can make your life easier.

STRAIGHT MAKEUP

The purpose of straight makeup is to make the actor look to the camera as if he or she is flawless without looking made up. Subtle makeup can hide blemishes, blend skin tones, enhance features, and take off any shine.

At least use some kind of base for everyone on camera. I prefer powder bases applied with a wide brush, but you and your actors may want to use cream. If they need, or want, more than basic makeup, most of the name brands are quite good.

HYGIENE

Each actor should use his or her own makeup kit, and each kit and the makeup within it should be clean. If it smells funny, throw it out. Wash your hands before and after applying makeup to each person. After each use, all brushes and sponges you plan to use again should be washed. Warm water and soap works fine for cream bases, but you'll need a good brush cleaner for oil-based products. Consider using disposable brushes and sponges.

Never use makeup directly from the container. Put a small amount on an artist's palette and use it from there. Do not apply makeup to broken or irritated skin and never, ever use the same mascara applicator on more than one person.

SAFETY

Before applying any makeup, ask whether the actor has ever had any reaction to any kind of makeup. Test products by dabbing a little on the actor's wrist. Remove the makeup and see whether there is any reaction. Some people are sensitive to scents and additives, so use makeups that are listed as nonallergenic and fragrance-free.

Ask whether the actor is wearing contacts. Contact wearers are much more prone to eye irritation and if you plan on using any chemicals with strong fumes, they should remove their contacts first. Be prepared to deal with possible problems from excessive tearing.

- Read all directions and warnings on packaging and follow them carefully.
- Use adequate ventilation at all times.
- Never use adhesives not approved for use on human skin.
- Never apply anything you do not know how to take off.

TECHNIQUES

Don't buy cheap makeup. It's hard to use, looks bad, and can cause skin problems for your actors. Get the good stuff. Name-brand and special makeup for motion pictures such as Ben Nye are your best options. In addition to foundations and bases, powders, eyeliners, mascara, and so on, consider getting several types of concealers.

A common mistake for straight makeup is choosing an incorrect shade for the skin tone. Choose a foundation shade closest to the actor's skin tone at the curve of the jaw line. After applying the foundation, finish by brushing out all over with a wide blending brush. This gives a more professional finish. Less is best.

Here are some other tips:

- Use Orajel or another over-the-counter toothache medication on eyebrows before plucking. It will hurt less.
- Lengthen eyes by extending the shadow beyond the outer corners.
- To make eyes seem farther apart, apply eye shadow lightly up from the outer edges of the eye and highlight the inner corners.
- Make eyes look larger by extending the shadow or eye color slightly above, beyond, and below the eyes. This can be helpful for someone wearing glasses.

- Use a lip liner to expand the curve of the lip and balance it with the opposite lip.
- To make a mouth appear larger, build out the sides of the upper and lower lips, and extend the corners of the mouth.

Bruises, grime, sweat, injuries, blood, scars, gray hair, mustaches, sideburns, and partial or complete balding can be accomplished with stunning realism. You'll need to test and plan before proceeding, and give your makeup artist time to get a good effect.

SPECIAL EFFECTS MAKEUP

Special effects makeup includes everything from simple contact lenses, fangs, wounds, and so on, to complex effects such as aging and full-body makeups. *Appliances* and *prosthetics* refer to a category of special effects in which latex or gelatin are used to create warts, noses, scars, arms, legs, heads, scales, and anything else you can attach to a human being.

There are many Web sites devoted to special effects makeups, created by professionals and enthusiastic amateurs. Check out the Society of Amateur and Professional Special Effects Makeup Artists (SAPSEMA) Web site at `www.geocities.com/rollie-tyler/index.html`. Bill Barto and crew keep things interesting with useful, detailed information.

Special effects makeup is addictive. After you read the information, you'll get the sudden impulse to start lifecasting everyone you know. Give yourself plenty of time to practice and be mindful of safety. Some of the materials require or generate heat, so wear protective clothing. Some materials give off fumes, so work in a well-ventilated area. You can purchase premade appliances and prosthetics, as well as fake blood, goo, blood capsules, fangs, and contacts online from many sources, or from a local theatrical supply, hobby, or Halloween shop. Several online sources are listed in the Resources section.

The contacts and fangs available online look pretty good. The appliances can look okay with some care, but if these special effects are an integral part of your show—and they should be or why would you be using them at all?—consider making your own.

NEVER APPLY WHAT YOU CAN'T TAKE OFF. Use the proper remover to take off any prosthetic or appliance. Whatever makeup adhesive you use requires a remover that's as good, or better, quality. Spend some money and get the good stuff, readily available online from many suppliers listed in the Resources section.

Start with a skin conditioner for your hands and the actor's face, hands, or any other body part to which you're applying special effects makeup. The skin cream will protect the actor's skin from irritation from adhesive, latex, or gelatin. For example, ADM Tronics, Inc. at www.admtronics.com sells aqua-cream, a lotion for this purpose. It makes skin smooth and soft, as well as making adhesive and makeup removal easier because it protects the pores. Spread evenly, rinse, and pat dry.

APPLIANCES AND PROSTHETICS

There are two basic steps in creating appliances:

1. Creating a mold
2. Creating the appliances based on the mold

Creating Molds

The goal of mold making is creating a mold that will result in a high-quality appliance. A good mold includes paper-thin edges for blending and is specifically made to fit an actor's face or body.

It's a fascinating and time-consuming effort, something you cannot do without practice. Give yourself enough time to create good molds and practice the techniques before committing to the process. Also, you might know someone who knows how to do this. Ask around—it's rather fun and people take it up as a hobby.

One of the most important techniques for good special effects makeup is the creating of a lifecast. Basically, you cast in alginate a mold of someone's face or other body part. Alginate is the only safe material for casting body parts. It's soft and flexible, won't stick to anything, even itself, and fast setting. Plaster bandages are used to support the alginate for a better result. See Resources for a listing of suppliers.

For example, let's say your actor needs a fake nose and chin. You would do a lifecast, beginning with the back of the head using alginate on all skin and plaster to support the alginate and the structure of the mold.

When removed, the mold, called *negative* because it's the reverse of the original, is put back together and used to cast in special plaster the lifecast. The plaster is extra tough to withstand a lot of use and often has acrylic additives to make it extra rugged.

You then use the lifecast as the form for smaller *snap molds*. Snap molds are small sections of the mold that you intend to cover with an appliance. You can create a single latex mask of the entire face, but for realistic appliances, use snap molds.

You can use alginate on the lifecast for the snap molds and cast plaster positives. For example, for your actor's fake nose, you would create a mold from the lifecast that would cover the nose and into the cheek area. You would then cast that alginate negative into a plaster positive.

The appliances themselves you sculpt with oil-based clay on the lifecast. You gently cut the clay sculpt from the lifecast, and place the clay pieces on the snap molds for further adjustments.

When the clay pieces look the way you want, you create a negative of the clay sculpture. After everything is thoroughly dry, you part the two plaster molds carefully and remove all the clay.

When the molds are fully dry after several days, you have two casts—a positive and negative. Run foam latex or gelatin into the casts, and then lock them together. When the material is set, you have a form-fitting appliance with very thin edges, called *flashing*, for blending. An appliance without those thin edges looks terrible and is useless, so be sure you have flashing on each side of each appliance.

If you want to do this yourself, research first and try it a few times. There are many books and Web sites that give the specific steps for this process. See the Resources section for listings.

Creating the Appliances

Casting for makeup effects is called *running*. Latex and gelatin are the most common materials run to make appliances. When using latex, follow the manufacturer's directions precisely and work in a well-ventilated area.

Gelatin is a great material from which to make fake flesh. It was the standard until latex and other plastics became available. Unfortunately, gelatin rots, melts at low temperature, and just isn't durable. It's also hygroscopic, meaning it absorbs moisture, so gelatin appliances may swell depending on humidity. Gelatin has seen a resurgence, though, as makeup artists have successfully experimented with other safe additives.

Gelatin

Academy Award–winning special effects makeup artist Matthew Mungle created interest in it again using gelatin for special effects makeup with his techniques in the 1996 motion picture, "Ghosts of Mississippi." His old-age makeup for James Woods used a gelatin appliance for cheeks, chin, and neck, a second appliance for the forehead and other appliances for the earlobes.

Matthew experimented with several additives to make the gelatin easier to use and developed formulas and methods he has gladly shared. Not only is the guy a gifted makeup artist, his generosity is an example for us all. See www.matthewmungle.com for more information about Matthew's career and special effects makeup techniques. Plus, he offers advice and tips from his discussion board.

Gelatin is cheap, available, easy to use, easy to blend, and can look good. You can use unflavored gelatin from the grocery store or order gelatin with greater strength. See the Resources section for a list of suppliers.

Gelatin strength is called its *bloom*. Bloom describes the relative hardness of the gelatin when cured. A higher bloom number means the stronger the gelatin. Gelatin with a bloom of 300 can be obtained from most special effects suppliers.

The unflavored gelatin you can get from the grocery stores has a bloom between 200 and 225, and is handy for experimentation.

Matthew Mungle's gelatin method produces a strong, elastic, semitranslucent appliance that is flexible, has inherently good resistance to perspiration and heat, and retains excellent detail from the mold.

Matthew Mungle's gelatin formula:

> 100 grams of Sorbitol
> 100 grams of glycerin
> 20 to 30 grams of gelatin (300 bloom)
> And not over 1 gram of zinc oxide

He also added flocking material (red, blue, brown, and tan) to the mixture and pigmented the gelatin with ground facial powders.

Glycerin is available in local pharmacies and grocery stores. It's used in everything including cosmetics, inks, perfumes, antifreeze, and the preservation and sweetening of food. In addition to its use in gelatin for makeup, glycerin is used to create perspiration and grease effects.

Sorbitol increases the structural rigidity of gelatin, improving its resistance to tearing. There are two forms of Sorbitol—liquid and powder. The liquid form of Sorbitol usually contains higher concentrations of Sorbitol to water, just enough to form the Sorbitol solution.

Zinc oxide results in a stronger gelatin prosthetic with a greater tolerance to temperature changes, and is a water-insoluble powder that can be found at any pharmacy. Unfortunately, the addition of zinc oxide will begin to affect the translucency of the gelatin in the final product. If you can't find powdered zinc oxide, experiment with the ointment.

To run the gelatin, put a microscopic layer of petroleum jelly on all plaster mold surfaces and keys.

Heat the gelatin in a double boiler or a microwave, stirring occasionally to avoid uneven heating and cooking. When the formula liquefies, add all the components and mix well.

Pour close to the mold to prevent splashing and air bubbles. After pouring the mixture into the mold, place the positive over the negative, and apply slow, constant pressure until the positive is seated firmly into the negative. Excess gelatin will overflow, but ignore that.

Set the mold aside to cool. You can put it in the freezer if you want to. When cooled, remove the appliance from the mold. Use baby powder or talc to keep the gelatin from sticking to itself.

You can also experiment with gelatin effects. Add a half-packet of yeast to a small amount of warm water and let it rise. Add it to your warm gelatin formula slowly and mix. You can create intrinsic color with Krylon Aquacolors and isopropyl alcohol.

Adhering gelatin appliances is another matter. Some artists use spirit gum, Pros-Aide, or Pros-Aide II. Regardless of which adhesive, be sure you are aware of the proper application and removal of the appliance.

To apply, first use skin cream to protect the actor's pores and protect from irritation. Stipple a thin layer of medical-grade adhesive onto the skin and let it dry. Do this again, and then powder. This helps seal the skin so sweat doesn't come through. Use a damp towel to remove the excess powder.

Apply adhesive to the back of the appliance, staying about 1/4" away from the blending edges. While the adhesive is still wet, put the gelatin piece on. After the adhesive is set, use witch hazel to melt the edges of the gelatin appliance and blend it into the skin. Allow it to dry, and then blend in the appliance with makeup.

BLOOD

Fake blood is messy and it stains. Keep this in mind when you work with it.

Most fake blood is created by mixing food coloring (red, green, and blue) into light corn syrup until it reaches the desired consistency and shade. You can also add Sorbitol and cornstarch to the mix for a better result.

If you need fake blood in someone's hair, consider diluting some clear hair gel and tinting it with food coloring. It's a lot easier to clean up.

Another good method is using A-B blood. A-B blood comprises two clear solutions, and when they touch, appear blood red. This is how it works: Apply solution A to the actor's skin. Apply solution B to the weapon. Touch the weapon to the anatomy, and the result is a spectacular streak of blood. You can also use A-B blood to create blood spatter effects.

You can get A-B blood from theatrical supply, Halloween, or special effects shops.

KEEPING TRACK OF WARDROBE

Theatrical costume designer Tara McGinnis has said, "The most creative work in the designs of all my shows are the result of having to fix a screw-up." You can find more advice about the art and craft of costume design at her Web site at `www.costumes.org/pages/indexm.htm`.

If you haven't determined wardrobe requirements during preproduction, deal with it now.

Use your wardrobe list to make sure everyone is wearing the correct clothing and accessories. Your actors may be willing to use their own clothes. Just be up front with them if there's a chance their clothes will get dirty or even ruined.

Consider buying used. Wardrobe from thrift stores or other shoots comes with a low price tag and a funny smell. Wash well and rub a couple of dryer sheets over them or spray them with Febreeze. You can easily and cheaply change their appearance by dyeing them with diluted RIT in spray bottles or highlighting them with fabric paint.

Depending on the type of show, you may need to rent or borrow costumes. Keep the rental contract with you to make sure you get everything and everything gets returned. In this case, you may also want to assign someone to handle wardrobe. Have the actors return their wardrobe to this person, who will make sure it is securely locked up when not in use.

Be sure to list clothing and accessories in your production script with every wardrobe change. Do not expect the actors to just remember what they were wearing; because you're probably shooting out of sequence, it's easy to get confused. Consider taking Polaroids of every outfit.

If you must buy new, keep the receipts and tags on everything until it's used. Everything unused can go back to the store for a refund. This way, you have a variety of outfits to choose from.

If you have stunts or physical effects, you will need multiple changes of the same outfit. These clothes will get very dirty very quickly. Keep track of continuity. For example, if there's a tear across the back of the shirt, make sure all the others match accordingly.

In any case, always keep needle and thread handy for quick repairs or alterations. You can always use tape if you have to.

EXPENDABLES

Makeup is always expendable. Assume you're going to have to spend a bit of money to get the basics. If you want more than the basics, you can spend a great deal.

For every actor, you'll need

- Base, also known as foundation, either powder or cream
- Brushes, sponges, and other applicators

You may also want to get

- Mascara
- Eyeliner
- Concealer

You'll also need	Number	Cost
Polaroid camera and film	_____	_____
Soap and hand lotion	_____	_____
Tissues	_____	_____
Cotton pads	_____	_____
Sea Breeze	_____	_____
Makeup remover	_____	_____
Baby wipes	_____	_____
Streaks and tips—black, brown, gray, and other shades	_____	_____
Hairspray	_____	_____
Mousse	_____	_____
Towels	_____	_____
Sewing kit	_____	_____
Fabric tape	_____	_____
Safety pins	_____	_____

EXPLOSIONS, GUNPLAY, AND FISTFIGHTS: WHEN TO CALL IN THE EXPERTS

Splatter and gore used to be the mainstay of low-budget movies. Then, Hollywood got into the act. Although you can still use gruesome effects, it's hard to compete with the big money. Still, if you want to have stunts and special effects, what follows may help you plan and execute them safely and effectively.

STUNTS

Generally, a *stunt* is any physical activity presented for camera where someone may get hurt. A *gag* is a sequence of controlled mechanical events that requires rigging. For each stunt, you need to ask

- Will it be performed by the actor?
- Will it be performed by a stunt double?

Depending on the skill and training of your actors, they may be comfortable performing some of the required stunts. Keep in mind, though, that an injury will affect your shoot and even your project. One lawsuit can ruin your whole day.

The stunt coordinator will choreograph the stunt, handle stunt equipment including props, and teach the moves to the actors or stunt doubles. The stunt coordinator is the only person who should touch stunt equipment and, other than the necessary actors, the only person who should handle stunt props.

This kind of choreography requires trust. Start slowly and gradually get up to speed only when everyone is comfortable. The actors need to know they can rely on one another, especially for blind moves—moves where one actor can't see another. Don't speed up until everyone is hitting the correct marks.

Consider shooting submasters so everyone can save their energy for the performance. Close shots make everything seem faster, so you don't necessarily need to go at top speed. Just be sure the actors complete the motion before calling cut. It will make editing easier.

ANIMALS

For any stunt that includes animals, you will probably need a wrangler. A wrangler is the animal's trainer. That person's sole job is to handle the animal. No one else. Consider using stunt doubles. You can ruin your shoot if your lead breaks a bone falling from a horse or needs stitches after a bite. When using animals, your insurance costs will go up and you will need extra time for those scenes.

We had a Great Dane named Wanda (shown in Figure 27.1) in "Music Appreciation." Wanda is very well trained and I've worked with her and her owner/handler before. Although Wanda's scene was less than three minutes long, we had to schedule four hours to shoot it.

FALLS AND FIGHTS

Falls are tricky. Unless your actors have some training and know how to fall, be careful. Make sure they're wearing padding under wardrobe. Use extra padding, such as mattresses, and empty boxes for landing. For any falls higher than a couple feet, use a dummy or a stunt professional. Judicious framing can also make things look higher, so you can always fake a fall by having the actor begin the move, cutting, and showing the landing.

FIGURE 27.1

Wanda.

Many actors have been trained in stage fighting and those skills may help. For fistfights, camera placement makes all the difference. Over-the-shoulder and similar shots can make a fake punch look very real.

FIRE

There is no safe way to set someone on fire. There are safer ways, but fire is dangerous. Anyone who thinks otherwise should never be in charge of anything more dangerous than making toast.

These kinds of stunts require flame retardant materials, special fuels, and fire safety equipment. It also requires experience, planning, and thought regarding sets, wardrobe, makeup, and other materials.

Be careful about advice you get from anyone regarding the use of flames. A trained stunt technician will never tell a neophyte these techniques in detail unless that technician is going to be on the set. If something goes wrong, that professional may be the target of a lawsuit. You may find practices on the Internet but think before you use them. Do you honestly believe that a trained and experienced person would give away this information?

A trained and experienced stunt coordinator is on the set to protect you from your own stupidity. If you need fire, hire.

SPECIAL EFFECTS

Special Effects: The History and Technique by Richard Rickitt is a beautifully illustrated and helpful guide to special effects. Although most of his illustrations are beyond most independent movie budgets, the book is filled with examples and practices that can be inspiring.

A special effect is any activity requiring special equipment to be presented to camera. There are two types of effects, those special effects created by mechanical means, and visual effects, which are computer-generated images (CGI).

Special effects include

- Physical effects
- Atmospherics
- Mattes and miniatures
- Cloud tanks
- Computer-generated imagery (CGI)

Cloud tank effects are shot on a special set and combined with live or computer-generated action in postproduction. CGI includes greenscreen techniques, as well as other image manipulation.

PHYSICAL EFFECTS

Physical effects are usually combined with stunts. One of the most common are bullet hits.

Bullet Hits

When a gun has been fired, the viewer expects to see a result. Depending on what you envision for your show, you can imply the effect by cutting to a fallen character. You can also reveal the outcome using a combination of bullet hits and acting. Raking a wall or the ground can often imply someone's been hit. Actors will fall quite dramatically if you give them the chance. They've been waiting all their lives to show off their technique.

If you need to show bullet hits, there are two ways of doing this.

- Pyrotechnic
- Nonpyrotechnic

Either way, if you need blood, you will probably have to buy or create blood packs. Blood packs are small bags that hold fake blood. You can practice safe effects and use condoms, although balloons will work. You can also make them.

Pyrotechnics   Pyrotechnics means explosives.

Professionals create bullet hits by using a small explosive charge triggered by a battery to make a blood pack burst outward. The charges are carefully rigged so no one gets a shock and actors are trained not to let their hands (or any other body part) pass in front of the charge because shredded cloth or other materials from the detonation can hurt someone.

Anytime you use explosives, you need a license and training. Laws regulating pyrotechnics vary from state to state, but for your and your ensemble's safety, find someone with a license, training, and experience.

To get your pyrotechnician license, you will need to contact your local Alcohol, Tobacco and Firearms office. Your state, city, and county may have other requirements. You will also have higher insurance costs for your show.

Many companies sell charges that can be used for bullet hits. One such device is called a *squib*. A squib is a small detonator used to set off a secondary charge such as black powder or other pyrotechnic compounds. They have many uses, but they're often used for pyrotechnic bullet hits.

A charge with an electric match or other igniter is taped to a sturdy 5"×4" metal plate that is cushioned with foam or leather to protect the actor. A blood pack is placed over the charge and secured in place with gaffer's tape.

The plate is rigged to the actor with gaffer's tape or a leather weightlifting belt, and concealed under clothing. Clothes should be prescored with a knife or rubbed with sandpaper to weaken the fabric.

Cable is run from the charge to a 9-volt battery carried by the actor or down the actor's leg to a device called a *clinker* or *clunker box,* which controls the charge detonation. Many professionals bypass the clinker box in favor of a simple nail board. The nail board has a series of nails fixed in a row. Each nail is connected to a terminal to which a single charge is wired. The special effects coordinator uses an isolated rod attached to a low-charge power supply to each nail to detonate each charge. Multiple hits are simulated by dragging the rod over the nails.

Strafing works the same way, although the charges are set into holes in the ground or wall.

NOTE

Making Blood Packs

You'll need

Plastic wrap, such as Saran Wrap

Aluminum foil

Gaffer's tape or duct tape

An iron set on high

A small block of wood

You'll need a clean work area with a work surface you can iron on.

Cut a piece of plastic wrap and fold it over. Take a strip of aluminum foil and fold it over.

Slip the edges of the plastic wrap into the aluminum. Heat the foil, not the plastic, with the iron on high for about 10 seconds.

Take the iron away. The plastic will be fused together.

Seal the pack on all sides. Tape the three edges to ensure a good seal on the seams. On the fourth seam, leave a corner open that's large enough for a piece of tubing or the metal wand of the pump sprayer. You'll fill the blood pack here as well.

Tape the front and back of the pack except for a small area in the front center toward the bottom. That's where the blood will spurt out.

Some pros prefer the nailboard method because they believe it allows for greater control of each charge. Detonation can run according to where the actors are and what they're doing. Before firing, everyone stands well clear of the charges, the actor avoids looking down at his or her chest, and the camera is a safe distance away.

You can purchase these charges from many suppliers. See your film commission for listings. Magician supply shops also have many devices that may be useful to you. Again, though, unless you are a trained and licensed pyrotechnician with experience rigging these kinds of effects, do not do this yourself. People can get hurt or killed using these things.

You don't have to do anything as dangerous or expensive to get good bullet hits.

Nonpyrotechnic   This is an old-fashioned way of creating bullet hits. If you make it a quick cut, it can work well. You'll need

> A blood pack, filled and sealed (do not tape the front surface)
> Small washers
> Fine black thread or fishing line
> A stick
> Surgical tape
> Alcohol swabs or Sea Breeze and cotton pads
> Masking tape
> Fast-setting Super Glue

Tape the filled blood pack to the actor. Use Sea Breeze or alcohol swabs to clean the actor's skin before attaching the tubing and blood pack. The actor may also want to shave the area before taping anything. It's better if the actor wears an undershirt.

Take the piece of wardrobe, such as a shirt, and carefully put it on the actor. Find the exact center of the bullet hit on the garment and carefully mark the spot with a tiny piece of tape.

Remove the shirt. Carefully cut a diagonal "X" in the cloth and feed the thread through. Put a small piece of masking tape on the backside of the cloth to keep it closed. Tie a small washer inside the shirt to the end of the thread.

Have the actor put on the shirt. Put a drop or two of Super Glue on the washer, and attach it to the center of the blood pack.

Have the actor take a couple feet of thread, while you or an assistant back out of camera view. Tie the thread to the stick and slowly spool the slack.

Have the actor drop the thread and carefully take it up until the stick is almost pointing at the actor.

Roll camera. Call "Action!" Snap the stick back hard. The washer and hunk of the blood pack will come flying.

What a mess.

You can also use compressed air with tubing attached to a pump sprayer or syringe. Syringes are very useful for small amounts of blood. I've used two methods with varying success.

The first doesn't require a blood pack. You'll need

> A pump sprayer
> Tubing that will fit tightly over the wand of the pump sprayer
> Surgical tape
> Alcohol swabs or Sea Breeze and cotton pads
> Gaffer's tape or duct tape
> Clamp
> 1 hot glue gun
> Sandpaper
> Scotch tape or masking tape

You can use different kinds of tubing. Polyethylene tubing is cheap, milky white, and easy to find. It's not very flexible, but it can withstand pressure. Vinyl tubing will withstand the pressure and is more flexible, but it's more expensive. Surgical silicone tubing is the best, but it costs. You can find it at medical supply stores.

Get your blood pack. Cut the untaped corner of the pack off and fill the bag with blood. You may want to use a syringe or funnel.

Slide about 1/2" of the tube into the pack and seal it and the blood pack with the hot glue gun. Tape the seam.

Prep the shirt (or whatever wardrobe) and put small pieces of scotch tape or masking tape lightly on the backside to hold it together.

Line up the untaped opening of the blood pack to the prepped cloth, and then tape the blood pack with the tubing in one of the upper corners into place. Use Sea Breeze or alcohol swabs to clean the actor's skin before attaching the tubing and blood pack. The actor may also want to shave the area before taping anything. It's better if the actor wears an undershirt.

Tape everything into place. If you're taping to skin, use surgical tape. For everything else, use gaffer's tape. Send the tubing down a pant leg.

Remove the adjustable nozzle at the end of the pump sprayer's wand. Pump the pump sprayer. Read the directions on it to make sure you get the right amount of pressure.

Slip the tubing onto the pump sprayer wand. Make sure it's tight.

Set the camera away from the area and zoom in. Have the assistant holding the pump sprayer step out of camera view. Roll camera. Call "Action!" Press the pump sprayer trigger.

What a mess.

You can always dip the metal end of the pump sprayer wand into red goo (such as Jello) and send it flying.

Practice each technique until you know which one you want to use. Instead of fake blood, load with water to make cleanup easier. You can create multiple hits with careful planning.

You can use these same techniques to make wall hits. Dip the wand in a damp mix of baby powder, sand, and coloring. You'll need to hide the tubing somewhere, either by drilling through a wall or behind furniture or wallhanging.

If you use a blood pack for a wall hit, instead of fake blood, fill it with sand and baby powder and follow the same procedure.

Finally, you can take some vinyl tubing and push the end into some sand and baby powder. Attach the end of the tube to the edge of a wall. On cue, have an assistant blow hard.

Although these techniques seem cheesy, it's not what you see that makes the effect so gory. Sound is most of the effect. It's the bang and splat that make them work.

ATMOSPHERICS

Atmospheric effects apply to natural events manufactured for the camera. No matter what your budget, these effects can be difficult to pull off on a wide shot. Keep the angles fairly close.

RAIN

One of the most common atmospheric effects is rain. Often, city streets at night will glisten as if a rain had just eased off. Professionals achieve that effect by hiring water trucks to wet down their sets.

Naturally, that's expensive.

I live in the Pacific Northwest. I love the rain. It's beautiful. At night it makes everything shiny and boosts illumination levels. Many DV cameras have a difficult time with low light, so I consider rain my friend.

If it starts raining and you're not in danger of hurting the gear, ensemble, or continuity, try to stay with it. Let it work for you. With a small mobile crew and well-rehearsed cast, you can make the rain work in your favor.

You can create rain effects for interiors. An easy way uses a pump sprayer filled with water. Adjust the nozzle and aim it right above an exterior window. Be sure to backlight it for maximum effect.

You can also create a more extensive rainmaker.

Get an 8' length of 1/2"-diameter PVC pipe. Drill 1/8" (or smaller) holes every 1/2" in a straight line down the length. Cap one end. Take a garden hose and cut off one end, but not the end with the water inlet. Connect the cut end to the PVC pipe and lock it into place with a hose clamp. That's the rain bar.

You need some supports to get the rain bar up and out of view. Clamp it to a pair of c-stands or other supports with the holes facing up and just a little to one side of your actors. Attach the hose to a water faucet and adjust as needed.

You may also be able to persuade the local fire department to come over and show off their fire trucks. The hoses can spray a lot of water, and the firefighters can adjust the flow to give you a mist that looks very much like rain.

SNOW

Fake snow is made out of plastic, foam, and potato starch, but the most common material is paper. For large areas, cover with white plastic. For snowdrifts, try papier-mâché painted white. For best effect, keep your depth of field fairly shallow. You may need to use ND filters.

You can rent machines that will produce foam that will dissipate in a few hours, or spray C-90. C-90 is a cellulose powder that's completely safe for the environment. Spray water on the area you want to coat, and then spray on the C-90. Wash the C-90 away with more water when you're finished. Your local grip house should have the foam machines or see Resources for a listing of suppliers.

To frost windows, you can use the frost-in-a-can sold in theatrical supply stores and hobby shops and discount stores. Just make sure the set is ventilated.

Falling snow can be created by using snow candles. These are handheld incendiary devices that will send plumes of white ash into the air. A cheaper alternative is the old standby: unbuttered potato flakes thrown into a huge fan. The flakes really do look like falling snow and are relatively easy to clean up. If you can't find unbuttered potato flakes, you can use torn paper tossed into the fan. You can find online suppliers of snow candles, unbuttered potato flakes, and torn paper. Check your local grip house for the fan.

Keep in mind that big fans are quite noisy and require an experienced operator to set up and run. Make sure everything is secured before turning on the fan—objects and people can go flying if everything isn't tied down tightly.

Consider placing your actors in small areas and using CGI to paint backgrounds. This will save you some money and time because you won't have to lay everything out and clean it all up.

WIND

Wind machines range from a small fan to the engine of a Boeing 707. If you absolutely need the effect, hire a professional to run professional equipment. Lock everything down and have materials such as leaves and dust blow into the shot.

You can always use small, powerful fans close up on the actors, while hidden crew members pull trees and other objects in the background using rope and wire. This actually works quite well as long as you don't linger too long.

FOG AND SMOKE

There are many ways to create fog and smoke effects. The machines range from handheld devices to truck-size. Most of these machines use a heating element that heats up mineral oil or ethyl glycol. The vapor condenses into plumes of smoke.

In windless areas, the smoke will hang in the air for quite a while. Wafting the smoke with a flag will dissipate it somewhat, creating a hazy mist. This works well in sunlit forest areas. If it's windy, though, you may have some problems keeping the smoke around.

In addition to oil-heating fog and smoke machines, there are dry ice machines. Dry ice is frozen carbon dioxide with a temperature of -79° Celsius, so handle with caution. You can usually get some from the meat and fish department of your local grocery store or an ice supply house in your area. You can rent the machine from a local rental or special effects shop.

The machine drops big pieces of dry ice into warm water and blows out the fog. The warmer the water, the thicker the smoke.

Dry ice fog is heavy and will hug the ground. If you have a large exterior you want to fog, you can hide buckets in holes or behind trees and stumps and drop dry ice into them to get the effect you want.

Ultrasonic humidifiers (also called cool-mist humidifiers) are electrical appliances you can find at local department stores. They're useful for localized fog, but don't expect much. The mist disappears after drifting a foot or two, but it's done with water and is very safe. You can add just a bit of glycerin to make the mist last a little longer.

To make windows look frosty or foggy, use Epsom salts, which you can get at a local drugstore, and water. Dissolve one cup of Epsom salts into one gallon of water. Apply the solution to the glass. When it dries, the salt will stay. Repeat until you have the look you want.

COBWEBS

You can purchase premade cobwebs from hobby and Halloween stores. Use these to put on people and fabric. You can also make cobwebs. Squirt a lot of hot glue or rubber cement onto two lengths of 2'×4' and squish them together. Pull the 2'×4's apart and the glue will form stringy webs. Lay them were you want them. Off-the-shelf rubber cement is messy. Be careful with it.

There's also a device you can rent from theatrical supply stores called a web-spinner, which attaches to a standard electric drill. You'll need web fluid. Some manufacturers include solvent for web removal—this should tell you something. The webs are sticky and some are flammable. Try to find fluid that's safer and easier to use. Also, experiment with the spinner before covering the room.

Pour the fluid into the hopper, turn it on, and the web spinner spins tiny strands that will stick to things. Consider tossing some dust or Fuller's earth on the cobwebs for extra texture. Fuller's earth is a very fine clay and can get into your lungs if you're not careful. Anyone working with the Fuller's earth should wear a respirator or dust mask. You can find them, and Fuller's earth, at hardware and garden stores.

CLOUD TANKS

Cloud tanks are tanks of water into which various liquids are poured to get certain effects, most often roiling clouds. Often a greenscreen is placed at the back to help with any compositing effects. This footage is then matched with live-action footage to create dramatic skies, with waterproof flash guns in the tank fired as lightning.

Paint, which is heavier than water, is often injected into the tank to create cloud effects, but any material that can be suspended in water can be used. Plagues of locusts have been created with coffee grounds suspended in water and then composited with live-action footage.

Models, especially of aircraft, can be hung in cloud tanks. Billows of paint create the illusion of moving clouds and remove the jerkiness of using wire-hung models in the air.

MATTES AND MINIATURES

I don't know many people experimenting with mattes and miniatures for DV, but that's no reason you can't do it. Watch your depth of field and be sure to light carefully for best effect.

Mattes are prepared frames or digital images that replace certain parts of the frame with another image. To use a matte for camera, you prepare the image on glass or masonite, leaving certain areas you want the viewer to see uncovered. For example, you may want two characters to step out of the door and into a futuristic big-city alley. You would paint the big-city alley on the glass or masonite, leaving blank the area where the viewer would see the characters stepping out the door, and then place this matte between the camera and the set you're shooting.

The painted images are then lit by the sun or sidelights at about 45 degrees from the matte. The camera sees the painting and the live action that shows through the unpainted areas. By carefully lining up the live action and the matte, you create an excellent illusion.

This matte technique has some limitations. You can't really track through the matte painting and you can't place moving elements in the painting. Still, you can create a definite visual style to support your story through your matte work. Matte painting may also work for faking foreign locations, grand landscapes, imaginary cities, and sets for which you have no location.

You can use masonite or inexpensive glass, such as that from picture frames, and paint on them. You can also use photos you've taken yourself, though be sure to back them with black construction paper so no light leaks through. Either tape or paste the pictures to the glass.

Hang the glass matte in its frame between the camera lens and the action. Keep the camera on a rock-solid tripod and lock it down. Any movement will ruin the illusion. If you need twinkling city lights or stars, you can use a glass matte painted accordingly. Where you need the twinkly lights, use a tack or push pin to scrape away some of the paint. Backlight carefully to get the full effect.

Digital matte work done in the computer combines the cleverness of painted mattes with the power of an infinite number of layers, three-dimensional motion, and ease of correction and replacement of composited elements. Please see Chapter 29, "Cutting Picture," for tips on rotoscoping and using digital mattes.

Using miniatures is the creation of scale models of a set or prop that is shot and composited into live action.

The art of miniatures is in the modeling and painting. It takes a great eye to design and execute a convincing miniature set, but if you enjoy that work, go to it. There are many online resources for people interested in modeling and miniatures, with tips and tricks. One of my favorites is using salt instead of water in a miniature waterfall. (Water is one natural element that's very hard to fake with miniatures.)

After you create your miniature set or prop, you need to proceed carefully to get a good illusion. Remember that objects tend to get rather hazy the farther away they are. You can help create the illusion of distance by using washes on the back pieces of the miniature set. Add some haze with a fog machine. Incense can also work quite nicely.

The best light, especially for an exterior miniature such as a city, is sunlight. You may be chasing light trying to match the light and shadows of the miniature with that of the live action, but it's worth it. Sunlight has a certain quality to it that really adds a level of reality. And be sure to match camera perspective.

One element of the illusion that you may want to consider is the sense of weight. For example, miniature cars just don't move down a miniature street the way real cars roll down a real street. Even when you have everything else right, the masses between the mini cars and real cars are so different that it can give away the illusion. You may want to work on using an extra wire for a slight upward or downward motion as the miniature vehicle slows down or speeds up. A little bit just may do the trick.

You need to be careful about your frame rate. Don't worry about it while shooting because it's unlikely you'll be able to overcrank your video camera. Overcranking is the process of causing the media to actually move through the camera faster than its normal rate. You can do this easily with a film camera, but not with a video camera. In post, however, you'll need to manipulate the frame rate so it matches the live action footage.

Do this by multiplying the normal frame rate (29.97 fps for NTSC, or 25 fps for PAL) by the square root of the inverse of the scale of the miniature. For example, you've built a model of a city with a scale of 1/25. This means that a street 250' long is 10' in the miniature. The inverse square of the scale (25) is 5. Round up 29.97 to 30 fps and multiply by 5 to get 150 fps.

In post, you will speed up the miniature's footage so it looks as if it were shot at 150 frames per second, or in slow motion. (Remember that the faster the frame rate, the slower the illusion of motion.) Your NLE software may allow you to slow down the footage by a factor of five. This will get you closer to the correct "look," helping you convey the illusion.

You may have to fuss with the frame rate and color saturation of the miniature to get it right. Test before committing to either mattes or miniatures.

CGI

More CGI is showing up in no- and low-budget shows. In addition to image correction and enhancement, DV moviemakers are creating sophisticated characters, sets, and props using hardware and software for their shows.

Compositing is multilayering motion pictures by painting, keying, matting, and so on. Other kinds of compositing include creating digital effects, color correction, creating opticals, and image repair.

One type is called rotoscoping. *Rotoscoping* uses frames of live footage as reference for painting animation. Rotoscoping has become easier with more powerful computers and software, although it still takes time, patience, and real talent to get a good result.

Chromakeying is replacing one video signal over another using a specific range of color. For this to work reliably, the chrominance must have sufficient resolution, or bandwidth. Many people will insist that you can't chromakey DV footage. This isn't true. DV works fine for a lot of typical greenscreen shots.

DV starts to fall apart with thin lines and subtle motion, but that applies to other formats as well. Generally, the chroma performance of 4:2:2 formats will be superior to 4:1:1, but that doesn't mean that you can't do very satisfactory work with a bit of care and planning.

Keying for DV requires a technique called greenscreen. *Greenscreen* works by gathering footage that can be easily manipulated in terms of layers. Background and foreground elements are treated separately and then these layers are composited into a single seamless whole.

If you want to combine CGI and live action, you will need to shoot greenscreen.

GREENSCREEN

Blue is the traditional color, but green backdrops work just a bit better for DV because of the higher luma content of green. Plus, green requires less light.

Start with a test before committing any CGI. Discuss all the issues regarding wardrobe, set dressing, screen color, and lighting before proceeding. Screen tests will often quickly reveal problems.

Paint the set with chromakey paint. You can buy chromakey paint from suppliers such as Rosco. Although it's a bit expensive, you know with Rosco you're getting a good product.

One way of getting inexpensive chromakey paint is to take a sample to your local hardware store. Have the paint department match the color. To get a nice seamless background, buy a sheet of the cheapest linoleum from your local hardware store, flip it over, and paint the white backing.

If painting is impractical, you can use green cloth stretched as wrinkle-free as possible. Make sure there are no seams. You can also buy inexpensive rolls of chromakey paper. Many video supply and grip houses sell it in varying widths and lengths.

The next issue is to light it properly. Light the wall as evenly as possible, because the best results will come from a smooth, even color. It's better to have the wall a little on the dark side to prevent spill and consider gelling the lights to match the greenscreen. Outdoor sunlight can provide excellent results. A wall of Kino-Flo fluorescents works great, though they can get costly. Many soundstages have greenscreen walls already in place that you can rent by the day.

Light your actors in front of the greenscreen to match the lighting color and direction of the composite background. Try to keep the actors at least six to eight feet away from the wall to prevent unwanted shadows and color spill. In addition to front lighting, make sure your side and back lighting match, avoiding hotspots on the wall.

Consider using an amber or straw gel on the fill light to minimize spill. It helps if you have a monitor with switchable guns so you can see how the R and G guns are affecting your greenscreen.

Regardless of what kind of lighting you need, make sure the image stays within the contrast ratio of DV.

STEP IV: POSTPRODUCTION:
DIRECTING THE MOVIE

OVERVIEW

Walter Murch's *In the Blink of an Eye* is a wonderful collection of short pieces on editing and sound design. Ignore what he says about editing on computer, but pay attention to his ideas about style and editorial choices.

My friend editor Margot Roth says, "Editing is by far the most fun part of the process. It's the reward for all your hard work."

I agree.

Because people emphasize production, they come into postproduction thinking they're at the end. They're not. Postproduction isn't a matter of assembly. Like every step in making movies, postproduction requires a plan.

Get some rest before diving into post. Coming to the material fresh can be difficult, especially if you had a rough production period. Still, catch up on your sleep, do some laundry, and start bathing regularly again.

Cutting picture and sound are designed according to the director's vision, the raw material accrued during production, and any additional material that will be created for the show. This combination takes into account three concerns:

- **Aesthetic**—What does the director believe will best convey his or her reading of the script given the existing material?

- **Technical**—What is the final version of the show, what equipment is required, and what are the restrictions of using DV?

- **Logistic**—What issues regarding scheduling and budgeting come into play?

Major motion pictures have a separate team to manage each aspect of postproduction. That team then handles a collection of other teams assigned to the show with a postproduction supervisor to manage the personnel, schedule, and budget of each job, a sort of assistant director of postproduction.

On many shows, the *editor* cuts the movie, while an *assistant editor* takes care of the organizational details. Though digital technology has made organizing and handling the material easier, some editors will not work unless they have an assistant. Be sure to budget accordingly. Titles and credits are handled by companies who specialize in creating them. Frankly, unless you have a very specific and intricate title sequence, or can get the work done for little or no money, you or your editor may be able to handle it.

Visual effects are handled by a *visual effects supervisor*. This person will locate companies and individuals to handle matte work, compositing, roto-scoping, CGI, and other postproduction effects. Get this person on your show while in preproduction to avoid costly overruns.

With post-audio, a *dialogue editor* repairs and replaces dialogue, a *Foley artist* records sound effects, and a *music supervisor* manages the music, including hiring a *composer* who writes and often performs music to fit the length of certain scenes, and clearing music for use with a motion picture.

After these elements have been cleaned up, edited, created, cleared, and placed, a *rerecording mixer* mixes them and places them into the final show.

You can hire experienced personnel to handle some or all of these tasks, or decide to do them yourself. Because you can manipulate DV in a computer for relatively little money, you may want to handle all of this yourself. Many independent producers have more time than money, and time is what really matters. Especially if you have little or no pressure regarding investors, interest rates, and deadlines, you can take the time to work on the material.

However, just because you can doesn't mean you should. Affordable equipment doesn't automatically make anyone an editor or sound designer. If the task is too much for you, or you're simply not interested in it, find someone who can handle it.

Chapter 28, "Postproduction Systems: Things to Consider," explores different configurations of systems for video and audio postproduction and can help you decide whether you have both the budget and the personality to handle postproduction tasks.

Chapter 29, "Cutting Picture," explains and illustrates techniques, tools, and philosophical approaches regarding editing motion pictures, including organizing the material, transitions between shots, scenes, and sequences, as well as common problems and solutions. This chapter also discusses the differences between *action safe* and *title safe* image areas, and tricks like compositing and rotoscoping.

Chapter 30, "Post-Audio," details how to handle post-audio tasks, such as sound designing, dialogue editing, narration and voiceovers, and creating soundbeds. This chapter also covers finding, creating, and using sound effects, music, and sound beds.

Finally, Chapter 31, "Finishing," covers what you'll need to do to complete, master, and duplicate your show so you can take it to market.

POSTPRODUCTION SYSTEMS: THINGS TO CONSIDER

You gave some thought to how you were going to handle your postproduction chores back in development. First, decide whether you want to change plans. Perhaps you had decided to build a nonlinear editing system to save money, but prices on turnkey systems have dropped, or maybe you want to concentrate on editing and not on tweaking your system. Maybe you wanted to compose and perform all the music, but you just don't know whether you have the time or the energy.

DV in a desktop-based nonlinear editor (NLE) works by handling data, not digitizing analog signals. As video is being shot, it is compressed and converted to digital form in the VTR part of the camera. What's on the tape are images that have been digitized and compressed using the DV codec.

Data, not video, is transferred electronically via a 1394 connection to the computer's hard disk. During transfer, the DV data is wrapped into a file format appropriate for the operating system.

You manipulate the DV data with any standard editing application that can work with DV file formats. Your computer will need a DV codec to display your video on your computer screen.

If you add filters or transitions to your show while editing, the editing software will call the DV codec, hand it compressed frames retrieved from the DV file, and receive uncompressed RGB bitmaps back from the codec. The software will then alter the necessary frames for the transition. When that's done, the finished RGB bitmap goes back to the DV codec, which compresses it to the correct DV file format and hands it back. The editing software then stores it in the target file.

After you've finished editing, the resulting file must be copied from the computer to a DV device. During this copying process, the file wrapper is removed.

The software and hardware required for DV nonlinear editing include

- Editing software
- 1394 card
- A second hard drive
- DV deck
- Monitor(s)

To transfer to an analog video format you may want the following:

- Analog deck
- Monitor
- Proc amp
- Waveform monitor and vectorscope

If at all possible, try as many systems as you can before making a decision. Local retailers have some simpler demo systems set up onsite for you to try. Local media organizations and colleges may offer classes and workshops where you can try the equipment.

The software and hardware required for editing digital audio include the following:

- Audio software
- Audio card
- Speakers and/or headphones

To digitize analog audio, you'll need

- Analog decks
- Analog-to-digital and digital-to-analog interface

VIDEO SOFTWARE

The best way to select an NLE is to first choose which editing application you want to use. Your choice really depends on what feels the most comfortable, your budget, and what you want to do. Most editing applications allow you to control your DV deck, select what you want from a DV tape, and transfer it.

From here, the differences are in the user interface and level of control. The number of transitions, although touted in the marketing material, is really not a terribly good indicator of usefulness.

Many applications have plug-ins from the manufacturers and other vendors that can greatly expand the power of the application. Consider the availability of support, books, training tapes, and user groups as you try them.

There are also several demos of editing software available on the DVD included with this book. Other manufacturers have demo versions of their software available for you to try. Often a demo or light version of an NLE application is bundled with the capture card or system you buy.

You may also find that after you outgrow the bundled version of the NLE software, you might want to invest in the full version, but be prepared for some serious sticker shock—professional-quality NLE software and effects packages can get very expensive.

TYPE 1 AND TYPE 2 AVI FILES

With Windows-based machines, there are two types of AVI files. Type 2, the sort of AVI file used by Video for Windows-, or *VfW-*, compatible applications, contains one video stream and one audio stream. The audio buried within the DV datastream is separated into its own track so audio tools in the computer can manipulate it. Because this audio stream is redundant, Type 2 files take up a bit more storage space.

Older applications read and write Type 2 AVIs. Because the boards must supply their own codecs and VfW utilities, they tend to cost a bit more.

A Type 1 DV AVI has a single interleaved video and audio stream. This is more efficient in terms of storage, but not many NLEs can deal with it yet. Starting with Windows 98 and Windows 2000, Microsoft is providing a standard DV codec as part of the DirectShow suite of technologies. The bad news is that this codec will handle only Type 1 AVI files.

Newer products have appeared at a fraction of the cost of seemingly identical older cards. Because they use the DirectShow infrastructure on Windows 98 and Windows 2000 for a DV codec, these cards aren't carrying the costs of creating software codecs. But because they rely on DirectShow, they read and write Type 1 files.

There's no quality difference between Type 1 and Type 2 files. Problems arise if you have a Type 1 file and want to work in an application that supports only Type 2 files. There's no easy way to go between them, although these will likely be developed by a third party at some point. Fortunately, Type 2 tools will install and run on Windows 98 and Windows 2000 platforms.

Make sure the output of inexpensive DV cards gives you the file type you need for the software you want to use. For more information, read Microsoft's official description at `http://www.microsoft.com/HWDEV/desinit/dvavi.htm`. Also, see Richard Lawler's always helpful Silver List at `http://www.well.com/user/richardl/SilverListFrameSet.html`.

THE COMPUTER

You may decide that you want a standalone system such as the DraCo Casablanca. These tools offer full DV editing and storage in one dedicated unit. You just plug in your deck and go. Some people really like them, and some rental houses have them available.

Buying an NLE that uses a desktop computer such as a PC or Mac requires the same sort of research as buying any computer. No one platform is best for everyone. Use what's comfortable for you and the best you can afford. If at all possible, try different systems and software before committing yourself. There are many products and configurations, and you can get a definite feel for what will work best for you if you give them a try.

When you've made your purchase, don't look back. Assume you'll be upgrading software at least every six months and either upgrading or replacing the hardware every 18–24 months.

Most manufacturers recommend you have one machine dedicated to video editing, another for audio, and a third for everything else you want to do on a computer. If that's how you want to do it and you can afford it, go ahead.

Some of us lack both the cash and the room for three separate systems. I use one computer for all of my work. I have a Sony 538DS with a second Maxtor hard drive in it on a 100BASE-T Ethernet network. I've transferred DV files from my deck to the server and edited using Premiere 5.1a without a problem.

I rarely have analog video that I need to digitize. When I do, I either use a friend's deck and go via S-video to miniDV using my Sony GV-D300 portable DV deck, or I send the analog material to a shop to be digitized to DV format.

For analog-to-digital audio recording, I often use a Toshiba laptop and a Roland UA-30 USB A/D interface. The material goes into a Behringer mixing board so I can control levels, and then into the UA-30. All the raw audio goes onto my 538 for manipulation using Cakewalk's Sonar and Syntrillium's Cool Edit 2000.

If I were editing video and audio every day for 12 hours, I'd insist on separate workstations built by reputable vendors. Because my time is divided among many tasks, this system works for me. I keep very good records and back up everything on a regular basis.

I'm not averse to opening up a computer to replace cards, add RAM and hard drives, and so on, but I'd rather be working on my show and not tidying up ribbon cable. But if you enjoy messing around with computers then building your own system may be really fun. There's good information about motherboards and chipsets available all over the Internet. Many of the available products are mature enough that the issues are listed on the manufacturers' Web sites. See Resources for listings.

Don't expect $100,000 worth of performance on a system that cost $5,000. And don't expect $5,000 of performance from a system that cost $899. You can do a lot with very little, but rendering will be a fact of life for some time yet, even with real-time cards for desktop computers.

You'll want a fairly robust system with plenty of drive space. Two gigabytes of hard-drive space will hold about 9:30 of DV footage. If you have an hour to transfer, you'll need about 13 gigs. Having more than one hard drive is a good idea—you place the editing software and scratch disks (the place where the editing application will hold temporary files) on the main drive, and your audio and video files on another.

Unless you have the technical skills to build an NLE, I recommend you buy one. You can always install a 1394 or digital audio card to an existing machine, but be sure to read the manufacturer's recommendations and instructions. Visit user Web sites and message boards for help and be prepared for things to go wrong.

To work effectively, you'll want a good chair and workspace, as well as a decent filing system and tape storage area.

DV ON THE COMPUTER

People talk of nonlinear editing as if it were a brand-new phenomenon. It's not. Film editing is nonlinear—you can grab any piece of film you want at any time and cut it on a flatbed, an upright, or any other film editor.

FIGURE 28.1

Bob Watson's home-editing suite.

Nonlinear video editing, however, is relatively new. In the past, analog video editing required you to assemble your show from beginning to end. That's *assemble editing*. If you made an error and needed to add or remove something, often you had to reassemble from your correction forward. If your error could be repaired in exactly the same amount of time, you could do an *insert edit*: Record over the error with the correction, without touching anything else in the assemble edit. In addition to being time-consuming, linear editing was hard on magnetic videotape because of constant shuttling of the deck.

Video editors came up with some ingenious methods of handling the technical shortcomings of the medium, including timecode and edit decisions lists (EDLs).

When proprietary computer systems came into the video-editing suite, manufacturers and video editors found the joys and hardships of going nonlinear. But the system was still analog-based. The video signal from an analog format, such as Beta SP, was digitized in the computer on-the-fly.

Because video requires a tremendous amount of hard-drive space, editors and technicians came up with offline editing and online editing. *Offline editing* means to digitize footage at a very low resolution to save space. After the show was cut, the editor would create an EDL with all the edits and transitions referenced by timecode.

He or she would take the original tapes and EDL and go into an online suite. An *online edit* is assembling the material at the highest resolution. The online suite would contain a series of high-end decks, all controlled by a central computer or computers. The source tapes were loaded into the decks, the EDL was loaded into the computer, and the computer assembled the show.

Another form of online editing is to take the completed EDL and original tapes and have a high-end, proprietary computer-based system digitize only the necessary footage (based on the EDL) into its hard drives and then send it back to tape as a completed show. This required very fast processors, massive amounts of disk space, and a serious investment.

People still use offline and online editing methods, especially with video that originated as analog and for digital forms such as Digital Beta and HD. Although Digital Beta, HD, and other digital video formats are digitized in the camera, the equipment for manipulating that video data is still outside the budget of most independent producers. They cut in a low-resolution (and relatively inexpensive) offline suite, and then finish in a high-resolution (and usually expensive) online suite.

DV, however, is within budget. In addition to being affordable, it's relatively simple to use and maintain. Plus, some producers editing with laptop and notebook computers will capture DV footage at a lower resolution, cut an offline version of the show, and then online it at full DV resolution. This saves disk space.

TWO-GIG LIMIT

Some operating systems have maximum sizes they allow. Windows 95 running the FAT16 file system can't access any more than 2GB on a drive.

Windows 95 OSR 2 or Windows 98 formats the drive with a FAT32 file system to avoid this limit. With Windows NT or Windows 2000, you can also use NTFS.

Mac OS 7.5 has a maximum partition size of 4GB starting with OS 7.5, whereas Mac OS 7.5.2 has a maximum partition size of 2TB.

The file format for video can also have a 2GB limit. On PC systems, the most common format is AVI, which stands for Audio/Video Interleave. AVI files are limited to 2GB. Some QuickTime files on both Mac- and Windows-based machines are limited to 2GB, regardless of hard-drive size.

There are tricks to get around these limits. Some involve using specialized codecs that use pointers to other files instead of raw data; others use a proprietary, non-AVI format for storage; and others use QuickTime reference files. The system I use automatically breaks larger files into a series of smaller ones, numbering them consecutively.

Already there have been repairs and redesigns to address this issue. See the product information of any system or component you're considering to determine whether this is an issue for you.

CAPTURE CARD

The capture card allows you to transfer to and from your DV source deck and your computer's hard drive. Check your computer's motherboard to see whether it has 1394 ports. There are two types of connectors: the six-pin and the four-pin. The six-pin connectors carry data as well as power to a 1394 device. The four-pin connectors only carry data. Most cameras and decks have four-pin connectors, whereas most computers have six-pin connectors. You can find a four-pin–to–six-pin connector at your local computer shop, at a video store, or online.

If your computer has 1394 ports, you may very well be able to start transferring and manipulating the footage right away. If it doesn't, you'll have to get a 1394 interface card.

The installed DV codec can be implemented in software or hardware. Software-based 1394 cards are cheaper than hardware codec cards because they use software implementations of the DV codec. A hard codec system has the same chips as the camera or deck and allows larger real-time video windows on the computer display and better real-time jogging, shuttling, and scrubbing. Hard codecs also allow scrubbing to a video monitor with no extra equipment. DV data goes into the codec, and the codec outputs the video and audio to a TV monitor.

It doesn't matter whether you use a hardware or software codec when transferring from or to DV VTRs using a 1394 connection. Both software and hardware codecs can give excellent if not identical results regarding picture quality, although minor differences in codecs can cause accumulated errors.

Generally, you'll never notice image-quality differences between codecs. If you take away information, such as using filters to blur or remove video noise, then the compression will likely be near transparent. If you use a filter that adds information, such as adding contrast or sharpening an image, then there will likely be more artifacts.

In either case, it's best to limit the number of passes the footage takes through the codec. Converting from one codec to another is called *transcoding*, and it always involves errors that degrade the overall picture quality.

For more information about codecs, see Codec Central at `www.icanstream.tv/CodecCentral/index.html`.

Strictly Digital or Digital/Analog Capture Cards

There are basically two types of video-capture systems for DV: IEEE 1394-only DV and DV/analog combinations. (There are some ultra–high-end systems that will take anything, but these are as expensive as they are cool.)

DV systems connect to and control the DV deck remotely via IEEE 1394. DV/analog systems accept input from either a DV deck by 1394 or an analog source. If you have a lot of analog video footage, you may want to consider using a combination system.

Composite analog video is carried by a single cable with a single connector. Consumer gear uses RCA connectors, whereas pro gear uses BNC. You will get better quality using a Y/C cable, also known as an S-video cable, that separates the luminance and chrominance elements for better-quality transmission.

The best quality is achieved through the use of component video cables. Component video separates the video signal into three signals that are carried by cables. You will pay a lot more for equipment with component video connections. Be sure you need it before writing that check.

Analog audio is carried in two cables joined together. Pro audio equipment uses XLR connectors for balanced audio. Balanced audio enables longer audio cable runs with little risk of interference or signal loss.

Realtime and Nonrealtime Capture Cards

Capture cards can also be broken down into realtime and nonrealtime. *Realtime* and *nonrealtime* refer to how effects are done, not how the cards capture video in the first place. Your software-based nonrealtime system will capture and lay back DV to tape just as well as a hardware realtime system does.

The advantage of a realtime system is that certain effects are done as you select—there's no rendering.

Rendering is the process of creating transitions and other effects in the NLE. When you place something that needs to be rendered, such as a dissolve, on the NLE timeline, you tell the editing software to make the transition. The editing software calls the DV codec, hands it compressed DV frames, and receives uncompressed RGB bitmaps back. The editing software alters the necessary frames for the transition, and when done, the finished RGB bitmaps go back to the DV codec. The codec compresses the bitmaps back to the correct DV file format and hands them to the editing software. The editing software then stores them.

Basically, it decompresses DV data to RGB, manipulates it, and recompresses to DV.

This process takes time. Nonrealtime systems require that just about everything but cuts must be rendered. Rendering can be 10–20 times the length of the show—several hours are not uncommon. The more titles, effects, and filters you use, the more processing power and time required.

Realtime systems don't require that all titles, effects, and filters be rendered, but handle it as you work. Most realtime systems are not fully realtime—not all the effects are completed immediately, just the easiest or more common ones. Full realtime systems are quite expensive. If you do a lot of effects work on a desktop computer–based NLE, you may find a realtime system worth every penny.

HARD DRIVES

EIDE hard drives are commonly found in many computers, not just those for video editing. Although not the fastest hard drives, they provide plenty of speed for DV editing. These days, you can buy a 30GB hard drive and larger, quite inexpensively.

Ultra-DMA is a further enhancement of EIDE. UDMA drives tend to be less expensive than SCSI-3 drives and are often capable of stutter-free capture and playback of DV. UDMA are backward-compatible with IDE/EIDE controllers, so you can install a UDMA drive into an older computer and it will work. For realtime DV, though, you may need to have a UDMA-compatible controller with BIOS and OS support.

There are several variations of SCSI, or Small Computer Systems Interface, drives. Fast-Wide SCSI uses a 16-bit data path for 20MB-per-second peak transfer rates, whereas Ultra SCSI, or SCSI-3, yields 20MB-per-second through faster data clocking. Fast-Wide and Ultra SCSI drives are fine for DV editing.

Wide Ultra SCSI claims a theoretical transfer rate of 40MB-per-second and Wide Ultra II claims maximum throughput rates of about 80MB-per-second. But even these SCSI numbers are only theoretical whereas the reality is most SCSI buses and hard drives can achieve sustainable read/write rates of only about 6MB–13MB-per-second.

Make sure that the SCSI drives are assigned unique ID numbers, connected to the computer with a robust cable, properly terminated, and in a well-ventilated case. You can avoid annoying problems with care.

RAID (Redundant Array of Independent Disks) arrays are hard drives striped with indexing information that allows the computer to treat the array as a single drive. The advantage is that the computer can interleave data, allowing it to read to one drive while writing to another. Many NLEs that handle analog or digital video requiring higher transfer rates use disk arrays.

DV DECK

You want a deck that allows you to transfer to and from your digital format via 1394. In Europe, DV cameras don't record via 1394. You can transfer from, but not to, a DV camera, requiring either a widget or a separate deck.

Many people use their cameras as decks to save money. If you don't shoot or edit often, you can do this, but I don't recommend it. You're placing undue wear on the tape transport and heads of the camera.

Some decks take different sizes of cassette. DV and DVCAM use two different types, whereas DVCPRO uses another two. The actual reel sprocket is the same for all cassette sizes, but decks that take more than one size move the hub carriers to fit. It is relatively easy to accommodate three sizes if you can already accommodate two. Nearly all pro decks now take all three sizes.

NOTE

Video Linear Editing

You can do linear editing with DV equipment. Sony and Canon prosumer cameras and some decks can be controlled remotely with the Sony Control-L (LANC) protocol. Some Panasonic cameras have Control-M ports. JVC DV cameras offer J-LIP ports for remote control and editing. These cameras and decks will work as edit sources, although they're not necessarily frame accurate.

There are inexpensive standalone edit controllers that can control any mixture of RS-232, RS-422, LANC, and Control-M VTRs, usually accurate to +/-1 frame.

FIGURE 28.2

Sony DSR-20 DVCAM and DV deck.

If you intend to dub your DV tapes to VHS or SVHS, a dual DV/VHS deck may fit your needs. They don't cost much more than low-end single-DV decks, and they offer brainless dubbing of your tapes. The main feature they lack is the ability to use the larger-size DV cassettes. Unless you need to create extremely long productions that you need to record to a single DV tape, you can probably do without the capability to use full-size DV cassettes.

At minimum, your DV deck should have an IEEE 1394 port, composite video in/out, Y/C or S-video in/out, and audio L/R in/out.

MONITOR(S)

In addition to the computer display, you may want to use a studio monitor. Like a field monitor, these tools are designed to be calibrated and used as a reference for your video. It can be handy to have all the screens for your software on the computer display and all the video on the studio monitor. It's not absolutely necessary, however.

If your system allows a second monitor, use it. See the documentation that came with your video-editing card and operating system software.

At minimum, consider using a studio or field monitor, properly set up, with your deck. You can review the footage when you lay it back. Also, consider using a regular television. You can review your show on the set to make sure everything looks all right.

AUDIO SOFTWARE

I recommend you use a separate application for editing your audio. Many NLE software applications have simple audio tools built in that are very helpful for basic postaudio tasks, but you'll probably want more flexibility. Video-editing software uses frames, and you can't manipulate the sound in a more discrete way than 1/29.97 or 1/25 of a second. That's a long time for audio, and you'll have a hard time filtering out pops, snaps, and other noise.

You want software that will allow you to see pictures as you manipulate the audio, can handle and resample different kinds of audio, has visual audio meters so you can keep an eye on the levels, and is easy to use. Most digital audio software allows you to record directly to your hard drive, provided you have a hardware interface.

Many applications have plug-ins from the manufacturers and other vendors that can greatly expand the power of the application. If you want to do MIDI, look for software that allows you to do that, although you can always have a separate application.

Avoid using audio at different sample rates. If you upsample your audio, you won't be adding any detail, but it will be easier to handle. For example, if your dialogue is recorded at 12-bit 32kHz but you have original music at 16-bit 48kHz, you may want to upsample the dialogue to avoid software glitches.

You can use any audio-editing software that will work with the DV format of 12-bit 32kHz or 16-bit 48kHz.

LOCKED AND UNLOCKED AUDIO

DV formats have two kinds of recorded audio: locked and unlocked.

Locked audio has the audio sample clock precisely locked to the video sample clock. For PAL, locked audio provides exactly the same number of samples per video frame with either 32kHz or 48kHz audio. For NTSC, 48kHz locked audio provides exactly the same number of audio samples for every 5 video frames, whereas 32kHz locked audio uses 15 video frames.

In *unlocked* audio, the slaving method used to keep the audio sampling in sync with the video sampling is looser, allowing the audio clock some imprecision. The sync may slip in unlocked audio +/–1/3 frame. However, it stays in sync over the long run.

Unlocked audio was chosen to keep costs down for DV cameras and VTRs. DVCAM and DVCPRO cameras and VTRs generate locked audio.

Some 1394 NLEs generate locked audio, some generate unlocked, and some allow you to choose. DV cameras and VTRs will record locked audio via 1394, and some DVCAM gear will record unlocked audio with a bit of coaxing.

Unlocked audio shouldn't be a problem with a 1394 DV-based NLE. However, when you make an edit using unlocked audio, you may hear two distinct sounds. A click or pop on the soundtrack during playback happens because of an audio buffer overrun, when the audio subsystem has to discard the extra data and resynchronize. You may also hear a dead spot caused by a buffer underrun. That means there are too few bits of sound to cover the time available.

The unlocked audio pop is different from the pop that happens when cutting between two locked audio streams without regard to synchronization.

You may run into trouble using unlocked audio with digital audio systems such as digital audio workstations (DAWs) and multitrack digital audio recorders such as ADAT and DA-88. If the receiving gear is trying to sync to the unlocked audio datastream, the entire audio chain can be rendered unstable.

Convert unlocked audio to locked audio. Transfer the footage into an NLE that outputs locked audio and use it to write out locked audio to a DV tape.

AUDIO HARDWARE

Digital audio requires

- An audio card
- Speakers or headphones
- A quiet room

If you want to work with DAT or DA-88 media, you'll need an appropriate deck and a digital audio card to handle the transfer of digital audio to your hard drive. DA-88 machines in particular offer eight separate tracks. To take full advantage, you'll want a card that allows you to connect directly to bring over all tracks separately.

AUDIO CARD

You can use the audio card that comes with any standard off-the-shelf system. For better quality, however, there are digital audio cards from Aardvark and other manufacturers that offer multitrack recording, better ADC, and more inputs. Some are just cards, whereas others have a card and breakout box. Prices vary, but these tools simply keep getting better.

You may also want to consider audio ADC products that use USB or 1394. If your system already has the inputs, you can then just add on the device.

SPEAKERS OR HEADPHONES

To monitor your audio, you'll need speakers or headphones.

Standard computer speakers just don't have the quality to give you a sense of the full sound. You may want to get a pair of matched full-size monitors. These should be flat-response, meaning they add little or no coloration to the sound. Make sure they're shielded so the magnets inside the speakers don't interfere with your computer equipment.

Go to a high-end music or electronics store and bring along an audio engineer if you know one. You can test the store's studio speakers in the quiet room, but if you can't hear the differences, that may not help you much.

Jay Rose recommends picking up a speaker. Because better speakers use better, heavier components, he argues that weight can often help you make a decision. I think this is a good argument.

Place speakers in an equilateral triangle with you as the apex and mounted solidly just above your ears and aimed slightly down.

You'll need to power the speakers with a decent amp. Decent amps tend to be heavier than cheap ones, so the weight test may help you out here.

Sony MDR-7506 headphones are my favorites. I use them on location and post-audio. Other people use Sennheiser and AKG with success. Just make sure your headphones are comfortable—you'll be wearing them for hours.

Headphones make everything so very close. You hear every change in volume, noise, sputter, and stop. You can spend hours trying to fix something that no one will ever notice. Also, dialogue is more intelligible in headphones than in speakers. I often do a middle mix, where I dump everything to a VHS tape and play it in a regular television to check the sound.

QUIET ROOM

F. Alton Everest's book *Sound Studio Construction on a Budget* may help you design an editing and digital audio suite that will help you get the best results from an existing room.

Check out your editing and audio suite by using the same location audio techniques from Chapter 14, "Scouting and Locking Locations."

Cut down reflections by angling your work area so no walls are directly parallel or perpendicular to the speakers. You can hang up furniture blankets, but they're pretty ugly. You can make a fiberglass foam board wainscot around the room. Use two layers of 2'×4'×2" yellow fiberglass boards. Cover the insulation with pretty fabric. Figure 28.3 shows an example of a post-audio suite.

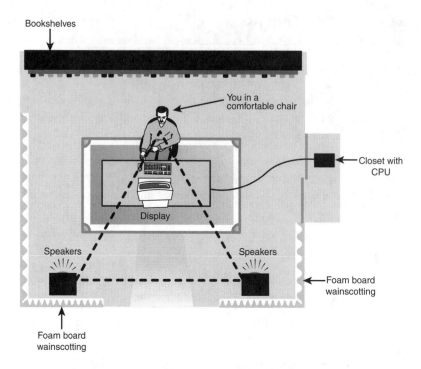

FIGURE 28.3

A home post-audio suite.

Have some shelves along the other walls to further cut reflections.

If you have a closet in the room, insulate it with the foam board and put your computer's CPU in it. It won't completely cut the sound of the fan, but it will help. If you have no closet or separate room, you may want to block out an area for the CPU using the foam boards. Don't shut them up completely, just three sides. You can always tuck the CPU behind a bookshelf.

DIGITIZING ANALOG

To digitize analog audio you'll need

- Analog decks
- Analog-to-digital and digital-to-analog interface

You'll need some kind of analog-to-digital converter. Many off-the-shelf audio cards will let you record by using the miniplug mic in on the back of the computer. That can work in a pinch, but you may want to use a more sophisticated interface for better results.

BEST PRACTICES

Getting the most from your post-audio equipment requires some basic computer practices:

- Add as much RAM as you can.

- Keep applications and program files on separate hard drives.

- Turn off screensavers while transferring footage and recording audio. Turn off virus-checking software, too.

- Read the manuals.

- Defragment your disks on a regular basis. Do NOT defragment a RAID—they don't work the same way as a single disk.

- Turn off all background operations.

- Virus check frequently—do NOT run virus software in the background of your system, but run manual virus checks on a regular basis. Update your virus software as well.

- Reboot often—rebooting often prevents some of the oddest behavior.

- Keep a log of new software installs and exactly what gets installed. You can save the installer logs for the software.

- Never upgrade in the middle of a project—you're asking for trouble.

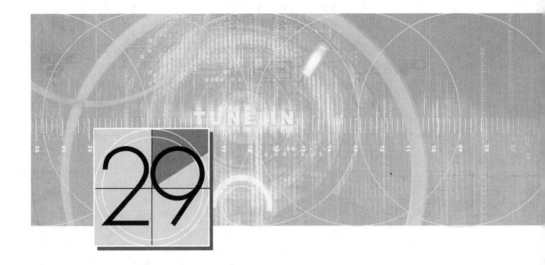

CUTTING PICTURE

Editing is the sort of job that when done well, no one notices.

To edit well requires talent, skill, and discipline. Talent is an unknown factor. You won't really know whether you can edit until you do it. Skill is both knowing your NLE and your experience with editing conventions. Discipline requires the ability to forget everything but what's in the frame as well as the guts to omit material you really like but just doesn't work.

First, decide whether or not you want to work with someone else. There are advantages to working with someone else, especially on your first serious project. In editing, what's outside of the frame doesn't exist—nothing matters but what's in the footage. If you don't have the ability to be ruthless, hire someone to cut your show.

ARE YOU AN EDITOR?

Just as owning a pencil doesn't make you a writer, owning the fanciest NLE on the market doesn't make you an editor. Despite the preoccupation with geegaws and gimcrackery, editing is an art.

Do you have the ability to hold five or six things in your head at one time? Figuring out a way to get from one shot to the next, one scene to the next, one sequence to the next, and building the entire arc is a demanding task. It requires what I call *lookahead*—the ability to see how every decision you make affects what has happened and what's coming. You have to think on the level of the frame as well as the level of the entire movie, all while running a computer, fending off distractions, and imagining additions and changes to audio. If you're easily distracted, maybe you should think of working with someone else.

Do you need a lot of attention? Are you easily bored? When editing, you spend a lot of time alone, wrapped up in single frames and story arcs. Self-reliance is required.

Are you enthralled with nuance? You'll be spending time studying the slightest, smallest changes in performance and meaning. If you have no interest in subtlety, consider hiring someone else.

Do you have the ability to forget all the pain you went through to get a scene so you can sacrifice it when it doesn't work? Your perceptions of a performance can be colored by what happened when you were trying to get that shot. This is, in my opinion, the number one reason to work with an editor. For that person, nothing exists for your show but the footage. Good behavior, atrocious behavior, expensive stunts, heartache, victory— none of that matters.

If you have some doubts about your ability to use your NLE and DAW system, consider taking a class. You may also want to hire someone to teach you how to use a certain piece of software. It doesn't take long to get the basics down.

WORKING WITH AN EDITOR

If you decide to hire an editor, look for one with enough equipment to handle the task with minimum fuss at a rate you can afford. I tend to emphasize personal chemistry over hardware—as long as the person can work comfortably with his or her equipment and the footage stays in DV. The editor who gets the story, fights fair, is creative, and loves the job is the person you want to work with.

You can find motion picture editors just about anywhere and in every configuration: from high-end postproduction houses to an iMac in the basement. Your local film commission should have some listings, as well as any motion picture arts organizations, independent film and video magazines, Web sites, and so on.

Many producers and directors are happy to recommend people they've worked with. Ask around.

You can request a sample reel from someone you're considering. Study the work and see whether you like the style. Listen carefully to how the editor describes the material. An editor who starts badmouthing the footage he or she had to work with may not be the person for you, no matter how affordable the day rate.

Reels are deceptive—it's hard to judge how well the editor did if you can't see the uncut material. Even better is to ask whether you can come in during a session and see the editor at work.

You'll want to meet in person at least once and may want to tour the editing suite. I find this useful and not just so I can count the pieces of hardware. An editor is often more comfortable in this place than anywhere else. You're going to be spending a lot of time with this person, and personal chemistry is important.

Most of the good editors I know are quite intelligent. Interestingly, many of them are or used to be musicians, although rarely would they ever front the band. They may or may not have experience working sets—in my opinion, every editor should be required to work an independent set to understand just how difficult it is to capture footage that's properly focused, much less coherent.

The good editors I know are very adept with language—they can summarize very quickly in concrete terms a shot, scene, sequence, or story arc, as well as articulate a problem and solution. They are diplomatic, until they relax, and then they let it rip. They have very strong egos and can be incredibly ruthless with the material. Telling the story takes precedence over showing off flawless (and often lifeless) editing technique.

The minimum equipment is an NLE that keeps the material in DV format with decent audio monitors and a deck. Anything beyond that is a bonus.

Editors who are sound designers can often sculpt some of the sound, or cut to scratch tracks. A *scratch track* is a temporary audio track on the timeline that is later replaced. It can be very useful for setting rhythm. You can always go elsewhere to handle your post-audio work, but an editor who is also skilled with audio can help you get the most out of combining sound and picture.

TERMS OF ENGAGEMENT

After you've chosen an editor, discuss the money before you start working together. You don't want your project held hostage, and your editor doesn't want to get stiffed. The editor should sign a contract, such as the Technical Services Contractor Agreement located in the Appendix. Usually, editors have set day rates, and most will lower the per day fee for projects lasting several weeks.

You may want to add language that says any failures of the editor's system should not be counted against you. For example, if the hard drive crashes and you lose an entire day's work, you shouldn't have to pay for that day. You will be expected to pay for capturing and rendering time.

You may want to bring your editor into the process early. Some editors may show up on the set to watch continuity. If you can afford it, this can be helpful. Many editors will begin organizing and cutting as soon as dailies arrive.

Some editors have assistant editors who log and order footage for them. You can be the assistant editor if you go in with the camera logs in shape and the material organized. It may be worth buying your own NLE just to handle this task.

If you decide to work with an editor, keep a few rules of conduct in mind:

- Take care of your editor. Make sure both of you get enough to eat. And take some breaks.

- Be prepared with your camera logs annotated and your material as much in order as possible.

- Don't take editing personally. You don't hire an editor to say nice things. You hire him or her to critically appraise every frame and solve problems on behalf of the viewer. Your editor won't be any harder on you than your critics will. The difference is that the editor will have solutions and ideas about how to make the piece stronger.

- Don't flatter yourself into thinking the editor is taking over your show. He or she is just doing the job—if your editor becomes passionate about the piece, it's because the editor wants your show to be as good as it can possibly be. This is the attitude you want.

- Fight fair. Remember these guidelines from a Hong Kong action flick: "No eyes. No groin."

- Don't ask for instantaneous miracles. If it took you weeks to shoot it, don't think an editor will be able to cut it in two days.
- Pay what you promised, when you promised.

EDITING YOURSELF

Most narrative movies use *continuity style* to tell stories. Continuity style is cause and effect, a photographic and editorial style that creates the illusion that a sequence of events appears to present action as it happens. It's also known as *découpage classique* and the *Hollywood style*.

Another style, called *dialectical montage* and promulgated by Sergei Eisenstein, sets up a question in the first two shots, asking for the connection between them, and answering in the third shot. Straight cuts and dissolves are the primary transitions.

The difference between continuity style and montage style involves mise-en-scène and continuity. Continuity style pushes the narrative along in chronological order while remaining within the mise-en-scène. Montage also pushes the narrative along but allows you to create atmosphere, mood, and emotional impact by using discontinuity—another scene in time, location, emotion, and so on, intercut with another scene. Montage allows you to cross-cut between radically different images so the viewer can find a new idea or relationship.

In the United States, montages are often used in dream sequences, flashbacks, or as filler to slow down or speed up sequences so the producer can hit a specific running time. For a movie that's running too long, the editor will use a montage to finish the denouement so the audience knows what happened to the main characters just before the ending. It's usually emotionally very unfulfilling and a cheap way to cover poor directing.

Some of the most interesting motion picture editing is not going on in features, but on television. Some series have a distinct visual style that challenges ideas about correct continuity style editing. If you're interested in short-form motion pictures, television commercials offer some of the finest experimental and conceptual examples.

CONTINUITY EDITING

The conventions of continuity editing use editing as a way to provide shots and nothing more. Changes in camera angle have little or no bearing emotionally on the substance of the scene. Meaning arises from what is being shown at any given moment, not in the contradictions caused by juxtaposing different shots next to another.

Continuity editing uses transitions by matching shots with similar framing, setting, rhythm, and motion.

Shots with similar framing have objects placed in roughly the same frame area regardless of camera position. Similar setting means the shots have the same, or very close to the same, spatial relationships. Similar rhythm means the shots are timed roughly according to focal length, whereas similar motion refers to matching moves either by a person or an object in the frame, or in the camera move.

Continuity style demands that shots must be continuous to create an illusion that what the viewer is seeing is happening in order of time and space.

Continuity in time means that each shot must match according to time when scenes are supposedly happening as they're being presented. For example, if two characters are arguing over money, a pool of sunlight does not change position between shots. If it does, this implies that the argument is not continuous, but has taken place over time. The illusion is broken.

Continuity in space refers to rigorously following the 180° rule. See Chapter 10, "Production Design," for an illustration. (The 180° rule seems to apply more to interiors than exteriors, especially those interiors with little or no movement. Even then, however, directors and editors violate the 180° rule if doing so achieves a desired effect.)

Continuity editing tends to make use of establishing shots to define the geography of the scene and usually at least one principal character. The establishing shot does not have to be first—its purpose is to define the general area of the action that will take place. A reestablishing shot is a reprise of the establishing shot, used if new characters or objects have entered the scene, time has passed, or action has occurred in the area, and you want to reestablish spatial relationships.

Continuity editing also follows the *rule of perception*. The rule of perception says that 30° is the minimum change of camera angle from one shot to another. Less than that can create confusion for the viewer.

Unconventional

Motion pictures seem to follow strict continuity style less and less. As directors and editors have become less literal, and viewers more sophisticated, editing styles are focusing less on continuity and more on conveying the meaning of the scene. Continuity hasn't been abandoned altogether (and I don't think it should be), but directors and editors have finally realized that viewers will follow the story faithfully provided we continue to offer emotional power, truthfulness to the beat, and excellent performances.

In *In the Blink of an Eye*, Walter Murch writes that he has six criteria for any transition:

- It is true to the emotion of the moment.
- It advances the story.
- It occurs at a rhythmically interesting place.
- It's concerned with the viewer's focus of interest.
- It respects the limits of the two-dimensional plane of screen, such as line of action and so on.
- It respects the three-dimensional continuity of the space.

These criteria are an excellent way to make decisions about transitions. Emotion is what should be preserved, sometimes at the expense of other features. Often, you'll be able to get all six aligned, but if you have to choose between emotion and the 180° rule, go with the emotion. Your viewers may notice but quite possibly won't care.

This is not to say you can completely ignore the other features of the transition. Some continuity errors are so tremendous that they can destroy the illusion you're trying to create. For example, you've cut a scene in which a character is buttoning a shirt. In one shot, the shirt is blue, whereas in the next, it's red. If you're trying to create a sense of continuous time, this sort of blivet will shove your viewers right out of the story—you will destroy their willing suspension of disbelief.

However, imagine in one shot the blue shirt is almost completely buttoned and matches continuity with the prior and following shot perfectly. In another take, with a better performance, the shirt is only half-buttoned, violating continuity. If you have to choose one, the more truthful emotion should take priority.

A lot of editors have a hidebound reliance on continuity. People emphasize continuity because it's something anyone can see. But sometimes you have to give up on continuity for the truer moment. Knowing when to compromise continuity for the sake of emotion requires talent, experience, and skill.

ACTION SAFE AND TITLE SAFE

As mentioned in Chapter 19, "The DV Camera," most pro field monitors have an underscan control that allows you to see the complete raster extending slightly beyond the physical edges of the CRT screen. The larger raster, or overscan, ensures that images will always fill the screen of a typical television set.

The amount of overscan is not consistent with all televisions, so it is best to keep important subjects within the Action Safe area and titles within the Title Safe Area (see Figure 29.1). For best results, play back the video on a television.

Engineers have defined Action Safe and Title Safe areas. The Action Safe area is what's visible on most TV sets, and is defined roughly as 90% of the image area. The Title Safe area is even smaller, or about 80% of the image area.

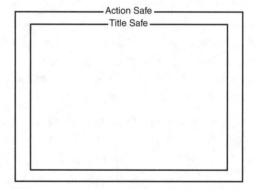

FIGURE 29.1

Action Safe and Title Safe areas.

See your NLE software's documentation for tools to help you keep your images in the proper screen location.

ORGANIZING THE MATERIAL

You have to organize all the material. You can hand over a crate of unlabeled tapes and incomplete logs, but your editor will spend at least a week just trying to find everything. This is not a good use of time or money.

Begin organizing the footage by logging.

LOGGING FOOTAGE

Logging footage means reviewing every frame and writing down where everything is. It's a necessary step and purely technical in nature. If you're working with an editor, discuss logging and paper edits before you're on the clock.

Because I cut my own movies, I do logging myself the old-fashioned way. As I'm watching dailies, I transfer the footage with timecode displayed to a VHS tape. When I start post, I obsessively watch the VHS tapes with the camera logs and put all my notes in my production script. I then write down the location of every piece of footage for every scene on a set of index cards. Each scene gets its own card. I put the cards in order and know where everything is.

If you're working with an editor, you can save yourself time and money by handling all the logging yourself. When I was working with editor Eric S. Anderson on *Amazing World,* I walked in with all the selected footage in scene order on a set of tapes. He didn't have to spend a week figuring out where it all was but could concentrate on doing what he's really good at— putting footage together to tell the story.

If you don't have the time, it may very well be better for you to hand over the camera logs and production script so the editor can start logging.

TRANSCRIPTS

For shows without a script, such as a documentary, you're going to need transcripts of all the materials. A *transcript* is a written version of the material. Don't skip this step. There are companies that will do transcribing. You can find them on the Web or in the Yellow Pages.

I do my own transcripts. I use my VHS tapes with the timecode burn, a set of headphones, and a laptop. I sit in a comfortable chair and start typing. I use the timecode as a reference for where everything is located.

I try to go in order, from the first to last tape. It takes me a long time, but like my index card method, I know the footage very well by the time I go to cut it. I make notes in my transcript about themes, possible sequences, repeated topics, funny things people do and say, and natural transitions.

For example, for my documentary *Family Business,* I was interviewing the children of the subject. I used their references to one another as a way to introduce or return to someone else. It really helped me to move from moment to moment, as well as build the sense of these people as a family.

FIRST PASS

A first pass is a complete look of all the material in one session after logging. This may take several days, but you need to see everything. This can be hard to do with fiction features, because they're usually shot out of order. Many editors have assistants assemble the footage in order. The editors then view that assembly. If you're working alone, you'll need to put it in order yourself.

DECISIVE MOMENTS

In his book, *In the Blink of an Eye*, Walter Murch writes that while watching and prepping dailies 6,000 miles from the set, he pulled a single representative frame from every camera setup. The frames distilled the essence of the thousands of frames making up the shot.

Not only were these still photos helpful for publicity and continuity, he assembled the single frames in scene order in a series of panels. Along with a record of each shot, the combination of frames suggested a series of relationships. Murch wrote: "So the juncture *between* those panels was an interesting thing to look at, because it juxtaposed frames that were never meant to go together and yet there they were.... And sometimes you got sparks out of that, it would cause you to think about things, editorial leaps, that otherwise you might never have thought of...."

Documentary editor Margot Roth uses a similar method. Taking her notes from the first pass, Margot separates individual moments by writing a brief, pithy paraphrase onto a series of index cards.

She includes everything she thinks is interesting: quotes, shots, scenes, silences—everything she may want to pursue. It is, she believes, a way of looking for relationships that you may not otherwise find.

Eric Anderson uses the same paraphrase technique, but he does it in his NLE. When transferring footage, you would think an editor would name the bins and files according to scene and shot number. Not Eric. He paraphrases the footage and uses that as the name. He has a list of scene order based on the paraphrases, but it's remarkably easy to tell where things belong based on his use of language.

I use both Margot's and Eric's methods. I like the speed and convenience of the index cards, but using my NLE helps me lessen my impatience to start cutting.

I take my index card file and begin transferring footage in order to my NLE. Depending on what the project is, I may lay back a chunk of the ordered footage and make another VHS with a timecode burn. For other shows, I only do a collection of selects. *Selects* are selected takes or material, culled from everything. I batch capture certain material and ignore the rest.

What I'm looking for are these key moments when the beat is expressed. Sometimes it's a reaction shot—I love reaction shots—sometimes a close-up, and often it's a certain line delivery.

PAPER EDITS

A paper edit is a way to precut footage using your production script or transcript. For movies with scripts, your production script is the paper edit and your job is to clarify any changes.

For shows with transcripts, though, a paper edit is really important. Audio is often more important than picture, and you may be editing to clarify what people are saying. This means you might want only one phrase from one section of an interview.

Different people have different ways of doing their paper edits. Some mark the pieces they want in the transcript, with a note in where it should go. Because I've done the transcripts, I have a pretty good idea of the beginning, the order of the material, and the ending.

I usually start by reading the entire transcript, concentrating on the really crucial information—single lines and phrases that I find insightful or striking. I then move to creating context for that word or phrase, creating scenes. Then I look for transitions to fit the topic or a facet of the topic so I can assemble the scenes into sequences. I then think about the order of the sequences and note any music I might need and ideas for title sequences, and so on.

If you're working with an editor, this method may still work, but you need to write clear and concise notes.

WORKING ORDER

After all the material is organized, I edit picture in this order:

- Footage review
- Rough cut
- Review
- Fine cut
- Polish

Although it may be tempting to dive into an action sequence or a love scene, what you need at this point is every scene in script order and as complete as possible. Resist the temptation to go in and repair, apply fancy transitions and filters, adjust cuts on frame, and so on. You'll refine as you go deeper.

Keep the movie in straight cuts as long as you can—at this point in the process there's no use in creating transitions that require rendering time. It's easier to change material when the elements remain simple.

FOOTAGE REVIEW

The editor's task is to figure out how to get from one shot to the next in a way that fits the director's vision and works for the viewer. These two goals are often distinctly at odds with each other. Remember that it isn't about you. Don't ask: *Can I make a movie?* Ask: *Is there a movie in all this stuff?*

You can begin to answer that question by analyzing the material. Chapter 9, "Locking and Prepping Your Script," discusses aspects about critical reading and analysis of your script. One of the key aspects is to figure out the givens of every sequence, scene, and beat. A given is specified in the screenplay as well as what's inferred through dialogue and action.

In postproduction, you also have to seek out the givens, but this time the givens are in the footage. Sit down with your camera logs, pen, and notebook, and watch all the footage, paying attention to

- Context
- Style
- Natural transitions
- Rhythm
- Errors
- Stunts and special effects

Context

Context is the meaning of something in relation to its surroundings. When editing all the material for your show, you're constantly referring back to the context of the beat, scene, sequence, show, and movies.

For example, a woman runs down the street. The meaning of her running will be determined by various factors, including what has come before, the circumstances surrounding the motion, the setting, and the music. Add to this the meaning of women running in movies belonging to the same genre as yours. For example, a woman running in a thriller may have a very different connotation from a woman running in a comedy.

In movies, meaning can be manipulated any number of ways. To help you make choices, just as you analyzed your script, analyze the footage by noting the context of each beat, scene, sequence, and story arc.

Style

The style of the footage can give someone an excellent idea about what kind of movie that director wants to make.

Chapter 10 discusses the various aspects of camera work and design you should consider when shooting your movie. Review your footage with these elements in mind: blocking, framing, lighting, props and sets, hair and makeup, stunts, and camera moves.

The look of the shots and the types of performances will give you an indication of what kind of transitions you may want to consider using. For example, an action movie may require a lot of fast cuts, a story of lost love may have more dissolves, and a detective story may use more inserts and action wipes.

Natural Transitions

Note where scenes and sequences offer natural transitions. For example, if the camera pans to follow an actor crossing the room, this implies that the next scene should start with a continuation of the camera move.

Note any blocking that offers opportunities for transitions. *Blocking* is the motion of characters and camera through the scene and includes entrance and exit, cross, lead-and-follow, and circular. Body wipes are moves done by actors who cross in front of the camera, giving you a place to cut.

Note common natural transitions that are completed actions—for example, when an actor sits in a chair. That moment after the actor has settled is a natural place to cut to another scene.

Note lighting and set elements, such as time of day, weather, location, and place in the story arc, as well as the director's aesthetic choices. Pay attention to the effect—not the intent. For example, you may have a graphic match between a night shot and a day shot that can be cross-dissolved to connote time passing.

Rhythm

You may find rhythms established by the blocking, a character's speech patterns, or lengths of shots. Note any patterns that seem to emerge. Also note any music cues—practical music often gives you an idea of what the scene's pacing should be.

Errors

In production, you're constantly making choices, and often the choices have more to do with logistics than aesthetics. Invariably, something gets a bit out of whack. In editing, you're solving problems by taking the greatest advantage of what's available.

Note any scenes that are missing or have technical problems.

Stunts and Special Effects

Write down which scenes have stunts or special effects that require special attention when editing. Before you spend time assembling an action sequence or creating a special effect, you'll want to make sure it fits with the story arc.

ROUGH CUT

Because you already have the material in script order, you now must eliminate everything but what you want to work with. Focus on the story arc and keep moving—get the entire rough cut into place. You can figure out how you're going to solve the inevitable problems, but there's no use reshooting a scene for a show that has no arc.

With the spine of the show in place, start again at the beginning. Edits, just like lighting and script beats, work best when they are motivated. Any transition can break your viewer's concentration and push that person right out of the story. The goal is to make it seamless: the invisible hand at work. To help achieve that, remember to cut on action. Even subtle action, such as a glance, will make the transition seem less obvious.

Placing Transitions

Placing transitions is a lot like placing lights: Where you don't put one is as important as where you do. The following concepts will help you determine where to place transitions and what kind will be most effective.

Basically, you're looking for images that you can match

- Graphically
- Spatially

- Temporally
- By eyeline
- On action

Graphic Matching   Graphic matching means comparing the characteristics of all the key objects in a frame with the characteristics of key objects in another frame. You then match the prior frame to the following frame. Generally, the narrower the difference in camera angle on the same subject in the same mise-en-scène, the more the cut will feel like a jump cut.

Graphic matching occurs when shots share a graphic element and the transition focuses on that element. Often called a *match cut,* usually you dissolve between the two shots for a smoother effect. For example, a scene ending with someone setting down a glass in a bar dissolves into another glass in the same position in the frame in a party across town.

A similar kind of cut is when the match is on action. For example, someone tosses a revolver on a hotel bed. A black-gloved hand reaches in, picks up the revolver. The scene cuts to someone you know was not in the room, picking up a different revolver in a different place.

Spatial Matching   You can determine transitions according to the space around key objects in one frame with those of another. This includes objects, props, set, and camera angle. Spatial relationships usually follow the 180° rule and use establishing shots to allow the viewer to understand the geometry of the scene.

Temporal Matching   Editing allows you to control time by determining the order, length, and frequency of the shots, as well as the rhythm of the transitions. If the scene jumps ahead in time, you can select a transition, such as a dissolve, to better express that change.

Eyeline Matching   If you have a shot where a subject is looking offscreen, the second shot tells the viewer what the subject was looking at. Also, you can make transitions based on the subject's eye movements. For example, even action as small as a blink or narrowing of the eyes gives you a place to cut.

Match on Action   A match on action is when movement in the frame of one shot continues into the following shot. For example, you may have a tracking shot following one character and then cut to the middle of a similar dolly shot with the same speed and screen direction.

Types of Transitions

Transitions are the way you get from here to there, the bridges between shots, scenes, and sequences. Some common transitions are

- Cut
- Dissolve
- Fade out and fade in
- Focus in and out
- Wipes
- Audio cues

Cut   There is an old saying in editing: If you can't say it with a straight cut, there is something wrong with your footage (see Figure 29.2).

FIGURE 29.2

A cut.

A cut is the end of one shot and the start of the next. It is the easiest and most common transition with no visual effect between shots, scenes, or sequences.

A *cross-cut* is a cut between two scenes in different locations happening simultaneously. For example, you may cut between characters talking on the telephone, or between one character doing something dangerous and another doing something innocuous.

A *jump cut* is a cut from the same shot with several frames removed. Jump cuts can be disturbing, and many editors will avoid them at all costs. But sometimes a jump cut is exactly what you want. They can serve almost as a parenthetical comment on the action.

For example, in a scene in *Amazing World*, editor Eric Anderson used a jump cut that wasn't just funny but absolutely right. In the scene, a burned-out rocker (Maleah Jacobs) is explaining that she channels long-dead musicians when writing and performing her music. We then cut to Maleah playing a synthesizer with no sound coming out of it. Smack in the middle of this, Eric cut in this funny head motion Maleah made. It doesn't match the rest of the scene, but it doesn't matter—it works.

Dissolve   A dissolve mixes one image or sound into the next (see Figure 29.3). You often see them as a way to convey the passing of time, dream sequences, fantasies and hallucinations, and so on. Dissolves come in and out of favor, but if you need them, use them. Dissolves have also been used to hide problem footage. As another old saying goes, "If you can't solve it, dissolve it."

FIGURE 29.3

A dissolve.

Editors are now using what I call a jump dissolve. A *jump dissolve* is very quick, usually just long enough to cover a change in audio. I see them used a lot in interviews to move quickly from one piece of narrative to another. It's not as much of a jolt as a jump cut and not as false as cutting to something else in the room. I think they work very well and help the moviemaker create a coherent narrative.

Fade Out and Fade In   A fade out has an image fade into a single color and is often associated with the end of a scene or the show (see Figure 29.4). A fade in is the opposite (see Figure 29.5). The image fades in from a single color and is often associated with the beginning of a sequence or show.

FIGURE 29.4

A fade out.

Fade out and fade in can be from or to any color and of any timing. Eric used a special fade for *Amazing World* that he called an *eyeblink fade*. The image would fade to black at one rate, but fade up much more quickly to the next scene. Because there's so much music in the movie, he often timed the fades on the beat of the music. The eyeblink fade, along with its placement, is also an example of creating a transition palette for the entire show.

FIGURE 29.5

A fade in.

Focus In and Out   Focus in and out can be a bit jarring. They're often used when a character passes out or is knocked unconscious and then slowly awakens.

I've seen some uses of focus changes made in postproduction that have been quite interesting. Using blur filters in the NLE, editors can create changes in depth-of-field and rack focus from one subject to another that are quite effective.

Wipes   A *wipe* is a physical change between two images. For instance, a line going from one side of the screen to the other pushes out the old image and introduces the new (see Figure 29.6). Wipes are often used as a bridge between noticeable gaps in time or location. Many editing applications and video mixers offer many, many kinds of wipes that call so much attention to themselves that they're rarely effective as transitions.

An *action wipe*, however, is a different kind of transition. An action wipe uses an element in the shot to make the transition, such as the motion of someone crossing the scene in a body wipe.

FIGURE 29.6

A common wipe, called a push.

Audio Cues   An audio cue transition uses sound from a previous or next scene. Usually, a cut comes somewhere after the audio cue has started in what is called an *L-cut*. I find these very effective, especially for reaction shots.

If you're both editor and sound designer on your project, consider working with sound as well as picture as you edit. Don't spend a lot of time repairing major audio problems or prepping the tracks, but place some music and effects scratch tracks.

> **NOTE**
>
> **Reading Inserts**
>
> An *insert* is a shot of an object, such as a spinning newspaper, inserted into the show to draw connections and advance the story. When you use inserts the viewer must read, such as signs, book covers, and so on, it's important to allow enough time so the viewer can read it. Set reading time for onscreen materials by timing how long it takes you to read the insert three times.

Because I usually write and perform some of the music for my shows, I often have it completed before I start shooting. Especially for short shows or sequences, I place the music first and often cut picture to it, rather than sticking the music in later. The music gives the images continuity and forward motion so I can concentrate on what is happening emotionally.

TRANSITIONS BETWEEN SCENES

With your notes from your footage review, consider how you want to handle changes in location and time. If your show has a lilting quality to it, you may want to use slow fades and dissolves or hold exit shots a bit longer before cutting to the next scene's entrance. If you want a more frenetic pace, consider how fast you want to go from one scene to the next and how you'll allow the viewer some breathing room.

Breathing room is a change from the current pace, a transition in rhythm that retains viewer interest and gives the viewer a chance to absorb what has happened. This usually occurs between scenes. Scenes that exist merely to give the viewer room to think are wasted screen time.

Place the natural transitions. The trick is to keep them tight, especially for action wipes. It takes about a quarter of a second, or about six frames, for the viewer's eyes to move from one side of the frame to the other. During this time, a viewer can become confused or distracted before refocusing on the scene. Try to place your transition as the subject's eyes pass the edge of the frame. Start the next scene about six frames before the person's eyes enter the frame.

Consider placing scratch music early in the process. Rhythm is extremely powerful, and it helps to have an ongoing beat for you to follow. If you don't have music for a scene or sequence, you may decide to follow the speech rhythms of a certain actor. Even if you have no soundtrack planned for this sequence, you may want to have scratch music anyway to help you build a visual rhythm.

TRANSITIONS WITHIN SCENES

The easiest way to approach editing within a scene is by following the pattern of shooting: from wider to closer. Begin with a momentary wide shot, cut to a medium shot, and then cut to close-ups. Some scenes will then return to the wide shot.

Remember the rule of perception: A new shot of the same subject is justified only if the camera angle changes by at least 30°.

Shot length is determined by how long it takes for the viewer to see the key elements. For example, a cityscape is a cityscape. You don't need to linger over that shot because the viewer will see it and know what it is. Unfamiliar elements, however, may need a longer establishing shot.

But after you've established it, you don't need to continually have long, lingering shots of that subject. For example, if you've created a spaceship, you may want to give the viewer an extra moment to look at the exterior. The next time the spaceship is shown, the viewer doesn't need that amount of time because he or she knows what it is.

Make use of cutaways. B-roll material, such as reaction shots and inserts, are often the most interesting material you have. By combining these with the dialogue, you allow the viewer to become part of the show. The viewer will make connections between what's being seen and heard, making the experience more interesting.

Many cuts often feel like things are moving quickly, whereas fewer cuts can imply leisure. Contrasting scenes and sequences with quick cuts and those with longer takes can be a very effective technique, provided the emotion of the scene requires it. Be careful not to shift rhythm too much—it can quickly begin calling attention to itself.

Cutting on action within scenes generally has the first third of the action in the first shot, whereas the following shot has the second two-thirds of the action. This is not always the case, but this is a very handy convention for cutting on action.

Most stunts and special effects follow an arc of action. For example, a fist-fight may begin with the first punch, shown in one shot, and then move on to a series of quick cuts as the fight continues. The pacing slows down toward the end, usually finishing on another completed action, such as another punch that sends the bad guy flying into a heap of priceless crystal figurines, where he lies unconscious. The action is complete.

Many transitions are used to control an element in the story such as perspective, time, and rhythm. You may want the viewer to get closer to the characters, so cut to closer shots. You may decide to stretch out a moment by not cutting a long take or compress time but cutting directly to the point. You may decide to use a long dissolve out of a scene or a dissolve between cuts to imply time is passing.

TECHNICAL TROUBLE

In a perfect world, you would have every bit of material you require, with perfect performances from subjects and camera, and utterly without technical problems.

It's not a perfect world.

Even big-budget shows have technical problems. The list is potentially endless: video problems, audio problems, continuity errors, dropped shots and missed scenes, and so on. You can ignore them or

- Cut around by using only the audio and footage that doesn't include, or minimizes, the error.
- Cut around the error by shortening the scene.
- Cut around the error by reordering the shots.
- Cut around the error by using excess footage that has been poached or recorded before "Action!" and after "Cut!"
- Omit the footage entirely and use black video to be replaced by footage from a reshoot.
- Omit the scene.

Video Problems

Video technical problems may include

- Color balance and exposure
- Unwanted objects in frame
- Focus problems and damage

Most viewers notice color balance differences, especially in images with faces. Even if you or your camera operator was very conscientious on the set, problems arise, especially if you're using multiple cameras.

If you have footage with major color differences between shots of the same scene, you may want to test color correction before you start editing. If you have software that will make changes in color balance, try it out on short lengths of footage.

You can try the same ideas in the preceding list with exposure differences, although they're harder to fix. Especially if a shot has a massive amount of video noise, you may have to either cut around or accept the imperfection. Some software will minimize video noise, but you'll get artifacting.

You can also contact a local postproduction house regarding tape-to-tape color correction. These systems can clean up a lot of unwanted video noise as well, which may help with shots of radically different exposure. Often the colorist can look at the footage and tell you immediately whether it's something they can fix.

Shots with unwanted objects in the frame can be repaired by applying a blur to everything in the frame but the subject. Basically, you apply a filter that mimics a shorter depth of field. If you can blur that lightstand in the back corner, it may be unrecognizable and not of any concern to the viewer.

You can also rotoscope. *Rotoscoping* is the process of painting on top of an existing image. You can paint out wires, gear that accidentally gets into the shot, unwanted people, and so on. You can also use a digital matte to block out unwanted parts of the image. See the section "Digital Visual Effects" for more detail.

Material that is out of focus or damaged is unfixable. Your choices are to not use the footage (although you may be able to use the audio) or rethink the shot. Sometimes mistakes have one second of very effective, messed-up images that can really work. For example, during an action sequence I was shooting with a SteadiCam, I tripped, blowing the take.

In editing, the footage with the trip was jarring and ugly. I had marked it as unusable, but when I looked at it again in context with other shots, it was right for the sequence.

You may want to consider using exaggerated effects. For example, you may completely blur, change the colors, add haze, or composite in other images. It's not ideal, and using exaggerated effects on half the shots in your romantic comedy will scream that someone was trying to rescue unacceptable footage. Still, you'd be surprised how well you can cover.

Audio Problems

Audio problems can be deceptive. While cutting picture, you need to be aware of certain audio issues, primarily what's an easy fix and what is more complicated.

An actor may have misread part of the scene or a line that you corrected in a later take. There may be part of that performance that's very powerful and right, but the rest won't work. You may have to live with it or schedule ADR for the entire scene.

A single muffled or missing word can be very hard to repair. Intense on-set performance can be hard for actors, even good ones, to match. Plan on spending time re-creating the line from existing material or doing ADR.

Audio continuity problems can be caused by variations in

- Mic characteristics
- Mic distance
- Levels
- Background sound

Different mics sound different. This is especially noticeable between shotgun mics and lavs. Usually, lavs are much closer than shotgun mics to the audio source, complicating the potential problems. Take a piece of intercut audio and try applying some filters, EQ, and reverb to see whether you can match the audio.

If not, you may want to talk with an engineer at a post-audio house. He or she may be able to match the sound.

Differences in mic distance may also result in changes in levels. The mic moved, allowing more background sound, for which the sound mixer had to adjust the recording level. An actor may just be louder than another, so the mixer adjusted to compensate. You can place room tone to help smooth out the differences, but most of these problems should be handled in post-audio.

Changes in background sound can sometimes be diminished by judicious use of filtering. You may also be able to mask some noise by laying in a soundbed of consistent background sounds. Some changes in audio, however, are next to impossible to repair. If a Harley roars by during one crucial close-up and you want to cut to another, the throaty motor, complete with Doppler effect, will disappear, calling attention to the cut.

Continuity Errors

Continuity errors by subjects or cameras cause big headaches.

If you have a blown line or missed camera move, you can cover it with another take. Use those reaction shots and cutaways.

Worse are errors with screen direction. For example, a character exits camera left, but then enters the next scene camera right. This isn't always a mistake, but it can certainly be jarring.

Your choices are to not use the exit or entrance. If you must use it, you can flip-flop the necessary shots. A *flip-flop* is taking an image and flipping it horizontally so the characters are facing or moving in the right direction. Keep an eye out for any lettering or other obvious clues that the cut was flip-flopped.

Dropped Shots and Missed Scenes

Dropped shots and missed scenes are those that were skipped during production either through a bit of disorganization or schedule constraints. With the unrealistic schedules of many independent shows, dropped shots and missed scenes are common. Add to this that often no one reviews the dailies or bothers to keep track of what has been done, so the producer has no idea whether everything is in place. Everyone goes home, and only in post do you realize something is terribly wrong.

If the shot or scene is integral to the story, it should be rescheduled and shot prior to the end of principal videography. If you didn't realize how important it was, schedule your reshoots after you have the rough cut in order. You may have other pickups, or may be able to reorder later scenes to lessen the impact of the missing material.

REVIEW

It's called a rough cut for a reason: It's rough to watch. You'll quickly find this out after your first review.

People respond differently to a show depending on how close to finished it is. A rough cut without sound effects and music may not be as well received as one with those elements in place. If you can scratch in your sound effects, music, and so on, do it.

It's okay to show your rough cut to friends, but also show it to people who had nothing to do with the show. Find five people you trust. Not five people you like or five friends, but five people who will tell you the truth. Ask these five people to a screening and be sure to make popcorn—remember that they're doing you a favor and not the other way around.

As they watch your show, you should watch them. Note any time they start shifting or look bored or confused. Any time someone says, "What?" make a note. You may have to repair or replace that audio.

Ask them what they thought of the movie. When you get their responses, take notes and keep your mouth shut. It's not about you—it's about the work. If you have specific questions, wait until the person has finished before asking. And don't apologize or explain—no matter how much you want to defend your show, don't. Just say thank you.

What you should listen for are points of common agreement—if everyone hates a character they're supposed to love, misses a major plot point, or laughs when they're supposed to be crying, you've got problems.

Some people are not going to like your movie no matter what. It simply may not be the kind of movie they like. This is not to say that their comments should be ignored, but listen critically as they respond. Sometimes people start talking about the movie they wanted to see and not the movie you just made.

Give yourself some time before reviewing your notes. Use what's helpful and ignore the rest. Revise as you see fit.

FINE CUT

A fine cut involves solving problems you couldn't take care of in the rough cut.

Minor tweaks include correcting rhythm and transitions that are a little too loose or a little too tight. You may swap out one take for another, but usually these are minor corrections and clarifications.

The most common fine cut revisions involve rhythm. Like a screenplay, come in late and leave early. Cut away the moment the visual statement has been made. If you're not sure a shot needs to be longer, leave it out. Your reviewers will tell you if they're confused or lost before you do the fine cut. Eliminate repetition. If you've said it once, you don't need to say it again.

Consider asking the editor to take a couple weeks off, and have one more review before clearing off the material.

DIGITAL VISUAL EFFECTS

There are two ways to consider digital visual effects: creative and corrective.

Creative effects are those that add to the shot or scene. This includes gunshots, explosions, animated characters, and virtual sets. If you need creative effects in your show, you can hire people to handle it. Bring them on early, and don't expect the work to be cheap or fast.

Corrective effects are applied to existing footage usually to remove unwanted objects in the frame.

If you want to do the work yourself, make sure you feel comfortable with your skills as a visual designer and creator. You can have the greatest software in the world, but if you have no eye for perspective, the result may be less than pleasing.

Remember that one second of video takes 29.97 frames of video. You may be applying effects to each individual frame, and that takes time. Still, if you're not under the gun regarding scheduling, give it a try. It may be the thing that saves you from having to reshoot a scene.

ROTOSCOPING AND MATTES

Rotoscoping is a process in which you paint directly on the frame. It was originally associated with animation. Animators would trace the movements of a subject on which to base animated characters. Since its inception, it's become an important tool for visual effects.

Digital rotoscoping uses a computer to manipulate individual frames, making this painstaking, highly demanding craft much easier. For removing unwanted parts of the image, you'll paint over each affected frame in a paint application such as Adobe Photoshop. You then reassemble the painted frames in your NLE.

FIGURE 29.7

Before (left) and after (right) rotoscoping. I put a little bit of light in John's hair to mimic a backlight.

You can also create and apply *mattes*. A *matte* is a mask that screens out areas of an image, leaving select areas visible. Most mattes are created using a combination of photographs, software filters, and drawn effects in the computer.

Mattes can help you block out unwanted objects in the frame. As long as the action doesn't cross into the matte area, you can cover a boom or boom shadow with a matte. It's a little faster than rotoscoping because you can often apply the matte to lengths of footage in your NLE, rather than place it on each individual frame manually.

Because color space for computers and video are different, you need to keep a sharp eye on your RGB values. The majority of computer graphics applications set black at 0% brightness with an RGB color value of 0,0,0, and white at 100 percent brightness, with an RGB color value of 255,255,255. Many digital video systems set black at just more than 6% brightness, with an RGB color value of 16,16,16 and white is just over 92% brightness and 235,235,235.

The DV datastream itself is based on 16/235 luminance. Determine whether your NLE allows you to select whether or not to have the luminance range clamped at 16/235 or stretched to 0/255. Some will make the change automatically, and others will clamp luminance at 16/235.

There are two ways to handle these differences in source luminance. The first is to set your NLE and animation to the video legal levels of 16 and 235 before combining them. The second option is to composite the material and then run a clamp on the edited footage to make sure the video is legal with black value at 16 and white value at 235.

Your NLE may have a filter that will lock the black and white values to 16/235. If your system doesn't have a filter, or you want more control, process each frame in a paint application such as Adobe Photoshop and apply Levels, with Output Black set to 16 and Output White to 235.

See Chapter 27, "Explosions, Gunplay, and Fistfights: When to Call In the Experts," for more discussion on CGI.

POLISH

Get yourself some time between the fine cut and a polish, and then watch the whole show from beginning to end. Tweak as necessary. After the material is in place, apply filters and render everything.

Drop in scratch sound effects. If you're not doing tape-to-tape color correction at a post house, place titles and credits. Be sure to proofread your credits. See Chapter 31, "Finishing," for more information.

MAKING IT LOOK LIKE FILM

You can process video footage to look more like film. This often requires a services bureau or plug-ins for your NLE to filter your footage. Some of the filtering includes deinterlacing, altering gray scales, color, and contrast, adding grain, and adding motion characteristics to mimic film.

The final image depends on how good the untreated video is. If it was well-lit, stays away from lots of camera movement, and is well-composed, you're going to get a better result. Stay away from higher shutter speeds and turn down the detail enhancement. Expose properly, and especially look out for overexposures and hot areas. Stay away from fast camera moves and transitions, and discuss with the service bureau if you need fast or slow motion.

Remember that if you plan on transferring to film, do not use any filmlook process on the footage. Use it only for home video, broadcast, or video display masters.

Generally, service bureaus will charge you per minute, with a minimum number of minutes, to run your footage through their systems. Many will use line doublers and digital up-converters to reduce some of the digital artifacts and simulate higher definition. See the Resources section for listings.

You don't have to go to a service bureau and spend tons of money. There are several vendors who sell third-party plug-ins for popular NLE applications. You'll have to render the resulting footage, but it's a lot cheaper than most bureaus and can look pretty good.

FIELD DOMINANCE

To make sure filters, transitions, titles, and digital visual effects work properly, select the proper field dominance. Field dominance determines what order the two fields, upper and lower, are in when a frame is made up for editing purposes.

All the video tracks in your NLE should have the same field dominance—for DV, that's lower field first. That way, the even fields get combined with the even fields and all the odd fields with the odd fields. If the video tracks have mixed field dominance, one of two things will happen:

- The NLE detects the difference and interpolates a new field, resulting in lower vertical resolution.

- The NLE doesn't detect the difference and gets the fields backward. When played, the fields come out in reverse temporal order. The frames are in the correct order, but the fields within the frames have been flipped. The result is ugly and choppy.

If your rendered transition or effects look awful, check the field dominance setting first.

WHAT TO DO WHEN IT'S JUST NOT WORKING

Sometimes it just doesn't work. The first task is to correctly identify the problem. Generally, most editing problems fall into certain categories:

- Story arc
- First act tempo
- Second act sag
- Third act confusion
- Scenes
- Shots
- Character
- Performance

STORY ARC

Story arc problems include pacing, duration, and structural problems.

If you don't have a scratch audio track, consider putting one in. If you have one, consider changing it. You'd be surprised at how often what appears to be a problem with pacing or rhythm is corrected by the right music.

Examine the transitions. Sometimes straight cuts are the best path, but if you just need to linger at a moment to let what happened sink in then use a dissolve or montage.

If the show is too long, you have to consider what crucial information must stay and how you'll convey it when you start removing scenes and sequences. If the show is too short, consider how you can add length. Review outtakes and poached material. Often you can find what you need.

If you need to add substantive material, consider first if you can make the addition with an audio cue. An offscreen comment can relay the necessary information for minimal expense. You can use a voiceover, although I find they are often obviously in place to avoid reshoots and are emotionally

NOTE

Desperate Measures

When you're trying to solve editing problems, try an idea, no matter how ridiculous it may seem. You can always undo it. Often the silly idea doesn't work, but it may lead you to try something else that does.

very unsatisfying. Still, if you don't have any money for a reshoot, a voiceover can do the trick.

Structural problems often involve mistimed events—for example, when the audience is expecting a conflict, but the tension and forward motion are put on hold because the movie moves to some insignificant subplot. Other structural problems may require that you reconsider the entire show. Sometimes letting go of what you think the movie should be and paying attention to what it is can help you revise.

I was asked to review the rough cut of a show that followed strict continuity-style editing. It had major problems, not the least of which was that it was chaotic and dull. When asked for any ideas on how to fix this mess, I responded that perhaps the editor and director may want to rethink the style of the show. A more expressionistic, montage approach may allow the viewer to at least empathize with the very dull main character. I also suggested they cut as much of the main character as possible to focus on some of the supporting characters, who were a lot more interesting to watch.

The editor then showed me footage of some backstage hijinx that was hysterical. I found out the DP had poached hours of material of extras and actors that was priceless. When I asked why they weren't using it, the editor replied that it wasn't in the script. "Forget the script," I responded impulsively. "This stuff is great."

The atmosphere of the room changed. I found out later the editor had been encouraging the director to do this very thing.

A few months after that, I was asked to take a look at the rough cut of another show. This one was also chaotic and dull, but for the opposite reason—the director/editor was using too many expressionistic, music-video style transitions. These choices resulted in characters too far removed to be recognizable, much less sympathetic. The director/editor was trying too hard for a visual style that made him look cool, not a visual style that conveyed the story the footage contained.

When asked for ideas on how to fix the show, I asked to see the script. The director/editor had no script, no notes, no camera logs—nothing. I suggested, gently, maybe he should review the material and organize it a bit better. His visual style was very powerful and could certainly work, as long as he had something substantive to hang it on.

FIRST ACT TEMPO

If you find yourself introducing your show by saying something like, "The first ten minutes are kind of slow, but it really picks up after that," you have a problem.

Cut redundancy. You don't need to show the character's family eating a complete breakfast if the point of the scene or sequence is to establish the character has a family.

Ask:

- What is it in the first act that is absolutely necessary to the story?
- Is there any way to convey this information in single, quick cuts to make those slow 10 minutes evaporate?
- Is there a way to shift this information to later parts of the movie?

If worse comes to worse, you can always run opening credits over the sequence. Just be sure the crucial plot and character points aren't buried under someone's name.

Other times, the beginning of the show is too fast. Many moviemakers rush the first act, even when the show has a leisurely, lush pace. I think a lot of this is the influence of commercial television, which requires speed and power to hook viewers in so they'll put up with the commercial breaks and not change channels. But sometimes the pace is the hook. Don't be afraid of deliberate, slower tempos if that's what your story requires. I'd love to see more DV movies with first acts that ease the viewer in, rather than the typical music video jumps and leaps.

SECOND ACT SAG

Features, regardless of budget, often suffer from second act sag. The movie seems to be treading water, and rarely in an interesting way. It's just a long slog of grafted-on subplots, forays into false starts, and the sex scenes.

If your show has second act problems, start chopping. If the subplots go nowhere, or the performances are weak and bring the entire show to a grinding halt, use that delete key. A tight 40 minutes will make a better show (and speak better of you) than a dull, sloppy 90 minutes.

Some movies, however, suffer from having no subplots. This is a script problem that can be very difficult to repair without getting on a set. If you want, or are obligated to deliver, a feature-length show, you may need to schedule some shoot days to gather material for your second act.

Ask yourself the following questions:

- Is the problem too much or too little material?
- Is there any way to convey this information in single, quick cuts?
- Is there a way to shift this information to later parts of the movie?
- Do I need to shoot additional footage?

THIRD ACT CONFUSION

Some movies just stop. Sometimes that is absolutely the best ending, and viewers have a chance to readjust as the credits roll.

More often, though, an ending is stuck on because the director thinks people will like that better. That may be true, but sticking on an ending completely antithetical to what has come before will leave many emotionally unsatisfied. If there's no way the hero is going to live happily ever after, why does the movie end there? If it's more likely the hero dies, or walks off alone, then do that. Be true to the story.

Some directors think they're being very clever by changing up at the end. For example, the lead character has been chasing a crook and at the very end, someone pops out of the woodwork to declaim that the hero has been chasing the wrong person all along. That's not the end of a movie—that's a beginning of a story. Unless you have set up this ending skillfully, it will leave your viewers confused and dissatisfied. They won't be impressed at your cleverness, but irritated at sloppy storytelling.

I worked a show where the second lead made a startling revelation at the climactic point in the script. The problem was that the show was about someone else. This character's revelation came out of nowhere and had little, if anything, to do with the lead. It was part of a setup for what was supposed to be a happy ending, and it was wrong for both the performances and the arc of the story. The viewer would simply not believe it.

Luckily, I caught it early enough to suggest another ending. We happened upon the perfect place for the new ending while waiting for the rest of the ensemble to arrive at a new location.

A lot of movies end with a voiceover or a card telling the viewers what happened. These can work to clarify things, but they are a bit heavy-handed and old-fashioned—but if that's what you want and it works, that may be appropriate. Consider parity—if you have a voiceover or card at the end, consider having one at the beginning to bookend the show.

Finally, consider moving the end to the beginning. For some stories, *what* happens is not as important as *how* it happens. This is especially true of stories based on fact—we all know the outcome; we just want to know why it happened the way it did.

Oddly enough, the way a character dies can be very revealing and an excellent way to establish who this was.

Ask yourself the following questions:

- Is the ending set up from the first frame of the show? If not, can I set it up with existing material? If not, what do I need to set it up?

- If another ending will work better, do I have existing material to cover? Do I need to shoot coverage?

- Is it possible to shift the chronological end of the story to the beginning of the show?

- Do I need title cards or a voiceover?

SCENES

Sometimes the problem has to do with specific scenes or sequences of scenes. Those that read well during prep and production may play as inconsequential or dull. Omit them.

If a scene seems repetitive, look at the prior scene that it seems to be repeating. You may be able to lose this one with little damage.

You can try reordering scenes, especially those that are cross-cut. Sometimes shaving off portions of scenes can make them flow better. As long as you establish where we are and who is there, you can do a lot with very little.

Documentary editor Margot Roth uses the term *contraposto*: putting images or audio that are opposites together to see the result. Juxtaposing contrary shots, reactions, and sound can often work for scenes and shots by creating a third meaning between the two opposites.

Other common techniques for solving problems with scene chronology is using flashbacks, dream sequences, and flights of the imagination. Moviemakers used to use wavy lines and harp music. Now many moviemakers use straight cuts, although they often treat the flashback or sequence with filters to set it off against the everyday life of the movie. Music and other sound effects can be very useful in marking images that belong to flashbacks, dreams, and the imagination.

You can also reorder a scene. Reordering a scene is often necessary when the dramatic beat has fallen somewhere else other than at or near the end. You have to be somewhat careful because continuity blivets can make the whole thing confusing, but this often works quite well.

SHOTS

Many problems with individual shots are technical, including problems with audio or something in the frame that shouldn't be there.

Shots that have the boom or a lightstand in the background can be corrected using rotoscoping or digital matte work.

Shots that have eyeline or screen direction problems can be flip-flopped. Just be sure there's nothing obvious that will give it away.

Some shots lack parity, but you need to move between them. This can be difficult to solve. Either cut to something else and then complete the shot sequence or don't worry about it.

Other shots may be very, very dark. You can apply filters and raise the overall illumination, but watch out for video noise. If you've decided on tape-to-tape color correction, you'll be surprised at what a good colorist can do. Still, you may want to discuss it and screen the material before committing. Although colorists can work magic, they can't yet perform miracles.

CHARACTER

If the main character is too passive or unlikable in an uninteresting way, you may have a very difficult time trying to fix it. I'd like to be clear that unlikable is not enough to be a problem. A main character can be downright hateful, yet fascinating. The problem is when the character is unsympathetic and dull. Viewers will forgive just about anything but dullness.

This could be a script problem. Passivity in particular is often a result of a script where things happen to the character, but the character does nothing on his or her own initiative. You can't really fix this.

Unlikability, though, can be made interesting. Don't try to dodge it. If you don't have the footage, consider shooting more that really shows the character as a real pig.

PERFORMANCE

Often viewers perceive a character based on the actor's traits, not on the character's. Make sure you're not affected by the actor's bad behavior and weakening that actor's scenes. You'd be surprised at how often it happens. The person onscreen may have caused you all kinds of problems or may be someone you don't like, and these attitudes can drift into editorial decisions. You may want someone unconnected with the show to review that actor's footage to get a more objective opinion of the material.

Some performances are just not good. The best you can do is limit the actor's onscreen time.

If the problem is with line readings, you can schedule a series of ADR sessions. You should plan on doing entire scenes, not single lines, to keep the audio consistent. For more information, see Chapter 30, "Post-Audio."

Consider reshooting the scene or take. If the actor is good, but just misread a line or was poorly directed, you may be able to get this easily. If the actor is poor, you may have to recast. If the actor is poor, but you can't recast, consider cutting the lines way back and having someone else onscreen say them.

PICKUPS AND RESHOOTS

If you need to reshoot certain shots, scenes, or sequences, handle it as if you were producing a short motion picture. You'll need to contact everyone, get the location, schedule, and let everyone know what's going to happen. Make sure you have matching wardrobe, props, and set design.

Keep it as simple as possible.

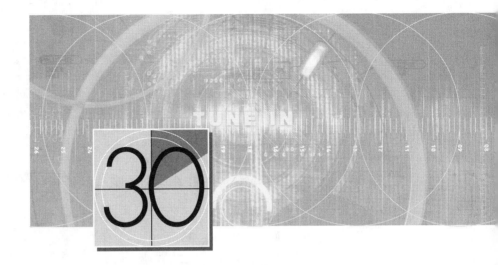

POST-AUDIO

Too often producers approach post-audio tired and broke. Get your post-audio people, especially composers and performers, involved early in your show. If you're handling your post-audio work yourself, try to get a bit of time between fine cut and audio to charge your creative batteries. Just don't try to handle any elaborate post-audio work before you've locked your picture—it can be frustrating, time-consuming, and expensive.

The priorities of any post-audio work are

- Dialogue
- Narration and voiceovers
- Sound effects
- Music
- Sound beds and ambience

Before you dive into the audio work, consider how much of the post-audio work to do yourself. Depending on your budget and interest in the work, you can handle all, none, or somewhere in between. I suggest you consider handling at least the most basic tasks (which we go into in this chapter). It may save you money, give you control over the audio aspect of your show, and give you a concrete example of why good location audio is so important.

Besides, as sound designer, producer, director, and my pal Peter B. Lewis says, "Sound is fun." It is fun. Even inexpensive digital audio software for desktop computers is amazingly powerful. You can experiment with changes in tone and volume, placement of effects, removing little clicks and breath sounds, adding footsteps and other sounds, and so on. Even the simplest, easiest audio tasks can be quite absorbing. Doing this work also teaches you why a good sound designer is worth every penny.

WORKING WITH A SOUND DESIGNER OR POST-AUDIO TECH

Sound designers, as in *directors of sound*, are a little more difficult to find than editor and camera operators. Some post-audio houses have people who are, or want to be, sound designers. Check your local film commission for listings, as well as any motion picture arts organizations, independent film and video magazines, Web sites, and so on.

Many producers and directors are happy to recommend people they've worked with. Ask around.

On a Hollywood show, the first postproduction sound person brought onto the project is the *supervising sound editor*. The supervising sound editor directs and coordinates the postproduction sound staff as well as handles related administrative duties.

In large productions, teams of mixers will handle every aspect of audio simultaneously. The *lead mixer* usually handles dialogue and ADR and may take care of music with another mixer. The *sound effects mixer* handles sound effects and Foley (see the following for a discussion of ADR and Foley). Most independent shows, however, have neither the personnel nor the need for the personnel to split up the tasks so completely. Many post-audio houses, in fact, have audio engineers who are also Foley artists, composers, and producers themselves.

What you want from a sound designer or post-audio technician is enough equipment to handle the task at a rate you can afford. As usual, I emphasize personal chemistry over boxes. As long as the sound designer can work to picture, has enough audio equipment to handle any audio format you may need, and has recording facilities for voiceovers, ADR, and Foley if you need them, you can get to work. This does not mean a huge recording studio and Neumann microphones, although if you can get that at an affordable rate then use it if that's what your show needs.

Consider that experience working with sound for picture is important. Audio for movies is different from music recording. A great music producer may simply not have the understanding to give you what you need. He or she may be able to record great vocal tracks for your theme music, but recording ADR requires a different set of skills.

For a sound designer, you need someone who fights fair, is creative, and loves the job. This is a person who considers sound in terms of creating and enhancing mood, atmosphere, and other aspects of picture.

With both a sound designer and post-audio tech, you're looking for someone who understands that recording sound is different from listening to sound. This person needs a solid foundation of the technical issues regarding digital audio for motion pictures.

The sound designer or tech should sign a contract, such as the Technical Services Contractor Agreement located in the Appendix. Usually, they have set day rates, and most will lower the per-day fee for projects lasting several weeks. Your sound designer should be brought into the project early—preferably before you start shooting. Often post-audio people have worked a number of sets and may have ideas that can save you time and money in post.

You go to a post-audio house when you're ready to do your post-audio work. Some sound designers work with assistants and composers. The assistants clean up the dialogue tracks and spot the audio. The composers write, and often perform, original music. You can be the assistant if you go in with the audio spotted, sound effects recorded or located from a library, music cleared and masters in hand, and everything organized.

If you have to take care of the music, dialogue, and sound effects gathering and editing, assume a minimum of eight weeks if you don't need extensive repair to your audio tracks. If you want to record ADR, narration or voiceovers, sound effects, Foley, and original music, you can spend months doing the post-audio.

Discuss the money before you start. You don't want your project held hostage, and your audio people don't want to get stiffed. You will be expected to pay for recording time and use of their sound effects library. You may want to add language to the agreement that says any failures of the post-audio tech's system should not be counted against you. For example, if the hard drive crashes and you lose an entire day's work, you shouldn't have to pay for that day.

Finally, go into your post-audio house prepared. Consider having your dialogue split out on discrete tracks, everything spotted, music and sound effects gathered, and everything cleaned up for use. That way the post engineer can concentrate on the big picture, orchestrating the entire soundtrack, and not on removing noise.

ARE YOU A SOUND DESIGNER?

Audio guy Steve Weiss says, "Ever wonder why when you get on a plane, they give you the picture for free but charge you $4.50 for the headphones?" People who say movies are a visual medium are half right. Picture and sound together make up the show. What happens when those two things collide is where the experience lies.

If you don't believe me then go to your local multiplex on a Saturday night and talk loudly throughout the show.

There are no silent movies. There are motion pictures with no dialogue, music, or sound effects, but you, the viewer, are still breathing, laughing, gasping, twisting in your seat, fighting with the guy sitting next to you for the armrest, and so on.

Adding sound to movies is another way to control the viewer's experience. Advances in motion picture technology don't happen just because this stuff is neat. Moviemakers want to offer better experiences to viewers, so search out ways to control all the elements of motion pictures for greater effect.

Like every other aspect of your show, your sound needs to be designed. Many people think of a sound designer as someone who conceives and creates particular sounds for a show—the voice of a cartoon grapefruit or the blast from a laser gun. But I think of sound design more like directing the sound, and a sound designer as the director of sound, similar to a director of photography. Sound design means thinking of every layer of sound through the entire movie and how they'll all work together with picture to convey the story. It's a combination of aesthetic and technical skills put to use to serve the director's intent.

It helps to have some musical training as a sound designer, but it isn't absolutely necessary. Do you have an ear for sound, a sense of rhythm, and incredible patience? Maybe you're a sound designer.

SOUND DESIGN

Sound design is so important that you should pay attention to it no matter who's going to press the buttons, be it you or a post-audio tech. If you decide to handle your sound design yourself, you may be able to compete with high-buck movies by carefully designing and executing your audio. In addition to technical aspects such as clean dialogue and a good mix, you can use the immense power of sound to enhance the viewer's experience.

Sound is tremendously subtle. It usually doesn't take much and especially if designed and used consistently, the viewer can have a deeper experience of the show. I would go so far as saying that sound is the crucial tool for creating and sustaining verisimilitude.

Sound has a direct storytelling role in a motion picture. Dialogue, narration, and narrative sound effects tell the story. Narrative sound effects are often written into the script because they affect when, where, and how actors respond. But sound also has a subliminal role. The score in particular is written to enhance the mood of a scene and underscore the action. The score tells the viewer how to feel about the scene, character, location, and so on in a subtle way.

Sound provides a form of continuity and can play a geographical role. If it remains constant before and after a cut, the audience understands that although the point of view has changed, the scene has not shifted—we're in the same place. It can also work as a transition—a change in sound clues the viewer that there's a change in geography or time.

A lot of directors and producers have a very narrow sense of what motion picture sound does. A director who takes tremendous risks with actors or camera will revert to being literal with audio. Sound seems like useless decoration stuck on as an afterthought, like extra frosting on a birthday cake. The director gets the dialogue repaired, a couple of sound effects thrown in, the music placed, and it's done.

These directors are missing a tremendous creative opportunity. For example, if you have a score with a theme for one of the lead characters, you can design the use of that theme to support the character's changing situation. Having a scene end on an unexpected note or chord can leave the moment feeling unresolved, and sometimes even asks a subtle question about how the character should respond to what's happening. The underscore can emphasize the emotional content and clarify the viewer's response to that moment.

Like any subtle craft for motion pictures, such as makeup and editing, sound is most noticeable when done poorly. Many people repeat the cliché that no- and low-budget movies suffer because of bad audio. If you ask the person to expand a little further, he or she may respond with technical issues: poor location audio that wasn't repaired or replaced, a bad mix, and so on. Basic techniques and practice can help you get better with the technical side.

They may respond regarding choice of music: It sounds canned. This is a real issue. Too many decisions about sound are made at the end of postproduction, when the producer has run out of money and time and just wants the thing done. It's easier to use library music or have someone perform a piece of music on a computer that really ought to be recorded using live players or better synthesizers.

A lot of it, though, is poor design. No one really thought through the entire show in terms of audio.

For *Amazing World* I worked with a musician and actor named Maria Mabra. She really understood the sensibility of the story and characters, created an aural concept of the show, and made choices based on that concept. I can't say we necessarily designed the sound, but I think we stumbled upon a sense of how things should go and Maria's talent took over from there. When she began seeking music, she was able to select songs that reflected a lot of the interior landscape of the characters.

In addition to finding and ordering the songs, Maria also wrote and performed the percussion for the chase sequence theme for the action sequence. She produced the recording session of cellist Lori Goldston that resulted in some remarkable sounds. Lori is an accomplished musician unafraid of experimenting with her instrument. Maria asked her to create sounds "like birds fighting—big birds."

That was an excellent piece of directing, and it freed Lori to play an array of tones and pitches that I'd never heard come out of a cello before. The sound mixer layered in these pieces along with a piece created by Wayne Flower of Icicle Bike Music for the action sequence that was quite effective.

For a short I did called "Winner, winner, winner," I designed the sound. When I went to shoot, I knew I wanted specific sounds that I would layer together for this piece. I collected a set of sounds using my Audio-Technica 4073 short shotgun and a Sony minidisk recorder. The recording quality was good enough for what I wanted to do and the recorder had the extra advantage of being small. I could take it on a roller coaster without fear of getting it damaged.

The raw audio was then added to audio I captured while shooting the images, and these layers served as the basis on which I built the flow of images. I wanted pieces of dialogue to rise and fall, like a carnival ride.

For "Music Appreciation," I knew the song the lead characters had in common would be one I wrote and performed and that it would also serve as the theme song. I wanted some sound effects added to certain scenes, but because the story was about two people struggling to talk with each other, silence would play a big part. So I created sets of sound palettes.

SOUND PALETTES

Like your color, camera shot, and lighting palettes, you can create sound palettes. These palettes include ambience, sound effects, and music for the story arc, characters, locations, scenes, and sequences. Using pattern and repetition can be very effective.

Even the most practical sound is manipulated in a show. For example, a ringing phone may have its pitch, placement, or length changed. Sometimes it's changed to fit the requirements of the onscreen action—the length of the ring may be shortened so the character answers the phone in mid-ring. Other times it's changed to work better with other sounds, such as changing the pitch so it fits harmonically with the score.

Thinking about it this way will help you orchestrate and arrange all the layers of audio as a cohesive whole.

Diegetic sound, or practical sound, is sound whose source is visible or implied in the story. *Nondiegetic* sound, also known as *commentary sound*, comes from a source outside the story. For example, mood music is nondiegetic.

Establishing sound is sound that establishes surroundings and characters. Establishing sound is usually cut or lowered in volume during dialogue but may return to reestablish the location or character. Most establishing sound is created using sound motifs.

Sound motifs are recurring patterns that condition the audience for what's coming. They're usually applied to characters. For example, the hero has a theme that recurs in different, yet recognizable, forms as the story progresses. But you can create motifs for locations that can be quite effective.

To begin creating motifs for your sound palette, watch the fine cut again, this time with audio in mind.

Story Arc

Regarding the story arc, write down the answers to these questions:

- What's the genre?
- What's the style?
- What are the pivot points of the story?

The genre of the show will determine a lot of your audio decisions. If you have an action movie, you may want a lot of sound, especially staccato bursts such as gunfire, and music with fast tempos.

The style of show will help you decide on what kinds of sound it will be. For example, a high-key action movie with a lot of comedy may have high-pitched gunfire or music with snappy melodies. The reverse may also be true: You may want fluffy pop music under horrifying special effects for a greater emotional impact.

Consider your pivot points:

- Conflict
- Inciting incident
- Complications
- Climax
- Outcome

You may decide to start with very little sound and add to it as the show progresses. Or you may begin with lower volume that gradually increases until the climactic moment. Conflicts and inciting incidents may require music with greater tension. Remember that tension requires some kind of resolution. A melody or musical texture that ends on a note that doesn't resolve the melody begs for an answer—your audience is waiting for a conclusion.

Characters

For every character, write down the answers to these questions:

- Does this character have a rhythm in speech or movement?
- Does this person speak loudly or softly, with a high- or a low-pitched voice?
- What kind of objects does the character handle?
- What's the character's backstory? Does it affect sound choices? For example, a character who was a jazz musician may need a jazz-styled theme.

- What does each character want?
- How should the audience view this character?

You may be able to develop a motif based on the way each character has of communicating. While you're analyzing the characters' voices, you can also make notes that'll help you during the mix. For example, if your lead character's voice records a bit thin, write down that you may need to manipulate it with some judicious equalization.

If the character has a personal object, consider what kind of sound that object would make. For example, if the character always carries keys in her pocket, do the keys need to make a sound as she walks or runs? You don't necessarily have to include this audio element in your sound design, but you'll find that sometimes a single small element can enhance the character or spark a response in the viewer.

What kind of clothes do the characters wear? Cloth often rubs against itself when characters move. Shoes squeak and sound differently on different surfaces. What sort of accessories does each wear? A jangling bracelet placed so as not to conflict with dialogue and set way back in the mix can really identify a character.

I think of these sounds as creating a signature for each character to convey the character's presence even when he or she is offscreen. Sometimes it's something subtle, such as pocket change, clothes rustling, or a kind of atmospheric sound such as a breeze. I've also tried using very low pitches such as rumbles deep in the background. By using audio signatures, you can further dress the characters.

Be sure to note any backstory elements that can help you develop a motif for the character.

Locations

For every location, write down the answers to these questions:

- What kind of place is it?
- What's the time of day?
- What's the weather?

Every place has its own sound. Listen to that one minute of room tone gathered at every set and you'll hear what I mean. You can add sound to further enhance the viewer's idea of the place. For example, the whirring of sewing machines can convey the idea of being in a garment factory, even though we never see the sewing machines.

Consider the place, time of day, and weather as you think about how you want to represent the location. If the characters are sweating in the jungle, you can infer that it's hot and muggy. Sound is different in hot, humid air than it is elsewhere, like on the shore of an Alpine lake. Sound effects are usually different, too. I haven't heard much yodeling in an Amazon rain-forest, either.

You can create establishing audio that will place the viewer geographically in your movie based on unique sounds of each location. For example, in *Amazing World*, we created a motif using sound beds with office sound effects and a type of music and disc jockey playing from an implied radio.

This motif was placed in the preceding scene as a foreshadowing that the next place we'd be is back at the office. I avoided the establishing shots I dislike so much, was able to move at a rapid pace the way I wanted, and still let the viewer know where he or she was at any given point.

Scenes

For every scene, write down the answers to these questions:

- How far is each character from the camera?
- What kind of shots make up the scene?
- What sound supports the character's emotional state?
- How does this scene relate to the scenes before and after it?
- Who is moving?
- When are they moving?
- Why are they moving?

The psychic or emotional distance of the character can be further support-ed by sound. For example, in a wide shot of a character walking by a drip-ping faucet, you may choose to bring the volume of the drips up to the forefront and the character's footsteps way down. This may convey how small the character feels or seems in relation to surroundings.

People expect dialogue in a wide shot to sound farther away. This can be accomplished with a bit of reverb on and filtering out some of the higher frequencies from the dialogue. It should be consistent. And remember: Just because it's a convention doesn't mean you have to follow it. Some direc-tors use very close audio on long shots to great effect.

Consider, too, how this scene fits into what's come before and what's com-ing after. The experience of sound is subjective—loudness and softness are relative. A loud battle scene with lots of sound effects and music will make a dialogue scene following seem very quiet, even though the volume levels are exactly the same.

In sequences like this, some sound designers will place a sound effect of something you normally wouldn't hear up front, to emphasize the quiet—for example, the tinkle of a single teacup on a saucer. Its level may be very high, but that single, isolated sound is so quiet compared to what's come before.

This is also true of pitch. The rattling of the saber may end on the same note as that of the tinkling of the teacup. These are subtle effects, but audio software has become so powerful and inexpensive, many no- and low-budget producers can control elements to this level.

Motion in the frame is often mirrored by the sound. This is especially true for music: The image of a running man often has up-tempo music as the score. You'll also soon realize that the tempo of the sound and music affects how you experience the scene. Fast music often makes the scene seem much quicker. This subjective experience of speed is a great way of controlling effect.

POST-AUDIO FOR DV

All sound elements can be placed in three categories:

- **Dialogue**—Any spoken word you want heard clearly, including location audio, ADR, and narration or voiceovers.
- **Sound effects**—Recorded or existing. You can record them wild, through Foley, or in the computer.
- **Music**—Original or existing, and is used as score or source. A score is theme and atmospheric music, whereas source music is music motivated by an onscreen or offscreen source, such as a radio, stereo, or jukebox.

Generally, you want to use 16-bit 48kHz recording whenever possible. If your show was recorded in 12-bit 32kHz, upsample to 16-bit 48kHz during or right after you've transferred it. Working at a higher sample rate will give you an improved noise floor and greater accuracy when doing mixing or processing.

You may run into problems when transferring digital audio files such as music and library sound effects from CDs, which are 16-bit 44.1kHz. As long as you're staying in the digital realm and plan to lie back to DV, convert everything to 16-bit 48kHz before you start working on it. You may get some distortion doing the conversion—it really depends on the quality of the software you're using. With most equipment there's no sonic difference between 44.1kHz and 48kHz sample rates, because they use the same filter settings.

You can test ahead of time to see whether you get distorted sound. You can decide to use only music and sound effects available at 16-bit 48kHz. These elements may be sold on DATs or available directly from the mixing house. For example, a band that is recording in a local studio may have a mixed version of a song you've licensed on a hard drive at the studio. The engineer can give you a file at the correct bit and sample rate. You can ask.

The crucial thing is to make sure everything is sampled at the same rates or converted to the same rates.

If you can't afford anything beyond the most basic digital audio-editing software, without reference picture, you can still handle some of your post-audio work. Place scratch versions of dialogue, sound effects, and music in the NLE. Export the motion picture audio using your NLE software and open it in your audio software. You can then replace all the temporary audio with better-quality material. When you've completed it, you can export it back to your NLE to make sure everything is in sync.

SPOTTING

Spotting is the process of locating all audio cues throughout the show. This includes what the sound is as well as its location and duration. You'll spot music and sound effects, as well as note any places where dialogue needs to be repaired or replaced. Spotting is a lot like a script breakdown, only you're going through the fine cut (see Chapter 12, "Locking the Schedule").

I have a hard time cutting footage with poor dialogue, so I tend to do some repair as I edit picture. It's very hard for me not to start fixing little audio problems, but don't do that. You can get bogged down repairing audio you end up not using.

I'll also place scratch music so I can time the cuts. I know several editors who work in similar fashion—often the director falls in love with the scratch music and ends up wanting to use it. Jay Rose points out that in Hollywood, the term for "scratch" music is "temp score," and when directors love that scratch track, they're in "temp love." This often leads to heartbreak because the scratch music or temp score is often unavailable, or too expensive, to include in the show.

I handle simple spotting tables with a window-burn VHS, production script, and comfortable chair. I have a chart on my laptop with every scene separated into different tables (see Table 30.1).

TABLE 30.1   SAMPLE SPOTTING TABLE FOR "MUSIC APPRECIATION"

Scene Name: ____   Vet Clinic Start: 00:00:10:00   End: 00:00:54:01

Dial.	MM:SS:FF	Music	MM:SS:FF	Length	Lib/Rec.	SFX	MM:SS:FF	Lib/Rec.	Ambience	MM:SS:FF	Lib/Rec.
						Wanda's feet	00:10:00	Dogfeet1.wav	Dog barking	00:10:00 to 00:15:11	Record
						Peggy Walking	00:10:00 to 00:15:11	Foley	Radio chatter	00:10:00 to 00:24:20	Record
						Betty Walking	00:10:00 to 00:19:28	Foley			
						CD Case down	00:25:07	Foley			
						Cabinet open	00:26:24	Existing or Foley			
						Cabinet close	00:28:27 to 00:29:00	Existing or Foley			
		Pop song	00:27:10 VOLUME UP 00:51:10	Record		Latex glove stretching and on	00:36:00	Foley			
						Latex glove SNAP!	00:42:14	Foley			
						Lube	00:45:00	Foley			
						Container down on self	00:49:20	Existing or Foley			
Mic noise	00:51:10										

A spot sheet will really speed up the process if you're working with someone else. Even if you're working alone, it will help you think about how all the sound should fit together.

SPLITTING

After spotting every audio element, split them out to separate tracks. You can do this in your NLE in this order:

- Dialogue, with one track per speaker and often a couple tracks for alternative takes
- Narration or voiceovers
- Music
- Sound effects recorded during production
- Library sound effects
- Foley effects
- Scratch sound effects marking sounds you need to create or find
- Artificial sounds
- Ambience

Splitting elements like this allows you to apply certain filters or additional modifications to only one track. For example, if you wanted to add a flanger or other special effect to a voice, you could apply it across a track. If you wanted to add a bit of reverb to an ambient sound bed, you could do that to only one set.

Your production dialogue should be mono. Audio for sound beds or atmosphere should be recorded stereo, but the sound of a car or train going past is best recorded mono. The sound will be positioned in the stereo field during mixing. Spot sound effects, such as telephones and doors, should be in mono.

If you want your final audio to be stereo, you can create a stereo track after everything is in place.

DIALOGUE

Dialogue is an important part of motion pictures—if it isn't then it should be cut. What remains is crucial to your story. Often, an actor's or a subject's voice makes the difference between what's believable and what isn't.

Regardless of how well your location audio has been recorded the tracks require work to get it absolutely clear. *Cleaning the tracks* or *checkerboarding* is further separating the dialogue from any sound effects or noise that was recorded during production. Splitting the dialogue out further is especially useful if your actors have different vocal dynamics—one is louder or quieter.

Do this splitting in your NLE. Be sure to leave handles. *Handles* are lengths of audio on each side of the material you want to use so you can make transitions smoothly, especially between disparate voices or sounds. If you're working with a post-audio technician, he or she will tell you how many frames of audio you should have for handles. If you're doing the post-audio, you may want an extra second on either side of the audio for clean transitions. In your NLE, stretch the handle on each side of the checkerboarded sound (see Figure 30.1).

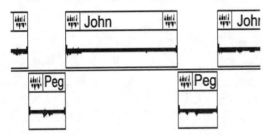

FIGURE 30.1

Checkerboarding audio is handled in the NLE. These pieces of dialogue have no handles yet.

With the dialogue tracks split out, mute everything but the dialogue and listen to the entire show from beginning to end. Note discrepancies and potential problems in your spot sheet. Discrepancies include changes in mic proximity and angle resulting in a different quality of sound, differences in levels between speakers, poor line readings and so on. Also note noise: pops, clicks, and other annoyances.

Note lip-sync problems. Some NLE applications have sync drift problems. Check your NLE's manual for information, as well as the manufacturer's Web site for any known issues, and online user groups for other tricks.

On larger shows, a *dialogue editor* preps the material. If you're doing the dialogue editing, get to it. Check sync, swap audio from one take with another, lay in room tone to cover all the cuts, and remove extra noise. For example, any hard cut between clips can cause a pop or click if the waveform of the audio at the cut point is mismatched. At this point of the prep, that pop should be removed (see Figure 30.2).

I tend to minimize sharp intakes of breath, but sometimes it can be quite effective as is.

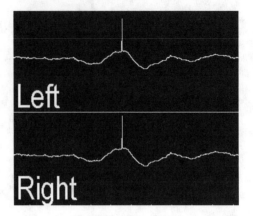

FIGURE 30.2

A pop in a stereo track.

For combining sound elements it's often best to use a cross-fade (see Figure 30.3), also called a *cross-dissolve,* to avoid clicks and pops. Basically, you lower the level of one sound, while raising the level of another. This is exactly like a dissolve transition for picture and is a standard technique.

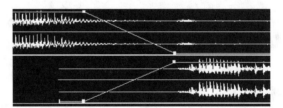

FIGURE 30.3

A cross-fade between a pair of stereo tracks.

One of the big advantages of using existing locations is that you can get a certain quality to the production audio that really brings a level of authenticity to the voices. Unfortunately, existing locations often present certain challenges to getting clear dialogue.

For example, that great factory you were able to use had compressors running continually through the scene. This presents problems to having intelligible dialogue. In addition to so much noise, the cuts may make the compressors mismatch, resulting in a jolt to the person watching your show.

Your first option is to see whether you can cut the picture to convey what is necessary without any dialogue at all. For example, Eric Anderson asked me to review a feature he was working on. In one scene, two characters are in a club. The director shot the scene with the music and other club noise at full blast, and it was impossible to hear what the characters were saying.

Eric had dropped in subtitles for the two necessary lines. But he didn't need to do that. Given the setting and the motion of the characters, it was pretty obvious that one character was telling another to go upstairs to buy some cocaine.

If the viewer only needs to know people are talking, and not what they're talking about, lower the levels of the lines so they're barely audible, or remove them completely.

If you don't have replacement audio, try filtering some of the noise using your audio software. With too much filtering, the voices start sounding strange.

Location audio usually has a lively feel, so take time to rescue as much as you can. If the existing take isn't working, see whether you have replacement audio you can drop in. If that still doesn't work, mark the section for ADR.

REPLACING

There are three reasons for replacing dialogue. The first is that track was recorded properly but in an unacceptably noisy location. The dialogue may sound acceptable to you—you've been listening to the lines multiple times and know what the actor or subject is saying, and, especially if you use headphones, you can get very close to the sound and hear every nuance. But this is not acceptable to your viewer.

The second reason is that the dialogue was not recorded correctly. For example, multiple mics were all sent to the same track, resulting in audio that's out of phase and unusable. Another common problem is audio that was recorded at too high a level at the recorder or at the mixer and has been compressed. Usually, it's too difficult to repair the clipped or distorted audio (Figure 30.4 shows a typical example of clipped audio).

The third reason is to change the performance. Technically everything may be fine, but you may not like the actor's line reading, or even the actor's voice.

One of the big benefits to cutting picture and sound yourself is that if you have to replace audio, you can recut the scene to make the replaced line appear to be in sync. For example, if a better line reading from another take is too long and out of sync with the actor speaking, you can cut to the reaction shot to cover. I find this to be especially true with ad-libs and interviews—sometimes what is said is the story and because I handle postproduction myself, I can make choices regarding sound and picture together.

Compressed audio appears flat in the audio wave.

FIGURE 30.4

Clipped digital audio often has a flat plateau instead of curved hills and canyons.

If you need to replace the dialogue, think about how people speak. You can replace lines, words, and syllables, but you need to think about language as sound, not as words.

With language, discretion happens in the brain, not in the mouth. What you hear is a bunch of sounds that you interpret for meaning. Speech starts when air leaves the lungs. That stream of air is then impeded and modified by the larynx, esophagus, windpipe, glottis, vocal cords, epiglottis, tongue, pharynx, nasal cavity, uvula, soft palate, hard palate, alveolar ridge, teeth, and lips. And what comes out is often a streak of sound—talking is nowhere near as tidy as the written word, and what looks like discrete units of meaning is smashed, mashed, and mumbled when spoken.

And often you have no problem understanding it. For example, "Jeetyet?" is supposed to be "Did you eat yet?"

One of the big problems in replacing audio is finding an appropriate spot to remove the offending sound. A lot of people will just look for a break in a phrase, and sometimes it's easiest just to do that. But be sure that you're getting the line reading you want. If you don't have an alternative take, or you want to keep the line reading the way it is but remove a small error, first locate the offending sound and a suitable replacement.

Because most people speak in one continuous streak, it can be hard to find the break. The offending sound and replacement are not single words, but a sound unrelated to meaning.

The components of speech are never the same, even when produced by the same speaker. We just treat certain sounds as identical. Sounds that never contrast significantly with one another—speakers treat them as the same sound—are *phonemes*, whereas noncontrastive variants comprising a phoneme are *allophones*. Every language has its own unique combination of phonemes and allophones.

Phonemes of all languages are subdivided into consonants and vowels because of the way consonants and vowels are produced and their different roles in the structure of syllables.

A consonant is defined by its place and manner of articulation. *Stops*, or *plosives*, are sounds produced by blocking the stream of air somewhere in the mouth, such as the /p/ in past and the /g/ in gum. *Fricatives*, also called *spirants*, are produced by impeding but not totally blocking the stream of air, such as the /f/ in fine, the /s/ in seal, and the /z/ in zeal. *Affricates* are a combination of a stop and fricative, with the air stopped briefly, and then released. Affricates are also diphthongs and frequently classed with them for editing purposes because you can treat the stop and fricative as separate phonemes, such as taking the initial /t/ from chill and using it elsewhere. Remaining consonants are known as *resonants*, and are grouped as *nasals*, *laterals*, *retroflex*, or *semivowels*.

If the vocal cords are moving, the consonant is considered voiced; if not, the consonant is voiceless. The benefit here is that intonation is less important when cutting unvoiced consonants. Unvoiced consonants can also be swapped between one piece of dialogue and another, or even between different speakers.

Vowels are normally classified as *high*, *mid*, or *low*, depending on the position of the tongue. Depending on where the highest part of the tongue is in the mouth, the vowel may be further divided as *front*, *central*, or *back*. If the tongue is tense, the vowel is considered *tense*; if the tongue is relaxed, the vowel is considered *lax*.

In addition, English has several diphthongs. *Diphthongs*, or *glides*, are a combination of two phonemes, such as /ah ih/ in sky. You can often find a place to edit a diphthong. Vowel diphthongs are produced while the tongue is moving from one position to another, such as in the words *toy* and *bough*. Most English vowels are diphthonized in actual speech and are very difficult to edit because they lack an initial or a final sound that you can manipulate cleanly.

Prosody refers to the stress patterns of language. In English, stress is found in individual words and in phrases, clauses, and sentences.

This little foray into phonetics isn't just because I like words such as fricative and diphthong. You quickly learn that it's difficult to edit vowels because people tend to slur the sounds with the surrounding consonants, creating a continuous sound. It's hard to edit continuous sound. Words and phrases are often continuous, and sentences can even be made continuous by the breath sounds of the speaker.

Cutting from a continuous sound to silence is abrupt—not like the abruptness of an interruption, but simply a stop that is jarring. Sounds often last longer than what you expect, and considering them not as words or parts of words, but as sound, will help you figure out where you can make a break.

Generally, you can cut audio on identical phonemes: Cut at the start of the phoneme in one word to the same sound in another. It may not work well if the identical phonemes are glides, such as /r/ or /l/ because they're influenced by the preceding sound.

Then listen to it. You'd be surprised at how well these manipulations can work.

ADR

Automatic dialogue replacement isn't automatic. It's a pain, honestly. After a replacement line of dialogue has been recorded, you check the sync and edit the audio to match it to the picture. You may have to process it a bit to match the rest of the audio as well.

Given that audio is difficult to match even with time, money, and experience, plan on doing ADR on a line or series of lines, rather than a single word. You may have to redo the entire scene and bring in multiple actors so it all matches, but often that works better than trying to get that one small word or phrase.

You can handle ADR at a post-audio house. They have the equipment and array of microphones, so it may be worth spending the money. Because the post-house will record the new lines directly into a DAW while watching the picture, you'll know whether the replacement is acceptably in sync.

Acceptably in sync varies according to how close the camera is to the person speaking. Many dialogue editors use specialized software such as VocAlign to make unacceptable ADR acceptable. If you don't have access to that software, however, acceptable ADR usually means that critical consonants are in the right place. You can make tiny adjustments to the less important sounds without too much difficulty. Also, being a little late is better than being early.

If you want to handle ADR yourself, you have some choices. Start with the same audio rig you used on location.

Have the actor record the line wild. Drop it in to match picture and hope it works. If you do this on the set right after a scene was shot during production, it often works remarkably well. And it doesn't cost anything.

Another technique is *audio-dominant* ADR. Basically, the actor listens to the audio over and over and over, and speaks along with it. There's no reference picture, just the line or scene repeated until the actor delivers the line.

You can also loop it to picture. See the following for the procedure. Have your actor sit or stand and adjust the mic to the same angle and placement as the original audio.

RECORDING ADR, FOLEY, NARRATION AND VOICEOVERS, AND OTHER ELEMENTS FOR POST-AUDIO

There are lots of ways to record replacement and supplementary audio for your show. If you have a DAW and a second video monitor out for picture, you can send original picture and audio to the actor, while checking sync in real-time. If not, and most of us don't, you have another possibility. You'll need

- A reference tape with the scene to be looped, narrated, Foleyed, and so on, recorded several times in a row with cueing beeps.
- A quiet room without sound reflections.
- A deck—the deck can be a VHS or your DV deck.
- A monitor—your field monitor will work nicely.
- Two pairs of headphones. You'll need one set, as will the person doing the ADR or Foley. You can split the headphone out of the

recorder with a Y-adapter or use headphone distribution amp to send audio to each pair.

- A microphone—preferably the one you used for the original audio for ADR and sound effects, and a nice cardioid for voiceovers and narration.

- A recorder—you can use a DAT, your DV camera, or a computer with analog-to-digital converter. If you have a DAW, record each take on separate tracks from the original audio.

- Pop filters, mic mounts, and stands.

- Cables.

Create the reference tape from your fine-cut picture by placing cueing beeps, also known as *streamers*, for reference prior to the point you want to start recording. I've seen two types of streamers. The first was a five-second countdown with a beep at every second. The other was a standard eight-second countdown with one beep exactly two seconds prior to the beginning of picture. That beep is known as a 2-pop and is always placed at exactly two seconds prior to picture start.

If your mic needs phantom power and you don't have a separate power supply or your recorder doesn't provide phantom power, you can use your field mixer. I always use a mixer for better control over the audio, but many people go directly into DATs and other recorders without one.

If the quiet room has some echo, use some furniture blankets to cut the reflections. You can even make a small isolation booth by creating a furniture blanket tent using PVC pipe or c-stands. If you don't have furniture blankets, use sofa cushions, cushy quilts and comforters, or sleeping bags. The idea is to control the noise.

Unfortunately, this type of sound dampening absorbs only high frequency audio, leaving low rumbles in the background. Eliminating low-frequency components takes mass and distance. Use a medium-size room, with carpeted floor and heavy drapes. Add furniture blankets and sofa cushions to control the high-frequency sounds. I typically use some light stands placed a foot or so away from the wall to hang quilts.

Treat the area like any audio location. Shut off all possible noisemakers during recording. If you're using a computer as your recorder or for playback, keep it in the next room—the fan noise is terrible.

In the quiet room, set up the monitor and set up the mic in its shock-mount and on the stand. You may want to use a pop filter for extra protection from plosives, but it's not absolutely necessary.

A *pop filter* is a round, two-layer disk of nylon gauze that you put between the speaker and the mic to stop the air blast from plosives from producing a distinct pop. It lets the speaker talk louder and get closer to the mic, minimizing reflections.

You can make one with a wooden embroidery hoop covered with a nylon stocking. You can buy some nylons and the hoop for a couple of dollars at a craft store. Attach a clamp and gooseneck so you can mount it to a stand and you're set. If the room has good acoustics and isolation, and you're working with a pro, you may not need the pop filter. If you're recording someone who doesn't have much training with microphone technique and voice control, you may want to have one ready.

Record in stereo at 16-bit 48kHz. Send the audio from the reference tape panned either hard right or hard left, and the new recording panned to the opposite channel. Set your levels and remember to EQ exactly as you had it on location. Be sure there's no audio leaking from the headphones into the mic.

Plug the monitor into the videotape deck. Insert the tape and go. If you have a second monitor or TV, you can watch picture as an actor loops or someone Foleys in a sound effect.

After you have the audio in your NLE, you'll separate the stereo tracks and resample so they're in mono. Line up the new audio with the original audio. Experiment with the audio using EQ, reverb, and filters to match the existing audio, but don't commit until you listen to the replacement dialogue on a decent set of speakers. You can always use pitch and time shifting to make everything work together if you have to. Be sure to extend room tone under the new audio so that it blends with the existing audio.

Narration and Voiceovers

Narration can be recorded in two different ways.

With *sync to picture*, the narrator watches a fine cut of the show and records commentary. *Wild narration* involves recording the narration separately from the show as isolated takes, either before or after the show has been edited. The narrator can concentrate on delivery of the script, rather than worry about matching what's onscreen, and an editor cuts in the desired lines opposite the footage. Wild narration gives you maximum creative control and greater flexibility should you need to make changes later.

A common technique is to narrate your own scratch version of the voiceover as reference while you edit the show. You then replace your version with the narration from a voiceover artist or actor. This gives you both the timing of the narration so you can match the audio and picture elements, plus the person doing the replacement narration has a reference track.

Which method you use depends completely on your budget and what you want to do. Narration tracks can physically be recorded either in a professional recording studio or on location. Not all studios are created equal. Some recording engineers have never recorded ADR or narration, only music. They may emphasize elements of the human voice that are not appropriate for what you're doing. The techniques aren't terribly difficult, but talk with the engineer before committing.

What you need is clean, dry recording that you can work with to match your show. This means that you want very little processing done while recording—you can add in appropriate reverb and EQ later. If the narration is supposed to be *voice of God* (VOG) style then recording in an isolated studio will probably get you the best result. But if the narration is supposed to be a part of the onscreen dialogue, then it may be easier for the actor or interview subject to just do it then and there. The sound quality should match that of the dialogue, since the goal is to create narration that sounds like a continuation of what's onscreen.

You can record VOG-style narration without spending exorbitant sums in a studio. You'll need a good mic. I have an Audio-Technica 4033 that I like for vocal recording. It's responsive and for the money, sounds pretty good. You can use a shotgun mic, but they often don't have the bottom end for a richer-sounding voice. I've been told that a lot of professional narrators with home studios use short shotgun mics to get a tighter sound in less-than-perfect rooms.

The person doing the voiceover may want to stand or sit on the edge of a stool. Have a music stand for script pages. Professional voiceover artists know proper breath technique and how to keep their voices in excellent shape. But even the pros may have problems with snaps and clicks when they get tired or their mouths are dried out from heating systems, nervousness, and lots of talking. Keep fresh water—not too cold—at hand.

If you need to do a voiceover quickly, one of the best places is to do it in an automobile. The newer ones particularly have excellent sound isolation and absorption.

EFFECTS

Sound effects, commonly abbreviated as *SFX*, refer to all sound other than dialogue and music in the movie. What a sound may be like in real life is not of much concern—emphasis is instead placed on what perception and practice deem right.

Natural sounds are sounds from an actual source, unadorned. Often, they're just not punchy enough for use in a movie. For example, recording gun-shots on a set rarely gives you good audio. They just don't sound right: Blanks don't sound like live ammunition, the distance between source and mic may not be right, and so on. They sound more like a crack than a real bang. Usually, sound effects mixers will replace, process, or layer natural sounds with other sounds for better effect.

Characteristic sounds are the sounds people expect to hear, regardless of reality—for example, explosions in outer space. Realistically, you wouldn't hear anything if a spacecraft exploded, yet viewers demand the sound.

Hard sound effects are upfront sounds that sync to events onscreen. They're further divided into *editorial* and *principal effects*. Editorial effects are every-day sounds such as doors closing, guns firing, and so on. Principal effects are the big, fancy production-specific sounds, such as laser blasts and explosions.

Background sound effects, also called *atmospheres*, *sound beds*, and *background loops* (abbreviated as BG), are sounds that are not synced to events onscreen. These are sounds that set mood and define geography. Backgrounds also come in two types: ambiences and stingers.

Ambiences are long, continuous recordings that set a mood, referring to and often creating the pervading atmosphere of a place. Not only can this be the physical place, but this can also be the emotional or psychological set-ting. Ambient sound may be created from the natural background sounds of the place or deliberately layered collections of sounds to create a sound bed for each location or change in mood.

One of the most commonly used elements for ambience is the room tone you recorded on the set. *Room tone* is a collection of nonspecific sounds used to match the production sound track so that it may be intercut with-out noticeable interruption. Presence and ambience help to sell the conti-nuity of a scene to the viewer.

Stingers or *specifics* are short elements added to the ambience tracks to liven things up. For example, you may create an ambience or a sound bed track of an office, but keep a collection of ringing phones for only specific points when the viewer sees a lot of people. The audio supports that the place is hopping.

Sound effects tracks are normally built from scratch. Even if you could record all the appropriate sound on the set, it still wouldn't sound right. Movies are not life. In everyday life, you select what you decide you're going to listen to and ignore everything else. In movies, the sound designer and director make those choices for you.

Many sound effects start from the location audio tracks. They may be processed or enhanced, or replaced all together. Many sounds are lifted from sound effects libraries purchased for this reason, though most sound editors and post-audio houses compile their own elaborate libraries of sound effects. If you're working with a post-audio house, you will be charged for each sound effect.

You can use sound effects libraries or start creating your own. You can also record audio through field recording or Foley work.

Try to create ambient tracks that are a minimum of one minute in stereo. Hard effects can be recorded in mono at the same bit and sample rate as the rest of the show. Remember that the crucial thing is to have everything at the same bit and sample rate.

LOCATION AUDIO SOUND EFFECTS

Many of your necessary sound effects may be recorded in sync with picture on the set. If the sound coincides with dialogue, often your sound mixer will try to record the sound effect wild after the take has been shot. This recorded effect retains most, if not all, of the same ambience and characteristics of the original. In my opinion, sound effects from the location audio have a certain quality that beats even the best library effect.

If you have these effects, place them in the audio tracks of your NLE. You can then decide what sort of processing you want to do and which sounds you want to replace.

SOUND LIBRARIES

Commercial sound-effects libraries can be very handy, but you get what you pay for. Cheap effects libraries often have cheap sounds and rarely include synchronization rights, limiting your ability to distribute your show. Good CD libraries can be pricey. The market is small, and each CD took some of the best sound designers in the world a lot of time to gather, process, and produce. Remember, too, that CD audio is at 16-bit 44.1kHz, so if you use CD sound effects, be sure to upsample them to 16-bit 48KHz to match the rest of your audio.

Instead of a complete library, you may want to use Web-based services. You can audition specific sound effects and then download and pay for just the ones you want. The benefit is that you use the power of the Web to find what you need in the format you want. The downside is that the per-piece pricing adds up quickly. Also, some sites have only low-resolution sounds that just aren't the quality you may require.

Many computers come with sound cards that have built-in synthesizers. Although the sounds may not be the most authentic, you can always combine and process them to get different effects.

See Resources for listings of sound effects Web sites.

RECORDING SFX

You can build your own audio library for your show by recording your own sound effects. Knowing how the sound is going to be used and how you want viewers to respond to beats, scenes, and characters really helps you sharpen up what you're looking for.

You can collect sounds through field recording. *Field recording* means taking a microphone and portable recorder out of your studio. The results are authentic and unique.

Unfortunately, you have to deal with unwanted noise, such as wind and intrusive human noise. When the air blows on the diaphragm of the mic, it creates low-frequency rumbles that ruin the recording. Blow directly on a mic and you'll hear what it sounds like. Try to avoid wind noise by recording on calm days or during times that the wind is not kicking up, such as close to sunrise and sunset. Use furries on your microphones to block and distribute the air pressure before it hits the mic. Place your mic carefully. Tuck it behind a tree or even close to your stomach. You'll still get bursts across the mic, but you can edit them out later.

Intrusive human noise is a bigger problem. Airplanes, cars, and other sounds will intrude on your quiet audio recording. I have a collection of "What you doing?" and "Is this going to be on TV?" from people who simply would not walk on by.

Try to do exterior field recording after midnight, when there's much less traffic and fewer people around. If you want specific sounds from one small source, use a shotgun microphone. The mic's hypercardioid pickup pattern cuts down any sound not directly in front of the diaphragm.

I often record with a collection of microphones, Behringer mixing board, Roland UA-30 USB digital-to-analog converter, and laptop computer. I've also used DAT decks and a minidisk recorder. Good mic technique and how carefully you set your levels are more important than which medium you record to.

Foley

Foley effects, named after Hollywood sound effects tech Jack Foley, are sounds that are created by recording human movement in sync with picture. A Foley mixer records the sounds the Foley artists create. After the effects are recorded, the Foley editor makes any adjustments necessary to ensure that they are in sync.

The scenes requiring Foley are shown over and over again for the Foley artist. The artist then mimics the action and rhythm using a variety of props, as well as creates sounds from rustling of clothes, punches, hugs, kisses, armpit scratching, and anything else that makes sound.

Before you start any Foley work, place your ambient or background tracks into your show and listen to everything. You may eliminate a lot of extra work because often the ambient sound will populate those areas you're thinking need Foley. You may want to place some of the music for the same reason.

See "Recording ADR, Foley, Narration and Voiceovers, and Other Elements for Post-Audio" for the procedure.

If you need a clean sound with little coloration, curtain off a small area and put the mic 6"–24" from the source. The quieter the sound you're recording, the closer the mic needs to be. Keep in mind that if the mic is really close, it will pick up the sound of your breathing.

Consider what a character is wearing, including jewelry and pocket contents. Just because something is out of sight doesn't mean it has to be out of hearing. What kind of fabric does this person wear? What kind of shoes and other accessories?

Consider the physical components that make up an object. What's it made of? Does it rattle? Is it squeaky?

Consider the physical space the character or object is in. Is it a small room or a large one? What kind of surfaces, especially floors, does it have?

After you think of what the sound should be, consider the sort of props that would work to create the audio elements. The prop doesn't need to be or even look like what it represents. Look around where you live for suitable materials. You can re-create a lot of sounds just using yourself. Your voice is capable of a lot more than arguing with distributors and singing in the shower, and the character of the voice will get viewer interest no matter how much manipulation it undergoes.

For other sounds, you may need to use some props, such as balloons, sandpaper, cloth, pieces of wood and brick, chain, and so on. Also check your local thrift stores for props.

You can re-create all the footsteps of each character, whether or not the viewer sees the steps in the show. You'll need an array of footwear and perhaps some Foley pits. *Foley pits* are rectangular boxes filled or covered with different materials, such as carpet, concrete, dirt, sand, hardwood flooring, and so on. You can build Foley pits to match your show. For example, you can cover a piece of plywood with carpet remnant. If you need the sounds of footprints in dirt or sand, you can either build a 4'×8'×6" pit or use wading pools filled with the appropriate material.

I Foleyed the audio for the first scene and an opening dolly shot for "Music Appreciation." For the first scene I Foleyed in footsteps, the sound of someone wiping her hands on a towel, the jingles of a dog collar, and the gooey sound of someone swirling KY-Jelly around in a jar.

In the dolly shot, Peggy and John are walking into the empty theater, looking for their seats. They come up the stairs, turn to the left, and walk down a long aisle.

I started with John's footsteps. I was wearing a pair of wingtips with heavy soles. I was in my living room and fake walked on the carpeting. When John stepped on a concrete surface. I stepped onto the kitchen floor that had a little salt on it to make it sound a bit grittier. I then took a pair of cotton pants and put them on my arms so I could better create the whish-whish sound of his pants as he walked. I then added the sound of keys in his coat pocket.

For Peggy, I wore a pair of light ankle-high boots and used a silk blouse to mimic the sounds of her clothing.

MANIPULATING SOUND EFFECTS

Effects may be based on real sounds that have been modified inside the DAW. You may do a bit of editing or EQ or apply filters and layers to create completely new sounds.

Editing is choosing the part of the sound you like and discarding the rest. You'll be cutting, pasting, and cross-fading between audio takes, sounds, and pieces of sound. Apply EQ, filters, and dynamics processing as needed, although keep an eye on the levels. You can easily clip the audio when adding and manipulating audio.

For sound effects outside of realism, you may want to use layers. Start with a sound that is the same as or similar to what is onscreen, and then continue to add portions of other sound to build up a structure. You can also distort the sound by changing its speed or pitch, running it backward, filtering out some of its frequencies, and so on.

Common techniques for modifying and recording sounds are

- Speeding up and slowing down original sound to alter pitch
- Reversing sounds
- Time-expanding or compressing the sound
- Compressing and expanding levels to manipulate the sound size and sustain
- Using filters to boost or reduce certain frequency in sounds

Equalization, or *EQ*, allows you to manipulate sets of frequencies. For sound effects, adjust the EQ controls to exaggerate or minimize the parts of a sound that provide its basic identity. Try that with a recording of wind rumble and get a wispy, airy sound.

You can also use reverb to build up a sound. Chorusing and very short delays can be useful for converting a mono file to stereo, just as in music, although if you're planning to release to broadcast TV, home video, or the World Wide Web, make sure your soundtrack is mono compatible when using delays. I like using flangers with sounds that should impart motion. Pitch and time shifting allow you to raise or lower the pitch and decrease or increase the duration of the sound separately or concurrently.

For "Music Appreciation," I had arranged for Catherine, my girlfriend, to hold Howie, one of our cats, so I could record him meowing. I wanted to place the meows in the background of the first scene. Naturally, this cat, who meows incessantly, simply would not meow into the mic. I then convinced Catherine to meow instead. I then sped up that original audio and cut some of the lower frequencies to make it sound a bit more catlike.

PLACING SOUND EFFECTS

Place your sound effects. Test your timing against the picture and adjust until it's how you want it. Hard sound effects need to be in sync, and once you've got them where you want them, lock them in place.

Listen to each sound element by itself with picture and in combination with the other sounds. Does the sound work with picture conceptually? If not, will editing or processing help? Is it too thin and does it require another layer? Is it too busy?

Repeat this process for all of your sound effects.

Keep everything neatly organized. I usually group the sounds according to use, with folders for specific scenes or sequences. Others organize material based on how similar the sounds are to one another. For example, all the footsteps are in one folder. Just be consistent and keep good notes, especially if you're going to a post-audio house for your mix.

MUSIC

Music for motion pictures falls into two general categories: score and source. The score is music specifically related to the events onscreen, although the characters are unaware of it. It can be composed or created by combining a series of existing songs or other music. Source music is music coming from an onscreen or implied device, such as stereo, radio, jukebox, and so on.

Some music is initially motivated by a source but then becomes more of a score as it's repeated and varied throughout the show. "Music Appreciation" uses its source song, "This Dancing Life," like this.

Music tells the audience what they're supposed to feel about a character, beat, or scene. Try this:

- Put on a video or DVD of one of your favorite movies.
- Turn down the sound.
- Play a track from a series of CDs.

You may feel a complete disconnect or read the scene in a different way. Different music will spark a different response.

Musical effects in motion pictures have a number of conventions. It speeds up during car chases and other action sequences, dissonance foreshadows danger, groups of violins hang on an unusual note to create tension, and so on. Music styles tend to match up to emotional events. For example, if the scene has swooping, lush, orchestral music and two characters are staring at each other, you're supposed to figure out that they're falling in love—despite whatever has come before.

On big-budget shows, a music editor will help a composer in the preparation of the dramatic underscore. The music editor will supply timings for the composer created during a spotting session in order to note the specific places needing score or source music. After the score is recorded and the source music gathered, the music editor edits or supervises the final sync of all music for the final mix.

A music supervisor often works closely with the music editor, locating and clearing music for use with the motion picture.

There's a lot of crossover in these tasks. A music supervisor may act strictly in an administrative capacity, although some actually supervise all the tasks regarding music for the movie, including hiring and firing the music crew. Some music editors compose, and many composers perform the music they've written.

If you're not under time and money pressure, you can handle these tasks yourself if you feel the inclination. Generally, these tasks include

- **Spotting**—Just as you spotted all of the dialogue and effects, you should spot the music. Include start and end times, duration, whether it's source or score, and the emotion you're trying to evoke.

- **Gathering**—You can get music for movies in a number of ways, including music libraries, having music composed and performed specifically for the show, and using existing music.

- **Editing**—Cutting music means editing it to make its timing match picture.

- **Clearing**—This means getting proper clearances from rights holders allowing you to sync the music to picture.

- **Creating a music cue sheet**—Music cue sheets have information that performance rights organizations use to gather fees for the rights holders of music in their catalogs.

GATHERING MUSIC

Canned music comes from a prerecorded music library. For a fee, a producer can purchase the rights to use selections of existing music in his or her production. Many companies produce volumes of high-quality, generic music for this purpose. The music is composed and recorded to be easily cut into different lengths. There are two types of canned music: buy-out and needle-drop.

Buy-out music allows you to use the songs on your projects. That grants you long time periods and few restrictions, unless there are large sums of money involved. The CDs cost anywhere from $10 to $150 or more. Most post-audio houses have extensive collections, although you can buy your own libraries. Just be sure you understand the restrictions before using a piece of music.

Needle-drop, or *cue,* music refers to paying for the music based on the selection, use, and length of the selection from a needle-drop library. Fees often take into account the purpose and market of the show—theatrical, educational, home video, broadcast, and so on. This term comes from when music libraries were distributed on vinyl. Now needle-drop music is available on CDs or over the Web. Each time you use a piece of a song, the rights holder gets a licensing fee. You can buy a blanket license to cover a single project or a contract that covers what you produce during a period of time.

You are required to submit reports that detail which songs you used and how long the cue was for each project that inpes music from the library.

ORIGINAL MUSIC

If you have any musical talent, why not put it to work for your show? You'll have to give yourself plenty of time, but it's pretty fun. You can

- Compose and perform the music yourself.
- Compose the music yourself and hire musicians to record it.
- Hire a composer to write and musicians to record original music.

Recording Music

Your post-audio house will probably have music recording capabilities. Just make sure the recording engineer has experience recording the kind of music you want to perform. A recording engineer who works with rock bands may have real problems trying to mic a string quartet. Conversely, someone who specializes in recording orchestral music may be a bit flabbergasted by pop and hip-hop recording techniques. Voiceover engineers may not have the ability to do much beyond recording a speaking voice.

This doesn't mean you shouldn't work with these people. If you have a good relationship, trust the person, and believe him or her competent, you may be able to get a lower hourly rate, or the services provided as part of the post-audio package, because you're giving the engineer the opportunity to try something new. You should ask about experience and pricing before proceeding.

You can handle the recording yourself. It's hard to engineer, produce, and perform simultaneously, but you can do it. Mic placement is so crucial to good recording, though, that if you want to play multiple instruments, ask a friend to help.

I write and perform a lot of the music I use with MIDI. MIDI, or Musical Instrument Digital Interface, is a LAN standardized by synthesizer manufacturers that sends messages to synthesizers and other devices to do certain things. The MIDI standard has been in use since the 1980s, and a lot of the issues regarding hardware and software conflicts have been ironed out. Plus, the sounds just keep getting better.

You can use MIDI software to write and perform music using your computer's audio card. By using a MIDI cable and interface in the computer, you can hook up synthesizers, samplers, and controllers that can do all sorts of wonderful things.

I use MIDI to create rhythm and synth tracks and then record all the guitar music using a separate effects box plugged into an analog-to-digital converter. All the recording happens on the laptop. Although it's not the most pristine audio chain, it's affordable and convenient. I can plug everything in and record wherever I need to.

Hiring Musicians

If you hire musicians to perform the music, they should sign a contract similar to the Technical Services Agreement in the Appendix. It must be very clear that this is a work-for-hire agreement. See Chapter 15, "Build the Ensemble," for more discussion about these contracts.

If you have an orchestral score, the musicians assemble in a large recording studio, known as a *scoring stage*. They play while the show is projected on a large screen. The conductor, who is often the composer, leads them through the entire piece. You may want to add a click track or streamers so the conductor can stay in sync with the picture.

I've never been on a scoring stage, although I have worked with musicians who play to picture. See "Recording ADR, Foley, Narration and Voiceovers, and Other Elements for Post-Audio" for the procedure.

Hiring a Composer

Start by signing a contract with the composer that clearly states this is a work for hire and you own all rights to the work. The piece will generate revenues from performance royalties if your show plays on television, in theaters outside of the U.S., or if the music is played separately, such as on the radio. Ownership of the composition and recording, as well as all fees, are negotiable.

The other possible revenue is from publishing income. It's common for independent producers to split publishing income with the composer 50%–50%. The money is paid to the holder of the rights by performance rights organizations such as ASCAP and BMI.

Your composer may want to handle all the music. In addition to composing, this includes arranging the music, hiring musicians and recording studio, and producing the sessions.

Common terms for a Composer or Music Package Agreement include the following:

- **Engagement**—This paragraph states that the producer is engaging the composer's services as a work for hire. It also includes whether you're hiring the composer to just compose or to take care of the recording and delivery of the music.

- **Compensation**—This includes the compensation and pay schedule. Generally, you'll pay the first half of the total on the start of the work, with the balance paid on delivery. If the composer is giving you the entire package, the balance is paid when you have the master recording in your hands.

  This clause will also state explicitly the publishing income or *publisher's share*. If you need to keep your fees low, you can make a 50%–50% arrangement. Otherwise, keep 100%.

- **Rights**—Don't forget this paragraph, which states that the composer is granting you all synchronization rights exclusively to the work in whatever media and in perpetuity.

- **Indemnification**—In this clause, the composer indemnifies you in any event of breach of copyright or other problem arising from the work. Don't forget this.

- **Credit**—This states the screen credit, which is always negotiable.

There are other issues, including representations and warranties, no obligation to exploit, notice, cure, remedies, and so on. Talk with your entertainment attorney.

After the contract is signed, send the composer a videotape of the fine cut with window-burn of the timecode and the spotting table. At some point, the composer and editor may want to create a *click track*. This is sound consisting of clicks placed opposite picture to convey cutting rhythm and climax. The click track serves to guide the composer and possibly the musicians in keeping beat with the show.

I've never created a click track. I've spent time with musicians discussing suggestions and ideas for music at certain points in the show and that has worked well. Still, a click track may be a handy way to convey pacing, especially if the composer is out of town.

Jay Rose suggests using a digital metronome or sequencing software to create a click track. Set the range to the tempo you and the composer have agreed to, lay it into the NLE, and you have a timing reference for montages.

The composer must orchestrate with instruments that do not overlap too much with the frequency of the human voice or dominant sound effects. This can be particularly difficult with music that has vocals. Luckily, multitrack recording and sequencing techniques will allow you to provide different mixes of any songs you've recorded. One version can be guitar only, another just the panpipe and nose flute version. Given what you can do with pitch and temporal shifting, you can shape a single melodic line to match the length of a scene almost exactly.

EDITING MUSIC

When cutting picture, you or your editor will place scratch music onto the timeline. Generally, the beginning of the piece should coincide with the start and end with the video segment.

I don't always follow this practice, but it's a good place to start.

If the music contains repetitions, take out measures to shorten it and repeat to lengthen it. You can also electronically speed up or slow down the music using your audio software +/–10% without glitches or affecting pitch. You probably don't want to change timing in your NLE because it will cause noticeable changes in pitch and timbre of the music, especially with acoustic instruments. You can also change the speed of the picture, but try to avoid this because it's so much more noticeable.

If the music is much too long for the picture, try backtiming. *Backtiming* is when you place the end or fade out of the music at the end of the sequence first. The music will fade in at some point in the song at the appropriate point in the show.

If you need to edit the music, it's all in the downbeat.

We may not all be musicians, but just about everyone can hear a beat. This is why music that is edited offbeat is so noticeable. Most, although not all, Western music is in 4/4 time. There are four beats in a measure, every quarter note gets a beat, and usually, but not always, the first beat is stressed.

If you've ever clapped along to a song, you've counted beats. You cut music by matching those beats between musical sections. Count out the music you want to use, "one and two and three and four...."

Your audio software should let you place markers in the audio track. As you count off the beat of the music, place a marker every time you count off a one. You can then cut a section out without disturbing the song's basic rhythm.

Another way to do this is to place two versions of the music into your NLE. You then slide the pieces backward and forward, using the rubber bands to cross-fade or silence portions of each copy, until it sounds right. Many NLE applications, though, have pretty weak audio tools, so you may have to export the music to an audio application to get this right.

For very simple music, this may work just fine. If you're getting hiccups, you may have placed the markers off the beat. It also may sound funny because the melody doesn't match or the sustain of an instrument or voice is crossing beats. You can move the markers to a different measure.

You may also want to cross-fade between the sections of music. Give yourself plenty of room on each side of the edit so you can make a smooth transition.

CLEARING MUSIC

Existing music is music not commissioned by you for your show. Existing music MUST BE CLEARED before you can use it legally. There is no special number of free notes that can be used in a show without written permission. Anyone who tells you otherwise is just plain wrong.

Don't be tempted to assume that "Fair Use" lets you use music without permission. Fair Use is determined by four standards: the purpose and character of the use of the material; the nature of the copyrighted work; the amount and substantiality of the portion used in relation to the copyrighted work as a whole; and the effect of the use upon the potential market for or value of the copyrighted work.

Just because you're a student, teacher, or first-time producer, or your show is on behalf of a noble cause has no bearing on whether Fair Use applies.

Fair Use is the exception, not the rule, regarding copyright protection and permissions. An attorney can help you figure out whether your use qualifies. "Reproduction of Copyrighted Works by Educators and Librarians" from the U.S. Copyright Office gives an excellent overview of Fair Use policies. You can find it online at `http://lcweb.loc.gov/copyright/circs/circ21.pdf`.

If you need specific music for your show then you should see whether the rights are available, and at what fees, before you even begin shooting. I know a few producers who thought getting the rights to certain pieces of music would be cheap and easy, only to find out someone else locked up the rights or the fees were incredibly high. One in particular ended up reshooting parts of her movie because she never bothered to check until the last minute.

Public Domain

You may be thinking about using an existing song that you believe may be in the public domain.

That a song is freely available on the Internet does not guarantee that it is in the public domain. That a song is given away for nothing doesn't guarantee that it is in the public domain. That you can't find a copyright notice doesn't guarantee that a song is in the public domain. The upshot is that even if you find material that is freely available at no cost and contains no copyright notice, don't assume it is in the public domain.

You must conduct a copyright search. Start with a visit to the U.S. Copyright Office online at `www.loc.gov/copyright` or at the Library of Congress, James Madison Memorial Building, 101 Independence Avenue, S.E., Washington, D.C. 20559-6000. For information on searching records from 1790 through 1978, see *How to Investigate the Copyright Status of a Work* (Circular 22) located online at `www.loc.gov/copyright/circs/circ22.html` or `http://lcweb.loc.gov/copyright/circs/circ22.pdf`, and *The Copyright Card Catalog and the Online Files of the Copyright Office* (Circular 23) `http://lcweb.loc.gov/copyright/circs/circ23.pdf`.

Although public domain status may apply to a song or composition, it may not apply to the recorded performance. You still need to negotiate for the Master Recording License to that recorded performance.

Even if your copyright search is very thorough, the results may not be conclusive. Consult with a copyright attorney before reaching any conclusions regarding the copyright status of a work.

You may not need licenses for an original score, but that really depends on what you negotiated with the composer and the score's producer. You may not need to clear music from a music library, but I highly recommend you read the fine print on the CD before proceeding. Some music libraries have specific terms of use that you're required to follow.

You may be able to hire a rights clearance service or music supervisor to handle the clearances for you, but it's always good to know what's going on and why. To properly clear music for movies, you need the expertise of an entertainment attorney and at least a basic understanding of the types of licenses required.

First, determine whether you'll use the music many times through the piece or just once and where it falls in the movie. If the music is rolling at the head, it may be construed as a theme song, which costs more. If the music is incidental, as if coming from a jukebox, it may cost less. If you're not using the whole song, be sure to mention that in your negotiations— you can save yourself some money. If you want to use the piece repeatedly throughout your show, that'll probably cost more.

With the changes in markets and outlets, your attorney may suggest that you get a broad grant of rights to cover all markets and any media, including those of the future, as well as the right to incidental use of a song in advertising, trailers, and other promo materials. You'll probably also want the license to be perpetual, especially for a feature.

Keep asking your lawyer questions until you understand the issues.

Sync and Master

There are two items you need to legally use a song and recording in your movie:

- **Sync License**—The written authorization to synchronize the recorded version of that song with visual images such as movies, TV, videos, Web sites, and so on. Sync Rights are usually, although not always, controlled by the music publisher.
- **Master Recording License**—This pertains to the recording of the performance itself. Master Use Rights are usually, but not always, controlled by the record label.

You need to find out whether the Sync and Master Recording licenses are available for the song you want to use. The first step is to find out who controls the licensing.

The CD packaging should list a performance rights organization for the song, such as the American Society of Composers, Authors, and Publishers

(ASCAP), Broadcast Music, Inc. (BMI), or the Society of European Stage Authors and Composers (SESAC). The performance rights organizations don't control these rights, but it can tell you who does.

For works in the ASCAP repertoire, see ASCAP Clearance Express (ACE) at `http://ascap.com/ace/ACE.html` or call the Clearance Desk at (212) 621-6160.

You can search the BMI HyperRepertoire Internet Song Title Database at `http://bmi.com/repertoire/about.asp`. You can also call (310) 659-9109 and ask for the Research Department.

The SESAC Repertory On-Line (SRO) at `www.sesac.com/repertory.htm` contains a listing of the SESAC repertory. You can also call (800) 826-9996.

When you call ASCAP, BMI, or SESAC, ask for the names, addresses, and phone numbers of the parties controlling the Sync Rights and the Master Use Rights for the song you need.

Because some copyrights are held by multiple entities, dealing with one agency can be a great timesaver. The Harry Fox Agency (HFA), which represents most of the major U.S. publishers, grants Master Recording and Sync licenses and collects the fees for them. If the song you want is handled by HFA, that's whom you need to speak to. You can find HFA at `http://www.harryfox.com` or by calling (212) 370-5330 and asking for the Theatrics Department.

Sync It Up

Call the organization controlling the Sync Rights. Ask to speak with someone in Rights, Permissions, or Licensing—each organization has a different name for this department. Write down that person's name. Ask whether the organization controls the Sync Rights and whether the Sync License is available. If the answer is yes, you're officially negotiating.

Because there are no set fees or standard practices for Sync Licenses, make obscurity and poverty work for you. Tell the publisher's rep that you're an independent producer with an independent flick at fine cut. They'll know immediately that you don't have any money. But that doesn't mean they'll just hang up. As everyone in the music business knows, your offer may be the only one for that song in the lifetime of the contract.

Be ready to tell them your music budget and offer to send them a dub of the fine cut. I've found that the smaller labels usually want one. The people at the megalith multinationals can't be bothered, but in the past, they liked it when I offered because it showed that I had the chutzpah to make a movie for less money than the cookie budget on a typical Hollywood show.

Ask how much the publisher wants for the Sync License. I had one publisher demand three times the entire budget for my feature for three obscure songs by a friend's band. Crazy. Say thank you, tell them you'll call back after you have spoken with your lawyer and counted your pennies, and GET OFF THE PHONE.

Repeat this process for every song you need to clear.

Now, spend a couple days getting over the shock and decide, realistically, what you can afford and what you'll accept. You're a creative person. Use negotiating tools other than cold hard cash: featuring the band or artist on your marketing collateral, setting up a concert for the world premiere, and so on.

After you know what you're willing to accept, call them back. Don't drink too much coffee beforehand because perkiness is irritating. Plus, there's nothing worse than desperately needing to use the bathroom in the middle of a delicate negotiation.

Make your counteroffer.

Listen to them sputter for a minute. It will happen, because it's that person's job to sputter. Be ready with all the reasons they should agree to your price: prestige of the song in an independent flick, it's such a great fit, your movie will be shown in festivals around the world, whatever. Appeal to the individual's desire to do something cool. Help them say yes.

Don't be afraid to walk away from an agreement that doesn't fit your needs or your budget. Just keep it friendly. They might call back tomorrow to accept your offer because you handled yourself really well. Stranger things have happened. And before accepting anything, remember that one of the best things you can say in any negotiation is, "Well, I have to talk to my lawyer about that."

Even if you get your Sync License for less than you budgeted, don't start jumping around in glee yet. You still need the Master Recording License.

Yes, Master

The problem with Master Recording Licenses is getting them at an affordable price, especially if the recording artist is famous. The record label will argue that the artist is more famous and recognizable than the song (which might be true), and because that's where the value is, that's what you should pay for.

This is one of the reasons you hear hit songs rerecorded by someone obscure. A producer gets the Sync License, but the Master Recording License is outrageously expensive. So, he or she hires a band to record the song. If you go this route, just be careful about soundalikes. See Chapter 4, "Don't Tread on Me: Intellectual Property and Other Thorny Issues," for further discussion and just make sure you have a written contract with the band you hired that states you own all the rights to the recording.

Call the company that controls the Master Use Rights and put to use all those skills you acquired getting your show to this point: charm, guts, and an insane level of optimism. Again, your lack of budget can work to your advantage. One record label exec I negotiated with decided to sign away the Sync and Master Recording Licenses to four songs for a token $1.00 each.

If the label isn't budging, use any pull you have with the band, artist, or producer. If they're unhappy, it's in the label's interest to make them happy, so the label may acquiesce now for profits later.

And remember: Wear comfortable shoes in case you have to walk away.

The Devil's in the Details

When you get the contracts from the music publisher and record label, have your entertainment attorney read through and explain every word on every piece of paper. One whiff of potential litigation will scare away a distributor, justified or not. "Is everything cleared?" is one of the first questions out of a distributor's mouth.

All of your deliverables, such as payment, music cue sheets, one or more copies of the movie, and so on, will be listed in the contract. Follow through on them conscientiously.

MUSIC CUE SHEETS

In the United States, when you license music, the publisher and record label will require you to deliver a cue sheet to them, shown in Figure 30.5. Usually, they'll hand it onto the performance rights organizations. These organizations will then compare your cue sheet with the lists of theaters and broadcasters to make sure the composers get their royalties.

	MUSIC CUE SHEET Program: AMAZING WORLD Producer: HOLY TOLEDO PICTURES, INC. Length: 91 MINUTES Air Date: Undetermined	19030 Lenton Place SE, Suite 242 Monroe, WA 98272-1353 360/793-7947 206/499-5796 425/827-2747 (fax) www.holytoledo.com
HOLY TOLEDO PICTURES, INC		

USAGES
VV: Visual Vocal VI: Visual Instrumental VD: Visual Dance
VB: Vocal Background IB: Instrumental Background

CUE. NO.	TITLE	COMPOSER (S)	PUBLISHER (S)	SOCIETY	USE	TIMING
1	Second Skin	Mia Zapata Mattew Dresdner Steve Moriarty Joe Spleen	Fishheadhotdog Burrito Music	ASCAP	VB	00:01: 32
2	Chiva Kneiva	Blind Marky Felchtone	Scooch Pooch Records,	None	VB	00:01: 02
3	1 Rose's Theme	Denise Ohio	Inc. Holy Toledo Music	None	IB	00:01: 23
4	Fire-cracker	Lisa Wright David McCarroll David Delong Jason Freeman Jeth Odom	Feel the Sting	ASCAP	VB	00:00: 46
5	Fire-cracker	Lisa Wright David McCarroll David Delong Jason Freeman Jeth Odom	Feel the Sting	ASCAP	VB	00:00: 07
6	Spear & A Magic Helmet	Mia Zapata Mattew Dresdner Steve Moriarty Joe Spleen	Fishheadhotdog Burrito Music	ASCAP	VB	00:00: 28

FIGURE 30.5

Music cue sheet sample from *Amazing World.*

The cue sheet can be on standard 8.5"×11" paper, printed on one side only.

Put your production company name in the upper-left box. In the center-top box, list the name of the program, producer, and length of the show, including titles and credits, in minutes. Then, list the air date. If you have no air date, put "Undetermined." In the upper-right box, list the production company contact information (see Figure 30.6).

[PRODUCTION COMPANY NAME]				[PRODUCTION COMPANY CONTACT INFORMATION]		
MUSIC CUE SHEET						
Program:						
Producer:						
Length:			**MINUTES**			
Air Date:						
USAGES **VV: Visual Vocal VI: Visual Instrumental VD: Visual Dance** **VB: Vocal Background IB: Instrumental Background**						
CUE. NO.	TITLE	COMPOSER (S)	PUBLISHER (S)	SOCIETY	USE	TIMING

FIGURE 30.6

Music cue sheet blank.

Under *Cue No.*, number each piece of music in order, including repeated uses. Under *Title*, list the title. Under *Composer(s)*, list everyone credited with writing the piece, including the arranger. Under *Publisher(s)*, list all publishers. Under *Society*, list the performance rights organization, usually ASCAP or BMI. If the piece isn't listed with a performance rights organization, write "None." Under *Use*, use the code under Usages. Music that is part of an on-camera performance, such as an actor singing a song or a band performance, would be either *Visual Vocal* or *Visual Instrumental*. *Background Vocal* and *Background Instrumental* is music without an on-camera performance, such as a score. Under *Timing*, list the duration of the piece in your show.

The cue sheet can be several pages for longer shows, so number all of them clearly.

Cue sheet information may be different in other countries.

MIXING

During the mix, the edited sound elements of dialogue, sound effects, and music are assembled and balanced to become the final soundtrack in stereo. The combined elements are adjusted in volume and tonal quality relative to one another and picture. It's during mix that the sum of the parts becomes greater than the whole.

First, decide whether you want to work with a sound mixer or handle the mix yourself.

WORKING WITH A SOUND MIXER

If you take care of all the sound editing chores, you can hire a mixer to put the piece together for you. Contact your mixer ahead of time so you know exactly how your sound mixer works and what video and audio formats the post-audio house accepts.

Your goal is to deliver master-quality audio so the post-audio house will not have to start from scratch.

Put a countdown at the start of your show. Many NLE applications will generate countdown leaders for you. If your show is over an hour and you're mastering on miniDV tapes, you'll need at least two tapes with a countdown on each. The countdown must include a 2-pop on every audio track. If you're working with a long piece, you may also want to place a tail pop. That's a beep at the end of every audio track placed on exactly the same frame.

If you need a music-and-effects (M&E) track, tell the post-audio house. An M&E mix has all the music and sound effects on one track and English language on another. This allows foreign language versions to be dubbed easily. If you need an M&E, it may add some dollars, but if you think you have a chance at a foreign release or sale, you'll need it. Do this now—it's a lot more expensive to do it later. If you're producing for a network, your contract may specify an M&E master, so check before going into the post-audio house that they can handle it and be sure to follow the network's technical requirements scrupulously.

Ask what video format they use. It's unlikely the post-audio house will have DV or DVCAM decks for their work. You may need to bring in a Beta SP or Digital Beta fine cut master. Some post-audio houses will let you bring your own DV camera and dub from your master to their deck. Depending on program length, this can be cheaper than buying a Beta dub elsewhere. Check with the post-audio house.

Some post-audio mixers will ask for a window-burn VHS tape. They're not using the sound on these masters—they just need to see the picture so they can make sure everything falls where it needs to. Have a scratch version of all the audio properly placed to help the mixer know where everything is supposed to go.

For the individual audio tracks, stay away from analog. Most sound mixers will prefer your audio on DTRS (also known as DA-88) or an ADAT, both of which are modular digital multitrackers (MDMs). They will probably accept timecode DAT and possibly a Digital Beta master.

DA-88 is a format from Tascam that has become a motion picture industry standard. You can have eight discrete tracks of audio, and as long as the deck has an optional timecode card, the timecode is stable. You need stable timecode if you're laying tracks from your NLE to keep multiple passes in sync. With a DA-88, the mixer can create sets of mixes for different uses. If you think you may be going to theatrical or want 5.1 surround sound, the mixer can use the first six tracks for that mix. For all other uses, the mixer will place a stereo mix on the last two tracks.

I've noticed more music studios taking on post-audio work. ADATs are standard in the music industry, and if you're using an ADAT, both you and the studio need BRCs or third-party converters to use timecode with ADAT. If you have an ADAT, you probably won't need to bring your deck to a typical music studio, but you will need it at a post-audio house.

Timecode DATs are standard tools in any pro studio. Digital Beta decks, however, are a bit more rare. You can bring one in if the post-audio house doesn't have one. To get a Digital beta master, you will need to have it converted from DV to Digital Beta at a post-production facility or duplication house.

If you're using a DA-88 or an ADAT, you may have to bring your deck. If you have a removable hard drive, your post-audio house may accept that instead of tape-based media. But ask first. Depending on your NLE and the studio DAW, you may be able to transfer everything in sync with a proprietary format. But talk with the post-audio house people before doing anything.

If you don't have access to the fancy equipment, you can bring in separated tracks burned as files onto a CD-ROM, Zip disk, or just about any other media. Windows WAV and Macintosh AIFF are standards and should be acceptable file formats. If you put everything on CD-ROM, be sure you're putting everything in as data files, not as audio that can be played in a CD player. That way, you can retain 16-bit 48kHz sample rates.

Make sure your sound elements are clean, are well-edited, and sync to picture. Everything should be sampled at 16-bit 48kHz. Keep all the sounds on separate tracks and don't EQ anything coming out of your system. When you are recording a stereo track to a mono track, don't combine both tracks during the edit. Your levels will be too high.

I usually send my audio files a couple days before the mixing session so the engineer can transfer everything when convenient. When I show up, everything is loaded on the drives and we're ready to go.

Bring your spotting and other notes, raw audio, and duplicates of the placed audio files. You may also want to create a cue sheet. A cue sheet is a chart showing exactly what's on every track lined up against timecode. The mixer will then line up all the 2-pops. Everything should sync correctly, but make sure. Let the mixer put the elements together and stay out of the way. Few shows can withstand a poor mix.

It will take longer than you think. Still, it's quite an experience to watch a talented mixer bring things together. Then listen carefully to the playback. Make some notes and have the mixer revise anything that didn't sound right. Even the most talented mixer may not be sure of your intent and won't know what to emphasize when there are multiple elements at the same time.

Your post-audio house may not be able to lay back the mix to picture or you may want to have the audio on a format the post-audio doesn't work with. If you don't have the equipment, you'll need to have your mixed soundtrack laid back to picture at a postproduction house. The post-audio engineer or sound mixer can give you the mixed soundtrack on a timecode DAT or DA-88.

You then take the soundtrack mix to the postproduction house, have them sync audio to picture, and replace the existing audio on your picture master with the mixed soundtrack. Speak with your post houses before proceeding. You can also have the mixer hand you a CD-ROM of the mix with a 2-pop and resync the mix to picture in your NLE for layback to a DV master.

SOUND MIXING BASICS

The mix can be the greatest source of satisfaction on a project. It can also be a heap of frustration, pain, and disappointment. Preparation is key.

Generally, you begin mix in this order:

- Dialogue, narration, and voiceovers
- Hard effects
- Music
- Ambiences
- Smaller sound effects

Arrange the individual tracks in a logical way. Many mixers create submixes of related sounds to make mixing easier, such as ringing phones, slamming drawers, bubbling water coolers, murmuring, and so on, into one office audio sound bed track. I rarely do this, preferring to keep the elements as separate as possible for as long as possible. Don't stint on tracks. Use as many as necessary to for maximum flexibility, but that will depend on what kind of system you're using.

Sound mixers place audio elements in the acoustic space in four ways:

- **Volume**—Louder sounds closer. Just don't make everything close and watch those levels. Dynamics processing, adjusting sounds in relation to themselves and one another, is the automatic form of volume control that can help you place audio elements.

- **Pan**—Adjusting the position of sounds in the stereo field left or right may help define physical space. Don't overdo this—the effect is often lost. Always keep the dialog and crucial sound effects straight up the middle.

- **Equalization**—EQ controls tone by manipulating the relative strength of certain frequencies. The midrange EQ control, especially between 1,200Hz and 2,500Hz, brings voices forward in the mix. If you notch your music, lowering the midrange frequencies, you can give the voices a bit more room. Frequencies between 100Hz and 250Hz add warmth to voices, but don't overdo the low frequencies. You can turn down some of the higher frequencies in exterior sounds to add a bit of distance.

- **Reverb**—Those echoes make things seem farther away. Use it carefully on interior sounds to make everything seem more three-dimensional.

Dynamics Processing

Dynamics processing varies the output level of a sound based on its input level. By compressing or limiting the dynamic range, perceived loudness is kept below a certain limit or the overall dynamic range is kept at about the same level.

Compressors reduce the dynamic range of an audio signal. They can eliminate the variations in the peaks of a signal by clamping them to a constant level. Compressors can compensate for variations in level of a signal of someone who moves a lot when being recorded or has an erratic dynamic range.

Limiters are compressors having very fast attack times and often, though not always, a compression ratio of 10:1. They allow the dynamic range to increase up to a certain threshold. Beyond this level, if the input continues to increase in gain, the output doesn't increase in volume. Watch out for "feed-forward" dynamics processors; they can introduce a delay for which you'll have to compensate if you want to keep sync.

Expanders expand the dynamic range of an audio signal, boosting high-level signals and attenuating low-level signals. *Noise gates* are a type of expander that can reduce or eliminate noise below a threshold level. Signals below a certain threshold are heavily attenuated and often totally cut off during a pause. This increases the perceived dynamic range.

The purpose of a compressor is to keep the level consistent. This can also add punch or body to a sound, but don't compress anything until the sound elements have been placed, layered, and roughly mixed. You don't know how much compression you'll need until you've got a mix in place.

One way to think of compressors and limiters is as an automatic volume control. As long as the signal remains below a certain, predetermined value (known as the *threshold*), the compressor won't trigger. If the signal reaches that value, the compressor will trigger, reducing the signal's volume level.

By cutting peak levels, a compressor lets you raise the level of the overall track. The threshold control sets how high the input level can rise before the compressor triggers. The ratio control tells how far the compressor should compress the signal. Judicious use of threshold and ratio allows you to set a stable level that will hold its position in the mix regardless of the complete soundtrack's overall volume level. In addition, you can often determine attack, release, and output settings.

Attack determines the speed of the compressor's response. Attack is the length of a sound from its beginning to its peak. Short attack times force the compressor to kick in as soon as the signal gets too high. A long attack will allow sound at the threshold level to slide by, provided it only lasts for a determined period of time. *Release* determines how quickly the compressor should return to its level after a loud signal has been compressed. The *output* control determines at what level the processed audio should be once the compressor or limiter is finished.

Many audio software packages have preset software compressors. Listen to them carefully—often these presets are for music mixing. Still, try them out on your system and experiment with these tools to understand what they do.

Reverb

Reverb is used to simulate acoustic space. It consists of early reflections and echoes spaced so that they are perceived as a single decaying sound. It's different from a basic echo in that the delays aren't repeated at regularly spaced intervals.

Reverb is often used to give the illusion of being in a particular space. Tracks without any reverb are referred to as *dry*, while tracks with reverb are referred to as *wet*. Using fairly short reverbs with a high wet/dry mix can work, although it's not quite the same as recording in the actual place.

Longer reverbs can add weight and drama to sounds that need heaviness. Have one track of the dry original sound and a track to which you apply the reverb. Raise the reverb at the tail portion of the sound for a pretty effective sound.

To adjust audio to match image size, such as a wide shot with audio that was recorded with the mic close to source, first determine the perspective. With audio, this means comparing the ratio of direct to reflected sound. *Direct sound* comes from the source itself, such as from an actor's mouth. When a person is close, you hear what comes from the person. As the person moves farther away, you hear more of the reflected sound.

Reflected sound is the direct sound bouncing off any structure, including you, in the vicinity of the direct sound. Reflected sound is more complicated than direct sound because surfaces at different distances have varying reflective properties.

For example, stand right in front of someone and ask the person to speak. Now, step into a large bathroom and step as far back as you can. In the first instance, the direct sound is coming right at you with very little reflection. You're hearing just about every part of the voice, including nasal and low-frequency chest tones, clicks and pops of the teeth, and so on.

In the second, the voice has to travel, bouncing off all of those surfaces. Bathrooms, in particular, have hard surfaces such as glass and tile that bounce the sound right back. Such rooms are considered live because of all the activity. Rooms that have a lot of cushy material, such as carpeting, drapes, and really comfortable sofas, are considered acoustically dead.

(*Live* and *dead* don't refer to good or bad when talking about acoustics. They're simply shorthand for describing acoustically what kind of space the sound is in.)

When you're trying to place a sound in a certain space, you have to consider what you need to remove and what you'll need to add to make the audio sound right. For example, you have a wide shot of your characters coming into a cave. You have replaced the original location audio with that of a closer shot because it was more intelligible.

Considering what kind of cave it is, you may want to add some delay and reverb to give the sounds a sense of space. If the cave is supposed to be very large with very hard rock, the reverb may be a bit bigger, with more reflected sound. Delays are great for making sounds bounce around, especially if they are panned around the stereo field. Use a bit of pitch shifting to make everything a bit livelier.

If the cave is small or has softer sides, such as a mineshaft with dirt sprinkling dangerously from the ceiling every few minutes, you may want to have less or no reverb. Short delays can mimic early reflection to evoke the feeling of a tight space without adding an echoey tail.

Worldizing

Although I will use dynamics processing, delays, and reverb to shape a sound for a certain scene, I'll often play the sound in a room and record it that way. It just sounds more alive to me. This is called *worldizing*.

For example, if you have to match music playing through a door that is opening, mic a room outside a closed door. Open the door and there you go.

THINKING ABOUT YOUR MIX

If your audio seems to be just too big, rethink your audio priorities. Dialogue is the most important audio element. You can sacrifice sound effects or music, but you want to avoid compromising dialogue. In some instances, the point of the scene may be that people are screaming at one another. What they are screaming is less important than that they are struggling to communicate. In this instance, obscuring the dialogue may work to your benefit.

Keep your dialogue panned equally left and right of the stereo mix. You may need to apply some compression and limiting to make it ride above the rest of the mix. EQ will also help to make sure that the other elements don't compete with the words. If a line isn't clear in the mix, turn everything else down a bit.

Face that you may lose that great effect or beautiful music in the mix. What matters is the mix, not the individual elements. Just keep in mind the dialogue takes precedence.

If you have a lot of sound elements converging on a point, make sure you leave headroom for the combined volume. Not only should you listen for distortion from levels that are too high, keep an eye out for peaking in the audio meters. Remember in digital audio, you don't want to go above 0 dB.

Mixing Tips

- Don't work nonstop for hours. Your hearing gradually becomes numbed.

- Don't monitor at high levels, especially when using headphones.

- Before you start, set your mixer to zero, pan controls centered, mutes and solo buttons off, and EQ controls set at zero.

- When EQing, it's usually better to cut frequencies than to boost them.

FINISHING

Finishing is the process of creating a single, finished show on an accepted format along with support materials. It combines aesthetic, technical, and legal issues, and may include

- Copyright
- Video sweetening
- Videotape-to-film
- Transferring to different formats, including any standards conversion
- Duplication

The accepted format depends on your show's destination. Distributors, film festivals, and broadcasters may have different requirements. Duplication houses may not accept any DV format, so you may have to transfer your finished show to a new format master. Check before delivering a duplication master.

COPYRIGHT

Register the work with the copyright office and place a proper copyright notice on the work. A copyright notice contains the word *copyright*, the abbreviation of the word copyright, or the copyright symbol ©. This is followed by the name of the copyright owner and date of publication.

Omission of the notice doesn't make the work public domain. However, the 1976 Copyright Act limits remedies against innocent infringement because the owner neglected to put a notice on the work. The innocent infringer is shielded from certain damages.

Although a work is covered when created, registration is important for further protection. To register copyright in the United States, send a properly completed application form, the appropriate fee, and a deposit copy of the work in one envelope.

Registrations take effect on the date of receipt in the copyright office.

See Chapter 4, "Don't Tread on Me: Intellectual Property and Other Thorny Issues," for more discussion on this subject. For copyright forms, visit www.loc.gov/copyright/circs/index.html#fl.

VIDEO SWEETENING

Video sweetening polishes your completed show through

- Tape-to-tape color correction
- Adding titles
- Clamping to legal colors
- Adding reference bars and tone

TAPE-TO-TAPE COLOR CORRECTION

Tape-to-tape color correction allows you to manipulate the color from shot to shot, scene to scene, and through the entire show for a consistent look. You can also correct and repair some exposure problems, and manipulate the footage in other ways.

Tape-to-tape allows you to get one more layer of consistency and control over your images. Some desktop video editing software will help you do some amazing things with color correction. For example, export a frame from your show to a still format and open that in a photo editor, such as

Adobe's ubiquitous and wonderful Photoshop. Start manipulating the levels, contrast, hue, and saturation of the image.

Many editing applications have filters that allow you to tweak your footage in similar ways. You can correct to make everything more consistent, or saturate or desaturate certain hues for a more unusual look. You'll probably have to render any footage you filter, but the results can be interesting.

For faster results and more options, consider going to a local postproduction house that offers tape-to-tape color correction on a DaVinci or other color enhancement system.

The colorist will be able to do some incredible things with your footage. Colorists can grab any color and manipulate it without affecting the rest of the picture, and change the brightness and even the perceived sharpness of an image. A colorist can darken backgrounds while keeping the subject bright, tone down overexposed areas, and perform other image manipulation.

Often the colorist can fix bad video. Footage that's too dark or has poor color rendition or other problems can be manipulated. But the best result from video sweetening happens to the best footage. It can enhance well-shot DV by further controlling color and exposure to make it consistent throughout the show.

Tape-to-tape costs. Usually it's an hourly rate and how long it takes depends on what needs to be done. You may be able to get a lower rate by going in at night, during times of the year when postproduction houses aren't as busy, and by calling around for pricing. Many postproduction houses will match their competitors.

You can assume that every 15 minutes of your show will require about two hours—maybe more, maybe less, depending on what needs to be done.

Talk to the colorist ahead of time, preferably before you shoot. Your postproduction house techs may also suggest camera settings so you will have the best footage for sweetening. Don't blow out the highlights or crush the blacks, but shoot so that you still have detail in highlight and shadow. As long as it's there, it can be brought out in sweetening. If it's gone in the original, it's gone forever.

NOTE

Closed Captioning

Many viewers require closed captioning to get the fullest experience of your show. You may want to add closed captioning. You can do this at a post-production house or your-self using

www.ccaption.com or http://dvguys.com/ fcptricks_vault.shtml.

Some postproduction houses don't handle DV formats and you may have to master to Beta SP, Digital Beta, or even HD. That's more time and expense for you, so be sure you've got the money in your budget.

Go in with your master and notes about what you want done. I work with the people at Modern Digital in Seattle. Usually, I tell the night colorist, Sam, to make the piece pretty. From my observation, he tends to correct by first making the skin tones consistent and bright, correcting any over- and underexposures, and then tweaking anything that annoys him. Only once have I disagreed with a choice he made.

ADDING TITLES

If you're going into a postproduction house for tape-to-tape color correction, leave the titles off your show. You'll add those at the post facility after the tape-to-tape.

If you're finishing on your NLE, in addition to keeping the colors clamped, consider the viewer's ability to read moving text on a relatively low-resolution display such as a TV screen. *Character generation*, or CG, for interlaced video can exhibit line twitter on static or moving text, as well as distortions on rolling text. If the video format is compressed, such as DV, you can see artifacting.

Line twitter happens when fine, single-line detail appears in one field but not in the other. The detail noticeably flickers at the frame rate of 29.97 for NTSC and 25 for PAL, while the rest of the image updates at the field rate. Use heavy fonts at bold, extrabold, or black, and avoid fine type. If you just have to use a light font, build up the lines using outline, glow, or extrusion in a similar color or brightness. Drop shadows in a similar color with minimal offset can help.

You can also create hardcopies and scan them in, treating the credits as graphics. You'll have a hard time getting multiple cards to roll properly, but you can crossfade, dissolve, overlay, and apply just about any other filter to them.

Consider shooting your credits rather than using a CG. One of my favorite no-budget credit sequences was done with sidewalk chalk. The director wrote the credits on a length of sidewalk outside his house, put the camera on a tripod, and then started the camera. He timed the shot by reading the credits aloud twice, then picked the camera up, while it was still running, and positioned it to the next card. I think he intended to cross-dissolve between cards, but the jiggling of the moving camera really brought a sense of humor to the entire sequence.

If you want to use your NLE's titling features, keep in mind that rolling credits can be a problem. A roll rate in lines per second, that's the same as the field rate of 59.94 for NTSC or 50fps for PAL, the roll looks terrible. The text will lose resolution and otherwise distort.

For NTSC, only two decent roll rates are slow enough to be read: 120 and 240. PAL is better because the roll rates are about 20% slower and there are almost 20% more active scanlines per frame. You can roll at 100, 200, and 300 lines per second with good results.

If you want to use other roll rates, use a good character generator that offers subpixel positioning, such as Chyron and Abeka machines, or the text will stutter up the screen. Software character generators may offer you more control than the titler included in your NLE software. If you're doing a tape-to-tape color correction, you may be able to do it during the same session.

If you're creating titles in your NLE, consider using applications such as Adobe Photoshop or Adobe After Effects to create them. Most NLE titlers render sharp text that work well on a computer screen and poorly on a TV set or when compressed.

In DCT-based codecs such as those for DV, you'll get mosquito noise, critters, or feathering artifacts, with visual noise scattered around the text. Put the text in a roll and the mosquito noise surrounding the text will fly around just like a flock of hungry mosquitoes.

You can correct this by filtering the text with a soften or blur. It will look worse on the computer screen but better after going through the codec.

Keep your titles legal colors. Set the peak white in your text at 80 IRE for NTSC or 80% in PAL. Watch out for text color bleeding onto the background and vice versa. It can get especially bad with composite display or analog transmission.

Back off the saturation and go for pastel tones. Try not to use colors in opposition to one another, such as green on magenta. One thing that does seem to work nicely is yellow text on blue or cyan backgrounds. Although the colors are opposites, or close to opposites, you can get a fairly saturated yellow without too many problems.

Watch the rendered text on a real, honest-to-goodness composite video monitor.

CLAMPING TO LEGAL COLORS

Remember that luminance is defined by a 1-254 scale inside the video stream. Systems that use the ITU-R 601 digital coding standard require black to be set at level 16 and white at 235.

As discussed in Chapter 18, "Making Video Digital," for analog video, the electrical reference for white is generally defined as 100 IRE regardless of format, whereas the electrical reference for black depends on what video format and standard you are using. For PAL, as well as the Japanese version of NTSC, black is 0 IRE. In the United States, composite video places black at 7.5 IRE. All the IRE black levels are digitized to a value of 16.

When you go from DV to an analog format, you must make sure that the luminance and chrominance are clamped to the correct electrical signals. DV specifically doesn't record the NTSC setup. It must be added while going to analog.

Different IRE setups do not change the way the DV data stream defines black and white. DV and DV-based formats use the 16/235 luminance range. Black is just over 6% brightness, with an RGB color value of 16,16,16, and white is just over 92% brightness at 235,235,235.

You can use a plug-in or application to do the clamping, and then lay back to DV. If you transfer to Beta SP, an analog format, have the transfer house be sure to run your video through a proc amp to adjust to legal colors. Do the same thing from the tape-to-tape color-correction machine to the analog deck.

Many postproduction houses automatically clamp to legal colors.

ADDING REFERENCE BARS AND TONE

Because the head and tail of a videotape are the most common places for physical damage to the tape or its coating, run two minutes of black leader before rolling picture. You then add reference SMPTE bars and 1kHz tone to the head of your tape so the duplication house can set its equipment.

Be sure to record the following:

- 30 seconds of bars and tone.
- 15-second slate with the title, director, and total runtime, or TRT, in real-time.
- 10-second countdown with a 2-pop. Many NLE software applications have a utility that will create one for you.

At 0, the show should start.

VIDEOTAPE-TO-FILM

Unless your show gets into a major festival, there's no reason for you to pay for a tape-to-film transfer. If a distributor wants to release your show theatrically, let the distributor pay for it.

You can find excellent articles on tape-to-film at 2-pop, at www.2-pop.com/library/articles/2000-03-09.html. 2-pop is a goldmine of great information about DV, moviemaking, and related technology, so spend some time checking the articles, archives, and message boards.

Robert Goodman's article in the August 2000 issue of *The Independent* from Association of Independent Video and Film (AIVF) is a well-written piece comparing tape-to-film facilities. AIVF members can read the full article at www.aivf.org/the_independent/archives/0008/mo/augsep00_goodman.html. Visit AIVF's Web site at www.aivf.org for more info about the organization and *The Independent*.

Steve Mullen also had an article on www.mindspring.com/~d-v-c.

DV tape-to-film requires advance planning. Contact the transfer house prior to shooting and try to get test transfers before committing. It's too expensive to let it go to the last minute. You can find a listing of tape-to-film houses in Resources.

Consider the different frame rates between video and film. NTSC runs at 29.97, whereas PAL runs at 25fps. Film, on the other hand, runs at 24fps. Transferring between NTSC video and film can cause artifacting. To avoid it, the ideal solution would be to shoot video at 24fps. Some manufacturers have built HD cams at 24fps progressive, but they are far beyond the budgets of most independent producers.

Another solution is to use PAL equipment and capture at 25fps. You can then transfer frame by frame to 35mm film. When video is slowed down to 24fps, the 35mm version will run four percent longer, so edit appropriately. Don't worry about the effect of the slowdown on audio—special equipment corrects for the speed change without changing the pitch of the sound.

Before you decide, talk with your transfer house. Some transfer houses handle only NTSC, some only PAL, some prefer frame movie mode—talk with them first.

Undoubtedly, you'll want a camera with the largest number of chips at the highest resolution, controls to manipulate image sharpness, and gain offset. Lower the detail setting, use dynamic contrast control, keep shutter speeds at or below 1/60 of a second, and turn off the digital zoom and electronic image stabilizer.

Shoot for transfer by keeping your eye on these issues:

- Light each shot with depth and modeling, using layers of lights.
- Don't use the zoom. Lock down your tripod or, for a moving camera, use a dolly. No tilts, and pans, especially digital artifact-riddled whip pans.
- Try out camera filters for a diffuse look. Some moviemakers prefer Tiffen Pro-Mist filters, such as the Black Pro-Mist #1 or Warm Pro-Mist 1/2. These knock off a bit of high-frequency detail and add a bit of halation around highlights, reducing hard-to-compress high-contrast edges and fewer "mosquito noise" artifacts.
- If you're using a camera that allows it, reduce the sharpness control. Use manual exposure and lock in once your exposure is set. Use wide apertures.
- In post, stick mostly to fades, cuts, and dissolves.
- Be sure to budget your time and money.

Try for a 3:1 lighting ratio, where the response curve of the CCDs is very similar to film. The contrast will be heightened during the transfer process, but it's important not to exceed the range of brightness the CCD can handle.

Some transfer houses prefer movie mode or frame mode for transfers for better resolution of DV footage. For PAL projects, there is no frame-rate conversion problem, so noninterlaced modes work better.

Aspect Ratios—Video and Film

Aspect ratio refers to the width of the frame versus the height. True 16:9 is either created with an anamorphic lens or 16:9 chips.

Decide whether to shoot your video in 4:3 or 16:9 aspect ratio. Anamorphic 16:9 material can be obtained from cameras in four ways:

- The camera's 4:3 image is masked in the viewfinder and field monitor, and then cropped in post.
- The 4:3 image is cropped in camera.
- An anamorphic lens is used on the camera.
- The camera allows true 16:9.

You'll need an aspect-ratio switchable viewfinder and field monitor.

Your film aspect ratio can be 1.33:1 (NTSC 4:3), 1.66:1 (European standard), 1.85:1 (Academy Standard), and 2.35:1 (Panavision/CinemaScope).

The video must be cropped or blanked at the top and bottom to fill the frame. Shooting 16:9 will reduce the cropping and increases apparent vertical resolution.

- 4:3 video transferred to 1.66:1 requires either cutting out a portion of the top and bottom of the frame or blanking off the right and left of the screen.
- If you shoot 16:9 and transfer to 1.66:1, a small portion of both sides will be blanked.
- If you shoot 16:9 and transfer to 1.85:1, either the top and bottom portions of the frame or the right and left portions will be blanked.

POSTING FOR TAPE-TO-FILM

If your NLE doesn't support different aspect ratios, use a monitor that operates in 16:9. Limit transitions to cuts, dissolves, and fades. The transfer house will tell you whether they want you to use any sort of filmlook process. Most don't, but each one has its idiosyncrasies.

You have to deal with reel changes. Film reels in theaters are changed every 20 1/2 minutes. It's your job to create reel change points and deliver a list of points with timecode. Don't have any sustained sound at these points—it will be noticeable.

Get the video sweetened for color correction prior to transfer. Your transfer house will tell you what format they prefer for delivery. Also ask the transfer house how they prefer to handle titles. Rolling titles, especially, should be shot on film for best results. If you create titles on video, stay away from motion, saturated color, and fine edges.

Transfer houses use a Kinescope, electron beam recorder, or film recorder to produce the film negative. Most send the film out for processing and printing—be sure you know what lab and check it out. A great film transfer, like any great film footage, can be damaged by sloppy handling.

After you have the negative, you will ask the lab to strike an answer print. This will be timed by the film printer. *Timing* is a process when the negative is examined to determine color and exposure settings.

You should sit in on the timing session. It may take a little longer, and cost a little more, but if you get it right the first time, it will save you money in the long run. After you have the timing the way you want it, you'll create an internegative, from which all projection prints will be struck. Don't use your original negative—if it's damaged, you'll have to pay to get it repaired.

POSTING FOR TAPE

Often the master for transfer won't look quite right as video. You may want to plan a separate video master session, with titles and even a film-look process applied.

If you shot in 16:9, you'll want to letterbox the master. If you used an anamorphic lens, you'll want to apply a vertical squeeze to the image in your NLE and then lay back to tape. If you shot 4:3, apply a 16:9 in post and lay that back to tape.

If you shot in PAL, send it out for a high-quality standards conversion to NTSC.

TRANSFERRING TO DIFFERENT FORMATS AND STANDARDS

Many duplication houses and buyers prefer formats other than DV for mastering. You can master to an analog format, such as Beta SP, or transcode to a digital format, such as Digital Beta or HD.

Transferring from one standard to another, such as going from NTSC to PAL, can present certain problems, the biggest being that of making the motion in the finished image look as smooth as possible. The only way to effectively perform such a conversion is to freeze a frame and hold it until it's the right time for it.

A digital standards converter does this very thing. Another solution mixes two adjacent images together to create an in-between frame where needed. Many industrial converters and some high-end domestic standards converters use this method. A third system uses motion tracking and stores a sequence of frames for processing, whereas extremely fast microprocessors analyze the motion. This is very expensive compared to other techniques.

Even the most advanced standards converters aren't perfect. Although they can find edges in the moving image and predict where they would be between two images, the more indistinct the motion, the more likely it will fail to predict correctly. Fine detail is problematic, and the different line structure of NTSC and PAL means that each line of the image is out of proportion in reference to its neighbor in the other system.

Simpler standards converters merely drop or repeat lines in the output picture, resulting in some slightly strange effects, but retaining definition.

DUPLICATION

If you need a few dupes, you can run them off a good VHS deck. You may want to use a proc amp, waveform monitor, and vectorscope for best results. See Chapter 18 for discussion on video levels and Chapter 19, "The DV Camera," for discussion of waveform monitors and vectorscopes.

I usually create a separate dupe tape clamped to correct levels in my NLE. It's not the best, but if I need a dupe fast, it's acceptable quality.Proper dubs start with a legal video signal. Reputable duplication houses will check your levels and run the video signal through. The dupe house will raise the black level, knock down the video level if overexposed, and reduce the chroma level.

If you need VHS dupes of a different standards format, it's easier to get a master in that standard and run dupes from that.

PROCESSING AMPLIFIERS

A proc amp sits between the source deck and recording deck, and allows you to change the actual video signal rather than just the display of the video. This way, you can correct the color and luminance elements of the video signal. Usually, a proc amp is used with both a waveform monitor and vectorscope to ensure that the changes you are making are what you think you are making.

TIME-BASE CORRECTORS

A time-base corrector, or *TBC*, is used to synchronize a tape machine with other machines in a studio. This includes all the cameras, character generators, and special effects generators. Each device is genlocked to a master sync generator. If they aren't, the picture will break up and roll every time a cut is performed, and dissolves and fades would be impossible.

TBCs are also used to adjust color and video levels of the tape playback. The four controls used are basically the same as those found on a monitor.

- Set up a waveform monitor with the black levels at either 0 IRE for PAL or 7.5 IRE for NTSC.
- Turn on the TBC and use the control on the TBC marked Set Up, Pedestal, or Black Level, to match the waveform monitor's black level.
- Adjust the video level peak white to 100 IRE using the control marked Gain, Level, Video, or Luminance.
- To adjust hue, turn the Phase or Hue control until the colors are lined up with their correct boxes.
- Turn the Chroma, Color, Chroma Gain, or Saturation knob until the colors are in the boxes.

NOTE

Genlocking a Genlock

Genlock the noun and *genlock* the verb refer to different things. A genlock is an RGB-to-video encoder designed to take a graphic, such as animation or titles, from a computer and superimpose it on video. It genlocks to an incoming video signal and keys in computer graphics.

PCs and Macs use progressively scanned RGB pictures, so genlocks for them need a scan line converter to convert the computer's RGB image to interlaced video and clock it out at the correct video frequencies.

STEP V: SELLING:
HOW TO KEEP YOUR SHIRT

OVERVIEW

This section covers all of the aspects of selling your show.

Chapter 32, "Whom You're Selling To," details the different buyers of shows, while Chapter 33, "Festivals and Markets," details the most popular festivals and markets, what happens at a festival or market, and how to go in ready to do business. Chapter 34, "What You Sell: The Shape of Distribution Agreements," covers common elements in a distribution agreement.

Before you dive in, however, you may want to review Step I, "Development: Hunting and Gathering." Selling isn't a one-time experience. The movie business is fueled by both deep friendships and equally deep animosity. The relationships cover the gamut. To sell your show means developing business relationships. The movie you just finished gives you some credibility—and a topic of conversation—with buyers across markets and territories.

Sell this show with the goal of finding distribution for the next.

SET YOUR GOALS

Set some goals for yourself. If you never plan to make another movie, then having a scorched-earth policy toward buyers may work. But if you want to continue making shows, you'll want to develop good relationships with buyers and other producers.

SELLER BEWARE

Some people have always been crooks and always will be. Your job is to find out enough about them so you can steer clear.

Unfortunately, many buyers live on the float—the interest earned on funds that accrues between the time they get paid and the time they have to pay you. Many have to use a rob-Peter-to-pay-Paul strategy to cover their bills. No matter how much money they make, they always owe somebody. It's easy to get swamped by thin profit margins, heavy debt and obligations, and an almost insane optimism that the next acquisition will solve all their problems.

As a producer, you must protect your show and reputation from getting involved in a sticky financial situation. You need to research your potential buyers to see how they've behaved in the past. Past behavior isn't always an exact prediction for future behavior, but it's a pretty good indicator.

For example, if you're considering an offer from a home video distributor and you find out that this particular buyer has been sued seven times in the past two years for nonpayment, you may want to rethink accepting anything beyond a free drink.

In the retail market, it's buyer beware; in the motion picture business, it's seller beware.

HANDLING REJECTION

As you know by now, a lot of producing requires being able to handle rejection. Buyers will say no, often for reasons that have nothing to do with your show. Rejection is part of the business and it's nothing personal. You may want to ask why they're giving you the ax, although brace yourself for an answer you won't like.

Still, don't argue. People have a right to their opinions, regardless of how shallow or ill-conceived they may be.

People will tell you there's no such thing as bad press, but I think that you have to keep in mind who's saying it. Some bad reviews won't even sting, but to get one from someone you respect can really hurt. Influential critics can make or break a movie.

That's the risk you run anytime you take something public. People will just shoot arrows at your project and some of them are bound to hit the target. You can take some consolation in that someone from the press watched your show, and then took the time to write about it. Take the high road—whether you get good press or bad, send a thank-you note. Better luck next time.

What can really sting, though, is when regular folks—like your friends—tell you they just don't like your show. It happens. You'll be standing around after a screening and people are muttering to themselves. Most won't look you in the eye and tell you your movie is terrible. The ones that do, though, deserve your thanks.

Pay attention to the things that can help you, and move on.

WHOM YOU'RE SELLING TO

You have to make a decision whether or not to pursue distribution. Used to be that you didn't have a choice—movies cost so much to make that you had to get distribution if you ever wanted to make another one.

Because many DV movies have tiny budgets, though, you now have a choice. If you're not interested in any of the markets, you don't have to sell to them. If you shot your movie for Webcast, for your personal enjoyment, or as a portfolio piece, then you don't have to chase distribution.

Most of us, though, have obligations to investors, or deferrals and debts to pay off. Others feel an obligation to the people who worked so hard to make the show, so it doesn't seem fair to not pursue distribution.

SELF-DISTRIBUTION

Some independent moviemakers have decided to distribute their shows themselves. As with any kind of motion picture distribution, you'll need to research the market and package your product the way any distributor would.

THEATRICAL

Getting your show into a movie theater yourself is called *four-walling*. Basically, you rent the theater for a length of the run, hire the staff, arrange advertising and promotion, and sell tickets. You can either rent the theater for a flat fee or offer to split the door with the theater owner. The theater owner keeps all concession stand money.

Although it's unlikely you'll get into any of the multiplexes, you may be able to book into independent movie and art houses. Factor in costs for a video projection system, which can be quite steep. It may be less expensive to do tape-to-film and strike a limited number of 35mm prints for film projection.

You'll need projection masters in the format appropriate for the projection system, posters, one-sheets, and ad slicks.

Microcinemas are usually set in the back room of a bar or coffeehouse. Customers may or may not pay an entrance fee to watch your movie—often it's up to you. This is an interesting way to screen independent shows. Some microcinemas have a regular screening series, with a programmer or curator who books and promotes each show. Contact the programmer to find out the procedure.

You could book microcinema screenings yourself. For example, if you have a movie for a special audience, such as gay/lesbian, art house, dance, and so on, you could contact clubs, bars, and other organizations across the United States to book your show. You could go on the road with a list of press contacts, a deck, a projector, a projection master, a box of tapes and DVDs to sell, posters, and enough money for food and gas, and travel from booking to booking.

I've often wondered what that would be like. I imagine it would be exhausting, but I think it would be quite an experience to meet the audience this way.

CABLE TELEVISION

With an independent one-off, you can just contact the programmer at the Independent Film Channel, Bravo, HBO, The Learning Channel, Discovery Channel, and others.

See Resources for contact information and more listings.

BROADCAST TELEVISION, INCLUDING PUBLIC TELEVISION

It's unlikely you'll even talk to anyone at the networks. Public television, however, does offer some outlets for independent producers. Two public television shows that get national carriage and accept independent movies are *Through the Lens* and *P.O.V.*

You can approach regional public television stations that carry independent work. WGBH in Boston, KQED in San Francisco, and WTTW in Chicago are known for their innovative programming. Local PBS stations may also be approachable provided your movie has an identifiable regional interest. Call one of the station producers and ask.

ITVS, an independent entity outside of the Corporation for Public Broadcasting, offers funding programs to independent producers twice a year. These are not grants but distribution deals. They provide production funds in exchange for exclusive domestic television distribution rights and a piece of any other sale you may make.

Each series, show, and station has specific guidelines regarding submission. Check the Web site `www.pbs.org/insidepbs/redbook/` for the online version of the PBS *Red Book.* This book details the packaging, deliverable, promotion, and legal guidelines for PBS broadcast programs. Read through this manual to make sure that you and your production and postproduction team familiarize themselves with the relevant sections.

See `www.pbs.org/insidepbs/guidelines` for information on funding guidelines. Guidelines for announcements promoting program-related goods and services can be found at `www.pbs.org/insidepbs/guidelines/index_onair.html`.

FOREIGN MARKETS

Selling to foreign markets can be difficult. You have to deal with customs, and some countries have restrictions on currency. Your funds may be unavailable to you. Copyright infringement is ongoing.

However, you may be able to approach programmers and buyers from stations in Western European countries and Great Britain. Channel 4 in London has a reputation for risky programming. You can contact them directly.

Keep in mind that you may have to dub or subtitle your show, although they should pay for it, as well as deliver a master in the appropriate standard. Be sure these requirements are listed clearly in the contract.

VIDEO, DVD, AND OTHER HOME-USE FORMATS

If you want to sell videotapes or DVDs, remember that it can be difficult to compete in the retail market. In addition to a method for payment and fulfillment, you'll need mailing lists of prospective buyers. This is especially true if you want to sell to libraries, universities, and other institutions. You'll need to design and mail flyers and one-sheets.

I'm not saying you can't do it—you most certainly can. If selling cassettes and DVDs directly is in your plan, there's no reason you can't do it. I just don't know whether you can expect to make much money at it.

There are rack jobbers who serve the video rental shops. Search the World Wide Web for listings.

EDUCATIONAL

The National Educational Media Network (NEMN) is dedicated to recognizing and supporting excellence in educational media. NEMN brings together leading professionals working in motion media and provides a crucial link to outstanding educational and nontheatrical films, videos, and interactive multimedia. NEMN's internationally acclaimed Apple Awards Competition is the premier event in the nation honoring outstanding achievement in educational media. See www.nemn.org for more information.

Under the auspices of the European Broadcasting Union (EBU), the Rotterdam Market for Educational Programs and Multimedia is a unique three-day market, where leading educational broadcasting organizations present their educational television and/or video productions and where broadcasters, educational publishers, the computer and telecom industry, and independent production and multimedia companies will present their multimedia and online products. It is a special initiative that is meeting the interest in high-quality educational material for both children and adults and is growing by the day. See www.rotterdammarket.org for more information.

INTERNET

You can approach Internet Webcasters yourself. If you want, you can even place your show on your own site. Whether you decide to stream the material or make it available as a download, face that you probably won't make any money.

You can always have a trailer on your Web site and then offer the show for sale on cassette or DVD. Again, it's unlikely you'll make much money, and fulfillment can be a problem. Still, there's no reason you can't do it.

FINDING A DISTRIBUTOR

If you've decided to pursue distribution, you need to do some homework.

First, you'll get a better deal if several buyers are competing for your show. If you haven't been apprising them of your progress throughout your project, alert them now. Also contact *Hollywood Reporter*, *Daily Variety*, *Weekly Variety*, *Screen International*, *Film Maker*, *Moviemaker*, *The Independent*, and other press, as well as place information on your Web site.

Generally, when you're trying to sell a movie, you'll meet agents, distributors, and television programmers.

Sales agents take movies and try to place them with different buyers. Some are specialized according to market and subject matter; others will sell anything. They go to the major film and television markets and earn a distribution fee on every sale. Because they usually work on commission, they don't offer postproduction funds, although some may be able to locate those funds according to your needs.

Distributors of movies, like distributors of any product, take your show, package it, market and promote it, and try to sell it to retailers. These retailers include multiplexes, art house theaters, theater chains, and video rental shops such as Blockbuster and Hollywood Video, and mom-and-pop shops, as well as television broadcasters. They may or may not work in foreign markets. Some, particularly specialty distributors, may sell directly to viewers or institutions such as universities and libraries.

Television programmers buy shows they think enough people will watch that they can sell advertising.

In this model, you begin to see that you are a wholesaler going to a middleman who sells to a retailer. It is in the interest of the middleman to get your product for as low a price as possible and then sell to a retailer for as high a price as possible.

If you want to skip the middleman, you can go directly to retailers or even the viewing market yourself. Often you can contact programmers from microcinema, pay-per-view and cable television, and Internet outlets yourself.

When you try to sell anything, you need to prepare yourself by doing

- Market research
- Packaging
- Marketing

MARKET RESEARCH: BUYERS AND HOW TO FIND THEM

I once read an interview with a high-profile cable programmer who said she expected producers to know not only what her company was looking for, as well as her name and face, but even her favorite color. She was exaggerating, but you get the idea: It's your job to know what your buyers are looking for.

Get out your list you made during development. Update it by scanning the *Hollywood Reporter*, *Daily Variety*, *Weekly Variety*, and *Screen International*. Check the AFMA for trends in the industry. You may want to purchase directories from NAB and research information about TV, radio, and other aspects of the broadcast industry. See Cinemedia at www.cinemedia.com for an alphabetical list of Web sites with more information.

You can also read the Announcements section of independent movie magazines for recent acquisitions and other information. You may want to note the names of producers who have made deals with specific buyers. If you get an offer, it can be enlightening to speak with someone who has worked with the buyer before.

The *AIVF/FIVF Guide to Film & Video Distributors* is a handy directory. The Bay Area Video Coalition's annual list of video distributors, included in their newsletter, *Video Networks*, and the National Educational Media Network have listings as well.

See Resources for listings.

Go to your local video rental store and look for videos similar to yours. Write down all the information you can from the back of the box. Look up titles in *Videolog*. This book has thousands of titles ranging across genres and budgets. You'll be able to flip through this book and find more titles similar to yours. Bowker's *Complete Video Directory* has extensive listings of Entertainment, Educational, and Special Interest titles.

Mark Litwak has continued to serve the independent moviemaking community with the Filmmaker's Clearinghouse, a Web site devoted to disseminating information about distributors similar to what the Better Business Bureau reports on merchants. A survey form and responses can be viewed at www.marklitwak.com.

See the Resources section for contact information and more listings.

Go to the Web sites of companies you're interested in and note any changes. People shift companies and jobs fairly often in the movie business. Letting someone talk about himself or herself will always kickstart a conversation.

Get out your potential distributors list and start dialing. If you don't already have copies of each distributor's catalog, request one. Also ask for press kits for movies it handled recently. Examine the materials—what kind of titles does each distributor sell? What's the price range? What's the style? Is this a good fit?

If your show is accepted into a festival or market, you'll probably receive a catalog of buyers. Research the companies and the individuals who are attending. Often, you can find news stories in magazines for independent movies, in the trades, and online. Pictures are good—matching a name to a face can give you a slight edge—but use this information for good and not for evil.

For each potential buyer, ask yourself:

- What genre are they looking for?
- What market do they specialize in?
- Do they handle shows with the same format and standard as mine?
- Whom are they affiliated with?
- What products have they released in the past year?
- Has anything interesting and positive happened to the company or any of its products recently?

Compare these answers with your goals and recategorize according to how closely to each buyer's philosophy and products mesh with yours. Your first tier is the dream distributors and television programmers. Your second tier contains listings of smaller, established distributors and buyers of less-prestigious television cablecasters and series. Your third tier is new distributors or programmers.

Selling to the Buyers

You're trying to sell to a certain, specialized market. How you approach someone has as great an impact as what you have to sell. Being clear and reasonable, and delivering on time, is the hallmark of the professional. This doesn't mean, however, you should let potential buyers walk all over you. Failure to return phone calls and blowing off appointments require immediate action on your part. But save the yelling for after the contract is signed.

First, identify what it is you're selling. The people who make up your market of distributors and programmers have certain needs. They need

- Product that's easy to sell
- Producers who make their lives easier
- A certain level of cool to enhance their reputations

Product That's Easy to Sell   Buyers are looking first for finished shows—a movie that can be turned with minimal fuss is preferred over a movie that needs time and money to be completed. A good, interesting show that's technically acceptable is also a big plus.

A movie with a great hook is easier to sell. So is one with press materials created and in place. The buyer won't necessarily use your posters and one-sheets, but it's easier to change what you've got than to create from scratch. To get a buyer's attention you should have

- A movie as close to finished as you can get it
- A movie that is technically correct for the markets' standards
- A great, catchy hook
- A press kit, including an EPK

Producers Who Make Their Lives Easier   A producer who comes in having done some retail market research, understanding the terms of distribution agreements and the distribution system, and has marketing collateral and a professional approach is a lot easier to work with than a disorganized slob. This is not to say that messy projects won't be sold—they may be. But part of what you're selling is yourself.

This doesn't mean you can't be creative. Of course you can. But that effort should fit an overall strategy. Showing up in a chicken suit may work for enticing potential viewers, but it won't say much to potential buyers. Buyers are a different market with different needs.

It's a fine line between clever and stupid.

You should also have reasonable expectations. I've heard some outrageous claims that producers have made for their shows that are completely out of touch with reality. You can certainly stand up for your show—confidence is appealing, but claiming your show will do better than recent flukes is a sign of an amateur.

Don't believe anything. Especially at festivals and markets, you'll hear moviemakers gabbing at cocktail parties about offers and interest their shows have received. Taking it with a grain of salt is too much salt.

Fulfill all of your obligations. Arrive on time for appointments, be available for phone conferences, and meet your contractual obligations on time.

To make the buyers' lives easier:

- Be prepared.
- Be clever, not stupid.
- Have reasonable expectations.
- Fulfill your obligations.

A Certain Level of Cool to Enhance Their Reputations   As you research the markets, you'll see a lot of deals that just don't seem to make sense. These deals serve another purpose.

A buyer may acquire a show because the company wants to get into digital video tape-to-film for the theatrical market. Someone's raise is riding on acquiring this kind of product, and he or she may take something that has bad acting but will transfer well.

Buyers may make offers because there's a hole in their catalogs, or a new genre or market they want to get into. A name actor will often bring a show offer. Name actors are marketable, regardless of the quality of the movie.

Buyers may bid fiercely for a movie because they hate one another. Winning the bidding is a way to humiliate the enemy. Conversely, jacking up the bidding is a way to cause pain.

A movie may be hip and have received all sorts of buzz or festival awards. Some buyers will swoop in because they want to protect or build a reputation as a distributor of quality.

PACKAGING: BUYERS AND YOUR BRAND

In the same way that you use light and sound to influence the viewer's perception of a character, you'll use your packaging to influence the buyers' view of you.

You need to package your show and yourself. This is not lying about anything—this is clearly communicating what you're offering potential buyers. Ask yourself:

- How is my show different from other movies currently on the market?
- How is it similar?

To just say that your movie's good isn't a hook—everyone says that. What makes this show unusual? A name actor or director? Geography or location? The way it was shot?

How is it the same? Were you influenced by classic films or television shows?

The answers to these two questions will help you develop a hook. Your hook needs to be short and punchy—think bumper stickers and you'll get the idea. They'll also help you write a 25-word pitch that describes the plot.

Now ask yourself how you are different from other moviemakers.

Saying that you want to make good movies, you hate Hollywood, and have a good sense of humor does not set you apart. Practically every independent moviemaker believes his or her movie is good, Hollywood sucks, and he or she has a great sense of humor.

Honestly assess your strengths and weaknesses. Be honest about what you bring to the table. You can then design how you want to present yourself to buyers. This doesn't have to be anything elaborate. What I'm asking you to do is to create a code of conduct for yourself and present it clearly and concisely in everything you do.

The code of conduct isn't something you tell people about—it's what helps you make good decisions for yourself over the long run. Your life has a longer run than any movie. Your business relationships should as well.

How you present yourself in the market is your brand. It speaks to your style of movies and ways of doing business, your reputation as a producer, and other public aspects of you and your endeavors.

Your design and strategy for promotion and marketing will come from these two things.

MARKETING TOOLS

For a business that requires creativity, you'll quickly learn that being too creative is a bad thing. It's your job to find the form buyers expect and fit into it. Buyers expect every producer to have screeners, a press kit with stills from the shoot, and a one-sheet or poster. They may also want an electronic press kit or EPK. You may want swag (discussed in detail later in this section).

A *screener* is a VHS tape in a cardboard slip case. You don't need hard cases or covers, as long as everything is neatly labeled.

Your press kit contains

- A one-page press release announcing the project with full contact information
- A 25-word pitch
- A two- to three-page treatment
- Résumés of key personnel
- Two or three stills of the actors taken on the set
- Photocopies of any reviews or interviews

Try to get quotes from notable sources. Pursue quotes and reviews from *Library Journal*, *Booklist*, and *Video Librarian*. Media librarians pay attention to them. If your show is subject specific, try to get reviews and quotes in media that cover the same topic.

These materials should all fit into a single folder or envelope. Make sure that everything is proofread and photocopied cleanly.

If you don't have stills, you can either schedule a photo shoot or pull frames from your show. The problem with pulling frames is that the resolution of a DV frame is about 72dpi–90dpi. You can convert the frame to higher resolution, but that doesn't give you any more detail.

If you use a color inkjet printer, you may be able to get away with it. The color inks tend to spread out as they go through the printer, which can soften the lack of resolution. If you're using Adobe's Photoshop software, deinterlace the video frame. That will get rid of some of the jaggies. You may have to go in and repair some other odd artifacting. This really isn't a good solution. The stills look poor.

You can try one of the plug-ins for software that will sample multiple frames to create a higher-resolution, more detailed single image. See Shortcut Software Development's S-Spline at `www.s-spline.com`, or the VideoPix plug-in from Redhawk Vision at `www.redhawkvision.com /demo_software.html`.

A *one-sheet* is a small color poster. Generally, they're usually 10"×12" and 18"×24", but they can be whatever size you want. Many people create them on standard U.S. paper sizes of 8 1/2"×11" and 11"×17" using color inkjet or color laser printers.

For a more professional look, design or have designed an array of printed collateral: one-sheets, flyers, and postcards. A good design that uses only two colors can unify all of your print material to very good effect. Also, you can use more conceptual treatments of video frames pulled from your show, so you can work around the poor print resolution of the frames.

If you want to make posters, they will have to be designed. There are some companies that offer a single price for bulk inkjet printing of one-sheets and posters. You can find listings in any magazine for independent moviemakers.

Four-color full-size posters printed with offset are pricey. It's just as much work to make one, or a hundred, as it is a thousand. If you just have to have them, though, call local printers for pricing and don't expect a quick turnaround.

An electronic press kit (EPK) is a video about the project with a trailer, interviews with key personnel, and some behind-the-scenes footage. If you can do it easily then do it. Just be sure to label the tape neatly. Instead of duplicating onto VHS, you could create video CDs that fit nicely in the folder with your other press material.

For *Family Business*, I created an audio CD of stories and snips that didn't fit in the documentary. The main subject had a distinctive accent from his boyhood in western Arkansas. He's also quite eloquent, and I thought people might enjoy hearing some of his stories. I burned the CDs on my system and included them in all press kits.

Swag is imprinted items such as caps, shirts, jackets, keychains, bags, and others. If you want people to wear clothing with your logo and name of your show on it, make the items good quality. A cheap cap with cheesy iron-on transfer isn't going to appeal to many people.

Other kinds of swag include useless, but funny, things. For *Amazing World*, I ordered a stack of temporary tattoos with the name of the movie on them. (Tattoos play a part in the show.) I don't know whether anyone other than my friend Sarah wore one, but people did get a chuckle out of it.

MARKETING: BUYERS AND HOW TO APPROACH THEM

Get out your list and start dialing.

Be clear about what you're asking for and whether that distributor handles that market. For example, if you want a theatrical release and will need money for a tape-to-film transfer, find out which distributors do that before you call. It can be embarrassing to be speaking with someone for 15 minutes about your action feature only to find out the distributor only handles documentaries on collecting porcelain figurines.

Do not tell anyone your budget. They will ask, several times. Be ready with some clever deflections—I use "How much do you think I spent?" as a response after someone has seen the show.

On the Phone

The person answering the phone may very possibly be earning the least amount of money. He or she doesn't deserve your rudeness on top of a paltry paycheck. Please and thank you mean something.

Many buyers are busy putting out fires on Mondays and Fridays, so try to call during the week and later in the day. Have patience. Someone who doesn't immediately call you back isn't trying to be rude.

Calling during the major festivals isn't a good idea. Many buyers are gone or in a fluster trying to get prepared to leave. Calling right after can be a bit of a problem, too. Be ready to answer why your show isn't at Sundance or one of the other major festivals. If you just finished then say that. If you didn't get in, it's up to you whether or not you want to tell them.

Stay calm. Confidence is good, but a hard-sell can be off-putting. Remember that you're trying to build a relationship. People in the movie business both like and fear independents. We can be funny, interesting, and make gems that can advance a distribution executive's career. We can also be unprofessional, unprepared, and have unrealistic expectations.

If a distributor asks to see the show, respond promptly. However, be careful about sending out rough cuts. People say they can watch them and imagine what will happen in fine cut and post-audio, but that just isn't true. The first impression is the one that will stick.

Only show your unfinished movie if you need finishing funds. Unfortunately, the terms you'll be offered will be less advantageous than for a completed show. If you have to show a work-in-progress, consider screening it in the edit bay. Label your work-in-progress screeners clearly so buyers are reminded of what they're watching.

At Festivals and Markets

Have your business stationery in order and always carry a stack of crisp business cards.

Consider your timing. At festivals and markets, buyers are often given color-coded badges that separate them from the moviemakers. Often there's an area for buyers only, and it's easier for the festival programmers to use a color-coded method to tell who is who. It doesn't take producers long to start circling someone with a buyer badge. One television programmer I know said she feels like chum in a swimming pool of sharks whenever she goes to a market.

You want to make contact, but it needs to be good contact. Years ago I met a high-profile television producer and programmer outside a pub in London. She was going in, I was going out, and a mutual friend introduced us. I met her almost 10 years later, reminding her we'd met under these circumstances. She was amazed I remembered, and it gave us something to talk about. What was scheduled for a 10-minute meeting went to almost 45.

It was fun to reminisce, plus I got the feeling that this was someone I could work with. I think she felt the same way. I haven't done business with her. Yet.

Don't expect an offer at a film festival or market. Unless your appointment is specifically about terms, don't bring it up. You can, and should, ask about a buyer's acquisition process, but don't expect anyone to pull out a checkbook.

Don't expect someone to take a video screener of your show. You may want to have a couple tucked away in your suitcase for other producers, but leave them in your hotel room. No one is going to haul around a stack of videotapes, and asking him or her to do so is unrealistic. However, when a distributor, buyer, or someone from the press requests a screener and press kit, respond promptly after the festival.

BUYERS AND HOW TO RESEARCH THEM

If you get a nibble, you need to do some in-depth research.

Start by checking the state and county where the distributor is incorporated to see whether there have been any lawsuits filed. It can be pretty disturbing to find out that the distributor has been sued for nonpayment.

Get the names of producers whose shows this buyer is handling from the buyer's catalog. You can track down the producers using the Internet. It's easier than you think.

Call, e-mail, or use regular mail to contact the producers. Ask them

- How well has this buyer done for you?
- What's the working relationship been like?
- Have there been any problems?
- Have there been any victories?
- Has this buyer been able to make sales you couldn't?
- Did you receive an advance? If so, may I ask the terms?
- Would you work with this buyer again?

FIVE THINGS YOU NEVER SAY TO A POTENTIAL BUYER

- **It only cost X dollars.** Don't ever tell anyone what your budget is. It is irrelevant to making a sale.

- **The sound's not very good.** Don't apologize for your show. If you're embarrassed about a technical issue, performance, or any other aspect of it, either fix it or shut up. You did what you could with what you had—that's all that matters.

- **No, dummy, that's not what happened at all.** Making someone feel stupid won't win you any friends. Besides, a buyer may see something in your show that really speaks to him or her and it might be enough for you to start negotiating. The time for arguing about packaging and advertising copy is after you've signed the contract, and you have the right to ax any ideas.

- **It's the next *Blair Witch Project*.** The *Blair Witch Project* was a fluke. More power to the people who made the movie and to the distribution company that snapped it up. Who knows when it will happen again? The distributors certainly don't.

- **My girlfriend/boyfriend really liked it.** And I'm sure your mom did, too. What does that have to do with anything? Unless your significant other is a prominent film critic or high-profile producer, this doesn't count for much.

LITERAL NEGOTIATING

The buyer is not your friend. You're not even business partners until the contract is signed. At this point, the buyer is trying to purchase product at the lowest possible price. Your interests may be to get the highest price, commitments for the next project, control of packaging materials, or any other possible goals. Just be sure that you look out for yourself.

You don't know the behind-the-scenes action going on with any buyer. You don't know whether the person you're speaking with is trying to look busy while updating her résumé. You don't know whether your show fits into a package of products the buyer plans to flog off at fire-sale prices. You don't know whether the distributor is tying you up in negotiations to stop another buyer from making an offer.

I had something like this happen with one of my shows. A distributor made an offer for my show, and we began negotiating. She kept returning to provisions in the contract we had already agreed upon, dragging out the negotiations. Then I got the ax. She told me that the company had decided to pass on my movie.

I sold the show to this buyer's competitor. It became clear afterward that the distributor's intention was to tie up my show so she could have a clear field when releasing a similar program she'd already acquired. I had no idea. And I don't think there's any way I could've known.

My point here is that you don't know what's going on in back rooms or inside someone else's head.

Take buyers literally:

- Only respond to what they say, not what you think they've said.
- If it isn't in writing, it doesn't count.
- Don't take it personally. Keep the emotional meltdowns away from the negotiation. Just as on the set, fall apart at home.
- Choose your battles. Put the provisions of the agreement in order of priority and fight for what is important to you.
- Let them talk.

FESTIVALS AND MARKETS

I've read that less than 25% of completed features will ever get festival exposure. Your show may or may not be in that 25%.

Although some markets have a festival and some festivals have markets, they're distinct categories. A festival is an opportunity for you to screen your show to just about anyone who buys a ticket. A film and video market, like any other kind of market, is a place where buyers and sellers meet to do business.

Festivals are, generally, open to the public. Markets are restricted to professionals, although the definition of professional is pretty loose—just about anyone can be credentialed as long as he or she paid the fees.

Some festivals in which prizes or cash are awarded are competitive. Different festival awards carry different levels of prestige. Acceptance into different festivals carries different levels of prestige. Markets are always competitive,

NOTE

Fun Fun Fun

Festivals are fun. If your movie has been accepted, and you attend, you can usually get comped into just about any show you want to see. I also make it a practice to spend time away from the festival. I love movies, but moviemakers can sometimes induce a frenzy of hustling in one another that's just no fun. Trust me, when a producer is talking to you, but constantly scanning the room for someone more important, it's time to go bowling.

but what you win isn't a pretty trophy. You get contacts with people in the business, offers from buyers, and invitations from festival programmers.

For many moviemakers, getting into a prestigious festival is the reward. Markets aren't curated—as long as you make the deadline and the check doesn't bounce, just about anything can be screened.

FESTIVALS

Certain festivals are more prestigious than others. Only you know what you want to accomplish with your show, so select your festival submission carefully.

Here are several of the higher-profile festivals and markets. Remember that these are fiercely competitive. This is only a partial list. There are more listings in the Resources section.

There are many, many others. See Kathryn Bowser's *The AIVF Guide to International Film & Video Festivals* for overviews of festivals and markets around the world. Also see the film festivals Web server at www.filmfestivals.com. In addition to listings, www.filmfestivals.com has interesting news. Check www.cinemedia.org for another extensive, alphabetical listing.

BERLIN

Berlinale: Internationale Filmfestspiele Berlin, Budapester Strasse 50, 10787 Berlin, Germany, Tel: (011) (49-30) 254-890; Fax: (011) (49-30) 254-89-249; Contact: Festival Director: Moritz de Hadeln; E-mail: info@berlinale.de; www.berlinale.de

Berlinale: Internationale Filmfestspiele Berlin, or Berlin International Film Festival, is a prestigious competitive festival and host to the European Film Market.

Held in February, the festival has a number of sections and has representatives in Athens, London, Los Angeles, Madrid, New York, Paris, Rio de Janeiro, and Rome.

The European Film Market is open only to producers, distributors, exhibitors, exporters, and importers of movies, as well as professionals active in the areas of video and television sales and acquisitions. The Market offers business representatives screening facilities on 16mm, 35mm, and on video in the usual systems. It also offers places for mounting promotional displays and constructing stands and furnished booths, as well as venues for meetings. It publishes and distributes a daily program, as well as a general catalog. In addition to the Festival accreditation, participants must also apply for accreditation to the Market. A Market badge will be provided on payment of a fee.

The European Film Market gives priority to theatrical features. Programs of short and medium-length films are presented only on the first two and last two days of the Market. Films to be screened must first be submitted on the official entry form of the Market, which must be duly completed and signed. A projection fee is charged at an hourly rate and must be settled in advance.

ROTTERDAM INTERNATIONAL FILM FESTIVAL

Rotterdam International Film Festival, P. O. Box 21696, 3001 AR Rotterdam, The Netherlands, Tel: (011) (31-10) 411-8080; Fax: (011) (31-10) 413-5132; Contact: Simon Field; E-mail: iffr@luna.nl; www.iffrotterdam.nl

Cinemart, P. O. Box 21696, 3001 AR Rotterdam, The Netherlands, Tel: (011) (31) 10 4118080; Fax: (011) (31) 10 4135132; Contact: Ido Abram; E-mail: iffr@luna.nl; www.iffrotterdam.nl

Rotterdam may be one step down in prestige compared to Berlin, but from all accounts, it's tremendously fun and often very lucrative for American independents. It's held at the same time as Sundance and although there is a market, it is pretty low key from all accounts. The Rotterdam Film Festival is one that glories in bringing world cinema in all its diversity to the screen.

Cinemart, the festival's market, revolves around the famous matchmaking technique of pairing up moviemakers and buyers. Cinemart does not present completed projects looking to be sold worldwide—instead, the market's organizers seek to help everyone involved forge friendships and alliances in order to get new movies made.

SAN FRANCISCO

San Francisco Film Society, 39 Mesa Street, Suite 110, The Presidio, San Francisco, CA 94129-1025; Tel: 415-561-5000, Fax: 415-561-5099; http://sfiff.org/

San Francisco International Film Festival is presented each spring by the San Francisco Film Society. The competitive section is for documentaries, shorts, animation, experimental, and television production. The invitational, noncompetitive section is for recent narrative features, archival presentations, retrospectives, and special awards and tributes recognizing individual achievement.

SUNDANCE

Sundance Film Festival, P. O. Box 16450, Salt Lake City, UT 84116; Tel: (801) 328-3456; Fax: (801) 575-5175; Contact: Geoff Gilmore; E-mail: sundance@xmission.com; www.sundance.org

Sundance is Mecca for many independent moviemakers. It's held in January and is often clogged with Hollywood movie stars and suits, the antithesis of the independent spirit.

The Sundance Film Festival accepts fiction (70+ minutes) or documentary (50+ minutes) features that have been previously screened at a maximum of two festivals. If the show is to be considered for competition, it can play at a maximum of two international festivals, but it must be a U.S. premiere. Regarding shorts, there is no maximum number of festivals at which the show may be screened.

The Sundance Film Festival accepts digital works as long as they are transferred to a 1/2" VHS videotape for submission. Those films selected for the Festival (whether they were made digitally or on film) can opt to project digitally in the Sony HDCAM format.

TORONTO

Toronto International Film Festival Group, 2 Carlton Street, Suite 1600, Toronto, Ontario, Canada M5B 1J3; Tel: 416-967-7371; Fax: 416-967-9577; www.e.bell.ca/filmfest

Unlike Berlin, the Toronto International Film Festival is not officially a competitive festival. However, prizes issued with the People's Choice Award voted upon by members of the audience are the most coveted.

For selection and programming consideration, the festival accepts 1/2" VHS videocassette transfers in either NTSC or PAL, or 16mm or 35mm prints of the complete work. If the show is invited, they require an NTSC Digital Betacam projection master. Although the festival intends to project digital video, there is absolutely no guarantee that this format will be available. Be prepared to transfer to 16mm or 35mm if your show is invited.

DOCFEST

New York Documentary Center, Inc., 159 Maiden Lane, New York, NY 10038; Tel: 212.668.1100; Fax: 212.943.6396; E-mail: mail@docfest.org; www.docfest.org/docfest.html

New York International Documentary Festival Selection for docfest is by invitation only. However, you can make the selection committee aware of your show by sending a short synopsis including technical specifications and contact information prior to the February deadline. Do not submit videocassettes unless requested.

SXSW

South by Southwest (SXSW) Film Festival, P.O. Box 4999, Austin, Texas 78765; Tel: (512) 467-7979; Fax: (512) 451-0754; Contact: Nancy Schafer; E-mail: sxsw@sxsw.com; www.sxsw.com

Austin's SXSW is film and video, interactive, and music festivals all rolled into one. The Film Conference features panels, mini-meetings, one-on-one mentor sessions, and equipment demos covering all aspects of the independent film industry from screenwriting through distribution, and everything in between.

SUNNY SIDE OF THE DOCS

Sunny Side of the Docs, 23, rue François Simon, 13003 Marseilles France; Tél: +33 (0)4 95 04 44 80; Fax: +33 (0)4 91 84 38 34; E-mail: contact@sunnysideofthedoc.com; www.tvfi.com/archives/2001/sunnyside2001/indexan.htm

Sunny Side of the Docs international documentary market is held in Marseilles at the Palais du Pharo in June. This market features three days of meetings with leading decision-makers, information sessions and coproduction breakfasts, and other activities.

HOT DOCS

Hot Docs Canadian International Documentary Festival, 517 College Street, Suite 420, Toronto, Ontario, Canada M6G 4A2; Tel: (1) 416-203-2155; Fax: (1) 416-203-0446; E-mail: pgrove@hotdocs.ca; www.hotdocs.ca

Hot Docs Canadian International Documentary Festival presents a selection of 80+ cutting-edge documentaries from Canada and around the world. The festival also hosts a full industry program, including the Toronto Documentary Forum, a two-day event for the international cofinancing and coproduction of new documentaries.

Hot Docs has quickly become a must-attend event for documentary moviemakers, buyers, distributors, and broadcasters from around the world. Hot Docs offers a stimulating market environment where delegates may examine issues, learn and enhance skills, meet colleagues, and locate interest and financing for their documentaries.

HOT SPRINGS

Hot Springs Documentary Film Institute, 819 Central Avenue, Hot Springs National Park, Arkansas 71902-6450; Tel: 501-321-4747; Fax: 501-321-0211; E-mail: hsdff@DocuFilmInst.org; www.docufilminst.org

Hot Springs International Documentary Film Festival requires NTSC VHS preview videos for the screening process. Foreign-language (non-English) motion pictures must be subtitled or dubbed in English.

PLANNING A FESTIVAL STRATEGY

You can't enter all the festivals. You need to develop a set of tiers listing the festivals you want to submit your show to. How you categorize the festivals into tiers depends on what you want to achieve.

Don't give away your festival premiere. If your show gets into a small festival, you may have disqualified it from the major ones. If you're going for the biggies, save the smaller ones for later. If submitting to the big festivals fits your goals, there's no reason not to do it.

If you get into a major festival, send out a press release to everyone on your media and distribution list. A distributor may make a deal before the festival even starts.

Should you go? It depends on whether or not you can pay for it.

Go through the festival directory for names of potential buyers. You can research the companies online and search for information about the individuals. Distributors are looking for different things at different times and it's your job to know what those are. Only invite buyers who sell to the market that fits your motion picture.

The festival programmers may or may not arrange meetings between moviemakers and buyers. If they do, show up on time and in clean clothes. Have your business card and pitch ready. Stay calm. The goal is to make contact, not to hard-sell your show.

No matter what the pressure is on you, remember that the person you're talking with has probably already had a dozen meetings, with more after you.

MARKETS

In addition to the directories, ads, and word of mouth about distributors, you may want to consider attending one of the film and video markets. Some of the major ones include

AMERICAN FILM MARKET (AFM)

AFMA, 10850 Wilshire Blvd., Ninth Floor, Los Angeles, CA 90024; Tel: (310) 446-1000; Fax: (310) 446-1600; Contact: Andrea Keldsen; E-mail: info@afma.com; www.afma.com/AFM/afm_home.asp

AFMA®, formerly known as the American Film Marketing Association, is the trade association for the independent film and television industry. AFMA's global membership distributes (and often produces) the films and programs made outside the major United States studios.

The AFMA sponsors the AFM. The AFM is a marketplace where deals exceeding $500 million in production and distribution revenues are closed annually. Each year, more than 7,000 people convene in Santa Monica for eight days of screenings, deal making, and hospitality. Participants come from more than 70 countries, and include leaders in motion picture production and distribution, directors, agents, writers, lawyers, bankers, and trade groups. The AFM is the annual Hollywood gathering for the global motion picture industry.

THE INDEPENDENT FEATURE PROJECT (IFP) MARKET

IFP Market, c/o Independent Feature Project, 104 West 29th Street, 12th Floor, New York, NY 10001-5310; Tel: (212) 465-8200; Fax: (212) 465-8525; See www.ifp.org for more information.

The IFP Market is a weeklong showcase, held each fall in New York, for features, works-in-progress, shorts, scripts, and documentary projects by independent filmmakers. For 22 years, the IFP Market has been the place to discover new talent and see films before they hit the festival circuit. Combining screenings, seminars and workshops, script-pitching sessions, and social events, the Market is an essential networking opportunity for filmmakers at any stage of a current project, and an early window for the film industry on upcoming independent work.

NOTE

DV Triumphs

In 1997, when I was submitting *Amazing World* to festivals, many programmers would sneer that they didn't accept video, even DV, and never would. I was told by a programmer at the Seattle International Film festival that I would have to transfer my video to film if I even wanted a chance at acceptance. SIFF didn't project video, he said.

(That programmer was wrong. I know because I was in the rental house the day the video decks and projectors came back.)

Luckily, this attitude has changed. Not only has the projection technology improved, but more and more moviemakers are using DV technology to shoot their projects. Many festivals have special DV sections specifically for movies shot using that format.

Sections include

- **Documentaries**—Documentaries at all stages of production and completion are eligible for the IFP Market's Features, Works-in-Progress, and Shorts sections.

- **Features**—Completed feature-length films (fiction and documentary), over 60 minutes, screened on 16mm, 35mm, and video. A limited number of features at the fine or rough cut stage will be considered for this long-form section.

- **Works-in-Progress**—Unfinished feature-length films (fiction and documentary) at any stage of production or postproduction seeking financing, finishing funds, or distribution.

- **Shorts**—Completed short films (fiction and documentary), less than 60 minutes in length, screened on 16mm and 35mm and video.

- **Scripts**—Scripts for feature-length fiction films are made available for onsite review by company attendees in the Script Library of the Company Lounge.

- **Video Library**—All projects screening in the Market are available in the Video Library for onsite review, along with feature films and shorts not screened in the main program because of space limitations.

The invitational sections include

- **No Borders**—A coproduction market held concurrently with the IFP Market that showcases United States and international projects in development or at a very early stage of production.

- **IFP Market Showcase at the European Film Market**—Ten feature-length works from the IFP Market will be selected to participate in AIM, IFP's annual showcase at the European Film Market during the Berlin International Film Festival.

MARCHÉ INTERNATIONAL DES FILMS ET PROGRAMMES POUR LA TÉLÉVISION, LA VIDEO, LE CABLE ET LE SATELLITE (MIPCOM)

See www.mipcom.com for extensive contact information.

International film and program market for television, video, cable, and satellite. Held in October in the Palais des Festivals in Cannes. MIPCOM brings together producers, distributors, broadcasters, Webcasters, worldwide cable and satellite operators, buyers, coproducers, and investors.

MARCHÉ INTERNATIONAL DES PROGRAMMES DE TÉLÉVISION (MIP-TV)

Reed Midem Organization, P.O. Box 572, 11 rue du Colonel Pierre Avia, 75726 Paris Cedex 15, France; Tel: (011) (33-1) 4190-4580; Fax: (011) (33-1) 4190-4570; Contact: André Vaillant; E-mail: webmaster@miptv.com; www.miptv.com; or www.miptv.com/explorer/index.shtml

MIP-TV International Television Program Market is one of the busiest international television markets and considered to be one of the most important markets for buying and selling television program rights and arranging coproduction deals. It is held in April in the Palais des Festivals in Cannes. Thousands of producers, television buyers, distributors, programmers, and others attend.

MERCATO INTERNAZIONALE FILME E DOCUMENTARIO (MIFED)

MIFED is organized by Rassegne spa—Foro Buonaparte, 65 20121 Milan, Italy; Tel: 39.0289012188; Fax: 39.0289011578; E-mail: mifed@rassegne.it; www. mifed.com/; or www.fmd.it/mifed/2000/cosa.asp

MIFED is an international audiovisual market for companies and professionals buying and selling rights for cinema, television, and home video. MIFED has been considered the world's first audiovisual market. It's now ranked among the three most important international markets. Participants come from more than 70 countries, with 80 percent from abroad. The European Union, through the Media Program, has found in MIFED the right vehicle to promote the European audiovisual industry.

MIFED keeps constant contacts with the main international organizations in the industry as well as with the foreign markets and festivals, thus fostering and promoting international business exchanges.

NATIONAL ASSOCIATION OF TV PROGRAMMING EXECUTIVES (NATPE)

National Association of TV Program Executives (NATPE) Conference, 2425 Olympic Blvd., Suite 550E, Santa Monica, CA 90404, Tel: (310) 453-4440; Fax: (310) 453-5258; Contact: Nick Orfanopoulos

European Offices: 454 Oakleigh Rd North, London N20 ORZ, UK; Tel: 44-81-361 3793; Fax: 44-81-368-3824; Contact: Pam Mackenzie; E-mail: Dee@natpe.org; www.natpe.com

The NATPE Conference & Exhibition is recognized worldwide as a key global media content event. Held in January, this event offers information, contacts, and possibilities, bringing together thousands of attendees in advertising, broadcast/cable, and other media from all over the world.

PLANNING A MARKET STRATEGY

The best time to approach distributors (if you haven't done it during development) is 60–90 days before a market, when they are hungriest for product. They need inventory to sell to other buyers so don't wait until a week before a market. Distributors need to plan a marketing strategy and create a trailer, one-sheet, poster, screeners, and advertising.

Set some goals for yourself. Chances are you won't walk into a market or a festival and make a sale, but you get to meet people, hear about new advances in technology or channels, and, best of all, watch movies.

FIVE RULES FOR SURVIVING A FESTIVAL OR A MARKET

- Carry breath mints. Between the coffee, drinks, and bad food, a breath mint can be a blessing.
- Watch movies. You'll get to see movies you'll never see in theaters or on television.
- Spend time away from the festival. An afternoon walking around a city or an art museum can really help you get some perspective and recharge your batteries.
- Wear good shoes.
- Get some sleep. You're in this for the long haul.

WHAT YOU SELL: THE SHAPE OF DISTRIBUTION AGREEMENTS

Do not sign anything until your entertainment attorney has explained the provisions of any offer and you understand it. I am constantly amazed by the carelessness of independent producers when it comes to contracts. They'll spend thousands, and even millions, on a movie, but won't spend a few hundred bucks to protect it.

No matter how well-intentioned other moviemakers are, their advice is no substitute for the knowledge and experience of an attorney. Following the suggestions you find in a book (even this one), in a conversation, or on a Web site is simply not wise. Talk with an entertainment attorney at length about any distribution contract offered to you.

There are different kinds of distribution agreements. Although you may be offered an outright purchase of all rights to your show, it's more likely you'll be offered a percentage deal. Any time the show is sold, you get a piece.

Usually, a distributor will offer a contract with the terms and conditions in place. Remember that every part of that contract is negotiable. To negotiate wisely, you should know what the terms mean.

These are some of the important aspects to a distribution agreement:

- Territory
- Licensing period
- Media
- Consideration
- Expenses
- Accounting
- Warranties and representations
- Deliverables
- Copyright
- E&O insurance
- Remedies
- Termination

TERRITORY

This refers to the country or region where the distributor may distribute your show. *Worldwide* means in any country in the world. *Domestic* is the United States and English-speaking Canada, although it may include all of Canada. *Foreign rights* are usually defined as the rest of the world.

Generally, you want to limit the distributor to as few territories as possible. Other than big studios, few distributors handle both foreign and domestic markets. They may, or may not, make a deal with a foreign distributor to handle international sales. The foreign distributor will take a bite out of any money from those sales, as will the domestic distributor.

However, if you can't exploit foreign markets yourself, you may want to grant worldwide rights. You can always place a cap on the total fees the distributor, foreign distributors, or subdistributors may take.

If you retain foreign rights, you'll probably need to find a foreign sales agent or international distributor to take the show to the major international markets. Just make sure you haven't promised the same thing to two different distributors.

The advantage to working with multiple distributors is to further exploit the possible sales. You'll also avoid having one distributor cross-collateralizing expenses and revenues. *Cross-collateralizing* means all expenses and revenue are pooled regardless of where they came from. For example, your show makes $37,000 in the United States, with distribution costs in the U.S. of $14,000. But in France, the distributor spent $21,000 trying to sell and made only $2,000.

If the distributor cross-collateralizes, the expenses and income are pooled. Basically, the movie made $39,000 and cost $35,000. Your piece of the money is based on the $4,000 difference. Without cross-collateralizing, though, income and expenses from each territory are figured separately. Your piece of the income from the United States is based on income minus expenses, or $23,000. Your income from the sales in France is zero, because the distributor lost money.

In addition to cross-collateralizing territories, the distributor may cross-collateralize media. For example, income from home video sales may be $27,000 with expenses of $12,000. But the distributor may have spent $54,000 on a webvideo effort that hasn't made any money at all. In this instance, you won't see a dime if the distributor cross-collateralizes across media.

If there were no cross-collateral, you'd get a piece of the income minus expenses of $15,000 from home video sales in the United States.

TERRITORY MINIMUMS

A schedule of minimums attached to the contract lists the licensing territories of the world with minimum amounts that the distributor can accept.

You may want to insist on a schedule of minimums to prevent the distributor from licensing your motion picture for a ridiculously small amount of money. If the distributor licenses a package of shows, the distributor will have to split the money among all the shows in the package. This is especially important when the term of the distribution agreement is about to expire and the distributor may want to unload the show at whatever price can be secured.

Usually, a schedule of minimums has asking and accept prices, and may be divided by media.

LICENSING PERIOD

This is the term the contract covers. Distributors tend to ask for long terms, often 10 years or even in perpetuity. Generally, it's not in your interest to have an unduly long term. If you have the enthusiasm, passion, and connections to further exploit the show, you may want to limit the distributor's licensing period.

One to three years is ideal, although you can understand that if a distributor spends large sums, he or she is going to want to milk the show for everything it's worth for the longest time possible.

One compromise is to give the distributor a short initial term followed by automatic extensions if certain milestones are met. For example, the initial term may be three years. If the distributor returns a certain dollar amount at the end of that period, the contract extends another two years. You can cap the extensions at a set period, such as eight or ten years.

MEDIA

Media is the means of exploitation. A show may be distributed and exploited in many markets, including

- Theatrical release, both general and art house—Although more DV movies are being projected, it's unlikely that an independent DV feature will get wide theatrical release. Art house or specialty theatrical release may be possible, although there's often very little money in the market to justify the effort.

- Pay-per-view television—Distributors who handle pay-per-view may be interested in obtaining media rights of your show for this market.

- Cable television—Distributors with connections to cable networks may be interested in obtaining these rights, although you may be able to make these sales yourself.

- Broadcast television, including public television—Few distributors will be able to sell an independent one-off to broadcast television. You may be able to make the sale to public television series or stations yourself. You may want to hold onto these rights.

- Foreign markets—You may want to work with a distributor with contacts and a track record selling independent shows to foreign markets.

- Video, DVD, and other home-use formats—This is a common market for independent DV motion pictures.

- Educational—A distributor with contacts and a track record can do amazingly well for you if your show fits the market.

- Internet—Distributors may request Internet rights along with everything else, but you may want to approach with caution. Internet distributors, on the other hand, often ask for a nonexclusive deal with no money.

See Chapter 5, "Who's Buying What: Surveying the Market," for more discussion about the markets.

Retain rights to media the distributor will not actively exploit. Many distributors ask for multimedia and interactive rights, but they have no idea how to sell them. Consider limiting the grant of rights to theatrical, television (pay-per-view, cable, and broadcast), and home video.

CONSIDERATION

The consideration is what you get in exchange for granting those rights. Consideration may be in the form of advances, guarantees, royalties, or a combination of these.

An advance is paid to the producer upon signing of the contract or delivery of materials. A guarantee is an assurance of the distributor to pay the producer a certain sum at a certain time. If royalties fall short, the distributor will advance money to cover the shortfall. Often the guarantee is recouped by the distributor from later royalties.

The royalty approach ensures that the producer shares in revenue even if sales are less than explosive. Because the royalty is based on the number of units sold (minus returns), there's less room for creative accounting.

Royalties are payable from revenues. There are different ways to define revenues and the contract should define the term clearly. *Revenues* may be defined as gross, adjusted gross, or net. *Gross* is the total receipts. *Adjusted gross* is total receipts minus specified expenses. *Net* is gross minus all expenses. Usually, royalty percentages against gross and adjusted gross are quite a bit lower than royalties on net deals. However, some distributors will start expensing everything against gross and you end up with less money.

Try to steer clear of net deals unless you can limit expenses. Define the terms clearly and without ambiguity. With a royalty deal based on gross or adjusted gross, the producer gets an amount in the range of 20%–25%, based on an agreed-upon price. This may change based on other terms in the contract.

For example, the distributor may sell cassettes or DVDs to a retailer at a sell-through price. A *sell-through* price is usually less than the agreed price because the distributor is trying to encourage the retailer to carry more of that product or to entice customers into buying rather than renting your show. Usually, the royalty rate is lowered to 10%–15% for sell-throughs.

Cassettes and DVDs may be sold to retailers on a revenue-sharing basis. The retailer pays a nominal amount per unit and agrees to share revenue from sales with the distributor. Most major studios and independent operators now supply shows to retailers with this deal.

ADVANCES AND GUARANTEES

Every producer wants an advance. You can pay off investors or deferral contracts, it may be the only money you ever see, and finally, a hefty advance forces the distributor to commit to your show. Think about it: If you've spent $25,000, you're going to work pretty hard to get it back.

A lot of time passes between the time distribution starts and the day you get your first check. Generally, revenues are applied first to pay distributor fees and expenses, so it may be a while before you see any money after the advance. That advance may help you be a bit more patient.

For home video and DVD, you can figure an advance by multiplying the projected sales per unit for the first year by the agreed-upon price, and then multiply by your percentage. For example, a distributor says it projects total unit sales to be 10,000 the first year of release. The cover price is $19.99. Projected gross revenues will be $199,900.

It's unlikely you'll have a deal based on gross. More likely, you'll be dealing with adjusted gross, so the gross amount will be adjusted according to accepted expenses. Let's assume the adjusted gross is $175,000. If your royalty is 10% of adjusted gross, your advance should be a minimum of $17,500.

You may ask for more if you think the distributor is underestimating projected sales or your show has a lot of buzz and you have other offers. You may accept less in exchange for a higher royalty rate or guarantee.

Advances are not refundable and are either paid on signing of the distribution agreement or after delivery and acceptance of materials. If you fail to deliver, or what you deliver is defective, the distributor may refuse to pay the advance.

Give the distributor a limited period to inspect materials and raise objections, and make sure you have some time to correct any problems should your deliverables be messed up. You don't want the distributor to wiggle out from the deal or withhold your money for a lengthy time.

You may want to include language that says if the deliverables are defective, and you either disagree, or you can't fix the problem, you can void the distribution deal and regain all rights to your show.

If an advance is paid in installments, the arrangement is a guarantee. Be sure to include payment deadlines and penalties if those funds are not forthcoming. Make the penalties specific. Should you have to sue, it's likely the court will uphold interest charges specific in an agreement. Remember: A guarantee is only as good as the financial health and integrity of the guarantor. If the distributor goes bankrupt, or sales are less than anticipated, the distributor may renege.

It's unlikely a no- or low-budget DV motion picture without name actors will receive an advance or a guarantee. Still, it doesn't hurt to ask.

DISTRIBUTION FEES

If the distributor wants television rights, you will probably have another section for distribution fees in the event of a television sale. Licensing a show for television may entail little more than contacting the cable channel and offering them the movie, so I'm not sure whether this is a route you want to take. The distribution fee is often 25% of the license fee, but it can vary, and if you can do it yourself, why give away a quarter of the money?

If you sell to a television outlet, the terms of the agreement should be quite specific. Review with your attorney before signing. I know a producer who agreed to deliver his show to a public television series, only to discover he would have to pay for closed captioning and E&O insurance. He lost money on the deal.

Delivery usually requires a video master, artwork, and perhaps chain-of-title paperwork. You'll probably need a music cue sheet as well as other documents.

Generally, television sales go pay-per-view, pay cable, network broadcast television, basic cable, and broadcast. Sometimes networks are willing to pay a premium to get the show sooner, but with independent DV movies, it's unlikely they'll return your phone calls, much less talk money.

EXPENSES

The distribution agreement should clearly define the nature and extent of expenses the distributor is allowed to recoup. Unfortunately, some distributors will take advantage of producers and try to expense everything against a motion picture's revenues.

Although you may not be able to control a distributor's expenses, you can restrict what a distributor can get back. You may want to separate expenses into three categories:

- Travel expenses—Costs to attend the markets such as AFM, MIP, MIP-COM, and NATPE, including airfare, hotel, shipping, telephone, and staff expenses. These expenses should be limited to the first year of distribution and only applied to those markets that the distributor attends. This applies to markets only, not festivals. Allowing the distributor to recoup money spent to sell your show is reasonable, but paying for the distributor to swan off to Aspen to go skiing is not.

- Promotional and marketing expenses—Costs incurred for preparing posters, one-sheets, trailers, and other promotional and advertising items. This does not include overhead and office expenses, but are limited to direct out-of-pocket expenses actually spent on behalf of the show.

- Distribution expenses—Costs in connection with the distribution and sale of your show may include long distance charges, photocopying and faxing, shipping, clearance and brokerage fees, insurance, bank transfers, taxes and duties, and the cost of manufacturing anything you fail to deliver. Duplication of screeners and masters, standards transfers, foreign language dubbing, and manufacturing of promotional material may also be recoupable as well, although these expenses should be paid by the territory buyer.

Precisely define each category and each amount must be reasonable and verifiable. The agreement should specify a minimum amount of money, known as the *floor*, and a maximum, known as the *cap*, for each category. The agreement should state that at the producer's request, the distributor will provide documentation for each expenditure or skip getting its money back.

You may want to include language that says your efforts will be counted as expenses. For example, if you create your own poster and one-sheet, the cap on expenses should be lower because you just saved the distributor some money.

Also, have language specifying that any advertising materials created by the distributor to promote the show should be created as a work-for-hire contract between you and whoever makes the items. This means you own the materials, not the distributor, designer, or photographer. The expenses for these items are recoupable by the distributor, and because you're paying for this stuff, you should own it.

ACCOUNTING

If you sell your show outright, it's unlikely you'll ever need to see the books unless the check bounces.

However, because most producers retain ownership and license rights for a term of years, distributors must account for a portion of the revenues generated by the show.

Make sure there's language that states the distributor must keep records regarding sales, rentals, sublicenses, and so on. Records should be kept in accordance with generally accepted accounting principles.

You'll want to require that monthly or quarterly accounting statements be sent along with any amounts due you. Include language so the distributor must deliver a detailed breakdown by territory and media of all licenses, with how much revenue has been received and what has yet to be collected. All expenses should be itemized. You may even want the distributor to include copies of all license agreements.

You'll want language specifying your right to audit the books on reasonable notice. You may have to review the distributor's accounting practices should something go awry. Some agreements specify that if you have been underpaid a specific percentage, usually 3–5%, the distributor must pay for the audit. If you haven't been underpaid by that amount, you pay for the audit.

Cut any language that says you accept the statements as accurate unless you initiate legal action within a year or two of receipt. Replace it with language that says you'll inform the distributor in writing of any objections before going to court. The distributor can review and resolve any disputes informally, while you retain your right to a remedy.

With a bit of vigilance, you can track sales through other means. For example, you can create a music publishing company that controls all the music on the soundtrack, and have your publishing company enter into an agreement with one of the performance rights organizations, such as ASCAP, BMI, or SESAC. These agencies collect public performance royalties when a show is shown on television in the United States and abroad. When royalties for the music are remitted from the broadcast of the show in another country, you know a sale was made. You can compare the music report with your distribution statements to make sure you're getting what you're owed.

WARRANTIES AND REPRESENTATIONS

The distributor wasn't there when you made your show and has no way of knowing for certain that you didn't violate anyone's right to privacy, copyright, or anything else. To ensure you have chain of title, and to protect it from lawsuits arising from your failure to clear anything, the distributor will ask you to warrant certain facts and indemnify the distributor for any losses or legal fees incurred from a breach.

This is a reasonable demand and it should be followed up by warranty demands of your own. You want mutual indemnification.

Include language stating that the distributor must obtain all rights needed to use artwork or advertising materials, and if in breach, you are indemnified from any damages and costs that may be incurred because of a lawsuit.

Also, get a provision stating that the distributor won't edit your show without your prior written approval and that the distributor will not accept any undisclosed compensation or favors in return for licensing the motion picture. Demand warranties that the distributor will not misallocate revenue from package sales, use hidden rebates, or mark up duplicating costs.

Include language so the distributor warrants to diligently promote and license the motion picture, that it's not in danger of bankruptcy, and that there are no outstanding suits that would obstruct the distributor from fulfilling its contractual obligations.

Warranties can be absolute or to the best of one's knowledge and belief. An absolute warranty means you're warranting a fact absolutely. You are as sure of it as you are of gravity. A good-faith mistake is no defense.

However, if you warrant a fact to the best of your knowledge and belief, you're stating that as far as you know, the statement is true. That's what you want. So many factors arise in moviemaking, that even when you're absolutely sure everything is all right, it isn't. For example, you have cleared a piece of music using a properly executed agreement, but the song-writer doesn't own the copyright to the work and has no power to enter into such an agreement. You didn't know that, and sadly, often the song-writer isn't even aware of it.

There's no advantage to offering an absolute warranty for anything. If the distributor insists on it, talk to your lawyer before signing on.

If you make an absolute warranty, you may be liable to the distributor for damages arising from breach of copyright. If you warrant that to the best of your belief and knowledge, you're saying you believed in good faith that you obtained the necessary rights and only promise that you have such a good-faith belief. You're not liable to the distributor.

DELIVERABLES

Distribution agreements often have extensive schedules and technical specifications for the master materials you're required to deliver. Examine these schedules closely. If your show is at fine cut and still needs post-audio work, you don't want to be caught having to deliver a finished show unless you have the time and money to complete it.

Some distributors will agree to advance the cost of completing deliverables, then recoup the expense from revenues. This language should be specifi-cally stated in the agreement.

I was recently on a collaborative project with other moviemakers for which the supervising producers insisted we all send our original releases to them. It never occurred to them what would happen if the masters were lost or that in the event of a dispute, their possession of those materials would put the moviemakers at a disadvantage.

Because you may be making several distribution deals, you may want to have multiple masters cloned. If the distributor needs it, you can ship it.

COPYRIGHT

You want to retain copyright in your show. If a distributor demands the copyright, the distributor should pay you a handsome sum of money. Even then, you should try to get language stating you were the producer, direc-tor, screenwriter, or whatever role you played, and that information will be included in every copy broadcast, or any other showing.

It's hard to control a show after you've given up copyright. Try to get lan-guage limiting what the new copyright owner can do to the show regarding reediting and so on. You may be able to argue that you have *droit moral*, or

⬚ WARNING

Never give a distributor your master materials. Clone and deliver all video masters and keep all of your releases, agreements, photos, and other important paper-work locked away. You can send duplicates, but never, ever, send your masters.

moral rights, to the work because you created it. Some countries recognize moral rights, which are separate from copyright. Moral rights include

- The right to be known as the author of the work.
- The right to prevent others from falsely attributing the work to someone who didn't create it.
- The right to prevent others from making changes to the work.
- The right to withdraw a work from distribution if it no longer represents the author's views.
- The right to prevent others from using the work or author's name in a way that reflects adversely on the author's professional standing.

United States copyright law does not mention moral rights, except for the fine arts. Several federal and state courts have noted that moral rights are not recognized in the United States. Still, if you're in the United States, you may be able to argue in favor of moral rights, or aspects of moral rights, in your deal.

E&O INSURANCE

One common delivery item is Errors & Omissions (E&O) insurance. Generally, domestic licensees, such as cable stations, will insist on E&O. Foreign buyers are not as concerned. E&O is essentially malpractice insurance that protects the insured from liability arising from failing to secure rights, permissions, and clearances for the motion picture. E&O won't protect you from intentional misconduct.

In addition to liability, E&O covers legal fees and cost of a defense. See Chapter 3, "I Mean Business," for more information on E&O insurance.

Many moviemakers can't afford E&O insurance. If that's the case for you, see whether the distributor will agree to purchase a policy and recoup the cost from gross revenues. If the distributor buys a policy, make sure you're added as an additional named insured. Some distributors have their own blanket E&O to cover all the films they distribute.

REMEDIES

You'll want language specifying remedies in the case of breach by either party.

Generally, there are two forms of remedy you'll find in a distribution agreement. One limits the resolution to disputes to arbitration, whereas the other states that either party has the right to go to court to seek injunctive relief.

Any remedies clause should provide that the prevailing party is entitled to reimbursement of costs and reasonable attorney's fees. Without this provision, the prevailing party may not recoup these expenses.

Also, the clause should specify the venue should a dispute arise. This is especially important if the parties reside in different states. Try to set the venue in your state and county; otherwise, you may be trekking cross-country to get your day in court.

ARBITRATION

Many entertainment attorneys recommend an arbitration clause. Because you probably are in a weaker financial position than the distributor, you probably won't be able to afford to pay attorney and court costs to enforce your rights. Without a viable means of protecting your interests, a distributor can blatantly breach the contract while you stand there stamping your feet.

Arbitration allows you to go before an impartial person or persons to arbitrate the issue. Most entertainment industry arbitrations are conducted either by the American Arbitration Association (AAA) or the American Film Marketing Association (AFMA). The AAA has a well-defined system of procedural rules, as well as offices in the United States and many other countries.

AFMA is a trade organization and organizes the American Film Market (AFM). AFMA arbitrations usually occur in Los Angeles, but they can be held during an international film market or in a foreign city. All AFMA arbitrators are experienced entertainment attorneys.

Under AFMA rules, if you win but the distributor refuses to comply with terms, you can have that distributor barred from participation in future American Film Markets. This threat may persuade an otherwise obstinate distributor to comply, although frankly, some distribution companies are shell corporations with no assets. Some people will dump the company and start a new one.

Regardless of what kind of remedies agreement you have, it is unlikely you'll be able to take action against an individual who works for a distribution company that is a corporation. One big benefit of a corporation is that it limits personal liability. See Chapter 3 for more information on business structures.

AFMA has a personal binder that can be enforced against distribution executives. If the individual executive has signed such a binder and the company fails to comply with an arbitration award, that person can be barred from future AFMs.

Consider this:

- If the distributor is in breach, you can't go to an arbitrator and demand an injunction to stop behavior that continues to damage you.

- If someone isn't going to pay up, whether you win or not, you'll end up going to court anyway to get your money.

- Because arbitrators are usually licensed attorneys, they're probably in private practice. Like anyone in private practice, they like to have repeat clients. Who is more likely to be a repeat customer: an independent producer who may never make another movie, or a distributor doing business all over the world?

- A distributor may know the arbitrators as colleagues, clients, or friends. You may not know any of them. This familiarity may result in unconscious bias.

One big advantage to arbitration is that an arbitrator experienced in the field may make a better decision, especially if the issue is only a monetary one. The arbitrator knows the issues and common practices, so may be able to get to the heart of the matter quickly. That can be a relief.

Neither you nor the distributor can reverse an arbitration award simply because you don't like it. If the loser doesn't comply with the arbitration award, the winner can have the award confirmed by the court, and once confirmed, the award is no different from any court judgment. The arbitration clause may also provide that the award is final, binding, and can't be appealed. Otherwise, you may incur large legal bills on appeal.

GOING TO COURT

Why limit your options? Just because you don't have an arbitration clause doesn't mean you can't enter into arbitration with another party. In some states, if the issue is monetary and less than a certain amount, the court may send you to arbitration before going any further.

What you get by keeping your options open is injunctive relief. You'll want language that allows you to go to court to file an injunction to order an individual or company to stop violating the terms of the contract. If the distributor continues violating the contract, you can go back and request the individual or company be found in contempt of court and that's a world of trouble. Judges don't like having their orders violated.

TERMINATION

You want language that specifies your right to terminate the distribution agreement. This includes conditions such as the distributor's failure to pay your share of revenue, the distributor declaring bankruptcy, or the distributor doing a poor job distributing the show.

The distributor won't want to give you broad termination rights because it may have contracted to deliver to other buyers and spent a lot of money promoting the motion picture. Many distribution agreements severely limit your termination rights, denying you everything but the right to take action for monetary damages. Often you're required to notify the distributor in writing to offer an opportunity to make good.

If the distribution agreement is terminated, licenses entered into by the distributor remain in force. The distributor may have a continuing right and obligation to serve these deals, and is usually allowed to take a distribution fee from revenue received after termination.

Think before you terminate. Other distributors may not be interested in you or your show after such an action.

RETURN OF MATERIALS

Upon expiration of the term, you should get all materials in the possession of the distributor, including artwork, tapes, promotional and marketing items, and so on. You may want language giving you the right to use these materials after the term, or even during the term outside the territory.

Be sure you have language addressing disposal of any existing product. For example, if the distributor has 100 DVDs sitting in a warehouse, the DVDs should be destroyed at the end of the term. You don't want your movie being sold when you're not making any money from it.

OTHER RIGHTS

Your attorney will undoubtedly have other issues for you to consider. You may want to discuss reservation of rights and the right to assign.

RESERVATION OF RIGHTS

You should expressly reserve all other rights to your show. The distributor will probably want limited radio and print publication rights to advertise the motion picture. Have this language specifically stated in the agreement.

RIGHT TO ASSIGN

You should include language that limits the distributor from licensing rights to third parties beyond the term you've granted that distributor. Without this language, near the end of the distribution agreement, the distributor may enter into a series of long-term agreements with third parties, often for little money.

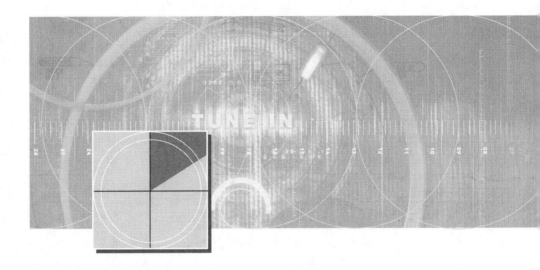

RESOURCES

DV

PRINT

Luther, Arch and Andrew Inglis. 1999. *Video Engineering*, Third Edition. New York: McGraw-Hill.

Ward, Peter. 2000. *Digital Video Camerawork*. Boston: Focal Press.

ONLINE-RECOMMENDED

Adam Wilt's Web site is a goldmine of good, solid information about DV and related technologies. See www.adamwilt.com.

2-pop abounds with great information on Final Cut Pro, DV, and moviemaking. See www.2pop.com.

DV Central is an ongoing e-mail discussion list on all aspects of DV, maintained by Bertel Schmitt and Alexei Gerulaitis. www.dvcentral.org/links.html. Subscribe to the DV-L e-mail list at www.dvcentral.org/thelist.html.

Great DV maintained by John Jackman has excellent articles on DV, lighting, and other aspects of production. See `www.greatdv.com`. He also has procedures for setting field monitors at `www.greatdv.com/video/smptebars.htm`.

Video University maintained by Hal Landon has information about video and many aspects of the video business. `www.videouniversity.com`. For procedures for setting field monitors, see `www.videouniversity.com/tvbars2.htm`.

DV.com has information on all aspects of DV. See `www.dv.com`. Articles by Chris and Trish Meyer on animation and special effects for DV and by Jay Rose on audio are terrific.

CyberCollege is an online cybertext on studio and field video production. Maintained by Ron Whittaker, Ph.D. See `www.cybercollege.com/tvp_ind.htm`.

Filmbiz.com has listings of many motion picture professionals. See `www.filmbiz.com`.

Jennings, Roger. 1998. "Consumer and Professional Digital Video (DV)." See `www.chumpchange.com/parkplace/Video/DVPapers/dv_formt.htm`.

_____. 1998. "Fire on the Wire: The IEEE 1394 High Performance Serial Bus." See `www.chumpchange.com/parkplace/Video/DVPapers/FireWire.htm`.

Charles Poynton's Color FAQ details color theory, digital technologies, and other subjects. See `www.inforamp.net/~poynton/notes/colour_and_gamma/ColorFAQ.html#RTFToC1`.

Guy Bonneau has an excellent article on DV and MJPEG on Adam Wilt's site. See `www.adamwilt.com/DVvsMJPEG.html`.

VidPro is a Web site and subscription list that covers many issues regarding video. See `www.vidpro.org/contents.shtm`.

ORGANIZATIONS

Advanced Television Systems Committee (ATSC) is an international organization that is establishing voluntary technical standards for advanced television systems. See `www.atsc.org`.

International Electrotechnical Commission (IEC), 3, rue de Varembé, PO Box 131, CH - 1211 Geneva 20, Switzerland. Phone 41 22 919 02 11, Fax 41 22 919 03 00. E-mail `info@iec.ch`, `www.iec.ch`.

International Standards Organization (ISO), International Organization for Standardization, 1, rue de Varembé, Case postale 56, CH-1211 Geneva 20, Switzerland. Phone 41 22 749 01 11, Fax 41 22 733 34 30. E-mail `central@iso.ch` `www.iso.ch`.

International Telecommunication Union (ITU), Place des Nations, CH-1211 Geneva 20, Switzerland. Phone 41 22 730 51 11, Fax 41 22 733 7256 or 41 22 730 6500. E-mail `itumail@itu.int`. See `www.itu.int/home/index.html`.

National Association of Broadcasters (NAB) is a full-service trade association that promotes and protects the interests of radio and television broadcasters in Washington D.C. and around the world. See `www.nab.org`.

National Association of Television Programming Executives (NATPE) is an association for content professionals. 2425 Olympic Boulevard, Suite 600E, Santa Monica, CA 90404. Phone 310-453-4440, Fax 310-453-5258. See `www.natpe.org`.

Society of Motion Picture and Television Engineers (SMPTE), 595 West Hartsdale Avenue, White Plains, NY 10607. Phone 914-761-1100, Fax 914-761-3115. E-mail `smpte@smpte.org`. See `www.smpte.org`.

Society of Operating Cameramen (SOC) was created to recognize and nurture excellence in the field of camera operation. SOC publishes *Operating Cameraman* magazine. Society of Operating Cameramen, P.O. Box 2006, Toluca Lake, CA 91610. Phone 818-382-7070. E-mail `info@soc.org`. See `www.soc.org`.

TV Technology is a Web site for video professionals covering many issues regarding video. See `www.tvtechnology.com`.

MOVIEMAKING

PRINT

Douglass, John S. and Glenn P. Harnden. 1996. *Art of Technique: An Aesthetic Approach to Film and Video Production*. Needham Heights, MA: Allyn & Bacon.

Film Threat. Editor Chris Gore sets the tone for a print and online independent movie magazine with some of the best short reviews around. Film Threat International Headquarters, 5042 Wilshire Blvd., P.M.B. 1500, Los Angeles, CA 90036. Phone 626-683-8245, Fax 626-683-3170. E-mail `input@filmthreat.com`. See `www.filmthreat.com`.

Goodell, Gregory. 1998. *Independent Feature Film Production: A Complete Guide from Concept Through Distribution*, Revised. New York: St. Martin's Press.

Lipton, Lenny. 1983. *Independent Filmmaking*. Revised. New York: Simon & Schuster.

Merritt, Greg. 1998. *Film Production: The Complete Uncensored Guide to Independent Filmmaking*. Hollywood, CA: Lone Eagle Publishing Co.

MovieMaker Magazine, 2265 Westwood Blvd., #479, Los Angeles, CA 90064. Phone 310-234-9234, Fax 310-234-9293.
E-mail `staff@moviemaker.com`. See `www.moviemaker.com`.

Pincus, Edward and Steven Ascher. 1984. *The Filmmaker's Handbook*. New York: Plume.

ONLINE-RECOMMENDED

Cinemedia is a collection of links organized according to topic. A great resource for listings of just about any company involved with any aspect of moviemaking. See `www.cinemedia.org`.

Digital Idiots.com has a collection of links and articles on many aspects of moviemaking. Maintained by Jason Tugman. E-mail `Jason@digitalidiots.com`. See `www.digitalidiots.com`.

IndieClub is a message board maintained by Eric Colley. It gets pretty lively, and most discussions are among new moviemakers. See `www.indieclub.com`.

ONLINE-OTHER

Filmmaker.com has a collection of articles, reviews, and other stuff. See `www.filmmaker.com`.

Global-DVC is Jan Van der Meer's DV Web site. Global Digital Video Club, Van der Meer Video/Global DVC, Box 276, 2040AG Zandvoort, The Netherlands. Phone 31-23-5717701 or local in Holland 023-5717701, Fax 31-23-5719798. See `www.global-dvc.org`.

Indiewire is an online magazine with film news and discussion boards. See `www.indiewire.com`.

ORGANIZATIONS

Association for Independent Video and Film (AIVF) was established by a group of independent filmmakers to offer support and resources to independent artists. AIVF offers 501(c)(3) sponsorship and publishes *The Independent*. Association for Independent Video & Filmmakers, 304 Hudson Street, Sixth Floor, New York, NY 10013. Phone 212-807-1400, Fax 212-463-8519. E-mail info@aivf.org. See www.aivf.org.

International Documentary Association (IDA) is a nonprofit association founded in 1982 to raise public consciousness of the importance of the documentary. IDA offers 501(c)(3) sponsorship and publishes *International Documentary*. International Documentary Association, 1201 W. 5th St., Suite M320, Los Angeles, CA 90017-1461. Phone 213-534-3600, Fax 213-534-3610. See www.documentary.org/index.html.

American Association of Producers (AAP) supports and represents the interests of professionals working in film, tape, and live television production, plus feature films and new media. American Association of Producers, 6363 Sunset Blvd., 9th Floor, Hollywood, CA 90028. Phone 323-467-2340, Fax 323-467-2293. E-mail info@tvproducers.org. See www.tvproducers.org.

American Film Institute (AFI) is dedicated to advancing and preserving the art of the moving image. American Film Institute, P.O. Box 27999, 2021 North Western Avenue, Los Angeles, CA 90027. Phone 213-856-7705/7729, Fax 213-467-4578. E-mail info@afionline.org. See http://afionline.org.

Association of Independent Feature Film Producers (AIFFP) is dedicated to the advancement of the art, science, and business of independent feature film production. Association of Independent Feature Film Producers, Inc., P.O. Box 38755, Hollywood, CA 90038. Phone 651-324-3255. E-mail info@aiffp.org. See www.aiffp.org.

British Academy of Film & TV Arts (BAFTA) is the U.K.'s leading organization promoting and rewarding the best in film, television, and interactive media. British Academy of Film & TV Arts, 195 Piccadilly, London W1J 9LN, UK. Phone 44 [0]20 7734 0022, Fax 44 [0]20 7734 1792. See www.bafta.org.

MARKET TRENDS AND THE BUSINESS

PRINT

Daily Variety, 5700 Wilshire Blvd., Suite 120, Los Angeles, CA 90036. Phone 323-857-6600, Fax 323-857-0494. New York Office: 245 West 17th Street, New York, NY 10011. Phone 212-645-0067, Fax 212-337-6977.

London Office: 6 Bell Yard, London WC2A 1EJ UK. Phone 44 20 7520 5222, Fax 44 20 7520 5217. Sydney Office: Level 1 Tower 2, 475 Victoria Street, Chatswood NSW 2067, Australia. Phone 61 2 9422 8630, Fax 61 2 9422 8635. Madrid/Latin America Office: Avenida de Burgos 39,-4 izda. Madrid 28036 Spain. Phone 34 91 766 1356, Fax 34 91 383 8671. See www.variety.com.

Hedlund, Patric. *A Bread Crumb Trail Through the PBS Jungle: The Independent Producer's Survival Guide*. Dendrite Forest Books. For more information about this title, see www.forests.com/breadcrumb/index.html.

Hollywood Creative Directory, as well as other directories from the same company, lists contact information for a variety of show business companies. Also searchable as an online database. Hollywood Creative Directory, 3000 W. Olympic Blvd., Suite 2525, Santa Monica, CA 90404-5041. Phone 800-815-0503 or 310-315-3815. See www.hollyvision.com.

Hollywood Reporter Blu-Book Directory lists vendors, service providers, agents, managers, and so on. *Hollywood Reporter Blu-Book*, c/o *The Hollywood Reporter*, 5055 Wilshire Blvd., Sixth Floor, Los Angeles, CA 90036. Phone 213-525-2000, Fax 213-525-2377.

Hollywood Reporter, 5055 Wilshire Blvd., Los Angeles, CA 90036-4396. Phone 323-525-2000, Fax 323-525-2377. See www.hollywoodreporter.com.

The Producer's Masterguide is a directory of movie picture financing, contracts, and so on. *The Producer's Masterguide*, NY Production Manual, Inc., 60 East Eighth St., 34th Floor, New York, NY 10003. Phone 212-777-4002, Fax 212-777-4101. See www.producers.masterguide.com.

Production Weekly is a weekly breakdown of projects in various stages covering Los Angeles, New York, and other major markets. *Production Weekly*, P.O. 15052, Beverly Hills, CA 90209. Fax 213-651-1916.

RealScreen is a print and online magazine about docs, infomags, and lifestyle programming. *RealScreen*, Suite 500, 366 Adelaide St. W., Toronto, Ontario M5V 1R9, Canada. Phone 416-408-2300, Fax 416-408-0870. See www.realscreen.com.

Screen International, c/o Alexis Grivas, PO Box 65132, Psyhikon, Athens, 15410 Greece. Phone 30 1 643 6384, Fax 30 1 643 6384. E-mail info@showbizdata.com.

ONLINE

ACNielsen EDI collects data from approximately 32,000 screens in the U.S., Canada, U.K., Germany, Spain, and France on a daily basis. ACNielsen EDI, 6255 Sunset Blvd., 20th Floor, Hollywood, CA 90028. Phone 323-860-4600, Fax 323-860-4610. See `www.acnielsenedi.com`.

Baseline.Hollywood.com is the entertainment industry's premiere resource for film and television information. 115 West California Blvd., #401, Pasadena, CA 91105. Phone 626-943-8075, Fax 626-943-8077. New York Office: 30 Irving Place, Fifth Floor, New York, NY 10003. Phone 212-254-8235, Fax 212-529-3330. E-mail `info@baseline.hollywood.com`. See `http://www.baseline.hollywood.com`.

FilmFinders tracks films for many distributors and has information about many buyers and distributors of motion pictures. 9056 Santa Monica, W. Hollywood, CA 90069. Phone 310-246-9202, Fax 310-246-9203. See `http://filmfinders.visualnet.com`.

Internet Movie Database has information on all kinds of movies. See `http://indie.imdb.com`.

ShowBizData.com's core business is entertainment industry data and consumer entertainment content. ShowBiz Data, Inc., 888 W. Sixth St., 15th Floor, Los Angeles, CA 90017. Phone 213-439-9830, Fax 213-439-9839. E-mail `info@showbizdata.com`. See `www.showbizdata.com/index_box.htm`.

Worldwide Box Office maintained by Chuck Kahn lists up-to-date box office totals for theatrical films. E-mail `chuck@worldwideboxoffice.com`. See www.worldwideboxoffice.com.

MARKETS

American Film Market (AFM), AFMA, 10850 Wilshire Blvd., Ninth Floor, Los Angeles, CA 90024. Phone 310-446-1000, Fax 310-446-1600. E-mail info@afma.com, See `www.afma.com/AFM/afm_home.asp`.

International Film Financing Conference (IFFCON) is presented by EBS Productions, a nonprofit organization designed to support and encourage adventurous filmmakers through global partnerships. 360 Ritch St., San Francisco, CA 94107. Phone 415-281-9777, Fax 415-495-2381. E-mail `Info@Iffcon.com`. See www.iffcon.com.

IFP Market, c/o Independent Feature Project, 104 West 29th Street, 12th Floor, New York, NY 10001-5310. Phone 212-465-8200, Fax 212-465-8525. See www.ifp.org.

Marché International des Films et Programmes pour la Télévision, la Video, le Cable et le Satellite (MIPCOM), MIPCOM brings together producers, distributors, broadcasters, Webcasters, worldwide cable and satellite operators, buyers, coproducers, and investors. See www.mipcom.com.

Marché International des Programmes de Télévision (MIP-TV), Reed Midem Organization, P.O. Box 572, 11 rue du Colonel Pierre Avia, 75726 Paris Cedex 15, France. Phone 011 33-1 4190-4580, Fax 011 33-1 4190-4570. André Vaillant. E-mail webmaster@miptv.com. See www.miptv.com or www.miptv.com/explorer/index.shtml

Mercato Internazionale Filme e Documentario (MIFED), Rassegne spa - Foro Buonaparte, 65 - 20121 Milan, Italy. Phone 39 0289012188, Fax 39 0289011578. E-mail mifed@rassegne.it. See www. mifed.com/ or www.fmd.it/mifed/2000/cosa.asp.

National Association of Programming Executives (NATPE), 2425 Olympic Blvd., Suite 550E, Santa Monica, CA 90404, Phone 310-453-4440, Fax 310-453-5258, Nick Orfanopoulos. European Offices: 454 Oakleigh Road North, London N20 ORZ, UK. Phone 44-81-361 3793, Fax 44-81-368-3824, Pam Mackenzie. E-mail Dee@natpe.org. See www.natpe.com.

CABLE AND NETWORK BROADCASTERS

The American Experience, WGBH, 125 Western Ave., Boston, MA 02134. Phone 617-300-5950, Fax 617-300-1020. See www.pbs.orx/amex.

Channel 4 is well-known for international coproductions and innovative programming. Channel Four, 124 Horseferry Road, London SW1P 2TX, UK. Phone 011 44 171 396 4444. See www.4producers.co.uk.

HBO America Undercover and **Cinemax Reel Life** acquire completed docs and offer finishing funds for partially completed projects. Send proposal or tape to Greg Rhem, HBO, 1100 Sixth Ave., New York, NY 10036. Phone 212-512-1670, Fax 212-512-8051. See www.hbo.com.

Independent Film Channel (IFC), managed and operated by Bravo Networks, is the alternative movie channel on television. Bravo/IFC, 150 Crossways Park West, Woodbury, NY 11797. See www.ifctv.com.

Independent Lens is a PBS series designed to showcase the works of independent film and videomakers. PBS—Independent Lens, 1320 Braddock Place, Alexandria, VA 22314. See www.pbs.org/independentlens.

The Independent Television Service (ITVS) was established by Congress "to encourage the development of programming that involves creative risks and that addresses the needs of underserved audiences." Independent Television Service, 51 Federal Street, Suite 100, San Francisco, CA 94107-1447. Phone 415-356-8383, Fax 415-356-8391. E-mail itvs@itvs.org. See www.itvs.org.

The History Channel, 235 East 45th Street, New York, NY 10017. Phone 212-210-9005, Fax 212-907-9481. See www.historychannel.com.

The Learning Channel, 770 Wisconsin Ave., Bethesda, MD 20814-3579. Phone 301-986-1999. See http://tlc.discovery.com.

Next Wave Films was established to help moviemakers from the U.S. and abroad launch their careers. Next Wave Films, 2510 7th Street, Suite E, Santa Monica, CA 90405. Phone 310-392-1720, Fax 310-399-3455. E-mail launch@nextwavefilms.com. See www.nextwavefilms.com.

PBS requires you submit your ideas with a TV proposal, Web proposal, treatments, scripts, tapes, and so on that should be mailed, e-mailed, or faxed to Cheryl Jones, Senior Director, Program Development & Independent Film, PBS Headquarters, 1320 Braddock Place, Alexandria, VA 22314. Phone 703-739-5150, Fax 703-739-5295. E-mail cjones@pbs.org. See www.pbs.org.

P.O.V., American Documentary, Inc., P.O. Box 5034, Bowling Green Station, New York, NY 10274-5034. Phone 212-344-3385, 212-344-3384, Fax 212-344-3386. E-mail pov@pov.org. See www.pbs.org/pov.

Showtime Networks Inc., A Viacom Company, 1633 Broadway, New York, NY 10019. Phone 212-708-1600, Fax 212-708-1217. See www.showtimeonline.com.

The Sundance Channel will consider unsolicited shows. Send a VHS copy of the completed motion picture, which they won't return, and an information packet on the project including (1) brief synopsis, (2) reviews (if you have any), (3) film festival history, (4) production notes, and (5) director/cast/crew backgrounds. Include your information such as your (1) name, (2) postal address, (3) telephone number, and (4) e-mail address. If they license your movie, you will need to supply and/or guarantee a master of the film in D1 or Digital Betacam formats. All rights and clearance to license the project for television. Larry Greenberg, Sundance Channel

Acquisitions, c/o Showtime Networks Inc., 10880 Wilshire Blvd., Suite 1600, Los Angeles, CA 90024. See www.sundancechannel.com.

WEBCASTING

Atom Films, www.atomfilms.com.

IFILM, www.ifilm.com.

MediaTrip, www.mediatrip.com.

New Venue, www.newvenue.com.

ReelShort, www.reelshort.com.

Underground Film, www.undergroundfilm.com.

UNIONS

Many software budgeting packages list day rates and requirements for union crews.

Industry Labor Guide has labor rates and working conditions for all union and guild agreements in the motion picture industry available as a book, online, or CD-ROM database. *Industry Labor Guide*, Entertainment Publishers, Inc., 11693 San Vicente Blvd., #206, Los Angeles, CA 90049. Phone 310-440-5800 or 800-820-7601, Fax 310-440-5812. E-mail epi@EntertainmentPublisher.com. See www.laborguide.com.

American Federation of Musicians (AFM), Los Angeles Office: 7080 Hollywood Blvd., Hollywood, CA 90028. Phone 323-461-3441. New York Office: 1501 Broadway, Suite 600, New York, NY 10036. Phone 212-869-1330. See www.afm.org.

American Federation of Television and Radio Artists (AFTRA), 260 Madison Ave., New York, NY 10016. Phone 212-532-0800, Fax 212-532-2242. See www.aftra.org.

Directors Guild of America, Inc. (DGA), Los Angeles Office: 7920 Sunset Blvd., Los Angeles, CA 90046. Phone 310-289-2000. New York Office: 110 W. 57th St., New York, NY 10019. Phone 212-581-0370. Chicago Office: 400 N. Michigan Ave., Suite 307, Chicago, IL 60611. Phone 312-644-5050. See www.dga.org.

International Alliance of Theatrical and Stage Employees (IATSE), IATSE General Office: 1515 Broadway, Suite 601, New York, NY 10036. Phone 212-730-1770. West Coast Office: 10045 Riverside Drive, Toluca Lake, CA 91602. Phone 818-980-3499, Fax 818-980-3496. See www.iatse.lm.com. Check the Web site for information on locals.

International Brotherhood of Electrical Workers (IBEW) 1125 15th Street N.W., Washington, DC 20005. Phone 202-833-7000, Fax 202-728-7664. See www.ibew.org/contact.htm. Check the Web site for information on locals.

National Association of Broadcast Employees and Technicians (NABET), Phone 800-882-9174, Fax 202-434-1426. E-mail nabet@nabetcwa.org. See http://union.nabetcwa.org/nabet. Check the Web site for information on locals.

Producer's Guild of America, 400 S. Beverly Dr., Suite 211, Beverly Hills, CA 90212. Phone 310-557-0807. See www.producersguild.org.

Screen Actors Guild (SAG), Los Angeles Office: 5757 Wilshire Blvd., Los Angeles, CA 90036-3600. Phone 323-954-1600. New York Office: 1515 Broadway, 44th Floor, New York, NY 10036. Phone 212-944-1030. Chicago Office: One East Erie, Suite 650, Chicago, IL 60611. Phone 312-573-8081. See www.sag.org.

Songwriters Guild of America, 1500 Harbor Blvd., Weehawken, NJ 07086. Phone 201-867-7603, Fax 201-867-7535. West Coast Office: 6430 Sunset Blvd., Suite 705, Hollywood, CA 90028. Phone 323-462-1108, Fax 323-462-5430, E-mail: LASGA@aol.com. Nashville Office: 1222 16th Avenue South, Suite #25, Nashville, TN 37212. Phone 615-329-1782, Fax 615-329-2623. E-mail: SGANash@aol.com. New York Office: 1560 Broadway, Suite #1306, New York, NY 10036. Phone 212-768-7902, Fax 212-768-9048. E-mail SongNews@aol.com. See www.songwriters.org/nashville2.htm.

GRANTMAKING INFORMATION

American Council for the Arts has information on more than 200 grantmakers. See www.artsusa.org.

The Chronicle of Philanthropy Web site offers the complete contents of the new issue, an archive of articles from the past two years, and more than four years' worth of grant listings—all fully searchable for subscribers. See http://philanthropy.com/index.html.

Council on Foundations is an organization for grantmakers—they don't make grants to anyone. However, you may want to take a look to understand what they go through to be able to give you money. Council on Foundations, 1828 L Street NW, Washington, DC 20036. Phone 202-466-6512. See www.cof.org.

The Foundation Center collects, organizes, and communicates information on U.S. philanthropy via the Web, print, and electronic publications. Subscribe to their online Foundation Directory. The Foundation Center, 79 Fifth Avenue/16th Street, New York, NY 10003-3076. Phone 212-620-4230 or 800-424-9836, Fax 212-807-3677. See `http://fdncenter.org`.

Foundation Center Online offers grantmaker information giving you access to hundreds of private and corporate foundations online and use of its search feature. See `www.foundationcenter.org`.

Foundations Online has directories, listings, news releases, and a lot of great information. See `www.foundations.org`.

National Assembly of State Arts Agencies has links to state arts councils that have online information. See `www.artswire.org`.

GRANTMAKERS

Arthur Vining Davis Foundations provide partial support for major educational series assured of airing nationally by PBS. Dr. Jonathan T. Howe, Executive Director, Arthur Vining Davis Foundations, 111 Riverside Ave., Ste. 130, Jacksonville, FL 32202-4921. Phone 904-359-0670. E-mail `arthurvining@msn.com`. See `www.jvm.com/davis`.

Artist Trust is a not-for-profit organization dedicated to supporting Washington State artists working in all creative disciplines. Artist Trust, 1402 Third Avenue, Suite 404, Seattle, WA 98101. Phone 206-467-8734, toll-free 866-21TRUST, Fax 206-467-9633. See `www.artisttrust.org`.

Artists' Fellowship, Inc., funds artists experiencing serious illness, crisis, or bereavement. Send SASE to Artists' Fellowship, Inc., Emergency Aid, c/o Salamundi Club, 47 Fifth Ave., New York, NY 10003. Phone 212-255-7740.

ArtsEdge is a compilation of funding opportunities and is sponsored jointly by the Kennedy Center and the National Endowment of the Arts. See `http://artsedge.kennedy-center.org/newsbreak/competitions.cfm`.

Center for Alternative Media and Culture supports independent media projects in postproduction that address the economy, class issues, poverty, women, war and peace, race, and labor. Center for Alternative Media and Culture, P.O. Box 0832, Radio City Station, New York, NY 10101. Phone 212-977-2096. E-mail `tvnatfans@aol.com`.

Center for Independent Documentary seeks proposals on an ongoing basis for the production of documentaries on contemporary issues. Center for Independent Documentary, 1608 Beacon St., Waban, MA 01268. Phone 508-528-7279. E-mail info@documentaries.org. See www.documentaries.org.

Corporation for Public Broadcasting (CPB) accepts proposals for the Public Television Future Fund. Corporation for Public Broadcasting, 901 E St. NW, Washington, DC 20004-2037. Phone 202-879-9734, Fax 202-783-1019. E-mail askus@cpb.org, www.cpb.org. Check the CPB guide to grant proposal preparation and writing at www.cpb.org/grants/grantwriting.html.

Creative Capital supports artists pursuing innovative approaches to form and content in the performing, visual, literary, and media arts. Creative Capital, 65 Bleeker St., Seventh Floor, New York, NY 10012. Phone 212-598-9900, Fax 212-598-4934. E-mail info@creative-capital.org. See www.creative-capital.org/.

Film Arts Foundation Grants encourages new and diverse works by film and video artists who have little likelihood of being supported through traditional funding sources. Film Arts Foundation, 346 Ninth Street, 2nd Floor, San Francisco, CA 94103. See www.filmarts.org.

Ford Foundation supports public broadcasting and the independent production of film, video, and radio programming. A letter of inquiry is advisable. Pamela Meyer, Director, Media Arts and Culture, Ford Foundation, 320 E. 43rd St., New York, NY 10017. See www.fordfound.org/grant/guidelines.html.

Hollywood Film Foundation awards grants in the following categories: Experimental, Digital Moviemaking, Post-Production, and Partial Budget Grants for up to 50% of budget. Projects must have a first- or second-time feature director and/or producer and must be budgeted under $5 million; 75% of the production must take place in the state of California. Hollywood Film Foundation, 433 N. Camden Dr., Ste. 600, Beverly Hills, CA 90210. See www.hff.org/grants/application.html.

Jerome Foundation operates a grant program for individual media artists. Applicants must be residents of New York City. The Jerome Foundation, 125 Park Square Ct., 400 Sibley St., St. Paul, MN 55101-1928. Phone 651-224-9431, Fax 651-224-3439.

John D. and Catherine T. MacArthur Foundation provides partial support for selected documentary series and independent films intended for national and international broadcast. The John D. and Catherine T. MacArthur Foundation, 140 S. Dearborn St., Chicago, IL 60603. Phone 312-726-8000. E-mail 4answers@macfdn.org. See www.macfdn.org.

The Kongsgaard-Goldman Foundation provides support to a wide range of nonprofit organizations in Washington, Oregon, Idaho, Alaska, Montana, and British Columbia. Initial contact must be made through a brief letter, complete with a description of the organization and project, summary budget, and 501(c)(3) status. Martha Kongsgaard, President, The Kongsgaard-Goldman Foundation, 1932 1st Avenue, Suite 602, Seattle, WA 98101. Phone 206-448-1874, Fax 206-448-1973. E-mail kgf@kongsgaard-goldman.org. See www.kongsgaard-goldman.org/who.html.

Latino Public Broadcasting (LPB) has an open call for proposals for programs to air on public television. The projects should center around themes and issues that are relevant to Latinos. Marlene Dermer, Executive Director, Latino Public Broadcasting, 6777 Hollywood Blvd., Ste. 500, Los Angeles, CA 90028. Phone 323-466-7110.

Minnesota Humanities Commission provides media grants to support humanities projects in radio, film, video, and multimedia. Minnesota Humanities Commission, Humanities Education Center, 987 East Ivy Ave., St. Paul, MN 55106. Phone 651-774-0105, Fax 651-774-0205. E-mail mnhum@thinkmhc.org. See www.thinkmhc.org.

National Endowment for the Arts (NEA) administers organizational grants program in several areas. NEA, 1100 Pennsylvania Ave., NW, Washington, DC 20506. Phone 202-682-5400, Fax 202-682-5611. E-mail webmgr@arts.endow.gov. See www.arts.endow.gov.

National Endowment for the Humanities supports films and videos with humanities content. See www.neh.fed.us/index.html.

Newton Television Foundation is a nonprofit foundation collaborating with independent producers on documentaries concerning contemporary issues. NTF, 1608 Beacon St., Waban, MA 02168. Phone 617-965-8477.

Pacific Pioneer Fund supports emerging documentary moviemakers who live and work in California, Oregon, and Washington. Pacific Pioneer Fund, P.O. Box 20504, Stanford, CA 94309. Phone 650-497-1133. See www.pacificpioneerfund.com.

Paul G. Allen Foundations has the Allen Foundation for the Arts that offers grants to strengthen the Pacific Northwest's cultural community and its services by supporting organizational and artistic excellence, innovation, diversity, and access. Paul G. Allen Foundations, 505 5th Ave. South, Suite 900, Seattle, WA 98104. See www.paulallen.com/foundations.

The Paul Robeson Fund for Independent Media supports media activism and grassroots organizing by funding the preproduction and distribution of film and video projects. The Paul Robeson Fund for Independent Media, Funding Exchange, 666 Broadway, #500, New York, NY 10012. See www.fex.org/robeson.

The Puffin Foundation Ltd. has sought to open the doors of artistic expression to those who are often excluded because of their race, gender, or social philosophy. Puffin Foundation, 20 East Oakdene Avenue, Teaneck, NJ 07666-4198. Phone 201-836-8923.
E-mail puffinmail@mindspring.com.
See www.angelfire.com/nj/PuffinFoundation.

Playboy Foundation supports media projects that help to foster open communication about and research into human sexuality, reproductive health, and rights, and protect and foster civil rights and civil liberties in the United States. Projects must have nonprofit fiscal sponsorship to be eligible. Playboy Foundation, 680 North Lake Shore Dr., Chicago, IL 60611. Phone 312-751-8000. See www.playboy.com/pd-foundation.

The Wallace Alexander Gerbode Foundation supports media projects proposed by 501(c)(3) organizations through its Arts and Culture Grants. Thomas C. Layton, President, The Wallace Alexander Gerbode Foundation, 470 Columbus Ave., #209, San Francisco, CA 94133-3930. Phone 415-391-0911. E-mail maildesk@gerbode.org.
See www.fdncenter.org/grantmaker/gerbode/.

BUSINESS AND LEGAL

PRINT

Donaldson, Michael C. 1996. *Clearance & Copyright: Everything the Independent Filmmaker Needs to Know.* Los Angeles: Silman-James Press. In addition to writing a very handy book, Donaldson is president of the IDA.

Levison, Louise. 1998. *Filmmakers and Financing: Business Plans for Independents,* Second Edition. Boston, MA: Focal Press. This is a good book.

Litwak, Mark. 1994. *Dealmaking in the Film and Television: From Negotiating to Final Contracts.* Los Angeles: Silman-James Press. Mark Litwak just can't help giving good information.

ONLINE

Circlelending.com can help with paperwork between friends, family, and so on. See www.circlelending.com.

Harris Tulchin & Associates, Attorneys at Law has a collection of helpful articles and listings. Trident Center, 11377 West Olympic Blvd., Second Floor, Los Angeles, CA 90064-1663. Phone 310-914-7979, Fax 310-914-7927. E-mail entesquire@aol.com. See www.medialawyer.com.

Hollywood Law CyberCenter hosted by entertainment attorney John W. Cones, contains information on financing and legal issues for moviemakers. See www.hollywoodnetwork.com/Law/Cones.

FindLaw provides access to a comprehensive and fast-growing online library of legal resources for use by legal professionals, consumers, and small businesses. See http://smallbiz.biz.findlaw.com.

Internal Revenue Service, www.irs.gov.

Lawgirl.com is an entertaining and helpful Web site maintained by Jodi Sax, an entertainment and news media attorney and Internet consultant. Phone 310-275-5721. See www.lawgirl.com.

Mark Litwak's Entertainment Law Resources for Film, TV and Multimedia Producers has great information on the legal aspects of producing motion pictures. See www.marklitwak.com.

Mycounsel.com is another legal information Web site. See www.mycounsel.com.

Nolo has do-it-yourself legal information and tools. See www.nolo.com.

E&O INSURANCE

C&S International Insurance Brokers, 20 Vesey Street, Suite 500, New York, NY 10007. Phone 800-257-0883 or 212-406-4499, Fax 212-406-7588. E-mail staff@csins.com. See www.csins.com.

D.R. Reiff & Associates, Inc., 320 W. 57th St., Second Floor, New York, NY 10019. Phone 212-603-0231 or 800-827-7363, Fax 212-247-0739. E-mail reiffd@tanhar.com. See www.reiffinsurance.com.

Mesirow Financial's Entertainment Group Phone 888-973-2323, Fax 312-595-7205. E-mail rfreeman@mesirowfinancial.com. See www.mesirowfinancial.com/insurance/independentfilms.

Near North Insurance Brokerage of New York, 777 Third Ave., 17th Floor, New York, NY 10017. Phone 212-935-7373 or 800-795-8075, Fax 212-935-7561. E-mail csadofsk@nnng.com. See www.nnng.com.

Speare & Company, 11620 Wilshire Blvd., Suite 900, Los Angeles, CA 90025-6820. Phone 310-914-9300. See www.speare.com/home.asp.

Truman Van Dyke Company, 6290 Sunset Blvd., Suite 1800, Hollywood, CA 90028. Phone 213-462-3300 or 415-386-8956.

United Agencies, 350 West Colorado Blvd., Suite 220, Pasadena, CA 91105-1855. Phone 626-792-1176, Fax 626-577-1346. See www.unitedagencies.com.

Walterry Insurance Brokers, 7411 Old Branch Avenue, Clinton, MD 20735. Phone 800-638-8791, Fax 301-868-2611. See http://www.walterry.com.

COPYRIGHT REPORT COMPANIES

Law Offices of Dennis Angel, 1075 Century Park Avenue, Suite 414, Scarsdale, NY 10583. Phone 914-472-0820.

Thomson and Thomson, 1750 K Street NW, Suite 200, Washington, DC 20006. Phone 800-356-8630.

501(C)(3) SPONSORSHIP INFORMATION

These organizations offer 501(c)(3) sponsorship, as well as other services, to independent producers.

Center for Independent Documentaries collaborates with independent moviemakers to create motion pictures on issues of contemporary social and cultural concern. Center for Independent Documentaries, 1608 Beacon Street, Waban, MA 02168. Phone 508-528-7279. See www.documentaries.org/index.htm.

Documentary Educational Resources is dedicated to the production, distribution, and promotion of quality ethnographic and documentary films from around the world. Phone 617-926-0491 or 800-569-6621, Fax 617-926-9519. See http://custwww.xensei.com/docued.

MediaRights.org encourages people working for social change and environmental protection to access the growing power of media to further their work. MediaRights.org, 104 W. 14th St., Fourth Floor, New York, NY 10011. Phone 646-230-6288. See www.mediarights.org.

National Video Resources has the goal to assist in increasing the public's awareness of and access to independently produced media through new digital technologies. National Video Resources, 73 Spring Street, Suite 606, New York, NY 10012. Phone 212-274-8080, Fax 212-274-8081. E-mail nvrinfo@nvr. See www.nvr.org.

PRESS CONTACTS

PRINT AND ONLINE

Bacon's Radio/TV/Cable Directory lists all U.S. radio and TV stations, including name, telephone numbers, program format, and target audience. Also available on CD-ROM. See www.bacons.com.

Booklist Magazine from the American Library Association is another terrific periodical read by librarians, distributors, store buyers, and others. *Booklist*, American Library Association, 50 E. Huron, Chicago, IL 60611. See www.ala.org/booklist.

Columbia Journalism Review online has a searchable database of newspapers and magazines. See www.cjr.org/database/papers.asp.

Editor & Publisher has directories and links of print and broadcast media from all over the world. *Editor & Publisher*, 770 Broadway, New York, NY 10003-9595. Editorial Phone 646-654-5270, Fax 646-654-5370. See www.mediainfo.com.

Library Journal is the oldest independent national library publication. Founded in 1876, this terrific periodical is read by more than 100,000 library directors, administrators, and others in public, academic, and special libraries. *Library Journal*, 245 West 17th Street, New York, NY 10011. Phone 212-463-6819, Fax 212-463-6734. E-mail lj@cahners.com. See www.libraryjournal.com.

Video Librarian, 8705 Honeycomb Ct. NW, Seabeck, WA 98380. I've never read this magazine, but a librarian friend of mine swears by it. Interesting Web site. Phone 360-830-9345, Fax 360-830-9346. E-mail vidlib@videolibrarian.com. See www.videolibrarian.com.

ORGANIZATIONS

The Association of Alternative Newsweeklies (AAN) is the trade organization for alternative newspapers in North America. Copies of the AAN directory, which contains demographics and information about each AAN member publication, are available. If you would like a copy of the directory, please call AAN at 202-822-1955, or send a check for $25 along with your return address to AAN, attn: Directory Sales, 1020 16th Street NW, Fourth Floor, Washington, DC 20036-5702. See www.aan.org.

Association of America's Public Television Stations (APTS) is a nonprofit membership organization that supports the continued growth and development of a strong and financially sound noncommercial television service. Association of America's Public Television Stations, 1350 Connecticut Ave. NW, Suite #200, Washington, DC 20036. Phone 202-887-1700, Fax 202-293-2422. See www.apts.org.

INTELLECTUAL PROPERTY

Copyright Web site provides real-world, practical, and relevant copyright information. See www.benedict.com.

United States Copyright Office, Library of Congress, Copyright Office, 101 Independence Avenue, S.E., Washington, DC 20559-6000. Phone 202-707-3000. www.loc.gov/copyright. To register a copyright, Register of Copyrights, Library of Congress, Washington, DC 20559-6000. Please see the Web site for current fees and forms.

World Intellectual Property Organization (WIPO) is an international organization dedicated to promoting the use and protection of intellectual property. World Intellectual Property Organization, 34, chemin des Colombettes, Geneva, Switzerland. Phone 022-338-9547, Fax 022-338-8810. www.wipo.int. U.S. Office: 2 United Nations Plaza, Room 560, New York, NY 10017. Phone 212-963-6813, Fax 212-063-4801. E-mail general wipo.mail@wipo.int, arbitration arbiter.mail@wipo.int, copyright copyright.mail@wipo.int.

PRODUCT PLACEMENT COMPANIES

A Creative Group, 1015 N. Hollywood Way, Suite 101, Burbank, CA 91505. Phone 818-842-9119, Fax 818-842-9568. See www.acreativegroup.com.

Entertainment Resources & Marketing Association (ERMA) is composed of corporations and agencies providing entertainment resources to the filmed entertainment community by product placement. Helpful information, including listings of members. Start here. See www.erma.org/nav/frame.html.

HERO Product Placement, Inc., 10777 Sherman Way, Sun Valley, CA 91352. Phone 818-764-7414, Fax 818-764-7415. See www.heroproductplacement.com.

I.S.M. Entertainment, Inc., 2601 41st Avenue, Suite A5, Soquel, CA 95073. Corporate Office Phone 831-475-1472, Fax 831-475-1473. Los Angeles Office Phone 310-281-8552, Fax 310-281-8553. E-mail ppinfo@ismentertainment.com. See www.ismentertainment.com.

International Promotions, 10725 Vanowen Street, Suite 113, North Hollywood, CA 91605. Phone 818-755-6333, Fax 818-755-6444. E-mail linda@productplacements.com. See www.productplacements.com.

Norm Marshall & Associates, 11059 Sherman Way, Sun Valley, CA 91352. Phone 818-982-3505, Fax 818-503-1936. E-mail info@normmarshall.com. See www.normmarshall.com/home.html.

SCREENPLAYS AND SCREENWRITING

PRINT

Field, Syd. 1994. *Four Screenplays: Studies in the American Screenplay*. New York: Dell Publishing.

_____. 1982. *Screenplay: The Foundations of Screenwriting*. Expanded Edition. New York: Delacorte Press.

Goldman, William. 1983. *Adventures in the Screen Trade*. New York: Warner Books.

Linda Seger answers your questions at the Hollywood Network Web site. See http://hollywoodnetwork.com/hn/writing/swls/chat/board.html.

Potter, Dennis. 1986. *The Singing Detective*. New York: Vintage Books.

Seger, Linda. 1992. *The Art of Adaptation: Turning Fact into Film*. New York: Henry Holt.

_____. 1988. *Making a Good Script Great*. Los Angeles: Samuel French.

ONLINE

There are hundreds of screenwriting Web sites and screenwriters groups around the world. Check your local arts organizations for listings and search the Web.

To purchase screenplays and books on screenwriting, budgeting, scheduling, and just about any other aspect of the motion picture industry, you can always contact

Cinema Books, 4653 Roosevelt Way NE, Seattle, WA 98105. Phone 206-547-7667.

Drama Book Shop, 723 Seventh Ave., New York, NY 10019. Phone 212-944-0595.

Larry Edmunds Bookshop, Inc., 6644 Hollywood Blvd., Hollywood, CA 90028. Phone 213-463-3273, Fax 213-463-4245.

Script City, 8033 Sunset Blvd., #1500, Hollywood, CA 90046. Phone 213-871-0707.

Theatrebooks, Ltd., 11 St. Thomas St., Toronto, Ontario M5S 2B7, Canada. Phone 416-922-7175.

Writer's Computer Store, 11317 Santa Monica Blvd., Los Angeles, CA 90025-3118. Phone 310-479-7774, Fax 310-477-5314. E-mail writerscom@aol.com. See http://writerscomputer.com.

ORGANIZATIONS

American Screenwriters Association (ASA) is organized for educational purposes, including the promotion of and encouragement of the public's participation in and knowledge of screenwriting as an art form. American Screenwriters Association, 269 S. Beverly Drive, Ste. 2600, Beverly Hills, CA 90212-3807. Fax 513-731-9212. E-mail asa@asascreenwriters.com. See www.asascreenwriters.com.

Writers Guild of America (WGA) offers screenplay registration, lists of literary agencies, and other information. They also publish *Written By*, a magazine about the screenwriting trade. West Coast Office: 7000 West 3rd St., Los Angeles, CA 90048. Phone 323-782-4520. East Coast Office: Writers Guild of America East, 555 West 57th St., New York, NY 10019. Phone 212-767-7800. See www.wga.org.

Writer's Guild of Canada offers script registration and other information. Send $20 Canadian and your script to Writer's Guild of Canada, 123 Edward St., Suite 1225, Toronto, ON M5G 1E2, Canada. Phone 416-979-7907.

PREPRODUCTION

PRODUCTION DESIGN

Arijon, Daniel. 1991. *Grammar of the Film Language*. Los Angeles: Silman-James Press.

Barclay, Steven. 2000. *The Motion Picture Image: From Film to Digital*. Boston, MA: Focal Press.

Katz, Steven D. 1991. *Film Directing Shot by Shot: Visualizing from Concept to Screen*. Studio City, CA: Michael Wiese Productions.

_____. 1992. *Film Directing—Cinematic Motion: A Workshop for Staging Scenes*. Studio City, CA: Michael Wiese Productions.

PRODUCTION MANAGEMENT

Cleve, Bastian. 2000. *Film Production Management*, Second Edition, Boston, MA: Focal Press.

Hart, John. 1999. *The Art of the Storyboard.* Boston, MA: Focal Press.

Singleton, Ralph. 1996. *Film Budgeting: Or, How Much It Will Cost to Shoot Your Movie?* Los Angeles, CA: Lone Eagle Publishing Co.

_____. 1991. *Film Scheduling: Or, How Long Will It Take to Shoot Your Movie?* Second Edition. Los Angeles, CA: Lone Eagle Publishing Co.

AssistantDirectors.com is a handy Web site listing production resources. See `http://assistantdirectors.com`.

The Badham Company brings you ShotMaster storyboard software. Demo available. See `www.badhamcompany.com`.

Easy Budget software is developed by John G. Thomas, who has been in the film and television business for more than 20 years. Easy Budget uses Microsoft Excel as its basis with updated rate sheets on its Web site. See `www.easy-budget.com/index.htm`.

PowerProduction Software offers software such as StoryBoard Quick, StoryBoard Artist, AutoActuals, CostumePro, and others. Nice folks, too. Phone 408-358-2358, Fax 408-358-1186. E-mail `info@powerproduction.com`. See `www.powerproduction.com`.

Screenplay Systems software products include Dramatica Pro, Movie Magic Scheduling, Movie Magic Budgeting, Movie Magic Contracts, and others. Some demos available on its Web site. See `www.screenplay.com/about/index.html`.

PERMITS

Check your local film commission for information on permits.

Association of Film Commissioners International, 7060 Hollywood Blvd., Suite 614, Los Angeles, CA 90028. Phone 213-462-6092, Fax 213-462-6091. See `www.afciweb.org`.

Media Services Toolbox has information on a state-by-state basis of interest to producers. See `www.media-services.com/toolbox/toolbox.htm`.

For a searchable directory of film commissions, see **U.S. & International Film Commissions**

`http://dir.yahoo.com/Entertainment/Movies_and_Film/`
`Organizations/Regional_Film_Commissions_and_Boards/`.

For permits to use United States national property, see

Institute of Museum Services, 1100 Pennsylvania Ave. NW, Room 510, Washington, DC 20506. Phone 202-786-0536.

United States Information Agency, Television and Film Service, Patrick Henry Bldg., Room 5118, 601 D St. NW, Washington, DC 20547. Phone 202-501-7764.

PRODUCTION

PRINT

Box, Harry C. 1997. *Set Lighting Technician's Handbook*. Boston: Focal Press.

Detmers, Fred H. 1986. *American Cinematographer Manual*, Sixth Edition. Hollywood, CA: The ASC Press.

Hines, William E. 1997. *Operating Cinematography for Film and Video: A Professional and Practical Guide*. Los Angeles: Ed-Venture Films/Books.

Kirk, John W. and Ralph A. Bellas. 1985. *The Art of Directing*. Belmont, CA: Wasworth, Inc.

Laszlo, Andrew. 2000. *Every Frame a Rembrandt: Art and Practice of Cinematography*. Boston: Focal Press.

Mascelli, Joseph V. 1965. *The Five C's of Cinematography*. Los Angeles: Silman-James Press.

Rabiger, Michael. 1989. *Directing: Film Techniques and Aesthetics*. Boston: Focal Press.

Ryan, Rod, ed. 1993. *American Cinematographer Manual*, Seventh Edition. Hollywood: The ASC Press.

Uva, Michael G. and Sabrina Uva. 1997. *The Grip Book*, Second Edition. Boston: Focal Press.

Weston, Judith. 1996. *Directing Actors: Creating Memorable Performance for Film and Television*. Studio City, CA: Michael Wiese Productions.

ONLINE

Abrupt Edge Film and Video Resources has information about the Sony VX-1000. See www.abruptedge.com.

Bob Stevers has a free Memory Stick full field color bars with PLUGE, plus articles on the Sony DVCAM PD-150 and other DV products. See www.BobStevers.com.

Chris Hurd's Web site is the home of the XL-1 Watchdog and lots more. See www.dvinfo.net.

Cinematography.com has links, articles, and discussion boards on cinematography. Tim Tyler, cinematography.com, 2026 NW Market Street, 2nd Floor, Seattle, WA 98107. Phone 206-686-7890. E-mail info@cinematography.com. See www.cinematography.com.

The Cinematography Mailing List is a closed discussion group promoting the free exchange of ideas among cinematographers, camera crews, manufacturers, rental houses, and other related businesses. To subscribe and for more information, contact www.cinematography.net.

The Golden List maintained by Ross Jones is dedicated to DV on the Mac platform. See http://desktopvideo.about.com.

The Silver List maintained by Richard Lawler is the spiritual twin of the Golden list, dedicated to DV for the Windows platform. See www.well.com/user/richardl/SilverListFrameSet.html.

Also see Usegroups rec.video.production and rec.art.movies.production for ongoing discussions.

FILTERS

Cokin Filters also has a range of filters for motion pictures using an innovative filter holder with various adapter rings. See www.cokin.fr.

Schneider Optics is the United States subsidiary of Schneider-Kreuznach, the German manufacturer of precision optics and filters for professional photography, cinematography, cinema projection, television, and industrial applications. Schneider Optics Inc., 285 Oser Ave., Hauppauge, NY 11788. Phone 631-761-5000, Fax 631-761-5090. E-mail info@schneideroptics.com. See www.schneideroptics.com.

Tiffen Company, LLC offers filters, tripods, lens accessories, storage systems, and digital camera accessories. The Tiffen Company, LLC, 90 Oser

Avenue, Hauppauge, NY 11788-3886. Phone 631-273-2500, Fax 631-273-2557. E-mail `techsupport@tiffen.com`. See `www.tiffen.com`.

CASES

Amphibico offers equipment for underwater film and video. 459 Deslauriers, Montreal, Quebec H4N 1W2, Canada. Phone 514-333-8666, Fax 514-333-1339. E-mail `info@amphibico.com`. See `www.amphibico.com`.

Light & Motion Industries offers a variety of underwater cases. Light & Motion Industries, 300 Cannery Row, Monterey, CA 93940. Phone 831-645-1525, Fax 831-375-2517. E-mail `sales@lmindustries.com`, `support@lmindustries.com`. See `www.lmionline.com`.

Pelican cases are excellent hard cases for all kinds of equipment. Search the Web or check your local Yellow Pages for a local retailer.

Portabrace is the leading designer and manufacturer of field cases for professional video, audio, and film production. I own at least four of their softcases—they are tough and affordable. PortaBrace/K&H Products, Ltd., Box 249, North Bennington, VT 05257. Phone 802-442-8171, Fax 802-442-9118. See `www.portabrace.com`.

CAMERA CONTROLLERS

Addenda Electronics makes adapters currently used in underwater camera housings and aboard the space shuttle. Addenda Electronics, PO Box 907, Monterey, CA 93942. Phone 831-372-6205, Fax 831-372-6192. E-mail `brucer@addenda.com`. See `www.addenda.com`.

Cool Contraptions is a place to find some of the coolest video and film accessories and devices, including the CoolZoom controller, as well as links to many other cool gadgets. Cool Contraptions, 25819 Anderson Lane, Stevenson Ranch, CA 91381-1211. Fax 661-288-1808. E-mail `sales@coolcontraptions.com`, `tech@coolcontraptions.com`. See `www.coolzoom.com`.

Varizoom offers controllers for just about every DV camera. Phone 888-826-3399, Fax 512-219-7724. See `www.varizoom.com`.

ADD-ON LENSES

Century Precision Optics makes add-on lenses. Century Precision Optics, 11049 Magnolia Blvd., North Hollywood, CA 91601. Phone 800-228-1254 or 818 766-3715, Fax 818 505-9865. E-mail `sales@centuryoptics.com`, `info@centuryoptics.com`. See `www.centuryoptics.com`.

OpTex International is one of the largest manufacturers and distributors of video and film equipment, with headquarters in North London and products distributed worldwide. E-mail info@optexint.com. See www.optexint.com.

CAMERA STABILIZERS

These are only some manufacturers of camera stabilizers and similar equipment for DV cameras. You'll be able to find Web sites with instructions for building your own stabilizers, dollies, jib arms, and other equipment.

Easyrig AB manufactures portable camera support for both film and video cameras. Ergonomically designed, the easyrig reduces the static load on the neck and shoulder muscles and distributes it to other parts of the body that are more capable of handling it. Easyrig AB, PO Box 6106, 906 04 Umeå, Sweden. Phone/Fax +46 90 77 60 01. E-mail info@easyrig.se. See www.easyrig.se.

EZ FX, Inc., makes a jib arm and controller for DV cameras. Phone 800-541-5706 or 407-877-2335. See www.ezfx.com.

Glidecam Industries makes a range of camera stabilization products. Glidecam Industries, Inc., Camelot Industrial Park, 130 Camelot Drive Bldg #4, Plymouth, MA 02360. Phone 800-600-2011 or 800-949-2089 or 508-830-1414, Fax 508-830-1415. E-mail glidecam@glidecam.com. See www.glidecam.com.

Glidecam Operators Network gives users of Glidecam professional systems the means to network and share their problems, solutions, and techniques. See www.glidecam-ops.net.

Habbycam sells stabilizers, cranes, and other interesting gear for DV cameras. Richard Haberkern, Ent., 3727 West Magnolia Blvd., Suite 159, Burbank, CA 91510-7711. Phone 818-554-0025. E-mail info@habbycam.com. See www.habbycam.com.

Hollywood Lite manufacturers and sells stabilizers of various configurations depending on your needs. See www.hollywoodlite.com.

MARzPAK from Marztech, Inc., is an over-the-shoulder stabilization system. Marztech, Inc., PO Box 513, Whitmore Lake, MI 48189. Phone 866-MARZTEC. E-mail info@marztech.com. See www.marztech.com.

Microdolly Hollywood makes grip equipment such as the Microdolly and Microdolly Jib. Microdolly Hollywood, 3110 W. Burbank Blvd., Burbank,

CA 91505-2313. Phone 818-845-8383, Fax 818-845-8384. See `www.microdolly.com`.

Sachtler sells terrific tripods and heads and is now offering a handheld camera stabilizer for prosumer cameras called Artemis DV. See `www.sachtler.com/seiten/products/cam_supp_eng/balance/artemis.htm`.

SkyCrane is a small crane for prosumer DV cameras. Nightshift Enterprises, 2255 Heritage Drive, Costa Mesa, CA 92627. Phone 949-631-6065, Fax 949-631-2922 E-mail `bjgoddard@skycrane.com`. See `www.skycrane.com`.

Steadicam The Tiffen Company now produces, markets, and sells the Steadicam line of manually held camera support systems. The Tiffen Company, LLC, 90 Oser Avenue, Hauppauge, NY 11788-3886. Phone (NY) 800-645-2522 (CA) 800-593-3331 or 631-273-2500, Fax 631-273-2557. E-mail `techsupport@tiffen.com`. See `www.tiffen.com`.

SteadyTracker ProMax now sells SteadyTrakcer and CobraCrane products from Classic Video Productions, Inc. ProMax Systems, Inc., 16 Technology Drive, Suite 106, Irvine, CA 92618. Phone 800-977-6629 or 949-727-3977. See `www.steadytracker.com`.

LIGHTING

These Web sites will get you started learning about the various manufacturers of lighting and lighting control equipment.

Arri Group, `www.arri.de`.

Cool-Lux, `www.cool-lux.com`.

De Sisti Lighting USA, `www.desisti.it`.

Frezzi Energy Systems, `www.frezzi.com`.

K5600, Inc., `www.k5600.com`.

Kino-Flo, `www.kinoflo.com`.

LightTech, `www.lighttech.com`.

Lowel-Light Manufacturing, Inc., `www.lowel.com`.

LTM Lighting, Inc., `www.ltmlighting.com`.

Mole-Richardson Co., `www.mole.com`.

Videssence, www.videssence.tv.

Rosco, www.rosco.com.

Cinemills, www.cinemills.com.

Matthews Studio Equipment, www.matthewsgrip.com.

SOUND

Rose, Jay. 1999. *Producing Great Sound for Digital Video*. San Francisco: Miller Freeman Books. Terrific resource about all aspects of audio for DV. Also see Jay's Web site, Digital Playroom, www.d-play.com.

David Moulton has a series of articles on audio at www.tvtechnology.com.

Cinema Audio Society (CAS) is an organization of mixers and boom operators with a message board and a journal available online. See www.ideabuzz.com.

Equipment Emporium is a retailer of audio equipment. In addition to selling you stuff, they have a collection of helpful articles online written by owner and location audio pro Fred Ginsburg. See www.equipmentemporium.com.

G. John Garrett and **Jay Rose** have an excellent article on using wireless rigs that I highly recommend. See "Dialog Unplugged: The Art of Wireless Mics" at www.dv.com/magazine/2000/1000/garret_rose1000.html.

Quantel Digital Fact Book is an online glossary about digital video and audio. Very handy. See www.quantel.com/dfb/index.html.

PROPS AND PROPMAKING

James, Thurston. 1989. *The Prop Builder's Molding & Casting Handbook*. Cincinnati, OH: Betterway Books.

Polytek, Inc., is a leading producer of liquid rubbers and plastics for molds and castings. Polytek, Inc., 55 Hilton Street, Easton, PA 18042. Phone 610-559-8620, Fax 610-559-8626. E-mail Sales@Polytek.com. See www.polytek.com.

The Prop Werx custom builds props. The Prop Werx, 101- 196 Rouge Hills Dr., Scarborough, Ontario M1C 2Z1, Canada. Phone 416-694-2717. E-mail Info@propwerx.on.ca. See www.propwerx.on.ca.

Sculpture House Casting Inc., 155 W. 26th St., New York, NY 10001. Phone 888-374-8665, Fax 212-645-3717. See www.sculptshop.com.

Smooth-On Company has moldmaking materials and how-tos on prop casting and making. Smooth-On Company, 2000 St. John Street, Easton, PA 18042. Phone 800-762-0744, 610-252-5800, Fax 610-252-6200. E-mail smoothon@smooth-on.com. See www.smooth-on.com.

HAIR, MAKEUP, AND WARDROBE

PRINT

Baker, Patsy. 1993. *Wigs and Make-Up for Theatre, Television and Film.* Boston: Focal Press.

Ingham, Rosemary and Elizabeth Covey. 1992. *The Costume Designer's Handbook: A Complete Guide for Amateur and Professional Costume Designers, Second Edition.* Portsmouth, NH: Heinemann Educational Books.

Kehoe, Vincent, J.R. 1995. *The Technique of the Professional Make-Up Artists,* Revised Edition. Boston: Focal Press.

Make-Up Artist Magazine is published six times a year. The Web site has a forum and articles. *Make-Up Artist Magazine,* P.O. Box 4316, Sunland, CA 91041-4316. Phone 818-504-6770, Fax 818-504-6257. See www.makeupmag.com.

ONLINE

The Costume Source is just one of many costume Web sites. See www.milieux.com/costume/source.html.

Maginnis, Tara. *The Costumer's Manifesto,* www.costumes.org/index.html. Although Tara primarily does costuming for theater, a lot of what she says applies to moviemaking.

MakeUpMania is a comprehensive virtual professional makeup store. See www.makeupmania.com.

Set the Pace Publishing Group has an online message board about make-up, hair, and styling. See www.setthepacepubgroup.com.

SPECIAL EFFECTS MAKEUP

The Complete Eejit's Guide to Film-Making has a section on blood and bullets for no-budget shows. See www.exposure.co.uk/eejit/blood/index.html.

Matthew Mungle's Web site with forum. See www.matthewwmungle.com.

Society of Amateur and Professional Special Effects Make-up Artists (SAPSEMA), maintained by Bill Barto, is a fun and interesting site. See www.geocities.com/rollie-tyler/index.html.

SPECIAL EFFECTS MAKEUP SUPPLIERS

Many of the online suppliers have how-to articles about their products.

ADMTronics, www.admtronics.com.

Anatomical Supply, www.anatomical.com.

Burman Industries sells foam latex kits, ultracal, clay, alginate, sculpting tools, silicone, gel effects, foam latex, trauma, aging and character appliances, Pros-Aide, training videos and books, and much more. 14141 Covello St., Suite 6A, Van Nuys, CA 91405. Phone 818-782-9833, Fax 818-782-2863. See www.burmanfoam.com.

Cybergraphic Designs sells materials and videos on special effects makeup. Cybergraphic Designs, 3202 Center Drive, Cleveland, OH 44134. Phone 440-888-8548, Fax 440-888-6638. E-mail customercare@getspfx.com. See www.getspfx.com.

Factor II, Inc., www.factor2.com.

GM Foam Company, makers of GM Foam, which is ideal for prosthetic makeup appliances and animatronic creature skins. GM Foam, Inc., 14956 Delano St., Van Nuys, CA 91411. Phone 818-908-1087, Fax 818-908-1262. See www.gmfoam.com.

Mehron, Inc., www.mehron.com.

Michael Davy Film & TV Makeup, www.bitstorm.net/mdftv.

Monster Makers, 7305 Detroit Ave., Cleveland, OH 44102. Phone 216-651-SPFX, Fax 216-631-4FAX. E-mail sales@monstermakers.com. See www.monstermakers.com.

Nightmare Factory, www.nightmarefactory.com/props.html.

If you need gafquat, www.ispcorp.com/products/hairskin/haircare/per7.html

LENSES AND ARTIFICIAL EYES

Custom Colors, www.customs.com.

Hamilton Eyes, Inc., www.vcnet.com/hamilton/default.html.

Lenses Online, www.lenses.com.

Oculo-Plastik, Inc., www.generation.net/~ocuplast/ocuproindex.htm.

Scotts' Ocularists of Florida, www.ocularist.com.

FANGS

Davis Dental Supply Company sells dental acrylics, plaster, alginate, bandages, clay, and other useful material. Davis Dental Supply Company, 13120 B Saticoy, North Hollywood, CA 91605. Phone 818-765-4994.

SPECIAL EFFECTS

PRINT

Baygan, Lee. 1988. *The Techniques of Three-Dimensional Makeup.* New York: Watson-Guptill Publications.

Cinefex, The Journal of Cinematic Illusions, P.O. Box 20027, Riverside, CA 92516. Fax 800-434-3339. See www.cinefex.com.

Corson, Richard. 2000. *Stage Makeup.* Second Edition. New Jersey: Prentice Hall.

Fleming, Bill. 1998. *3D Photorealism Toolkit.* New York: John Wiley & Sons.

Rickett, Richard, 2000. *Special Effects: The History and Technique.* New York: Billboard Books.

Tarassuk, Leonid and Blair, Claude, eds. 1982. *The Complete Encyclopedia of Arms and Weapons.* New York: Simon and Schuster.

ONLINE

Chris Hillman's Robotics/Animatronics/SPFX links page has lots of good sites. See http://members.aol.com/c40179/index.html.

The Journal of Pyrotechnics, www.jpyro.com.

Special Effect Supply Co., supplies and information at www.fxsupply.com.

The Student Club of Realistic Effects, Animatronics and Make-up (SCREAM) dedicated to students interested in special effects. See www.geocities.com/Hollywood/Lot/9373/SCREAM/main.html.

The Truly Dangerous Company is made up of two people—Trey Stokes and Maija Beeton—to provide production and design services to the entertainment industry. Good articles. See www.trudang.com.

VFX Pro, www.vfxpro.com.

Visual Effects Headquarters, www.vfxhq.com.

Visual Effects Society, www.visual-effects-society.org.

Visual Effects Resource Center, www.visualfx.com/home.htm.

ORGANIZATIONS

Alliance of Special Effects & Pyrotechnic Operators (ASEPO) is a non-profit created to promote the science and improve the methods of special effects and pyrotechnic operators. See www.ASEPO.org.

Bureau of Alcohol, Tobacco, and Firearms (ATF), www.atf.treas.gov.

STUNTS

STUNTNet, www.stuntnet.com.

Stuntwomen's Association of Motion Pictures Inc., www.stuntwomen.com.

COMPOSITING AND MATTES

Chris and Trish Meyer have ongoing articles at DV.com that will tell you everything you need to know to do compositing and matte work for DV. See www.dv.com.

Steven Bradford's Blue Screen Page, www.seanet.com/Users/bradford/bluscrn.html.

SPECIAL EFFECTS SUPPLIERS

Alfonso's Breakaway Glass, 8070 San Fernando Road, Sun Valley, CA 91352. Phone 866-768-7402 or 818-768-7402, Fax 818-767-6969. E-mail info@alfonsosbreakawayglass.com. See www.alfonsosbreakawayglass.com.

American Science & Surplus sells really great stuff. American Science & Surplus, 3605 Howard St., Skokie, IL 60076. E-mail info@sciplus.com. See www.sciplus.com.

Edmund Scientific sells wonderful science equipment and optics. Request a catalog. See www.edsci.com.

FX Warehouse has supplies and how-tos. FX Warehouse Inc., 3500 Aloma Ave. #F17, Winter Park, FL 32792. Phone 407-679-9621, Fax 407-679-5609. E-mail info@fxwarehouseinc.com. See www.fxwarehouseinc.com.

McMaster-Carr Supply Company sells all sorts of hardware and materials for many different tasks. McMaster-Carr Supply Company, P.O. Box 740100, Atlanta, GA 30374-0100. Phone 404-346-7000, Fax 404-349-9091. E-mail `atl.sales@mcmaster.com`. See `www.mcmaster.com`.

Special Effects Unlimited, 1005 N. Lillian Way, Hollywood, CA 90038. Phone 323-466-3361, Fax 323-466-5712. E-mail `seuefx@aol.com`. See `www.specialefxunltd.com`.

Tri-Ess Sciences has all sorts of supplies for many kinds of special effects. Tri-Ess Sciences, 1020 W. Chestnut Street, Burbank, CA 91506. Phone 800-274-6910 or 818-848-7838, Fax 818-848-3521. E-mail `science@tri-esssciences.com`. See `www.tri-esssciences.com`.

FAKE BODY PARTS AND ANIMATRONICS

All Effects, 17614 Lahey St., Granada Hills, CA 91344. Phone 818-366-7658, Fax 818-366-3768. E-mail `eric@allfx.com`. See `www.allfx.com`.

Animal Makers make puppets and suits. Animal Makers, 12473 Gladstone Ave., Sylmar, CA 91342. Phone 818-838-3440. E-mail `mailto:info@animalmakers.com`. See `www.animalmakers.com/index.html`.

Backstage Prosthetics, Phone 800-977-8749 or 416-977-8703. E-mail `mail@backstageprosthetics.com`. See `www.backstageprosthetics.com`.

Bodytech Special Effects Makeup, 13659 Victory Blvd. #145, Van Nuys, CA 91401. Phone 818-342-6886, Fax 818-342-2337. `madamec@bodytek.com`. See `www.bodytek.com`.

The Character Shop is an award-winning special effects company working in animatronics, makeup effects, puppets, and robotics. The Character Shop, P.O. Box 4777, Chatsworth, CA 91311. See `www.character-shop.com`.

WEAPONRY

Creative Effects Inc., rents firearms. Phone 818-365-0655. E-mail `ceifx@creative-effects.com`. See `www.creative-effects.com`.

IAR, Inc., offers collectible replica firearms and blank firing guns. IAR, Inc., 33171 Camino Capistrano, San Juan Capistrano, CA 92675. Phone 949-443-3642, Fax 949-443-3647. E-mail `sales@iar-arms.com`. See `www.iar-arms.com`.

Imperial Weapons has a selection of swords, knives, and martial arts equipment. Imperial Weapons, 40 Casey Jones Lane, Suite 1, Jackson, TN 38305. See `www.imperialweapons.com`.

Iron Wolf Armouries provides props and equipment for the entertainment industry. Iron Wolf Armouries, 9540 Assiniboine Rd SE, Calgary, Alberta T2J 0Z6, Canada. Phone 403-371-4439 or 403-255-9163. E-mail `ironwolfarmouries@home.com`. See `www.ironwolf.com`.

Superfoots, from Bill "Superfoot" Wallace, is an online martial arts supply store selling rubber knives and other weapons. Martial Arts Enterprises, Inc., 2225 E. Weldon Ave., Phoenix, AZ 85016. Phone 602-840-8776. E-mail `admin@superfoots.com`. See `www.superfoots.com`.

Tactical Edge Group is a motion picture production services company specializing in firearms safe handling and rental to the film and television industries. Tactical Edge Group, 2911 Winona Avenue, Burbank, CA 91504. Phone 818-361-5569. E-mail `movie.guns@gte.net`. See `www.propguys.com`.

TherionArms sells antique and reproduction arms and armory. TherionArms, 2002-A Guadalupe St. #123, Austin, TX 78705. E-mail `therion@therionarms.com`. See `www.therionarms.com`.

Western Stage Props is the premier source of Australian and American whips, bullwhips and specialty whips, Western stage props, instructional books and videos, blank firing guns and blank ammo, and more. Phone 800-858-5568. E-mail `wsprops@aol.com`. See `www.westernstageprops.com`.

EDITING PICTURE

PRINT

Dmytryk, Edward. 1988. *On Film Editing*. Boston: Focal Press.

David Bordwell, Kristin Thompson, Janet Staiger. 1985. *The Classical Hollywood Cinema*. London: Routledge.

Eisenstein, Sergei. 1942. *Film Sense*. New York: Harcourt Brace Jovanovich.

_____. 1949. *Film Form*. New York: Harcourt, Brace and World, Inc.

Murch, Walter. 1995. *In the Blink of an Eye*. Beverly Hills, CA: Silman-James Press.

Monaco, James. 1981. *How to Read a Film*. Oxford: Oxford University Press.

ONLINE

EditorsNet is an electronic magazine on editing. See
`www.editorsnet.com`.

ORGANIZATIONS

American Cinema Editors (ACE) is a motion picture editors organization
that publishes *Cinemeditor* magazine, American Cinema Editors, Inc., 100
Universal City Plaza, Building 2282, Room 234, Universal City, CA
91608. Phone 818-777-2900, Fax 818-733-5023. E-mail
`amercinema@earthlink.net`. See `www.ace-filmeditors.org`.

The Motion Picture Editors Guild, 7715 Sunset Blvd. Suite 200,
Hollywood, CA 90046. Phone 800-705-8700 or 323-876-4770, Fax 323-
876-0861. See `www.editorsguild.com`.

ORGANIZING THE MATERIAL

C.A. Childers created freeware Slate 2.0 for the Palm platform. See
`http://homepage.mac.com/engine16/palmslate.html`.

Eidria makes e-trim for the Palm platform. See `www.eidria.com`.

Production Magic Inc.'s Production Magic Shot Logger for the Palm platform. See `www.productionmagic.com/shot/shot.html`.

Square Box Systems Ltd. makes CatDV for Windows-based computers.
See `www.catdv.com`.

SOFTWARE

In addition to manufacturers' Web sites, WWUG Forums cover many
applications. See `www.wwug.com`.

When the people who maintain **Codec Central** say, "Your one-stop source
for educational information on streaming technologies," they mean it.
Codec Central is an informational resource created and maintained by
Media 100 Inc., makers of Cleaner 5. See
`www.icanstream.tv/CodecCentral/index.html`.

Adobe Systems Inc., `www.adobe.com`.

Apple's Final Cut Pro, `http://finalcutpro.com`.

Autodesk has signed an agreement to acquire the software product line
from Media 100. This includes the Cleaner family of products: Cleaner 5,
Cleaner EZ, Cleaner Live, Charger, and SuperCharger and the editing and
dynamic streaming media production software of CineStream,
EventStream technology, EditDV, and IntroDV. See `www.autodesk.com`.

Avid Technology, Inc., www.avid.com.

CineStream (EditDV), www.media100.com/product/cinestream.

Discreet Logic, www.discreet.com.

DPS, www.dps.com.

Fast, www.fast-multimedia.com.

in-sync, www.in-sync.com. in-sync distributes one of my favorite plug-ins for Premiere: ViXen. They also offer other great products, including Big FX's FilmFX, a filmlook plug-in.

Ulead, www.ulead.com.

PLUG-INS

Boris FX, plug-ins for Mac and Windows platforms. www.borisfx.com.

CrystalGraphics, www.crystalgraphics.com.

CSB-Digital offers AlamDV special effects tools for both Mac and Windows platforms. See http://www.csb-digital.com/alamdv.

DigiEffects, digital special effects tools for Mac and Windows platforms, including Cinelook, a filmlook plug-in. See www.digieffects.com.

Digigami, Inc., products for Mac and Windows platforms. See www.digigami.com.

Digistudio offers Digital Video Stabilizer to repair shaky video images. See http://digistudio.netfirms.com.

Digital Mediaworks VScope is a software-only waveform monitor/vectorscope for the Windows platform. It is accurate and about $30 delivered to your e-mail. 30-day free trial. See http://hotfiles.zdnet.com/cgi-bin/texis/swlib/hotfiles/search.html.

Eveological offers many plug-ins and applications for the Mac platform. See www.evological.com.

Pixelan Software, www.pixelan.com.

StageTools develops and sells MovingPicture, which enables pans and zooms on still images. Available as a standalone app or a plug-in for most NLEs. See www.stagetools.com/index.htm.

Synergy International, Inc., www.synergy1.com.

Synthetic Aperture makes a series of plug-ins and tools for DV on Mac and Windows platforms. See www.synthetic-ap.com.

Terran Interactive has products for Web streaming and compression. See www.terran.com.

HARDWARE

Apple, www.apple.com.

ATI Technology Inc., www.atitech.com.

JVC, www.jvc.com.

Matrix of 1394 NLE cards, maintained by Pat Leong at www.geocities.com/dvnle/matrix.html.

Matrox, www.mtrox.com.

Media 100, www.media100.com/index.html.

miro/Pinnacle, www.pinnaclesys.com.

NewTek, www.newtek.com.

Panasonic, www.panasonic.com.

Scitex, www.scitexdv.com/index.html.

Softimage, www.softimage.com.

Sony, http://bpgprod.sel.sony.com/home.bpg.

Truevision, www.truevision.com.

Videonics, www.videonics.com.

EDITING SOUND

PRINT

Altman, Rick, ed. 1992. *Sound Theory/Sound Practice*. New York: Routledge.

Chion, Michel. 1994. *Audio-Vision: Sound on Screen*. Edited by Claudia Gorbman. New York: Columbia University Press.

Forlenza, Jeff and Terri Stone, eds. 1993. *Sound for Picture: An Inside Look at Audio Production for Film and Television*. Emeryville, CA: MixBooks.

LoBrutto, Vincent. 1994. *Sound-on-Film: Interviews with Creators of Film Sound*. Westport, CT: Praeger Publishers.

Millward, C.M. 1996. *A Biography of the English Language*. Ft. Worth, TX: Harcourt Brace.

Pinker, Steven. 1994. *The Language Instinct*. New York: William Morrow.

Schneider, Arthur. 1990. *Electronic Post-Production Terms and Concepts*. Boston: Focal Press.

Weis, Elisabeth and John Belton, eds. 1985. *Film Sound: Theory and Practice*. New York: Columbia University Press.

ONLINE

Audio Engineering Society, 60 East 42nd St., New York, NY 10165. Phone 212-661-8528, Fax 212-682-0477. See `www.aes.org`.

Cinema Audio Society (CAS) consists of more than 400 sound mixers and associates from the film and television industries. They publish a journal and have a terrific online discussion board. Cinema Audio Society, 12414 Huston Street, Valley Village, CA 91607. E-mail `cinaudso@aol.com`. See `www.ideabuzz.com/cas`.

Film Sound Design, created and maintained by Sven E Carlsson, is dedicated to the art and analyses of film sound. Lots of great articles, including several by Walter Murch and Randy Thom. Check out the film sound cliches list. See `http://filmsound.studienet.org`.

Film Sound has a collection of articles on sound design and editing. See `www.filmsound.org/new.htm`.

Motion Picture Sound Editors (MPSE), an organization for professional sound and music editors who work in motion pictures and television. Motion Picture Sound Editors, P.O. Box 55725, Sherman Oaks, CA 91413. Phone 818-789-3813, Fax 818-789-3862. E-mail `join@mpse.org`. See `www.mpse.org/home.html`.

SOFTWARE

Arboretum, `www.arboretum.com`.

BIAS, Inc., `www.bias-inc.com`.

Cakewalk develops and markets software for music and sound production, including Sonar. Cakewalk, 51 Melcher Street, Boston, MA 02210. Phone 617-423-9004, sales 888-CAKEWALK, Fax 617-423-9007. See `www.cakewalk.com`.

Digidesign offers an array of products, including Pro Tools. E-mail dpninfo@digidesign.com. See www.digidesign.com.

Sonic Desktop, www.smartsound.com.

Sonic Foundry, www.sfoundry.com.

Syntrillium Software Corporation, headquartered in Scottsdale, Arizona, develops, publishes, and markets computer software products that enhance individual creativity in the manipulation of sound and visual effects. Of particular note is Cool Edit 2000, an inexpensive four-track software mixer. Syntrillium Software Corporation, P.O. Box 62255, Scottsdale, AZ 85082-2255. Phone 888-941-7100 or 480-941-4327, Fax 480-941-8170. See http//www.syntrillium.com.

PERFORMANCE RIGHTS ORGANIZATIONS

ASCAP Clearance Express (ACE), Clearance Desk, Phone 212-621-6183. See http://ascap.com/ace/ACE.html.

BMI HyperRepertoire Internet Song Title Database, Research Department, Phone 310-659-9109. See http://bmi.com/repertoire/about.asp.

Harry Fox Agency (HFA), Theatrics Department, Phone 212-370-5330. See www.harryfox.com.

SESAC Repertory On-Line (SRO), Phone 800-826-9996. See www.sesac.com/repertory.htm.

LIBRARIES

Digital Pro Sound has a collection of articles and links. See www.digitalprosound.com.

EarthStation1.com has a collection of audio and video files available online. See www.earthstation1.com.

FindSounds.com is a search engine for finding sound effects on the Web. See www.findsounds.com.

Image-Line Software offers fruityloops, a collection of sound effects and music libraries. Image-Line Software, Kortrijksesteenweg 281, B-9830 Sint-Martens-Latem, Belgium. Phone 32 (900) 10 292, Fax 32 9 281 15 01. E-mail info@fruityloops.com. See www.fruityloops.com/English/frames.html.

Partners in Rhyme offers free music and sound effects from its Web site, as well as inexpensive CD collections. See www.partnersinrhyme.com.

Sounddogs.com has thousands of sounds available online or on CD. Web site has a search engine. Sounddogs.com, Inc., 2411 Third Street #J, Santa Monica, CA 90405. Phone 877-315-3647. See www.sounddogs.com.

Sound-Effects-Library.com allows you to search the collection for the audio you need. See www.sfx-gallery.co.uk.

Synthzone has patches and music files, articles. and a discussion board. See www.synthzone.com.

FINISHING

Leapfrog Productions offers CCaption. Closed captioning software for adding captions to digital video and streaming data. Leapfrog Productions, P.O. Box 4189, San Rafael, CA 94913-4189. Phone 415-499-5609, Fax 415-472-6620. See www.ccaption.com.

TAPE-TO-FILM

2-pop. See the articles at www.2-pop.com/library/articles/2000-03-09.html. 2-pop is a goldmine of great information about DV, moviemaking, and related technology, so spend some time checking the articles, archives, and message boards.

Goodman, Robert. August 2000. *The Independent.* See www.aivf.org/the_independent/archives/0008/mo/augsep00_goodman.html.

DV Film Transfers FAQ, www.dvfilm.com/faq.htm.

Video for Film Release, www.zerocut.com/tech/vid_film.html.

TAPE-TO-FILM HOUSES

Cineric, 630 Ninth Avenue, Suite 508, New York, NY 10036. Phone 212-586-4822, Fax 212-582-3744. See www.cineric.com.

DuArt Film and Video, 245 West 55th, New York, NY 10019. Phone 800-52-DUART or 212-757-4580 x690. See www.duart.com.

EFILM: Electron Filmworks, 1146 N. Las Palmas Ave., Hollywood, CA 90038. Phone 323-463-7041, Fax 323-465-7342. E-mail efilm_info@efilm.com. See www.efilm.com.

Film Craft Lab, 23815 Industrial Park Drive, Farmington Hills, MI 48335. Phone 248-474-3900. See www.gracewild.com/filmcraft.

Four Media Company has locations all over the world. Check its Web site for the one nearest you. Phone 818-840-7144. See www.4mc.com/studio/Strans.html.

Hokus Bogus ApS., Pilestræde 6-8, DK-1112 Copenhagen K., Denmark. Phone 45 33 32 78 98, Fax 45 33 32 88 48. E-mail info@hokusbogus.dk. See www.hokusbogus.dk.

Soho Digital Films, Soho Digital Film, 26 Soho Street, Toronto, Ontario M5T 1Z7, Canada. Phone 888-SOHO-DIG or 416-591-8408, Fax 416-591-3979. See www.sohodigital.com.

Sony High Definition, Sony Pictures High Definition Center, 10202 W. Washington Blvd., Capra 209, Culver City, CA 90232. Phone 310-244-7434, Fax 310-244-3014. See www.sphdc.com/index1.html.

Swiss Effects, Thurgauerstr. 40, CH-8050 Zurich, Switzerland. Phone 41 1 307 10 10, Fax 41 1 307 10 19. E-mail info@swisseffects.ch. Paris Phone 33 6 07 10 42 82. New York 212-727-3695. E-mail jpoynton@swisseffects.ch. See www.swisseffects.ch.

Tape House Digital Film, 305 East 46th Street, New York, NY 10017. Phone 212-319-5084. See www.tapehousedigitalfilm.com.

FESTIVALS

PRINT

Bowser, Kathryn. 1996. *The AIVF Guide to International Film & Video Festivals*. New York: Foundation for Independent Video and Film.

Gore, Chris. 2001. *Ultimate Film Festival Survival Guide*, Second Edition. Hollywood: Lone Eagle Publishing Co.

Langer, Adam. 2000. *The Film Festival Guide: For Filmmakers, Film Buffs, and Industry Professionals*. Chicago: Chicago Review Press.

Film Festival Server, www.filmfestivals.com.

SOME FESTIVAL LISTINGS

Berlinale: Internationale Filmfestspiele Berlin is a prestigious competitive festival and host to the European Film Market. Berlinale: Internationale Filmfestspiele Berlin, Budapester Strasse 50, 10787 Berlin, Germany. Phone 011 49-30 254-890, Fax 011 49-30 254-89-249. E-mail info@berlinale.de. See www.berlinale.de.

Docfest, New York Documentary Center, Inc., 159 Maiden Lane, New York, NY 10038. Phone 212-668-1100, Fax 212-943-6396. E-mail mail@docfest.org. See www.docfest.org/docfest.html.

Hot Docs Canadian International Documentary Festival, 517 College Street, Suite 420, Toronto, Ontario M6G 4A2, Canada. Phone 416-203-2155, Fax 416-203-0446. E-mail pgrove@hotdocs.ca. See www.hotdocs.ca.

Hot Springs Documentary Film Institute, 819 Central Avenue, Hot Springs National Park, AR 71902-6450. Phone 501-321-4747, Fax 501-321-0211. E-mail hsdff@DocuFilmInst.org. See www.docufilminst.org.

Rotterdam International Film Festival and **Cinemart**, the festival's market. Rotterdam International Film Festival, P.O. Box 21696, 3001 AR Rotterdam, The Netherlands. Phone 011 31-10 411-8080, Fax 011 31-10 413-5132. E-mail iffr@luna.nl, www.iffrotterdam.nl. Cinemart, P.O. Box 21696, 3001 AR Rotterdam, The Netherlands. Phone 011 31 10 4118080, Fax 011 31 10 4135132. E-mail iffr@luna.nl. See www.iffrotterdam.nl.

San Francisco International Film Festival, San Francisco Film Society, 39 Mesa Street, Suite 110, The Presidio, San Francisco, CA 94129-1025. Phone 415-561-5000, Fax 415-561-5099. See http://sfiff.org.

South by Southwest (SXSW) Film Festival, P.O. Box 4999, Austin, TX 78765. Phone 512-467-7979, Fax 512-451-0754. Nancy Schafer. E-mail sxsw@sxsw.com. See www.sxsw.com.

Sundance Film Festival, P.O. Box 16450, Salt Lake City, UT 84116. Phone 801-328-3456, Fax 801-575-5175. E-mail sundance@xmission.com. See www.sundance.org.

Sunny Side of the Doc is an international documentary market. Sunny Side of the Doc, 23, rue François Simon, 13003 Marseille, France. Phone 33 (0)4 95 04 44 80, Fax 33 (0)4 91 84 38 34. E-mail @sunnysideofthedoc.com. See www.tvfi.com/archives/2001/sunny-side2001/indexan.htm.

Toronto International Film Festival, Toronto International Film Festival Group, 2 Carlton Street, Suite 1600, Toronto, Ontario M5B 1J3, Canada. Phone 416-967-7371, Fax 416-967-9577. See www.e.bell.ca/filmfest.

DISTRIBUTION

PRINT

Bowser, Kathryn. 1996. *The AIVF Guide to Film and Video Distributors.* New York: Foundation for Independent Video and Film.

Warshawski, Morrie, ed. 1995. *The Next Step: Distributing Independent Films and Videos.* New York: Foundation for Independent Video and Film.

Bay Area Video Coalition (BAVC) is the nation's largest noncommercial media arts center dedicated to providing access to media, education, and technology. BAVC includes an annual list of video distributors in its newsletter, *Video Networks.* Bay Area Video Coalition, 2727 Mariposa Street, Second Floor, San Francisco, CA 94110. Phone 415-861-3282, Fax 415-861-4316. E-mail bavc@bavc.org. See www.bavc.org.

ONLINE

There are hundreds of Web sites of distributors and directories online. Use your favorite search engine.

Docos.com is an online documentary information system listing buyers and sellers from around the world. Docos.com, 14 Buxton Road, Brighton BN1 5DE, U.K. Fax 44 1273 508 841. E-mail info@docos.com. See www.docos.com.

National Educational Media Network, 510-465-6885. See www.nemn.org.

Rotterdam Market for Educational Programs and Multimedia, www.rotterdammarket.org.

SELF-DISTRIBUTION

Mookas, Ioannis, ed. *The AIVF Self-Distribution Toolkit.* New York: Foundation for Independent Video and Film.

Directory of Media Funding Sources/Mediamaker Handbook, published by Bay Area Video Coalition, 2727 Mariposa Street, Second Floor, San Francisco, CA 94110. Phone 415-861-3282, Fax 415-861-4316. E-mail bavc@bavc.org. See www.bavc.org.

Media Market distributor list and profile from the National Educational Media Network. 510-465-6885. See www.nemn.org.

UC Media Center Director Gary Handman's Distributor List, www.lib.berkeley.edu/MRC/Distributors.html.

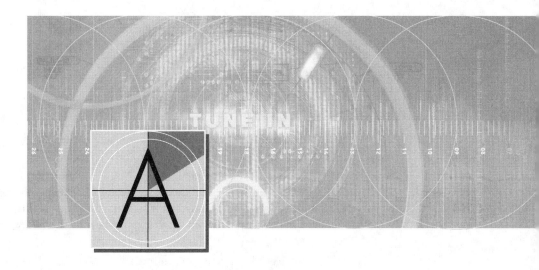

BUSINESS FORMS AND LICENSING AGREEMENTS

All of these documents are for your use. Customize as needed and photocopy as many as you want. For your convenience, they are included on the DVD. Reproduction of these forms for your use is encouraged. However, you are prohibited from copying and disseminating these documents in any form.

The Script Breakdown Sheet blank can be photocopied onto 50 sheets of yellow, green, white, and blue paper to help you complete your script breakdown.

Photocopy and fill out the Budget forms as completely as possible.

Fill out a Production Schedule Estimating Sheet for every scene in your script. Fill out a Location Sheet for every location change you anticipate during your shoot. Filling out these sheets will help you schedule your shoot.

On your scouts, take a copy of the Location Scouting Sheet, along with

- Still camera (digital or film)
- Compass
- Tape measure (electronic is helpful)
- Pad and pens
- Grid paper
- Circuit tester
- Flashlight

Fill out an Audition Sheet for every actor who auditions for you, and have each actor fill out an Actor Information Sheet.

Fill out a daily Callsheet using this form. You can photocopy a completed Contact Sheet on the back of each Callsheet, so everyone has the important phone numbers at all times. Be sure your camera crew fills out the Camera Log during production. It will make organizing and preparing for post a lot easier.

There are several legal documents as well. Be sure to have them reviewed by an entertainment attorney before using them.

Life Story Consent and Release Agreement applies to nonfiction movies, such as documentaries.

Use the Location Release at every location. Be sure the person who signs it is empowered to do so. Use the Personal Release for anyone who appears on camera as an extra or walks into camera view while you are shooting.

The Technical Services Contractor Agreement is for everyone who works on your show who is not on camera. Use the Actor Services Agreement for all actors who appear on camera or perform as voice talent. These are both deferral contracts. The Amendment to Agreement document allows you to offer to buy out one of these agreements. For example, if a DP wants you to buy his or her contract for a percentage of its deferred value, that person would have to sign this Amendment to Agreement on accepting payment.

The Master Recording License Agreement grants you the right to use the master recording of a specific recorded performance. You must have the signature of everyone who has a claim of copyright ownership in the recording: performers, producers, arrangers, and possibly others. Attachment A lists the exact information of the recording so you can list credits and fill out a Music Cue Sheet.

The Sync License Agreement grants you the right to use a specific musical composition. Just like the Master Recording License Agreement, you must have the signature of everyone who has a claim of copyright ownership in the composition: composers, arrangers, lyricists, and so on. Attachment A lists the exact information of the recording so you can list credits and fill out a Music Cue Sheet.

The Master Recording and Sync License Agreement combines both the master recording and sync license in one document. This is handy if you're dealing with performers who write and record their own music and have no record or distribution deal. You must have the signature of everyone who has a claim of copyright ownership in the master recording and composition. Attachment A lists the exact information of the recording so you can list credits and fill out a Music Cue Sheet.

If you want to create a soundtrack album for your show, you'll need everyone with a claim of copyright ownership to sign the Soundtrack Licensing Agreement. This agreement assumes your production company will act as the record label. Have each person fill out the Exhibit A—Credit Sheet so you can properly credit everyone on the album.

Remember to have an entertainment attorney examine these documents before you start signing anything. Laws vary according to city, county, and state. It's a lot cheaper to get the correct documents taken care of before there are any legal problems.

SCRIPT BREAKDOWN SHEET

Day Ext.–Yellow
Night Ext.–Green
Day Int.–White
Night Int.–Blue

Scene number: _____
Date: _____

Script Breakdown Sheet

Page number: _____

Title: _____ Int./Ext.: _____

Scene Number: _____ Scene name: _____ Day/Night: _____

Description: _____ Page count: _____

CAST—SPEAKING	CAST—SILENT BITS	CAST—ATMOSPHERE
	STUNTS	
SPECIAL EFFECTS	**SOUND EFFECT/MUSIC**	**PROPS**
WARDROBE	**MAKE-UP/HAIR**	**VEHICLES/ANIMALS**
SPECIAL EQUIPMENT	**PRODUCTION NOTES**	

BUDGET SHEETS

TOP SHEET

Producer fees and expenses		
Director fees and expenses		
Writer fees and expenses		
Script fees and expenses		
Talent fees and expenses		
	Total ABOVE-THE-LINE	
Development	**Total A**	
Preproduction	**Totals B & D**	
Production		
Crew labor	**Total C**	
Travel and location expenses	**Total E**	
Props & wardrobe	**Total F**	
Soundstage and set expenses	**Totals G**	
Equipment purchase and rentals	**Total H**	
Tape stock	**Total I**	
Talent fees and expenses	**Total J**	
Pick-ups		
Insurance (rental)		
Insurance (CGL)		
Insurance (E&O)		
Insurance (other)		
	Subtotal	
Postproduction		
Editorial	**Total K**	
Music	**Total L**	
Post-audio	**Total M**	
	Subtotal	
Selling		
Marketing	**Total N**	
Deliverables		
	Subtotal	
	Total BELOW-THE-LINE	
Contingency at	**(percentage)**	
	TOTAL	

DEVELOPMENT FEES AND EXPENSES

	Rate	Number	Total
Business stationery			
Web site development			
Business plan development and writing			
Press release writing			
Photocopying			
Deliveries and postage			
Office expenses			
Long distance calls			
Software purchase			
Hardware purchase			
Legal expenses			
Filing expenses			
		Subtotal A	

ABOVE-THE-LINE FEES AND EXPENSES

	Rate	Days	Total
PRODUCER'S FEES AND EXPENSES			
Development			
Preproduction			
Travel			
Production			
Postproduction			
Per diem			
		Subtotal	
DIRECTOR'S FEES AND EXPENSES			
Preproduction			
Travel			
Production			
Postproduction			
Per diem			
		Subtotal	
WRITER'S FEES AND EXPENSES			
Preproduction			
Travel			
Production			
Postproduction			
Per diem			
		Subtotal	
SCRIPT EXPENSES			
Option			
Option Execution			
Life Story			
Copyright search			
Copyright report			
Legal expenses			
Preproduction		**Subtotal**	
ABOVE-THE-LINE TALENT FEES AND EXPENSES			
Travel			
Production			
Per diem			
		Subtotal	
		Subtotal A	

PRODUCTION CREW FEES AND EXPENSES

		Prep			Production	
	Rate	Days	Total	Rate	Days	Total
DP						
Camera Op.						
UPM						
AD						
Art Director						
Props						
Gaffer						
Best Boy						
Key Grip						
Grip						
Sound Mixer						
Boom Operator						
Makeup						
Hair						
Wardrobe						
Script Supervisor						
SPFX Supervisor						
Still Photo.						
Loc. Scout						
PA						
PA						
Craft Services						
Prod. Coord.						
		Subtotal B			**Subtotal C**	

PREPRODUCTION FEES AND EXPENSES SHEET

	Rate	Number	Total
Office expenses			
Deliveries and postage			
Photocopying			
Long distance			
Scheduling expenses			
Budgeting expenses			
Cast/crew call expenses			
Casting/interview location fees			
Casting callbacks			
		Subtotal D	

TRAVEL AND LOCATION FEES AND EXPENSES

	# Units/People	Rate	Days	Total
Air fares				
Per diem				
Car rentals				
Motorhome/trailer				
Parking, tolls & gasoline				
Other vehicles				
Location fees				
Street sign rental				
Craft services (meals × people × days)				
Security guards				
Hotel/motel				
			Subtotal E	

PROPS AND WARDROBE EXPENSES

	Rate	Days	Total
Prop rental			
Prop purchase			
Wardrobe rental			
Wardrobe purchase			
Picture vehicles			
		Subtotal F	

SOUNDSTAGE AND SET EXPENSES

SOUNDSTAGE	Rate	Days	Total
Build days			
Pre-rig days			
Shoot days			
Strike days			
Generator and operator			
Total power charge and bulbs			
Misc. soundstage charges			
Meals			
Craft services			
SET	# Items	Cost Per	
Set dressing purchase			
Set dressing rental			
Lumber			
Paint			
Hardware			
Special effects			
Special construction			
		Subtotal G	

EQUIPMENT RENTAL AND PURCHASE EXPENSES

	Buy or Rent	#	Rate	Days	Total
Camera package					
Camera					
Lenses					
AC power supply					
Batteries and charger					
Tripod and plates					
Monitor					
Filters					
Other equipment					
Expendables					
Audio package					
Audio adapter					
Field mixer					
Boom					
Shotgun mic					
Lav mic					
Other mic					
Filters					
Wireless units					
Mic mount					
Mic zeppelin					
Mic furry					
Headphones					
Other equipment					
Expendables					
Lighting package					
Open face					
Fresnel					
Soft lights					
Chimera					
PAR					
HMI					
Fluorescent					

Other equipment				
Expendables				
Grip package				
C-stand				
Flags, nets, silks, etc.				
Reflectors				
Overheads				
Other equipment				
Expendables				
Gaffer package				
Stingers				
Dimmers				
Distribution gear				
Batteries				
Generator				
Other equipment				
Expendables				
Walkie-talkies, bull horns				
Dolly				
Crane				
Camera car				
Helicopter/plane				
Production supplies				
Expendables				
			Subtotal H	

TAPESTOCK AND MISCELLANEOUS FEES AND EXPENSES

	Rate	Number	Total
Tapestock			
Petty cash			
Still film, processing, and printing			
Animals and wranglers			
		Subtotal I	

BELOW-THE-LINE TALENT FEES AND EXPENSES

	Prep			Production			Per Diem		
	Rate	Days	Total	Rate	Days	Total	Rate	Days	Total
Principal									
Principal									
Principal									
Principal									
Supporting									
Supporting									
Supporting									
Supporting									
Extras— silent bits #:									
Extras— atmosphere #:									
Voiceover									
Wardrobe allowance									
Other									
		Subtotal			**Subtotal**			**Subtotal**	
								Subtotal J	

PICTURE EDITING FEES AND EXPENSES

	Rate	Days	Total
Editor			
Hardware rental			
Hardware purchase			
Software rental			
Software purchase			
Transcripts			
CGI			
Animation/rotoscope			
Titles			
Tapestock			
Facility rental			
Shipping			
Tape-to-tape color correction			
Filmlook			
Tape-to-film transfer			
Audio transfer			
Internegative			
Answer print			
Release print			
Release print shipping			
		Subtotal K	

MUSIC FEES AND EXPENSES

	Rate	Days	Total
Composer/arranger			
Studio rental			
Musicians			
Singer(s)			
Recording engineer			
Sync license			
Master use rights			
Tapestock and transfer			
		Subtotal L	

POST-AUDIO FEES AND EXPENSES

	Rate	Days	Total
Sweetening			
ADR			
Foley			
Sound effects			
Stock music fee			
Voiceover recording			
Mixing			
		Subtotal M	

SELLING AND MARKETING FEES AND EXPENSES

	Rate	Days	Total
Legal fees			
Festival entries			
Tape mastering			
Film market entries			
Travel			
Hotel/motel			
Meals			
Press kits			
EPK			
VHS/DVD dubs			
One-sheets			
Posters			
Flyers			
Shipping and mailing			
		Subtotal N	

PRODUCTION SCHEDULE ESTIMATING

SCENE NUMBER: _____

SCENE DESCRIPTION:

_____

Runtime: _____ **Number of set-ups:** _____ **(Min.: 1)**

Time per set-up: _____ **(Min.: 20 min.) # of takes:** _____ **(Min.: 1)**

Action	Est. time (in minutes)
Blocking time (runtime × 3)	
Set and tech rehearsal time (runtime × 3)	
Subtotal	
(set-ups × time per set-up) For night scene: × 1.5	
(runtime × set-ups) (time per set-up × takes)	
Subtotal	
Actor prep time Min.: 10 minutes	
Set dressing time Min.: 10 minutes	
Extra sound capture Min.: 10 minutes	
Subtotal	
Total A	

Total A = Estimated time to shoot this scene.

FOR EVERY LOCATION

Action	Est. time (in minutes)
Time for everyone to arrive on location	
(# of people × 5 minutes)	
(# of boxes × 5 minutes)	
Subtotal	
Staging time Min. 30 minutes	
Breakdown and tidy up Min. 30 minutes	
Mealtimes (number of meals × time per meal)	
Subtotal	
Total B	

Total B = Estimated time for staging and breakdown on each location change.

For greater accuracy, consider complex blocking, complex camera moves, extra lighting, rigging, set dressing, wardrobe, special effects, stunts, and additional factors.

LOCATION SCOUTING

Location:			
Date:	Time:		Fee:
Travel time:		People around:	
Days available:			
Times available:			
Cover or remove signs or features:			
Access:			
Parking			
Multiple angles of view			
Floorplan dimensions:			

	Number	Type	Location
Roads			
Doors			
Windows			
Surfaces			
Furniture			
Window treatments			
Appliances			
Other			

Power supply voltage:			
Circuit box location:			
Amps available:			
Power supply voltage			

	Number	Type	Location
Voltage			
Outlets			
Light switches			
Appliances and switches			
Cooling/heating and switches			
Other electrical			

Existing light				
	Number	Type	Location	Size
Fixtures				
Lamps				
Windows				
Audio				
	Number	Type	Location	
Vents				
Surfaces				
Interior sounds:				
Appliance hum:				
Traffic:				
Machinery:				
Airplanes:				
Other:				

AUDITION SHEETS

Audition sheet

Actor's name:_____ Date:_____

Audition material:_____

On time	yes	no			
Interpretation	1	2	3	4	5
Professionalism	1	2	3	4	5
Confidence	1	2	3	4	5
Take direction?	1	2	3	4	5

Special skills:_____

Favorite way to work:_____

Impression/notes:_____

✄ -

Audition sheet

Actor's name:_____ Date:_____

Audition material:_____

On time	yes	no			
Interpretation	1	2	3	4	5
Professionalism	1	2	3	4	5
Confidence	1	2	3	4	5
Take direction?	1	2	3	4	5

Special skills:_____

Favorite way to work:_____

Impression/notes:_____

ACTOR INFORMATION SHEET

Actor Information

Thanks for coming in to audition!

Name:_____

Phone:_____

Fax:_____

Email:_____

Please list the days and times you're available.

SUNDAY: _____

MONDAY:_____

TUESDAY:_____

WEDNESDAY:_____

THURSDAY:_____

FRIDAY:_____

SATURDAY:_____

Please list any exceptions to your schedule:

_____

_____

_____

_____

CALLSHEET

Title:_____**Date:**_____

Crew Call:_____**Shoot Day:**_____

Location	Sc. #	P#	I/E	D/N	Cast	Call Time	Props	Wardrobe	Makeup/ Hair

Sound FX/Music	Vehicles/Animals
Special Equipment	Production Notes

Location Address	Phone

CALLSHEET

	Crew	Phone	Cast	Phone
Director				
Producer				
DP				
Camera Op.				
UPM				
AD				
Art Director				
Props				
Gaffer				
Best Boy				
Key Grip				
Grip				
Sound Mixer				
Boom Operator				
Makeup				
Hair				
Wardrobe				
Script Supervisor				
SPFX Supervisor				
Still Photo.				
Loc. Scout				
PA				
PA				
Craft Services				
Prod. Coord.				

CAMERA LOG

Page:_____

Production:_____**Camera:**_____

Production Company:_____

Roll	Timecode	Sc.	Shot	Take	Notes
	: :				
	: :				
	: :				
	: :				
	: :				
	: :				
	: :				
	: :				
	: :				
	: :				
	: :				
	: :				
	: :				
	: :				
	: :				
	: :				

LIFE STORY CONSENT AND RELEASE AGREEMENT

From

Subject's Name

_____

Address _____

To

Production Company

_____

Address _____

I understand that you desire to use all or parts of the events of my life in order to do any or all of the following: write one or more books or publications of any kind, write or create one or more screenplays, produce, distribute, exhibit and exploit one or more motion pictures of any length in any and all media now known or hereafter devised and sound recordings in any and all media now known or hereafter devised, which are based upon, derived from, or suggested by all or parts of the events of my life. I have agreed to grant you certain rights in that connection. This Agreement confirms our agreement to the terms stated below.

1. <u>CONSIDERATION:</u> I acknowledge the receipt of $_____ and such other good and valuable consideration consisting of the publicity and notoriety that may result from your exercise of the grant of rights listed below. I affirm that this shall be sufficient consideration for my entering into this Agreement with you.

2. <u>GRANT OF RIGHTS</u>: (a) With regard to the above stated consideration granted to me, with full knowledge I hereby grant you, perpetually and irrevocably, the unconditional and nonexclusive right throughout the world to use, simulate, and portray my name, likeness, voice, personality, personal identification and personal experiences, incidents, situations, and events which have previously occurred or later occur (in whole or in part) based upon or taken from my life or otherwise, as well as my filmed image, my recorded voice (whether or not coupled with any visual image), and any printed materials, audiotapes, audio-visual tapes, photographs, drawings or similar items I may provide to you, in and in connection with motion pictures, sound recordings,

publications, and any and all other media of any nature whatsoever, whether now known or hereafter devised.

(b) Without limiting the generality of the foregoing, it is understood and agreed that said nonexclusive rights include theatrical, television, dramatic stage, radio, sound recording, music, publishing, commercial tie-up, merchandising, advertising, and publicity rights in all media of every nature whatsoever whether now known or later devised. I reserve no rights with respect to such uses. All said rights are hereinafter referred to as the "Granted Rights." It is further understood and agreed that the Granted Rights may be used in any manner and by any means, whether now known or hereafter devised.

(c) I acknowledge that I am to receive no further payment with respect to any matter referred to in this Agreement other than the consideration outlined in Paragraph 1 above. Any or all of the Granted Rights shall be freely assignable by you.

3. <u>RELEASE:</u> I agree hereby to release and discharge you, your employees, agents, licensees, successors and assigns from any and all claims, demands or causes of action that I may now have or may hereafter have for libel, defamation, invasion of privacy or right of publicity, infringement of copyright or violation of any other right arising out of or relating to any utilization of the Granted Rights or based upon any failure or omission to make use of them.

4. <u>NAME-PSEUDONYM:</u> You have informed me and I agree that in exercising the Granted Rights, you, if you so elect, may refrain from using my real name and may use a pseudonym which will be dissimilar to my real name. However, such agreement does not preclude you from the use of my real name should you in your sole discretion elect to do so. In connection with the use of my real name, I shall have no claim arising out of the so-called right of privacy and/or right of publicity.

5. <u>FURTHER DOCUMENTS:</u> I agree to execute such further documents and instruments as you may reasonably request in order to effectuate the terms and intentions of this Agreement, and in the event I fail or am unable to execute any such documents or instruments, I hereby appoint you as my irrevocable attorney in fact to execute any such documents or instruments, provided that said documents and instruments shall not be inconsistent with the terms and conditions of

this Agreement. Your rights under this Paragraph 5 constitute a power coupled with an interest and are irrevocable.

6. <u>WARRANTY AND INDEMNIFICATION</u>: I hereby warrant that I am completely free to give to you any information, and any printed materials, audiotapes, audio-visual materials, photographs, drawings or similar items (hereafter referred to as the "Granted Materials") I have that relate to the Granted Rights. I further warrant that none of the information or Granted Materials I give you will infringe on the rights of any other person, or will libel, defame, or invade the privacy of any other person. I agree to indemnify and hold you (and any assignee of yours) harmless from any and all claims and expenses (including court costs and attorney's fees) that may arise which are in violation of this Paragraph.

7. <u>REMEDIES:</u> (a) No breach of this Agreement shall entitle me to terminate or rescind the rights granted to you herein. I hereby waive the right, in the event of any such breach, to equitable relief or to enjoin, restrain, or interfere with the production, distribution, exploitation, exhibition, or use of any of the Granted Rights granted, it being my understanding that my sole remedy shall be the right to recover damages with respect to any such breach.

(b) Should any dispute arise concerning this Agreement and either of us finds it necessary to commence legal action to resolve such dispute, the prevailing party in such legal action shall be entitled to have the other party pay the attorney's fees, court costs, and expenses of the prevailing party incurred in such dispute and legal action, in addition to any other damages or legal relief awarded.

(c) The interpretation and enforcement of this Agreement shall be governed by the laws of the State of
_____. We agree that venue for any legal action shall be the courts of _____ County, _____. We both agree to be subject to the jurisdiction of the courts of
_____ County, _____ for purposes of any legal proceedings.

8. <u>PUBLIC DOMAIN MATERIAL:</u> Nothing in this Agreement shall ever be construed to restrict, diminish, or impair the rights of either you or me to utilize freely, in any work or media, any story, idea, plot, theme, sequence, scene,

episode, incident, name, characterization, or dialogue which may be in the public domain from whatever source derived.

9. <u>ENTIRE UNDERSTANDING:</u> (a) This Agreement expresses the entire understanding between you and me, and I agree that no oral understandings have been made with regard thereto. This Agreement may be amended only by a written agreement signed by you and me.

(b) I acknowledge that in granting the Granted Rights I have not been induced to do so by any representations or assurances, whether written or oral, by you or your representatives relative to the manner in which the Granted Rights may be exercised and I agree that you are under no obligation to exercise any of the Granted Rights and agree I have not received any promises or inducements other than as stated in this Agreement. The provisions of this Agreement shall be binding upon us and our respective heirs, executors, administrators, and successors.

(c) I acknowledge that you have explained to me that this Agreement has been prepared by your attorney and that you have recommended to me that I consult with my attorney in connection with this Agreement. I acknowledge that I have either consulted with an attorney of my own choosing or have voluntarily chosen not to do so.

ALL TERMS ACCEPTED AND AGREED

Date _____   Date _____

PRODUCTION

NAME _____   COMPANY _____

Social Security
Number_____

By _____   By _____

on behalf of the
corporation

LOCATION RELEASE

This agreement (hereinafter referred to as the "Agreement")
is entered into on this the _____ by and between
_____ (the "Production Company"),
and the agent/owner/proprietor (the "Proprietor") of the
property or premises described below:

_____

_____

_____

_____

This Agreement, signed and executed, confirms that the undersigned Proprietor has agreed and grants permission to
Production Company to use the property or premises described
as follows:

For the purpose of being photographed, filmed and/or videotaped by the Production Company during the production of
_____("the Project") for use as
the Production Company sees fit, and that the Production
Company will own any and all rights in said photography,
filming and/or videotaping. The undersigned Proprietor now
waives to the Production Company, its assigns and licensees,
all personal rights and objections to any use to be made of
such photography, filming or videotaping of the property or
premises, the Proprietor's name or likeness in connection
with the use of the photography, filming, or videotaping containing images of the property or premises or the likeness
of the Proprietor, for any and all motion picture, radio,
and television purposes, and performances thereof, accompanied by any narration and dialogue whatever, and the publicity in connection therewith, and/or for any other trade and
advertising purposes, in perpetuity and throughout the world.

The undersigned Proprietor warrants that he/she is legally
empowered to make such agreements. The Proprietor hereby represents that he or she understands that in proceeding with
said photography, filming, or videotaping, the Production
Company will do so in full reliance on the foregoing permission. The undersigned is acting as an independent contractor
during all participation in the rehearsal and shooting of the
project and hereby releases the Production Company from all
liability for all personal injury or property damage during
all participation in the making of the project.

In consideration of the above release, the undersigned Proprietor agrees that the Production Company will provide monetary compensation in the amount of $1.00.

This Agreement constitutes the only agreement between the Proprietor and the Production Company.

ALL TERMS ACCEPTED AND AGREED

Date _____   Date _____

By _____   PROPRIETOR _____
                              on behalf of the
                                 corporation

PERSONAL RELEASE

This agreement (hereinafter referred to as the "Agreement") is entered into on this the _____ by and between _____, whose offices are located at _____ (the "Production Company") and _____ (the "Interviewee").

This writing, signed and executed confirms that the undersigned has agreed to be photographed, filmed and/or videotaped by the Production Company during production of the project, _____ and that the Production Company will own any and all rights in said photography, filming and/or videotaping. The undersigned Interviewee now waives to the Production Company, its assigns and licensees, all personal right and objections to any use to be made of such photography, filming, or videotaping of the undersigned, the undersigned's name or the undersigned's likeness in connection with the use of the photography, filming, or videotaping containing the likeness of the undersigned, for any and all motion picture, radio, and television purposes, and performances thereof, accompanied by any narration and dialogue whatever, and the publicity in connection therewith, and/or for any other trade and advertising purposes, in perpetuity and throughout the world.

The undersigned Interviewee hereby represents that the undersigned understands that in proceeding with said photography, filming, or videotaping, the Production Company will do so in full reliance on the foregoing permission. The undersigned Interviewee understands that he/she will commit himself/herself in participating, as needed, during the Project. The undersigned Interviewee is acting as an independent contractor during all participation of the Project and hereby releases the Production Company from all liability for all personal injury or property damage during all participation in the Project.

In consideration of the above release, the Production Company agrees to provide monetary compensation in the amount of $_____.

This Agreement constitutes the only agreement between the Interviewee and the Production Company.

ALL TERMS ACCEPTED AND AGREED

Date _____   Date _____

By _____   SUBJECT INTERVIEWEE _____
    on behalf of the
      corporation

                Address _____

                        _____

                        _____

TECHNICAL SERVICES CONTRACTOR AGREEMENT

This agreement (hereinafter referred to as the "Agreement") is between _____ (the "Company"), a _____ corporation, and _____ (the "Contractor"). This Agreement will set forth the terms under which Company has agreed to engage Contractor to render services to Company in connection with the motion picture currently titled _____ (hereafter referred to as the "Picture").

1. <u>SERVICES</u> (a) Contractor shall render services to Company in the capacity as

_____. Services shall be rendered on the Picture commencing on or about the date of _____, or such other date as Company shall specify in advance Services shall continue until the completion of principal photography, or until such later date as Company shall specify.

(b) Contractor shall render all services as Company may require in connection with the capacity listed above regarding the Picture. Said services shall be rendered at the times and places required by Company and in a conscientious and professional manner.

(c) In connection with the exploitation of the picture, Company shall also have the right to record, produce, reproduce, amplify, enlarge, broadcast, use, perform, and distribute pictures of Contractor's work or product of any kind or nature, whether the same shall have been created by Contractor or others.

2. <u>COMPENSATION</u> Company shall pay Contractor at the rate of $_____ per day for _____ days, for a total compensation of $_____. This total compensation shall be paid entirely as deferred compensation. Such deferred compensation shall b payable only if all expenses and costs of any kind incurred in connection with the Picture are first recovered in full by the Company. If Company never receives full reimbursement of all expenses and costs incurred in connection with the Picture then contractor shall never receive the stated deferred compensation. Contractor understands that the possibility exists that Contractor may never receive any portion of the stated deferred compensation, and Contractor expressly agrees to these terms. If Company receives full reimbursement for all

expenses and costs incurred in connection with the Picture, Contractor shall receive the stated deferred compensation in a manner proportionate to all other person who are entitled to deferred compensation. While Company shall be obligated to pay such deferred compensation once all expenses and costs incurred by Company in connection with the Picture have been fully reimbursed, the actual frequency of the payment of such deferred compensation shall be at the discretion of the Company.

3. CREDIT Provided Contractor substantially renders the services contemplated in the Agreement on the Picture, renders them in a professional manner satisfactory to Company and further provided that Contractor is not in breach of any of the terms of this Agreement, then Contractor shall be accorded credit on the master(s) in a manner customary within the motion picture industry. The size and placement of such credit shall b at the sole discretion of Company.

4. TAXES As Contractor is an independent self-employed party, Contractor shall be solely liable for the payment of all income and other taxes that may be due on the compensation that Company has paid for Contractor.

5. PAYMENT All payments and notices to Contractor shall be personally delivered or mailed via United States mail to contractor at the following address:

_____

_____

_____

_____Contractor
shall be responsible for notifying Company in writing of any change in Contractor's address.

6. RESULTS AND PRODUCT (a) In addition to Contractor's services rendered hereunder, Company shall solely and exclusively own all results, product, and proceeds thereof (including, but not limited to, all rights of whatever kind and character throughout the world, in perpetuity in any and all languages of production, manufacture, recordation, reproduction, performance, and exhibition in any manner and by any art, device, or method, now known or hereinafter devised), whether such results, product, and proceeds consist of literary, dramatic, musical, motion picture, mechanical, or any other form of works, themes, ideas, compositions, creations, or products. Company's acquisition hereunder shall also include all rights generally known in

the field of literary and musical endeavor as the "moral rights of the authors" in and/or to any musical and/or literary proceeds of Contractor's services. Company shall also have the right in respect to such product, to add to, subtract from, change, arrange, revise, adapt, rearrange, translate into any and all languages, change the sequence, change the characters and the descriptions thereof, change the title of the same, record and photograph the same with or without sound (including spoken words, dialogue and music synchronously recorded), use said title or any of its components in connection with works or motion pictures wholly or partially independent thereof, to vend, copy, and publish the same as Company may desire. Contractor hereby assigns to Company all of the foregoing without reservation, conditions, or limitation and no right of any kind, nature, or description is reserved by Contractor.

(b) Company shall always have the sole and exclusive right, but only in connection with the Picture or in connection with the services rendered by Contractor with regard to the Picture, to use and display Contractor's name and likeness in advertising, publicizing, and exploiting the Picture, including without limitation souvenir programs, commercial tie-ups, paperback editions of the literary property directly related to and on which the Picture is based, or any sound recordings.

7. PUBLICITY AND ADVERTISING Contractor hereby specifically grants to Company the right to use Contractor's name, likeness, and biography in connection with the production, exhibition, advertising, and other exploitation of the Picture. Contractor shall not circulate, publish, or otherwise disseminate any news stories or articles, books, or other publicity containing Contractor's name relating directly of indirectly to Contractor's services, the subject matter of this Agreement, the Picture or the services to be rendered by Contractor or others for the Picture unless the same are first approved by Company.

8. CONTRACTOR DEFAULT If Contractor fails or refuses to perform or comply with any material terms or conditions for any reason including but not limited to Contractor's physical or mental incapacity then Company shall have the right to terminate this Agreement upon written notice thereof to Contractor. Except as indicated below, prior to termination of this Agreement by Company based upon Contractor Default, Company shall notify Contractor, specifying the nature of

the Contractor Default. Contractor shall have 48 hours after the giving of such notice to cure the Default. If the Contractor Default is not cured within the 48-hour period, Company may terminate this Agreement forthwith. However, if Contractor's default is that Contractor has failed to appear for a scheduled shoot for which Contractor has been given prior notice then Company may terminate this Agreement without sending Contractor written notice of the default. Such termination, solely in this case, shall be effective immediately upon the giving of notice of termination by Company.

9. EFFECT OF TERMINATION of this Agreement, whether by lapse of time, mutual consent, operation of law, exercise of a right of termination or otherwise shall terminate Company's obligation to pay Contractor any further compensation. Neither Company nor Contractor shall be deemed to have waived any other rights they may have or alter Company's rights or any of Contractor's agreements or warranties in connection with the rendition of Contractor's services prior to termination.

10. REMEDIES CUMULATIVE (a) All remedies accorded herein or otherwise available to either Company or Contractor shall be cumulative, and no one such remedy shall be exclusive of any other. Without waiving any rights or remedies under this Agreement or otherwise, Company or Contractor may from time to time recover, by action, any damages arising out of any breach of this Agreement by Contractor or Company, as applicable, and may constitute and maintain subsequent actions for additional damages which may arise from the same or other breaches. In particular, Company may recover from Contractor all costs incurred by Company as a result of Contractor failing to appear for a scheduled shoot for which Contractor is given advance notice. This shall be one, but not the sole measure of damages to Company. The commencement or maintaining of any such action or actions by Company shall not constitute or result in the termination of Company's use of Contractor's services hereunder unless Company shall expressly so elect by written notice to Contractor. The pursuit of Company of a remedy under this Agreement or otherwise shall not be deemed to waive any other or different remedy which may be available under this Agreement or otherwise, either at law or in equity. If any litigation is commenced in connection with this Agreement, the prevailing party in such litigation shall be entitled to an award of the court costs, expenses and attorney's fees

incurred in such litigation, in addition to any other damages or legal relief awarded.

(b) Contractor agrees that in the event of breach by Company, Contractor's sole remedy shall be limited to the right to recover damages, if any, in an action at law. Contractor agrees that in no event shall Contractor be entitled by reason of such breach by Company to terminate this Agreement or seek or be entitled to enjoin or restrain in any manner the exhibition or other usage of the Picture in any manner.

11. ASSIGNMENT This Agreement at Company's election, shall inure to the benefit of its successors, assigns, licensees, grantees, and associated, affiliated, and subsidiary companies, and Contractor agrees that Company and any subsequent assignee may freely assign this Agreement and grant the rights obtained hereunder, in whole or in part, to any person, firm, or corporation.

12. GOVERNING LAW AND VENUE The Agreement shall be construed in accordance with the laws of the State of
_____. Both Contractor and Company agree that the venue for any litigation regarding this Agreement shall be in _____ County, _____. Both Contractor and Company agree to be subject to the jurisdiction of the courts of _____ County,
_____.

13. CONTRACTOR STATUS All of Company's obligations herein are expressly conditioned upon Contractor's warranty and guarantee to Company that Contractor is properly licensed to do business in the state of _____ and render the services contemplated in the Agreement. By signing this Agreement, Contractor does so warrant guarantee the same to Company. Contractor acknowledges that Company has informed Contractor that the Picture will be a nonunion shoot. Contractor further warrants and guarantees Company that this will not prevent Contractor from rendering the Company the services specified under the terms of this Agreement. Contractor agrees to indemnify and hold the Company harmless from any costs (including attorney's fees) incurred by Company as a result of any claim that are inconsistent with the promises made by Contractor to Company in this Agreement.

<u>14. ENTIRE AGREEMENT</u> This Agreement shall replace and supersede all previous arrangements, understandings, representation, or agreements, either oral or written, regarding the subject matter hereto and expresses the entire agreement between the Contractor and Company with reference to the terms and conditions for the rendition of Contractor's services for Company for Company in connection with the Picture.

<u>15. PROMOTIONAL COPIES</u> Contractor may purchase, at Company's cost, one full copy of the picture. Contractor agrees to use this copy of the Picture solely for promotional use. Contractor will not duplicate or copy the Picture in any manner. Contractor will ensure that full credit for Company is given with regard to the usage of the copy of the Picture.

By signing in the spaces provided, Contractor and Company accept and agree to all terms and conditions of this Agreement.

ALL TERMS ACCEPTED AND AGREED

Date _____ Date _____

By _____ CONTRACTOR _____

    on behalf of the
      corporation Federal Tax ID _____

              State Business Lic.___

_____

Your name as it should appear in the credits:

_____

ACTOR SERVICES AGREEMENT

This agreement (hereinafter referred to as the "Agreement") is between _____ (the "Company"), a _____ corporation, and _____ (the "Actor"). This Agreement will set forth the terms under which Company has agreed to engage Contractor to render services to Company in connection with the motion picture currently titled _____ (hereafter referred to as the "Picture").

1. <u>SERVICES</u> (a) Actor shall render services to Company in the capacity as _____. Services shall be rendered on the Picture commencing on or about the date of _____, or such other date as Company shall specify in advance Services shall continue until the completion of principal photography, or until such later date as Company shall specify.

(b) Actor shall render all services as Company may require in connection with the capacity listed above regarding the Picture. Said services shall be rendered at the times and places required by Company and in a conscientious and artistic manner.

(c) In connection with the exploitation of the Picture, Company shall also have the right to record, produce, reproduce, amplify, enlarge, broadcast, use, perform, and distribute pictures of Actor's image, voice and all other sound of any kind or nature, whether such sounds shall have been created by Actor or by others. Company shall have the right to substitute the voice of another or others for actor's voice, when Company deems necessary. If applicable, Company shall also have the right to use a "double" for Actor's acts, poses, plays and appearances to such extent as Company may desire.

2. <u>COMPENSATION</u> Company shall pay Actor at the rate of $_____ per day for _____ days, for a total compensation of $_____. This total compensation shall be paid entirely as deferred compensation. Such deferred compensation shall be payable only if all expenses and costs of any kind incurred in connection with the Picture are first recovered in full by the Company. If Company never receives full reimbursement of all expenses and costs incurred in connection with the Picture then actor shall never receive the

stated deferred compensation. Actor understands that the possibility exists that Actor may never receive any portion of the stated deferred compensation, and Actor expressly agrees to these terms. If Company receives full reimbursement for all expenses and costs incurred in connection with the Picture, Actor shall receive the stated deferred compensation in a manner proportionate to all other persons who are entitled to deferred compensation. While Company shall be obligated to pay such deferred compensation once all expenses and costs incurred by Company in connection with the Picture have been fully reimbursed, the actual frequency of the payment of such deferred compensation shall be at the discretion of the Company.

3. CREDIT Provided Actor substantially renders the services contemplated in the Agreement on the Picture, renders them in a professional manner satisfactory to Company and further provided that Actor is not in breach of any of the terms of this Agreement, then Actor shall be accorded credit in a manner customary within the motion picture industry. The size and placement of such credit shall be at the sole discretion of Company.

4. TAXES As Actor is an independent self-employed party, Actor shall be solely liable for the payment of all income and other taxes that may be due on the compensation that Company has paid to Actor.

5. PAYMENT All payments and notices to Actor shall be personally delivered or mailed via United States mail to actor at the following address:

_____

_____

_____

_____

Actor shall be responsible for notifying Company in writing of any change in Actor's address.

6. RESULTS AND PRODUCT (a) In addition to Actor's services rendered hereunder, Company shall solely and exclusively own all results, product, and proceeds thereof (including, but not limited to, all rights of whatever kind and character throughout the world, in perpetuity in any and all languages of production, manufacture, recordation, reproduction, performance, and exhibition in any manner and by any art, device, or method, now known or hereinafter devised),

whether such results, product, and proceeds consist of literary, dramatic, musical, motion picture, mechanical or any other form of works, themes, ideas, compositions, creations or products. Company's acquisition hereunder shall also include all rights generally known in the field of literary and musical endeavor as the "moral rights of the authors" in and/or to any musical and/or literary proceeds of Actor's services. Company shall also have the right in respect to such product, to add to, subtract from, change, arrange, revise, adapt, rearrange, translate into any and all languages, change the sequence, change the characters and the descriptions thereof, change the title of the same, record and photograph the same with or without sound (including spoken words, dialogue, and music synchronously recorded), use said title or any of its components in connection with works or motion pictures wholly or partially independent thereof, to vend, copy, and publish the same as Company may desire. Actor hereby assigns to Company all of the foregoing without reservation, conditions, or limitations and no right of any kind, nature, or description is reserved by Actor.

(b) Company shall always have the sole and exclusive right, but only in connection with the Picture or in connection with the services rendered by Actor with regard to the Picture, to use and display Actor's name and likeness for advertising, publicizing and exploiting the Picture, including without limitation souvenir programs, commercial tie-ups, paperback editions of the literary property directly related to and on which the Picture is based, or any sound recordings.

7. PUBLICITY AND ADVERTISING Actor hereby specifically grants to Company the right to use Actor's name, likeness, voice, still publicity photographs, actual appearance in the Picture (in any manner) and biography in connection with the production, exhibition, advertising, and other exploitation of the Picture. Actor shall not circulate, publish, or otherwise disseminate any news stories or articles, books, or other publicity containing Actor's name relating directly of indirectly to Actor's services, the subject matter of this Agreement, the Picture or the services to be rendered by Actor or others for the Picture unless the same are first approved by Company.

8. ACTOR DEFAULT If Actor fails or refuses to perform or comply with any material terms or conditions for any reason

including but not limited to Actor's physical or mental incapacity, then Company shall have the right to terminate this Agreement upon written notice thereof to Actor. Except as indicated below, prior to termination of this Agreement by Company based upon Actor Default, Company shall notify Actor, specifying the nature of the Actor Default. Actor shall have 48 hours after the giving of such notice to cure the Default. If the Actor Default is not cured within the 48-hour period, Company may terminate this Agreement forthwith. However, if Actor's default is that Actor has failed to appear for a scheduled shoot for which Actor has been given prior notice, then Company may terminate this Agreement without sending Actor written notice of the default. Such termination, solely in this case, shall be effective immediately upon the giving of notice of termination by Company.

9. EFFECT OF TERMINATION Termination of this Agreement, whether by lapse of time, mutual consent, operation of law, exercise of a right of termination, or otherwise shall terminate Company's obligation to pay Actor any further compensation. Neither Company nor Actor shall be deemed to have waived any other rights they may have or alter Company's rights or any of Actor's agreements or warranties in connection with the rendition of Actor's services prior to termination.

10. REMEDIES CUMULATIVE (a) All remedies accorded herein or otherwise available to either Company or Actor shall be cumulative, and no one such remedy shall be exclusive of any other. Without waiving any rights or remedies under this Agreement or otherwise, Company or Actor may from time to time recover, by action, any damages arising out of any breach of this Agreement by Actor or Company, as applicable, and may constitute and maintain subsequent actions for additional damages which may arise from the same or other breaches. In particular, Company may recover from Actor all costs all costs of reshooting footage in which Actor appears if Actor's services are terminated before shooting is completed. This shall be one, but not the sole measure of damages to Company. The commencement or maintaining of any such action or actions by Company shall not constitute or result in the termination of Company's use of Actor's services hereunder unless Company shall expressly so elect by written notice to Actor. The pursuit of Company of a remedy under this Agreement or otherwise shall not be deemed to

waive any other or different remedy which may be available under this Agreement or otherwise, either at law or in equity. If any litigation is commenced in connection with this Agreement, the prevailing party in such litigation shall be entitled to an award of the court costs, expenses and attorney's fees incurred in such litigation, in addition to any other damages or legal relief awarded.

(b) Actor agrees that in the event of breach by Company, Actor's sole remedy shall be limited to the right to recover damages, if any, in an action at law. Actor agrees that in no event shall Actor be entitled by reason of such breach by Company to terminate this Agreement or seek or be entitled to enjoin or restrain in any manner the exhibition or other usage of the Picture in any manner.

11. <u>ASSIGNMENT</u> This Agreement at Company's election, shall inure to the benefit of its successors, assigns, licensees, grantees, and associated, affiliated, and subsidiary companies, and Actor agrees that Company and any subsequent assignee may freely assign this Agreement and grant the rights obtained hereunder, in whole or in part, to any person, firm, or corporation.

12. <u>GOVERNING LAW AND VENUE</u> The Agreement shall be construed in accordance with the laws of the State of _____. Both Actor and Company agree that the venue for any litigation regarding this Agreement shall be in _____ County, _____. Both Actor and Company agree to be subject to the jurisdiction of the courts of _____ County, _____.

13. <u>ACTOR STATUS</u> Actor hereby warrants and guarantees to Company that actor is free to enter into this agreement and render the services specified. Actor hereby warrants and guarantees to Company that Actor is under no restriction that would prevent Actor from entering into this Agreement and rendering the services specified, including any unions rules or restrictions. Actor acknowledges that Company has informed Actor that the Picture will be a nonunion shoot. Actor agrees to indemnify and hold the Company harmless from any costs (including attorney's fees) incurred by Company as a result of any claims that are inconsistent with the promises made by Actor to Company in this Agreement.

14. ENTIRE AGREEMENT This Agreement shall replace and supersede all previous arrangements, understandings, representation, or agreements, either oral or written, regarding the subject matter hereof and expresses the entire agreement between Actor and Company with reference to the terms and conditions for the rendition of Actor's services for Company for Company in connection with the Picture.

15. PROMOTIONAL COPIES Actor may purchase, at Company's cost, one full copy of the picture. Actor agrees to use this copy of the Picture solely for promotional use. Actor will not duplicate or copy the Picture in any manner. Actor will ensure that full credit for Company is given with regard to the usage of the copy of the Picture.

By signing in the spaces provided, Actor and Company accept and agree to all terms and conditions of this Agreement.

ALL TERMS ACCEPTED AND AGREED

Date _____ _____

Date

By _____ _____

ACTOR   on behalf of the corporation

                           Federal Tax ID _____

                           State Business Lic. _____

                           Your name as it should appear in
                           the credits

                           _____

AMENDMENT TO AGREEMENT

This agreement (hereinafter referred to as the "Agreement")
is between _____ (the "Company"), a
_____ corporation, and
_____, hereafter referred to as
"Deferring Party." The parties acknowledge that they had previously entered into an agreement dated _____
(referred to as the "Original Agreement"), which under certain rights were granted to Company and/or services were rendered to Company. The parties further acknowledge that in the
Original Agreement, all compensation due to the Deferred
Party was to be deferred and paid at a later date. The parties now agree to amend the Original Agreement as follows:

1. COMPENSATION (a) The Deferring Party now agrees to accept
the amount of $_____, as the full and complete compen-
sation due to the Deferred Party under the Original
Agreement. This payment shall be in lieu of the deferred
compensation due to the Deferring Party, as detailed in the
Original Agreement. The Deferring Party accepts the stated
compensation as the full and sole compensation and payment in
full due to the deferring Party. The Deferring Party hereby
forever waives and releases any claims of any kind to any
additional compensation in connection with the Original
Agreement, the Picture (as defined in the Original Agreement)
or Company.

(b) The above stated compensation shall be paid to the
Deferring Party upon return of a signed copy of this
Amendment to Agreement to the offices of the Company.

2. REMAINING TERMS OF ORIGINAL AGREEMENT The compensation
terms of the Original Agreement have been modified by this
Agreement. All other terms and provisions of the Original
Agreement shall remain in full force and effect and shall
remain fully and completely legally binding on both the
Deferring Party and the Company. All rights granted by the
Deferring Party to the Company in the Original Agreement
shall remain in full force and effect.

ALL TERMS ACCEPTED AND AGREED

Date _____   Date _____

By _____   DEFERRING
   on behalf of the
     corporation   PARTY_____

                          PRINT NAME

                          _____

MASTER RECORDING LICENSE AGREEMENT

This Agreement is between _____ hereafter referred to as "Licensor" and _____, hereafter referred to as "Licensee."

1. Licensor warrants and represents that Licensor is the owner of valid United States copyrights in the master recordings listed in Attachment A. Licensor warrants and represents that Licensor has the right to allow Licensee to use the master recordings in the manner specified in this Agreement. Licensor further warrants and represents that Licensor has the right to grant the license and all rights covered in this Agreement.

2. Licensor grants to Licensee the nonexclusive, irrevocable right, privilege and license, to use the master recordings listed in Attachment A in synchronism or timed-relation with the following video, television program, motion picture or film (hereafter referred to as the "visual image"):

_____

The length of time of usage for master recording shall be as specified in Attachment A. The method of usage and transmission of the visual image shall be: in all forms of motion picture, film, television broadcast of any kind, videocassette and any other formats or transmissions of said visual image whether currently in existence or later created or discovered, including advertising and promotion of the visual image.

3. This license is granted upon the express condition that the master recordings are to be used solely in synchronism or timed-relation with the above listed visual image. No sound recordings produced or licensed under this license are to be manufactured, sold, licensed, or used separately or apart from the visual image. The visual image shall not be used, transmitted, or exhibited except as specifically noted in this Agreement.

4. If the method of usage and transmission of the visual image is one that is subject to performing rights granted to any performing rights society then the exercise of recording rights granted in this license are subject to the broadcaster having a valid performing rights license. Licensee shall have no claim against Licensor if the broadcaster which Licensee intends to broadcast through does not have, or is unable to obtain, a valid performing rights license.

5. This license is granted for the geographic territory of the World.

6. The term of this license shall be for as long as the copyrights in the master recordings remain valid and in force. At the end of this period, all rights given from the Licensor to the Licensee shall terminate, including the right to make or authorize any use or distribution whatsoever of the master recordings, subject to those rights which the Licensee may then be able to obtain with regard to public domain compositions.

7. For the rights granted in this Agreement, Licensee shall pay compensation to Licensor at the rate of $_____ per musical composition for compositions, for a total of $_____. This total compensation shall be paid entirely as deferred compensation. Such deferred compensation shall be payable only if all expenses and costs of any kind incurred in connection with the Picture are first recovered in full by Licensee. If Licensee never receives full reimbursement of all expenses and costs incurred in connection with the Picture then Licensor shall never receive the stated deferred compensation. Licensor understands that the possibility exists that Licensor may never receive any portion of the stated deferred compensation, and Licensor expressly agrees to these terms. If Licensee receives full reimbursement for all expenses and costs incurred in connection with the Picture, Licensor shall receive the stated deferred compensation in a manner proportionate to all other persons who are entitled to deferred compensation. While Licensee shall be obligated to pay such deferred compensation once all expenses and costs incurred by Licensee in connection with the Picture have been fully reimbursed, the actual frequency of the payment of such deferred compensation shall be at the discretion of Licensee. The failure of Licensor to receive compensation because Licensee has not been fully reimbursed for its expenses and costs shall not be grounds to terminate or revoke the rights granted by Licensor to Licensee in this Agreement.

8. Licensee shall inform Licensor of the necessary format and technical requirements for the master recordings. Should Licensor fail to deliver master recordings that are satisfactory to Licensee, Licensee may either require Licensor to supply new master recordings that are satisfactory, or

Licensee may cancel a portion of this Agreement and adjust fees due to Licensor accordingly, whichever Licensee so chooses.

9. Licensor indemnifies and shall hold Licensee harmless from all loss, damage, or expense (including legal expenses and attorney's fees) arising out of, or connected with any claim by a third party which is inconsistent with any of Licensor's promises or warranties in this Agreement, or by reason of any adjudication invalidating the copyright in the master recordings.

10. Licensee shall give Licensor credit in the credit section of the visual image. While Licensee shall endeavor to give such credit in the form noted in Attachment A, Licensee reserves the right to edit such credit as may be necessary due to space limitations or other production constraints.

11. Licensee may assign this Agreement without the written consent of the Licensor, but only to the extent necessary or advisable to properly effect the distribution, exhibition, or transmission of the visual image. This Agreement shall be binding upon the heirs, legal representatives, successors, and assigns of the parties. The execution of this Agreement by Licensee shall constitute and is accepted by Licensor as full compliance with all obligations of Licensee to Licensor, statutory and otherwise, which arise from or are connected with Licensee's use of the musical compositions as stated in this Agreement.

12. This Agreement is subject to Licensee obtaining all necessary rights and permissions for use of the underlying musical compositions embodied in the master recordings, in the manner desired by Licensee. Should Licensee be unable to obtain all necessary rights and permissions for use of the underlying musical compositions, Licensee may terminate all or part of this Agreement, and then proportionately reduce or eliminate entirely the fees due to Licensor. In the event Licensee is unable to obtain the necessary rights and permissions for the use of the underlying musical compositions, Licensee will notify Licensor of the same in writing.

13. The persons signing below guarantee that they are authorized to sign this Agreement on behalf of the parties, and bind the parties to all terms of this Agreement.

ALL TERMS ACCEPTED AND AGREED

Date _____   Date _____

LICENSEE   LICENSOR

Print Name

_____   _____

By _____   _____

  on behalf of the
    corporation

Social Security
Number _____

Address

_____

_____

ATTACHMENT A

Song Title: _____

Time: _____

Performed by: _____

Courtesy of: _____

From the album: _____

Written by: _____

Publishing company: _____

Other: _____

Song Title: _____

Time: _____

Performed by: _____

Courtesy of: _____

From the album: _____

Written by: _____

Publishing company: _____

Other: _____

Song Title: _____

Time: _____

Performed by: _____

Courtesy of: _____

From the album: _____

Written by: _____

Publishing company: _____

Other: _____

SYNC RIGHTS AGREEMENT

This Agreement is between _____ hereafter referred to as "Licensor" and _____,
hereafter referred to as "Licensee."

1. Licensor warrants and represents that Licensor is the
owner of valid United States copyrights in the musical compositions listed in Attachment A. Licensor acknowledges that
Licensor is the sole writer of each of the original musical
compositions listed in Attachment A. Licensor warrants and
represents that Licensor has the right to grant the license
and all rights covered in this Agreement.

2. Licensor grants to Licensee the nonexclusive, irrevocable
right, privilege and license, to record the above named and
copyrighted musical composition in synchronism or timed-relation with the following video, television program, motion
picture, or film (hereafter referred to as the "visual
image"):

_____

The length of time of usage for each composition shall be as
specified in Attachment A. The method of usage and transmission of the visual image shall be: in all forms of motion
picture, film, television broadcast of any kind, videocassette and any other formats or transmissions of said visual
image whether currently in existence or later created or
discovered, including advertising and promotion of the visual image.

3. This license is granted upon the express condition that
the recording is to be used solely in synchronism or timed-
relation with the above-listed visual image. No sound
recordings produced or licensed under this license are to be
manufactured, sold, licensed, or used separately or apart
from the visual image. The visual image shall not be used,
transmitted, or exhibited except as specifically noted in
this Agreement.

4. If the method of usage and transmission of the visual
image is one that is not subject to performing rights granted to any performing rights society then this Agreement
shall constitute a valid performing rights license from the
Licensor to the Licensee.

If the method of usage And transmission of the visual image
is one that is subject to performing rights granted to any

performing rights society then the exercise of recording rights granted in this license is subject to the broadcaster having a valid performing rights license. Licensee shall have no claim against Licensor if the broadcaster through which Licensee intends to broadcast does not have, or is unable to obtain, a valid performing rights license.

5. This license is granted for the geographic territory of the World.

6. The term of this license shall be for as long as the copyrights in the musical compositions remain valid and in force. At the end of this period, all rights given from the Licensor to the Licensee shall terminate, including the right to make or authorize any use or distribution whatsoever of said recordings of the musical composition, subject to those rights which the Licensee may then be able to obtain with regard to public domain compositions.

7. For the rights granted in this Agreement, Licensee shall pay compensation to Licensor at the rate of $_____ per musical composition for compositions, for a total of $_____. This total compensation shall be paid entirely as deferred compensation. Such deferred compensation shall be payable only if all expenses and costs of any kind incurred in connection with the Picture are first recovered in full by Licensee. If Licensee never receives full reimbursement of all expenses and costs incurred in connection with the Picture then Licensor shall never receive the stated deferred compensation. Licensor understands that the possibility exists that Licensor may never receive any portion of the stated deferred compensation, and Licensor expressly agrees to these terms. If Licensee receives full reimbursement for all expenses and costs incurred in connection with the Picture, Licensor shall receive the stated deferred compensation in a manner proportionate to all other persons who are entitled to deferred compensation. While Licensee shall be obligated to pay such deferred compensation once all expenses and costs incurred by Licensee in connection with the Picture have been fully reimbursed, the actual frequency of the payment of such deferred compensation shall be at the discretion of Licensee. The failure of Licensor to receive compensation because Licensee has not been fully reimbursed for its expenses and costs shall not be grounds to terminate or revoke the rights granted by Licensor to Licensee in this Agreement.

8. Licensor indemnifies and shall hold Licensee harmless from all loss, damage, or expense (including legal expenses and attorney's fees) arising out of, or connected with any claim by a third party which is inconsistent with any of Licensor's promises or warranties in this Agreement, or by reason of any adjudication invalidating the copyright in the musical compositions.

9. Licensee may assign this Agreement without the written consent of the Licensor, but only to the extent necessary or advisable to properly effect the distribution, exhibition, or transmission of the visual image. This Agreement shall be binding upon the heirs, legal representatives, successors, and assigns of the parties. The execution of this Agreement by Licensee shall constitute and is accepted by Licensor as full compliance with all obligations of Licensee to Licensor, statutory and otherwise, which arise from or are connected with Licensee's use of the musical compositions as stated in this Agreement.

10. Licensee shall give Licensor credit in the credit section of the visual image. While Licensee shall endeavor to give such credit in the form noted in Attachment A, Licensee reserves the right to edit such credit as may be necessary due to space limitations or other production constraints.

11. The persons signing below guarantee that they are authorized to sign this Agreement on behalf of the parties, and bind the parties to all terms of this Agreement.

ALL TERMS ACCEPTED AND AGREED

Date _____   Date _____

LICENSEE   LICENSOR
Print Name

_____   _____

By _____   _____
on behalf of the
     corporation

                        Social Security
                        Number _____
                        Address

                        _____

                        _____

ATTACHMENT A

Song Title: _____

Time: _____

Performed by: _____

Courtesy of: _____

From the album: _____

Written by: _____

Publishing company: _____

Other: _____

Song Title: _____

Time: _____

Performed by: _____

Courtesy of: _____

From the album: _____

Written by: _____

Publishing company: _____

Other: _____

Song Title: _____

Time: _____

Performed by: _____

Courtesy of: _____

From the album: _____

Written by: _____

Publishing company: _____

Other: _____

MASTER RECORDING AND SYNC RIGHTS AGREEMENT

This Agreement is between _____ hereafter referred to as "Licensor" and _____,
hereafter referred to as "Licensee".

1. Licensor warrants and represents that Licensor is the
owner of valid United States copyrights in the musical compositions listed in Attachment A. Licensor acknowledges that
Licensor is the sole writer of each of the original musical
compositions listed in Attachment A. Licensor warrants and
represents that Licensor has the right to allow Licensee to
use the master recordings of the same musical compositions
in the manner specified in this Agreement. Licensor further
warrants and represents that Licensor has the right to grant
the license and all rights covered in this Agreement.

2. Licensor grants to Licensee the nonexclusive, irrevocable
right, privilege and license, to use the master recordings
of the above named and copyrighted musical compositions in
synchronism or timed-relation with the following video,
television program, motion picture, or film (hereafter
referred to as the "visual image"):

_____

The length of time of usage for each composition shall be as
specified in Attachment A. The method of usage and transmission of the visual image shall be: in all forms of motion
picture, film, television broadcast of any kind, videocassette, and any other formats or transmissions of said visual
image whether currently in existence or later created or
discovered, including advertising and promotion of the visual image.

3. This license is granted upon the express condition that
the recording is to be used solely in synchronism or timed-
relation with the above-listed visual image. No sound
recordings produced or licensed under this license are to be
manufactured, sold, licensed, or used separately or apart
from the visual image. The visual image shall not be used,
transmitted, or exhibited except as specifically noted in
this Agreement.

4. If the method of usage and transmission of the visual
image is one that is not subject to performing rights granted to any performing rights society then this Agreement

shall constitute a valid performing rights license from the Licensor to the Licensee.

If the method of usage and transmission of the visual image is one that is subject to performing rights granted to any performing rights society then the exercise of recording rights granted in this license are subject to the broadcaster having a valid performing rights license. Licensee shall have no claim against Licensor if the broadcaster through which Licensee intends to broadcast does not have, or is unable to obtain, a valid performing rights license.

5. This license is granted for the geographic territory of the World.

6. The term of this license shall be for as long as the copyrights in the musical compositions remain valid and in force. At the end of this period, all rights given from the Licensor to the Licensee shall terminate, including the right to make or authorize any use or distribution whatsoever of said recordings of the musical composition, subject to those rights which the Licensee may then be able to obtain with regard to public domain compositions.

7. For the rights granted in this Agreement, Licensee shall pay compensation to Licensor at the rate of $_____ per musical composition for compositions, for a total of $_____. This total compensation shall be paid entirely as deferred compensation. Such deferred compensation shall be payable only if all expenses and costs of any kind incurred in connection with the Picture are first recovered in full by Licensee. If Licensee never receives full reimbursement of all expenses and costs incurred in connection with the Picture, then Licensor shall never receive the stated deferred compensation. Licensor understands that the possibility exists that Licensor may never receive any portion of the stated deferred compensation, and Licensor expressly agrees to these terms. If Licensee receives full reimbursement for all expenses and costs incurred in connection with the Picture, Licensor shall receive the stated deferred compensation in a manner proportionate to all other persons who are entitled to deferred compensation. While Licensee shall be obligated to pay such deferred compensation once all expenses and costs incurred by Licensee in connection with the Picture have been fully reimbursed, the actual frequency of the

payment of such deferred compensation shall be at the discretion of Licensee. The failure of Licensor to receive compensation because Licensee has not been fully reimbursed for its expenses and costs shall not be grounds to terminate or revoke the rights granted by Licensor to Licensee in this Agreement.

8. Licensee shall inform Licensor of the necessary format and technical requirements for the master recordings. Should Licensor fail to deliver master recordings that are satisfactory to Licensee, Licensee may either require Licensor to supply new master recordings that are satisfactory, or Licensee may cancel a portion of this Agreement and adjust fees due to Licensor accordingly, whichever Licensee so chooses.

9. Licensor indemnifies and shall hold Licensee harmless from all loss, damage, or expense (including legal expenses and attorney's fees) arising out of, or connected with any claim by a third party which is inconsistent with any of Licensor's promises or warranties in this Agreement, or by reason of any adjudication invalidating the copyright in the musical compositions.

10. Licensee may assign this Agreement without the written consent of the Licensor, but only to the extent necessary or advisable to properly effect the distribution, exhibition or transmission of the visual image. This Agreement shall be binding upon the heirs, legal representatives, successors and assigns of the parties. The execution of this Agreement by Licensee shall constitute and is accepted by Licensor as full compliance with all obligations of Licensee to Licensor, statutory and otherwise, which arise from or are connected with Licensee's use of the musical compositions as stated in this Agreement.

11. Licensee shall give Licensor credit in the credit section of the visual image. While Licensee shall endeavor to give such credit in the form noted in Attachment A, Licensee reserves the right to edit such credit as may be necessary due to space limitations or other production constraints.

12. The persons signing below guarantee that they are authorized to sign this Agreement on behalf of the parties, and bind the parties to all terms of this Agreement.

```
ALL TERMS ACCEPTED AND AGREED
Date _____    Date _____
LICENSEE                 LICENSOR
Print Name

_____    _____

By _____   _____
    on behalf of the
        corporation

                         Social Security
                         Number _____
                         Address

                         _____

                         _____
```

ATTACHMENT A

Song Title: _____

Time: _____

Performed by: _____

Courtesy of: _____

From the album: _____

Written by: _____

Publishing company: _____

Other: _____

Song Title: _____

Time: _____

Performed by: _____

Courtesy of: _____

From the album: _____

Written by: _____

Publishing company: _____

Other: _____

Song Title: _____

Time: _____

Performed by: _____

Courtesy of: _____

From the album: _____

Written by: _____

Publishing company: _____

Other: _____

SOUNDTRACK LICENSING AGREEMENT

This Agreement is between _____ here-
after referred to as "Label" and the group or artist
consisting of the following individual members:

_____

_____,

hereafter referred to as "Artist."

1. PROJECT DESCRIPTION Artist agrees to participate in the
following recording project to be produced by Label:

_____

which shall be referred to as the "Album." Artist has or
will record the following songs for the album:

1.	6.
2.	7.
3.	8.
4.	9.
5.	10.

2. PAYMENT OF COSTS (a) Artist agrees to pay all costs that
are incurred in creating a master recording tape of the
above-noted songs. Artist shall supply Label with a completed DAT master copy of the above song or songs, at Artist's
sole expense. Such master shall meet the technical requirements specified by Label. Label shall have the right to make
technical adjustments of each song (such as equalization),
in order to ensure the overall balance of all songs on the
Album.

(b) Label shall arrange for pressing and distribution of
retail copies of the Album. Other than the costs incurred in
creating the master recording tape of the above-noted songs,
Label shall be responsible for paying all other costs of the
recording project.

3. OWNERSHIP OF ALBUM Artist will be the sole owner and
copyright holder of all master recording tapes licensed to
Label under the terms of this Agreement. Label will be the
sole owner and copyright holder with regard to the entire
album in its form as a compilation of various recorded
songs. If the songs recorded by Artist were also written by
Artist then Artist shall retain full ownership of such songs
as written musical compositions. In such a case, Artist

grants to Label a mechanical license for the term of this Agreement to reproduce such written musical compositions as sound recordings, in all forms and configurations, whether now known, or later created. In return for the grant of this mechanical license, Artist shall receive no additional compensation other than that stated in Paragraph 6 of this Agreement.

4. <u>DELIVERY OF MASTER</u> Artist shall deliver to Label the master recordings of the songs noted above at the time and place requested by Label, and within the specific technical requirements requested by Label. Failure of Artist to deliver masters in accordance with all these requirements shall be a breach of this Agreement. Label shall have the sole and final authority to determine whether the recordings by Artist are of sufficient technical and commercial quality, and whether Label will use any recordings by Artist on the album. If Label does not use the master recordings, they shall be returned to Artist, within 90 days of delivery of the DAT master copy to Label.

5. <u>TERM AND TERRITORY</u> Label shall have the right to manufacture, produce, sell, and distribute copies of the Album. The rights granted to Label in this Agreement shall continue for as long as the copyrights in the sound recordings or written musical compositions shall remain valid, whichever is longer. The territory in which Label shall be able to exercise the rights granted in this Agreement shall be the World.

6. <u>ARTIST ROYALTIES</u> (a) Label shall pay Artist a royalty equal to _____ % of the net profits generated by sales of the album, multiplied by a fraction in which the numerator is the number of songs recorded by Artist appearing on the album, and the denominator is the total number of songs appearing on the album. (For example, if Artist records one song on the album, and there are 15 songs on the album then Artist's royalty shall be 1/15 of % of the profits.)

(b) As used in this Agreement, the term "net profits" shall mean those sums remaining after all costs of any kind incurred by Label have first been fully recovered by Label. Such costs shall include, but not be limited to: recording costs, pressing, manufacturing and distribution costs, mechanical license fees, legal fees, promotion and advertising expenses, mailing and shipping expenses, fees to third-party distributors and licensees, art and graphic costs.

(c) Label shall pay royalties to Artist twice a year, within 60 days of each June 30 and December 31. No payments shall be due to Artist until Label shall have achieved any net profits. Along with each payment, Label shall send Artist a statement of account, providing information on revenues and expenses of the recording project.

7. <u>PROMOTION, ADVERTISING, AND CREDIT</u> (a) Artist grants to Label the right to use Artist's name, likeness, photographs, biographical material, recorded performances, and similar material as Label deems necessary with regard to the promotion and advertising of the album. If any song recorded by Artist appears on the album, Artist shall receive credit on the album as a recording artist, as such credit is commonly given in the recording industry. To ensure proper credit, Artist shall complete the Credit Sheet attached as Exhibit A to this Agreement. Label shall retain complete control and authority over the packaging and artwork for the Album.

(b) Label will provide five free copies of the album to Artist at no charge, in a configuration to be determined by Label. Artist shall have the right to use these copies of the album for promotional purposes only, and shall not make additional copies of the album.

(c) Artist shall have the right to purchase additional copies of the album from Label, at a price to be determined by Label, which shall be less than the retail price. Artist may resell these copies of the album at live performances only. Artist shall not sell, trade, or consign the copies of the album given to or purchased by Artist at any retail outlet of any kind, or to any distributor, vendor, or catalog. Any violation of this Paragraph by Artist shall be considered a material breach of this Agreement. In the case of such breach, in addition to any remedies available at law or in this Agreement, Label shall have the right to cancel any outstanding orders of additional album copies to Artist (with a refund of any deposits taken on such orders), the right to refuse to sell any additional album copies to Artist, and the right to withhold royalties due to Artist in the amount of damages suffered by Label until the matter is settled by the parties or resolved in litigation.

8. <u>ARTIST WARRANTIES</u> Artist warrants and guarantees to Label that

(a) Artist has the legal right and ability to enter into this Agreement and grant the rights to Label stated in this Agreement.

(b) If Artist is under any contract or agreement that in any way restricts Artist's right to grants the rights to Label stated in this Agreement, Artist will obtain written permission that gives Artist the right to grant such rights to Label and provide Label with a copy of such document, upon the signing of this Agreement;

(c) All songs recorded by Artist that are written by Artist are Artist's own original compositions and such songs do not in any way infringe on, imitate, or copy other songs in which other parties have copyrights.

9. INDEMNIFICATION Artist agrees to indemnify and hold Label harmless from any claims and costs whatsoever (including attorney's fees) arising from the breach by Artist of any of the terms of this Agreement. Label agrees to indemnify and hold Artist harmless from any claims and costs whatsoever (including attorney's fees) arising from the breach by Label of any of the terms of this Agreement.

10. TAXES Both parties shall be solely liable for the payment of any income taxes or other taxes that may be due on that parties' share of net profits. Payments to Artist shall be sent to the following:

Name: _____

Soc. Sec. or Tax I.D. No.: _____

Address: _____

11. REMEDIES AND ATTORNEY'S FEES Should either party to this Agreement find it necessary to commence legal action to resolve a dispute regarding this Agreement, or to enforce the terms of this Agreement, the prevailing party shall be entitled to an award of court costs, expenses and attorney's fees incurred in such legal action, in addition to any other damages or legal relief awarded. In addition to the right to seek damages for breach, each party shall have the right to seek the remedy of specific enforcement of this Agreement, or the right to obtain injunctive relief to enforce the terms of this Agreement or prevent the further breach of this Agreement. Any party commencing legal action shall have the right to pursue any and all legal remedies herein mentioned or otherwise available at law.

12. GOVERNING LAW, VENUE AND MODIFICATION (a) The effect and interpretation of this Agreement shall be governed by the laws of the State of _____. Both parties agree

that the venue for any litigation regarding this Agreement shall be in _____, _____. Both parties agree to be subject to the courts of _____ County, _____.

(b) The parties acknowledge that this Agreement is the full and complete agreement between Artist and Label. Any modification, alteration, or termination by mutual consent applicable to this Agreement shall not be valid unless made in writing, dated, and signed by both Artist and Label.

<u>13. ARTIST LIABILITY</u> Should Artist consist of a group of individuals, each member of Artist shall be jointly and severally liable for carrying out all obligations of the Artist under the terms of this Agreement. This shall also apply to any new member of the Artist who joins after the signing of this Agreement. The breach of this Agreement by any one member of the Artist shall be considered a breach of this Agreement by all members of the Artist. In such a case, Label shall have the right to terminate this Agreement as to the entire group or pursue any other remedies available at law.

ALL TERMS ACCEPTED AND AGREED

Date _____ Date _____

LABEL   ARTIST
Print Name

_____   _____
By _____   _____
    on behalf of the
       corporation
                           Social Security
                           Number _____

                           Print Name _____
                           Signature _____
                           Social Security
                           Number _____

Print Name

_____

Signature _____

Social Security
Number _____

Print Name

_____

Signature _____

Social Security
Number_____

EXHIBIT A—CREDIT SHEET

1. Group Name:_____

2. Individual Member Names   Instruments Performed

_____

_____

_____

_____

_____

3. Song Titles and Writer Credits:

Song Title   Length   Lyrics   Music

_____

_____

_____

_____

_____

4. Publishing Company Name (if any): _____

5. ASCAP or BMI affiliation: _____

6. Produced by: _____

7. Engineered by: _____

8. Mixed by: _____

9. Recorded at: _____

10. Mixed at: _____

11. Contact name, address, and phone number: _____

_____

Label reserves the right to limit the credits listed, due to
space limitations.

INDEX

SYMBOLS

A

ABOUT THE DVD

The DVD that comes with this book contains three parts:

- Software
- Templates
- Video

To access this material on your computer, please make sure you have the most recent versions of your Internet browser.

- **Microsoft Internet Explorer 6** is available at `http://www.microsoft.com/windows/ie/default.asp`.
- **Netscape 6.1** is available at `http://home.netscape.com/browsers/6/index.html?cp=dowpod6`.

Also, be sure to have Windows Media Player loaded on your machine.

- **Windows Media Player** can be downloaded from
  www.microsoft.com/windows/windowsmedia/en/download/default
  .asp. (While you're here, you might want to download Windows
  Media Encoder for encoding audio and video for the Web.)

SOFTWARE

- **Adobe Premiere Demo** for Windows and Mac. One of the best-
  selling video editing applications on the market. Integrates well with
  other Adobe products, such as After Effects and Photoshop. From
  Adobe Systems Inc., 345 Park Ave., San Jose, CA 95110-2704.
  Phone 800-833-6687. www.adobe.com.

- **Adobe After Effects Demo** for Windows and Mac. After Effects
  really is as cool as everyone says. After Effects is used for producing
  motion graphics and visual effects for film, video, multimedia, and
  the Web. Integrates well with other Adobe products such as
  Premiere and Photoshop. From Adobe Systems Inc., 345 Park Ave.,
  San Jose, CA 95110-2704. Phone 800-833-6687. www.adobe.com.

- **Ulead Media Studio Pro Trial Version** for the Mac. This 30-day
  trial includes Video Editor, Video Paint, CG Infinity, Video Capture,
  and Audio Editor, which makes up the MediaStudio Pro 6.0 digital
  video editing suite. The demo does not include technical support,
  has limited transitions and effects, marks footage with a big red "X,"
  limits video capture to 20 seconds, and doesn't support ASF streaming video. However, you'll get enough of a taste of this product to
  consider paying for it. Ulead Systems, Inc., 20000 Mariner Ave.,
  Suite #200, Torrance, CA 90503. Phone 310-896-6388, fax 310-896-
  6389. E-mail sales@ulead.com, www.ulead.com.

- **Storyboard Artist Demo** for Windows and Mac. Storyboarding software. Nice application from nice people. From PowerProduction
  Software, 432 Los Gatos Blvd., Los Gatos, CA 95032. Phone 408-
  358-2358, fax 408-358-1186. E-mail info@powerproduction.com,
  www.powerproduction.com.

- **MovieMagic Scheduling Demo** for Windows and Mac. Movie sched-
  uling software to help you get a handle on scheduling your show.
  From Creative Planet, 5700 Wilshire Blvd., Suite 600, Los Angeles,
  CA 90036. Phone 323-634-3400. www.MovieMagicProducer.com.

- **MovieMagic Budgeting Demo** for Windows and Mac. Budgeting
  software to help you manage the money for your project. From

Creative Planet, 5700 Wilshire Blvd., Suite 600, Los Angeles, CA 90036. Phone 323-634-3400. `www.MovieMagicProducer.com`.

- **The Consolidator** for Windows and Mac. Use the Consolidator with Adobe Premiere to manage preview files and rendering—a useful plug-in for anyone using Adobe Premiere. From MadCat Software, LLC, 9170 Chetwood Dr., Colorado Springs, CO 80920. Phone 719-282-1783. E-mail `sales@PremiereTools.com`, `www.premieretools.com/Consolidator.asp`.

- **CatDV** for Windows and Mac. Power tools for logging and cataloging digital video. From Square Box Systems Limited, Brookland, The Green, Snitterfield, Stratford-upon-Avon CV37 0JG, United Kingdom. Phone 44 7050 372230. E-mail `info@squarebox.co.uk`, `www.squarebox.co.uk`.

TEMPLATES

All of these documents are for your use. Reproduction of these forms for your use is encouraged. However, you are prohibited from copying and disseminating these documents for mass distribution.

Remember to have an entertainment attorney examine any contract or agreement before you start signing anything. Laws vary according to city, county, and state. It's a lot cheaper to get the correct documents taken care of before there are any legal problems.

CONTRACTOR AGREEMENTS AND RELEASES

The **Technical Services Contractor Agreement** is for everyone who works on your show who is not on camera. The **Actor Services Agreement** is for everyone who appears on camera in a principal, supporting, or cameo role, as well as voice talent. These are both deferral contracts. The **Amendment to Agreement** document allows you to offer to buy out one of these agreements. For example, if a DP wants you to buy his or her contract for a percentage of its deferred value, that person would have to sign this Amendment to Agreement on accepting payment.

Life Story Consent and Release Agreement applies to nonfiction movies, such as documentaries.

Use the **Location Release** at every location. Be sure the person who signs is empowered to do so. Use the **Personal Release** for anyone who appears on camera as an extra.

MUSIC AGREEMENTS

The **Master Recording License Agreement** grants you the right to use the master recording of a specific recorded performance. You must have the signature of everyone who has a claim of copyright ownership in the recording: performers, producers, arrangers, and possibly others. **Attachment A** lists the exact information of the recording so you can list credits and fill out a Music Cue Sheet.

The **Sync Rights Agreement** grants you the right to use a specific musical composition. Just like the Master Recording License Agreement, you must have the signature of everyone who has a claim of copyright ownership in the composition: composers, arrangers, lyricists, and so on. **Attachment A** lists the exact information of the recording so you can list credits and fill out a Music Cue Sheet.

The **Master Recording and Sync Rights Agreement** combines both the master recording and sync license in one document. This is handy if you're dealing with performers who write and record their own music and have no record or distribution deal. You must have the signature of everyone who has a claim of copyright ownership in the master recording and composition. **Attachment A** lists the exact information of the recording so you can list credits and fill out a Music Cue Sheet.

If you want to create a soundtrack album for your show, you'll need everyone with a claim of copyright ownership to sign the **Soundtrack Licensing Agreement**. This agreement assumes your production company will act as the record label. Have each person fill out the **Exhibit A—Credit Sheet** so you can properly credit everyone on the album.

WORKSHEETS

These worksheets will help you correctly format your screenplay and break it down for budgeting and scheduling, as well as create callsheets.

- Screenplay Template
- Script Breakdown Sheet
- Callsheet
- Budget Sheets

CHECKLISTS

These checklists will help you budget, purchase or rent, and track equipment and expendables for your show.

- Lighting Expendables Checklist
- Gels and Diffusion Checklist
- Electrical Lighting Equipment Checklist
- Nonelectrical Lighting Equipment Checklist
- Rigging Expendables Checklist
- Rigging Equipment Checklist
- Makeup Expendables Checklist

VIDEO

There are two types of video on the DVD—one set plays in a DVD player and one set can be viewed on a computer using Windows Media Player.

"MUSIC APPRECIATION" FOOTAGE

These movies give you the rough version of "Music Appreciation," which you can compare to the fine-cut version. You'll notice differences because of color correction and some frame blending. You'll also hear differences in audio levels, dialogue editing, sound effects, and music.

The footage from behind the scenes gives you an idea of some of the activities on the set.

- **"Music Appreciation" Fine Cut** (5:31:22).
- **"Music Appreciation" Rough Cut** (6:58:13).
- **Behind-the-Scenes** (2:23:09) footage from "Music Appreciation," with Peggy Gannon, John Bianchi, Betty Marshall, Matt Lambert, Chris Beug, Sarah Johnson, Rich Phelps, and Denise Ohio. Shot by Shawn Telford.

INTERVIEWS AND DEMOS

These interviews and demos explain some of the issues you face as an independent motion picture producer.

- **Legal Tips** (10:06:13) with entertainment attorney Neil Sussman from the Law Offices of Neil Sussman. Neil covers some of the legal aspects of producing movies. While Neil is a fine attorney, this is not a substitute for having your own legal advisor experienced in entertainment law. Phone 206-363-8070.
  E-mail neilsussman@mindspring.com.

- **Location Audio Tips, Part 1** (7:48:03) and **Location Audio Tips, Part 2** (8:33:22) with location and post-audio professional and sound designer Scot Charles. That is Scot's latest Emmy Award sitting over his right shoulder. Scot has many such awards, but he doesn't brag about them. He doesn't have to. Blue Charles Productions, Inc. Phone 206-783-6797. E-mail info@bluecharles.com, www.bluecharles.com.

- **How to Set Up a C-Stand** (1:44:28) with grip-camera operator Matt Lambert. In addition to being one of the nicest guys I've ever met, Matt has the best work ethic. He knows the gear, pays attention, and hustles. Shooters Broadcast Services, Inc. Phone 206-768-9828. E-mail matt@shootersbroadcast.com.

- **Film Office** (5:56:15) with Lanie McMullin, City of Everett Film Office representative. Lanie is great. She's as professional, approachable, and helpful as she is in this interview. City of Everett, Washington. Phone 425-257-7100.

- **Post-Audio Tips** (8:09:29) with producer-director sound designer Peter B. Lewis. Peter is warm, funny, and creative. A fine fellow who also has a bunch of awards he doesn't have to brag about. AUDISEE. E-mail audisee@audisee.com, www.audisee.com.

- **Rental Houses** (3:43:20) with rental manager Jeremy Brown. Jeremy is another great, helpful guy. He really wants your show to make you a zillion dollars so you can come back and rent more cool stuff. Seattle Grip and Lighting. Phone 206-285-0840.

Please read this before opening the DVD (begins on page 815).